Rethinking Securities Law

Rethinking Securities Law

MARC I. STEINBERG

OXFORD
UNIVERSITY PRESS

OXFORD
UNIVERSITY PRESS

Oxford University Press is a department of the University of Oxford. It furthers the University's objective of excellence in research, scholarship, and education by publishing worldwide. Oxford is a registered trade mark of Oxford University Press in the UK and certain other countries.

Published in the United States of America by Oxford University Press
198 Madison Avenue, New York, NY 10016, United States of America.

Library of Congress Cataloging-in-Publication Data
Names: Steinberg, Marc I., author.
Title: Rethinking securities law / Marc I. Steinberg.
Description: New York : Oxford University Press, [2021] |
Includes bibliographical references and index.
Identifiers: LCCN 2021000011 (print) | LCCN 2021000012 (ebook) | ISBN 9780197583142 (hardback) |
ISBN 9780197583166 (epub) | ISBN 9780197583159 (updf) | ISBN 9780197583173 (online)
Subjects: LCSH: Securities—United States.
Classification: LCC KF1439 . S7329 2021 (print) | LCC KF1439 (ebook) | DDC 346.73/0922—dc23
LC record available at https://lccn.loc.gov/2021000011
LC ebook record available at https://lccn.loc.gov/2021000012

DOI: 10.1093/oso/9780197583142.001.0001

Note to Readers

This publication is designed to provide accurate and authoritative information in regard to the subject matter covered. It is based upon sources believed to be accurate and reliable and is intended to be current as of the time it was written. It is sold with the understanding that the publisher is not engaged in rendering legal, accounting, or other professional services. If legal advice or other expert assistance is required, the services of a competent professional person should be sought. Also, to confirm that the information has not been affected or changed by recent developments, traditional legal research techniques should be used, including checking primary sources where appropriate.

(Based on the Declaration of Principles jointly adopted by a Committee of the American Bar Association and a Committee of Publishers and Associations.)

This book is dedicated to the many individuals who have been instrumental in my professional career in corporate and securities law. Foremost, I thank my parents, Phyllis and Gerald Steinberg, and my sister, Nancy Burman, for their love, encouragement, and support. Their unwavering support and confidence have been a steadying presence in my life, providing me needed confidence that I could succeed. My grandmothers, Anne Marblestone and Belle Steinberg, like my parents and sister, instilled in me that the quest for excellence is attainable and worthy of pursuit. From my professional life, Judge Stanley Sporkin, who as Director of the Enforcement Division hired me at the SEC and was my mentor, was the person responsible for initiating my career as a securities law academician and practitioner. Justice Arthur J. Goldberg, whom I had the honor of assisting in connection with his position on the SEC's Advisory Committee on Tender Offers, imparted to me high standards of professionalism, integrity, and diligence. Judge Stanley N. Barnes of the U.S. Court of Appeals, whom I clerked for after law school, perhaps was the most successful person I've ever known as he achieved excellence in so many facets of his life—as an accomplished jurist, a superb trial lawyer, a star football player who was inducted into the collegiate football hall of fame, a master bridge player, a world traveler, and a successful family man. By his actions, Judge Barnes communicated to me that one can attain excellence in both one's professional career and personal life. And last, Senator Robert P. Griffin, whom I served as legislative counsel during his last term as the senior senator from Michigan. A man of integrity and sound values, Senator Griffin gave me what remains still true today as the most exciting position I've ever had in my career, particularly as a junior attorney in my twenties. I express my deep appreciation to all these individuals. Their affection, guidance, and support have meant so very much to me.

Summary Contents

Detailed Contents

Acknowledgments

I am delighted that this project has come to fruition. It certainly was challenging and interesting. As the contents of the book indicate, a wide array of subjects are explored and scores of recommendations are proffered for adoption. The analysis herein hopefully will be useful to legislators, regulators, judges, academicians, practitioners, and students.

My research assistants provided tremendous support, and I thank them: Ms. Devon Poage, Mr. Taylor Santori, and Ms. Kaitlyn Thorson.

From the faculty, I thank Dean Jennifer Collins for her strong support of this project. For their invaluable research assistance, I express my appreciation to Mr. Greg Ivy, Associate Dean for Library and Technology, and Mr. Timothy Gallina, Research and Faculty Services Librarian. In addition, Ms. Carolyn Yates, law school administrative assistant, merits kudos for her diligent and superb contribution.

During this project, I am fortunate to have received two summer research grants. These grants were the Fred E. Tucker Endowment for Faculty Excellence (summer 2019) and the Robert B. Rowling Center for Business Law and Leadership (summer 2020). I very much thank the donors for their generous support of my scholarship.

I also express my appreciation for the strong support I have received for over three decades as a faculty member of this superb law school.

About the Author

MARC I. STEINBERG is the Rupert and Lillian Radford Chair in Law and Professor of Law at the Southern Methodist University (SMU) Dedman School of Law. He is the Director of the SMU Corporate Counsel Externship Program, the former Director of SMU's Corporate Directors' Institute, the former Senior Associate Dean for Academics, and the former Senior Associate Dean for Research at the Law School. Prior to becoming the Radford Professor, Professor Steinberg taught at the University of Maryland School of Law, the Wharton School of the University of Pennsylvania, the National Law Center of the George Washington University, and the Georgetown University Law Center. His experience includes appointments as a Visiting Professor, Scholar, and Fellow at law schools both in and outside the United States, including at UCLA as well as universities in Argentina, Australia, China, England, Finland, France, Germany, Israel, Italy, Japan, New Zealand, Scotland, South Africa, and Sweden. In addition, he has been retained as an expert witness in several significant matters, including Enron, Martha Stewart, Belnick (Tyco), Mark Cuban, and the National Prescription Litigation.

In addition to his university appointments, Professor Steinberg has lectured extensively both in the United States and abroad, including at the Lauterpacht Centre of International Law at the University of Cambridge, Heidelberg University, University of Auckland, University of Tokyo, Peking University, UCLA, the Aresty Institute of Executive Education at the University of Pennsylvania, the American Bar Association's Annual Meeting, the PLI Annual Institute on Securities Regulation, the University of Texas Annual Securities Law Conference, the International Development Law Institute in Rome, the Hong Kong Securities and Futures Commission, the Taiwan "SEC" in Taipei, the New Zealand Securities Commission, the Australian Law Council Section on International Law in Melbourne, the David Hume Institute in Edinburgh, the German-American Lawyers' Association in Munich, the International Law Society of South Africa, the Buenos Aires Stock Exchange, the Finnish Banking Lawyers Association in Helsinki, the Swedish Banking Lawyers Association in Stockholm, and the

Ministry of Internal Affairs, Economic Crimes Department of the Russian Federation in Moscow. He also has served as a member of the FINRA National Adjudicatory Council (NAC).

Professor Steinberg received his undergraduate degree at the University of Michigan and his law degrees at the University of California, Los Angeles (JD) and Yale University (LLM). He clerked for Judge Stanley N. Barnes of the U.S. Court of Appeals for the Ninth Circuit, extern clerked for Judge Anthony J. Celebrezze of the Sixth Circuit, was legislative counsel to U.S. Senator Robert P. Griffin, and served as the adviser to former U.S. Supreme Court Justice Arthur J. Goldberg for the Federal Advisory Committee Report on Tender Offers.

Professor Steinberg was an enforcement attorney at the U.S. Securities and Exchange Commission, and thereafter became special projects counsel. In that position, he directly assisted the SEC's General Counsel in a wide variety of projects and cases and served as the General Counsel's confidential legal adviser.

Professor Steinberg has authored approximately 40 books and 150 law review articles, is editor-in-chief of *The International Lawyer*, editor-in-chief of *The Securities Regulation Law Journal*, and is an adviser to *The Journal of Corporation Law*. Professor Steinberg is a member of the American Law Institute.

1

Rethinking Securities Law—Laying the Groundwork

I. Introduction

This book focuses on an important and timely subject that merits comprehensive analysis: "rethinking" the federal securities laws, with particular emphasis on the Securities Act of 1933[1] and the Securities Exchange Act of 1934.[2] Since the passage of these Acts during the midst of the Great Depression,[3] Congress periodically has enacted significant revisions.[4] These

[1] 15 U.S.C. § 77(a) *et seq.*

[2] 15 U.S.C. § 78(a) *et seq.*

[3] *See Cyan, Inc. v. Beaver County Employees Retirement Fund*, 138 S. Ct. 1061, 1066 (2018) ("In the wake of the 1929 stock market crash, Congress enacted two laws, in successive years, to promote honest practices in the securities markets."); Securities and Exchange Commission (SEC), *50 Years of the U.S. Securities and Exchange Commission* (1984) ("The Great Crash dramatized the need for federal intervention in establishing and maintaining higher standards of business conduct in the capital markets.").

[4] *See, e.g.*, Maloney Act of 1938, Pub. L. No. 75-719, 52 Stat. 1070 (1938) (creating the National Association of Securities Dealers (NASD)—a predecessor of the Financial Industry Regulatory Authority (FINRA)—to regulate the over-the-counter securities markets); Securities Acts Amendments of 1964, Pub. L. No. 88-467, 78 Stat. 565 (1964) (extending the Securities Exchange Act's periodic reporting, proxy, and insider short-swing trading provisions to over-the-counter companies as well as strengthening qualification standards and administrative disciplinary controls with respect to broker-dealers and their associated persons); Williams Act, Pub. L. No. 90-439, 12 Stat. 454 (1968) (insofar as procedures and disclosures, establishing requirements in the going-private and tender offer contexts); Securities Acts Amendments of 1975, Pub. L. No. 94-29, 89 Stat. 97 (1975) (directing the SEC to "facilitate the establishment of a national market system for securities"); Foreign Corrupt Practices Act of 1977 (FCPA), Pub. L. No. 95-213, 91 Stat. 1494 (1977) (prohibiting the payment of bribes to foreign officials in seeking to obtain or retain business as well as requiring Exchange Act reporting companies to maintain reasonably accurate books and records and internal accounting control practices); Securities Enforcement Remedies and Penny Stock Reform Act of 1990, Pub. L. No. 101-429, 104 Stat. 931 (1990) (enhancing the SEC's enforcement remedies, including the levying of money penalties, cease-and-desist orders, and officer and director bars); Private Securities Litigation Reform Act of 1995, Pub. L. No. 104-67, 109 Stat. 737 (1995) (PSLRA) (providing for securities class action reform, imposing stricter pleading requirements, enhancing protection for forward-looking statements by publicly-held companies, and enacting a proportionate liability framework); National Securities Markets Improvement Act of 1996 (NSMIA), Pub. L. No. 104-290, 110 Stat. 3416 (1996) (preempting state regulation of securities registration and exemptions thereto in regard to "covered" securities as specified therein); Securities Litigation Uniform Standards Act of 1998 (SLUSA), Pub. L. No. 105-353, 112 Stat. 3227 (1998) (with certain carve-outs, mandating that securities class actions against nationally traded companies must

Rethinking Securities Law. Marc I. Steinberg, Oxford University Press. © Marc I. Steinberg 2021.
DOI: 10.1093/oso/9780197583142.003.0001

amendments have spanned a period of over eighty-five years encompassing a broad array of securities regulatory matters.[5] Invoking its expansive authority, the Securities and Exchange Commission (SEC)[6] has been an active regulator in this process.[7]

Over forty years ago, the American Law Institute (ALI) adopted the Federal Securities Code.[8] Having the eminent Professor Louis Loss as its Reporter and premier consultants,[9] the Code was a grand project with three principal objectives: "(1) simplification of an inevitably complex body of law . . . ; (2) elimination (so far as possible) of duplicative regulation; and (3) reexamination of the entire scheme of investor protection with a view to increasing

be brought in federal district court with only federal law applying); Sarbanes-Oxley Act of 2002, Pub. L. No. 107-204, 116 Stat. 745 (2002) (enhancing federal regulation by, *inter alia*, mandating that chief executive officers and chief financial officers of subject companies certify the accuracy of SEC periodic reports, federalizing aspects of corporate governance (such as the composition and functions of audit committees), mandating real-time disclosure by Exchange Act reporting companies, enhancing government enforcement, and focusing on professional (accountant and attorney) standards of conduct); Dodd-Frank Wall Street Reform and Consumer Protection Act, Pub. L. No. 111-203, 124 Stat. 1376 (2010) (with respect to federal securities law coverage, enhancing federal corporate governance by mandating greater disclosure of executive officer compensation as well as subject company governance structure, a non-binding shareholder "say-on-pay" vote, and an independent compensation committee as a condition of national stock exchange listing); Jumpstart Our Business Startups Act of 2012 (JOBS Act), Pub. L. No. 112-106, 126 Stat. 306 (2012) (facilitating capital raising by relatively smaller enterprises by relaxing a number of obstacles and creating a new type of registrant—the emerging growth company).

[5] Subjects addressed by these legislative amendments include, by way of example, disclosure mandates, capital raising, enhanced corporate governance, financial intermediary regulation, SEC enforcement powers, and private litigation. *See* sources cited *supra* note 4.

[6] The Securities and Exchange Commission was created pursuant to the Securities Exchange Act of 1934. *See* § 4 of the Securities Exchange Act, 15 U.S.C. § 78(d).

[7] Examples include the SEC's promulgation of the shareholder proposal rule in 1942, the issuance of the seminal *Cady, Roberts* decision in 1961 prohibiting insider trading under federal law, and the undertaking of its "Volunteer Program" (under the leadership of SEC Enforcement Director Stanley Sporkin) whereby corporations self-reported illicit payments which culminated with the enactment of the Foreign Corrupt Practices Act. *See Report of the Securities and Exchange Commission on Questionable and Illegal Corporate Payments and Practices*, Submitted to the Committee on Banking, Housing and Urban Affairs, U.S. Senate (May 1976) (SEC Report to U.S. Senate regarding self-reporting illicit payment practices by publicly-held companies); *SEC 50 Year Publication*, *supra* note 3 (stating that pursuant to this Volunteer Program "some of the world's largest corporations had admitted to questionable payments of some form"); In re Cady, Roberts & Company, 40 S.E.C. 907 (1961) (federalizing illegal insider trading based on "access" approach); Securities Exchange Act Release No. 3347 (1942) (adopting the SEC shareholder proposal rule now contained in SEC Rule 14a-8, 17 C.F.R. § 240.14a-8).

[8] American Law Institute, *Federal Securities Code* (1978) (published by the ALI in 1980).

[9] *See id.* at 5. The Assistant Reporter was Professor Victor Brudney. The consultants were Mr. Milton H. Cohen, Professor Vern Countryman, Mr. Theodore H. Focht, Mr. Ray Garrett, Jr. (who formerly served as Chairman of the SEC), Mr. L.C.B. Gower, Mr. Alton B. Harris, Mr. David S. Henkel, Mr. Charles Jackson, Jr., Professor Homer Kripke, Mr. Milton P. Kroll, Professor Robert H. Mundheim, and Professor David S. Ruder (who subsequently served as SEC Chairman).

its efficiency."[10] To date, the ALI Code has not been enacted by Congress, and its prospects are dim.[11] Nonetheless, certain aspects of the Code, such as the promulgation of uniform disclosure requirements, incorporation by reference of information from Exchange Act periodic reports into Securities Act registration statements, the concept of shelf registration, and the expansion of the intrastate offering exemption have been implemented pursuant to SEC directive.[12] Hence, although a number of the Code's principles have been adopted, the fact remains that the project was a massive undertaking that did not attain its ultimate purpose—namely, the federal codification of a coherent and simplified statutory framework that enhances investor protection without imposing undue impediments to capital formation and honest business.[13]

Thus, the framework of securities regulation that prevails today in the United States is one that is comprised of piecemeal federal legislation, judicial decisions, SEC action, state "blue sky" activity, and self-regulatory organization oversight.[14] As a consequence, the presence of consistent and logical regulation all too often is absent. With frequency, in both transactional and litigation settings, mandates apply that are erratic and antithetical to sound public policy. The principal objective of this book is to identify key deficiencies, address their failings, provide recommendations for rectifying these shortcomings, and proffer a thorough analysis for remediation in an effort to prescribe a consistent and sound public policy framework.

---

[10] *Id.* at xix. An objective also was to do so "with the least possible interference to honest business." *Id.*, *quoting*, President Franklin D. Roosevelt, S. Rep. No. 47, at 607, and H.R. Rep. No. 85, at 1–2, 73d Cong., 1st Sess. (1933).

[11] Indeed, in the first edition of my securities regulation textbook, the following is stated: "At this juncture, enactment of the ALI Code appears unlikely." Marc I. Steinberg, *Securities Regulation* 7 (1986). Today, this observation remains accurate.

[12] *See, e.g.*, SEC Regulation S-K, 17 C.F.R. § 229.10 *et seq.* (regulation setting forth uniform requirements for non-financial statement disclosures for such SEC filings as Securities Act registration statements and Exchange Act periodic reports); Securities Act Release No. 6383 (1982) (integrating the disclosure systems of the Securities Act and the Exchange Act); Securities Act Release No. 6499 (1983) (adoption of "shelf" registration rule). The ALI Code has similar (though not identical) provisions. *See, e.g.*, ALI Federal Securities Code, *supra* note 8, §§ 402, 505, 602.

[13] For commentary on the ALI Federal Securities Code, *see, e.g.*, Securities and Exchange Commission, *Statement Concerning Codification of the Federal Securities Laws*, Securities Act Release No. 6242 (1980); Symposium, *The Federal Securities Code*, 33 U. Miami L. Rev. No. 5 (1979); Symposium, *The American Law Institute's Proposed Federal Securities Code*, 30 Vand. L. Rev. 311 (1977) (Part 1); 32 Vand. L. Rev. 455 (1979) (Part 2); Louis Loss, *The American Law Institute's Federal Securities Code Project*, 26 Bus. Law. 555 (1970); Louis Lowenfels, *The Case Against the Proposed Federal Securities Code*, 65 Va. L. Rev. 615 (1979); Carl Schneider, *Reform of the Federal Securities Laws*, 115 U. Pa. L. Rev. 1023 (1967).

[14] *See generally* Marc I. Steinberg, *Securities Regulation* (7th ed. 2017); Marc I. Steinberg, *Understanding Securities Law* (7th ed. 2018).

In this regard, this book does not seek to address the entire subject matter of securities regulation.[15] To do so would constitute a far more ambitious undertaking than this endeavor. This book's goal is to identify important problematic aspects of the securities laws, focusing principally on the Securities Act of 1933 and the Securities Exchange Act of 1934 (and, of course, subsequent congressional legislation and SEC pronouncements impacting these Acts). The targeted analysis provided herein hopefully will serve as a useful resource for implementing an improved securities regulation framework in this country.[16]

II. The Preeminence of the U.S. Securities Law Framework

This book focuses on rethinking securities law in the United States, with principal focus on the Securities Act of 1933 and the Securities Exchange Act of 1934—as amended through the decades.[17] There are many deficiencies and inconsistencies in the current regimen. Nonetheless, the U.S. securities law framework remains preeminent in the domestic and global marketplaces. The following discussion succinctly identifies many of the characteristics that facilitate the effectuation of this achievement.

If soundly implemented, the regulatory framework is impressive, having a sophisticated and comprehensive structure. This structure is comprised of at least the following components: *First*, the presence of an all-encompassing statutory framework—as exemplified by the Securities Act of 1933 and the Securities Exchange Act of 1934—that addresses the multi-faceted aspects of securities regulation. *Second*, the role of an active government regulator, the SEC—that is charged with overseeing the securities markets, financial intermediaries, subject issuer conduct (usually focused on disclosure practices), key actors integral to this regimen (such as officers, directors, and control persons), other participants in the process (such as proxy advisory

[15] For the most comprehensive treatise covering securities regulation, *see* Louis Loss, Joel Seligman, and Troy Paredes, *Securities Regulation* (6th ed. 2020). With respect to state securities regulation, the seminal treatise is Joseph C. Long, Michael J. Kaufman, and John M. Wunderlich, *Blue Sky Law* (2020). For two other comprehensive works, *see* Thomas Lee Hazen, *Treatise on the Law of Securities Regulation* (7th ed. 2019); Louis Loss, Joel Seligman, and Troy Paredes, *Fundamentals of Securities Regulation* (7th ed. 2019).

[16] In this regard, the reader may be interested in another recent book with Oxford University Press: Marc I. Steinberg, *The Federalization of Corporate Governance* (2018).

[17] *See* sources cited *supra* notes 1–4.

firms, active investors, and professionals who render services to their clients), and miscreants who engage in illegal conduct. An additional layer is the specter of criminal prosecution that resides with the U.S. Department of Justice. *Third*, the so-called self-regulatory organizations (including the Financial Industry Regulatory Authority, the Public Company Accounting Oversight Board, and the Municipal Securities Rulemaking Board) play an instrumental role in seeking to promote the integrity of the financial markets (such as through enunciating standards of conduct for broker-dealers, accounting firms, and their associated persons). *Fourth*, the state securities laws (also called "blue sky" laws)—through their state securities commissions—provide an important level of protection, particularly with respect to policing sharp practices perpetrated by smaller publicly-traded and privately-held enterprises, their insiders, and market professionals. And, *fifth*, the presence of a vibrant private remedial framework whereby aggrieved investors can seek to recoup their financial losses allegedly caused by defendant misconduct. This multi-faceted regulatory framework, when effectively implemented, serves the U.S. securities markets and the investing public in an admirable manner.[18]

Another significant attribute of this framework is its flexibility to adapt in order to fulfill the objectives of securities regulation. One poignant example is the definition of the term "security."[19] Although criticism has been levied on determinations made regarding the appropriate scope of what constitutes a security,[20] overall, the analysis used is laudable. For example, stock having the typical attributes of that instrument will always be within the scope of the federal securities laws—thereby enhancing commercial

---

[18] For discussion, *see, e.g.*, Marc I. Steinberg, *Securities Regulation: Liabilities and Remedies* (2020); Marc I. Steinberg and Ralph C. Ferrara, *Securities Practice: Federal and State Enforcement* (2d ed. 2001 and annual supp.); treatises cited *supra* note 15.

[19] The term "security" is defined in Section 2(a)(1) of the Securities Act and Section 3(a)(10) of the Exchange Act. *See* 15 U.S.C. § 77b(a)(1), § 78c(a)(10). The term includes a broad range of instruments, including notes, bonds, stock, investment contracts, and "in general, any instrument commonly known as a 'security.'" Significantly, the definition is prefaced with the language "unless the context otherwise requires"—signifying that economic reality controls over the name given to an instrument. *See, e.g.*, *United Housing Foundation, Inc. v. Forman*, 421 U.S. 837 (1975) (holding stock in a cooperative housing project not stock under the federal securities laws as the instrument did not bear the necessary characteristics).

[20] For example, criticizing the U.S. Supreme Court's decision in *Marine Bank v. Weaver*, 455 U.S. 551 (1982), Harold S. Bloomenthal—a premier securities law expert—opined: "The Court's rationale for its holding, if an answer to a law examination including the identical question, would probably have been graded F by 95% of the securities regulation professors in the United States." Harold S. Bloomenthal, *1982 Securities Law Handbook* xlvii (1982). *See* Marc I. Steinberg and William E. Kaulbach, *The Supreme Court and the Definition of "Security": The "Context" Clause, "Investment Contract" Analysis, and Their Ramifications*, 49 Vand. L. Rev. 489 (1987).

certainty.[21] Although greater uncertainty exists with respect to the status of notes, generally notes that are widely offered or sold for investment purposes are deemed securities.[22] Last, with respect to unincorporated enterprises (such as limited liability companies,[23] limited partnerships,[24] and perhaps even general partnerships[25]), the investment contract test has been applied to bring many of these ventures within the ambit of the securities laws.[26] Indeed, for over seventy-five years, this test has been flexibly interpreted to

---

[21] *Gould v. Ruefenacht*, 471 U.S. 701 (1985); *Landreth Timber Co. v. Landreth*, 471 U.S. 681 (1985). The attributes typically associated with common stock are "(i) the right to receive dividends contingent upon an apportionment of profits; (ii) negotiability; (iii) the ability to be pledged or hypothecated; (iv) the conferring of voting rights in proportion to the number of shares owned; and (v) the capacity to appreciate in value." *Landreth*, 471 U.S. at 686.

[22] *See Reves v. Ernst & Young*, 494 U.S. 56 (1990) (adopting the "family resemblance" test in determining whether a note is a security: assessing the motivations that would persuade a reasonable purchaser and seller to engage in the transaction, the instrument's plan of distribution, the reasonable expectations of the investing public, and whether a risk reducing factor exists thereby lessening the risk of loss). For further discussion, *see* Marc I. Steinberg, *Notes as Securities: Reves and Its Implications*, 51 Ohio St. L.J. 675 (1990).

[23] *Cf. United States v. Leonard*, 529 F.3d 83 (2d Cir. 2008) (finding that LLC interests were securities as members in fact were passive investors), *with Avenue Capital Management II, L.P. v. Schaden*, 843 F.3d 876 (10th Cir. 2016) (because LLC members exercised meaningful efforts, the interests were not securities).

[24] Because limited partners ordinarily do not exercise meaningful efforts, interests in limited partnerships typically are deemed securities pursuant to the investment contract test. *See, e.g., Liberty Property Trust v. Republic Properties Corp.*, 577 F.3d 335 (D.C. Cir. 2009). On the other hand, no securities coverage exists when the limited partners have pervasive control over the investment. *See Steinhardt Group, Inc. v. Citicorp*, 126 F.3d 144 (3d Cir. 1997).

[25] Interests in general partnerships ordinarily are not securities because general partners as co-owners exercise meaningful control. *See, e.g., Hirsch v. du Pont*, 396 F. Supp. 1214 (S.D.N.Y. 1975), *aff'd*, 553 F.2d 750 (2d Cir. 1977). On the other hand, when the general partnership agreement allocates control as if the venture were a limited partnership or where a general partner otherwise, in practicality, cannot exercise control over the investment, a number of courts hold that the interests are securities. *See, e.g., Williamson v. Tucker*, 645 F.2d 404 (5th Cir. 1981). Moreover, interests in limited liability partnerships (LLPs) may well be securities because, due to the partners' limited liability, there is less incentive for passive partners to monitor their investments. *See, e.g., Securities and Exchange Commission v. Merchant Capital*, 483 F.3d 747 (11th Cir. 2007). *See generally* Elaine Welle, *When Are Limited Liability Partnership Interests Securities?*, 27 J. Corp. L. 63 (2001).

[26] *See Securities and Exchange Commission v. W.J. Howey Co.*, 328 U.S. 293 (1946) (holding that an investment contract exists if there is an investment of money in a common enterprise with the expectation of profits to be derived solely from the efforts of others). Through the years, the *Howey* test has been refined. For example, an investment contract may be found even if the investors exert some efforts so long as the essential entrepreneurial or managerial efforts are performed by others. *See, e.g., Securities and Exchange Commission v. Glenn W. Turner Enterprises, Inc.*, 474 F.2d 476, 482 (9th Cir. 1973). In addition, the Supreme Court subsequently expanded the meaning of "profit" under the *Howey* test. *See Securities and Exchange Commission v. Edwards*, 540 U.S. 389 (2004) (defining profit for investment contract analysis to encompass the receipt of periodic payments).

In addition, a number of states have adopted a more expansive test—the risk capital test—to ascertain whether an investment contract exists. *See, e.g., Silver Hills Country Club v. Sobieski*, 361 P.2d 906, 908 (Cal. 1961) (stating that the defendants "are soliciting the risk capital with which to develop a business for profit [and that an investor] risks his capital along with other purchasers"); *State Commissioner of Securities v. Hawaii Market Center, Inc.*, 485 P.2d 105 (Haw. 1971) (adopting a broad risk capital test, relying on Ronald Coffey, *The Economic Realities of a "Security": Is There a More Meaningful Formula?*, 18 Case. W. Res. L. Rev. 367 (1967)).

encompass interests in a broad spectrum of investments, including, for example, citrus groves,[27] condominiums,[28] viatical settlements,[29] and, more recently, virtual currencies.[30] Thus, the status of an instrument being deemed a security has witnessed a flexible approach coupled with the objective of enhancing both investor protection and commercial certainty. As an overall characterization, the approach that has evolved, although subject to criticism at times,[31] is successful.[32]

Accordingly, the U.S. securities framework is impressive in many ways and merits kudos. Taking into account the five components set forth earlier,[33] there is much to be said for the belief that the U.S. regimen is premier. Nonetheless, serious lapses occur with regularity—to which the scandals during the past two decades attest.[34] Unacceptable gaps persist in what ought to be regulated—but is not.[35] And the lack of zeal by the government to pursue enforcement actions against "reputable" persons in situations involving catastrophic investor loss has been a subject of popular

[27] *See, e.g., Securities and Exchange Commission v. W.J. Howey Co.*, 328 U.S. 293 (1946). In *Howey*, the sale of citrus groves coupled with a service contract came within federal securities law coverage. The aggregation approach adopted by the *Howey* Court has been applied in other settings, such as the sale of condominium units coupled with a rental pool arrangement. *See infra* note 28.

[28] *See, e.g., Hocking v. Dubois*, 885 F.2d 1449 (9th Cir. 1989) (en banc); Securities Act Release No. 5347 (1973). *But see Salameh v. Tarsadia Hotel*, 726 F.3d 1124 (9th Cir. 2013) (concluding that investors retained sufficient control, thereby precluding securities law coverage with respect to sales of condominiums coupled with rental service agreements).

[29] *See, e.g., Securities and Exchange Commission v. Mutual Benefits Corp.*, 408 F.3d 737 (11th Cir. 2005) (holding fractional interests in viatical settlements are investment contracts and, hence, securities). *But see Securities and Exchange Commission v. Life Partners, Inc.*, 87 F.3d 536 (D.C. Cir. 1996) (concluding that "the combination of [the promoter's] pre-purchase services . . . and its largely ministerial post-purchase services is not enough to satisfy the third requirement in *Howey* [that] the investors' profits were generated predominantly from the efforts of others").

[30] *See, e.g.*, Securities Exchange Act Release No. 81207 (2017) (stating that the federal securities laws apply "regardless whether those securities are purchased using U.S. dollars or virtual currencies"); Hayden Baker, *Tales from the Crypt: The Securities Law Implications of Initial Coin Offerings and a Framework for a Compliant ICO*, 47 Sec. Reg. L.J. 309 (2018).

[31] *See* sources cited *supra* note 20.

[32] The flexible definition of security, focusing on the economic realities, has enabled courts and the SEC to invoke securities law coverage for a wide variety of ventures whereby promoters seek to raise funds from passive investors. *See, e.g., Continental Marketing Corp. v. Securities and Exchange Commission*, 387 F.2d 466 (10th Cir. 1967) (holding that sales of live beavers coupled with service arrangements were investment contracts and, hence, securities); sources cited *supra* notes 21–30 and accompanying text.

[33] *See supra* note 18 and accompanying text.

[34] These debacles brought about the passage of two instrumental Acts—the Sarbanes-Oxley Act of 2002 and the Dodd-Frank Wall Street Reform and Consumer Protection Act of 2010. *See supra* note 4. *See also* Barney Frank, *What We Did Last Crisis*, 50 Loy. U. Chi. L.J. 523 (2019).

[35] These gaps are discussed later in this book. For example, huge gaps exist with respect to insider trading regulation. The fiduciary duty rationale adopted by the U.S. Supreme Court stands apart from other developed markets and has given rise to disparate and unpredictable enforcement. *See generally* Marc I. Steinberg, *Securities and Exchange Commission v. Cuban—A Trial of Insider Trading* (2019).

commentary.[36] This book now focuses on rethinking the securities laws with the objective of facilitating the effectuation of necessary changes in a manner that promotes investor protection, honest business practices, and the integrity of the U.S. securities markets.[37]

III. The Need for Rethinking the Securities Laws

While the U.S. securities law framework is laudable, significant pitfalls prevail. Key components must be revised to ameliorate the deficiencies that exist. In a preliminary manner, this section of the chapter highlights several of the problematic areas that should be revisited and remedied.

The following chapter (Chapter 2) explores a crucial aspect of securities regulation—the disclosure regimen of the federal securities laws. The mandatory disclosure framework (and its abandonment by the SEC in certain settings) is addressed in the context of offerings under the Securities Act as well as pursuant to the periodic and current reporting requirements of the Securities Exchange Act. Analysis focuses on the type of information required to be disclosed, the contexts in which such disclosures are made, the effectiveness of the SEC's uniform disclosure framework, and the rationales underlying the integrated disclosure system.[38] When deemed useful, comparisons will be made with disclosure mandates adhered to by other developed trading markets (such as the European Union).[39]

Chapter 3 addresses exemptions from Securities Act registration—with respect to both non-registered offerings and resales of securities. The current exemptive framework is premised on such problematic concepts as "affiliate" status, distinguishing a "distribution" from a "transaction," "underwriter status," and "accredited investor" qualification.[40] The chapter

[36] For example, the movie *The Big Short* (2015) portrays this situation. *See* Michael Lewis, *The Big Short* (2010).

[37] *See* sources cited *supra* notes 3, 4.

[38] I have addressed these concepts from a general standpoint throughout my career. *See, e.g.*, Marc I. Steinberg, *Corporate Internal Affairs—A Corporate and Securities Law Perspective* (1983); Marc I. Steinberg, *Securities Regulation* (1986 and 7th ed. 2017); *Understanding Securities Law* (1989 and 7th ed. 2018).

[39] Although other developed securities markets implement similar standards as those that prevail in the U.S. securities framework, they opt in some areas for significantly different standards that are worthy of serious consideration. *See generally* Marc I. Steinberg, *International Securities Law—A Contemporary and Comparative Analysis* (1999).

[40] This point is exemplified by the American Law Institute's treatment of such terms as "affiliate," "control," and "distribution." *See* ALI Federal Securities Code, *supra* note 8, at § 202(3), (29), (41).

analyzes Congress's and the SEC's determinations, identifying deficiencies and proposing solutions that hopefully accommodate the interests of investors as well as facilitate capital formation.[41]

Chapter 4 focuses on the SEC's registration process. During the last three decades, the SEC has sought to "modernize" that Act's stringent requirements.[42] At times, Congress itself has enacted legislation in efforts to enhance capital raising by subject issuers.[43] Given the challenges presented, Congress and the SEC generally have acted in a manner not inconsistent with investor protection. Nonetheless, critical gaps prevail that should be remedied. Moreover, the contours of the due diligence defense provided by Section 11 of the Securities Act[44] remains a major concern for certain actors, particularly outside directors and underwriters. This chapter seeks to provide resolutions to these problematic subjects.

Chapter 5 explores the expansive subject of corporate governance within the framework of the federal securities laws. Indeed, this subject is the focus of my recently published book with Oxford University Press, *The Federalization of Corporate Governance*.[45] Issues addressed in this chapter include the haphazard way that Congress and the SEC have federalized certain aspects of corporate governance—while other equally if not more troubling aspects are left untouched. While this federalization process generally has been beneficial for effectuating law compliance and enhancing investor protection, significant gaps remain.[46] This chapter provides recommendations with respect to harmonizing current federal

[41] A theme of this book is that, without adequate justification, Congress and the SEC too frequently seek to enhance capital raising at the expense of investor protection. The financial debacles that have occurred during the past twenty-five years may be traced, at least in part, to such lax regulation.

[42] *See, e.g.*, Securities Act Release No. 8591 (2005) (adopting numerous rules allowing conduct that otherwise would violate § 5 of the Securities Act, including Rule 163 permitting well-known seasoned issuers to make offers to sell prior to the filing of a subject registration statement); Securities Act Release No. 10699 (2019) (adopting Rule 163B permitting any issuer (or any person acting on its behalf so authorized) to engage in written and oral communications to specified institutional investors prior to the filing of its registration statement—such conduct otherwise would violate § 5 of the Securities Act).

[43] *See, e.g.*, Jumpstart Our Business Startups Act of 2012 (JOBS Act), *supra* note 4 (facilitating capital raising by relatively smaller enterprises by relaxing a number of obstacles and creating a new type of registrant—the emerging growth company).

[44] 15 U.S.C. § 77k (providing, *inter alia*, an express private right of action for those persons who purchased a security pursuant to a Securities Act registration statement that contained a material misrepresentation or half-truth against certain specified parties and providing such parties (except for the issuer) with a due diligence defense to avert liability).

[45] *See* Steinberg, *supra* note 16.

[46] *See id.* at 264–84 (addressing a number of these gaps and recommending solutions).

corporate governance mandates with suggested measures set forth in that chapter.

Chapter 6 examines private litigation under the securities laws. The litigation structure contained in the federal Securities Acts was adopted in a different era and is not suitable for the modern securities markets. Seeking to address perceived faults, Congress has legislated on an episodic basis but has failed to provide a coherent and fair liability framework.[47] The consequence is that the private securities litigation regimen is in need of clarification, greater uniformity, and better assessment of public policy implications. This chapter makes recommendations seeking to effectuate an improved framework—focusing on corporate fiduciaries, financial intermediaries, and gatekeepers.

Chapter 7 focuses on the key problematic area of insider trading, which is characterized by SEC regulatory activism, judicial ambiguity, and disparate treatment of similarly-situated individuals.[48] To date, Congress has declined to enact a statute specifically prohibiting insider trading.[49] The result is the application of federal law premised on state law concepts of fraud[50] and zealous SEC rulemaking that seeks effectively to enforce what the Commission views as improper insider trading.[51] A better approach, as the discussion in the chapter proposes, is that Congress enact an insider trading framework that compares favorably to standards adopted by other developed securities markets.[52]

Chapter 8 addresses mergers and acquisitions (M&A) under the federal securities laws. At the time of the passage of the federal Securities Acts in 1933 and 1934, the subject of mergers and acquisitions was not given prominence. Indeed, it was not until the going-private and tender

---

[47] Examples of such piecemeal legislation include the Private Securities Litigation Reform Act of 1995 (PSLRA), the Securities Litigation Uniform Standards Act of 1998 (SLUSA), and the Sarbanes-Oxley Act of 2002. *See supra* note 4 for citations to these Acts.

[48] For a treatise coauthored by the author on this subject, *see* Marc I. Steinberg and William K.S. Wang, *Insider Trading* (3d ed. 2010).

[49] Recently, the U.S. House of Representatives passed a bill addressing insider trading. *See* Insider Trading Prohibition Act, H.R. 2534, 116th Cong., 1st Sess. (2019); H.R. Report No. 116-219, Committee on Financial Services (2019). This bill is discussed in Chapter 7 herein.

[50] *See, e.g., United States v. O'Hagan*, 521 U.S. 642 (1997); *Dirks v. Securities and Exchange Commission*, 463 U.S. 646 (1983); *Chiarella v. United States*, 445 U.S. 222 (1980).

[51] Examples include the SEC's adoption of Rule 10b5-2, 17 C.F.R. § 240.10b5-2 (expanding the misappropriation theory to encompass confidentiality agreements even absent a preexisting relationship of trust and confidence) and Rule 14e-3, 17 C.F.R. § 240.14e-3 (applying a parity of information approach to illegal insider trading in the tender offer context).

[52] The enactment of a comprehensive insider trading statutory framework would bring the United States in line with other developed securities markets that have adopted this approach.

offer craze of the 1960s–1980s that Congress and the SEC focused on these transactions.[53] Today, federal statutes and SEC rules cover M&A transactions of publicly-held enterprises.[54] Yet, although Congress elected to federalize certain aspects of M&A regulation, it has declined to enact a federal statute encompassing substantive standards in this context. The discussion in this chapter sets forth the contours of a proposed approach.

Chapter 9 focuses on government enforcement. The SEC and the U.S. Department of Justice have far-reaching authority to enforce the federal securities laws—dating from the passage of the Securities Acts and amendments to these Acts through the decades.[55] Nonetheless, all too frequently, the government faces strong criticism for its failure to detect major frauds[56] and its neglect to pursue high-level executives with vigor.[57] The chapter addresses these failures and provides recommendations to ameliorate these shortcomings.

Chapter 10 summarizes my analysis and recommendations in regard to "rethinking" the securities laws. It explores how federal law should be restricted or expanded, made more uniform, and treat like actors in a similar manner. In doing so, the chapter focuses as well on policy perspectives from the standpoint of law compliance, corporate governance, and investor protection—while not unduly impeding capital formation and customary business practices.

---

[53] The key federal legislation, the William Act, was enacted in 1968 to address the processes and disclosures in the going-private and tender offer settings. *See supra* note 4.

[54] The SEC has adopted several rules addressing these transactions. *See, e.g.*, SEC Regulation M-A, 17 C.F.R. § 229.1000 *et seq.* (setting forth disclosure requirements with respect to cash merger, going-private, and tender offer transactions).

[55] The author has coauthored a treatise on securities enforcement practice. *See* Steinberg and Ferrara, *supra* note 18.

[56] *See, e.g.*, Eamonn Fingleton, *Madoff and the SEC: The Story You Don't Know*, Forbes, June 4, 2013, available at https://www.forbes.com/sites/eamonnfingleton/2013/06/04/heres-one-reason-why-east-asians-think-america-is-a-basket-case/#70a82f1829a7 (stating that "the SEC emerges from the [Madoff] affair not so much as incompetent, as many have charitably assumed, but corrupt").

[57] As then Commissioner Luis Aguilar pointed out, SEC enforcement actions in this context "are so infrequent that the agency does not currently maintain statistics on cases that are brought against directors." Luis A. Aguilar, *Remarks at the 12th Annual Boardroom Summit and Peer Exchange: The Important Work of Boards of Directors* (Oct. 14, 2015), available at https://www.sec.gov/news/speech/important-work-of-boards-of-directors.html. As another example, even though used with regularity in private federal class action lawsuits, the SEC in the aftermath of the financial crisis refused to invoke the control person provision in its enforcement actions seeking to hold chief executive officers, chief financial officers, audit committee chairs, and board of director chairs liable. *See* Steinberg, *supra* note 16, at 282–84; Marc I. Steinberg and Forrest C. Roberts, *Laxity at the Gates: The SEC's Neglect to Enforce Control Person Liability*, 11 U. Va. L. & Bus. Rev. 201 (2017).

IV. Conclusion

Hopefully, the contents of this book will generate meaningful dialogue focusing on the many ways in which the U.S. securities laws and regulatory oversight can be improved. This country may still have the preeminent securities markets in the world. To maintain that status, significant substantive changes should be made. Such changes are needed to enhance the integrity of the U.S. securities markets and the protection of investors. If not, it is only a matter of time before a precipitous bear market ensues, accompanied by massive financial frauds that will redound in financial calamity—reverberating globally.

2

The Disclosure Regimen of the Federal Securities Laws

I. Introduction

This chapter focuses on the disclosure regimen of the federal securities laws by exploring the benefits as well as drawbacks of the current framework and recommending measures that should be implemented to enhance its efficacy. Subjects addressed include the securities laws' focus on adequate disclosure rather than substantive fairness, the concept of materiality, the mandatory disclosure framework, the integrated disclosure system, the Securities and Exchange Commission's (SEC's) dismantling of the mandatory disclosure framework in certain contexts, application of the disclosure mandates in different situational settings, and the disclosure obligations placed upon subject companies by the national stock exchanges.

From a general perspective, Congress and the SEC have effectively implemented a comprehensive and impressive disclosure framework. Nonetheless, significant gaps and drawbacks exist that should be remedied. The ensuing discussion seeks to provide adaptable solutions that should meaningfully improve the disclosure regimen, thereby enhancing both market efficiency and investor protection.

II. Focus on Disclosure—Not Substantive Fairness

Unlike state corporation law, which traditionally has focused on the fairness of transactions[1] as well as numerous state securities laws that

[1] *See, e.g.*, *Santa Fe Industries, Inc. v. Green*, 430 U.S. 462, 477–79 (1977) (stating that the fairness of a transaction is a matter of state company law and only a tangential concern of the federal securities laws); *Cort v. Ash*, 422 U.S. 66, 84 (1975) ("Corporations are creatures of state law, and investors commit their funds to corporate directors on the understanding that, except where federal

Rethinking Securities Law. Marc I. Steinberg, Oxford University Press. © Marc I. Steinberg 2021.
DOI: 10.1093/oso/9780197583142.003.0002

engage in merit regulation of securities offerings,[2] the federal securities laws are premised on disclosure concepts.[3] The objective is to provide investors and the securities markets with accurate disclosure of material information so that informed decisions can be made.[4] At least in theory, fairness normally is of only tangential concern under the federal securities laws.[5]

A. Rejection of a Federal Fairness Approach

The seminal U.S. Supreme Court decision of *Santa Fe Industries*[6] illustrates the disclosure focus of the federal securities laws. There, in a cash-out

---

law expressly requires certain responsibilities of directors with respect to stockholders, state law will govern the internal affairs of the corporation.").

[2] Generally, pursuant to merit regulation, the state securities administrator may prevent a subject offering from going forward or impose conditions on the offering (such as requiring the escrow of insider proceeds for a specified period of time or until certain contingencies are met) on the basis that such offering is not "fair, just and equitable." Note that the state securities laws also focus on disclosure. *See* Joseph C. Long, Michael J. Kaufman, and John M. Wunderlich, *Blue Sky Law* § 1.04 (2020); Symposium, *Blue Sky Anniversary Edition*, 50 Washburn L.J. No. 3 (2011) (commemorating the 100th anniversary of the Kansas securities laws); American Bar Association, Section of Corporation, Banking and Business Law, *Report on State Regulation of Securities Offerings*, 41 Bus. Law. 785 (1986); Richard B. Tyler, *More About Blue Sky*, 39 Wash. & Lee L. Rev. 899 (1982). Note, however, that state merit regulation has limited reach: If the subject securities to be offered are or will be traded on a national securities exchange, such as the New York Stock Exchange, federal preemption prohibits the application of state registration requirements. *See* § 18(b)(1) of the Securities Act, 15 U.S.C. § 77r(b)(1).

[3] *See Ernst & Ernst v. Hochfelder*, 425 U.S. 185, 195 (1976) (stating that the Securities Act of 1933 "was designed to provide investors with full disclosure of material information concerning public offerings of securities" and that the Securities Exchange Act of 1934 "was intended principally to protect against manipulation of stock prices . . . and to impose regular reporting requirements on companies whose stock is listed on national securities exchanges"). *Accord, Securities and Exchange Commission v. Zandford*, 535 U.S. 813, 819 (2002) (stating that "Congress sought to substitute a philosophy of full disclosure for the philosophy of caveat emptor"). Note that the 1964 amendments extended the periodic reporting requirements to enterprises whose securities trade over the counter provided the subject company meets the asset and shareholder thresholds—§ 12(g) of the Securities Exchange Act, 15 U.S.C. § 78l(g). *See* Securities Acts Amendments of 1964, Pub. L. No. 88-467, 78 Stat. 565 (1964).

[4] *See, e.g., Basic, Inc. v. Levinson*, 485 U.S. 224, 230 (1988) (stating that "[t]his Court repeatedly has described the fundamental purpose of the [Securities Exchange] Act as implementing a philosophy of full disclosure"); Securities Act Release No. 10825 (2020) (stating that the SEC's "disclosure requirements, while prescriptive in some respects, are rooted in materiality and facilitate an understanding of a registrant's business, financial condition and prospects through the lens through which management and the board of directors manage and assess the performance of the registrant").

[5] *See Schreiber v. Burlington Northern, Inc.*, 472 U.S. 1, 12 (1985) (focusing on "Congress' consistent emphasis on disclosure"); *Santa Fe Industries, Inc. v. Green*, 430 U.S. 462, 478 (1977) (stating that "once full and fair disclosure has occurred, the fairness of the terms of the transaction is at most a tangential concern of the statute");

[6] *Santa Fe Industries, Inc. v. Green*, 430 U.S. 462 (1977).

merger,[7] the parent company valued the shares of the subsidiary at an allegedly egregiously unfair price.[8] Rather than seek appraisal[9] or initiate an action for breach of fiduciary duty in state court,[10] the plaintiff minority shareholder sought to invoke Section 10(b) of the Securities Exchange Act[11] and SEC Rule 10b-5 promulgated thereunder,[12] asserting that these provisions extend beyond disclosure to encompass substantive fairness.[13] Although prevailing in the U.S. Court of Appeals,[14] this argument met its demise before the Supreme Court.[15] Examining pertinent statutory language, legislative history, and the traditional functions of state corporation law, the Court held that a cause of action under Section 10(b) and Rule 10b-5 must be premised on deficient disclosure rather than substantive fairness.[16]

If the Court had not so decided, the specter would have been raised that, so long as a purchase or sale of a security was involved, the federal securities laws could have been invoked to cover a broad range of alleged corporate fiduciary self-dealing matters.[17] Such a holding would have facilitated the embracement of a federal corporation law to complement the duties of care and loyalty under state company law.[18] Given the perceived laxity with which

---

[7] In a cash-out merger, the minority shareholders receive cash as the consideration for their equity—typically for their shares of common stock—and no longer have any ownership stake in the enterprise. *See, e.g., Weinberger v. UOP, Inc.*, 457 A.2d 701 (1983).

[8] *See* 430 U.S. at 466–67 (offering minority shareholders $150 per share, while the complainant asserted the stock was worth $772 per share).

[9] *See, e.g.*, 8 Del. Code § 262 (stating that shares in an appraisal proceeding shall be determined at "their fair value"). *See generally* Marc I. Steinberg, *Short-Form Mergers in Delaware*, 27 Del. J. Corp. L. 489 (2002).

[10] *See, e.g., Weinberger v. UOP, Inc.*, 457 A.2d 701 (Del. 1983). *See generally* Marc I. Steinberg and Evalyn N. Lindahl, *The New Law of Squeeze-Out Mergers*, 62 Wash. U. L.Q. 351 (1984).

[11] 15 U.S.C. § 78j(b).

[12] 17 C.F.R. § 240.10b-5.

[13] 430 U.S. at 466–67.

[14] *Green v. Santa Fe Industries, Inc.*, 533 F.2d 1283, 1292 (2d Cir. 1976) (stating that "[w]hether full disclosure has been made is not the critical inquiry since it is the merger and the undervaluation which constitutes the fraud [and that] [i]f there is no valid purpose for the merger, then even the most brazen disclosure of that fact to the minority shareholders in no way mitigates the fraudulent conduct"), rev'd, 430 U.S. 462 (1977).

[15] 430 U.S. 462 (1977).

[16] *Id.* at 477–79 (also expressing the view that § 10(b)'s expansion to reach constructive fraud would present a danger of "vexatious litigation").

[17] *See id.* at 478 ("It is difficult to imagine how a court could distinguish, for purposes of Rule 10b-5 fraud, between a majority's stockholder's use of a short-form merger to eliminate the minority at an unfair price and the use of some other device . . . or indeed how a court could distinguish the alleged abuses in these going-private transactions from other types of fiduciary self-dealing involving transactions in securities [thereby] bring[ing] within the Rule a wide variety of corporate conduct traditionally left to state regulation."). *See generally* Ralph C. Ferrara and Marc I. Steinberg, *A Reappraisal of Santa Fe: Rule 10b-5 and the New Federalism*, 129 U. Pa. L. Rev. 263 (1980).

[18] For discussion on the introduction of proposed federal incorporation or proposed federal minimum standards legislation, *see, e.g.*, Marc I. Steinberg, *The Federalization of Corporate Governance* (2018); William L. Cary, *Federalism and Corporate Law: Reflections on Delaware*, 83 Yale L.J. 663

state legislatures and courts assess alleged fiduciary misconduct,[19] the extension of the federal securities laws to reach such behavior may have benefitted investors and served as a deterrent.[20]

B. Episodic Application of Fairness Approach

At times, Congress and the SEC have regulated substantive fiduciary conduct otherwise solely within the confines of state law. Two examples are provided. Traditionally, a loan provided to a publicly-held company's executive officer and duly authorized by the board of directors (or appropriate board committee) was a matter within the purview of state corporate law.[21] Although the terms of the loan may trigger obligatory disclosure under the federal securities laws,[22] the granting and terms of the subject loan were solely a matter of state corporate law with application of the duties of care and loyalty to assess the diligence and fairness of the

(1974); Melvin I. Urofsky, *Proposed Federal Incorporation in the Progressive Era*, 26 Am. J. Legal Hist. 160 (1982); discussion in Chapter 5 herein.

[19] For example, with respect to interested director transactions, state courts and legislatures give great, if not conclusive, discretion for these matters to be approved by disinterested and informed directors without a judicial assessment of fairness. *See, e.g.*, 8 Del. Code § 144; *Marciano v. Nakash*, 535 A.2d 400 (Del. 1987). With the specter of structural bias, the actual presence of detached disinterested director assessment of related party transactions may be questioned. *See* Note, *The Business Judgment Rule in Derivative Suits Against Directors*, 65 Cornell L. Rev. 600 (1980). Likewise, state court scrutiny of executive compensation arrangements may be viewed as unduly lax. *See, e.g.*, *Seinfeld v. Verizon Communications, Inc.*, 909 A.2d 117 (Del. 2006); *In re The Walt Disney Company Derivative Litigation*, 906 A.2d 27 (Del. 2006); Marc I. Steinberg and Matthew D. Bivona, *Disney Goes Goofy: Agency, Delegation, and Corporate Governance*, 60 Hastings L.J. 202 (2008). A third example is the lax treatment with respect to the liability of directors for their failure to adequately adhere to their oversight obligations. *See, e.g.*, *Stone ex rel. AmSouth Bancorporation v. Ritter*, 911 A.2d 362, 370 (Del. 2006) (emphasis supplied) ("articulat[ing] the necessary conditions predicate for director oversight liability: (a) the directors *utterly failed* to implement any reporting or information systems or controls; or (b) having implemented such a system of controls, *conclusively failed* to monitor or oversee its operations thus disabling themselves from being informed of risks or problems requiring their attention"). A last example—the state exculpation statutes that permit a corporation to amend its articles of incorporation to eliminate director monetary liability for breach of the duty of care. *See, e.g.*, 8 Del. Code § 102(b)(7).

[20] A contrary position is that an extension of the federal securities laws in this manner would have exacerbated the presence of vexatious litigation instigated by plaintiffs' lawyers seeking an expeditious settlement of the claims. *See Blue Chip Stamps v. Manor Drug Stores*, 421 U.S. 723, 739–44 (1975) (expressing concern of vexatious litigation as a rationale supporting its decision to recognize the purchaser-seller standing rule in private actions brought for alleged violations of § 10(b) and Rule 10b-5). With respect to further discussion on mergers and acquisitions, *see* Chapter 8 herein.

[21] *See, e.g.*, 8 Del. Code § 143 (authorizing interest-free loans by any corporation to any officer or employee of such corporation or one of its subsidiaries, "whenever, in the judgment of the directors, such loan . . . may reasonably be expected to benefit the corporation").

[22] *See, e.g.*, Item 404 of SEC Regulation S-K, 17 C.F.R. § 229.404.

transaction.[23] The standards applied by the state courts all too often were permissive, signifying that such loans were given minimal scrutiny.[24] In the aftermath of the financial scandals two decades ago, this lack of meaningful review drew the attention of Congress when it was apprised of the millions of dollars of interest-free loans that were granted to corporate insiders of these troubled companies.[25] Responding to these episodes of self-dealing, the Sarbanes-Oxley Act of 2002 generally prohibits any publicly-held company from making a loan to any of its directors or executive officers.[26] This piecemeal federal prohibition of this aspect of fiduciary self-dealing illustrates that Congress in fact may legislate with respect to substantive fairness when the prevailing political winds and public policy call for such a measure.[27]

A second example focuses on the Delaware Supreme Court's opinion in *Unocal*[28] upholding the decision by the target company's board of directors to exclude the hostile bidder from participating in the target's defensive self-tender offer made to its own shareholders.[29] The court ruled that the use of

---

[23] *See, e.g., Aronson v. Lewis*, 473 A.2d 805 (Del. 1984).

[24] *See id.* at 817 (with respect to interest-free loans totaling $225,000 to a shareholder owning 47% of the company's stock, stating "beyond the bare allegations that [the loans] were made, the complaint does not allege facts indicating the wastefulness of such arrangements [and] the mere existence of such loans, given the broad corporate powers conferred by Delaware law, does not even state a claim").

[25] *See* Douglas M. Branson et al., *Business Enterprises: Legal Structures, Governance, and Policy* 636 (4th ed. 2020) (commenting that, with respect to Enron, "CEO Kenneth Lay did not even take out bank loans in order to pay the strike price on options he exercised [as] [w]ags called the Enron treasury 'Ken Lay's ATM' [and, as for] WorldCom, mostly to meet margin calls in a rapidly falling market, WorldCom lent CEO Bernard Ebbers $405 million of corporate funds").

[26] Section 402 of the Sarbanes-Oxley Act, *adding*, § 13(k) of the Securities Exchange Act, 15 U.S.C. § 78m(k). To a limited extent, Section 402 excludes certain loans from its ban. Stated generally, specified types of loans to corporate directors and executive officers are allowed if they are granted pursuant to the subject company's ordinary course of business and are extended to the recipient-fiduciary on the same terms as loans made to the general public. 15 U.S.C. § 78m(k)(2); Robert E. Buckholz, Jr., Marc R. Trevino, and Glen T. Schleyer, *Public Company Deskbook: Complying with Federal Governance & Disclosure Requirements* § 5:5 (3d ed. 2018).

[27] Although not directly focusing on substantive fairness, congressional authorization for the SEC to procure officer and director bar orders provides another example of federal corporate governance impacting the internal affairs doctrine under state law. *See* §§ 8A, 20(e) of the Securities Act, §§ 21(d)(2), 22C of the Securities Exchange Act. These provisions authorize the Commission to seek to bar an individual from serving as a director or officer of any publicly-held enterprise if such individual is deemed "unfit" and has engaged in fraudulent conduct under the federal securities laws. *See* discussion in Chapter 5 herein. *See generally* Marc I. Steinberg and Ralph C. Ferrara, *Securities Practice: Federal and State Enforcement* §§ 6:1–6:19 (2d ed. 2001 & ann. supp.).

[28] *Unocal Corp. v. Mesa Petroleum Co.*, 493 A.2d 946 (Del. 1985).

[29] *Id.* at 958 (concluding that "there was directorial power to oppose the Mesa tender offer and to undertake a selective stock exchange made in good faith and upon a reasonable investigation pursuant to a clear duty to protect the corporate enterprise").

such an exclusionary tender offer for the purpose of fending off the overtures of a known "greenmailer"[30] was in compliance with the directors' fiduciary duties.[31] Disagreeing with the court's approbation of this substantive defensive tactic, the SEC responded by promulgating rules requiring that both issuer and third-party tender offers must be open to all shareholders.[32] The Commission's determination in effect "overruled" the Delaware Supreme Court's holding. Hence, although the legitimacy of tender offer maneuvers is within the province of state law,[33] this situation illustrates that occasionally the SEC will venture into this realm when it believes it has the statutory authority to do so and such activism is consistent with its perception of public policy.[34]

C. Enhancing Fairness through the Guise of Disclosure

Similarly, at times, the SEC has mandated disclosure, seeking to impact substantive conduct. A clear example is the Commission's adoption of Rule 13e-3[35] following the U.S. Supreme Court's decision in *Santa Fe* discussed

---

[30] *Id.* at 956 (characterizing the corporate raider in the case at bar as having "a national reputation as a 'greenmailer'"). Generally, "greenmail" may be defined as "[t]he purchase of a substantial block of the subject company's securities by a (potentially) unfriendly suitor with the primary purpose of inducing the subject company to repurchase the block at a premium over the amount paid by the potential suitor." Marc I. Steinberg, *Understanding Securities Law* 486 (7th ed. 2018). *See* discussion in Chapter 8 herein.

[31] *See* 493 A.2d at 958 (stating that "there was directorial power to oppose the Mesa tender offer and to undertake a selective stock exchange made in good faith and upon a reasonable investigation pursuant to a clear duty to protect the corporate enterprise [and that] the selective stock repurchase plan chosen by Unocal was reasonable in relation to the threat that the board rationally and reasonably believed was posed by Mesa's inadequate and coercive two-tier tender offer").

[32] Rules 13e-4 (issuer tender offer), 14d-10 (third-party tender offers), 17 C.F.R. §§ 240.13e-4, 14d-10. These rules also provide that the best price paid to a tendering shareholder must be paid to any other tendering shareholder. For example, Rule 13e-4(f)(8) provides: "No issuer or affiliate shall make a tender offer unless: (i) The tender offer is open to all security holders of the class of securities subject to the tender offer; and (ii) The consideration paid to any security holder for securities tendered in the tender offer is the highest consideration paid to any other security holder for securities tendered in the tender offer."

[33] *See, e.g., Schreiber v. Burlington Northern, Inc.*, 472 U.S. 1 (1985).

[34] As the SEC reasoned when adopting the all holders and best price rules:

> [M]any commenters have asserted that the Commission's authority under this provision [namely, § 13(e) of the Securities Exchange Act] is limited to regulating disclosure. It is clear, however, that in adopting the Williams Act, Congress granted to the Commission broad rulemaking authority in Section 13(e) to determine the most appropriate regulatory scheme for issuer tender offers, and that the exercise of this authority could include adoption of substantive regulations.

Securities Exchange Act Release No. 23421, 1986 WL 703866 at *6 (1986).

[35] 17 C.F.R. § 240.13e-3.

earlier.[36] Foreclosed from regulating substantive fairness by that decision's ruling, the SEC responded by mandating disclosure as to whether the subject going-private transaction is fair or unfair to unaffiliated minority shareholders and the reasons supporting this position.[37] Material misrepresentation that is contained in such a communication expressing that the going-private transaction is fair (when in fact it is not) gives rise to SEC enforcement and private actions.[38] This indirect way of seeking to regulate substantive fairness through the guise of disclosure has been utilized by the Commission on an episodic basis for several decades.[39]

D. Propriety of Federal Law Regulating Substantive Conduct

The foregoing examples attest that, to some extent, the federal securities laws regulate substantive fiduciary conduct. Of course, this observation is not to suggest that fairness is a primary focus of the federal securities laws. But it does signify, to the dismay of some sources,[40] that Congress and the SEC occasionally will act in this arena when they determine that the circumstances merit such intervention. This approach is beneficial as it signals to state legislatures and courts that unduly permissive treatment favoring corporate officers and directors as well as outside professionals (such as accountants, attorneys, and investment bankers) may trigger federal action, either preempting or significantly regulating matters that previously had been largely if not solely within the purview of state law.[41]

---

[36] *See* discussion *supra* notes 6–20 and accompanying text.

[37] Hence, the subject company or affiliate must disclose in its Schedule 13E-3 filed with the SEC whether it "reasonably believes that the Rule 13e-3 transaction is fair or unfair to unaffiliated security holders" and the "material factors" upon which such belief is based. *See* Rule 13e-3, 17 C.F.R. § 240.13e-3; SEC Schedule 13E-3; Item 8, SEC Regulation M-A, Item 1014.

[38] *See, e.g., Howing Co. v. Nationwide Corp.*, 826 F.2d 1470 (6th Cir. 1987); *In the Matter of FSC Corp.*, 22 SEC Docket 1374 (SEC 1981).

[39] For example, for decades the SEC has sought to deter excessive fiduciary self-dealing through the guise of mandating disclosure of executive compensation and related party transactions. *See, e.g.*, Items 402, 404 of Regulation S-K, 17 C.F.R. §§ 229.402, .404; *In re Franchard Corp.* 42 S.E.C. 163, [1964–1966 Transfer Binder] Fed. Sec. L. Rep. (CCH) ¶ 77,113 (1964); *infra* notes 83–92 and accompanying text; discussion in Chapter 5 herein.

[40] *See* Roberta Romano, *The Sarbanes-Oxley Act and the Making of Quack Corporate Governance*, 114 Yale L.J. 1521 (2005).

[41] From a historical perspective, the law of insider trading provides such an example. As stated by this author in a recent book published by Oxford University Press:

> Insider trading ought to be a fundamental aspect of state corporation law as such conduct implicates the duties of care and loyalty that corporate officers and directors owe to their subject corporations and shareholders. Yet, the states generally declined to set forth comprehensive principles proscribing this practice. . . . This inaction by the states

Such a reaction is most likely to occur during times of financial crisis, as evidenced by the Sarbanes-Oxley Act of 2002 and the Dodd-Frank Act of 2010.[42]

Moreover, there exist situations where federal action is necessitated to resolve important issues that the states either decline or are incapable of adequately addressing.[43] On occasion, Congress and the SEC respond to these situations by adopting a federal framework that seeks to regulate, at least to a significant degree, the pertinent subject matter areas.[44]

As discussed later in this book, Congress and the SEC should engage in this federalization of corporate governance process in a more vigilant manner.[45] If prohibition of loans to corporate fiduciaries in publicly-held enterprises can be a component of federal law, then the inquiry may be made why shouldn't the validity of executive compensation agreements and related party transactions also be subject to federal regulation? Although this inquiry may seem far-fetched, the same could have been said regarding loans to corporate insiders two decades ago.[46] With the abundance of arguably egregious levels of compensation paid to some corporate executives[47]

> left a distinct gap that federal law has filled. As stated by the U.S. Court of Appeals for the Second Circuit, "a director's common law liability for trading on inside information has been largely mooted by the advent of a federal cause of action under § 10(b) and Rule 10b-5."

Marc I. Steinberg, *The Federalization of Corporate Governance*, *supra* note 18, at 115–16, *quoting Treadway Companies, Inc. v. Care Corp.*, 638 F.2d 357, 375 n. 35 (2d Cir. 1980).

42 The Sarbanes-Oxley and Dodd-Frank Acts contain numerous provisions impacting corporate governance, including, for example, audit and compensation committees comprised solely of independent directors, codes of ethics, shareholder say-on-pay advisory votes, prohibition of loans to directors and executive officers, and executive clawbacks. For discussion, *see* Steinberg, *supra* note 41, at 191–224; discussion in Chapter 5 herein.

43 Insider trading, as discussed in *supra* note 41, provides such an example. The SEC shareholder proposal rule, promulgated in 1942, may be viewed as providing another example from a historical perspective. *See* Rule 14a-8, 17 C.F.R. § 240.14a-8; Securities Exchange Act Release No. 3347 (1942). Pursuant to Rule 14a-8, shareholder proposals are precatory and thus not binding on the corporation. For further discussion, *see* Steinberg, *supra* note 41, at 157–90; Marilyn B. Cane, *The Revised SEC Shareholder Proxy Proposal System: Attitudes, Results and Perspectives*, 11 J. Corp. L. 57 (1985); Alan R. Palmiter, *The Shareholder Proposal Rule: A Failed Experiment in Merit Regulation*, 41 Ala. L. Rev. 879 (1994); Patrick J. Ryan, *Rule 14a-8, Institutional Shareholder Proposals and Corporate Democracy*, 23 Ga. L. Rev. 97 (1988); discussion in Chapter 5 herein.

44 *See* discussion *supra* notes 21–43 and accompanying text.

45 *See* discussion in Chapters 5–9 herein.

46 *See* discussion *supra* notes 21–26 and accompanying text.

47 By way of example, the 2018 compensation for the five highest paid chief executive officers for U.S. companies was as follows: Elon Musk—Tesla—$513 million, Brendan Kennedy—Tilray—$256 million, Bob Iger—Walt Disney—$146 million, Tim Cook—Apple—$141 million, and Nikesh Arora—Palo Alto Networks—$130 million. *The Highest Paid U.S. CEOs of 2018: Bloomberg Pay Index*, available at https://www.bloomberg.com/graphics/2019-highest-paid-ceos.

and the undue permissiveness of state laws with respect to upholding related party transactions,[48] these subjects may be ripe for federalization during the next major financial catastrophe.[49]

III. The Concept of Materiality

The concept of materiality is one of the core principles of securities regulation in the United States.[50] Under federal as well as state securities law, the status of a statement's or omission's materiality significantly impacts disclosure obligations as well as liability exposure.[51] For example, numerous provisions of the federal securities laws render disclosure deficiencies actionable only if they are deemed material.[52] The same holds true under the state blue sky laws.[53]

A. Meaning of Materiality

Therefore, the definition of materiality and its application to the pertinent facts and circumstances are of fundamental importance. In this country, materiality generally signifies that a reasonable investor or shareholder would consider such information important in making one's investment or voting decision.[54] This definition does not require a "but for" showing—that the disclosure deficiency, if accurately and sufficiently disclosed, would have changed the decision.[55] This seemingly expansive

---

[48] *See* discussion *supra* notes 19–24 and accompanying text.

[49] Just prior to the emergence of the financial scandals, a comparable position was taken by the author. *See* Marc I. Steinberg, *Curtailing Investor Protection Under the Securities Laws: Good for the Economy?*, 55 SMU L. Rev. 347 (2002).

[50] *See, e.g.*, *Matrixx Initiatives, Inc. v. Siracusano*, 563 U.S. 27 (2011); *Basic, Inc. v. Levinson*, 485 U.S. 224 (1988); *TSC Industries, Inc. v. Northway, Inc.*, 426 U.S. 438 (1976).

[51] *See, e.g.*, §§ 11, 12(a)(2), 17(a) of the Securities Act, 15 U.S.C. §§ 77k, 1(a)(2), q(a); §§ 10(b), 18(a) of the Securities Exchange Act, 15 U.S.C. §§ 78j(b), r(a); SEC Rule 10b-5, 17 C.F.R. § 240.10b-5; § 410 of the Uniform Securities Act; Calif. Sec. Laws § 25401; Texas Sec. Act Art. 581-33A.

[52] *See, e.g.*, federal law sources cited *supra* note 51. *See generally* Marc I. Steinberg, *Securities Regulation: Liabilities and Remedies* (2020).

[53] *See, e.g.*, state law sources cited *supra* note 51. *See generally* Long, Kaufman, and Wunderlich, *supra* note 2.

[54] *See, e.g.*, *TSC Industries, Inc. v. Northway, Inc.*, 426 U.S. 438 (1976).

[55] *Id.* at 449 (stating that the standard adopted "does not require proof of a substantial likelihood that [accurate] disclosure of the [misstated or] omitted fact would have caused the reasonable investor to change his [mind]").

terminology is narrowed by the U.S. Supreme Court opining that "there must be a substantial likelihood that the [accurate] disclosure of the [misstated or] omitted fact would have been viewed by the reasonable investor as having significantly altered the total mix of information made available."[56]

With respect to situations involving uncertain or contingent events, such as in the product development, business combination, and government investigation contexts,[57] the presence of materiality depends "at any given time upon a balancing of both the indicated probability that the event will occur and the anticipated magnitude of the event in light of the totality of the company activity."[58] This standard thus signifies that a contingent event having huge magnitude may be material even if there exists only a relatively small probability that it will eventuate.[59] For example, in the closely-held corporation context, the signing of a nondisclosure agreement (NDA) with a publicly-traded company for the purpose of conducting due diligence to assess the feasibility of the target's acquisition by such prospective suitor may well be material—even though the likelihood of the acquisition's consummation under custom and practice is relatively minimal.[60]

---

[56] *Id. Accord, Matrixx Initiatives, Inc. v. Siracusano*, 563 U.S. 27, 38 (2011); *Basic, Inc. v. Levinson*, 485 U.S. 224, 232 (1988). *See* SEC Rule 12b-2, 17 C.F.R. § 240.12b-2 (defining material to mean "those matters in which there is a substantial likelihood that a reasonable investor would attach importance in determining whether to buy or sell the securities registered").

[57] As examples, with respect to product development, whether a highly touted new product will be timely launched; with respect to a business combination, whether preliminary merger negotiations have reached a more definitive level; and, with respect to a government investigation, whether it is reasonable to believe that a Federal Trade Commission enforcement action will ensue.

[58] *Basic, Inc. v. Levinson*, 485 U.S. 224, 238 (1988), *quoting, Securities and Exchange Commission v. Texas Gulf Sulphur Co.*, 401 F.2d 833, 849 (2d Cir. 1968) (en banc) (appellate court adopting this materiality standard in the context of a preliminary mineral discovery). The Second Circuit's decision is viewed as one of the most important decisions interpreting the federal securities laws. *See generally* Symposium, *Texas Gulf Sulphur 50th Anniversary Symposium Issue*, 71 SMU L. Rev. No. 3 (2018).

[59] *See, e.g., Securities and Exchange Commission v. Geon Industries, Inc.*, 531 F.2d 39, 47–48 (2d Cir. 1976) ("Since a merger in which it is bought out is the most important event that can occur in a small corporation's life, to wit, its death, we think that information, as regards a merger of this sort, can become material at an earlier stage than would be the case as regards lesser transactions—and this even though the mortality rate of mergers in such formative stages is doubtlessly high."). The U.S. Supreme Court gave its approbation to this approach in *Basic*. *See* 485 U.S. at 238.

[60] *See* sources cited *supra* note 59. In one case in which the author served as an expert witness, an arbitration panel determined that the signing of the NDA in a privately-held company involving its possible sale to a much larger enterprise (which in fact was consummated) constituted a failure to disclose a material fact when insiders purchased the minority shareholder's stock without informing him of the NDA's existence.

Many developed markets deem a statement (or omission) to be material if its accurate and adequate disclosure would generate significant price impact.[61] In this country, although occasionally employed by courts with respect to materiality,[62] this terminology most often is used by courts in the loss causation context—namely, that the disclosure deficiency proximately caused the financial loss.[63] While this definition of materiality may be appropriate when the subject corporation's stock is traded in an efficient market,[64] it clearly is not when an enterprise is privately-held or when its equity interests are traded in an inefficient market.[65] Moreover, in certain contexts, such as with respect to disclosures concerning the integrity of management and directors in the shareholder suffrage setting, a misstated or omitted fact (such as nondisclosure of a lucrative self-dealing transaction benefitting the chief executive officer and approved by the board of directors) may be viewed as significant by a reasonable shareholder, even assuming such fact has minimal or no price impact.[66]

---

[61] *See, e.g.*, Regulation (EU) No. 596/2014, of the European Parliament and of the Council of 16 April 2014 on Market Abuse Regulation at art. 7, para. 4 (focusing on whether the subject information "would be likely to have a significant effect of the prices of financial instruments"); Australia Corporations Act 2001 (Cth) §§ 1042C, 1042D, 1043A (focusing on whether the information, if it were generally available, would have a material effect on the price or value of the subject securities); Province of Ontario Securities Act, R.S.O. 1990, c. S.5 §§ 1(1), 126.2(1)(b) (setting forth that information is material if it "would reasonably be expected to have a significant effect on the market price or value of the securities") (Canada does not have national securities legislation).

[62] *See, e.g.*, *Christine Asia Co. v. Ma*, 2017 WL 6003340, at *2 (2d Cir. Dec. 5, 2017) ("The importance of this information to investors is illustrated by the fact that, when [the allegedly omitted information] was revealed four months subsequent to the IPO [initial public offering], Alibaba's stock dropped 13% in two days, erasing $33 billion in market capitalization.").

[63] *See, e.g.*, *Dura Pharmaceuticals, Inc. v. Broudo*, 544 U.S. 336, 347 (2005) (referring to "the complaint's failure to claim that Dura's share price fell significantly after the truth became known"). Note that, by showing an allegedly deficient disclosure's failure to generate price impact, defendants can rebut the fraud on the market theory of reliance. *See Halliburton Co. v. Erica P. John Fund, Inc.*, 134 S. Ct. 2398, 2414 (2014) (holding that defendants "must be afforded an opportunity before class certification to defeat the presumption [of reliance under the fraud on the market theory] through evidence that an alleged misrepresentation [or omission] did not actually affect the market price of the stock").

[64] *See, e.g.*, *Halliburton Co. v. Erica P. John Fund, Inc.*, 134 S. Ct. 2398 (2014); *Basic, Inc. v. Levinson*, 485 U.S. 224 (1988). For case law defining the characteristics of an efficient market, *see, e.g.*, *Unger v. Amedisys, Inc.*, 401 F.3d 316 (5th Cir. 2005); *Freeman v. Laventhol & Horwath*, 915 F.2d 193 (6th Cir. 1990); *Cammer v. Bloom*, 711 F. Supp. 1264 (D.N.J. 1989); discussion *infra* notes 122–123 and accompanying text.

[65] Such securities inherently trade in an inefficient market. *See* Alan R. Bromberg, Lewis D. Lowenfels, and Michael J. Sullivan, *Securities Fraud & Commodities Fraud* § 8.6 (2020); Geoffrey C. Rapp, *Proving Markets Inefficient: The Variability of Federal Court Decisions on Market Efficiency*, 10 U. Miami Bus. L. Rev. 303 (2002); discussion *infra* notes 129–134 and accompanying text.

[66] *See* Ralph C. Ferrara, Richard M. Starr, and Marc I. Steinberg, *Disclosure of Information Bearing on Management Integrity and Competency*, 65 Nw. U. L. Rev. 555 (1981).

B. Qualitative Economic Materiality

Being a mixed question of fact and law, materiality determinations represent one of the more difficult advisory tasks for the securities attorney.[67] As the U.S. Supreme Court has emphasized, sole reliance on solely quantitative analysis is misplaced.[68] This holding is consistent with commercial reality. For example, when a corporation's earnings miss analysts' forecasts, even by a small amount, its stock price frequently is adversely impacted.[69]

Thus, in court decisions and SEC pronouncements, the doctrine of qualitative economic materiality has been embraced.[70] Under this approach, even though a misstatement or omission may be quantitatively small, its impact nonetheless may be significant to the corporation and its stock price.[71] Thus, it is perplexing why the Commission continues to

---

[67] *See TSC Industries, Inc. v. Northway, Inc.*, 426 U.S. 438, 450 (1976) (stating materiality is a mixed question of fact and law). The role of the securities attorney has been addressed by the author in several books and articles. *See, e.g.*, Marc I. Steinberg, *Attorney Liability After Sarbanes-Oxley* (2018); Marc I. Steinberg, *Symposium on the Corporate Attorney—Ethical and Practical Lawyering with Vanishing Gatekeeper Liability*, 88 Fordham L. Rev. 1575 (2020).

[68] *See, e.g., Matrixx Initiatives, Inc. v. Siracusano*, 563 U.S. 27 (2011) (holding that the number of adverse drug reports received by the subject corporation need not reach the degree of being statistically significant for such information to be considered material under § 10(b) of the Securities Exchange Act).

[69] *See* Corrie Driebusch, *This Earnings Season, A Miss Hurts Even More*, Wall St. J., April 24, 2019, available at https://www.wsj.com/articles/this-earnings-season-a-miss-hurts-even-more-11556107202.

[70] *See, e.g., Matrixx Initiatives, Inc. v. Siracusano*, 563 U.S. 27 (2011); *Ganino v. Citizens Utilities Co.*, 228 F.3d 154 (2d Cir. 2000); SEC Staff Accounting Bulletin (SAB) 99, 64 Fed. Reg. 45, 150 (1999).

[71] In *Ganino*, the Second Circuit found SAB 99 to be "thoroughly reasoned and consistent with existing law" and hence of "persuasive guidance for evaluating the materiality of an alleged misrepresentation." 228 F.3d at 163. Accordingly, the following considerations may result in a quantitatively small misrepresentation or omission being deemed material:

- Whether the misstatement arises from an item capable of precise measurement or whether it arises from an estimate and, if so, the degree of imprecision inherent in the estimate;
- Whether the misstatement masks a change in earnings or other trends;
- Whether the misstatement hides a failure to meet analysts' consensus expectations for the enterprise;
- Whether the misstatement changes a loss into income or vice versa;
- Whether the misstatement concerns a segment or other portion of the registrant's business that has been identified as playing a significant role in the registrant's operations or profitability;
- Whether the misstatement affects the registrant's compliance with regulatory requirements;
- Whether the misstatement affects the registrant's compliance with loan covenants or other contractual requirements;
- Whether the misstatement has the effect of increasing management's compensation, for example, by satisfying requirements for the award of bonuses or other forms of incentive compensation; and
- Whether the misstatement involves concealment of an unlawful transaction.

SAB 99, *approved in*, *Ganino*, 228 F.3d at 163.

adhere in certain contexts to quantitative benchmarks. For example, with respect to the disclosure of legal proceedings to which the subject corporation or any of its subsidiaries is a party, disclosure generally is not mandated unless the claim for damages exceeds ten percent of current assets on a consolidated basis.[72] The use of this quantitative benchmark (and one that is of a relatively large percentage) is challenging to reconcile with Supreme Court precedent[73] and the Commission's adherence to qualitative materiality assessments in comparable circumstances.[74] Such use of quantitative standards should be rejected in favor of applying fluid materiality thresholds consistent with judicial precedent and the SEC's own disclosure mandates in comparable situations.

C. Application of Different Materiality Thresholds

Another troublesome development is the application of different materiality thresholds depending on the disclosure requirement triggered. Such an approach was disfavored by the U.S. Supreme Court in the *Basic* decision over three decades ago.[75] Yet the SEC and the courts today apply different materiality assessments with respect to disclosures required by Item 303 of SEC Regulation S-K (Management Discussion and Analysis—MD&A) as contrasted with the antifraud and remedial provisions of the federal

---

[72] *See* Item 103 of SEC Regulation S-K and Instruction 2 thereto, 17 C.F.R. § 229.103 ("No information need be given with respect to any proceeding that involves primarily a claim for damages if the amount involved, exclusive of interest and costs, does not exceed 10 percent of the current assets of the registrant and its subsidiaries on a consolidated basis."). Certain exceptions exist such as with respect to a "material bankruptcy" and environmental litigation. The SEC recently determined to maintain this ten percent threshold. *See* Securities Act Release No. 10825 (2020).

[73] *See* cases cited *supra* note 56.

[74] *See, e.g., Securities and Exchange Commission v. Leslie*, [2012 Transfer Binder] Fed. Sec. L. Rep. (CCH) ¶ 96,711 (N.D. Cal. 2012); SAB 99, *supra* note 70. Note that although SAB 99 focuses on disclosure in financial statements, its principles as seen in *Ganino*, apply to the narrative portions of SEC filings. On the other hand, a number of courts continue to focus on quantitative assessments to the exclusion of qualitative analysis. *See, e.g., Securities and Exchange Commission v. Hoover*, 903 F. Supp. 1135 (S.D. Tex. 1995) (misstatement of 3% held immaterial as a matter of law). *See generally* Clarissa Hodges, *The Qualitative Considerations of Materiality: The Emerging Relationship Between Materiality and Scienter*, 30 Sec. Reg. L.J. 4 (2002).

[75] *Basic, Inc. v. Levinson*, 485 U.S. 224, 240 n. 18 (1988) ("We find no authority in the statute [namely, § 10(b)], the legislative history, or our previous decisions, for varying the standard of materiality depending on who brings the action or whether insiders are alleged to have profited").

securities laws.[76] Pursuant to the MD&A, where a trend, commitment, demand, event, or uncertainty is *known* to the company, the following assessment must be made:

1. Is the known trend, demand, commitment, event, or uncertainty likely to come to fruition? If management determines that it is not reasonably likely to occur, no disclosure is required.
2. If management cannot make that determination, it must evaluate objectively the consequences of the known trend, demand, commitment, event, or uncertainty, on the assumption that it will come to fruition.

Disclosure is then required unless management determines that a material effect on the registrant's financial condition or results of operations is not reasonably likely to occur.[77]

The foregoing inquiry arguably is consistent with applicable materiality assessments that apply in the antifraud context when determining whether a subject disclosure deficiency is actionable. Yet the SEC and a number of courts hold that the standard of materiality under the MD&A disclosure mandate is broader than the Section 10(b) standard.[78] As a result, a misstatement or omission in the MD&A context can violate the SEC reporting requirements yet not be actionable by investors seeking redress.[79] Although materiality is not a bright-line test, disclosure deficiencies in the MD&A setting ordinarily are important to reasonable investors and significantly alter the total mix of information provided.[80]

---

[76] *See, e.g.*, *In re NVIDIA*, 768 F.3d 1046, 1054–56 (9th Cir. 2014) (opining that the standard of materiality under Item 303 is "much broader" than for § 10(b)); *Oran v. Stafford*, 226 F.3d 275, 288 (3d Cir. 2000) (stating that "the materiality standards for Rule 10b-5 and Reg SK-303 differ significantly"); SEC 1989 Interpretive Release, Financial Reporting Release No. 36, 6 Fed. Sec. L. Rep. (CCH) ¶ 73,193, at 62,842 (1989) (stating that the "probability/magnitude standard for materiality . . . is inapposite to Item 303 disclosure"). *See also* Concept Release, Business and Financial Disclosure Required by Regulation S-K, Securities Act Release No. 10064 (2016).

[77] SEC Financial Reporting Release No. 36, 6 Fed. Sec. L. Rep. (CCH) ¶ 73,193, at 62,843 (1989). For more recent SEC releases on the MD&A, *see, e.g.*, Securities Act Release No. 9106 (2010) (interpretive release addressing the MD&A with respect to climate change); Securities Act Release No. 8350 (2003) (providing guidelines to assist registrants and issuers to undertake more compliant MD&A disclosure).

[78] *See, e.g.*, sources cited *supra* note 76.

[79] *See* sources cited *supra* notes 76–77. *See generally* Denise Crawford and Dean Galaro, *A Rule 10b-5 Private Right of Action for MD&A Violations*, 43 Sec. Reg. L.J. 245 (2015).

[80] *See, e.g.*, *In the Matter of Caterpillar, Inc.*, AAER-363, 50 S.E.C. 903, 910 (1992) (stating that "Regulation S-K requires disclosure of information necessary to understand the registrant's financial statements [and that] Caterpillar's failure to include required information . . . in the MD&A left investors with an incomplete picture of Caterpillar's financial condition and results of operation").

As troubling, the fragmentation of such a key concept (namely, that of materiality) underlying the securities laws impairs commercial certainty and investor protection. For different definitions to apply to the same key concept for narrative disclosure purposes[81] invites further ambiguity and undisciplined practices. Accordingly, the term materiality should be applied as a facts and circumstances approach pursuant to U.S. Supreme Court precedent as well as recognition of qualitative materiality assessments. Succinctly stated, a narrative disclosure misrepresentation or omission should be judged by identical materiality standards irrespective of the statutory or regulatory provisions applicable. Holding that a material disclosure deficiency in the MD&A setting may not be material for Section 10(b) and other antifraud provisions signifies that allegedly aggrieved purchasers or sellers of the subject company's securities may have no right of action for damages caused by such misstatements or omissions.[82]

D. Materiality Analysis—Management Integrity

On a related theme, qualitative materiality analysis encompasses an assessment of information that may not be necessarily economically material but nonetheless is of significance to reasonable shareholders. Although economic loss may not be shown, SEC enforcement actions and requests for equitable relief by affected shareholders may be at issue.[83] For example, when determining whether to cast their votes in favor of director-nominees, many shareholders consider important such factors as the level of executive remuneration authorized by the board of directors, the specter of unethical or illegal conduct transpiring under the board's oversight, and the presence of unseemly self-dealing by corporate fiduciaries. This perception likely is heightened in the benefit corporation

[81] Clearly, the MD&A is focused on disclosure of financial information but nonetheless it is a component of narrative disclosure pursuant to Regulation S-K. Generally, Regulation S-X, 17 C.F.R. § 240.210, focuses on the contents of financial statements contained in specified SEC filings. *See* discussion in Chapter 4 herein.

[82] *See, e.g.*, cases cited *supra* note 76.

[83] *See, e.g.*, *Gaines v. Haughton*, 645 F.2d 761 (9th Cir. 1981) (shareholder suit seeking injunctive relief and to invalidate past elections of directors based on nondisclosure of questionable payments); *Securities and Exchange Commission v. Savino*, [2005–2006 Transfer Binder] Fed. Sec. L. Rep. (CCH) ¶ 93,705 (S.D.N.Y. 2006) (alleged nondisclosure of kickbacks to corporate insider held actionable). Note that the SEC may institute enforcement proceedings based on alleged violations of certain reporting provisions, such as Section 13(a) of the Securities Exchange Act (15 U.S.C. § 78m(a)), which do not require that an alleged disclosure deficiency be material.

setting.[84] Recognizing the importance of these matters to shareholders, the SEC has required disclosure for decades relating to executive compensation and fiduciary self-dealing transactions.[85] For example, in an enforcement proceeding brought in 1964, with respect to a subject company's failure to disclose the diversion of funds benefitting its chief executive officer, the Commission reasoned that this omission was material to investors because it was "germane to an evaluation of the integrity of management."[86] Notably, requiring disclosure of these types of matters may play a positive role in regard to improving standards for normative conduct. For example, mandatory disclosure of an excessive contemplated self-dealing transaction that would trigger activist shareholder dialogue may prompt the independent directors, comprising the majority of the board,[87] to oppose or modify the contemplated transaction.[88] In such situations, the SEC's focus on qualitative materiality substantively influences corporate governance practices.[89]

Nonetheless, significant gaps exist with respect to qualitative materiality. For example, one appellate court ruled that a chief executive officer's fabrication of his academic background was not material to investors.[90] As another example, if not economically material, a number of courts have held that a company is not required to disclose uncharged criminal conduct by its directors or executive officers.[91] These holdings present obstacles to the effectuation of a consistent disclosure rationale premised on qualitative materiality. To rule as a matter of law that reasonable

---

[84] Generally, a benefit corporation may seek to serve specified social objectives as well as to increase shareholder wealth. For an excellent discussion of benefit corporations, *see* Mark J. Loewenstein, *Benefit Corporations: A Challenge in Corporate Governance*, 68 Bus. Law. 1007 (2013).

[85] *See, e.g.*, Items 402, 404 of Regulation S-K, 17 C.F.R. §§ 229.402, .404.

[86] *In re Franchard Corp.*, 42 S.E.C. 163, [1964–1966 Transfer Binder] Fed. Sec. L. Rep. (CCH) ¶ 77,133, at 82,043 (1964).

[87] As a condition of stock exchange listing, with certain exceptions, a company must have a majority of independent directors. *See In the Matter of Self-Regulatory Organizations*, Securities Exchange Act Release No. 48745, 2003 WL 22509738 (Nov. 4, 2003); discussion in Chapter 5 herein.

[88] Nonetheless, independent directors with frequency approve lucrative compensation packages and other attractive perquisites benefitting senior executive officers, particularly the chief executive officer. *See supra* note 47.

[89] *See* discussion in Steinberg, *supra* note 18, at 133–36.

[90] *See Greenhouse v. MCG Capital Corp.*, 392 F.3d 650 (4th Cir. 2004). For a different perspective, *see* Floyd Norris, *Radio Shack Chief Resigns after Lying*, N.Y. Times, Feb. 21, 2006, at C1 (reporting that corporation's CEO resigned after "revelation that he had lied to the company about his education by claiming two college degrees when he had none").

[91] *See, e.g.*, *Gaines v. Haughton*, 645 F.2d 761 (9th Cir. 1981); *In re Axis Capital Holdings Ltd. Securities Litigation*, 456 F. Supp. 2d 576 (S.D.N.Y. 2006); *Amalgamated Clothing & Textile Workers v. J.P. Stevens & Co.*, 475 F. Supp. 328 (S.D.N.Y. 1979), *vacated as moot*, 638 F.2d 7 (2d Cir. 1980).

shareholders would not consider important a CEO's misrepresentation/ nondisclosure of his educational background or violations of law by corporate fiduciaries is difficult to comprehend. The solution to this inconsistency is straightforward—namely, the SEC should adopt regulations that specifically set forth disclosure mandates in response to these problematic rulings.[92] In this way, the Commission can rectify much of the inconsistency in the qualitative disclosure framework. This activism is unlikely to transpire in the current political climate and with the composition of the current SEC commissioners. But political winds change and, in times of financial crisis accompanied by massive frauds, a more protective shareholder climate may emerge.

E. Flexible Standards of Materiality

In many situations, the determination of materiality is an elusive and challenging process. Its assessment must take into account the surrounding facts and circumstances. Although inviting ambiguity at times, this approach is superior to a definition that focuses on bright-line standards and does not overload affected constituents with insignificant information.[93] As the Supreme Court has recognized, the recognition of a rigid standard of materiality carries the risk of generating inequity and gamesmanship.[94] If flexibly interpreted and vigilantly overseen by the SEC, the concepts of

[92] *See In re Axis Capital Holdings Ltd. Securities Litigation*, 456 F. Supp. 2d 576, 587 (S.D.N.Y. 2006) (stating that a duty to disclose uncharged illegal conduct "arises when it is necessary to disclose this conduct under the terms of a statute or regulation"). *Cf.* the SEC's rules adopting proxy disclosure enhancements. *See* Securities Exchange Act Release No. 61175 (2009). As an example of the Commission's activism in this area in a different era, the SEC stated the following in its amicus brief supporting the (unsuccessful) petition for rehearing en banc in the *Gaines* case (*see supra* note 91):

> Plaintiff alleges that certain of Lockheed's officers and directors knew and participated in substantial and pervasive illegal practices. Such allegations of illegal conduct of corporate affairs certainly are not so obviously unimportant to a reasonable shareholder's evaluation of the fitness of nominees to serve as directors that they may be dismissed as a matter of law. These alleged practices raise substantial questions regarding the "character and integrity of the officers relevant to their management of the corporation," which shareholders might well consider important.

[93] *See generally* Kurt S. Schulzke and Gerlinde Berger-Walliser, *Toward a Unified Theory of Materiality in Securities Law*, 56 Colum. J. Transnat'l L. 6 (2017).

[94] *See, e.g., Basic, Inc. v. Levinson*, 485 U.S. 224 (1988) (rejecting the existence of an agreement as to price and structure as too rigid a standard to ascertain materiality).

materialitysetforthhereinshouldprovebeneficialtoinvestorsandthesecurities markets.[95]

IV. The Mandatory Disclosure Framework

With the passage of the Securities Act of 1933 and Securities Exchange Act of 1934, a mandatory disclosure framework was established.[96] Through the filing with the SEC of Securities Act registration statements for public offerings of securities[97] and periodic reports with the Commission,[98] specified information is required to be set forth in these documents.[99] The central repository for these disclosure items is Regulation S-K (and for accounting items, Regulation S-X). These Regulations thus act as the principal sources for determining the disclosures required to be made and for ensuring that disclosure in the various documents filed with the Commission are as uniform as practicable.[100]

---

[95] *See generally* Troy A. Paredes, *Blinded by the Light: Information Overload and Its Consequences for Securities Regulation*, 81 Wash. U. L.Q. 417 (2003); James J. Park, *Assessing the Materiality of Financial Misstatements*, 34 J. Corp. L. 513 (2009); Schulzke and Berger-Walliser, *supra* note 93.

[96] 15 U.S.C. § 77a *et seq.*; 15 U.S.C. § 78a *et seq. See* Louis Loss et al., *Fundamentals of Securities Regulation* 50–54 (7th ed. 2018) (identifying mandatory disclosure as core function of the federal securities acts); Paul G. Mahoney, *The Exchange as Regulator*, 83 Va. L. Rev. 1453, 1465 (1997) (stating that "[t]he most prominent feature of securities regulation in the United States is the mandatory disclosure system"); Andrew A. Schwartz, *Mandatory Disclosure in Primary Markets*, 2019 Utah L. Rev. 1069, 1078 (2019) (asserting that "[t]he core feature of [the 1933 and 1934 Acts] was, and remains, mandatory disclosure").

[97] *See, e.g.*, §§ 2(a)(10), 5, 6, 7, 10, 11, 12, Schedule A of the Securities Act, 15 U.S.C. §§ 77b(a)(10), e, f, g, j, k, l, aa; *Herman & MacLean v. Huddleston*, 459 U.S. 375, 381–82 (1983) (stating that "Section 11 of the 1933 Act allows purchasers of a registered security to sue certain enumerated parties in a registered offering when [materially] false or misleading information is included in a registration statement [and that] the section was designed to assure compliance with the disclosure provisions of the Act by imposing a stringent standard of liability on the parties who play a direct role in a registered offering").

[98] *See, e.g.*, §§ 12(b), (g), 13(a), 15(d) of the Securities Act, 15 U.S.C. §§ 77l(b), (g), (m)a, o(d), SEC Forms 10-K, 10-Q, 8-K, 17 C.F.R. §§ 249.308, .308a, .310.

[99] This information includes, for example, description of the registrant's business and property, specified legal proceedings involving the registrant or any of its subsidiaries, description of the registrant's securities, information relating to the market price and dividends of the registrant's common stock, selected financial data for the registrant, management's discussion and analysis of financial condition and results of operation, changes in and disagreements with the registrant's accountants on accounting and financial disclosure, quantitative and qualitative disclosures regarding market risk, specified information focusing on the registrant's directors, executive officers, and control persons, executive compensation, and, with respect to Securities Act registered offerings, as examples, the furnishing in Form S-1 of a prospectus summary, use of proceeds, determination of offering price, plan of distribution, and identification of selling security holders. *See* SEC Regulation S-K, 17 C.F.R. § 229.101 *et seq.*

[100] Regulations S-K, S-X, 17 C.F.R. §§ 210, 229 *et seq. See* Securities Act Release No. 6383 (1982) (stating that "[s]ince its initial adoption, Regulation S-K has evolved beyond a source of certain

A. Established Presence of a Mandatory Disclosure System

The presence of a mandatory disclosure framework under the federal securities laws is firmly entrenched. Established with the enactment of the federal securities acts in 1933 and 1934 and as administered by the SEC for nearly a century,[101] compulsory disclosure may be viewed as the foundational component of the regulatory process. Although this framework has been challenged by critics who posit that market incentives are sufficient to induce subject corporations and their insiders to voluntarily disclose an appropriate amount of information to securities markets and investors,[102] this assertion generally has not gained acceptance.[103] Stated

---

standardized registrant-related disclosure provisions to become a more complete compendium of disclosure requirements applicable to Securities Act and Exchange Act filings"); Securities Act Release No. 6231 (1980) (stating that uniformity in disclosure has been achieved by, among other measures, "amending Regulation S-X").

[101] *See, e.g., Federal Regulation and Regulatory Reform*, Report by the Subcommittee on Oversight and Investigation of the Committee on Interstate and Foreign Commerce, U.S. House of Representatives, 94th Cong., 2d Sess. (1976) (stating that "[t]he Securities and Exchange Commission (SEC) has responsibility for implementing and enforcing the Federal securities laws [with] the [principal] statutes [being] the Securities Act of 1933 and the Securities Exchange Act of 1934").

[102] For criticisms of the mandatory disclosure framework, *see, e.g.*, Homer Kripke, *The SEC and Corporate Disclosure: Regulation in Search of a Purpose* 119 (1979) ("A disclosure will be supplied voluntarily by issuers interested in the capital markets when there is a consensus among suppliers of capital or other transactors in the capital markets that this information is necessary to them for lending and investment decisions."); George J. Benston, *Required Disclosure and the Stock Market, An Evaluation of the Securities Exchange Act of 1934*, 63 Am. Econ. Rev. 132 (1973) (in empirical analysis finding that mandatory disclosure did not significantly impact stock prices); Roberta Romano, *Empowering Investors: A Market Approach to Securities Regulation*, 107 Yale L.J. 2359, 2374 (1998) ("Because firms need capital and investors need information, firms have powerful incentives to disclose information if they are to compete successfully for funds against alternative investment opportunities."). *See generally* Omri Ben-Shahar and Carl E. Schneider, *The Failure of Mandated Disclosure*, 159 U. Pa. L. Rev. 647 (2011) ("explor[ing] the spectacular prevalence, and failure, of the single most common technique for protecting personal autonomy in modern society: mandated disclosure"); Kevin S. Haeberle and M. Todd Henderson, *A New Market-Based Approach to Securities Law*, 85 U. Chi. L. Rev. 1313, 1390 (2018) (proposing that, in lieu of the current mandatory disclosure regimen, the adoption of "a new approach to securities law: permit a market for the public-company information that sits at the center of modern securities law" and that "[d]eploying this market . . . would trigger incentives for firms to disclose more information of value").

[103] *See, e.g.*, House Comm. on Interstate and Foreign Commerce, 95th Cong., 1st Sess., *Report of the Advisory Committee on Corporate Disclosure to the Securities and Exchange Commission*, Comm. Print 95-29 (1977) (quoting cover letter at Two) (asserting that "the disclosure system established by Congress in the Securities Act of 1933 and Securities Exchange Act of 1934, as implemented and developed by the Securities and Exchange Commission since its creation in 1934, is sound and does not need radical reform or renovation"); John C. Coffee, Jr., *Market Failure and the Economic Case for a Mandatory Disclosure System*, 70 Va. L. Rev. 717 (1984) (positing that mandatory disclosure efficiently responds to the underproduction of information and agency costs which market forces alone would not be sufficient); Elisabeth de Fontenay, *The Deregulation of Private Capital and the Decline of the Public Company*, 68 Hastings L.J. 445, 473 (2017) ("For several decades now the majority view has been that, in theory, the cost-benefit analysis of mandatory disclosure in federal securities regulation is a favorable one."); Hilary A. Sale, *Disclosure's Purpose*, 107 Geo. L.J. 1045, 1051 (2019) (asserting

succinctly, the propriety of a mandatory disclosure regimen is premised on several key rationales, including that without adoption and implementation of such a framework: (1) more enterprises and their insiders would engage in fraudulent conduct; (2) insider remuneration and perquisites as well as financial intermediary costs would be higher; (3) oversight by the SEC, state securities authorities, and self-regulatory organizations of proscribed practices would be inadequate for effective enforcement; (4) the specter of civil and criminal sanctions would not be sufficient to induce an appropriate level of disclosure; and (5) market confidence would decline, resulting in an increase in the cost of raising capital, a decrease in market liquidity, less efficient securities markets, and a retreat or withdrawal by investors from the capital markets.[104]

B. Effectiveness of the Mandatory Disclosure Framework

Given that the mandatory disclosure framework is firmly ensconced, the question arises whether this system is functioning at a desired level. As other sources have addressed, more information is not necessarily better and investors are besieged by disclosure documents that can run hundreds of pages—thereby generating information overload.[105] And to whom are disclosure documents addressed: by way of example, to the amorphous reasonable investor or the financially savvy institutional investor or financial analyst?[106]

---

that "despite calls for changes and overhauls, the [disclosure] system has remained firmly in place—at least in part because market issues and situations involving significant greed and fraud provide regular counterweights to proponents of deregulation").

[104] *See* Steinberg, *supra* note 30, at 162–63 (setting forth justifications for mandatory disclosure framework); Joel Seligman, *The Historical Need for a Mandatory Corporate Disclosure System*, 9 J. Corp. L. 1, 5–9 (1983) (asserting that "generally the recent critics have ignored or underestimated the evidence concerning securities fraud, excessive underwriters' or insiders' compensation, and [lack of] public confidence in the securities markets that persuaded Congress in 1933, 1934 and 1964 to create the legislative basis for the present mandatory corporate disclosure system").

[105] *See, e.g.*, Paredes, *supra* note 95, at 420 (as a future SEC Commissioner, stating that "[w]hether or not the SEC is, or ever will be, prepared to cut back disclosure requirements meaningfully, the federal securities laws could be improved by accounting for how investors actually process information and make decisions [and] [a]t the very least, the specter of information overload casts doubt on the long-held belief and policy choice that more disclosure is better than less").

[106] For discussion on this subject, *see, e.g.*, Business and Financial Disclosure Required by Regulation S-K, Securities Act Release No. 10064, at 51 (2016) (concept release inquiring whether "registrants [should] assume some level of investor sophistication in preparing their disclosures"); Homer Kripke, *Fifty Years of Securities Regulation in Search of a Purpose*, 21 San Diego L. Rev. 257,

The specified disclosure provisions in SEC Regulation S-K are exhaustive and detailed. Yet registrants frequently engage in generic boilerplate disclosure with respect to important items (such as "risk factors"),[107] use laudatory language (known as "puffery"),[108] and increasingly express

276 (1984) (criticizing that the SEC's disclosure "system was founded not on disclosure of 'all material facts,' but on disclosure of events in the past which the Commission could objectively verify"); Amanda M. Rose, *The "Reasonable Investor" of Federal Securities Law: Insights from Tort Law's "Reasonable Person" & Suggested Reforms*, 43 J. Corp. L. 77, 113 (2017) (rather than embracing "particular definitions of the reasonable investor . . . highlight[ing] the need for policymakers to develop some explicit definitions, preferably ones that fit with the regulatory goals of the federal securities laws and market realities"); Margaret V. Sachs, *Materiality and Social Change: The Case for Replacing "the Reasonable Investor" with "the Least Sophisticated Investor" in Inefficient Markets*, 81 Tulane L. Rev. 473, 473 (2006) (proposing "an alternative standard for courts to apply in inefficient markets . . . replac[ing] 'the reasonable investor' with 'the least sophisticated investor'").

[107] Broad risk factors that are used by companies include, for example, the following: (1) We have not been profitable historically and may not achieve profitability; (2) The company's debt could materially and adversely affect our financial condition and prospects; (3) Each of our customer contracts may be terminated under certain conditions; (4) The company's use of hedging may adversely affect our liquidity or future operating results; (5) The company may not be successful in implementing our proposed business strategy; (6) Cost overruns and delays in completing specified projects may adversely affect our business, financial condition, cash flow, and prospects; (7) The company's inability to obtain additional funding may adversely impact the completion of certain projects; (8) Tornados, hurricanes, or other disasters could result in a material interruption of the company's operations; (9) The company's failure to obtain government approval for the implementation of our projects could have a material adverse effect; (10) Various political and economic factors could negatively affect the development of the company's facilities; (11) The industries in which the company competes are highly competitive and it may not be able to compete effectively with our competitors that have greater financial resources which could have a material adverse effect on our business, results of operation, or financial condition; (12) Existing and future environmental and related laws and regulations could result in increased compliance or operating costs; (13) The company's lack of diversification could have a material adverse effect on our financial condition, operating results, cash flow, liquidity, and prospects; (14) Due to past significant fluctuations in the market price of the company's common stock that are likely to continue, stockholders could lose all or part of their investment; and (15) The company's industry is affected by global economic factors, including risks associated with volatile economic conditions. The SEC recently has sought to address this situation by: "requiring summary risk factor disclosure of no more than two pages if the risk factor section exceeds 15 pages; refining the principles-based approach of Item 105 [of Regulation S-K] by requiring disclosure of 'material' risk factors; and requiring risk factors to be organized under relevant headings in addition to the subcaptions currently required, with any risk factors that may generally apply to an investment in securities disclosed at the end of the risk factor section under a separate caption." SEC Press Release No. 220-192 (2020), announcing amendments to "modernize disclosures of business, legal proceedings, and risk factors under Regulation S-K," Securities Act Release No. 10825 (2020).

[108] Generalized positive or optimistic statements, not phrased as guarantees, are deemed not actionable by courts as they are viewed as "puffery." Such statements, these courts hold, lack materiality and are not relied upon by reasonable investors. *See, e.g.*, *Anderson v. Spirit AeroSystems Holdings, Inc.*, 827 F.3d 1229 (10th Cir. 2016) (company's generalized statements lauding its "productivity and efficiency improvements" held to be puffery); *Lloyd v. CVB Financial Corp.* 811 F.3d 1200 (9th Cir. 2016) (characterizing as puffery subject company's generalized statements concerning its largest creditor's ability to repay its debt to the company as well as its description of its "sound credit culture and underwriting integrity"); *City of Edinburgh Council v. Pfizer, Inc.*, 754 F.3d 159 (3d Cir. 2014) (pharmaceutical company's optimistic statements regarding clinical trial data viewed as puffery). *But see In re Vivendi, S.A.*, 838 F.3d 223 (2d Cir. 2016) (corporation's statements concerning its net income and available cash deemed material and not puffery). The puffery doctrine has been

optimistic statements of "belief" (after the Supreme Court's decision in *Omnicare*, which provides significant protection from liability exposure with respect to such statements).[109] Engaging in unduly optimistic expressions, whether asserted generally or as an expression of belief, is unduly insulated from liability under current law.[110] Corporate directors and officers should not be accorded the same protection as pre-owned automobile salespersons.[111] Fiduciaries who owe duties of care and loyalty to their respective corporations and shareholders should be held to a higher standard of accountability.[112] Generalized lies and exaggerations, if undertaken with the requisite culpability,[113] should be actionable in

---

criticized by numerous commentators. *See, e.g.*, Jennifer O'Hare, *The Resurrection of the Dodo: The Unfortunate Re-Emergence of the Puffery Defense in Private Securities Fraud Actions*, 59 Ohio St. L.J. 1697 (1998); Stefan Padfield, *Is Puffery Material to Investors: Maybe We Should Ask Them*, 10 U. Pa. J. Bus. & Emp. L. 339 (2008); discussion in Chapter 6 herein.

[109] *Omnicare, Inc. v. Laborers District Council Construction Industry Pension Fund*, 135 S. Ct. 1318 (2015) (holding that statements of opinion can be actionable in two situations: first, when the company (or other speaker) sets forth an opinion that it does not actually believe; and second, if the opinion omits material facts regarding the company's (or other speaker's) inquiry into or knowledge regarding such statement of opinion, and if those facts are in conflict with how a reasonable investor would view the statement). *Omnicare* addressed statements of belief or opinion in the context of Section 11 of the Securities Act (15 U.S.C. § 77k) based on an alleged disclosure deficiency in a registration statement. *Omnicare*'s rationale has been extended to actions alleging violations of Section 10(b) of the Securities Exchange Act (15 U.S.C. § 78j(b)). *See, e.g.*, *City of Dearborn Heights v. Align Technology, Inc.*, 856 F.3d 605 (9th Cir. 2017). For commentary, *see, e.g.*, Allison Cook, *"I Believe" Omnicare Falls Short: An Analysis of the Supreme Court's Latest Attempt to Clarify Opinion-Statement Liability*, 46 Sec. Reg. L.J. 19 (2018); James D. Cox, *We're Cool Statements After Omnicare: Securities Fraud Suits for Failures to Comply with the Law*, 68 SMU L. Rev. 715 (2015); Hilary A. Sale and Donald C. Langevoort, *"We Believe": Omnicare, Legal Risk Disclosure and Corporate Governance*, 66 Duke L.J. 763 (2016); discussion in Chapter 6 herein. Another example is the frequent practice of a number of oil companies to inflate their oil reserves in excess of realistic levels. *See* Rachel Adams Heard, *Culture of Inflating Oil Reserves Helped Stoke U.S. Shale Boom*, Bloomberg (June 23, 2020), available at https://www.bloomberg.com/news/articles/2020-06-23/shale-oil-stocks-investors-question-industry-s-performance (discussing "rosy estimates" by companies of their oil reserves and referencing SEC enforcement actions over a decade ago against two major corporations alleging disclosure of inflated reserves but observing that since those actions, "high-profile fines and penalties have been noticeably absent . . . .").

[110] *See* articles cited *supra* notes 109–110, *infra* note 111.

[111] *See* Sarah K. Lee, *The Puffery Defense: From Used Car Salesman to CEO*, 30 Sec. Reg. L.J. 440 (2002).

[112] *Cf. Meinhard v. Salmon*, 249 N.Y. 458, 164 N.E. 545, 546 (1928) (Cardozo, Ch. J.) (opining that "[m]any forms of conduct permissible in a workaday world for those acting at arm's length, are forbidden to those bound by fiduciary ties [and that] [n]ot honesty alone, but the punctilio of an honor the most sensitive, is then the standard of behavior").

[113] In an action brought for violation of Section 10(b) of the Securities Exchange Act and SEC Rule 10b-5 (17 C.F.R. § 240.10b-5) promulgated thereunder, scienter (namely, knowing or intentional conduct) must be proven in both private and government actions. *See Aaron v. Securities and Exchange Commission*, 446 U.S. 680 (1980); *Ernst & Ernst v. Hochfelder*, 425 U.S. 185 (1976). Generally, except for forward-looking statements in the context of private litigation (where the defendant enjoys greater protection from liability), reckless conduct is sufficient to constitute the requisite intent. *See, e.g.*, *In re Ikon Office Solutions, Inc. Securities Litigation*, 277 F.3d 658, 667 (3d Cir. 2002) (applying the prevailing definition of recklessness in this context as constituting "an extreme

private and SEC actions (provided, of course, that the elements of the underlying claim are satisfied).[114]

On a related theme, the length of certain disclosure items, such as "executive compensation," frequently entails several charts, tables, and narratives amounting to dozens of pages.[115] Unless an investor or market professional has good reason to digest this information, there is little incentive to undertake this cumbersome task.[116] Information "overload" of information that is not material prevails in the SEC disclosure framework.[117] Clearly, the length of disclosure documents should be significantly shortened while implementing the universal mandate that, absent justifiable business reason, all material information must be sufficiently disclosed.[118]

departure from the standards of ordinary care to the extent that the danger was either known to the defendant or so obvious that the defendant must have been aware of it").

[114] The requisite elements of a private Section 10(b) claim include the plaintiff's standing as a purchaser or seller of the subject securities, presence of a material disclosure deficiency (misrepresentation or omission), the defendant's scienter, the alleged misconduct occurred in connection with the purchase or sale of the subject securities, reliance by the plaintiff on the alleged disclosure deficiency, loss causation shown by the plaintiff, and damages caused by the alleged violation. *See Dura Pharmaceuticals, Inc. v. Broudo*, 544 U.S. 336, 341–42 (2005). *See generally* Bromberg, Lowenfels, and Sullivan, *supra* note 65; discussion in Chapter 6 herein.

[115] This point is illustrated by the fact that Item 402 of Regulation S-K itself covers dozens of pages. *See* Stephen J. Choi and A.C. Pritchard, *Securities Regulation—Statutory Supplement* 268–302 (2020) (containing the instructions for Item 402). Item 303 of Regulation S-K, the MD&A, provides another example of the expanding degree of the length of the disclosures made pursuant to this directive. *See* Paredes, *supra* note 95, at 427–28.

[116] *See* Schwartz, *supra* note 96, at 1081 (asserting that "anyone who has actually looked at a securities filing in the primary market knows that these filings are so arcane and densely written as to be almost completely impenetrable to an ordinary retail investor").

[117] *See* Paredes, *supra* note 95, at 446 (stating that "concerns that investors are becoming overloaded with information have intensified"). As Warren Buffett stated: "For more than forty years, I've studied the documents that public companies file. Too often, I've been unable to decipher just what is being said." Warren E. Buffett, Preface to Office of Investors' Education & Assistance, Securities and Exchange Commission, *A Plain English Handbook: How to Create Clear SEC Disclosure Documents* 1 (1988). To some degree, the SEC has sought to address this situation. *See* Securities Act Release No. 10825 (2020) (stating that the adopted amendments to Regulation S-K "update" Items 101, 103, and 105 of Regulation S-K, "improve disclosure for investors, and simplify compliance for registrants").

[118] Accordingly, the manner in which information overload may be ameliorated is by reducing the complexity and length of narrative disclosures that concern matters that are not material. Indeed, the impact of such lengthy disclosures as well as the use of boilerplate language may have the detrimental effect of "burying" facts that are important to investors. *See Werner v. Werner*, 267 F.3d 288, 297 (3d Cir. 2001) (stating that "under the 'buried facts' doctrine, a disclosure is deemed inadequate if it is presented in a way that conceals or obscures the information sought to be disclosed"). *See generally* Jeremy McClane, *Boilerplate and the Impact of Disclosure in Securities Dealmaking*, 72 Vand. L. Rev. 191 (2019).

C. Incorporation by Reference—Informational Disparities

Incorporation by reference from an eligible registrant's periodic 1934 SEC reports into its Securities Act registration statements[119] exacerbates the actual informational delivery disparities. Such incorporation by reference signifies that generally the only information that the issuer must disclose in the registration statement addresses the terms of the offering (and the securities issued pursuant thereto) and information reflecting material changes in the issuer's affairs since the filing of its last periodic (and current) reports.[120] Understandably, ordinary investors do not as a matter of practice review the annual, quarterly, and current reports that are incorporated by reference into the subject registration statement. Generally, only institutional investors and market professionals have the wherewithal to engage in this analysis. As such, there is a sharp distinction between the institutional investor and the market professional as compared to the ordinary investor when assessing the actual information that is reviewed prior to making one's investment or voting decision.[121]

When the SEC adopted the integrated disclosure framework four decades ago,[122] it relied on the efficient market theory[123] to support "maximum use of incorporation by reference of Exchange Act reports [into 1933 Act registration statements.]"[124] At that time, such incorporation by reference was authorized to be used in certain primary equity offerings by an eligible

[119] *See* Securities Act Release No. 6331 (1981) (integration of Securities Act disclosure systems); Securities Act Release No. 6235 (1980) (proposing release). *See generally* Milton H. Cohen, *"Truth in Securities" Revisited*, 79 Harv. L. Rev. 1340 (1966) (supporting the adoption of an integrated disclosure framework).

[120] *See* Securities Act Release No. 10003 (2016) (implementing Congress's directive in the FAST Act (Fixing America's Surface Transportation Act), allowing a smaller reporting company to incorporate by reference into its registration statements from its SEC Exchange Act periodic reports); Securities Act Release No. 6383 (1982) (authorizing incorporation by reference for Form S-3 issuers and stating: "Information concerning the registrant will be incorporated by reference [in a Form S-3 prospectus] from its Exchange Act reports [and that] the prospectus will not be required to present any information concerning the registrant unless there has been a material change in the registrant's affairs which has not been reported in an Exchange Act filing.").

[121] *See* Paredes, *supra* note 95, at 431–32 (pointing out that average individual investors do not focus in any detail on the information publicly disclosed in SEC filings but that nonetheless these disclosures are "filtered" through financial intermediaries and securities professionals "who research and process the information and whose trades and recommendations ultimately set securities prices").

[122] *See* Securities Act Release No. 6331 (1981).

[123] As stated by the U.S. Supreme Court, "the market price of shares traded on well-developed markets reflects all publicly available information." *Halliburton Co. v. Erica P. John Fund, Inc.*, 134 S. Ct. 2398, 2408 (2014), *quoting*, *Basic, Inc. v. Levinson*, 485 U.S. 224, 246 (1988).

[124] Securities Act Release No. 6383 (1982) (stating that "Form S-3, in reliance on the efficient market theory, allows maximum use of incorporation by reference of Exchange Act reports").

company whose common stock likely traded in an efficient market—namely, in 1980s dollars, by requiring that the subject issuer have at least $150 million of voting stock held by non-affiliates ("float") or, alternatively, have at least a $100 million float and a three million share annual trading volume.[125] Through the years, the Commission and Congress have decreased these thresholds.[126] Today, generally provided it has filed its periodic reports and such reports are readily accessible on a website, an eligible smaller reporting company[127] may incorporate by reference into its subsequent Form S-1 registration statement any SEC reports that were filed before the subject registration statement's effective date.[128]

This development is antithetical to the Commission's principal rationale for prescribing incorporation by reference: namely, "reliance on the efficient market theory, allow[ing] a maximum use of incorporation of Exchange Act reports and requir[ing] the least disclosure to be presented in the prospectus and delivered to investors."[129] Clearly, the integrated disclosure process entailing incorporation by reference now encompasses companies whose securities trade in inefficient markets, thereby dismantling the rationale for this framework in this context. For such issuers, incorporation by reference is the norm even though many of these companies are not widely followed by financial analysts and market intermediaries. Therefore, to a significant degree, the information set

---

125 *Id.* (stating that "the Commission has determined to adopt the $150 million float transaction requirement for the use of Form S-3 by certain registrants and to add an alternative test of $100 million float and 3 million share annual trading volume").

126 *See, e.g.*, Securities Act Release No. 8878 (2007); Securities Act Release No. 10003 (2016).

127 *See* Rule 405, 17 C.F.R. § 230.405; Securities Act Release No. 10513 (2018) (generally defining a "smaller reporting company" to encompass "registrants with a public float of less than $250 million, as well as registrants with annual revenues of less than $100 million for the previous year and either no public float or a public float of less than $700 million"). Enterprises that are ineligible to be deemed a smaller reporting company include an asset-backed issuer, investment company, and majority-owned subsidiary of a parent corporation which is not itself a smaller reporting company. *See* Rule 405.

128 *See* Securities Act Release No. 8591 (2005); Securities Act Release No. 10003 (2016). In Securities Act Release No. 10003 (2016), the SEC stated that "to be eligible to use forward incorporation by reference, smaller reporting companies will be required to be current by having filed (a) an annual report for its most recently completed fiscal year; and (b) all required Exchange Act reports and materials during the 12 months immediately preceding filing of the Form S-1 (or such shorter period that the smaller reporting company was required to file such reports and materials).... In addition, the ability to forward incorporate by reference will be conditioned on the smaller reporting company making its incorporated Exchange Act reports and other materials readily available and accessible on a web site maintained by or for the issuer and disclosing in the prospectus that such materials will be provided upon request." Note that incorporation by reference is not permitted when the issuer is a blank check company, shell company, or an issuer conducting a penny stock offering. *Id.*

129 Securities Act Release No. 6383 (1982).

forth in periodic reports filed by these registrants has not been impounded into market price.[130] To exacerbate this dilemma, as will be discussed in Chapter 4 herein, specified disclosure and internal control requirements for so-called smaller reporting companies have been markedly decreased in recent years, resulting in significant gaps in the regulatory framework.[131] Given that these smaller publicly-held companies frequently are more inclined to engage in lax oversight and disclosure practices, this policy determination unduly favors short-term capital growth over that of adequately informed securities markets.[132] Granted that the impediments and costs of going-public and public company reporting status are significant,[133] thereby dissuading certain companies from entering the public

[130] Clearly, the common stock of many of these smaller reporting companies do not trade in an efficient market. Factors applied in determining whether the market for a particular security is efficient include: "(1) the average weekly trading volume expressed as a percentage of total outstanding shares; (2) the number of securities analysts following and reporting on the stock; (3) the extent to which market makers and arbitrageurs trade in the stock; (4) the company's eligibility to file SEC registration Form S-3 (as opposed to Form S-1) . . . [less important today in view of the Commission's expansion of the Form S-3 eligibility thresholds]; (5) the existence of empirical facts showing a cause and effect relationship between unexpected corporate events or financial releases and an immediate response in the stock price [probably the most important criterion]; (6) the company's market capitalization; (7) the bid-ask spread for stock sales; and (8) float, the stock's trading volume without counting insider stock." *Unger v. Amedisys, Inc.*, 401 F.3d 316, 323 (5th Cir. 2015). Generally, the common stock of smaller reporting companies lack many of the foregoing factors. *See* Russell Robinson, *Fraud on the Market and Thinly-Traded Securities under Rule 10b-5: How Does a Court Decide If a Stock Market Is Efficient?*, 25 Wake Forest L. Rev. 223 (1990).

[131] *See, e.g.*, Securities Exchange Act Release No. 88365 (2020) (exempting certain smaller reporting companies from the requirement to obtain a separate attestation from an outside auditor relating to management's assessment of the effectiveness of the subject issuer's internal control over financial reporting); Securities Act Release No. 10513 (2018) (adopting amendments to expand the number of registrants eligible to use the scaled disclosure requirements in Regulation S-K and Regulation S-X to encompass publicly-held companies having a public float of less than $250 million as well as those that have less than $100 million of revenues and a public float less than $700 million); SEC Press Release No. 2018-116 (June 28, 2018) (setting forth that the amendments will allow an additional 966 registrants to become a smaller reporting company and thus eligible to use scaled disclosure). The scaled disclosure items include: selected financial data, description of the registrant's business, MD&A, information regarding market risk, corporate governance, and executive compensation. For the definition of smaller reporting company, *see supra* note 127; discussion in Chapter 4 herein.

[132] *See* Steinberg, *supra* note 30, at 157 (stating that these congressional and SEC actions, such as the FAST Act and Commission amendments, "may be viewed as an effort to facilitate capital raising while rationalizing implicitly that any security listed on a national securities exchange is by definition traded in an efficient market [but] this rationalization contravenes established doctrine that the critical inquiry is the market for that particular stock, not the location where such stock trades"); John L. Orcutt, *The Case Against Exempting Smaller Reporting Companies from Sarbanes-Oxley Section 404: Why Market-Based Solutions Are Likely to Harm Ordinary Investors*, 14 Ford. J. Corp. Fin. L. 325, 357 (2009) (stating that smaller reporting companies "are more prone to inaccurate financial disclosure" and "receive less collective information-gathering and monitoring services to cope with this increased level of inaccuracy, due to their reduced institutional and secondary support").

[133] *See* Securities Act Release No. 10513 (2018); Stuart R. Cohn and Gregory C. Yadley, *Capital Offense: The SEC's Continuing Failure to Address Small Business Financing Concerns*, 4 N.Y.U. J.L.

markets,[134] these hurdles may be viewed as necessary conditions to minimize the perpetration of fraud and other aberrational conduct that redound to the detriment of investors and the U.S. securities markets.[135]

D. Proposed Adoption of a Mandatory "Summary" Section in SEC Filings

A suggested solution to enable the ordinary investor to have better access to meaningful and understandable information in a subject company's Securities Act registration statement, Exchange Act periodic report (including the Forms 10-K, 10-Q, and 8-K) and other SEC filing (such as the proxy statement) is to require a sufficiently comprehensive "Summary" Section at the beginning of each such document. For example, in the Securities Act registration context, whether incorporation by reference is utilized by a blue chip issuer by means of shelf registration[136] or by a relatively

---

& Bus. 1 (2007); Carl Schneider et al., *Going Public: Practice, Procedure, and Consequences*, 27 Vill. L. Rev. 1 (1981).

[134] *See* Securities Act Release No. 10513 (2018) (commenting that "a lower disclosure burden [for smaller reporting companies (SRC)] could spur growth in the registrants that newly qualify for SRC status to the extent that the compliance cost savings and other resources (e.g., managerial effort) otherwise devoted to disclosure and compliance are effectively deployed in alternative ways [and] also could encourage capital formation because companies that may have been hesitant to go public may choose to do so if they face reduced disclosure requirements").

[135] *See* Paredes, *supra* note 95, at 472 (stating that less demanding disclosure obligations, such as "scaling back the mandatory disclosure system," would facilitate "bad" issuers to "mimic" the conduct of "good" issuers, thereby undermining "its usefulness in solving the lemons problem in capital markets"); Robert Prentice, *Wither Securities Regulation?: Some Behavioral Observations Regarding Proposals for Its Future*, 51 Duke L.J. 1397, 1403 (2002) (asserting that the presence of a more permissive regulatory environment signals that fraud is "more acceptable and therefore more likely to occur"); Edward Rock, *Securities Regulation as Lobster Trap: A Credible Commitment Theory of Mandatory Disclosure*, 23 Cardozo L. Rev. 675, 686 (2002) (asserting that the mandatory disclosure framework "provides a credible and specialized enforcement mechanism which warrants both the comprehensiveness and quality of the information disclosed"); discussion in Chapter 4 herein.

[136] Generally, under shelf registration, securities are offered or sold on a delayed or continuous basis in the future. *See* Rule 415, 17 C.F.R. § 230.415. In such offerings, information contained in Exchange Act reports is incorporated by reference into the shelf registration statement. *See* Amici Curiae Brief of the Securities Industry Association and the Bond Market Association at pages 1, 3, in *In re Worldcom, Inc., Securities Litigation*, 346 F. Supp. 2d 628 (S.D.N.Y. 2004) (stating that "shelf registration offerings have become an essential part of the capital raising markets in the United States [and that such offerings] allow for more rapid and repeated access to the markets [due to that] an issuer [can] access the markets at any time and on extremely short notice, often as little as a few hours, without any further SEC review"). Moreover, with respect to well-known seasoned issuers (generally, reporting companies that have a public float of common stock of at least $700 million or have registered and issued at least $1 billion of non-convertible securities (other than common stock during the past three years)), the shelf registration statement immediately becomes effective upon its filing with the SEC. *See* Securities Act Release No. 8591 (2005).

recent publicly-held company,[137] the ordinary investor should have ready access to meaningful information regarding the company and other material facts in an understandable and plainly-written format. Mandating that the Summary contain the requisite material information in a succinct and user-friendly format should not prove unduly onerous for subject companies. The presence of a sufficiently comprehensive Summary in SEC registration statements and periodic filings—including shelf registered offerings by large-cap companies as well as certain Exchange Act filings (such as proxy statements and Forms 10-K and 10-Q)—should facilitate a more disciplined disclosure process and provide ordinary investors with better access to the material information necessary to make informed decisions.[138] In this regard, mandating that each Exchange Act reporting company have a disclosure committee comprised solely of independent directors who may retain separate legal counsel on the committee's behalf should help to effectuate this objective.[139]

---

[137] Many of these registrants are smaller reporting companies. *See supra* note 127 for the definition of smaller reporting company. There are thousands of these companies that may implement the scaled disclosure requirements. *See supra* discussion notes 131–135 and accompanying text.

[138] *See* Item 503(a) of Regulation S-K, 17 C.F.R. § 229.503(a) (stating that the registrant "must furnish in plain English . . . a summary of the information in the prospectus where the length or complexity of the prospectus makes a summary useful [and] should be brief"). Although useful, this item does not specify the type of information to be disclosed and does not extend to Exchange Act periodic filings.

The plain English disclosure rules adopted by the SEC focus on clarity of prospectus disclosure. Pursuant to these rules, the prospectus summary (as well as certain other portions of the prospectus) must be written in plain English. *See* Rule 421, 17 C.F.R. § 230.421; Securities Act Release No. 7497 (1998). The proposal set forth herein is to expand this requirement to mandate that a more comprehensive Summary must be provided not only in registered offerings but also in all SEC filings, including Exchange Act periodic reports (such as the Forms 10-K, 10-Q, and 8-K).

[139] Many publicly-held companies have disclosure committees comprised of corporate officers and other senior employees who typically report to the company's chief executive officer or chief financial officer. The committee is tasked with assessing the materiality of information and the company's disclosure obligations as well as playing an important role in maintaining adequate disclosure controls and procedures. *See* KPMG, *Transparency and Management's Disclosure Committee* (2016). As proposed in the Report of the Advisory Committee on the Capital Formation and Regulatory Processes, a disclosure committee comprised of outside directors would be formed to help ensure the integrity of corporate disclosures. This delegation would improve the disclosure process and provide some level of comfort that directors have met their statutory obligations. *See* [1996–1997 Transfer Binder] Fed. Sec. L. Rep. (CCH) ¶ 85,834, at 88,427–28 (1996) (positing that use of such a disclosure committee would be beneficial by: "ensur[ing] more continuous oversight of the disclosure preparation process and, over time, improv[ing] the quality and integrity of periodic and secondary market reporting and disclosure generally"; "provid[ing] a focus at the board level for due diligence in the context of primary offerings by issuers, thereby ensuring greater involvement by outside directors as one set of monitors"; and "provid[ing] a practical means for greater outside director involvement with the due diligence activities of other gatekeepers, such as underwriters"). The proposal set forth herein recommends that the disclosure committee be comprised solely of outside directors who, when appropriate, have the statutory entitlement to retain separate legal counsel—as is the situation currently with respect to audit committees. *See* § 10A of the Securities Exchange Act, 15 U.S.C. § 78j-1; Securities Exchange Act Release No. 48745 (2003); discussion in Chapter 4 herein.

E. Partial Dismantling of the Mandatory Disclosure Framework

Nonetheless, without much ado, the Commission has dismantled the mandatory disclosure framework in certain contexts.[140] This abandonment is most visibly seen with respect to Rule 506 offerings sold solely to accredited investors.[141] In these offerings, no compulsory disclosure requirements are specified.[142] Extending beyond institutional investors and financially sophisticated individual investors, the term "accredited investor" encompasses persons who with one's spouse or spousal equivalent have a net worth of $1 million (exclusive of one's primary residence) as well as those who generally earn $200,000 (or $300,000 joint) annual income.[143] With respect to each such individual, an irrebuttable presumption arises that he or she is financially sophisticated and can meaningfully bargain for registration-type information, thereby being able to fend for oneself.[144] Such a presumption is unwarranted and belies reality. The frauds that have been perpetrated upon such unwitting investors in Rule 506 offerings attest to the short-sightedness of the Commission's approach, which seeks to facilitate capital raising at the expense of investor protection.[145]

---

[140] For further discussion on this subject, *see* Chapter 3 herein.

[141] Rule 506(b), (c), 17 C.F.R. § 230.506(b), (c). Pursuant to the National Securities Market Improvements Act of 1996 (NSMIA), state regulation of Rule 506 offerings is preempted. *See* § 18(b)(4)(D), 15 U.S.C. § 77r(b)(4)(D); *Brown v. Earthboard Sports USA, Inc.*, 481 F.3d 901 (6th Cir. 2007); Jill Meyer, *Federal Preemption of the Rule 506 Exemption*, 37 Sec. Reg. L.J. 122 (2009); discussion in Chapter 3 herein.

[142] *See* Securities Act Release No. 6389 (1982) (stating that "if an issuer sells securities . . . only to accredited investors, then Regulation D does not mandate any specific disclosure"). Note that the antifraud provisions apply, signifying that disclosure of certain information ordinarily will be made.

[143] This accredited investor income level is income made for the prior two years with the reasonable expectation of reaching the requisite income level in the current year. Generally, other than individuals, having total assets exceeding $5 million qualifies such organization as an accredited investor. *See* Rule 501(a), 17 C.F.R. § 230.501(a); Securities Act Release No. 10824 (2020) ("add[ing] new categories of natural persons that may qualify as accredited investors based on certain professional certifications or designations or other credentials or their status as a private fund's 'knowledgeable employee' "); discussion in Chapter 3 herein.

[144] *See* Rule 506(b), (c), 17 C.F.R. § 230.506(b), (c). *Cf. Securities and Exchange Commission v. Ralston Purina Co.*, 346 U.S. 119, 124 (1953) (interpreting the statutory private offering exemption, stating that its availability should turn upon "whether the particular class of persons affected needs the protection of the [Securities] Act"); *Doran v. Petroleum Management Corp.*, 545 F.2d 893 (5th Cir. 1977) (opining that under the § 4(2) (now § 4(a)(2)) statutory private offering exemption, wealth does not render an individual financially sophisticated).

[145] *See* Luis A. Aguilar, *Increasing the Vulnerability of Investors* (SEC Public Statement 2012) (dissenting from the Commission's action regarding proposed amendments to Rule 506, then SEC Commissioner Aguilar stating: "When general solicitation is combined with an offering exemption such as Rule 506, no information statement or disclosure is required to be given to investors [and]

The solution to this dilemma is straightforward. In addition to financial wealth (such as having substantial net worth), to be deemed an accredited investor, an individual must have the requisite financial sophistication or be advised by his or her representative who has such financial acumen.[146] Such financial sophistication may be established through such indicia as education, work experience, and prior investing history. Absent such a showing, the mandatory disclosure framework should apply to entitle the subject investor to the receipt of registration-type information.[147]

To irrebuttably hold that an individual with $1 million net worth or annual income of $200,000 has sufficient leverage to bargain successfully to access material information belies reality. Yet, with the objective of enhancing capital formation, the SEC engages in this endeavor knowing full well that such investors often lack financial sophistication as well as the wherewithal to induce the issuer and its promoter to disclose registration-type information. Mandating that registration-type information be disclosed to those who are not financially sophisticated (or that meaningful access to such information be provided) should be a condition for a subject issuer to access the securities markets. Although this condition may adversely impact capital raising to a certain degree, it should reduce the frequency and severity of financial harm that occurs.[148]

---

thus, fraud can be easier to effect and much harder to detect"), available at https://www.sec.gov/news/public-statement/2012-spch082912laahtm.

[146] Basically, this proposal is a similar standard to that existing prior to the promulgation of Rule 506 in 1982 which generally required both prospective investor access to (or actual delivery of) registration-type information as well as financial sophistication (or the use of an offeree representative who had the requisite sophistication). *See, e.g., Lawler v. Gilliam*, 569 F.2d 1283 (4th Cir. 1978); *Doran v. Petroleum Management Corp.*, 545 F.2d 893 (5th Cir. 1977); former SEC Rule 146 (rule promulgated under the then § 4(2) (now § 4(a)(2)) private offering exemption).

[147] *See* Marc I. Steinberg, *Corporate Internal Affairs—A Corporate and Securities Law Perspective* 44–49 (1983); Marc I. Steinberg, *The Securities and Exchange Commission's Administrative, Enforcement, and Legislative Programs and Policies—Their Influence on Corporate Internal Affairs*, 58 Notre Dame L. Rev. 173, 209–14 (1982); discussion in Chapter 3 herein.

[148] This point was made in a letter submitted by the author to the SEC in response to the Commission's request for public comment regarding ways to simplify, enhance, and harmonize the Securities Act's exemptive framework. In that letter, the author asserted:

> The objective of this letter is to emphasize that the SEC's primary role is that of *investor protection—not* enhancing capital formation. Undoubtedly, while reducing undue impediments to the formation of capital should be an important Commission objective—the focus should be on providing sufficient investor safeguards. Unfortunately, the SEC has failed repeatedly in this task since the promulgation of Regulation D in the early 1980s. There, the Commission unilaterally overruled established appellate case law (*see, e.g., Lawler v. Gilliam*, 569 F.2d 1283 (4th Cir. 1978)) to dismantle the mandatory disclosure framework when an eligible offering is made solely to so-called wealthy individual

F. Requirement to Disclose All Material Information

Perhaps the most distressing characteristic of the current disclosure framework is the failure to require that companies disclose all material information in their SEC registration statements and periodic filings. Although the Regulation S-K disclosure items are comprehensive, with some frequency, they fail to capture all the material information which investors ought to receive.[149] Hence, the knowing failure by a company and its executives to disclose clearly important information to investors in its SEC filings is excused because the particular event or situation is not called for by a specified SEC disclosure item.[150] As stated by one appellate court: "There is no

---

"accredited investors." Unfortunately, with respect to individuals, this "financial" sophistication is based on wealth alone—and was set at the amount of $1 million of one's net worth. The result was that unsophisticated individuals invested in these offerings—all too frequently without adequate disclosure. Although misrepresentation/fraud claims may be brought after the fact, the likelihood of satisfactory recovery plus the uncertainty and costs of litigation are unacceptable ramifications. . . .

Through the decades, the Commission has declined to increase this $1 million net worth standard—even after the scandals of the 1990s. It took Congress in the Dodd-Frank Act of 2010 to enact legislation directing that this $1 million amount is exclusive of one's primary residence. That legislation also called for the SEC to revisit this monetary amount and increase such amount if deemed appropriate. The Commission has not done so—again, favoring capital formation over its primary mission of investor protection. In one of my prior articles, I criticized the Commission for this failure. *See* Steinberg, *The "Accredited" Individual Purchaser under SEC Regulation D: Time to Up the Ante*, 29 Sec. Reg. L.J. 93 (2001). As of today, my understanding is that $1 million in 1982 dollars is now the equivalent of approximately $2,650,000. In seeking to fulfill its statutory mandate, the SEC needs to remedy this situation. Thus, any revision of the Commission's exemptive framework impacting individual accredited investors should include an increased amount for both the net worth and individual/joint income criteria.

Public Comment Letter Submitted by Marc I. Steinberg, File Number S7-08-19, Concept Release on Harmonization of Securities Offerings (August 5, 2019), available at https://www.sec.gov/comments/s7-08-19/s70819-5914776-188970.pdf.

[149] *See, e.g.*, *Cooperman v. Individual, Inc.*, 171 F.3d 43 (1st Cir. 1999) (holding that, while material to investors, a conflict between the company's chief executive officer and its board of directors regarding corporate growth strategy was not required to be disclosed).

[150] In this context, the duty to disclose and the timing of disclosure is within the good faith judgment of the company's board of directors and management. *See, e.g.*, *Chiarella v. United States*, 445 U.S. 222, 230 (1980) (absent a duty to disclose, silence under § 10(b) of the Securities Exchange Act not actionable); *Shaw v. Digital Equipment Corp.*, 82 F.3d, 1194, 1202 (1st Cir. 1996) (stating that "the mere possession of material nonpublic information does not create a duty to disclose it"); *Securities and Exchange Commission v. Texas Gulf Sulphur Co.*, 401 F.2d 833, 850 n. 12 (2d Cir. 1968) (en banc) (stating that "the timing of disclosure is a matter for the business judgment of the corporation within the affirmative disclosure requirements promulgated by the exchanges and the SEC"). *See generally* Jeffrey D. Bauman, *Rule 10b-5 and the Corporation's Affirmative Duty to Disclose*, 67 Georgetown L.J. 935 (1979).

general duty on the part of a company to provide the public with all material information."[151]

Such a rule makes no sense: it incentivizes issuer nondisclosure, adversely impacts efficient markets, and contravenes investor expectations. Not surprisingly, other developed securities markets reject this arbitrary approach.[152] These countries mandate that, absent meritorious business justification, prompt disclosure must be made by a subject issuer to investors and the securities markets of all material information.[153] Consistent with this position, the national securities exchanges in the United States require a listed company, absent the existence of a valid business reason, timely to disclose material information.[154] Nonetheless, these stock exchange rules

[151] *J & R Marketing SEP v. General Motors Corp.*, 549 F.3d 484, 496–97 (6th Cir. 2008) (also opining that "[w]e are not authorized to impose a wide-ranging duty to disclose anything that a person can allege was nonpublic, material information"). *See Cooperman v. Individual, Inc.*, 171 F.3d 43, 49 (1st Cir. 1999) (stating that "although in the context of a public offering there is a strong affirmative duty of disclosure, it is clear that an issuer of securities owes no absolute duty to disclose all material information").

In a bygone era, the SEC exhorted registrants to disclose all material nonpublic information. For example, in a 1970 release, the Commission stated: "Notwithstanding the fact that a company complies with [its] reporting requirements, it still has an obligation to make full and prompt announcements of material facts regarding the company's financial condition." Securities Act Release No. 5092 (1970). In another release, the SEC stated: "Investors have legitimate expectations that public companies are making and will continue to make prompt disclosure of significant corporate developments." Securities Exchange Act Release No. 18271 (1981).

[152] *See, e.g.*, Corporations Act of 2001 (Cth) S 674(2) (Australia); Province of Ontario Securities Act, R.S.O. 1990, c. S. 5, § 75 (Ontario—Canada has no federal securities law); Council Regulation (EU) No. 596/2014 of the European Parliament and of the Council of 16 April 2014 on Market Abuse Regulation at art. 17 (providing that in addition to having a justifiable reason for delaying disclosure, the subject company also must establish that such delay will likely not mislead investors and that the confidentiality of the particular information will be maintained). *See generally Market Abuse Regulation—Commentary and Annotated Guide* (Marco Ventoruzzo and Sebastian Mock eds., 2018).

[153] *See* sources *supra* note 152; Timothy J. Johnston, *Is Mandatory Real-Time Disclosure Really Mandatory? A Comparison of Real-Time Disclosure Frameworks and Enforcement*, 47 Sec. Reg. L.J. 44, 56–57 (2019) (observing that "[t]he more widely adopted continuous disclosure framework is one that affirmatively requires companies to report all material nonpublic information in real time as soon as reasonably possible unless the information falls within one of the minor exceptions"); Marc I. Steinberg, *Insider Trading, Selective Disclosure, and Prompt Disclosure: A Comparative Analysis*, 22 U. Pa. J. Int'l Econ. L. 635, 670 (2001) (stating that "[u]nder the laws of other jurisdictions, absent sufficient business justification, publicly-held issuers on a continuous basis must promptly and timely disclose material matters to the securities marketplace").

This adequate business justification exception should be narrow, such as when "immediate disclosure is likely to prejudice the legitimate interests of the issuer." Market Abuse Regulation (MAR) art. 17(4). *See* European Securities and Markets Authority MAR Guidelines: Delay in the Disclosure of Inside Information (2016), available at https://www.esma.europa.eu/sites/default/files/library/2016-1478_mar_guidelines_-_legitimate_interests.pdf. (A non-exhaustive list of such possible situations was issued by the European Securities and Markets Authority to include negotiations focusing on major transactions (such as a merger), plans to acquire a substantial equity interest in another enterprise, and required approval of a contemplated contract by an unrelated party where confidentiality is necessary.); Timothy J. Johnston, *supra*, at 58 (discussing situations where disclosure of material information may be delayed pursuant to the EU MAR Regulation).

[154] *See, e.g.*, New York Stock Exchange (NYSE), Listed Company Manual §§ 202.01–.06; Nasdaq Listing Rules, Disclosure of Material Information Rule, IM-5250(b)(1). With certain exceptions,

may be viewed as more rhetoric than substance as the exchanges rarely issue sanctions against listed companies for such noncompliance, and, as held by the courts, investors have no private right of action for damages based on an alleged violation of a stock exchange rule.[155]

Indeed, even with respect to the filing of the current report on Form 8-K, which focuses on significant developments impacting the subject registrant during the interval between periodic reports,[156] the SEC declines to mandate that all material information known to such registrant, absent sufficient business justification, be disclosed.[157] For example, a major customer's termination of a clearly material contract need not be disclosed in the subject company's Form 8-K.[158] This failure to require that all material information be disclosed in the Form 8-K impedes the effectuation of adequately informed securities markets.[159]

NYSE Manual Section 202.05 provides in part: "A listed company is expected to release quickly to the public any news of information which might reasonably be expected to materially affect the market for its securities." Similarly, Nasdaq Listing Rule IM-5250(b)(1), with certain exceptions, requires that "Nasdaq Companies disclose promptly to the public through any Regulation FD compliant method (or combination of methods) of disclosure any material information that would reasonably be expected to affect the value of their securities or influence investors' decisions."

Generally, Regulation FD prohibits selective disclosure by issuers of material nonpublic information. *See* 17 C.F.R. § 243.100 *et seq.*; Securities Exchange Act Release No. 43154 (2000) (adopting release). In this country, publicly-held companies may disclose material nonpublic information even though not required by SEC rule or statute in order to meet the expectations of financial intermediaries, market analysts, institutional investors, and active shareholders. *See generally* Marc I. Steinberg and Jason B. Myers, *Lurking in the Shadows: The Hidden Issues of the Securities and Exchange Commission's Regulation FD*, 27 J. Corp. L. 173 (2002).

155 *See, e.g.*, *Harris v. TD Ameritrade, Inc.*, 805 F.3d 664 (6th Cir. 2015); *Walck v. American Stock Exchange*, 687 F.2d 778 (3d Cir. 1982); *State Teachers Retirement Board v. Fluor Corp.*, 654 F.2d 843 (2d Cir. 1981); *Jablon v. Dean Witter & Co.*, 614 F.2d 677 (9th Cir. 1980). Over fifty years ago, a number of courts did imply a private right of action in this context. *See, e.g.*, *Buttrey v. Merrill Lynch, Pierce, Fenner & Smith, Inc.*, 410 F.2d 135 (7th Cir. 1969). These older decisions evidently no longer are followed. Occasionally, the securities exchanges will levy sanctions against non-compliant listed companies. *See, e.g.*, Jing Yang, *Luckin Is on Brink of Nasdaq Delisting*, Wall St. J., May 20, 2020, at B3 (reporting that the Nasdaq Stock Market has determined to delist company due to disclosure of fabricated sales and company's "past failure to publicly disclose material information").

156 17 C.F.R. § 249.308.

157 *See* Securities Exchange Act Release No. 49424 (2004). The SEC amended the Form 8-K in 2004 in response to legislative directive set forth in the Sarbanes-Oxley Act of 2002. *See* § 409, Pub. L. No. 107-204, 116 Stat. 745 (mandating that "[e]ach issuer reporting under Section 13(a) and 15(d) [of the Securities Exchange Act] shall disclose to the public on a rapid and current basis such additional information concerning material changes in the financial condition or operations of the issuer, in plain English, which may include trend and qualitative information and graphic presentations, as the Commission determines by rule, is necessary or useful for the protection of investors and in the public interest").

158 *See* Securities Exchange Act Release No. 49424 (2004) (reasoning that requiring a registrant to disclose this information would present difficulties in determining when the subject contract was in fact terminated and could induce customers to engage in negotiation ploys). This rationale is subject to criticism. The irretrievable loss of a significant contract presumptively is material to investors and the securities markets. *See* Marc I. Steinberg, *Securities Regulation* 857 (7th ed. 2017).

159 Since the market price of a company's stock supposedly reflects all material information that is in the public domain, nondisclosure of such information signifies that the market price of the stock is misinformed. *See* discussion *supra* notes 122–135 and accompanying text.

G. Proposed Mandate to Disclose All Material Information

Hence, the failure to require disclosure of all material information (absent a justifiable reason) by publicly-held companies signifies that, with frequency, the securities of these companies do not trade at prices that accurately reflect their value. This situation thus adversely impacts the integrity of the securities markets—specifically, that while the market price of a company's stock in an efficient market reflects all publicly available information,[160] that price does not reflect undisclosed material information that has a reasonable likelihood of significant price impact. Undue delay in providing such information means that all too often the market prices of even well-known seasoned issuers[161] lack price accuracy. To alleviate this situation, publicly-traded companies should be required to disclose (absent meritorious justification) all material information within one business day after becoming aware of the materiality of such information.[162]

The implementation of this mandate also would provide another tangible benefit: it would drastically reduce opportunities for engaging in illegal insider trading.[163] By substantially closing the window for undisclosed material information to be embargoed by a subject company and its agents, incidents of impermissible insider trading should drastically decrease.[164] Despite the

---

160 *See, e.g.*, *Halliburton Co. v. Erica P. John Fund, Inc.*, 134 S. Ct. 2398, 2408 (2014), *quoting*, *Basic, Inc. v. Levinson*, 485 U.S. 224, 246 (1988) (stating that "the market price of shares traded on well-developed markets reflects all publicly-available information").

161 Among other requirements, well-known seasoned issuers either "(1) have a worldwide common equity (*e.g.*, common stock) market capitalization of at least $700 million [held by non-affiliates], or (2) have issued at least $1 billion of non-convertible securities, other than common equity, in registered primary offerings for cash (not exchange offers) in the last three years." Steinberg, *supra* note 30, at 128–29, *discussing*, Securities Act Release No. 8591 (2005).

162 As discussed in the text, a key exception would allow for delayed disclosure if a justifiable business reason existed. Generally, this one business day period follows the practice adopted by SEC Regulation FD. Pursuant to Regulation FD, if the selective disclosure of material nonpublic information is not intentional, the subject company must publicly disclose such information "promptly" meaning "as soon as reasonably practicable (but in no event after the later of 24 hours or the commencement of the next day's trading on the New York Stock Exchange)." Rule 101(d) of Regulation FD 17 C.F.R. § 243.101(d). *See* sources cited *supra* note 154.

163 For more coverage of insider trading, *see* Chapter 7 herein.

164 With respect to the impact of continuous disclosure obligations on the frequency of insider trading, the authors of one study found that "large abnormal gains to insiders came 'largely from transactions involving delayed disclosure' whereas 'transactions involving immediate disclosure earn[ed] insignificant returns' [thereby implying] that well-crafted disclosure rules have a significant impact on the incidence of insider conduct." George W. Walker and Andrew F. Simpson, *Insider Conduct in New Zealand: Exploring the Enforcement Deficit*, 2013 New Zealand L. Rev. 521, 542 (2013) (also stating that "[a]n effective continuous disclosure regime reduces the incidence of insider conduct by narrowing the information asymmetry between insiders and the market generally"), *quoting study by* Ahmad Etebari et al., *Disclosure Regulation and the Profitability of Insider Trading: Evidence from New Zealand*, 12 Pacific-Basin Finance Journal 479 (2004).

SEC's focus on combatting illegal insider trading,[165] the Commission nonetheless declines to remedy this disclosure gap.[166] The consequence is that the securities markets and investors lack material information, while miscreants have far greater wherewithal to illegally trade.

The solution to this unacceptable situation is clear. The SEC should adopt the following new disclosure item within Regulation S-K that would apply, by way of example, to all SEC registration statements, periodic filings (including Form 8-K current reports), and proxy statements:[167]

By analogy, the Sarbanes-Oxley Act amended the Securities Exchange Act to require that directors, officers, and ten percent shareholders of a publicly-held company must report their trades of an equity security to the SEC within two business days. *See* § 403(a) of the Sarbanes-Oxley Act, *amending*, §16(a) of the Securities Exchange Act, 15 U.S.C. § 78p(a); Securities Exchange Act Release No. 47809 (2003). Prior to this amendment, such insiders were able to delay reporting their trades until the tenth day after the end of the month in which the subject trades were made. *See generally* Peter J. Romeo and Alan L. Dye, *Section 16 of the Securities Exchange Act of 1934: Treatise and Reporting Guide* (5th ed. 2019). One key impact of this amendment is that it significantly reduced, if not largely eliminated, the opportunity for insiders to engage in stock option backdating. *See generally Ryan v. Gifford*, 918 A.2d 341 (Del. Ch. 2007) (addressing stock option backdating). For additional discussion, *see* Chapter 7 herein.

[165] *See, e.g.*, Marc I. Steinberg and William K.S. Wang, *Insider Trading* 639 (3d ed. 2010) (stating that the SEC is "waging its 'war' on insider trading"); David A. Vise and Steve Coll, *Eagle on the Street* 53 (1991) (quoting then SEC Chairman John Shad as stating that the Commission "was about to 'come down with hobnail boots' on illegal insider trading"). The subject of insider trading is addressed in Chapter 7 herein.

[166] The SEC's refusal is consistent with its long-standing practices in related situations. For example, until the enactment of the Sarbanes-Oxley Act directing the Commission to adopt rules requiring publicly-traded companies to adhere to current reporting obligations (§ 409 of the Sarbanes-Oxley Act, *amending*, § 13(l) of the Securities Exchange Act), the Commission declined to require such current disclosure except for a few events (namely, changes in control of the registrant, acquisition or disposition of specified assets, bankruptcy or receivership, changes in the company's certifying accountant, and resignation of a company director). This void left major gaps in the continuous reporting regime with respect to which Congress directed the SEC to fill. In performing this task, although enhancing the continuous reporting framework, the Commission elected to leave significant loopholes. For an article addressing this issue prior to the enactment of the Sarbanes-Oxley Act, *see* Steinberg, *supra* note 153, at 661 (stating that, with certain narrow exceptions, "the SEC should amend Form 8-K so as to mandate prompt disclosure of any event which a company knows or has reason to know will have a material impact on that enterprise"). For further discussion, *see* Chapter 9 herein.

[167] Note that the American Law Institute's *Federal Securities Code* would require company registration—rather than registration of securities. *See* American Law Institute, *Federal Securities Code* xxvii (1980) ("Under the Code there will be no more registration of securities. Instead, a company will register as such when it first reaches [a specified asset amount and number of holders of its securities] . . . or when the first 'distribution' is made of any of its securities."). The Report of the Advisory Committee on the Capital Formation and Regulatory Processes, [1996–1997 Transfer Binder] Fed. Sec. L. Rep. (CCH) ¶ 85,834, at 88,409 (1996), took a similar approach (stating that "the focus of the regulatory process in the post-initial public offering context should be shifted from registering transactions to registering companies with a corresponding emphasis on better ensuring the accuracy and integrity of continuing disclosures [and that] once a company is registered and filing the required public reports, all the securities that the company or its affiliates sell thereafter would be deemed registered for purposes of the Securities Act"). The SEC has declined to adopt this approach. Rather, through incorporation by reference and the shelf registration process, the Commission has endeavored to make the disclosure system more uniform and effective. While this objective has been somewhat achieved, as addressed in this section of the chapter, significant gaps remain.

> In addition to the information required to be included in the subject document, there shall also be provided any further material information, irrespective of whether such material information is or is not called for by any other item of this Regulation S-K. Omission of such material information is permitted provided that the issuer (or registrant) can establish a justifiable business reason for such omission.[168]

This proposed rule is consistent with the approach adhered to by other developed securities markets as well as by the U.S. stock exchanges.[169] By setting forth a meritorious business justification for nondisclosure, the burden on subject issuers and registrants should not be unduly burdensome. Importantly, adoption of this rule in conjunction with vigilant enforcement by the SEC should prove beneficial to market efficiency and investor interests.[170]

V. Conclusion

This chapter has focused on the disclosure framework of the federal securities laws. It has explored the benefits and drawbacks of the current regime and

---

[168] In an earlier era, by its rhetoric, the SEC suggested that registrants must disclose (absent justifiable business reason) all material information. *See, e.g.*, Securities Act Release No. 5092 (1970) (stating that "[n]otwithstanding the fact that a company complies with its reporting requirements, it still has an obligation to make full and prompt announcements of material facts regarding the company's financial condition"); discussion *supra* note 151; discussion in Chapter 4 herein.

In 2018, President Trump requested that the SEC review whether to shift from a quarterly public reporting mandate to semiannual reports with the objectives of easing regulatory costs, ameliorating short-term focus of companies, and generating growth. *See* Dave Michaels et al., *Trump Asks SEC to Ease Earnings Reporting*, Wall St. J., Aug. 18–19, 2018, at A1. *See also* W. Randy Eaddy, *A Case for Eliminating Quarterly Periodic Reporting: Addressing the Malady of Short-Termism in U.S. Markets with Real Medicine*, 74 Bus. Law. 387 (2019). At this point, President Trump's idea will not be implemented. *See* Dave Michaels, *SEC Won't Change Quarterly Reporting Rule*, Wall St. J., Oct. 12, 2018, at B1. The idea was met with criticism. *See* Review & Outlook, *Trump and Quarterly Capitalism*, Wall St. J., Aug. 23, 2018, at A16 (opining that "regular corporate earnings reports enhance accountability"); James J. Park, *Do the Securities Laws Promote Short-Termism?*, 10 U.C. Irvine L. Rev. 991 (2020) (stating that focus on short-term results largely was due to earnings projections issued by research analysts and urging that the SEC not eliminate quarterly disclosures); Jason Zweig, *Cutting Back on Corporate Disclosure Isn't the Answer*, Wall St. J., Aug. 18–19, 2018, at B1 (asserting that disclosure should not be dialed back). Regardless whether a quarterly or semiannual reporting framework ultimately emerges, a key point is that the information required to be included in the Form 8-K current report must be sufficiently comprehensive to keep the securities markets and investors adequately apprised, calling for the disclosure of all material information (absent adequate business justification otherwise).

[169] *See* discussion *supra* notes 152–154 and accompanying text.

[170] Unfortunately, with some frequency, the SEC has declined to pursue possible violators although having clear authority to do so. One such example is the Commission's failure on even one occasion to invoke the control person provision (§ 20(a) of the Securities Exchange Act, 15 U.S.C. § 78t(a)) in the aftermath of the financial crisis. For further discussion, *see* Steinberg, *supra* note 41, at 282–84; discussion in Chapter 9 herein.

recommended measures that should be implemented to improve its efficacy. As developed in this chapter, significant deficiencies currently exist that should be expeditiously remedied. While Congress and the SEC deserve kudos for effectively implementing a comprehensive disclosure framework, shortcomings continue to prevail that merit the prompt adoption of corrective action.[171]

---

[171] With respect to foreign companies issuing and listing their securities in the United States, the question arises what, if any, accommodations should be made. Generally, two approaches have been advanced to harmonize such regulation on an international basis: First, commonality which seeks to implement a common set of requirements, including standardized disclosure documents to be applicable in international offerings. Second, reciprocity which provides mutual recognition by one country of the regulatory framework and disclosure materials of foreign subject companies provided that minimum standards are satisfied. Clearly, harmonization through reciprocity is the more feasible approach. In this assessment, the regulatory authorities must weigh such factors as making their markets more advantageous to domestic and foreign investors versus the overriding concern that the lack of equivalent disclosure and the perpetration of fraud by foreign companies will redound to the detriment of their securities markets and citizenry. *See* Marc I. Steinberg, *International Securities Law—A Contemporary and Comparative Analysis* 1–51 (1999).

To some degree, in this country, the SEC provides non-U.S. issuers with greater flexibility in adhering to U.S. disclosure documents. Provided that these accommodations are prudently adopted and that vigorous enforcement prevails against foreign companies and their insiders, this approach is the most sensible. The SEC has been criticized for applying unduly lax standards for foreign private issuers from relatively unregulated markets accompanied by lenient enforcement against such issuers. *See, e.g.*, Steven M. Davidoff, *Rhetoric and Reality: A Historical Perspective on the Regulation of Foreign Private Issuers*, 79 U. Cin. L. Rev. 619 (2011); Yuliya Guseva, *The SEC and Foreign Private Issuers: A Path to Optimal Public Enforcement*, 59 Bos. Coll. L. Rev. 2055 (2018). For SEC accommodations to foreign private issuers, *see, e.g.*, *Simplification of Registration and Reporting Requirements for Foreign Companies*, Securities Act Release No. 7053 (1994) (setting forth accommodations made for foreign companies to include: not requiring quarterly reports, exempting from the proxy rules and § 16 reporting and short-swing profit recovery, executive compensation provided on an aggregate basis if reported in this manner in the issuer's home country, and updating of offering document financial statements on a semiannual basis instead of quarterly); Securities Act Release No. 8879 (2007) (adopting amendments to the cross-border exemptions expanding these exemptions to allow U.S security holders to participate in business combination transactions and rights offerings for foreign companies on the same basis as other target security holders); Securities Act Release No. 8957 (2008) (adopting amendments to accept use of financial statements prepared in compliance with International Financial Reporting Standards by foreign private issuers in SEC filings without requiring reconciliation to generally accepted accounting principles as applied in the United States). For a recent example of the SEC applying lax standards, *see* Dave Michaels and Akane Otani, *U.S. Seeks to Audit Chinese Firms, Stirring New Worries for Investors*, Wall St. J., May 27, 2020, at A1 ("For more than a decade, Chinese companies raised billions of dollars by listing their shares on U.S. stock exchanges while avoiding the accounting quality checks that other public firms endure.").

Note that the United States and Canada have adopted the Multijurisdictional Disclosure System, which is based on reciprocity. *See* Securities Act Release No. 6902 (1991).

See generally International Organization of Securities Commissions, *Objectives and Principles of Securities Regulation* (1998), available at https://www.iosco.org/library/pubdocs/pdf/IOSCOPD82.pdf; Daniel A. Braverman, *U.S. Legal Considerations Affecting Global Offerings of Shares in Foreign Companies*, 17 Nw. J. Int'l L. & Bus. 30 (1996); Kenneth B. Davis, Jr., *The SEC and Foreign Companies—A Balance of Competing Interests*, 71 U. Pitt. L. Rev. 457 (2010); Marc I. Steinberg and Lee E. Michaels, *Disclosure in Global Securities Offerings: Analysis of Jurisdictional Approaches, Commonality and Reciprocity*, 20 U. Mich. J. Int'l L. 207 (1999); Manning Gilbert Warren III, *Global Harmonization of Securities Laws: The Achievements of the European Communities*, 31 Harv. Int'l L.J. 185 (1990); Samuel Wolff, *Recent Developments in International Securities Regulation*, 23 Denv. Int'l L. & Pol. 347 (1995).

3

Exemptions from Securities Act Registration

I. Introduction

Through the last four decades, with the Securities and Exchange Commission (SEC) engaging in piecemeal amendments seeking to facilitate capital raising, the exemption framework has become convoluted and problematic. With respect to both primary exemptions as well as exemptions in the secondary trading markets, Congress and the Commission have dismantled established criteria in the exemption regimen. The result is a framework that unduly favors capital formation at the expense of investor protection.[1]

Particularly where state oversight of exempt offerings is preempted,[2] the specter of fraud perpetrated upon unknowing investors prevails. This lack of state regulation, coupled with the SEC's minimal presence with respect to Rule 506 Regulation D offerings,[3] may be viewed as key reasons underlying the widespread perpetration of financial scams upon unsophisticated investors,[4] including elder fraud.[5] The SEC's continued

[1] In 2019, $2.7 trillion was raised pursuant to exempt offerings contrasted with $1.2 trillion for registered offerings. *See* Securities Act Release No. 10824 (2020). *See generally* Jennifer J. Johnson, *Private Placements: A Regulatory Black Hole*, 35 Del. J. Corp. L. 151 (2010); Marc I. Steinberg and Joseph P. Kempler, *The Application and Effectiveness of SEC Rule 144*, 49 Ohio St. L.J. 473 (1988); Manning G. Warren III, *A Review of Regulation D: The Present Exemption Regimen for Limited Offerings Under the Securities Act of 1933*, 33 Am. U. L. Rev. 355 (1984).

[2] For example, the states are preempted from overseeing Rule 506 and Regulation A, Tier 2 offerings. *See* § 18(b)(4) of the Securities Exchange Act, 15 U.S.C. § 77r(b)(4).

[3] Pursuant to Rule 503, a notice of sales on Form D generally is required to be filed with the SEC "no later than 15 calendar days after the first sale of securities in the [Regulation D] offering." Rule 503(a)(1), 17 C.F.R. § 230.503(a)(1).

[4] Pursuant to a number of these exemptions, "fraud can be easier to effect and much harder to detect." Luis A. Aguilar, Commissioner, Securities and Exchange Commission, *Increasing the Vulnerability of Investors* (Aug. 29, 2012), available at https://www.sec.gov/news/public-statement/2012-spch082912laahtm; https://clsbluesky.law.columbia.edu/2013/09/18/facilitating-general-solicitation-at-the-expense-of-investors.

[5] *See* Stephen Deane, Office of the Investor Advocate, Securities and Exchange Commission, *Elder Financial Exploitation* (2018), available at https://www.sec.gov/files/elder-financial-exploitation.pdf;

Rethinking Securities Law. Marc I. Steinberg, Oxford University Press. © Marc I. Steinberg 2021.
DOI: 10.1093/oso/9780197583142.003.0003

quest to expand the exemption framework will likely accentuate this predicament.[6]

This chapter examines the exemption framework for both primary offerings and resales of securities. Its objectives are to explain why the current regimen is incompatible with the best interests of investors and the securities markets as well as to recommend the implementation of a revised framework that better serves the multi-faceted interests at issue.

II. Primary Exemptions from Securities Act Registration

The primary exemptions from Securities Act registration are characterized by inconsistencies and undue solicitousness for capital raising at the expense of investor protection. Examples follow to illustrate this assertion.

A. The Traditional Rule 506 Exemption

When the SEC adopted the Rule 506 exemption of Regulation D in 1982,[7] it did so as a safe harbor to the Section 4(2) (now 4(a)(2)) private offering exemption.[8] The incongruity is that the Rule 506 safe harbor exceeds the scope of Section 4(a)(2). As a matter of established authority, the parameters of an administrative rule cannot exceed the scope of the statute upon which it is based.[9] Yet the Commission did precisely that in promulgating Rule 506. Rule 506 is more expansive than Section 4(a)(2) in three major ways.

Larissa Lee, *The Ban Has Lifted: Now Is the Time to Change the Accredited-Investor Standard*, 2014 Utah L. Rev. 369, 385 (2014).

[6] *See* Securities Act Release No. 10844 (2020). *See also Lindeen v. Securities and Exchange Commission*, 825 F.3d 646, 648 (D.C. Cir. 2016) (rejecting a challenge by two state chief securities regulators to the validity of the SEC's promulgation of Regulation A, Tier 2 offerings that preempts state regulation of such offerings and stating that the challenge was based on the Commission's alleged failure "to adopt a qualified-purchaser definition limited to investors with sufficient wealth, revenue or financial sophistication to protect their interests without state protection").

[7] *See* Securities Act Release No. 6389 (1982).

[8] *Id.* (stating that "Rule 506 relates to transactions that are deemed to be exempt under Section 4(2)"). In 2019, $1.56 trillion was raised pursuant to Rule 506 offerings. *See* Securities Act Release No. 10824 (2020).

[9] *See, e.g., Ernst & Ernst v. Hochfelder*, 425 U.S. 185, 214 (1976) (stating that Rule 10b-5's "scope cannot exceed the power granted the Commission by Congress under § 10(b)"). Note that, with its more recent exemptive power provided by Section 28 of the Securities Act, 15 U.S.C. § 77bb, the Commission today has the requisite authority. The SEC's use of its exemptive authority under Section 28 is addressed in Chapter 4 herein.

First, under Section 4(a)(2), all offerees must be financially sophisticated or advised by an offeree representative who has the requisite sophistication.[10] By contrast, the Rule 506 exemption focuses on purchaser financial sophistication, rendering the degree of offeree sophistication irrelevant.[11] Second, pursuant to Section 4(a)(2), financial wealth alone does not make one financially sophisticated.[12] Departing from this requirement, under Rule 506, an individual who (with one's spouse or spousal equivalent) has a net worth of $1 million (exclusive of primary residence) or earns $200,000 annually (or joint income of $300,000) is irrebuttably deemed to be financially sophisticated,[13] thereby qualifying as an accredited investor.[14] Third, Section 4(a)(2) case law makes clear that the disclosure requirements can be satisfied either by providing the offeree with registration-type information[15] or by providing such person access to this information.[16] Notably,

---

[10] *See* former SEC Rule 146 (predecessor to Rule 506, providing a safe harbor to the § 4(2) private offering exemption); Securities Act Release No. 5913 (1974) (among other conditions, requiring that "offers [can] be made only to persons the issuer reasonably believes have the requisite knowledge and experience in financial and business matters or who can bear the economic risk [and] sales [can] be made only to persons as described above except that persons meeting the economic risk test must also have an offeree representative capable of providing the requisite knowledge and experience").

[11] *See* Rule 506(b)(2)(ii), (c)(2), 17 C.F.R. § 230.506(b)(2)(ii), .506(c)(2).

[12] *See, e.g.*, *Lawler v. Gilliam*, 569 F.2d 1283 (4th Cir. 1978); *Doran v. Petroleum Management Corp.*, 545 F.2d 893 (5th Cir. 1977); *Lively v. Hirschfeld*, 440 F.2d 631 (10th Cir. 1971). Notably, a position paper by the ABA's Federal Regulation of Securities Committee recognized that one's financial wealth did not render one financially sophisticated. *See* American Bar Association, *Section 4(2) and Statutory Law—A Position Paper by the Federal Regulation of Securities Committee*, 31 Bus. Law. 485, 491 (1975) ("We might have serious reservations about including a very wealthy person as an offeree in a highly risky private placement, based solely upon his ability to assume the risk, if he had no understanding of financial matters, and no competent advisor.").

[13] *See* Rule 501(a)(6), 17 C.F.R. § 230.501(a)(6). The income test also encompasses the two most recent years, providing: "Any natural person who had an individual income in excess of $200,000 in each of the two most recent years or joint income with that person's spouse in excess of $300,000 in each of those years and has a reasonable expectation of reaching the same income level in the current year." This income test is not "keyed to the federal income tax return, . . . permit[ting] the inclusion of certain deductions and additional items of income." Securities Act Release No. 6389 (1982). *See* Thomas M. Selman, *Protecting Retail Investors: A New Exemption for Private Securities Offerings*, 14 Va. L. & Bus. Rev. 41, 49 (2020) ("Whereas before [the adoption of Regulation D], private purchasers had to be smart, now they need only be rich"), *citing* C. Edward Fletcher, *Sophisticated Investors Under the Federal Securities Laws*, 1988 Duke L.J. 1081, 1123 (1988).

[14] *See* Rule 501(a), 17 C.F.R. § 230.501(a).

[15] *See Securities and Exchange Commission v. Ralston Purina Co.*, 346 U.S. 119, 124 (1953) (stating that "the design of the statute is to protect investors by promoting full disclosure of information thought necessary to informed investment decisions"); *Doran v. Petroleum Management Corporation*, 545 F.2d 893, 903 (5th Cir. 1977) ("The requirement that all offerees have available the information registration would provide has been firmly established by this court as a necessary condition of gaining the private offering exemption.").

[16] *See* 346 U.S. at 125 (opining that "some employee offerings may come within § 4(1) [now § 4(a)(2)], *e.g.*, one made to executive personnel who because of their position have access to the same kind of information that the Act would make available in the form of a registration statement"); ABA Position Paper, *supra* note 12, at 487 (stating that pursuant to the § 4(2) exemption, each offeree must be provided with information about the issuer or have access to such information).

to have effective access, the individual or entity must have sufficient leverage to induce the issuer to make available the type of information that would be provided in a registration statement. Ordinarily, only the issuer's insiders (and perhaps their family members) and investors whose financial contribution is central to the consummation of the offering will have such leverage.[17] By contrast, Rule 506 implies that any accredited investor conclusively has access to registration-type information.[18] Accordingly, an individual who meets the financial thresholds for being an accredited investor or, as recently adopted by the SEC, satisfies certain testing or certification requirements, is irrebuttably deemed to have access to registration-type information.[19] The same rationale applies to institutional investors, such as entities and other organizations, that meet specified monetary thresholds.[20] That an accredited investor who invests $25,000 in a Rule 506 offering of $10 million has the requisite leverage belies common sense.

The SEC has engaged in this fallacy in order to facilitate the conducting of Rule 506 offerings made solely to accredited investors. If any purchaser in a Rule 506 offering is not accredited, then registration-type information as called for in Regulation D must be provided to all non-accredited purchasers.[21] The costs of preparing this package of information can be substantial and is accompanied by greater liability exposure.[22] Focusing on its objective of facilitating capital raising, the SEC has favored issuer and

[17] *See* 545 F.2d at 906 (stating that "when an issuer relies on 'access' absent actual disclosure, it must show that the offerees occupied a privileged position relative to the issuer that afforded them an opportunity for effective access to the information registration would otherwise provide").

[18] *See* Rule 502(b)(1), 17 C.F.R. § 230.502(b)(1) (stating that the subject issuer must furnish specified information under Rule 506(b) "to any purchaser that is not an accredited investor" but "is not required to furnish the specified information when it sells securities under Rule 504, or to any accredited investor").

[19] *See* Securities Act Release No. 10824 (2020) ("add[ing] new categories of natural persons who may qualify as accredited investors based on certain professional certifications or designations or other credentials or their status as a private fund's 'knowledgeable employee'"); Paul Kiernan, *SEC Eases Access to Private Markets*, Wall St. J., Aug. 27, 2020, at A1 (stating that the amendments were adopted by a 3–2 vote and that critics "point out that due diligence is impossible without corporate disclosure about an investment").

[20] *See* Rule 501(a), 17 C.F.R. § 230.501(a); sources cited *supra* notes 10–19. This approach was criticized by this author four decades ago. *See* Marc I. Steinberg, *The Securities and Exchange Commission's Administrative, Enforcement, and Legislative Programs and Policies—Their Influence on Corporate Internal Affairs*, 58 Notre Dame L. Rev. 173, 209–14 (1982).

[21] *See* Securities Act Release No. 6389 (1982) (stating that if securities are sold pursuant to Rule 506 "to investors that are not accredited, then Rule 502 requires delivery of the information specified in [that Rule] to all [non-accredited] purchasers").

[22] Liability exposure based on alleged disclosure violations in a private offering memorandum (POM) may be premised on Section 10(b) of the Securities Exchange Act and, more likely, state securities and common law. *See* Marc I. Steinberg, *The Emergence of State Securities Laws: Partly Sunny Skies for Investors*, 62 U. Cin. L. Rev. 395 (1993).

financial intermediary interests over those of investors. This point is illustrated by the Commission's refusal to increase the individual accredited investor net worth amount of $1 million since Regulation D's promulgation four decades ago.[23]

As adopted by the SEC, the net worth amount for qualifying as an accredited investor included one's personal residence.[24] With the enactment of the Dodd-Frank Act in 2010,[25] Congress prescribed that one's primary residence must be excluded from an investor's net worth calculation[26] and directed the SEC periodically to revisit the $1 million amount to determine whether this amount should be increased.[27] In the decade since this directive, the Commission has declined to do so, maintaining the current $1 million level—with such irreplaceable assets as pension and retirement accounts included within this calculation.[28] With four decades of inflation since Regulation D's adoption, today approximately thirteen percent of U.S. households qualify as accredited investors.[29] While the Commission has been active in raising the issuer offering amounts of a number of exemptions from registration,[30] it has declined to raise the financial thresholds for qualification as an accredited investor. The Commission's rationale is clear, explaining that increasing these financial thresholds "could have disruptive effects on the Regulation D market" and "may result in a higher cost of capital for companies."[31]

This reasoning is detrimental to investors. Unlike registered offerings that have comprehensive disclosures, audited financial statements, and undergo SEC staff review, these virtues are ordinarily absent in private offerings made solely to accredited investors. As viewed by the President of the North American Securities Administrators Association (NASAA), "private offerings are often characterized by opaque disclosures, related party transactions, illiquidity, minimal financial information and, unfortunately,

---

[23] *See* Securities Act Release No. 10734 (2020) (proposing amendments to the definition of accredited investor but not with respect to the individual financial thresholds for qualifying as an individual accredited investor).

[24] *See* Securities Act Release No. 6389 (1982).

[25] The Dodd-Frank Wall Street Reform and Consumer Protection Act, Pub. L. No. 111-203, 124 Stat. 1376 (2010).

[26] *See* § 413(a) of the Dodd-Frank Act; Securities Act Release No. 9287 (2011).

[27] *See* § 413(a) of the Dodd-Frank Act.

[28] *See* Rule 501(a)(5), 17 C.F.R. § 230.501(a)(5).

[29] Securities Act Release No. 10734 (2020). When Regulation D was adopted in 1982, approximately 1.6 percent of U.S. households met the accredited investor qualification standards. *Id.*

[30] For example, since 1982, the Commission has significantly raised the monetary amount for offerings pursuant to the Regulation A and Rule 504 exemptions.

[31] Securities Act Release No. 10734 (2020).

fraud."[32] To enable privately-held issuers and their promoters to access this expansive pool of so-called accredited investors, many of whom are financially unable to withstand substantial losses in these investments, is antithetical to sound public policy.[33]

B. The JOBS Act Rule 506 Exemption

The Jumpstart Our Business Startups (JOBS) Act of 2012[34] provides an even more expansive version of Rule 506 by permitting issuers and their agents to engage in advertising and general solicitation provided that all purchasers are accredited investors.[35] Pursuant to this exemption, issuers and their agents can engage in such techniques as: "cold calling" prospective investors; advertising on the internet, billboards, radio, and television; and mass mailing promotional materials for the prospective offering to strangers.[36] Viewed

---

[32] Letter from Christopher Gerold, NASAA President, Chief, New Jersey Bureau of Securities dated March 16, 2020, to the Securities and Exchange Commission, Regarding Proposed Amendments Amending the "Accredited Investor" Definition, available at https://www.sec.gov/comments/s7-25-19/s72519-6960323-212740.pdf.

[33] *Id.* (asserting that "expanding the pool of accredited investors to include investors who may be financially unable to withstand losses in such investments serves no policy interest"). As this author stated in a comment letter dated January 23, 2020, to the SEC regarding this proposal, available at https://www.sec.gov/comments/s7-25-19/s72519-6684984-205887.pdf:

> This comment letter is submitted by me expressing solely my individual views with respect to the Securities and Exchange Commission's (SEC or Commission) proposed amendments to the "accredited investor" definition. While certain aspects of the proposal are beneficial, one glaring and inexplicable deficiency prevails: namely, the Commission's maintenance of the current financial thresholds for individual accredited investors. Simply put, to assert that merely on the basis of $200,000 individual income (or $300,000 joint income) for a relatively short time period or $1 million net worth (exclusive of primary residence) renders one conclusively to have financial sophistication—without entitlement to mandatory disclosure of material information relating to the contemplated investment—contravenes common sense and reality. Moreover, by expanding categories for one's qualification as an accredited investor while maintaining the current financial thresholds tellingly points to the SEC's priority—clearly, seeking to enhance capital formation at the expense of investor protection.
>
> As the agency charged with protecting investors, the Commission's position is perplexing. Financial scams, elder fraud, and ponzi schemes are all too common in purported Regulation D offerings. As the states are preempted from regulating Rule 506 offerings, the SEC should be vigilant in seeking to ensure that investors are not defrauded. After all, private damages actions and regulatory enforcement proceedings frequently occur when the money already is lost.

[34] The Jumpstart Our Business Startups Act of 2012, Pub. L. No. 112-106, 126 Stat. 306 (2012).

[35] *See* § 201(a) of the JOBS Act; Rule 506(c), 17 C.F.R. § 230.506(c); Securities Act Release No. 9415 (2013).

[36] *See* Phillip R. Sanders, *Understanding the New Rule 506(c) Exemption*, 42 Sec. Reg. L.J. 347 (2014).

as a private offering exemption, there is nothing private about engaging in these types of activities. In one of the more vivid oxymorons in the annals of securities regulation, Congress in the JOBS Act amended Section 4 of the Securities Act to provide: "Offers and sales exempt under Rule 506 . . . shall not be deemed public offerings under the Federal securities laws as a result of general advertising or general solicitation."[37] From this legislative fiction, the inquiry arises how an issuer and its agents can engage in such activities as the use of the internet, radio, and television—and yet the subject offering "shall not be deemed public."[38]

The availability of accessing thousands of investors by utilizing advertising and general solicitation should prove attractive to the least attractive of Regulation D issuers. Established promoters and their financial intermediaries already have preexisting relationships with large numbers of accredited investors, thereby providing them with broad outreach within the traditional Rule 506 exemption. Moreover, the use of mass general solicitation to strangers may pose greater confidentiality concerns as proprietary information may find its way to competitors.[39] As a result, issuers who are more likely to use the JOBS Act Rule 506 exemption are those entities that lack substantial relationships with accredited investors and reputable financial intermediaries.[40] This absence of meaningful connections provides a fertile opportunity for miscreants to engage in misconduct, which clearly does not bode well for transparency and honest conduct.[41]

To exacerbate this situation, state regulation is preempted in all Rule 506 offerings, including the JOBS Act version.[42] With no government review except for the filing of a Form D,[43] the commission of fraudulent practices is

---

[37] Section 4(b) of the Securities Act, 15 U.S.C. § 77d(b).

[38] *See* Marc I. Steinberg, *Understanding Securities Law* 64 (7th ed. 2018).

[39] *See* Manning G. Warren, *The Regulatory Vortex for Private Placements*, 45 Sec. Reg. L.J. 9 (2017).

[40] *Id.* at 14.

[41] *See* Aguilar, *supra* note 4 (stating that "[w]hen general solicitation is combined with an offering exemption such as Rule 506, no information statement or disclosure is required to be given to investors [and, hence,] fraud can be easier to effect and much harder to detect").

[42] *See* § 18(b)(4) of the Securities Act, 15 U.S.C. § 77r(b)(4). *See generally* Robert G. Bagnell and Kimble Cannon, *The National Securities Markets Improvement Act of 1996: Summary and Discussion*, 25 Sec. Reg. L.J. 3 (1997); Jill Meyer, *Federal Preemption of the Rule 506 Exemption*, 37 Sec. Reg. L.J. 122 (2009). Note that, if the Rule 506 exemption is not perfected for an offering, the states may oversee the offering and exemption criteria for that offering. *See, e.g., Brown v. Earthboard Sports USA, Inc.*, 481 F.3d 901, 910 (6th Cir. 2007) (holding that "offerings must actually qualify for a valid securities registration exemption in order to enjoy NSMIA preemption").

[43] *See* Rule 503(a), 17 C.F.R. § 230.503(a) (requiring the filing of a Form D with the SEC generally "no later than 15 calendar days after the first sale of securities in the offering"). Commissioner Aguilar asserted that a Form D filing should be mandated prior to the commencement by the issuer

likely to increase. Government enforcement and investor lawsuits after the proceeds are misappropriated or otherwise irretrievably lost through Ponzi schemes and other sharp practices ordinarily provide insufficient recompense to aggrieved persons.[44]

C. The Regulation A, Tier 2 Exemption

Pursuant to the JOBS Act and the 2020 amendments, the SEC amended the Regulation A offering exemption to permit offerings under Tier 2 of the exemption for up to $75 million annually, with the states being preempted from regulating these offerings.[45] The exemption has a number of beneficial attributes, including subjecting these issuers to a continuous reporting regime and to file with the Commission audited financial statements.[46] Nonetheless, significant gaps in investor protection arise, including that prospective issuers in all Regulation A (Tier 1 and Tier 2) offerings are authorized to "test the waters," engaging in advertising and general solicitation to determine the degree of investor interest prior to going forward with the contemplated offering.[47] In view that many of these offerings are speculative in nature and involve

or its agents of engaging in general solicitation. *See* Aguilar, *supra* note 4. Further, failure by an issuer to file the required Form D does not destroy an otherwise available exemption. Rather, if an issuer is subject to an injunction for failing to comply with this provision, it is disqualified from using Regulation D in the future unless the SEC determines to waive such disqualification. *See* Rule 507, 17 C.F.R. § 230.507; Securities Act Release No. 6825 (1989). Note that, if a Rule 506 offering is sold either to accredited or non-accredited individual investors, Rule 5123 of the Financial Industry Regulatory Authority (FINRA) requires a broker-dealer to provide to FINRA any Private Placement Memorandum or other offering document that is used in that offering.

[44] *See* Aguilar, *supra* note 4 ("In most cases, much of investors' monies are long gone by the time a fraud is identified and an action can be brought").

[45] *See* § 3(b)(2) of the Securities Act, 15 U.S.C. § 77c(b)(2); Rule 251(a)(2), 17 C.F.R. § 230.251(a)(2); Securities Act Release No. 10844 (2020); Securities Act Release No. 9741 (2015). The maximum annual amount that may be raised pursuant to Regulation A, Tier 1 is $20 million. *See* Rule 251(a)(1), 17 C.F.R. § 230.251(a)(1). The 2020 amendments raised the maximum amount that can be sold by affiliates during a twelve-month period under Tier 2 to $22.5 million. *See* Rule 241(a)(2); Securities Act Release No. 10884 (2020). The maximum amount for sales by affiliates under Tier 1 during a twelve-month period is $6 million. *See* Rule 251(a)(1).

[46] *See* sources cited *supra* note 45. The requirements that an issuer file audited financial statements annually with the SEC is specifically set forth in Section 3(b)(2)(F).

[47] *See* § 3(b)(2)(E): "The issuer may solicit interest in the offering prior to filing any offering statement, on such terms as the Commission may prescribe in the public interest or for the protection of investors." Rule 255 of Regulation A permits such solicitation in both Tier 1 and Tier 2 offerings. *See* 17 C.F.R. § 230.255. Similarly, the SEC in 2020 adopted Rule 241, 17 C.F.R. § 230.241, which permits "an issuer to use generic solicitation of interest materials to 'test the waters' for an exempt offer of securities prior to determining which exemption it will use for the sale of the securities." SEC Press Release No. 2020-273 (2020). *See* Securities Act Release No. 10844 (2020).

companies that have been previously subject to minimal state or federal regulation,[48] this laxity in allowing such conduct is inappropriate. After all, for an issuer to be eligible in a Securities Act registered offering to make offers to sell in the pre-filing period to any investor, whether accredited or not, it must meet the "gold standard," namely, qualifying as a well-known seasoned issuer.[49] Other companies can only engage in such communications with qualified institutional buyers and institutional accredited investors in the pre-filing period.[50]

Make no mistake that, although these communications by prospective Regulation A issuers are not defined by Congress and the SEC to constitute offers to sell triggering the provisions of Section 5 of the Securities Act, in reality, they are.[51] This status is evidenced by the Commission declaring in Regulation A that these test the waters communications "are deemed to be an offer of a security for sale for purposes of the antifraud provisions of the federal securities laws."[52] The government's approach that the identical conduct constitutes an offer to sell when the fraud provisions are at issue but not for purposes of the Section 5 registration provisions is illogical. Yet this fiction is implemented in order to promote the capital-raising objectives of these largely unknown and less than stellar companies.[53]

Traditionally, state preemption with respect to registration and qualification of public offerings occurs when the subject company's securities are

---

48 *See* Rod Turner, *These 32 Companies Raised $396 Mill Using Regulation A+, Entrepreneurs: You Have a New Option*, Forbes, March 14, 2017, available at https://forbes.com/sites/rodnturner/2017/03/14/how-they-did-it-32-companies-successfully-raised-capital-via-regulation-a/#4f88506c7cde; Rod Turner, *These 107 Companies Raised $1.5 B via Regulation A+; New Metrics*, Medium, June 5, 2019, available at https://medium.com/@IamRodTurner/these-107-companies-raised-1-5-b-via-regulation-a-new-metrics-7b60ec41958b.

49 *See* SEC Rule 163, 17 C.F.R. § 230.163; discussion in Chapter 4 herein.

50 *See* Section 5(d) of the Securities Act, 15 U.S.C. § 77e(d) (applying to emerging growth companies); Rule 163B, 17 C.F.R. § 230.163B (extending the legality of these pre-filing communications to all issuers). This expansive rule was adopted by the SEC in 2019. *See* Securities Act Release No. 10699 (2019) ("adopting a new communications rule under the Securities Act of 1933 that permits issuers to engage in oral or written communications with certain potential investors [namely, QIBs and institutional accredited investors], either prior to or following the filing of a registration statement, to determine whether such investors might have an interest in a contemplated registered securities offering"); discussion in Chapter 4 herein.

51 *See* sources cited *supra* note 50.

52 Rule 255(a), 17 C.F.R. § 230.255(a). Similarly, solicitations of interest permitted under Rule 241, 17 C.F.R. § 230.241, "are deemed to be an offer of a security for sale for purposes of the antifraud provisions of the Federal securities laws." *See* Securities Act Release No. 10884 (2020).

53 *See* Abraham J.B. Cable, *Mad Money: Rethinking Private Placements*, 71 Wash. & Lee L. Rev. 2253, 2263 (2014); Rod Turner, *Why Companies Are Raising Capital Via Regulation A+ Instead of Venture Capital*, Medium, Oct. 29, 2019, available at https://medium.com/@IamRodTurner/why-companies-are-raising-capital-via-regulation-a-instead-of-venture-capital-ba9f3fa75077.

listed, or authorized for listing, on a national securities exchange.[54] From a general perspective, this preemption makes good sense. With respect to these companies, there exists the presence of SEC regulation, self-regulatory organization oversight, and market analyst evaluations.[55] In addition, the rigors of a company going public pursuant to a registered offering and having its securities listed on a national securities exchange entails substantial auditor and underwriter diligence.[56] To subject securities trading in a national market system to state registration and qualification likely would result in several states requiring additional disclosures and undertakings, thereby impairing the capital raising, liquidity, and market for such securities.[57]

To expand this preemption to Regulation A Tier 2 offerings where there is no comparable market following and vetting makes little sense. Although state regulation will add costs to the raising of capital and may deter some companies from accessing the public markets,[58] these downsides are outweighed by the benefits of sound state oversight that incentivizes issuers, insiders, and others involved in the offering process to adhere to law-compliant conduct.[59]

D. Integration of Securities Offerings

The doctrine of integration of securities offerings has been controversial for over fifty years.[60] Under this doctrine, purportedly separate offerings are determined to be one integrated offering. Because each exemption has distinct conditions to satisfy, otherwise exempt offerings may not meet the criteria

---

[54] *See* § 18(b)(1)(A), 15 U.S.C. § 77r(b)(1)(A); discussion in Chapter 4 herein.

[55] *See* discussion in Chapter 4 herein.

[56] *See, e.g.*, Charles J. Johnson, Jr. et al., *Corporate Finance and the Securities Laws* (6th ed. 2019); Carl Schneider et al., *Going Public: Practice, Procedure and Consequences*, 27 Vill. L. Rev. 1 (1981).

[57] *See, e.g.*, Rutherford B. Campbell, *An Open Attack on the Nonsense of Blue Sky Regulation*, 10 J. Corp. L. 553, 579 (1985) (asserting that "millions of dollars are spent each year on a system of [state] regulation that provides no significant protection to investors and retards capital formation").

[58] *See* American Bar Association, Section of Corporation, Banking and Business Law, *Report on State Regulation of Securities Offerings*, 41 Bus. Law. 785 (1986).

[59] *See* Richard B. Tyler, *More About Blue Sky*, 39 Wash. & Lee L. Rev. 895 (1982). The U.S. Court of Appeals rejected a challenge brought by two state chief securities regulators to the validity of state preemption of Regulation A, Tier 2 Offerings. *See Lindeen v. Securities and Exchange Commission*, 825 F.3d 646 (D.C. Cir. 2016). *See generally* Joseph C. Long, Michael J. Kaufman, and John M. Wunderlich, *Blue Sky Law* § 5:30 (2019); Michael Andrews, *The Regulation A+ Exemption: Provider of Practical Tiers or Pointless Tears?*, 44 Sec. Reg. L.J. 221 (2016).

[60] *Cf.* Rutherford B. Campbell, *The Overwhelming Case for Elimination of the Integration Doctrine Under the Securities Act of 1933*, 89 Ky. L.J. 289 (2000–2001), *with* Daniel J. Morrissey, *Integration of Securities Offerings—The ABA's "Indiscreet" Proposal*, 26 Ariz. L. Rev. 41 (1984).

for an exemption once these offerings are integrated. Similarly, if a supposed exempt offering is integrated with a Securities Act registered offering, the exemption may be lost.[61] The consequence is that failure to qualify for an exemption results in a violation of Section 5 of the Securities Act, a strict liability provision, that gives rise to government enforcement and provides purchasers a right of rescission.[62]

The policy in favor of integration of offerings is to prevent issuers and promoters from avoiding Securities Act registration by raising capital through several apparently separate offerings that in substance constitute a single offering.[63] Critics assert that the doctrine "continues to frustrate issuers engaged in the capital formation process, engulfing them in a sea of ambiguity, uncertainty, and potential liability."[64] Clearly, sufficiently concrete integration rules should be promulgated to provide clear standards for issuers and their agents without subverting the policies underlying the registration mandate.

During the last two decades, the SEC has adopted several accommodations that significantly diminish the prospect of integration.[65] Indeed, with the adoption of Rule 152 in 2020, the Commission largely has nullified the integration doctrine. As discussed in the following, although definitive clarification of the integration of offerings doctrine should be effectuated, large-scale nullification is not the correct solution.[66] Rather, specifically tailored safe

---

[61] *See* Securities Act Release No. 4552 (1962).

[62] 15 U.S.C. § 77e. A purchaser's right of rescission for a registration violation is set forth in Section 12(a)(1) of the Securities Act. 15 U.S.C. § 771(a)(1). *See Pinter v. Dahl*, 486 U.S. 622 (1988).

[63] *See* Darryl B. Deaktor, *Integration of Securities Offerings*, 31 U. Fla. L. Rev. 465, 473 (1979).

[64] Perry E. Wallace, Jr., *Integration of Securities Offerings: Obstacles to Capital Formation Remain for Small Businesses*, 45 Wash. & Lee L. Rev. 883, 889 (1988). Professor Wallace was nationally known and admired for a far more important principle of integration. *See* Phil Taylor, *Exploitation or Opportunity?*, Sports Illustrated, Aug. 12, 1991, at 46, 52 (profiling Professor Perry Wallace "who [as a student at Vanderbilt University] in the winter of 1967–68 became the Southeastern Conference's first black varsity basketball player").

[65] *See, e.g.*, Rule 155, 17 C.F.R. § 230.155 (providing integration safe harbors with respect to a private offering following an abandoned registered offering or a registered offering following an abandoned private offering); Rule 502(a), 17 C.F.R. § 230.502(a) (providing an integration safe harbor in Regulation D offerings); Rule 147A(g), 17 C.F.R. § 230.147A(g) (providing an integration safe harbor for Rule 147A offerings). *See generally* J. William Hicks, *Exempted Transactions Under the Securities Act of 1933* (2d ed. 2001); Theodore W. Jones, *The Doctrine of Securities Act "Integration,"* 29 Sec. Reg. L.J. 320 (2001).

[66] *See* Rule 152, 17 C.F.R. § 230.152; Securities Act Release No. 10884 (2020); Statement of Commissioner Allison Herren Lee, Statement on Amendments to the Exempt Offering Framework (2020), available at https://www.sec.gov/news/public-statement/lee-harmonization-2020-11-02 (stating that the Commission's adoption of Rule 152 effectively renders the integration doctrine "hollow but for a requirement to wait 30 days between offerings"); discussion *infra* notes 129–149 and accompanying text.

harbors to the integration doctrine should be prescribed which would enable issuers and their agents to have clear guidance while preserving the objectives underlying Securities Act registration.

III. A Proposed Framework for Primary Securities Act Exemptions

The current primary Securities Act exemption framework needs a more balanced approach. The SEC's approach of promoting capital raising at the expense of investor protection is misguided. The following discussion provides a regimen that seeks to meet investor interests while not posing undue impediments upon issuers and their agents in their capital raising activities.

A. Private Offerings

Today, for out-of-state offerings, the Section 4(a)(2) private offering exemption generally will be used when an offering of over $10 million is made to a small number of non-accredited investors who are provided access to registration-type information;[67] or when the issuer is not eligible to use the Rule 504 or Rule 506 exemption due to a bad actor qualification.[68] The application of Section 4(a)(2) in these contexts is good policy, enabling those entities that cannot feasibly invoke another exemption to resort to this well-established statutory provision.[69] Significantly, with respect to the Section 4(a)(2) exemption, the states have authority to oversee these offerings and may prescribe additional conditions, thereby providing a greater measure of investor protection as these offerings may be promoted by unsavory characters.[70]

---

[67] Otherwise, pursuant to Rule 506, delivery of specified information to non-accredited purchasers is required. Providing access to such investors is not an option under Rule 506. *See* Rule 502(b)(1), 17 C.F.R. § 230.502(b)(1). The maximum annual amount that may be raised pursuant to the Rule 504 exemption is $10 million. *See* Rule 504(b)(2), 17 C.F.R. § 230.504(b)(2); Securities Act Release No. 10884 (2020).

[68] Bad actor disqualification provisions are contained in Rule 504(b)(3) and Rule 506(d), 17 C.F.R. §§ 230.504(b)(3), .506(d).

[69] In other words, in situations where there is an out-of-state purchaser, the issuer is subject to a bad actor disqualification, or an informational package is not financially feasible to prepare, Section 4(a)(2) is the remaining federal exemption from registration that may be employed in these contexts.

[70] *See* § 18(b)(4)(F) of the Securities Act, 15 U.S.C. § 77r(b)(4)(F) (preempting from state regulation SEC rules or regulations issued under § 4(a)(2) (namely, Rule 506 but not preempting the statutory § 4(a)(2) exemption)).

On the other hand, the Rule 506 traditional exemption (currently Rule 506(b)) needs to be revamped to better balance safeguarding investors and facilitating capital raising. The components of the revised rule should consist of the following:

(1) With no monetary limit to the amount that may be raised, the exemption should permit sales to no more than thirty-five non-accredited investors and an unlimited number of accredited investors.
(2) In order for an investor to be accredited, in addition to having the requisite financial wherewithal, the investor (or its representative) must be financially sophisticated. The requisite financial amounts would be based upon the levels as they were in 1982 (when Rule 506 was adopted) adjusted for inflation. For example, $200,000 annual income in 1982 to qualify an individual as an accredited investor is the equivalent of $546,753 in 2020 dollars.[71] In addition to one's primary residence, certain other irreplaceable assets also should be excluded from calculating an individual's net worth, including amounts vested in pension and retirement accounts. Likewise, entities and other organizations should not be deemed accredited investors based solely on meeting specified monetary thresholds, such as having $5 million in total assets. Assuming that an individual or entity has the requisite monetary wherewithal, the issuer still must qualify that prospective investor (or its representative) as being financially sophisticated. Such sophistication may be shown through such indicia as prior investments made, work experience, educational background, and financial industry certifications.[72]
(3) Advertising and general solicitation of prospective investors would be prohibited with the exception of accredited investors and qualified institutional buyers. These prospective investors can only be solicited after they are qualified as having attained that status (as set forth herein). To facilitate this process, an online data bank may be established whereby an individual or institutional investor may

[71] As calculated by https://dollartimes.com/inflation.

[72] This position is based on the premise that, with frequency, financial wealth does not equate with financial sophistication. *See* Martha C. White, *Are Millionaires Smarter Than the Rest of Us?*, Money.com, December 14, 2016, available at https://money.com/are-millionaires-smarter-than-the-rest-of-us/; Ohio State University, *You Don't Have To Be Smart To Be Rich, Study Finds*, ScienceDaily, April 25, 2007, available at https://www.sciencedaily.com/releases/2007/04/070424204519.htm.

provide adequate information and attest to the status of accredited investor.[73] As another alternative, generic questionnaires may be mailed or delivered electronically by a prospective issuer or its financial intermediaries to prospective investors requesting that they provide the requisite information and certification of being an accredited investor.[74] For entities having as a matter of public record an active investment history with total assets exceeding $13 million (adjusted for inflation from the $5 million 1982 level),[75] these entities would be automatically qualified as accredited investors.

(4) With respect to informational delivery requirements, an offering that is made to non-accredited investors must be accompanied by an informational package that contains specified disclosure pursuant to SEC rule.[76] For offerings made solely to accredited investors (as proposed herein), a number of these investors should have the leverage to induce the issuer to make meaningful disclosure. Once disclosure of substantive information is made to any accredited investor, this same information must be provided to all investors. As selective disclosure already has been made by the issuer, this approach protects those accredited investors who do not have the negotiating strength to induce the issuer to make disclosures which it would prefer avoiding. When deemed appropriate, a nondisclosure agreement may be executed to help ensure that the issuer may protect its confidential information.[77]

(5) Additional requirements would include: First, the issuer must take specified steps to guard against a distribution occurring. These measures include disclosing restrictions on resale in writing to prospective investors, obtaining investment letters from purchasers, and

---

[73] This qualification procedure is similar to that provided in the *Citizen VC No-Action Letter*, 2015 WL 4699193 (SEC Div. of Corp. Fin. 2015) (setting forth a procedure whereby a prospective investor becomes certified to receive private placement investment opportunities).

[74] This qualification procedure is similar to that provided in the *H.B. Shaine & Co., Inc., SEC No-Action Letter*, 1987 SEC No-Act. LEXIS 2004 (SEC Div. of Corp. Fin. 1987) (delivery to potential customers of a questionnaire "generic in nature [with] . . . sufficient time hav[ing] elapsed between the [prospective customer's] completion of the questionnaire and the completion or inception of any particular offering").

[75] As calculated by https://dollartimes.com/inflation.

[76] *See* Rule 502(b), 17 C.F.R. § 230.502(b).

[77] *See generally* E.J. Dickson, *What, Exactly, Is an NDA?*, Rolling Stone, March 19, 2018, available at https://www.rollingstone.com/culture/culture-features/nda-non-disclosure-agreements-809856/; Richard Harroch, *The Key Elements of Non-Disclosure Agreements*, Forbes, March 10, 2016, available at https://www.forbes.com/sites/allbusiness/2016/03/10/the-key-elements-of-non-disclosure-agreements/#8bb2ced627dd.

notification of resale limitations placed as a legend on the certificates.[78] Second, bad actor disqualifications would apply.[79] Third, a Form D would be required to be filed with the SEC and with each applicable state at least seventy-two hours before: the use of advertising or general solicitation (in Rule 506(c) offerings); and the making of any offer or sale (in Rule 504 and 506(b) offerings). In addition, a Form D would be required to be filed at the close of the offering.[80] Fourth, a substantial compliance standard would apply in private litigation to prevent investors unhappy with their investment from rescinding their purchases based on a technical inadvertent violation.[81]

(6) Provided that a law-compliant Rule 506(b) exemption has been perfected, the states would be preempted from regulating these offerings.[82] As is currently the situation, the states would retain their enforcement authority with respect to unlawful practices, such as deficiency in disclosure and manipulative practices.[83] In this regard, the

---

[78] *See* Rule 502(d), 17 C.F.R. § 230.502(d).

[79] The bad actor disqualification includes, among others: "the issuer; any predecessor of the issuer; any affiliated issuer; any director, executive officer, other officer participating in the offering, general partner or managing member of the issuer; any beneficial owner of 20% or more of the issuer's outstanding voting equity securities, calculated on the basis of voting power; any promoter connected with the issuer in any capacity at the time of such sale; . . . [and] any person that has been or will be paid (directly or indirectly) remuneration for solicitation of purchasers in connection with such sale of securities." Rule 506(d), 17 C.F.R. § 230.506(d). Disqualification events include criminal convictions, SEC injunctions, bar orders issued by another regulatory body (such as the Commodity Futures Trading Commission or a state securities commission), SEC cease and desist orders based on fraud or a Securities Act registration violation, and suspension or expulsion orders issued by a registered national securities exchange. *Id.*

[80] This proposal expands the current Form D filing requirement. *See* Rule 503, 17 C.F.R. § 230.503 (generally requiring that a current Form D be filed with the SEC "no later than 15 calendar days after the first sale of securities in the offering"). Requiring that a Form D be filed prior to the commencement of the offering (or in Rule 506(c) offerings prior to the conducting of general solicitation) would provide a mechanism to better enable regulators to decipher possibly sketchy offerings. *See* Aguilar, *supra* note 4 (asserting that in Rule 506(c) offerings there should be the "requirement that notice on Form D be made before general solicitation begins").

[81] *See* Rule 508, 17 C.F.R. § 230.508. As with the current provision, meeting the substantial compliance standard would be a defense in private litigation, not government enforcement proceedings. Generally, any failure to comply with a term, condition, or requirement of an exemption would not be actionable in private actions if such term, condition, or requirement was not meant to specifically protect the plaintiff, the defect was relatively minor, and there was a reasonable good faith effort to comply with all mandates of the exemption. Nonetheless, the substantial compliance defense is not available if there is impermissible general solicitation, the number of non-accredited purchasers in Rule 506 offerings is more than thirty-five, or the dollar limit in Rule 504 offerings is exceeded. *Id. See* Mark A. Sargent, *The New Regulation D: Deregulation, Federalism, and the Dynamics of Regulatory Reform*, 68 Wash. U. L.Q. 225 (1990).

[82] This is the current situation. *See* § 18(b)(4)(F) of the Securities Act, 15 U.S.C. § 77r(b)(4)(F). The states retain their authority to impose notice filing requirements similar to those that the SEC mandates. *Id.*

[83] *See Brown v. Earthboard Sports USA, Inc.* 481 F.3d 901, 912 (6th Cir. 2007) (observing that Congress preempted state law regulation of prescribing requirements for the Rule 506 exemption).

> Form D filings with the applicable states are important to enable their respective securities regulators to be apprised of ongoing offerings and be alerted to the possibility of fraud or other illegal conduct.[84]

The revamped Rule 506 meets both investor and issuer interests. As proposed, no longer would there be the need for the JOBS Act Rule 506(c) exemption as its objectives largely are met—with greater investor safeguards.

B. Limited and Exempt Public Offerings

This discussion focuses on the Rule 504, Regulation A, and intrastate offering exemptions. Although not comprising all of the transactional exemptions from registration (such as the Rule 701 and crowdfunding exemptions),[85] these three exemptions (Rule 504, Regulation A, and the intrastate offering exemptions)—along with the Rule 506 exemption—are among the most frequently used by issuers in the exempt primary offering setting.[86]

1. Rule 504

Under the Rule 504 exemption, state regulation is the focus. Companies that are Exchange Act reporting companies or investment companies may not use the exemption.[87] During a twelve-month period, a privately-held issuer may raise up to $10 million.[88] General solicitation is permitted only if the securities are state registered or sold exclusively to accredited investors under applicable state law;[89] if sold in this manner, the securities are not restricted.[90]

---

[84] *See* discussion *supra* note 80.

[85] By way of example, other exemptions include the Rule 147, 147A, and 701 exemptions as well as the crowdfunding exemption. The Rule 147 and 147A exemptions focus on intrastate offerings and are discussed later in this chapter. *See infra* notes 112–126 and accompanying text. The Rule 701 exemption, limited to companies that are not Exchange Act reporting companies, is designed for offerings made for the purpose of compensation for employees, directors, officers, advisers, and consultants of an eligible issuer. 17 C.F.R. § 230.701. The crowdfunding exemption is set forth in Section 4(a)(6) of the Securities Act, 15 U.S.C. § 77d(a)(6). *See* C. Steven Bradford, *The New Federal Crowdfunding Exemption: Promise Unfulfilled*, 40 Sec. Reg. L.J. 195 (2012); Stuart R. Cohn, *The New Crowdfunding Exemption: Good Idea, Bad Execution*, 64 Fla. L. Rev. 1433 (2012); Andrew A. Schwartz, *Crowdfunding Securities*, 88 Notre Dame L. Rev. 1457 (2013).

[86] *See* Securities Act Release No. 10763 (2020). The largest amounts were raised pursuant to the traditional Rule 506(b) exemption—in 2019, $1.492 billion. *Id.*

[87] *See* Rule 504(a), 17 C.F.R. § 230.504(a).

[88] *See* Rule 504(b)(2), 17 C.F.R. § 230.504(b)(2); Securities Act Release No. 10884 (2020).

[89] *See* Rule 504(b)(1), 17 C.F.R. § 230.504(b)(1).

[90] *See* Rule 502(d), 17 C.F.R. § 230.502(d). The Rule 504 exemption is subject to the bad actor disqualification. *See* Rule 504(b)(3), 17 C.F.R. § 230.504(b)(3).

Two concerns arise under this exemption. First, based on the discussion earlier in this chapter, the definition of accredited investor should be enhanced to encompass updated monetary amounts as well as financial sophistication.[91] Second, securities issued in public offerings under Rule 504, with some frequency, have witnessed pump-and-dump schemes and other unlawful practices.[92] While the existence of a bad actor disqualification provision is helpful in Rule 504 offerings,[93] more is needed. That responsibility rests principally with the states. Too many states have securities divisions that lack adequate funding, sufficient personnel, and other key resources to fulfill their missions.[94] This situation must be changed if aberrant conduct is to be detected and prosecuted. As a key step in this direction, more revenues must be raised to ameliorate these shortcomings. Clearly, with financial needs pressing from other sectors, state legislatures do not consider funding for their respective securities commission a top priority. The most feasible solution is for the NASAA to adopt a recommended schedule of fees for the state securities commissions to charge their users, including issuers, financial intermediaries, and investment companies. The respective state securities agencies would implement this recommended schedule and retain all or a sufficient portion of these fees to fund their operating costs. Although the amount of these fees may deter capital raising activities to a certain degree, the benefits of a more vigilant presence to combat the perpetration of fraud upon a state's residents should be paramount.[95] In addition, monetary fines levied upon violators may be deployed for this purpose.

2. Regulation A

As currently formulated, Regulation A has two tiers. The first tier allows up to $20 million to be raised in a twelve-month period with an offering circular containing specified information required to be filed with the SEC and the

---

[91] *See* discussion *supra* notes 10–33, 71–72 and accompanying text.

[92] *See* Securities Act Release No. 7644 (1999). Securities Act Release No. 7541 (1998); Howard Friedman, *Securities Regulation in Cyberspace* 5–22 (3d ed. 2004). These securities generally are characterized by low prices per share, thin capitalization, relatively sparse public information, and limited, if any, analyst coverage.

[93] *See* Rule 504(b)(3), 17 C.F.R. § 230.504(b)(3).

[94] *See* Manning Gilbert Warren III, *Reflections on Dual Regulation of Securities: A Case Against Preemption*, 25 Bos. Coll. L. Rev. 495, 496–97 (1984).

[95] In the past, this author has suggested that the monetary fines levied by blue sky authorities be directed to alleviating the lack of adequate funding in our public schools. *See* Marc I. Steinberg, *Enhanced "Blue Sky" Enforcement: A Path to Help Solve Our Public School Funding Dilemma*, 50 Washburn L.J. 563 (2011) (published as part of the 100th anniversary of the Kansas securities laws).

applicable state regulators.[96] Securities acquired pursuant to either Tier 1 or Tier 2 of Regulation A are not restricted.[97] Issuers subject to the bad actor disqualification cannot use either Tier.[98] Generally, Tier 1 may be attractive to privately-held issuers that elect to conduct a public offering seeking to raise funds greater than the monetary amount permitted under Rule 504.[99]

Key components of Tier 2 of Regulation A are discussed earlier in this chapter.[100] Expanding upon that discussion, the revised Regulation A structure should consist of the following:

(1) Serious consideration should be given to whether Tier 1 of Regulation A should be rescinded. With an increase in the offering amount for Rule 504 offerings to $10 million in a twelve-month period,[101] smaller issuers can engage in mini-public offerings under the purview of state registration requirements.[102] Issuers seeking to raise a greater amount of capital in a public offering, frequently accessing larger pools of investors, should be subject to the more rigorous mandates of Regulation A, Tier 2.

(2) Up to $75 million may be raised pursuant to Regulation A, Tier 2 during a twelve-month period, with no more than twenty percent of that amount constituting sales by affiliated security holders.[103]

---

[96] *See* Rules 251(a), 253, 17 C.F.R. §§ 230.251(a), .253.

[97] *See* § 3(b)(2)(C), 15 U.S.C. § 77c(b)(2)(C); Securities Act Release No. 9741 (2015).

[98] *See* Rule 262, 17 C.F.R. § 230.262.

[99] The maximum amount currently permitted to be raised annually under Rule 504 is $10 million. *See* Rule 504(b)(2), 17 C.F.R. § 230.504(b)(2). The SEC increased this amount to $10 million annually from $5 million. *See* Securities Act Release No. 10884 (2020).

[100] *See supra* notes 45–59 and accompanying text.

[101] This $10 million annual amount was adopted by the SEC in 2020. *See* Rule 504(b)(2), 17 C.F.R. § 230.504(b)(2); Securities Act Release No. 10884 (2020).

[102] These public offerings ordinarily are registered under applicable state law. A number of states continue to apply merit regulation whereby adequate disclosure is not sufficient. Rather, the subject offering also must be deemed "fair, just, and equitable." Hence, "in addition to requiring full disclosure, [state merit regulation statutes] have granted their administrators power to analyze the securities to be offered, the terms of the offering, and the business of the issuer for purposes of determining . . . whether the securities are too speculative for public sale." James Mofsky, *Blue Sky Restrictions on New Business Promotions* 7–8 (1971). Accordingly, in situations where, for example, promoters themselves have invested inadequate equity capital, underwriter's commissions are excessive, or an inappropriate number of warrants and options are issued to insiders, offerings may be rejected or certain conditions imposed, such as escrowing insider proceeds until specified contingencies are satisfied. *See* Tyler, *supra* note 59, at 903.

[103] This $75 million annual amount is the amount adopted by the SEC in Securities Act Release No. 10884 (2020) (for Regulation A, Tier 1 offerings $20 million annually—*see supra* note 45). Currently, up to thirty percent of the amount raised ($22.5 million in Tier 2 offerings) may be sold by security holders who are affiliated with the subject issuer. *See* Rule 251(a), 17 C.F.R. § 230.251(a). This is excessive. Capping sales by selling security holders at twenty percent provides significant liquidity to such holders while directing the vast bulk of the funds raised for issuer needs.

(3) Once an issuer has a public float of $75 million and the requisite number of holders of a class of equity securities, it would have a two-year transition period to become an Exchange Act Section 12(g) reporting company.[104]

(4) For all issuers using the Regulation A, Tier 2 exemption, the present disclosure requirements for Tier 2—including being subject to the continuous reporting regime and the delivery of audited financial statements—should be mandated.[105]

(5) There should be no state preemption of Regulation A offerings. However, to ensure that uniform disclosure requirements apply without the presence of state merit regulation,[106] federal standards would govern the exemption's parameters on the state level. The presence of state regulators is important in this setting as SEC personnel may not be sufficiently focused on these relatively smaller public offerings.

(6) Advertising and general solicitation or testing-the-waters prior to the filing of an issuer's offering circular with the SEC and the applicable states would be confined to accredited investors and qualified institutional buyers. These investors may be solicited after they are qualified (as proposed herein).[107]

(7) Unlike current Regulation A, Tier 2 offerings, there would be no limit on the monetary amount that a non-accredited investor may purchase in a Regulation A offering.[108] As there are no such

---

[104] This condition implements current practice. *See* SEC News Release 2015-49 (2015) ("An issuer that exceeds the dollar and Section 12(g) registration thresholds would have a two-year transition period before it must register its class of securities, provided it timely files all of its ongoing reports required under Registration A.").

[105] *See* Rule 257, 17 C.F.R. § 230.257. The continuous reporting regime is crucial to maintain. Otherwise, the securities of these non-reporting Exchange Act companies would normally be traded having the availability of only Rule 15c2-11 information, a clearly inferior alternative. For discussion of Rule 15c-11, *see infra* notes 172–179, 195–200 and accompanying text.

[106] The application of state merit regulation in this situation likely would impair the undertaking of Regulation A offerings as well as adding significant monetary costs. For discussion of state merit regulation, *see supra* note 102.

[107] Similarly, in prospective Securities Act registered offerings, an issuer may test-the-waters in the pre-filing period, engaging in oral or written communications with QIBs and institutional accredited investors. *See* § 5(d) of the Securities Act, 5 U.S.C. § 77e(d); Rule 163B, 17 C.F.R. § 230.163B. In the registered offering setting, only well-known seasoned issuers are allowed to make offers to sell to any potential investor in the pre-filing period. *See* Rule 163, 17 C.F.R. § 230.163B; discussion in Chapter 4 herein. The proposal set forth herein requires that solicitation may occur prior to the offering circular being filed with the SEC only after these prospective investors are qualified as being financially sophisticated.

[108] After all, no such limitations apply in other exempt offerings, including Section 4(a)(2) as well as 504 and 506 offerings.

limitations in other offering contexts, including Rule 504 and Rule 506 offerings, it makes little sense to impose these conditions in Regulation A offerings where relatively robust disclosure is called for with the presence of federal and (as proposed herein) state oversight.

(8) Consistent with current Regulation A, the exemption would not be available to specified issuers, including those entities that: are not U.S. or Canadian companies; have not filed their periodic reports with the Commission for the preceding two years; or are subject to the bad actor disqualification rules.[109]

These revisions to Regulation A are appropriate and evenly balanced. They are necessary so that the securities of these companies do not publicly trade in secondary markets that lack minimal standards, hence calling for the availability of at least Rule 15c2-11 information (as proposed herein) for securities that are issued pursuant to Regulation A, Tier 1.[110] Without the presence of a continuous disclosure mandate and active government oversight, the prospect of fraud drastically increases. Regulation A, as proposed herein, enables companies to raise substantial amounts of capital in public offerings while avoiding Exchange Act Section 12(g) status.[111] It thus serves as a valuable capital-raising resource while providing the structure for effective government oversight.

For the monetary limits that a non-accredited investor may purchase in a Regulation A, Tier 2 offering, *see* Rule 251(d)(2)(C) ("no more than ten percent of the greater of such purchaser's: (1) Annual income or net worth if a natural person . . . ; or (2) Revenue or net assets for such purchaser's most recently completed fiscal year end if a non-natural person").

[109] *See* Rule 251(b), 17 C.F.R. § 230.251(b) (also providing additional situations where an issuer is ineligible to use the Regulation A exemption). Note that, pursuant to the Economic Growth Regulatory Relief and Consumer Protection Act, Pub. L. No. 115-174, 132 Stat. 1296 (2018), the SEC more recently amended Regulation A, Tier 2 to permit Exchange Act companies to use this exemption. *See* Rules 251(b), 257, 17 C.F.R. §§ 230.251(b), .257; Securities Act Release No. 10591 (2018).

[110] Issuers utilizing Regulation A, Tier 2 are subject to continuous public reporting requirements. *See supra* note 105 and accompanying text. For discussion of the inadequacy of Rule 15c-11 information as currently adopted, *see infra* notes 172–179, 195–200 and accompanying text.

[111] An Exchange Act reporting company is subject to significantly more regulation and requirements than a Regulation A issuer. By way of example, Exchange Act reporting companies are required to: file quarterly reports; comply with the SEC's proxy rules as well as mandates set forth by the Sarbanes-Oxley and Dodd-Frank Acts; and adhere to the internal accounting controls and record keeping mandates of the Foreign Corporate Practices Act. In addition, insiders, including directors and officers of Exchange Act reporting companies, are subject to the short-swing trading provisions of Section 16 of that Act.

3. Intrastate Offerings

The objective of the intrastate offering exemption is to facilitate the raising of capital by local enterprises from in-state residents.[112] As viewed by the SEC, "Congress apparently believed that a company whose operations are restricted to one area should be able to raise money from investors in the immediate vicinity without having to register the securities with a federal agency."[113] Investors would be sufficiently protected, Congress reasoned, due to the presence of state regulation and the proximity of the issuer.[114]

The Section 3(a)(11) statutory exemption and Rule 147 promulgated thereunder can be vitiated by a single offer to an out-of-state resident.[115] Among other conditions, pursuant to Rule 147, the issuer must: be incorporated or organized in the offering state; offer and sell the securities solely to residents of that state; have its principal place of business located in that state; and satisfy the "doing business" in the offering state requirement set forth in the Rule.[116]

Because of the internet and other mass means of communication to conduct an offering, Rule 147 is of limited utility due to its prohibition of out-of-state offers.[117] In addition, the requirement that an issuer must be incorporated or organized in the offering state signifies that the exemption cannot be used by enterprises that elect to incorporate in Delaware or another favorable state, such as Nevada.[118] Seeking to make the intrastate exemption more attractive, the SEC adopted Rule 147A invoking its Section 28 authority.[119] Under this exemption, the issuer is not required

---

[112] *See* Securities Act Release No. 5450 (1974).

[113] *Id. See* Daniel J. Morrissey, *Think Globally, Act Locally: It's Time to Reform the Intrastate Exemption*, 20 Sec. Reg. L.J. 59 (1992); Fredrich Thomforde, *Exemptions from SEC Registration for Small Businesses*, 47 Tenn. L. Rev. 1 (1979).

[114] *See* Securities Act Release No. 5450 (1974).

[115] *See* American Law Institute, *Federal Securities Code* § 1904 Comment, at 969 (1980) ("No matter how carefully the issuer checks on the residence of each offeree, the exemption is lost if the issuer slips once, and absolute civil liability results under § 12(1) [today § 12(a)(1)].").

[116] *See* Rule 147, 17 C.F.R. § 230.147. With respect to the "doing business" requirement, the issuer must meet one of the following conditions: (1) the entity derives at a minimum eighty percent of its gross revenues "from the operation of a business . . . or from the rendering of services within that state"; (2) the entity has at least eighty percent of its assets located within that state; (3) the entity will use at a minimum eighty percent of the amount raised in the offering to conduct its operations within that state; or (4) a majority of the entity's employees are based in that state. Rule 147(c)(2).

[117] *See* Securities Act Release No. 10238 (2016) ("We believe offers over the Internet that can be viewed by a significant number of out-of-state residents are not consistent with Section 3(a)(11) and Rule 147.").

[118] *Id.*

[119] 17 C.F.R. § 230.147A. *See* Securities Act Release No. 10238 (2016) ("We are adopting new Rule 147A pursuant to our general exemptive authority under Section 28 of the Securities Act, and, therefore, new Rule 147A will not be subject to the statutory limitations of Section 3(a)(11)."). The Commission's use of its exemptive authority under Section 28 is addressed in Chapter 4 herein.

to be incorporated or formed in the offering state and offers may be made to out-of-state residents so long as all sales are made to residents of the offering state.[120] Among other requirements, the issuer must have its principal place of business in that state and meet the "doing business" requirement.[121] The more attractive features of Rule 147A as compared to Section 3(a)(11) and Rule 147 make it likely that in the foreseeable future the latter two exemptions rarely will be used. Indeed, for the time being, as the SEC recognized, their current utility is "to preserve the continued availability of existing state exemptive provisions that are specifically conditioned upon issuer reliance on Section 3(a)(11) and Rule 147."[122]

The SEC's resourcefulness in promulgating the Rule 147A exemption merits kudos. However, the more pointed question is whether the intrastate offering exemption should survive. The exemption was adopted in a different era.[123] Today, issuer capital needs ordinarily may be aptly met by means of the Rule 504, Regulation A, and Rule 506 exemptions, which all provide for offers and sales to out-of-state residents irrespective of the subject issuer's domicile.

Pursuant to the Rule 504 exemption, the individual states retain their authority to promulgate their respective offering criteria, including disclosure and merit-based standards.[124] If the maximum monetary amount for Rule 504 offerings is deemed insufficient, the SEC can appropriately increase that limit.[125] Moreover, when a Rule 504 offering is made in multiple states where

---

[120] Pursuant to Rule 147A(d), the issuer must reasonably believe that the subject purchasers are residents of the offering state. Advertising and general solicitation are permitted under the exemption. *See* Rule 147A(b), 17 C.F.R. § 230.147A(b).

[121] The doing business requirement is the same as that contained in Rule 147. *See* Securities Act Release No. 10238 (2016); *supra* note 116.

[122] Securities Act Release No. 10238 (2016). *See generally* Sarah Aboukhair, *The "Modernized" Rule 147 and 147A: An Analysis of the Potential Market Response to the SEC's Attempt to Revise and Modernize the Intrastate Offering Exemption*, 45 Sec. Reg. L.J. 421 (2017).

[123] After all, it should be remembered that the blue sky laws predated the federal securities laws. Kansas enacted the first state securities law in 1911. *See* 1911 Kan. Sess. Laws 210; Amy Deen Westbrook, *Blue Sky Laws for 100 Years: Introduction to the Special Issue on Corporate and Blue Sky Law*, 50 Washburn L.J. xxv (2011) (stating "that the financial markets in 2011 are profoundly different from the markets in 1911 [and that] the 1911 Act was passed under a specific combination of politics, economics, technology, and social forces at work in Kansas in 1911").

[124] The Rule 504 exemption thus allows for state registered public offerings that adhere to the disclosure and merit standards of the applicable states. *See* Securities Act Release No. 10238 (2016).

[125] In 2020, the SEC increased the annual amount that can be raised in Rule 504 offerings to $10 million. *See* Securities Act Release No. 10884 (2020). This $10 million annual level is appropriate. It provides the opportunity for enterprises to engage in regional state registered public offerings to raise a relatively significant amount of capital. If an issuer seeks to raise up to $20 million annually in a public offering, Regulation A, Tier 1 provides a feasible option. Either of these alternatives enables an issuer to avoid the ongoing disclosure requirements set forth by Regulation A, Tier 2. *See* discussion *supra* notes 45–59 and accompanying text. As set forth herein, serious consideration should be given to whether Tier 1 of Regulation A should be rescinded. *See* discussion *supra* notes 101–102 and accompanying text.

state registration is required, there is a greater likelihood that the offering will be vetted by at least one regulator. Hence, the specter of inadequate state review, as may exist in certain blue sky jurisdictions, is lessened. Although review by multiple state securities regulators likely will increase costs to some extent, issuers and their representatives will be more inclined to engage in sound practices. Further, the coordinated review protocols adhered to by the states should substantially reduce these costs.[126]

The intrastate offering exemption accordingly should be rescinded. The benefits of the exemption are outweighed by the availability of alternative exemptions that better meet issuer and investor needs. While the exemption was useful in the days of yesteryear, the time has arrived for its revocation.

4. Summation

While the preceding discussion does not address all SEC primary exemptions from SEC registration,[127] it does focus on the ones that are most frequently used. For example, the traditional Rule 506 exemption is the most frequently invoked exemption.[128] As proposed in this Section, the SEC's exemption framework should be restructured with the exemptions tailored in a balanced manner to meet both issuer and investor needs. The framework set forth herein would streamline the exemption process, benefitting investors while not unduly impeding capital raising by issuers.

C. Integration of Primary Exempt Offerings

As discussed earlier in this chapter, the SEC has adopted several accommodations that drastically decrease the prospect of integration of securities offerings.[129] Indeed, the Commission's adoption of Rule 152 in

---

[126] *See* Securities Act Release No. 10238 (2016). In raising the Rule 504 annual amount from $1 million to $5 million in 2016, the SEC stated in that release: "We . . . believe that our amendments to increase the aggregate offering amount limit in Rule 504 to $5 million may bolster efforts among the states to enter into, or revise existing, regional coordinated review programs that are designed to increase efficiencies associated with the registration of securities offerings in multiple jurisdictions without increasing risks to investors." *See* NASAA, Coordinated Review, available at https://www.nasaa.org/industry-resources/securities-issuers/coordinated-review/.

[127] For a listing of other exemptions, *see supra* note 85.

[128] *See* Securities Act Release No. 10763 (2020) (in 2019, $1.492 billion was raised in traditional Rule 506 offerings, more than any other exemption).

[129] *See* Rule 152, 17 C.F.R. § 230.152; Securities Act Release No. 10884 (2020); *supra* notes 60–66 and accompanying text.

2020, in practical effect, nullifies the integration doctrine except in relatively rare situations.[130] This consequence was recognized by SEC Commissioner Allison Herren Lee, who asserted that the SEC has "effectively rendered the [integration] doctrine hollow but for a requirement to wait 30 days between offerings."[131]

Up until recently, although the SEC contemplated decreasing the safe harbor period, it declined to take final action, such as the Commission's 2007 rule proposal to shorten the safe harbor to ninety days.[132] The Commission's 2020 ultimate adoption of Rule 152,[133] in practical effect, dooms the integration doctrine unless the subject issuer both fails to meet any of the Rule's

---

[130] *See* Rule 152, 17 C.F.R. § 230.152; Securities Act Release No. 10884 (2020). As set forth in the SEC's "Fact Sheet" describing the November 2020 amendments:

> The amendments establish a new integration framework that provides a general principle that looks to the particular facts and circumstances of two or more offerings, and focuses the analysis on whether the issuer can establish that each offering either complies with the registration requirements of the Securities Act, or that an exemption from registration is available for the particular offering.
>
> The amendments additionally provide four non-exclusive safe harbors from integration providing that:
>
> [1] any offering made more than 30 calendar days before the commencement of any other offering, or more than 30 calendar days after the termination or completion of any other offering, will not be integrated with such other offerings(s); provided that:
> - in the case where an exempt offering for which general solicitation is prohibited follows by 30 calendar days or more an offering that allows general solicitation, the issuer has a reasonable belief, based on the facts and circumstances, with respect to each purchaser in the exempt offering prohibiting general solicitation, that the issuer (or any person acting on the issuer's behalf) either did not solicit such purchaser through the use of general solicitation or established a substantive relationship with such purchaser prior to the commencement of the exempt offering prohibiting general solicitation;
>
> [2] offers and sales made in compliance with Rule 701, pursuant to an employee benefit plan, or in compliance with Regulation S will not be integrated with other offerings;
>
> [3] an offering for which a Securities Act registration statement has been filed will not be integrated if it is made subsequent to:
> - a terminated or completed offering for which general solicitation is not permitted,
> - a terminated or completed offering for which general solicitation is permitted that was made only to qualified institutional buyers and institutional accredited investors, or
> - an offering for which general solicitation is permitted that terminated or was completed more than 30 calendar days prior to the commencement of the registered offering; and
>
> [4] offers and sales made in reliance on an exemption for which general solicitation is permitted will not be integrated if made subsequent to any terminated or completed offering.

SEC Press Release No. 2020-273 (2020).

[131] *See* Allison Herren Lee, SEC Commissioner, Statement on Amendments to the Exempt Offering Framework, *supra* note 66.

[132] *See* Securities Act Release No. 8828 (2007).

[133] 17 C.F.R. § 230.152. *See* Securities Act Release No. 10884 (2020).

expansive safe harbor provisions and acts in a patently careless manner in seeking to perfect an exemption from registration.[134]

With the SEC's distinct policy of dismantling the bulk of the integration doctrine, the question arises whether this doctrine should be eliminated in its entirety.[135] On one hand, issuers should not be allowed within a relatively short time period to raise capital through the use of exemptions in several apparently separate offerings that in substance constitute a single offering. In such event, integration is in order to determine whether the integrated offering is law compliant.[136] If an exemption from registration is not available when the purportedly separate offerings are integrated, a registration violation has been committed. A law-compliant course of action would: time the alleged individual offerings in intervals so that they are sufficiently far enough apart; restructure the purportedly separate offerings into one offering that satisfies an exemption from registration; or file a Securities Act registration statement.[137]

On the other hand, it may be asserted that the integration doctrine serves little useful purpose today. So long as an issuer meets the criteria for perfecting an applicable exemption, it should be entitled to raise capital in simultaneous and concurrent offerings as it pleases. As each supposedly separate offering has its own exemption from registration, the alleged harm to investors is rather opaque. Moreover, for many of the exemptions, such as Rule 504 and Regulation A, a maximum monetary amount is specified that may be raised by an issuer during a twelve-month period.[138] So long as the

---

[134] In proposing a thirty-day safe harbor provision from integration (Securities Act Release No. 10763 (2020)), the Commission reasoned: "In light of the changes in technology, the markets, and the securities laws since 1982, we preliminarily believe a shortened 30-day safe harbor time period would enhance an issuer's flexibility and expand the capital raising options available to issuers under the Securities Act to access capital when needed, while still providing a sufficient length of time to impede what integration seeks to prevent: improperly avoiding registration by artificially dividing a single offering into multiple offerings." *Id.* Decreasing the safe harbor from six months to one month is unduly expansive, providing substantial opportunity to, in the words of the Commission, "artificially divid[e] a single offering into multiple offerings." A better approach is to lower this safe harbor from six months to ninety days as proposed by the SEC in 2007. *See* Securities Act Release No. 8828 (2007).

[135] This position was advocated by Professor Rutherford Campbell two decades ago. *See* Rutherford B. Campbell, *The Overwhelming Case for Elimination of the Integration Doctrine Under the Securities Act of 1933*, 89 Ky. L.J. 289 (2000–2001).

[136] *See* Darryl B. Deaktor, *Integration of Securities Offerings*, 31 U. Fla. L. Rev. 465 (1979).

[137] *See* Perry E. Wallace, Jr., *Integration of Securities Offerings: Obstacles to Capital Formation Remain for Small Businesses*, 45 Wash. & Lee L. Rev. 883 (1988).

[138] *See* Securities Act Release No. 10763 (2020) (proposing release) ("consider[ing] changes in the informational environment that have occurred [since] Regulation D was adopted . . . in 1982 and the accelerating speed and consumption of electronically disseminated information in today's financial marketplace," thereby making "a 30-day [safe harbor] time frame . . . sufficient to mitigate concerns

applicable offering amount is not exceeded and the other requirements of that exemption are satisfied for each purported offering, whether an issuer has one or fifteen offerings during that time period ordinarily would not be material to investors. As an additional consideration, the sanction for a registration violation is severe: strict liability with purchasers entitled to rescind their transactions with the specter of government enforcement proceedings, including criminal liability exposure.[139]

Both of the foregoing positions have merit. The better course of action is to first inquire whether the ostensibly separate offerings are for the same general purposes.[140] If they are for different purposes, then the offerings should not be integrated, even if they occur simultaneously. One example is the Rule 701 exemption (which is utilized for compensation purposes for a subject issuer's employees and consultants)[141] and exemptions whose main objective is capital raising (such as the Rule 504, 506, and Regulation A exemptions).[142] If the purportedly separate offerings, however, are part of a single plan of financing and occur in close proximity with one another,[143] the integration doctrine's objective becomes prominent: "to prevent an issuer from avoiding

---

that an exempt offering may condition the market for a subsequent registered offering or undermine the protections of a subsequent exempt offering"). With respect to the maximum monetary amounts that can be raised annually pursuant to Rule 504 and Regulation A, *see supra* notes 45, 88, 99, 103 and accompanying text.

[139] Purchasers are entitled under Section 12(a)(1) of the Securities Act, 15 U.S.C. § 77l(a)(1), to rescission (or damages if the securities have been sold) when the seller violates Section 5 of that Act, 15 U.S.C. § 77e. Indeed, several state statutes impose criminal liability premised on strict liability for registration violations. *See, e.g., Buffo v. State*, 415 So. 2d 1158 (Ala. 1982); *Cox v. Garvin*, 607 S.E. 2d 549 (Ga. 2005); *State v. Casper*, 297 S.W. 3d 676 (Tenn. 2009). *See generally* Mark A. Sargent, *A Blue Sky State of Mind: The Meaning of "Willfully" In Blue Sky Criminal Cases*, 20 Sec. Reg. L.J. 96 (1992).

[140] This is a key inquiry in the traditional five-factor test that has been replaced by the SEC with the adoption of Rule 152. *See* Securities Act Release No. 10884 (2020) (stating that "the final rules replace the five-factor test"). These five factors are: "whether the offerings are part of a single plan of financing; whether the offerings involve issuance of the same class of security; whether the offerings have been made at or about the same time; whether the same type of consideration is received; and whether the offerings are made for the same general purposes." Securities Act Release No. 4552 (1962).

[141] Rule 701 is available only to issuers that are not Exchange Act reporting companies or investment companies. The maximum amount that can be offered and sold during a twelve-month period pursuant to this exemption is the greatest of the following: "(1) $1 million, (2) 15 percent of the company's total assets, or (3) 15 percent of the outstanding securities of the class of securities issued." Securities Act Release No. 7645 (1988). Specified information, including financial statements, must be provided to the prospective purchaser "if the aggregate sales price or amount of securities sold during any 12-month period exceeds $10 million." Rule 701(e). Because Rule 701 is designed as an exemption for compensation purposes, it may not be invoked for capital raising activities. *See supra* note 85. The Commission has adopted a broad safe harbor from integration rule with respect to Rule 701 offerings. *See* Rule 152, 17 C.F.R. § 230.152.

[142] *See* discussion *supra* notes 7–66 and accompanying text.

[143] These are key inquiries in the traditional five-factor test set forth in *supra* note 140.

registration of a nonexempt transaction by accomplishing the transaction through two or more ostensibly distinct offerings each of which, if treated as a separate transaction, would conform to [an applicable exemption]."[144]

The Commission's determination not to integrate certain offerings irrespective of their relative proximity is misplaced:[145] offerings launched or consummated in relatively close proximity to one another pursuant to exemptions from Securities Act registration may be made for the same general purposes and comprise part of a single plan of financing. Moreover, when these offerings occur in close proximity with one another, solicitation of subject investors in one offering may spill over to other offerings.[146]

The proposed framework is straightforward and is comprised of two safe harbors: first, when separate offerings are for different purposes, they will not be integrated; second, a ninety-day safe harbor would apply with respect to offerings that have the same general purposes. This ninety-day period provides certainty to issuers while being sufficiently protective for investors and implements the time period that was proposed over a decade ago by the SEC.[147] The previous six-month safe harbor period that was adopted by the SEC in certain contexts prior to the 2020 amendments is excessive in today's markets, resulting in loss of capital-raising opportunities for issuers.[148] In addition, as is current practice, the SEC may adopt additional safe harbors in defined circumstances where it is clear that the objectives of the integration doctrine are not impaired. Otherwise, where purportedly separate offerings are made within ninety days of one another and are made for the same general purposes, the traditional five-factor test

---

144 Deaktor, *supra* note 63, at 473. *See also* Morrissey, *supra* note 60, at 77 ("If a combination of offerings will place the total issuance outside the well-considered exemptions to registration, an SEC registration filing is in order.").

145 *See* Lee, *supra* note 66.

146 To some extent, Rule 152, 17 C.F.R. § 230.152, addresses this matter in situations involving general solicitation. *See supra* note 130. Moreover, the Commission was aware of the potential of Rule 506(b) offerings being made every thirty-one days to non-accredited investors, resulting in potentially over 375 such investors during a one-year period. Accordingly, in adopting the November 2020 amendments (Securities Act Release No. 10884 (2020)), the SEC amended Rule 506(b)(2) to provide that there can be "no more than, or the issuer reasonably believes that there are no more than, 35 purchasers of securities from the issuer in offerings under this section [Rule 506(b)] in any 90-calendar-day period."

147 *See* Securities Act Release No. 8828 (2007). Proposing to shorten the safe harbor in Regulation D offerings to ninety days, the Commission stated in that Release: "We believe that 90 days is appropriate, as it would permit an issuer to rely on the safe harbor once every fiscal quarter [and] should provide additional flexibility to issuers, while still requiring them to wait a sufficient period of time before initiating a substantial similar offer in reliance on the safe harbor."

148 *See supra* note 134.

would apply to determine whether they will be integrated and deemed a single offering.[149]

IV. A Proposed Framework for Resales of Securities

The current framework with respect to exemptions from Securities Act registration for resales of securities is convoluted and often nonsensical. For decades, critics have urged that significant changes should be implemented.[150] The availability of accessing an exemption depends on such concepts as distinguishing a transaction as compared to a distribution, whether the seller is an affiliate, the presence (or absence) of underwriter status, and whether a security is deemed restricted or non-restricted.

With respect to security holders seeking to resell their securities, the same general principle applies as in the issuer offer or sale setting: absent the perfection of an exemption, any offer or sale of a security must be registered.[151] The key statutory provision in this context is Section 4(a)(1) of the Securities Act that provides an exemption from registration for "transactions by any person other than an issuer, underwriter, or dealer."[152] For brokers, Section 4(a)(4) provides the applicable source, exempting from registration "brokers' transactions executed upon customers' orders on any exchange or in the over-the-counter market but not the solicitation of such orders."[153]

The SEC has provided guidance in this area by promulgating Rule 144.[154] Provided that its provisions are met, the exemption serves as a safe harbor under Section 4(a)(1) for security holders reselling their securities and under Section 4(a)(4) for brokers who effect such transactions.[155] In addition,

---

[149] The five-factor test (which has been abandoned by the SEC) is set forth in *supra* note 140.

[150] *See, e.g., ALI Federal Securities Code, supra* note 115, §§ 501–515, at § 502 Comment (1) (stating that the ALI Code "abandon[s] the illogical and difficult 'control' test of the 1933 Act, whether primary or secondary").

[151] *See* § 5 of the Securities Act, 15 U.S.C. § 77e; *Securities and Exchange Commission v. Chinese Consolidated Benevolent Association*, 120 F.2d 738 (2d Cir. 1941).

[152] 15 U.S.C. § 77d(a)(1).

[153] 15 U.S.C. § 77d(a)(4).

[154] 17 C.F.R. § 230.144. Rule 144 was adopted in 1972. *See* Securities Act Release No. 5223 (1972). The Rule 144 safe harbor is not exclusive, permitting the security holder, for example, to invoke the statutory Section 4(a)(1) exemption. *See* Preliminary Note to Rule 144.

[155] *See* Rule 144. With respect to the Section 4(a)(4) exemption, *see* Rule 144(g) (providing a safe harbor for the term brokers' transactions in § 4(a)(4)). *See also* Securities Act Release No. 8869 (2007) ("Rule 144 under the Securities Act of 1933 creates a safe harbor for the sale of securities under the exemption set forth in Section 4(1) [now § 4(a)(1)] of the Securities Act.").

pursuant to SEC no-action letters and other Commission pronouncements, the so-called "Section 4(1½)" exemption has been recognized, providing an exemption in private resale transactions.[156] Bringing more clarity to private resales, Congress in 2015 enacted Section 4(a)(7) of the Securities Act, providing an exemption from registration for resales of securities under specified conditions to accredited investors.[157] As a last example, the SEC has promulgated Rule 144A, which provides a Securities Act registration exemption for resales of restricted securities to qualified institutional buyers (QIBs).[158]

These multi-faceted exemptions from registration in the resale context and their complexity are not comprehensively analyzed herein. This has been done by this author as well as several other academicians and practitioners.[159] Rather, the objective of the following discussion is to identify ambiguities, inconsistencies, and improper effects of the current regimen. Thereafter, a proposal setting forth a revised framework will be recommended.

A. The Unacceptable Current Resale Exemption Framework

The following examples illustrate the unacceptable status of the current provisions with respect to exemptions from Securities Act registration when security holders seek to resell their securities:

(1) The distinction between a transaction versus a distribution is problematic. For example, a control person (such as a chief executive officer) who sells during a seventy-five-day period over the New York Stock Exchange securities which she has owned for ten years, constituting two percent of the shares of common stock outstanding of that company, may be engaged in a distribution (and thereby

---

[156] *See* Securities Act Release No. 6188 (1980). For SEC no-action letters on this subject, *see, e.g.*, *Bank of New Hampshire Corporation*, 1981 WL 26188 (SEC No-Act. Letter 1981); *Optelcom, Incorporated*, 1982 WL 30378 (SEC No-Act. Letter 1982); *Candela Laser Corporation*, 1987 WL 108552 (SEC No-Act. Letter 1987).

[157] 15 U.S.C. § 77d(a)(7). This statute was enacted as part of the FAST Act (Fixing America's Surface Transportation Act), Pub. Law 114-94, 129 Stat. 1312 (2015).

[158] 17 C.F.R. § 230.144A.

[159] *See, e.g.*, Thomas Lee Hazen, *Treatise on the Law of Securities Regulation* (7th ed. 2020); J. William Hicks, *Exempted Transactions Under the Securities Act of 1933* (2020); Louis Loss, Joel Seligman, and Troy A. Paredes, *Securities Regulation* (2019); Marc I. Steinberg, *Understanding Securities Law* (7th ed. 2018).

violate Section 5 of the Securities Act).[160] By contrast, a disgruntled shareholder who has owned his securities for two years and is not an affiliate of the subject company may sell all of his common stock, constituting eight percent of the shares outstanding and be deemed to have perfected the statutory Section 4(a)(1) exemption.[161] The rationale is that the chief executive officer, as a control person, has "the power to direct or cause the direction of the management and policies" of the company,[162] including the leverage to cause the company to file a registration statement for the sale of her shares.[163] Nonetheless, a key consideration in this setting is the impact of the trades on the trading markets.[164] Frequently, an unaffiliated shareholder's unloading of eight percent of the common shares outstanding has a greater impact on the trading markets than a chief executive officer selling a far lesser amount.[165]

---

[160] Generally, Rule 144(e), 17 C.F.R. § 230.144(e), permits an affiliate, such as the subject company's chief executive officer, to sell pursuant to the rule (together with all other sales of the same class of securities) during any three-month period the greater of "one percent of the shares or other units of the class outstanding as shown by the most recent report or statement published by the issuer, or the average weekly reported volume of trading in such securities on all national securities exchanges and/or reported through the automatic quotation system of a registered securities association during the [preceding] four calendar weeks." Hence, in the example provided in the text, if the chief executive officer's sale constituting two percent of the company's outstanding shares exceeded the average weekly reported volume criterion set forth above, the safe harbor of Rule 144 would not be available. In such event the chief executive officer would need to rely on the murky Section 4(a)(1) statutory exemption. Note that the volume limitations with respect to the resale of debt securities and certain other securities under Rule 144 are set at a greater level. *See* Rule 144(e)(2)–(3).

[161] *See, e.g., United States v. Sherwood*, 175 F. Supp. 480 (S.D.N.Y. 1959) (holding that the statutory § 4(1) exemption was available to a non-affiliate who sold eight percent of the company's outstanding stock after owning these securities for a minimum of two years). A two-year holding period is deemed sufficient to find that the subject person did not purchase the securities from an issuer with a view to distribution. *See* § 2(a)(11), 15 U.S.C. § 77b(a)(11) (defining the term underwriter); *Securities and Exchange Commission v. Big Apple Consulting USA, Inc.*, 783 F.3d 786, 807 (11th Cir. 2015) ("Courts have generally agreed that a two-year holding period is sufficient.").

[162] *See* Rule 405, 17 C.F.R. § 230.405 (defining control as "the possession, direct or indirect, of the power to direct or cause the direction of the management and policies of a person, whether through the ownership of voting securities, by contract, or otherwise").

[163] *See Pennaluna & Company v. Securities and Exchange Commission*, 410 F.2d 861, 865 (9th Cir. 1969) (inquiring whether the individual is in a position to obtain the necessary signatures for the filing of a registration statement), *quoting*, 1 L. Loss, *Securities Regulation* 557 (2d ed. 1961).

[164] *See, e.g., United States v. Wolfson*, 405 F.2d 779 (2d Cir. 1968). For an insightful article on Louis Wolfson, *see* Alan M. Weinberger, *What's in a Name?—The Tale of Louis Wolfson's Affirmed*, 39 Hofstra L. Rev. 645 (2011).

[165] The impact of the insider's sales, however, may be significant if this information is leaked prior to the occurrence of these transactions or after these transactions become publicly known due to the executive officer filing a Form 4 within two business days of the trades. *See* § 16(a)(2)(C), 15 U.S.C. § 78q(a)(2)(C). Otherwise, sales of eight percent of a company's outstanding shares may well be more likely to have a greater impact than sales of one-quarter of that amount.

(2) In the foregoing example, the facts assume that the selling security holder of the eight percent of the common shares outstanding is not an affiliate of the company. The determination of affiliate or control status frequently is uncertain.[166] It is based on such factors as officer or director position, percentage of stock ownership, and relationships with the company's insiders.[167] Question, for example, whether the following individuals are control persons: an outside director who has served in the role of director for less than two years and is not a member of the audit, compensation, nomination, or other important board committee; the company's in-house general counsel who does not serve as a director and whose principal functions are to oversee the legal department and give legal advice to her client; the company's long-standing investment banking firm that has lent substantial funds to the company with onerous covenants and has served as lead underwriter or placement agent for all of the company's securities offerings; a shareholder who has a nine percent equity interest in the enterprise but who holds no director or officer positions; and a shareholder who owns 500 shares out of several million shares outstanding who does not serve as a director or officer but is viewed by the board of directors as Yoda in view of his sage advice and astute business acumen.[168]

(3) As a matter of logic, non-restricted securities (such as common stock purchased in a registered offering) would be more liquid and have fewer restrictions on resale than restricted securities (such as limited liability company interests purchased in a Rule 506 offering).[169] In certain ways, this in fact is the case. For example, non-restricted securities have no holding period, while purchasers of restricted securities must hold their securities for six months from the date of acquisition from the issuer (or from an affiliate of such issuer) with respect to an Exchange Act

[166] *See, e.g.*, A.A. Sommer, Jr., *Who's "In Control"?*, 21 Bus. Law. 559 (1966) (explaining the "imprecise limits" of the meaning of control and the importance of that determination).

[167] *See* Rutherford B. Campbell, *Defining Control in Secondary Distributions*, 18 Bos. Coll. Ind. & Comm. L. Rev. 37 (1976); Alexander Poor and Michelle A. Rees, *The "Control" Quagmire: The Cumbersome Concept of "Control" for the Corporate Attorney*, 44 Sec. Reg. L.J. 101 (2016).

[168] *See, e.g.*, *Pennaluna & Company v. Securities and Exchange Commission*, 410 F.2d 861 (9th Cir. 1969) (individual, not having a director or officer position and owning a minimal number of shares, held to be a control person based on his relationships with the company's insiders); sources cited *supra* notes 166–167.

[169] An illustration to support this proposition is Rule 504. Securities sold under Rule 504 that are restricted have a one-year holding period while non-restricted securities sold pursuant to that rule have no holding period. *See* Rules 144(d), 504(b)(1), 17 C.F.R. §§ 230.144(d), .504(b)(1).

reporting issuer or twelve months if the issuer is a non-reporting company in order to invoke Rule 144's safe harbor.[170] Once a holder who is not an affiliate satisfies this holding period for its restricted securities, it may sell under Rule 144 all of its restricted securities during a short interval, even if such holdings constitute a large percentage of the issuer's equity securities, such as over twenty percent.[171] On the other hand, Rule 144 does not address the non-affiliate who owns non-restricted securities. Because there is no safe harbor rule or other source (such as established judicial precedent) providing the non-affiliate with sufficient comfort in this setting, the non-affiliate who sells all of its non-restricted securities on a national securities exchange, constituting a sizable percentage (such as ten percent) of the issuer's outstanding securities, incurs the risk of being engaged in a distribution (rather than a transaction), and thereby violating Section 5 of the Securities Act.[172]

(4) As mentioned earlier, for whatever unknown reason, the SEC has declined to extend Rule 144 to cover the non-affiliated security holder who is selling its non-restricted securities. As a result, there is no safe harbor provided for these security holders when they sell their shares in an impersonal trading market, such as the over-the-counter market or on a securities exchange.[173] This lack of guidance is inexplicable and should be remedied.

---

[170] *See* Rule 144(d), 17 C.F.R. § 230.144(d); Securities Act Release No. 8869 (2007).

[171] *See* Rule 144(b), 17 C.F.R. § 230.144(b). In the adopting release, the SEC stated that the rule "permit[s] non-affiliates to resell their restricted securities freely after meeting the applicable holding period requirement (i.e., six months with respect to a reporting issuer and one year with respect to a non-reporting issuer), except that non-affiliates of reporting issuers still would be subject to the current public information requirement in Rule 144(c) for an additional six months after the end of the initial six-month holding period." Securities Act Release No. 8869 (2007). The Commission's requirement that a non-affiliate be subject to the current public information requirement for an additional six months seems nonsensical because the non-affiliate is not a control person and does not have sufficient leverage to cause the company to make this undertaking. The only practical way that a non-affiliate can comply with this provision, if the company otherwise would not engage in this undertaking, is by way of contractual commitment, ordinarily entered into at the time of the non-affiliate's (or its predecessor(s)') purchase of the subject securities from the company.

[172] It may be asserted that the SEC implicitly has taken the position that a non-affiliate's sale of its non-restricted securities is compliant with the Section 4(a)(1) exemption. Nonetheless, the Commission has not addressed this issue in Rule 144 or by way of any other SEC rule or regulation. Moreover, in *United States v. Sherwood*, 175 F. Supp. 480 (S.D.N.Y. 1959), the percentage of shares sold was eight percent of the outstanding shares. A significantly larger percentage, such as fifteen percent, may have been perceived differently by the court.

[173] *See* Steinberg, *supra* note 159, at 207 (stating that, when a non-affiliate sells a large percentage of the outstanding shares in the public markets, these trades have a "detrimental effect on the capital trading markets and the investing public . . . , irrespective of whether one has [or has not] affiliate status when reselling large quantities of stock"); *supra* note 172. Note that for a person to have the status as a non-affiliate, such person must "not [have] been an affiliate during the preceding three months." Rule 144(b)(1)(i), 17 C.F.R. § 230.144(b)(1)(i).

(5) In order for a broker or dealer to publish or submit any quotation for a security, it must have in its records specified information regarding the subject issuer as set forth in Exchange Act Rule 15c2-11.[174] With respect to non-reporting issuers, the information required is relatively minimal and prone to be outdated, generally requiring that it be within twelve months prior to the publication or submission of such quotation.[175] The result is that secondary trading in the over-the-counter market lacks adequate transparency.[176] It is incongruous that the SEC has taken significant measures in mandating meaningful disclosure in the issuer offering context but has declined to sufficiently address the provision of adequate disclosure with respect to non-reporting issuers whose securities trade in the over-the-counter market.[177]

(6) Pursuant to SEC no action and other pronouncements, the Section "4(1½)" exemption has come into being.[178] This exemption, while within the parameters of the Section 4(a)(1) exemption, looks to criteria within the issuer Section 4(a)(2) exemption to determine its conditions for qualification.[179] Nonetheless, as the SEC has declined to set forth all the requirements for the exemption, uncertainty

---

[174] 17 C.F.R. § 240.15c2-11.

[175] *See* Rule 15c2-11(b)(5)(i); Securities Exchange Act Release No. 89891 (2020) (adopting amendments to Rule 15c2-11). Yet, under the 2020 amendments, information generally is deemed to be current "as of a date within 12 months prior to the publication or submission of the quotation." Rule 15c2-11(b)(5)(i).

[176] On the other hand, the Rule aptly defines the breadth of the term "publicly available." See Rule 15c2-11(e)(4): "Publicly available shall mean available on EDGAR, or on the website of a qualified interdealer quotation system, a registered national securities association, an issuer, or a registered broker or dealer."

[177] The Commission's release adopting amendments to Rule 15c2-11 stated that the amendments "are designed to modernize the Rule, promote investor protection, and curb incidents of fraud and manipulation." Securities Exchange Act Release No. 89891 (2020). An important revision narrows the "piggyback exception." As described by the SEC in the proposing release:

> The Commission is proposing to limit eligibility for an existing exception, known as the "piggyback exception," which allows broker-dealers to publish quotations for a security in reliance on the quotations of another broker-dealer that initially performed the review of the issuer's information. Under its existing formulation, this exception has been used by broker-dealers to continuously quote a security over many years, even when the issuer of the security no longer exists. The proposed amendments would limit the use of the exception.

Securities Act Release No. 87115 (2019). Under the amended Rule 15c2-11, the piggyback exception is narrowed. *See* Securities Exchange Act Release No. 89891 (2020); discussion *infra* notes, 191–192, 197–202 and accompanying text.

[178] *See* sources cited *supra* note 156.

[179] *See, e.g., Ackerberg v. Johnson*, 892 F.2d 1328, 1335 n. 6 (8th Cir. 1989) (observing that compliance with the informal "4(1½)" exemption signifies that the subject person meets the § 4(1) [now § 4(a)(1)] statutory exemption, stating "it is clear that the exemption for private resales of restricted securities is § 4(1)").

prevails.[180] With the specter of strict liability looming for the selling security holder and its broker if the exemption is not perfected,[181] the Commission should rescind this informal exemption or promulgate a rule specifying the conditions necessary for its invocation.

(7) The Rule 144A resale exemption is directed at arguably the most sophisticated of purchasers—QIBs.[182] The exemption provides a market for resales of securities in generally two settings: (1) the sale of debt securities to QIBs by placement agents who themselves had purchased the securities from the subject issuer; and (2) resales to QIBs of the securities of foreign companies that were originally sold outside of the United States, including sales pursuant to SEC Regulation S.[183] Irrespective that these Rule 144A securities trade on a centralized

---

[180] *See, e.g.*, Christopher Olander and Margaret Jacks, *The Section 4(1½) Exemption—Reading Between the Lines of the Securities Act of 1933*, 15 Sec. Reg. L.J. 339 (1988).

[181] *See, e.g.*, *Securities and Exchange Commission v. Ralston Purina*, 346 U.S. 119, 126 (1953) (stating that the party's "motives, laudable though they may be, fade into irrelevance"). Also, the burden is placed on the party claiming the exemption to establish that the requirements of the exemption have been satisfied. *See, e.g.*, *Ralston Purina*, 346 U.S. at 126; *Securities and Exchange Commission v. Culpepper*, 270 F.2d 241 (2d Cir. 1959).

[182] 17 C.F.R. § 230.144A. Generally, a qualified institutional buyer is defined to include a specified entity (such as an insurance company within the meaning of Section 2(a)(13) of the Securities Act), "acting for its own account or the accounts of other qualified institutional buyers, that in the aggregate owns and invests on a discretionary basis at least $100 million in securities of issuers that are not affiliated with the entity"; "[a]ny dealer registered pursuant to Section 15 of the Exchange Act, acting for its own account or the accounts of other qualified institutional buyers, that in the aggregate owns and invests on a discretionary basis at least $10 million of securities of issuers that are not affiliated with the dealer" (however, securities comprising part of such dealer's unsold allotment as a participant in a public offering are excluded from this $10 million amount); and "[a]ny dealer registered pursuant to Section 15 of the Exchange Act acting in a riskless principal transaction on behalf of a qualified institutional buyer". Rule 144A(a)(1)(i)–(iii).

[183] *See* Securities Act Release No. 6862 (1990); Anita Raghaven, *Private Placement Market Is Proving Popular*, Wall St. J., April 1, 1997, at C14; Marc I. Steinberg and Daryl L. Lansdale, Jr., *Regulation S and Rule 144A: Creating a Workable Fiction in an Expanding Global Securities Market*, 29 Int'l Law. 43 (1995). Generally, Regulation S, 17 C.F.R. §§ 230.901–.905, provides that the registration provisions of the Securities Act do not apply to offers and sales of securities that occur outside of the United States and sets forth criteria for ascertaining whether a subject offer or sale occurs outside of this country. The Regulation has two safe harbor provisions—an issuer safe harbor and a safe harbor for resales of securities. *See* Securities Act Release No. 6863 (1990). From a general perspective, note the following:

> In Regulation S the SEC embraced a territorial approach to the extraterritorial application of the Securities Act. This approach is based on the notion that the registration requirements of the Securities Act are intended to protect U.S. capital markets and all investors in such markets, whether U.S. or foreign nationals. Regulation S represents a change in emphasis, from attempting to regulate U.S. persons irrespective of where they are located, to protecting the integrity of the U.S. capital markets. For registration purposes, the Commission decided to rely upon the laws in the jurisdictions in which the transactions occur rather than the U.S. Securities Act.

Steinberg and Lansdale, *supra*, at 47.

automated trading system,[184] significantly, the widespread reselling of the securities to QIBs is deemed not to constitute a distribution, thereby providing an exemption from Securities Act registration.[185] Perhaps the most bizarre aspect of the rule is that the holder of the securities and the prospective purchaser upon request are entitled to receive from the subject issuer certain specified information, including such issuer's financial statements.[186] Ironically, while the SEC takes the position that individual accredited investors under Rule 506 have the leverage to induce the issuer to disclose registration-type information,[187] the "big players," the QIBs, need the Commission to protect their interests.[188] To the contrary, under custom and practice, information regarding the subject issuer in Rule 144A offerings ordinarily would be disclosed to sophisticated institutional investors pursuant to contractual rights that have been negotiated.[189]

---

[184] *See Nasdaq's Rule 144A Platform Approved by SEC for Launch*, 39 Sec. Reg. & L. Rep. (BNA) 1214 (2007). With frequency, the filing of a Securities Act registration statement follows the Rule 144A offering, whereby the Rule 144A holders exchange their securities for the securities offered pursuant to such registration statement (called an A/B exchange). *See* Edward Greene et al., *U.S. Regulation of the International Securities and Derivative Markets* § 7.01 (12th ed. 2017) (stating that "investors often require the issuer to provide 'registration rights'—a prompt avenue to resell in the public market via either a subsequent resale registration statement or a subsequent A/B exchange offer"); Randall W. Bodner and Peter L. Welsh, *Institutional Buyer Beware: Recent Decisions Reinforce Narrow Range of Remedies Available to QIBs in Rule 144A Offerings*, 36 Rev. Sec. & Comm. Reg. 1728 (2004) (stating that "roughly two-thirds to three-quarters of high-yield offerings are now accomplished by a Rule 144A private placement, often followed by an A/B exchange").

[185] *See* Securities Act Release No. 10649 (2019) (stating that "a selling security holder can conduct a Rule 144A offering using general solicitation after purchasing the securities in a private placement or other exempt offering [and that as a result] market participants use [Rule 144A] to facilitate capital raising by issuers by means of a two-step process, to which the first step is a primary offering on an exempt basis . . . to one or more financial intermediaries, and the second step is a resale to QIBs pursuant to Rule 144A").

[186] *See* Rule 144A(d)(4)(i), 17 C.F.R. § 230.144A(d)(4)(i) (setting forth that the information that must be provided consists of "a very brief statement of the nature of the business of the issuer and the products and services it offers; and the issuer's most recent balance sheet and profit and loss and retaining earnings statements, and similar financial statements for such part of the two preceding fiscal years as the issuer has been in operation").

[187] *See* discussion *supra* notes 13–23 and accompanying text.

[188] *See* Securities Act Release No. 6862 (1990) (Fleischman, Commissioner, dissenting in part) ("Critics of this requirement say the requirement is inconsistent with the SEC's theory that large institutions can fend for themselves and do not need the SEC prescribing what information they need in order to make an investment decision.").

[189] *See* Greene et al., *supra* note 184, at § 7.01; Bradley Berman, *Conducting Due Diligence in Rule 144A, Reg. S Offerings*, Lexis Practice Advisor (2013), available at https://www.law360.com/articles/460924/conducting-due-diligence-in-rule-144a-reg-s-offerings; Alicia S. Davis, *A Requiem for the Retail Investor?*, 95 Va. L. Rev. 1105, 1110 (2009); Howell E. Jackson and Eric J. Pan, *Regulatory Competition in International Securities Markets: Evidence from Europe*, 3 Va. L. & Bus. Rev. 207, 255–7 (2018). *See generally* Gary M. Lawrence, *Due Diligence in Business Transactions* (2019); discussion *infra* notes 220–226 and accompanying text.

The foregoing discussion illustrates the unacceptable framework that currently exists with respect to exemptions from Securities Act registration for resales of securities. Inconsistencies, ambiguities, and erroneous policies prevail. The analysis that follows seeks to provide a more compatible and simplified process for this challenging area.

B. A Proposed Framework for Resale Exemptions

The distinctions between a transaction as compared to a distribution, affiliate and non-affiliate status, and restricted and non-restricted securities create undue complexity in the resale exemption framework. The proposals set forth herein seek to provide significantly greater certainty to this process while balancing the multi-faceted interests at issue.

From a general perspective, there should exist three separate exemptions that provide comprehensive safe harbors in three major contexts: public resales of securities, private resales of securities, and resales to QIBs. This restructuring may be effected under the current regimen by amending Rule 144, Section 4(a)(7) of the Securities Act, and Rule 144A. The language of Section 4(a)(1) and 4(a)(4) would be amended to accommodate these revisions.

1. Public Resales of Securities

With respect to public resales of securities, the key criteria should be whether the subject entity is an Exchange Act reporting company and the amount of securities that a security holder seeks to resell. For reporting companies, material information is regularly disseminated to the public.[190] On the other hand, for non-reporting issuers, only Rule 15c2-11 information is mandated.[191] As a result, the securities of these companies trade in inefficient markets with relatively minimal market following.[192] Consequently, greater flexibility should be accorded to publicly-held companies in the public resale setting. Regarding the amount of securities that may be resold, rather than

---

[190] *See* discussion in Chapters 2 and 4 herein.

[191] 17 C.F.R. § 240.15c2-11. *See* discussion *supra* notes 174–177 and accompanying text.

[192] Characteristics of these enterprises are thin capitalization, relatively limited public information and minimal, if any, analyst coverage. *See generally* Securities Act Release Nos. 7644 (1999), 87115 (2019); J. William Hicks, *Exempted Transactions Under the Securities Act* § 7:183 (2020); Jeffrey J. Haas, *Small Issue Public Offerings Conducted Over the Internet: Are They "Suitable" for the Retail Investor*, 72 S. Cal. L. Rev. 67 (1998).

focusing on whether a prospective seller is an affiliate, the inquiry should center on whether the subject enterprise is an Exchange Act reporting company. Again, due to that: these enterprises regularly report material information; their securities trade in more developed markets; and the trade(s) must be reported with the SEC,[193] a more expansive safe harbor is warranted. Implementing concrete criteria, this framework thus accords broader resale parameters for Exchange Act companies.

Because an abundance of information already is in the public domain for reporting companies and these securities generally trade in more developed markets, resales of securities should be allowed with no holding period, regardless whether the securities were initially purchased in a Securities Act registered offering or pursuant to an exemption, such as Rule 506. The current quantity limitations of Rule 144 for the resale of equity securities should be increased to provide: during any three-month period resales by a stockholder cannot exceed the greater of: (1) three percent of the shares of the class outstanding; or (2) the average weekly trading volume for the four weeks preceding the trade that is reported on the exchanges "and/or reported through the automated quotation system of a registered securities association."[194] The resale of common stock in this quantity should provide greater flexibility to those persons seeking to dispose of their securities in the public markets without unduly impacting the trading markets for that security.[195] If the security holder opts to resell a greater percentage during this three-month period, the private resale exemption of Section 4(a)(7) is the practical alternative.[196]

For enterprises that are not Exchange Act reporting companies, stricter resale provisions would apply. For securities of these companies to be publicly traded, Rule 15c2-11 should be revised to provide for more complete and updated information.[197] Rather than the general twelve-month period

---

193 *See* discussion in Chapters 2 and 4 herein.

194 This proposal increases the current percentage of one percent in Rule 144 to three percent. *See* Rule 144(e)(1). This increase should provide greater flexibility to insiders, institutional shareholders, and individual shareholders to resell their shares in a developed market without having a significant likely impact on the market for that security. Of course, when the market is apprised of these sales, it may react negatively. This reaction may be due to the market's negative perception of the subject security holder's exit from the enterprise or disposal of a substantial amount of such person's shares. Resales of debt securities would be set at a higher level. *See* current Rule 144(e)(2).

195 *See supra* note 194. Note that, where applicable, similar requirements would apply to the resale provisions of Rule 145, 17 C.F.R. § 230.145, involving resales of securities received in registered business reorganizations, including mergers. *See generally* Rutherford B. Campbell, Jr., *Rule 145 Mergers, Acquisitions and Recapitalizations Under the Securities Act of 1933*, 56 Fordham L. Rev. 277 (1987).

196 15 U.S.C. § 77d(a)(7). *See* discussion *infra* notes 210–219 and accompanying text.

197 *See* discussion *supra* notes 174–177 and accompanying text.

that currently exists, the information required pursuant to the rule should be updated and provided every three months.[198] Moreover, the rule should be expanded to mandate more specific information than merely "a description of the issuer's business; a description of products or services offered by the issuer; [and] a description and extent of the issuer's facilities."[199] Indeed, until the 2020 amendments, the Rule did not even require that the name of the company's chief financial officer be disclosed.[200] Investors should have access to adequate information when making their investment decisions. Indeed, an issuer's balance sheet pursuant to Rule 15c2-11 is deemed "current" if it is "of a date less than 16 months before the publication or submission of the quotation."[201] To define that a balance sheet of such age is "current" slights reality. Rather, as a quid pro quo for having its securities trade in a public market, the subject company should adhere to meaningful standards to enable investors and other market participants to have comfort in the sufficiency and timeliness of the information provided.[202]

Assuming that the Rule 15c2-11 information requirements as proposed herein are met, the current Rule 144 volume limits should apply.[203] There would be no holding period for either restricted or non-restricted securities.[204] Limiting resales every three months in the over-the-counter market

[198] The SEC's 2020 amendments retain the general twelve-month period. *See* Rule 15c2-11(b)(5)(i).

[199] *See* Rule 15c2-11(b)(5)(i)(H)–(J).

[200] *See* Rule 15c2-11(b)(5)(i)(K), (e)(1) (requiring disclosure of "any officer or director of the issuer, or a person that performs a similar function, or any person who is, directly or indirectly, the beneficial owner of more than 10 percent of the outstanding units or shares of any class of any equity security of the issuer"). Former Rule 15c2-11(a)(5)(xi) required disclosure of "the name of the chief executive officer and members of the board of directors."

[201] Rule 15c2-11(b)(5)(i)(L).

[202] With the SEC's failure to significantly improve the quality of disclosure required of non–Exchange Act reporting companies, irrespective of the Commissions hyperbole, there exists too little substantive and up-to-date information with respect to these issuers. As a result, fraudulent and manipulative practices involving the securities of these enterprises likely will ensue with frequency.

In its proposal to amend Rule 15c2-11, the Commission gave the impression that investors will have sufficient and timely information. *See* Securities Exchange Act Release No. 87115 (2019), where the Commission stated: "[R]etail investors, who might not have the same level of access to information available to other market participants, such as those having a relationship with the issuer, would benefit from having access to . . . information that is current." What the Commission omitted was that "current" information under the proposal (that was thereafter adopted) has the same meaning as under then Rule 15c2-11, namely, that the information is "of a date within 12 months prior to the publication or submission of the quotation." *See* Rule 15c2-11(b)(5)(i); Securities Exchange Act Release No. 89891 (2020). In the securities marketplace, information eleven months and twenty-nine days old is not "current." Moreover, as discussed herein, the information that is required to be provided, with few exceptions such as financial statements, lacks sufficient specificity and substance.

[203] *See* Rule 144(e), 17 C.F.R. § 230.144(e); *supra* note 160.

[204] Under Rule 144, restricted securities have a holding period: for Exchange Act reporting companies, six months from the date of acquisition of the securities from the issuer or an affiliate of the issuer (or twelve months for non-reporting companies). *See* Rule 144(d), 17 C.F.R. § 230.144(d).

to the greater of one percent of the company's outstanding equity securities or the average weekly trading volume during the preceding four weeks prior to the trade would enable most investors to sell all of their holdings during this three-month period.[205] For holders who own a greater amount, they would have two alternatives to come within a safe harbor: first, sell the maximum amount permitted during each three-month interval until all of their securities are disposed of; or second, come within the Section 4(a)(7) private resale exemption.[206]

Critics may well argue that the limitations on the amount of securities that may be sold are unduly restrictive and will impair capital raising.[207] These points minimize that fraudulent and manipulative practices occur with regularity in the over-the-counter market for thinly-traded securities.[208] Indeed, these quantity limitations may have the salutary effect of reducing the frequency of such misconduct.[209] Moreover, prospective sellers would have the revamped Section 4(a)(7) private exemption (as proposed herein) to resell all of their securities pursuant to the criteria as set forth in that exemption.

2. Private Resales of Securities

In 2015, Congress enacted Section 4(a)(7) of the Securities Act, providing an exemption from registration under specified conditions for resales of securities to accredited investors.[210] This exemption should be expanded and

---

[205] It is not uncommon, however, for one or a few shareholders to own a substantial percentage of a company's stock, including, of course, in the case of a parent company's subsidiary whose stock is publicly traded. *See generally* OECD Capital Market Series, *Owners of the World's Listed Companies* (2019), available at https://www.oecd.org/corporate/Owners-of-the-Worlds-Listed-Companies.htm; David Peelz and Georgina Murray, *Who Owns the World? Tracing Half the Corporate Giants' Shares to 30 Owners*, TheConversation.com., April 11, 2017, available at https://theconversation.com/who-owns-the-world-tracing-half-the-corporate-giants-shares-to-30-owners-59963.

[206] The Section 4(a)(7) exemption is covered *infra* notes 210–219 and accompanying text.

[207] *Cf.* Rutherford B. Campbell, *Resales of Securities: The New Rules and the New Approach of the SEC*, 37 Sec. Reg. L.J. 317 (2009).

[208] *See, e.g., Industry Bars and Fines for Microcap Fraudsters*, Fed. Sec. L. Rep. (CCH) No. 2757 (2017); *Prosecutors, SEC Name Individuals, Companies in Alleged Penny Stock Schemes*, 45 Sec. Reg. & L. Rep. (BNA) 1524 (2013); *SEC Fraud-Fighting Initiative Expels 37 Dormant Shell Companies*, SEC Press Release No. 2012-91 (2012); *SEC Suspends Trading in 17 Companies to Prevent Potential Microcap Stock Fraud*, 43 Sec. Reg. & L. Rep. (BNA) 1223 (2011).

[209] With limitations on the amount of securities that may be sold, the opportunity to engage in stock manipulation and other fraudulent practices is decreased to some extent. Of course, this comment assumes that prospective sellers would seek to engage in law-compliant conduct, a questionable assumption when applied to miscreants.

[210] 15 U.S.C. § 77d(a)(7). This statute was enacted as part of the FAST Act (Fixing America's Surface Transportation Act), Pub. Law 114-94, 129 Stat. 1312 (2015).

serve as the sole safe harbor in the private resale setting.[211] While a number of the exemption's conditions should remain intact,[212] two key revisions are in order.

First, for an issuer that is not an Exchange Act reporting company, Section 4(a)(7) requires that, upon the request of the seller, the company generally must provide the same information as that specified in Rule 15c2-11.[213] As discussed earlier, this information is inadequate and outdated.[214] For example, disclosure regarding the nature of the company's business and its products and services is "presumed reasonably current if the statement is as of 12 months before the transaction date."[215] This type of disclosure is too little and too late. To view information that is eleven months old as reasonably current in the hurly-burly entrepreneurial world is a misnomer. Rather, more comprehensive and timely disclosure should be mandated.[216]

Second, under specified conditions, the Section 4(a)(7) exemption should allow sales to be made to both accredited and non-accredited investors. In many privately-held enterprises, there may not be an adequate presence of accredited investors. Accordingly, provided that the prospective purchaser (or its representative) is qualified as being financially sophisticated and has access to the registrant's Exchange Act periodic reports or, if not an Exchange Act reporting company, to Rule 15c2-11 information (as proposed herein), sales to non-accredited investors should be allowed.[217]

As revised, Section 4(a)(7) provides an attractive private resale exemption in a broad range of contexts. As proposed, the exemption: encompasses

---

211 Accordingly, the informal Section "4(1½)" exemption would be rescinded. *See supra* notes 178–181 and accompanying text.

212 For example, advertising and general solicitation should continue to be prohibited in Section 4(a)(7) resale transactions and financial statements should continue to be provided. In addition, disclosure of the nature of the issuer's business as well as its products and services (but with more substantive information) should continue to be provided along with disclosure of the names of the issuer's directors and officers. *See* § 4(d)(2)–(3) of the Securities Act.

213 *Cf.* Section 4(a)(7) (and the information specified in Section 4(d)(3) of the Securities Act) to Rule 15c2-11.

214 *See* discussion *supra* notes 197–202 and accompanying text.

215 Section 4(d)(3)(G) of the Securities Act, 15 U.S.C. § 77d(d)(3)(G). Note that Section 4(a)(7) exempts from the provisions of Section 5 of the Securities Act "transactions meeting the requirements of subsection (d)."

216 *See* discussion *supra* notes 197–202 and accompanying text.

217 In primary exempt offerings pursuant to Section 4(a)(2) and Rule 506, sales may be made to non-accredited investors under specified conditions. *See* discussion *supra* notes 7–33 and accompanying text. There is no sound reason why such sales should not be permitted with respect to resales of securities, provided that the financial sophistication and delivery of information (or access thereto) conditions are satisfied.

the securities of Exchange Act reporting companies as well as privately-held enterprises; applies both to restricted and non-restricted securities; mandates the disclosure of meaningful and timely information; and permits the resale of securities to both accredited and non-accredited investors so long as specified conditions are met.[218] Hence, this flexible exemption may be used both by an institutional investor seeking to dispose of its entire holdings constituting four percent of the common stock of a New York Stock Exchange company as well as a controlling shareholder in a closely held corporation who is selling her fifty-one percent interest to non-accredited purchasers.[219] The broad range of this proposed exemption aptly serves the interests of investors, issuers, and resellers of securities, while not significantly impeding capital raising. Given its substantial benefits, the Section 4(a)(7) exemption as revised herein is worthy of implementation.

3. Resales to Qualified Institutional Buyers

Rule 144A provides a market for resales of securities in two key settings: the sale of debt securities by an issuer to a placement agent who in turn sells these securities to QIBs; and, with respect to securities of foreign companies that originally were sold outside of the United States (such as pursuant to Regulation S), the resale of these securities to QIBs.[220] With one exception, the requirements of Rule 144A are appropriate, including: the criteria for defining QIB status; the seller's (or its agent's) obligation to "reasonably believe" that the prospective purchaser qualifies as a QIB; the unavailability of fungible securities to be sold pursuant to Rule 144A; and a notice requirement whereby the seller must take reasonable steps to inform the QIBs that it is relying on the Rule 144A exemption.[221]

Surprisingly, with respect to non-reporting Exchange Act companies, Rule 144A requires that, upon request to the subject issuer, certain basic information regarding the issuer as well as financial statements must be provided to the security holder and to the prospective purchaser.[222] This

---

[218] *See generally* Taylor Anthony, *Navigating the New Section 4(a)(7) Private Resale Exemption—Compliance, Utilization, and Market Implications*, 44 Sec. Reg. L.J. 317 (2016).

[219] The flexibility of the proposed Section 4(a)(7) exemption would facilitate widespread usage while providing adequate safeguards for prospective purchasers.

[220] *See* discussion *supra* notes 182–183 and accompanying text.

[221] *See* Rule 144A(d), 17 C.F.R. § 230.144A(d); Securities Act Release No. 6862 (1990).

[222] See Rule 144A(d)(4), 17 C.F.R. § 230.144A(d)(2). The definition of information being "reasonably current" has the same drawback as that contained in Rule 15c2-11—namely, generally providing that information within twelve months prior to the resale transaction is deemed "reasonably current." *See* discussion *supra* notes 197–202, 213–216 and accompanying text.

requirement has been criticized and for good reason.[223] In its adoption of Rule 506, the SEC created an irrebuttable presumption that individual accredited investors (e.g., having a net worth of $1 million exclusive of primary residence) have access to registration-type information.[224] In the Rule 144A context, however, the Commission takes the position that these more well-heeled players cannot fend for themselves. This position is misplaced. As a matter of custom and practice, security holder(s) in Rule 144A transactions negotiate with the issuer for contractual rights of disclosure at the time of issuance.[225] Accordingly, Rule 144A's provision of information mandate should be rescinded. Otherwise, Rule 144A provides a workable framework with respect to resales of securities to QIBs.[226]

V. Conclusion

This chapter addressed the exemption framework for both primary offerings and resales of securities. It identified significant shortcomings, including the application of standards that with frequency are inconsistent, illogical, and detrimental to sound public policy. As proposed in this chapter, the exemption framework should be restructured with the exemptions tailored in a balanced manner to satisfy both issuer and investor needs. The proposals set forth herein accordingly would provide a coherent exemption framework, benefitting investors as well as the transparency of the securities markets without unduly impairing capital raising.

---

223 *See supra* notes 188–189 and accompanying text. *See also* Floyd Norris, *The SEC and the Death of Disclosure*, N.Y. Times, June 9, 1991, at C5 (asserting that, because of Rule 144A, "institutional investors can buy privately placed securities and trade them freely with other institutions . . . [a]fter minimal financial disclosure").

224 *See* discussion *supra* notes 18–20 and accompanying text.

225 *See supra* note 189 and accompanying text.

226 When the safe harbors of proposed Rule 144, Section 4(a)(7), and Rule 144A are not available, statutory exemptions in the resale context should provide an additional source. The objective of these statutes is to enable those persons engaged in resales of securities and their brokers to avail themselves of an exemption from registration in the event that a safe harbor has not been perfected. Like several other statutory exemptions, there will exist some degree of uncertainty regarding their application. In amending the Section 4(a)(1) and 4(a)(4) exemptions, Congress should focus on such criteria as: whether the issuer is an Exchange Act reporting company; the percentage of securities that the security holder seeks to resell; whether the resale occurs in the public markets or by means of a private transaction; whether general solicitation is employed in connection with the resale; the financial sophistication of the purchasers; and the quality of issuer-related information that is provided. With these statutory exemptions having no safe harbor, a facts and circumstances approach would apply.

4

The Securities Act Registration Framework

I. Introduction

Although a number of respected sources have advocated in favor of a company-based registration system,[1] the Securities and Exchange Commission has declined to implement this proposal. Rather, through the decades, the SEC has adhered to a transaction-based Securities Act registration framework, prescribing accommodations that seek to promote capital raising without adversely impacting investors.[2] To a large extent, the Commission has met its objective of designing a flexible and progressive transaction-based Securities Act registration system, thereby avoiding the adoption of a company-based registration regimen that inevitably would have raised uncertainties and novel applications.[3] Recognizing that the

[1] *See, e.g.*, Report of the Advisory Committee on the Capital Formation and Regulatory Processes, Securities and Exchange Commission, [1996–1997 Transfer Binder] Fed. Sec. L. Rep. (CCH) ¶ 85,834, at 88,409 (1996) (stating that "the focus of the regulatory process in the post-initial public offering context should be shifted from registering transactions to registering companies with a corresponding emphasis on better ensuring the accuracy and integrity of continuing disclosures [and that] once a company is registered and filing the required public reports, all the securities that the company or its affiliates sell thereafter would be deemed registered for purposes of the Securities Act"); American Law Institute, *Federal Securities Code* xxvii (1980) ("Under the Code there will be no more registration of securities. Instead, a company will register as such when it first reaches [a specified asset amount and number of holders of its securities] . . . or when the first 'distribution' is made of any of its securities.").

[2] *See* discussion *infra* notes 15–59 and accompanying text.

[3] *See* Report of the Advisory Committee, *supra* note 1, at 88,415 (recommending that the SEC establish a voluntary "pilot program" for company registration for seasoned issuers that subsequently would "with appropriate modifications, be made available to a broader class of issuers [and having] sufficiently demonstrated its benefits during the pilot, regulatory simplification could be completed through rulemaking and/or legislative changes, as necessary or appropriate"). The Advisory Committee lauded the benefits of company registration, asserting:

> If the regulatory focus is shifted to a company registration model that would replace the transactional registration requirements, issuers would benefit from the elimination of the increasingly complex, but often ineffective, series of regulations and concepts fashioned over the years to preserve those transactional requirements. Eligible companies would have easier access to the capital markets with lower regulatory and transaction

Rethinking Securities Law. Marc I. Steinberg, Oxford University Press. © Marc I. Steinberg 2021.
DOI: 10.1093/oso/9780197583142.003.0004

Securities Act registration framework overall is sound but in need of revision in view of securities market developments, the Commission has prescribed meaningful amendments that have significantly enhanced the process while largely maintaining its overall integrity.[4]

In its determination to maintain a transaction-based Securities Act registration framework while making necessary adjustments, the SEC has made the correct decision. With the improvements made, the registration framework functions in a relatively efficient manner and generally provides investors with adequate safeguards. Nonetheless, significant shortcomings exist. Several of these inadequacies are addressed in this chapter.

This chapter focuses on the Securities Act's registration framework. First, the chapter reviews several fundamental principles that were first addressed in Chapter 2 herein. Second, many of the multi-faceted issues that are implicated in the registration statement process are addressed. Last, the chapter focuses on the contentious subject of due diligence in the registered offering setting.

II. Fundamental Principles—The Need for Revision

A. Mandatory Disclosure of Material Information

From the discussion in Chapter 2 herein, certain inadequacies prevail with respect to the disclosure regimen (including in the context of registered offerings) that should be remedied. The foremost is that, absent a justifiable business reason, all material information should be required to be disclosed.[5] When investing in an enterprise, an investor should be entitled to the receipt of all material information. That a particular event, even though material, is not required to be disclosed because it is not specified in Regulation S-K

> costs, enabling companies to tap the equity markets far more often than they do now. Equally as important, adoption of a company registration system would allow the Commission to eliminate those anomalies under the current system that function to deny investors the protections originally contemplated by the Securities Act, and to make the necessary adjustments to secondary market disclosure practices and due diligence responsibilities that would benefit investors and provide better continuous disclosures to the markets.

Id. at 88,414. The SEC generally has achieved these objectives by use of incorporation by reference and (automatic) shelf registration.

[4] *See* discussion *infra* notes 15–59 and accompanying text.

[5] *See* discussion in Chapter 2 herein, at notes 149–170 and accompanying text.

is unacceptable.[6] The solution is for the SEC to prescribe a new item under Regulation S-K that mandates that, in addition to the disclosures called for by that Regulation, all other material information (absent the existence of a justifiable business reason) must be contained in the subject disclosure document, including in the statutory prospectus of a registration statement. This improvement would be consistent with the approach adopted by other developed markets.[7]

B. Uniform Standards of Materiality

Second, narrative disclosure should be assessed by identical standards of materiality irrespective of the regulatory or statutory provisions applicable. As currently applied, such as with respect to Item 303 MD&A disclosure, by using a broader definition of materiality under this item than under Section 10(b), further ambiguity prevails.[8] Fragmentation of this crucial concept also makes little sense from an investor protection standpoint: the board of directors of a subject company with scienter can make materially misleading statements in the MD&A, yet such misrepresentations may not be actionable by investors who relied on these disclosures in purchasing their securities in a registered offering. Hence, the current position embraced by the SEC and several courts is antithetical to meritorious investor redress.[9]

---

[6] *See, e.g., J & R Marketing SEP v. General Motors Corp.*, 549 F.3d 484, 396–97 (6th Cir. 2008) ("There is no general duty on the part of a company to provide the public with all material information."); *Cooperman v. Individual, Inc.*, 171 F.3d 43, 49 (1st Cir. 1999) ("[A]lthough in the context of a public offering there is a strong affirmative duty of disclosure, it is clear that an issuer of securities owes no absolute duty to disclose all material information.").

[7] *See* discussion in Chapter 2 herein, at notes 152–153 and accompanying text. As set forth in Chapter 2 (note 168 and accompanying text), this new item of Regulation S-K would provide:

> In addition to the information required to be included in the subject document, there shall also be provided any further material information, irrespective of whether such material information is or is not called for by any other item of this Regulation S-K. Omission of such material information is permitted provided that the issuer (or registrant) can establish a justifiable business reason for such omission.

[8] *See, e.g., In re NVIDIA*, 768 F.3d 1046, 1054–56 (9th Cir. 2014) (opining that the standard of materiality under Item 303 is "much broader" than for § 10(b)); *Oran v. Stafford*, 226 F.3d 275, 288 (3d Cir. 2000) (stating that "the materiality standards for Rule 10b-5 and Reg. SK-303 differ significantly"); SEC 1989 Interpretive Release, Financial Reporting Release No. 36, 6 Fed. Sec. L. Rep. (CCH) ¶ 73,193, at 62,842 (1989) (stating that the "probability/magnitude standard of materiality . . . is inapposite to Item 303 disclosure").

[9] *See* discussion in Chapter 2 herein, at notes 75–82 and accompanying text.

C. Incorporation by Reference Based on Efficient Markets

Third, the key rationale for the adoption of incorporation by reference of Exchange Act periodic reports into a subject company's registration statement is the efficient market theory.[10] This approach is commendable when applied to companies whose securities in fact trade in efficient markets. Yet, through the decades, the eligibility thresholds have been drastically reduced, resulting in companies using incorporation by reference in their registered offerings when their securities trade in inefficient markets.[11] With respect to these companies, the information contained in their periodic reports has not been impounded into market price. This anomaly should be corrected: incorporation by reference from Exchange Act reports into a company's registration statement should be allowed only if such company can establish that the securities (e.g., common stock) that it is registering for sale under the Securities Act trade in an efficient market.[12]

D. Mandatory Inclusion of Summary Section

Last, in view that ordinary investors (particularly, many individual investors) do not read the Exchange Act periodic reports that are

---

[10] *See, e.g.*, Securities Act Release No. 6235 (1980) ("To the extent that the market . . . acts efficiently, and information [contained in Exchange Act reports] is adequately reflected in the price of a registrant's outstanding securities, there seems little need to reiterate this information in a prospectus."); Securities Act Release No. 6383 (1982) (stating that "Form S-3, in reliance on the efficient market theory, allows maximum use of incorporation by reference of Exchange Act reports"). As stated by the U.S. Supreme Court in *Halliburton Co. v. Erica P. John Fund, Inc.*, 134 S. Ct. 2398, 2408 (2014), "the market price of shares traded on well-developed markets reflects all publicly available information."

[11] *See* Securities Act Release No. 8591 (2005); Securities Act Release No. 10003 (2016). As set forth in the 2016 release:

> [T]o be eligible to use forward incorporation by reference, smaller reporting companies will be required to be current by having filed (a) an annual report for its most recently completed fiscal year; and (b) all required Exchange Act reports and materials during the 12 months immediately preceding filing of the Form S-1 (or such shorter period that the smaller reporting company was required to file such reports and materials). . . . In addition, the ability to forward incorporate by reference will be conditioned on the smaller reporting company making its incorporated Exchange Act reports and other materials readily available and accessible on a web site maintained by or for the issuer disclosing in the prospectus that such materials will be provided upon request.

Securities Act Release No. 10003 (2016). Blank check companies, shell companies, and issuers conducting penny stock offerings are not allowed to incorporate by reference. *Id.*

[12] *See* discussion in Chapter 2 herein, at notes 122–135 and accompanying text.

incorporated by reference into the registration statement, there should be required a sufficiently comprehensive Summary Section in the prospectus.[13] The mandatory inclusion of such a Summary would enable an ordinary investor to have better access to meaningful and understandable information when making its decision whether to purchase the securities. Such information, for example, would include—in a succinct and user-friendly presentation—material terms of the offering, risk factors, and company-specific information. The presence of such a Summary in all SEC registered offerings should enhance the quality of the disclosure process and provide ordinary investors with useful information.[14]

E. Summation

In conclusion, four overriding changes should be made: first, absent a justifiable business reason, requiring that all material information must be disclosed; second, with respect to narrative disclosure, the application of a uniform definition of materiality; third, the use of incorporation by reference from SEC periodic reports into a subject company's registration statement should be permitted only for those companies whose securities in fact trade in an efficient market; and fourth, the addition of a Summary Section in prospectuses for all SEC registered offerings. These measures should prove beneficial for investors, align this country's approach with that adhered to by other developed markets, and enhance the efficiency of our securities markets.

---

[13] A prospectus summary is permissive under Item 503(a) of Regulation S-K but is without adequate specification. *See* Item 503(a) of Regulation S-K, 17 C.F.R. § 229.503(a) (emphasis supplied) (stating that the registrant "must furnish in plain English . . . a summary of the information in the prospectus *where* the length or complexity of the prospectus *makes a summary useful* [and] should be brief"). The instruction to Item 503(a) states that, in providing "a brief overview of the key aspects of the offering," the issuer should "[c]arefully consider and identify those aspects of the offering that are the most significant and determine how best to highlight these points in clear, plain language." Although this general language is helpful, a prospectus summary with specification of the disclosures required would be an important and readily available resource for ordinary investors to access.

[14] *See* discussion in Chapter 2 herein, at notes 136–138 and accompanying text.

III. Multi-faceted Issues Implicated in the Registration Statement Process

During the past four decades, the SEC has sought to facilitate the registration process without adversely impacting investor protection. The integrated disclosure framework was a major step in this quest, enabling eligible companies to incorporate by reference their Exchange Act periodic reports into their Securities Act registration statements.[15] With respect to regulating conduct during a registration statement's time periods—pre-filing, waiting, and post-effective[16]—the Commission's 2005 amendments provide much needed clarity to market participants.[17] Setting forth specified conduct that is permitted, the rules enable issuers, underwriters, and other participants to engage in conduct that is conducive to capital raising without (for the most part) significantly impairing investor interests.[18] The number of rules are far too many to be addressed in this chapter.[19] Instead, several examples are provided.

A. Well-Known Seasoned Issuers

First, well-known seasoned issuers[20] are permitted to make offers to sell at any time, including during the pre-filing period.[21] Prior to the adoption of this

[15] *See* Securities Act Release No. 6383 (1982) (authorizing incorporation by reference for Form S-3 issuers and stating: "Information concerning the registrant will be incorporated by reference [in a Form S-3 prospectus] from its Exchange Act reports [and] the prospectus will not be required to present any information concerning the registrant unless there has been a material change in the registrant's affairs which has not been reported in an Exchange Act filing.").

[16] Section 5 of the Securities Act, 15 U.S.C. § 77(e), covers three different time periods for regulating offers and sales. Generally: (1) Under Section 5(c), unless an exemption is available, no offers to sell may be made before a registration statement is filed with the SEC (pre-filing period). (2) Pursuant to Section 5(a), absent an exemption, no sales may be made until after the effectiveness of a registration statement (post-effective period). (3) Pursuant to Section 5(b), absent an exemption, after the registration statement is filed, written offers are permitted in accordance with the provisions of that subsection (waiting period). *See* Marc I. Steinberg, *Understanding Securities Law* 127–46 (7th ed. 2018).

[17] *See* Securities Act Release No. 8591 (2005).

[18] *See generally* Antonio Pena, *The Free-Writing Prospectus: A Six Question Approach for Issuers*, 35 Sec. Reg. L.J. 36 (2007).

[19] For a more comprehensive discussion, *see* Steinberg, *supra* note 16, at 127–46.

[20] Generally, a well-known seasoned issuer: has filed its Exchange Act reports; satisfies the registrant requirements for use of Form S-3 (or Form F-3), including for at least a twelve-month period being current and timely with respect to its Exchange Act reporting obligations; is not an ineligible issuer (such as having filed for bankruptcy or being a blank check or shell company); and has either worldwide common equity (such as common stock) held by non-affiliates of $700 million or greater or has issued a minimum of $1 billion of non-convertible securities (excluding common equity) in registered primary offerings for cash in the past three years. *See* Rule 405, 17 C.F.R. § 230.405; Securities Act Release No. 8591 (2005).

[21] *See* Rule 163, 17 C.F.R. § 230.163.

rule, such conduct violated Section 5 of the Securities Act.[22] In view that these companies frequently use automatic shelf registration,[23] are widely followed by market analysts,[24] and have their securities trade in efficient markets,[25] relaxation of the pre-filing rigor of Section 5 is warranted. At least two downsides exist, however, with respect to this approach. First, without a requirement that publicly-held companies must promptly disclose all material information absent a justifiable reason for withholding such information, this gap enables issuers to engage in general solicitation to prospective investors without adequate and accurate information being in the public domain. Second, a well-known seasoned issuer, who is experiencing severe financial struggles,[26] may be incentivized to market its forthcoming securities offering with hyperbole and misstatements. Although the antifraud provisions are available in this situation, the strict liability provisions of Section 5 no longer are applicable.[27] When an issuer and its associated persons engage in such misconduct, the Commission has an attractive enforcement resource available—namely, Section 17(a)(2) and 17(a)(3) of the Securities Act.[28] Under these provisions,

---

[22] Prior to the 2005 amendments, irrespective of the capitalization and compliant conduct by a blue chip issuer, Section 5(c) prohibited offers to sell in the pre-filing period. *See, e.g.*, Securities Act Release No. 4697 (1964) (stating that "Section 5 of the Securities Act prohibits offers to sell and offers to buy a security before a registration statement is filed [and that] publicity about an issuer, its securities or the proposed offering prior to the filing of a registration statement may constitute an illegal offer to sell"). Note that Section 2(a)(3) of the Securities Act, 15 U.S.C. § 77b(a)(3), exempts from the definition of offer to sell and offer to buy preliminary negotiations and agreements between an issuer "and any underwriter or among underwriters who are or are to be in privity of contract with [such] issuer."

[23] Pursuant to automatic shelf registration, the shelf registration statement becomes effective immediately upon its filing with the Commission. *See* Securities Act Release No. 8591 (2005) ("Under our automatic shelf registration process, eligible well-known seasoned issuers may register unspecified amounts of different specified types of securities on immediately effective Form S-3 or Form F-3 registration statements.").

[24] *See* Securities Act Release Nos. 6383 (1982), 6499 (1983).

[25] When the SEC adopted Form S-3, it did so "in reliance on the efficient market theory." Securities Act Release No. 6383 (1982).

[26] These financial struggles may be due to the subject company's specific financial woes, a downturn in the industry, general economic conditions, or a global catastrophe, such as the impact of the coronavirus. *See generally* Rebecca Spalding and Joshua Franklin, *Bankers Try to Keep IPO Party Going Amid Coronavirus Market Jitters*, Reuters (March 5, 2020), available at https://www.reuters.com/article/us-health-coronavirus-ipos/bankers-try-to-keep-ipo-party-going-amid-coronavirus-market-jitters-idUSKBN20S2YU.

[27] For example, Section 10(b) and Rule 10b-5 are available where intent can be proven along with the other requisite elements of the claim. For further discussion, *see infra* note 83; Chapter 6 herein. Section 5 is a strict liability provision. *See, e.g.*, *Securities and Exchange Commission v. Manor Nursing Centers, Inc.*, 458 F.2d 1082 (2d Cir. 1972).

[28] 15 U.S.C. § 77q(a)(2), (a)(3). *See Aaron v. Securities and Exchange Commission*, 446 U.S. 680 (1980) (holding that scienter is required to be proven by the SEC to prove violations of § 17(a)(1) of the Securities Act and § 10(b) of the Exchange Act while negligence is sufficient for § 17(a)(2) and (a)(3)). *See generally* Marc I. Steinberg and Abel Ramirez, Jr., *The SEC's Neglected Weapon: A Proposed*

negligence is actionable misconduct.[29] The vigilant implementation of this statute should deter violations in this context,[30] including those committed during an initial public offering.

B. Testing the Waters

Second, the SEC now permits all issuers to test the waters in the pre-filing period to gauge investor interest, entitling these issuers to communicate during this time period with qualified institutional buyers (QIBs)[31] and institutional accredited investors.[32] Prior to the Commission's 2019 rule, this practice was confined to emerging growth companies pursuant to the Jumpstart Our Business Startups (JOBS) Act.[33] In view of the costs

---

Amendment to Section 17(a)(3) and the Application of Negligent Insider Trading, 19 U. Pa. J. Bus. L. 239 (2017).

[29] *See Aaron*, 446 U.S. at 696–700. *See United States v. Naftalin*, 441 U.S. 768 (1979) (holding, *inter alia*, that § 17(a) encompasses misconduct in the secondary trading markets). *See generally* Marc I. Steinberg, *Section 17(a) of the Securities Act of 1933 After Naftalin and Redington*, 68 Geo. L.J. 163 (1979).

[30] With some frequency, the SEC is utilizing Section 17(a)(2) and (a)(3) in its enforcement actions alleging negligent misconduct. *See Securities and Exchange Commission v. Haswell*, 654 F.2d 698 (10th Cir. 1981); *In re Bolan*, 2015 SEC LEXIS 2201 (SEC 2015); *In re Flannery and Hopkins*, 2014 WL 7145625 (SEC 2014), *rev'd on other grounds*, 819 F.3d 1 (1st Cir. 2015).

[31] *See* Rule 163B, 17 C.F.R. § 230.163B; Securities Act Release No. 10699 (2019) ("adopting a new communications rule under the Securities Act of 1933 that permits issuers to engage in oral or written communications with certain potential investors [namely, QIBs and institutional accredited investors], either prior to or following the filing of a registration statement, to determine whether such investors might have an interest in a contemplated registered securities offering"). *See* Michael Zeidel et al., *SEC Expansion of "Testing-the-Waters" Communications to All Issuers*, Harv. Law School Forum on Corp. Gov. (Oct. 4, 2019), available at https://corpgov.law.harvard.edu/2019/10/04/sec-expansion-of-testing-the-waters-communications-to-all-issuers ("expand[ing] the permitted use of 'testing-the-waters' communications to all companies regardless of size or reporting status, including business development companies and other registered investment companies").

Generally, a qualified institutional buyer is an entity, "acting for its own account or the accounts of other qualified institutional buyers, . . . in the aggregate owns and invests on a discretionary basis at least $100 million in securities of issuers that are not affiliated with the entity." Rule 144A(a), 17 C.F.R. § 230.144A(a). Different QIB requirements apply for broker-dealers, banks, and savings and loan associations.

[32] Generally, institutional accredited investors have total assets exceeding $5 million. *See* Rule 501(a) of Regulation D, 17 C.F.R. § 230.501(a).

[33] The JOBS Act added Section 5(d) to the Securities Act, 15 U.S.C. § 77e(d), permitting emerging growth companies to "engage in oral or written communications with potential investors that are qualified institutional buyers or institutions that are accredited investors . . . to determine whether such investors might have an interest in a contemplated securities offering, either prior to or following the date of filing of a registration statement."

Generally, as enacted, an emerging growth company is an entity that has less than $1 billion (adjusted annually) in annual revenues in its previous fiscal year and did not have an initial public offering (IPO) of equity securities on or before December 8, 2011. Upon certain events, an entity ceases

of going public and the uncertainties of procuring financial intermediary and investor interest,[34] this approach generally presents a sensible balance. Ordinarily, institutional accredited investors are sufficiently savvy to make their investment decisions after receiving what they deem to be adequate information. Pre-selling the offering is unlikely to occur when dealing with sophisticated institutions.[35]

C. Unduly Broad Definition of Accredited Institutional Investor

Nonetheless, the definition of "accredited institutional investor" is broad, encompassing, for example, business organizations that have greater than $5 million in total assets.[36] Similar to individuals who are deemed accredited investors because they attain a specified level of net worth or annual income,[37] defining an organization as financially sophisticated, based on the elusive term "total assets," likewise is problematic. Similar to individual investors, with some frequency, these organizations lack financial sophistication. Unless they qualify as a sophisticated investor due to their past investment experience, expertise of their executives, or other indicia of financial acumen, these organizations should not be solicited in initial public offering (IPO) and related settings prior to having access to a preliminary statutory prospectus.[38] Accordingly, absent these organizations having the requisite

---

to be an emerging growth company, such as five years subsequent to its IPO or when such entity over a three-year period issues non-convertible debt securities exceeding $1 billion. *See* § 2(a)(19) of the Securities Act, 15 U.S.C. § 77b(a)(19).

[34] *See, e.g.*, Steinberg, *supra* note 16, at 148–49; Carl Schneider et al., *Going Public: Practice, Procedure and Consequences*, 27 Vill. L. Rev. 1 (1981).

[35] *See* Securities Act Release No. 10699 (2019) (recognizing the high level of financial sophistication of QIBs and institutional accredited investors). *See generally* Gary M. Lawrence, *Due Diligence in Business Transactions* (2019).

[36] *See* Rule 501(a)(1)–(3) of Regulation D, 17 C.F.R. § 230.501(a)(1)–(3). In 2020, the SEC expanded the "list of entities that may qualify as accredited investors [as well as adding] entities owning $5 million in investments [and eligible] family offices with at least $5 million in assets under management." Securities Act Release No. 10824 (2020).

[37] Generally, an individual along with his/her spouse having a net worth (exclusive of primary residence) exceeding $1 million or having annual income of $200,000 (or $300,000 joint income) qualifies as an accredited investor. *See* Rule 501(a)(5)–(6) of Regulation D, 17 C.F.R. § 230.501(a)(5)–(6); discussion in Chapters 2 and 3 herein.

[38] Without further indicia of financial acumen, the asset threshold alone should not be sufficient to deem a business organization an accredited investor. *Cf. Doran v. Petroleum Management Corp.*, 545 F.2d 893 (5th Cir. 1977) (under statutory private placement exemption, individual's wealth not equivalent to financial sophistication).

financial sophistication, "testing the waters" or otherwise engaging in offers to sell to such organizations in the pre-filing period should be prohibited by issuers that are not well-known seasoned issuers.[39]

D. Individual Investors—Registered Offerings Compared to Rule 506 Offerings

Ironically, Congress and the SEC provide greater protection to individual investors in the registered offering context than in exempt offerings. For example, pursuant to Rule 506(c), as discussed in Chapter 3, advertising and general solicitation are authorized to the world so long as all purchasers are individual or institutional accredited investors.[40] Because Rule 506 offerings are largely unregulated as compared to registered offerings,[41] miscreants have greater opportunities to engage in fraud.[42] By contrast, in registered offerings, including IPOs, there ordinarily is significantly greater regulatory

---

[39] Accordingly, the applicable rule would revert to the standard prior to the SEC's 2005 amendments, with two exceptions: first, well-known seasoned issuers would be allowed to make offers to sell in the pre-filing period; second, all other companies would be permitted to engage in "test the waters" communications with qualified institutional buyers and institutional accredited investors (provided that such institutions have the requisite financial sophistication).

[40] In the JOBS Act, Congress directed the SEC to permit issuers to engage in advertising and general solicitation in Rule 506 offerings, provided that all purchasers of the securities sold are accredited investors. As discussed in Chapter 3 herein, the SEC's 2020 amendments continue this approach. For example, Rule 241 permits an issuer, under specified conditions, to "communicate orally or in writing [to prospective investors] to determine whether there is any interest in a contemplated offering of securities exempt from registration under the [Securities] Act." Rule 241(a), 17 C.F.R. § 230.241(a). *See* Securities Act Release No. 10884 (2020).

[41] Indeed, pursuant to the National Securities Markets Improvement Act of 1996 (NSMIA), Pub. L. No. 104-290, 110 Stat. 3416 (1996), Congress preempted Rule 506 offerings. Other than the filing of a Form D with the SEC, the Commission engages in no oversight of the subject offering. Note, however, that with respect to a Rule 506 offering sold to non-accredited and/or accredited individual investors, the Financial Industry Regulatory Authority (FINRA) requires, with certain exceptions, that a member broker-dealer provide to FINRA a copy of the Private Placement Memorandum and other offering documents that are used for selling purposes in such offering. *See* FINRA Rule 5123.

More recently, the SEC preempted Regulation A, Tier 2 offerings from state regulation. *See* Securities Act Release No. 9741 (2015). The Commission's action was upheld in *Lindeen v. Securities and Exchange Commission*, 825 F.3d 646 (D.C. Cir. 2016). For further discussion, *see* Chapter 3 herein.

[42] *See, e.g.*, Luis A. Aguilar, Commissioner, Securities and Exchange Commission, *Increasing the Vulnerability of Investors* (2012) (then SEC Commissioner opining that permitting general solicitation in Rule 506 offerings "exacerbates investor vulnerability to fraudsters"), available at https://www.sec.gov/news/public-statement/2012-spch082912laahtm; Thomas M. Selman, *Protecting Retail Investors: A New Exemption for Private Securities Offerings*, 14 Va. L. & Bus. Rev. 41, 54 (2020) (asserting that "Rule 506 provides little assurance that non-accredited investors have reliable information, or the knowledge and experience necessary to evaluate the business and market risks associated with a private placement").

oversight; moreover, individual investors (irrespective of being accredited) cannot be solicited in the pre-filing period (other than in offerings by well-known seasoned issuers).[43] Although logic would dictate that greater risks are present in the exempt offering setting, it is in this setting that greater laxity prevails.

E. Certainty of Rules, Conditioning the Market Concerns

Prior to the SEC's amendments in 2005,[44] uncertainty prevailed as to whether certain activities, such as the making of forward-looking statements in a Form 10-Q, in the pre-filing period constituted offers to sell, thereby violating Section 5(c) of the Securities Act.[45] To the Commission's credit, the rules provide significant clarity to this situation. For example, as discussed earlier, offers to sell (both written and verbal) are permitted by well-known seasoned issuers during the entire offering period.[46] Communications made by other issuers more than thirty days prior to the filing of a registration statement are not deemed offers to sell, provided specified conditions are met.[47] Likewise, subject to certain conditions, reporting companies may continue to disseminate factual business information as well as forward-looking statements, subject to the antifraud provisions.[48] In addition, as has been the

---

[43] Such solicitation would constitute an offer to sell in the pre-filing period, thereby violating Section 5(c) of the Securities Act. The SEC exempted well-known seasoned issuers from this prohibition pursuant to the adoption of Rule 163. *See supra* notes 20–25 and accompanying text.

[44] *See* Securities Act Release No. 8591 (2005).

[45] *See, e.g.*, Guidelines for the Release of Information by Issuers Whose Securities Are in Registration, Securities Act Release No. 5180 (1971) (stating that "[t]he determination of whether an item of information or publicity could be deemed to constitute an offer—a step in the selling effort—in violation of Section 5 must be made by the issuer in the light of all the facts and circumstances surrounding each case").

[46] *See* Rule 163, 17 C.F.R. § 230.163; discussion *supra* notes 20–30 and accompanying text.

[47] *See* Rule 163A, 17 C.F.R. § 230.163A. In this regard, such communications cannot reference the forthcoming offering, must be made by or on behalf of the subject issuer (but cannot be made by an offering participant that is an underwriter or dealer), and "reasonable steps within its control [are taken by the issuer] to prevent further distribution or publication of such communication during the 30 days immediately preceding the date of filing the registration statement." Rule 163A(a).

[48] Rule 168, 17 C.F.R. § 230.168. Under Rule 168, such communications cannot reference the contemplated offering and must be made by or on behalf of the subject issuer (but cannot be made by an offering participant that is an underwriter or dealer). Hence, after Rule 168's adoption, issuers may continue to provide forward-looking information within the parameters of the rule without such information being viewed as conditioning the market and thereby constituting an impermissible offer to sell in the pre-filing period.

Note that non-reporting issuers may use Rule 169, 17 C.F.R. § 230.169, which, provided its conditions are met, allows such issuers to continue to publish in the pre-filing and other periods regularly released factual business information. The communication must be "released or disseminated

situation for several decades, companies may make a public announcement with respect to a contemplated registered offering in conformance with the specifications of the applicable rule.[49]

While these rules enhance commercial certainty and therefore are beneficial to capital raising, a number of provisions may provide impetus for smaller publicly-held companies to condition the market for a forthcoming registered public offering.[50] For example, simply one previous public release by a subject issuer may establish that the company "regularly" releases the same type of information in substantially the same manner in the ordinary course of its business.[51] To define a regular course of conduct by an issuer as engaging in one prior type of behavior belies common perceptions of reality.[52] Rather, to constitute a regular practice, one must engage in that conduct in a constant or definite pattern.[53] Accordingly, to deter these companies from creating an exaggerated impression among investors and the securities markets prior to the effective date of a registered offering, such optimistic information should be required to have been disseminated on a frequent and prolonged basis, such as on at least three such occasions during the past twelve months.[54]

---

for intended use by persons, such as customers and suppliers, other than in their capacities as investors or potential investors in the issuer's securities, by the issuer's employees or agents who historically have provided such information." Rule 169(d)(3).

[49] Rule 135, 17 C.F.R. § 230.135. Rule 135 sets forth that the issuer's notice must state that it does not constitute an offer to sell securities and must include "no more" than the information specified in the rule, including such information as "the title, amount and basic terms of the securities offered; the anticipated timing of the offering; [and] a brief statement of the manner and purpose of the offering, without naming the underwriters." Other than well-known seasoned issuers, if an issuer's communication goes beyond what is permitted in Rule 135, it may well constitute an impermissible offer to sell in the pre-filing period. *See Chris-Craft Industries, Inc. v. Bangor Punta Corporation*, 426 F.2d 569 (2d Cir. 1970) (en banc).

[50] *See* Securities Act Release No. 5180 (1971) (stating that "the publication of information and statements, and publicity efforts, made in advance of a proposed financing which have the effect of conditioning the public mind or arousing public interest in the issuer or in its securities constitutes an offer [to sell] in violation of the Act").

[51] *See* Securities Act Release No. 8591 (2005) ("While the Rule does not establish or require any minimum time period to satisfy the regularly released element, the safe harbor requires the issuer to have some track record of releasing the particular type of information. One prior release or dissemination could establish this track record."). As Rule 168 includes forward-looking information, this interpretation facilitates the making of unduly optimistic statements of future performance by subject companies.

[52] A regular course of conduct means "recurring, attending, or functioning at fixed, uniform, or normal intervals; orderly, methodical." Merriam-webster.com, available at https://www.merriam-webster.com/dictionary/regular.

[53] *Id.*

[54] Another example is that Section 105 of the JOBS Act allows brokers and dealers to publish research reports focusing on an emerging growth company at any time—prior to and during an initial public offering—even if these financial intermediaries are participating in the offering. *See* Section 2(a)(3) of the Securities Act, 15 U.S.C. § 77b(a)(3) (excluding such research reports from

F. "Scaled" Disclosure and Smaller Reporting Companies

With respect to disclosures required in registered offerings (as well as in Exchange Act reports), the SEC has made significant steps in eliminating duplicative and immaterial information.[55] This intended reduction and simplification of disclosure requirements constitute measures to ease regulatory burdens and information overload.[56] Nonetheless, the question arises whether the Commission went too far in relaxing these requirements with respect to smaller reporting companies. Pursuant to the 2018 amendments, by significantly expanding the criteria for qualifying as a smaller reporting company,[57] the SEC allows nearly an additional 1,000 publicly-held companies to use "scaled" disclosure documents.[58] As a consequence, these companies' disclosure requirements are significantly reduced, such as, for example: "two

being deemed an offer to sell for purposes of §§ 2(a)(1) and 5(c) of the Securities Act). Similarly, although not as expansive, Rule 139 permits brokers and dealers participating in a registered offering of an eligible publicly-held company to generate issuer-specific research reports that "upgrade" the subject securities from, for example, "hold" to "buy." These rules unduly incentivize financial intermediaries to hype a forthcoming registered offering. As Professor Joseph Morrissey points out, "it seems that a financially interested broker or dealer will be able to take advantage of this [Rule 139] safe harbor to inflate its rating of [a subject] security . . . having great financial incentive to condition the market to increase the price of the securities being offered." Joseph Morrissey, *Rhetoric and Reality: Investor Protection and the Securities Regulation Reform of 2005*, 56 Cath. U. L. Rev. 561, 579 (2007).

[55] *See, e.g.*, Securities Act Release No. 10825 (2020) (stating that the amendments to Items 101, 103, and 105 of Regulation S-K "are intended to improve the readability of disclosure documents, as well as discourage repetition and the disclosure of information that is not material"); Securities Act Release No. 10618 (2019) ("adopting amendments to modernize and simplify certain disclosure requirements in Regulation S-K, and related rules and forms, in a manner that reduces the costs and burdens on registrants while continuing to provide all material information to investors"). These amendments were mandated by the Fixing America's Surface Transportation Act (FAST Act), Pub. L. No. 114-94, 129 Stat. 1312 (2015).

[56] *See* Securities Act Release No. 10618 (2019) (stating that the amendments, "consistent with the Commission's mandate under the FAST Act, are intended to improve the quality and accessibility of disclosure in filings by simplifying and modernizing our requirements [as well as] clarify[ing] ambiguous disclosure requirements, remove redundancies, and further leverage the use of technology"). Nonetheless, as discussed in Chapter 2 herein, investor overload of information that is not material prevails in the SEC disclosure framework. *See* Troy A. Parades, *Blinded by the Light: Information Overload and Its Consequences for Securities Regulation*, 81 Wash. U. L.Q. 417, 446 (2003) (stating that "concerns that investors are becoming overloaded with information have intensified"); discussion Chapter 2 herein, at notes 96–118 and accompanying text.

[57] *See* Securities Act Release No. 10513 (2018) (adopting amendments to expand the number of registrants eligible to use the scaled disclosure requirements in Regulation S-K and Regulation S-X to encompass publicly-held companies having a public float of less than $250 million as well as those that have less than $100 million of revenues and a public float of less than $700 million).

[58] *See* SEC Press Release No. 2018-116 (June 28, 2018) (setting forth that the amendments will allow an additional 966 registrants to become a smaller reporting company and thus eligible to use scaled disclosure).

years of MD&A comparison rather than three; no quantitative and qualitative disclosures about market risk; two years of financial statements rather than three; executive compensation disclosure significantly reduced—three named officers rather than five; two years in summary compensation table rather than three; and no disclosure and analysis of the compensation committee report."[59]

To the extent that scaled disclosure substantially eases regulatory costs and investor overload, it makes good sense. If indeed the information now excluded is not material, then it may be posited that all companies (irrespective of size) also should be allowed to elect scaled disclosure. On the other hand, to the extent that scaled disclosure results in the withholding of material information to investors and the securities markets, it is unacceptable. The benefits of providing this information far outweigh the harm that investors may incur without being privy to such information. The lack of rigorous analysis by Congress and the SEC in their determinations to relax fundamental items of disclosure (e.g., with respect to MD&A, financial statements, and risk disclosure) is disconcerting.[60] Absent justifiable business reason, if information is material, then disclosure should be mandatory irrespective of the size of the subject company.[61]

G. The SEC's Undue Emphasis on Capital Formation

A final point in this section: As discussed earlier, the SEC has been active in relaxing the requirements of Section 5 of the Securities Act in an effort to ease regulatory burdens and facilitate capital raising.[62] With respect to many of these amendments, the Commission has relied on Section 28 of the Securities Act, which gives the Commission expansive authority to exempt any security, transaction, or person from any provision of that Act or any

---

[59] Hillary H. Holmes and Jordan G. Rex, *Updates to the Public Company Disclosure Rulebook*, 52 Rev. Sec. & Comm. Reg. 173, 179 (2019), *interpreting*, Securities Act Release No. 10513 (2018).

[60] In addition to the Congress's directive to the SEC pursuant to the FAST Act, the JOBS Act significantly lessened the disclosure obligations of emerging growth companies. By way of example, an emerging growth company may: provide two years (rather than three years) of audited financial statements; opt for less extensive disclosure in the Management's Discussion and Analysis of Financial Condition and Results of Operation; decline to obtain an auditor's report regarding the reliability and quality of its internal control over financial reporting; provide reduced disclosure concerning executive compensation; and decline to provide its shareholders with advisory "say-on-pay" votes. *See* Marc I. Steinberg, *Securities Regulation* 269 (7th ed. 2017).

[61] *See* discussion *supra* notes 5–7 and accompanying text.

[62] *See* discussion *supra* notes 15–54 and accompanying text.

rule or regulation thereunder.[63] Pursuant to this authority, the Commission has engaged in deregulatory practices in order to further these objectives.[64] In doing so, the SEC has slighted the last phrase of Section 28—namely, the requirement that the exercise of this exemptive authority "is necessary or appropriate in the public interest, and is consistent with the protection of investors."[65]

While the Commission engages in hortatory sayings when adopting these rules,[66] the fact is that many of these rules are not consistent with investor protection. Allowing pre-conditioning the market, or what has been coined gun-jumping, to override the prohibition against offers to sell in the pre-filing period may be beneficial to capital raising—but it is not consistent with investor protection. Stated succinctly, investors are worse off after the adoption of many of these rules than before their adoption. Rather than focusing primarily on facilitating capital raising,[67] the SEC should have a more balanced perspective. In applying this approach, there should be two overriding principles: first, if investors would be worse off if the contemplated measure were adopted, then such measure is not consistent with "the protection of investors"[68] and should not be adopted; second, if any proposed reduction in

---

[63] 15 U.S.C. § 77bb. Section 28 provides: "The Commission, by rule or regulation, may conditionally or unconditionally exempt any person, security, or transaction, or any class of persons, securities, or transactions, from any provision or provisions of this title or of any rule or regulation issued under this title, to the extent that such exemption is necessary or appropriate in the public interest, and is consistent with the protection of investors."

[64] Several of the 2005 amendments (*e.g.*, Rule 163) as well as the SEC's recent adoption of Rule 163B permitting any issuer to communicate with qualified institutional buyers and institutional accredited investors to test the waters in the pre-filing period are examples.

[65] *See* the language of Section 28 *supra* note 63.

[66] *See, e.g.*, Securities Act Release Nos. 8591 (2005), 10513 (2018), 10064 (2019).

[67] *See* sources cited *supra* note 66.

[68] *See* Morrissey, *supra* note 54, at 604 (stating that "there are many areas where the [2005 offering] reforms on their face seem to oppose the interests of investor protection and instead are more concerned with providing ease of access to the capital markets for issuers and a relaxation of liability that would have otherwise applied to offering participants").

With respect to nationally traded securities, state regulation with respect to the registration or qualification of such securities is preempted pursuant to Section 18(b)(1) of the Securities Act, 15 U.S.C. § 77r(b)(1). This provision grants the SEC exclusive authority over the qualification and registration of all securities that are "listed, or authorized for listing, on the New York Stock Exchange or the American Stock Exchange, or listed, or authorized for listing, on the National Market System of the Nasdaq Stock Market (or any successor to such entitles)." *Id.* This preemption was added as a provision of the National Securities Markets Improvement Act of 1996 and effectively federalized the then existing blue sky law exemptions. *See* Robert G. Bagnell and Kimble Cannon, *The National Securities Markets Improvement Act of 1996: Summary and Discussion*, 25 Sec. Reg. L.J. 3 (1997). This approach clearly is correct. The regulation of qualification, listing, and disclosure requirements involving nationally traded securities should be a matter of federal regulation—with the self-regulatory organizations having a prominent role overseen by the SEC. State regulation, with a myriad of diverse requirements imposed by many states, would adversely affect the efficiency and functioning of individual listings as well as the markets from a general perspective. This

disclosure signifies that certain material information no longer will be available to investors and the securities markets, that proposed measure likewise should be rejected.

IV. Due Diligence in Registered Offerings

Since *BarChris* was handed down over fifty years ago,[69] the issue of establishing the due diligence defense[70] for outside directors and underwriters in Securities Act registered offerings has been a subject of controversy.[71] Under Section 11 of the Securities Act,[72] if a material

preemption, however, is inconsistent with Congress's determination not to preempt maneuvers undertaken in the merger and acquisition (M&A) settings that materially impact companies whose securities trade on the national exchanges. These M&A "deals" ordinarily have national and global ramifications and, accordingly, should be within the sole province of federal law. For further discussion, *see* Chapter 8 herein. *See generally* Marc I. Steinberg, *The Federalization of Corporate Governance* (2018).

[69] *Escott v. BarChris Construction Corporation*, 283 F. Supp. 643 (S.D.N.Y. 1968).

[70] There is no affirmative obligation to conduct due diligence. However, if the registration statement contains a material misrepresentation or omission, the exercise of due diligence is an effective defense. Consequently, conducting due diligence often is viewed as a practical necessity. Note, however, that the issuer has no due diligence defense under Section 11. For non-experts, including directors and underwriters, the due diligence defense is set forth in Section 11(b)(3), 15 U.S.C. § 77k(b)(3):

> [N]o person, other than the issuer, shall be liable . . . who shall sustain the burden of proof—
>
> . . .
>
> (3) that (A) as regards any part of the registration statement not purporting to be made on the authority of an expert . . . he had, after reasonable investigation, reasonable ground to believe and did believe, at the time such part of the registration statement became effective, that the statements therein were true and that there was no omission to state a material fact required to be stated therein or necessary to make the statements therein not misleading; . . . and (C) as regards any part of the registration statement purporting to be made on the authority of an expert (other than himself) . . . he had no reasonable ground to believe and did not believe, at the time such part of the registration statement became effective, that the statements therein were untrue or that there was an omission to state a material fact required to be stated therein or necessary to make the statements therein not misleading.

Generally, an expert, such as the auditor who certifies the subject company's financial statements, is required to exercise the same standard of diligence as a non-expert with respect to the non-expertised portion of the registration statement. *See* Section 11(b)(3). Experts may incur liability under Section 11 only for the portion of the registration statement that they expertised.

The standard of reasonableness set forth in the statute is strict: "In determining for the purpose of [establishing the due diligence defense], what constitutes reasonable investigation and reasonable ground of belief, the standard of reasonableness shall be that required of a prudent man in the management of his own property." Section 11(c).

[71] *See, e.g.*, Report of the Advisory Committee, *supra* note 1, at 88,483–85 (and sources cited therein).

[72] 15 U.S.C. § 77k.

misstatement or omission is contained in a registration statement, potentially liable parties may avoid liability by proving they exercised due diligence (except the issuer, which has no due diligence defense).[73] In satisfying one's due diligence, one must not rely solely on information communicated by insiders;[74] rather, a subject party must conduct an appropriate investigation in view of its position with the issuer, its involvement in the preparation of the registration statement, and the type of offering implicated.[75]

A. Due Diligence and the Integrated Disclosure System

The integrated disclosure framework has exacerbated due diligence concerns. In the registered offering setting, Exchange Act reports (including 10-Ks, 10-Qs, and 8-Ks) previously filed by an eligible company are incorporated by reference into its Securities Act registration statement.[76] When these Exchange Act reports were filed with the SEC, the underwriters may have had no relationship with the company.[77] With

---

[73] *See* discussion *supra* note 70.

[74] *See, e.g.*, *In re Software Toolworks Inc. Securities Litigation*, 38 F.3d 1078 (9th Cir. 1994); *In re Worldcom, Inc. Securities Litigation*, 2005 U.S. Dist. LEXIS 4193 (S.D.N.Y. 2005); *Feit v. Leasco Data Processing Equipment Corp.*, 332 F. Supp. 544 (E.D.N.Y. 1971); *Escott v. BarChris Construction Corporation*, 283 F. Supp. 643 (S.D.N.Y. 1968).

[75] *See* SEC Rule 176, 17 C.F.R. § 230.176; discussion *infra* notes 76–116 and accompanying text.

[76] *See* discussion *supra* notes 10–12, 15 and accompanying text; Chapter 2 herein, at notes 119–131 and accompanying text.

[77] *See* Circumstances Affecting the Determination of What Constitutes Reasonable Investigation and Reasonable Grounds for Belief under Section 11 of the Securities Act, Securities Act Release No. 6336 (1981). In this release, underwriter concerns were set forth as follows:

> Underwriters and others have expressed concern regarding their ability to discharge fully their responsibilities under Section 11 with respect to registration statements incorporating substantial information from periodic reports. Historically, preparation of the traditional Form S-1 registration statement began many weeks in advance of the proposed offering due to the time required to assemble and verify the information required to be set forth in the registration statement and prospectus. . . . In contrast, integrated short form registration statements rely, to the maximum extent possible, on information contained in previously filed Exchange Act reports or in the annual report to security holders. Information actually set forth in the short form registration statement pertains primarily to the proposed transaction, the use of proceeds and the updating of information in incorporated documents. Preparation time is reduced sharply, as is the period of time between the issuer's decision to undertake a securities offering and the filing of the registration statement with the Commission. [Today, shelf registration allows an issuer to launch a public offering on extremely short notice, frequently in a few hours.] . . .
>
> Some underwriters also object to utilizing information in periodic reports for registration purposes, because it has been composed by persons without consultation with the underwriters who may, in turn, be held, in the context of a registration statement, to a

respect to the outside directors, the same measure of discipline may not have been applied to these reports as compared to a traditional registered offering.[78]

The situation presented in this context is that the integrated disclosure process drastically shortens the time period between the filing and effectiveness of a subject registration statement. Indeed, in the context of shelf offerings,[79] and particularly for well-known seasoned issuers,[80] an offering frequently is brought to market within a few hours.[81] Within this short time period, in practical effect, it is impossible for underwriters to perform customary due diligence practices.[82] With respect to liability exposure, the problem is clear: rather than plaintiffs in a class action having to allege and prove scienter and other challenging requirements under Section 10(b) of the Exchange Act[83]—once these same documents are

---

> higher standard of civil liability than that to which the original preparers may have been subject. . . .
>
> [Subsequently adopted Rule 415], allowing shelf registration, also has caused apprehension. Commentators on the rule believed that insufficient consideration had been given to the responsibilities of the persons involved in a shelf registration . . . under the Rule. For example, a shelf offering involve[s] automatic incorporation by reference into the registration statement of Exchange Act reports for a substantial period of time because the offering may be made on a delayed or continuous basis. In addition, if an underwriter is brought into a shelf offering after the initial effective date of the registration statement, the late-arriving underwriter would be responsible for the accuracy of the contents of the registration statement as of the time of his entry into the transaction.

[78] The Commission recognized this disparity and sought to largely correct this situation by requiring that a majority of a company's directors sign the Form 10-K. *See* Securities Act Release No. 6231 (1980) (By mandating this signature requirement, "the Commission anticipates that directors will be encouraged to devote the needed attention to reviewing the Form 10-K and to seek the involvement of other professionals to the degree necessary to give themselves sufficient comfort.").

[79] *See* SEC Rule 415, 17 C.F.R. § 230.415. The shelf registration rule permits eligible companies to register their securities on a delayed or continuous basis in the future. A more expansive version of shelf registration (automatic shelf registration) enables a well-known seasoned issuer to register its securities on a Form S-3 registration statement which becomes effective immediately upon filing with the SEC. *See supra* note 23.

[80] For the definition of well-known seasoned issuer, *see supra* note 20.

[81] *See* Amici Curiae Brief of the Securities Industry Association and the Bond Market Association at pages 3–4, in *In re Worldcom, Inc. Securities Litigation*, 346 F. Supp. 2d 628 (S.D.N.Y. 2004). *See generally* Barbara Banoff, *Regularity Subsidies, Efficient Markets and Shelf Registration—An Analysis of Rule 415*, 70 Va. L. Rev. 135 (1984).

[82] *See In re Worldcom Inc. Securities Litigation*, 346 F. Supp. 2d 628, 670 (S.D.N.Y. 2004) (observing the SEC's acknowledgment that "different investigatory methods would be needed in view of the compressed preparation time and the volatile nature of the capital markets").

[83] Plaintiffs have rigorous hurdles when bringing suit for alleged violations of Section 10(b), including: establishing the defendant's scienter (*Ernst & Ernst v. Hochfelder*, 425 U.S. 185 (1976)); pleading fraud with the requisite particularity (§ 21D(b)(2) of the Securities Exchange Act, *Tellabs, Inc. v. Makor Issues & Rights, Ltd.*, 551 U.S. 308 (2007)); showing loss causation (§ 21D(b)(4) of the Securities Exchange Act, *Dura Pharmaceuticals, Inc. v. Broudo*, 544 U.S. 336 (2005)); and proving the damages suffered (*see* Michael Kaufman, *Securities Litigation: Damages* (2019)). For further discussion, *see* Chapter 6 herein.

incorporated into a Securities Act registration statement—the plaintiff-friendly provisions of Section 11 of the Securities Act apply.[84] In a Section 11 action, plaintiffs need not prove such key elements as reliance, loss causation, mental culpability (such as negligence), and damages.[85] The consequence is that liability exposure is magnified, particularly in the shelf registration context.[86]

Underwriters and, to a lesser extent, outside directors assert that the rigorous liability standard of Section 11 is inappropriate in this setting.[87] They argue that more lenient standards should apply.[88] Although these assertions have been met with some support,[89] for the most part, the SEC (while adopting Rule 176) and the courts hold that

---

[84] To state a claim under Section 11, a plaintiff ordinarily must show that: the security purchased was bought pursuant to the subject registration statement; a means of interstate commerce was used in connection with the purchase; the registration statement contained a material misrepresentation or omission; and suit was brought within the applicable statute of limitations. Nonetheless, some lower courts have imposed rigorous tracing requirements that nullify the Section 11 right of action if the subject company has securities outstanding in the aftermarket in addition to those that were sold pursuant to the subject registration statement. *See, e.g.*, *Krim v. pcOrder.com, Inc.*, 402 F.3d 489, 495–96 (5th Cir. 2005) (denying a § 11 right of action for lack of satisfying the tracing requirement when the pool of shares in the secondary trading market contained 99.85 percent of shares that were traced to the subject registration statement). For further commentary, *see* Marc I. Steinberg and Brent A. Kirby, *The Assault on Section 11 of the Securities Act: A Study in Judicial Activism*, 63 Rutgers L. Rev. 1 (2010).

[85] With certain exceptions, Section 11(e) sets forth a formulaic measure of damages focusing on the difference between what the plaintiff "paid for the security (not exceeding the price at which the security was offered to the public)" and its value at three different intervals: (1) at the time suit was instituted, (2) the price that the plaintiff sold the security before suit, or (3) the price the plaintiff sold the security after suit but before judgment. Defendants have an affirmative loss causation defense under Section 11(e) of proving that the subject misrepresentation(s) did not cause all or a portion of the security's decrease in price. *See, e.g.*, *Akerman v. Oryx Communications, Inc.*, 810 F.2d 344 (2d Cir. 1987). In limited situations, a plaintiff must show reliance in Section 11 actions. For further sources on Section 11, *see, e.g.*, *supra* notes 71, 74, 84; discussion in Chapter 6 herein.

[86] *See In re Worldcom, Inc. Securities Litigation*, 346 F. Supp. 2d 628 (S.D.N.Y. 2004); Securities Act Release No. 6335 (1981); Securities Act Release No. 6499 (1983).

[87] *See* Report of the Advisory Committee, *supra* note 1, at 88,485 (stating that "outside directors of public corporations currently are not always well positioned to perform a full investigative function [and that] because of timing constraints characteristic of shelf takedowns, outside directors may not have sufficient time to review any disclosure documents other than the Form 10-Ks"). With respect to underwriter concerns, *see, e.g.*, sources cited *supra* notes 77–82.

[88] For example, the Securities Industry Association asserted that the underwriter due diligence defense should be met if: (1) such underwriter read the registration statement, the exhibits thereto, and the materials incorporated therein; (2) discussed these materials with representatives of the issuer and the named experts; and (3) after engaging in these steps, was not aware of any material misrepresentation or omission in the registration statement. Because this proposed standard does not include the element of verification as mandated by the statute and case law, the SEC summarily rejected it. *See* Securities Act Release No. 6335 (1981).

[89] *See, e.g.*, *Task Force Report on Seller's Due Diligence and Similar Defenses Under the Federal Securities Laws*, 48 Bus. Law. 1185, 1239 (1993) (asserting that the "integrated disclosure system and the expansion of shelf registration statements have called into question whether underwriters any longer 'sponsor' an issue in a meaningful way").

meaningful due diligence must be conducted for this defense to be successful.[90]

The argument that liability exposure is unduly onerous in the Section 11 integrated disclosure context is reasonable. As discussed earlier, plaintiffs must hurdle challenging requirements to state a viable case under Section 10(b) based on materially false statements in Exchange Act reports.[91] Once those very same Exchange Act reports are incorporated by reference into a registration statement, the plaintiff-friendly provisions of Section 11 apply whereby the due diligence defense presents a challenging burden for underwriters and outside directors to satisfy.[92] As addressed in Chapter 6 herein, the liability framework under the federal securities laws should be revised along the lines as suggested therein. Assuming, however, that the present regimen remains intact, the question arises how the due diligence defense should be interpreted.

B. Due Diligence—Outside Directors

With respect to outside directors, the suggested approach is to require that publicly-held companies, as a condition of listing on a national securities exchange, have a disclosure committee of the board of directors comprised solely of independent directors.[93] Given that the directors' own

[90] *See, e.g.*, sources cited *supra* note 86. Rule 176, 17 C.F.R. § 230.176, is discussed *infra* notes 98, 103–104, and accompanying text.

[91] *See supra* note 83.

[92] As the court observed in *In re Worldcom, Inc. Securities Litigation*, 348 F. Supp. 2d 628, 670 (S.D.N.Y. 2004), "academics and practitioners alike have asserted that the current regime for underwriter liability under Section 11 no longer makes sense." The court quoted the following sources: John C. Coffee, Jr., *Brave New World? The Impact(s) of the Internet on Modern Securities Regulation*, 52 Bus. Law. 1195, 1211 (1997) (stating that "it is not clear that the underwriter today still performs the classic gatekeeping function"); Donald C. Langevoort, *Deconstructing Section 11: Public Offering Liability in a Continuous Disclosure Environment*, 63 Law & Contemp. Probs. 45, 67 (2000) (stating that "there is a strong practical case to be made for absolving underwriters of all inquiry obligations short of recklessness"); Frank Partnoy, *Barbarians at the Gatekeepers? A Proposal for a Modified Strict Liability Regime*, 79 Wash. U. L.Q. 491, 522 (2001) (stating that "for shelf registrations, disinterested advance due diligence is the exception not the rule").

[93] Typically, publicly-held corporations have disclosure committees comprised of corporate officers and other high-level personnel. Most often, the committee reports to the company's chief executive officer or chief financial officer. A key objective is to assist the CEO, CFO, and the audit committee with respect to the company's adherence to the proper implementation and maintenance of adequate disclosure controls and principles. In this regard, the disclosure committee is tasked with assessing the materiality of information and the company's disclosure obligations as well as playing an important role in maintaining adequate disclosure controls and procedures. *See* KPMG, *Transparency and Management's Disclosure Committee* (2018), available at https://boardleadership.kpmg.us/relevant-topics/articles/2016/transparency-and-managements-disclosure-committee.

liability is at issue, rationally there should be sufficient impetus for these directors to focus diligently on their committee obligations. The committee should meet with company personnel (including inside counsel and accounting staff as well as the company's outside accounting firm) on a regular basis to review topical disclosure issues as well as recent and forthcoming SEC filings. Similar to the audit committee mandate, the disclosure committee should have the authority to retain its own advisers, including legal counsel.[94] Requiring independent counsel, however, may be cost prohibitive for smaller publicly-held companies and duplicative of the work performed by other attorneys (in-house and outside counsel) that are engaged to undertake the preparation of SEC filings.[95] Nonetheless, with some frequency, matters are likely to arise that raise thorny disclosure issues. On those occasions, the disclosure committee must have the authority to retain independent counsel to render a "second

---

html. A growing number of committees also assess these disclosure controls and procedures to encompass cybersecurity risk. *See* Pamela L. Marcogliese, *Cleary Partner Moderates Panel on Disclosure Committees* (June 26, 2018), available at https://www.clearymawatch.com/2018/06/cleary-partner-moderates-panel-disclosure-committees/.

The SEC's Advisory Committee on the Capital Formation and Regulatory Processes recommended that a disclosure committee of outside directors be formed that would "conduct an investigation of the issuer's disclosures." The efficient functioning of this committee would improve the disclosure process and provide some level of comfort that directors have met their statutory obligations. *See* Report of the Advisory Committee, *supra* note 1, at 88,427–28 (asserting that use of such a disclosure committee would be beneficial by: "ensur[ing] more continuous oversight of the disclosure preparation process, and over time, improve the quality and integrity of periodic and secondary market reporting and disclosure generally"; "provid[ing] a focus at the board level for due diligence in the context of primary offerings by issuers, thereby ensuring greater involvement by outside directors as one set of monitors"; and "provid[ing] a practical means for greater outside director involvement with the due diligence activities of other gatekeepers, such as underwriters"). *See* John C. Coffee, Jr., *Company Registration Approach Would Modernize the 1933 Act*, Nat'l L.J., Sept. 11, 1995, at B4 (stating that "other outside directors could rely on a committee of directors—tentatively called the 'disclosure committee'—which would review the company's [Exchange] Act filings, such as its Form 10-K and 10-Qs, and consider the need for additional disclosures to cover material developments").

[94] *See* § 10A(m)(5) of the Exchange Act, 15 U.S.C. § 78j-1(m)(5) ("Each audit committee shall have the authority to engage independent counsel and other advisers, as it determines necessary to carry out its duties."); Rule 10A-3(b)(4), 17 C.F.R. § 240.10A-3(b)(4) (setting forth, as a condition of listing on a national securities exchange, that the audit committee have the authority to engage independent counsel as well as other advisers).

[95] For a smaller publicly-held company, the compliance costs are extensive and have dissuaded several companies from going public. *See* Securities Act Release No. 10513 (2018). Requiring independent counsel for the disclosure committee would exacerbate this situation. Nonetheless, in appropriate situations, the committee must have the authority to retain independent counsel.

Aside from the size of the subject company, the presence of an independent law firm may generate disagreements with the company's general inside as well as outside counsel. Due to the extent that independent counsel is objective and proficient, this conflict ultimately may better serve the company's best interests. Where conflicts arise because of technical or egocentric disagreements, however, the presence of independent counsel is problematic.

opinion."[96] In such circumstances, it is unacceptable for the committee to rely on inside counsel whose jobs and salaries depend on pleasing executive personnel or on incumbent outside counsel whose continued retention and receipt of lucrative fees are likewise dependent on maintaining good relations with high-level executives.[97] Implementation of this proposal would enable outside directors to perform ongoing due diligence in a proactive manner. In addition to attending board of director meetings (and audit committee meetings for those directors who are members), the presence of a sound disclosure committee enables outside directors to take greater control of the disclosure function. By being apprised of disclosure issues and developments on an ongoing basis, these directors will be in a far superior position to engage in adequate due diligence. Moreover, by holding sessions attended by the other outside directors who do not serve on the committee (along with support personnel such as legal counsel), a more meaningful discussion regarding substantive disclosure matters is likely to occur. Accordingly, the functioning of a sound disclosure committee should instill greater discipline to the disclosure process, enhance the quality of disclosures made, and (with respect to conducting a reasonable investigation under case law and Rule 176) serve as a valuable source for outside directors to satisfy their due diligence defense.[98]

[96] Through the decades, the use of a second opinion in the attorney-client setting has significantly increased. My mentor and good friend, the Honorable Stanley Sporkin (who served as SEC enforcement director, CIA general counsel, and a U.S. federal district court judge), and I coauthored a piece on this subject four decades ago. *See* Stanley Sporkin and Marc I. Steinberg, *Second Opinion for Lawyers—The "Consultative Attorney,"* N.Y. L.J., Jan. 3, 1983, at 1.

[97] These conflicts of interest prevail when law firms and individual attorneys derive lucrative fees from preferred clients. For in-house counsel, there is the specter of loss of employment. In such situations, the retention of independent counsel becomes critical. For my books on this subject, *see, e.g.*, Marc I. Steinberg, *Attorney Liability After Sarbanes-Oxley* (2018); Marc I. Steinberg, *Lawyering and Ethics for the Business Attorney* (5th ed. 2020); Marc I. Steinberg and Stephen B. Yeager, *Inside Counsel—Practices, Strategies, and Insights* (2d ed. 2020).

[98] The presence of a diligent and functioning disclosure committee comprised of outside directors should be a significant criterion in establishing that the Section 11 due diligence defense is met. For those outside directors who do not serve on the committee, Rule 176(f) is helpful in that it provides that a relevant circumstance in determining whether a director's conduct "constitutes a reasonable investigation or a reasonable ground for belief" is whether there was "[r]easonable reliance on officers, employees, and others whose duties should have given them knowledge of the particular facts." 17 C.F.R. § 230.176(f). As stated by the SEC's Advisory Committee on the Capital Formation and Regulatory Processes:

> The disclosure committee could conduct this investigation, just as a board of directors may appoint a committee to engage in other types of specialized inquiries, so long as (a) the delegating directors reasonably believe that the member(s) of the disclosure committee are sufficiently knowledgeable and capable of discharging due diligence obligations on behalf of the outside directors (if necessary, with the assistance of their professional advisers) and are provided with adequate resources to conduct the

C. Due Diligence—Underwriters

To meet their due diligence defense, underwriters must engage in verification.[99] They simply cannot rely on corporate filings and communications with the company's personnel.[100] While this task of verification is entrenched in the traditional initial public offering and related settings,[101] its implementation in the shelf registration context is a source of contention.[102] While continuing to support the concept that verification is a necessary measure for establishing the due diligence defense, the SEC promulgated Rule 176, which applies a more flexible standard in the integrated disclosure framework.[103] One of the factors set forth in Rule 176

> requisite investigation—that is, the delegation must be reasonable; (b) the delegating directors maintain appropriate oversight of the disclosure committee (which would entail requiring the disclosure committee to report periodically to the Board on the procedures followed to ensure the integrity of the disclosure) and reasonably believe that the disclosure committee's procedures are adequate and were being performed; and (c) the delegating directors reasonably believe that the disclosure is not materially false or misleading.

Report of the Advisory Committee, *supra* note 1, at 88,427. *See* discussion *supra* notes 69–92 and accompanying text.

[99] *See, e.g., Escott v. BarChris Construction Corporation*, 283 F. Supp. 643, 696 (S.D.N.Y. 1968) (holding that the underwriters failed to show that they had made a reasonable investigation and stated "it is clear that no effectual attempt at verification was made").

[100] *See, e.g., In re Software Toolworks Inc. Securities Litigation*, 38 F.3d 1078, 1088 (9th Cir. 1994) (reversing summary judgment in favor of the underwriters when they "did little more than rely on [the company's] assurances that the transactions were legitimate").

[101] *See, e.g., In re Facebook, Inc. IPO Securities and Derivative Litigation*, 312 F.R.D. 332 (S.D.N.Y. 2015); *Weinberger v. Jackson*, [1990–1991 Transfer Binder] Fed. Sec. L. Rep. (CCH) ¶ 95,693 (N.D. Cal. 1990); *Feit v. Leasco Data Processing Equipment Corp.*, 332 F. Supp. 544 (E.D.N.Y. 1971). *See also Chris-Craft Industries, Inc. v. Piper Aircraft Corp.*, 480 F.2d 341, 380 (2d Cir. 1973) ("No greater reliance in our self-regulatory system is placed on any single participant in the issuance of securities than upon the underwriter."); Securities Exchange Act Release No. 26100 (1988) (stating that an underwriter has "a vital position in the offering . . . [and that by] participating in an offering, an underwriter makes an implied representation about the securities").

Nonetheless, direct listings that take place on a national securities exchange, such as the New York Stock Exchange, lack the involvement of traditional underwriters in the IPO process. Critics assert that this absence enables subject corporations to circumvent the protections traditionally present in this setting, thereby impairing investor protection. *See* Securities Exchange Act Release No. 89684 (2020) (approving NYSE's proposed rule permitting companies to raise capital by means of direct listings); Alexander Osipovich, *NYSE's New Alternative to an IPO Wins a Green Light from the SEC*, Wall St. J., Aug. 27, 2020, at B1 ("the SEC approved the NYSE's plan despite objections from some groups that warned it could harm investors by letting companies circumvent the protections of the IPO process.").

[102] *See, e.g., In re Worldcom, Inc. Securities Litigation*, 346 F. Supp. 2d 628 (S.D.N.Y. 2004) (and sources cited therein); sources cited *supra* notes 81, 92.

[103] As observed by the court in *Worldcom*, Rule 176 "largely mirrors Section 1704(g)" of the American Law Institute's Federal Securities Code. 346 F. Supp. 2d at 669. In determining whether a subject defendant (other than the issuer which has no due diligence defense) conducted a reasonable investigation (non-expertised portion of the registration statement) or a reasonable ground for belief (expertised portion), relevant circumstances include:

in determining whether requisite due diligence has been performed is whether the subject person, such as an underwriter, "had any responsibility for the fact or document at the time of the filing from which it was incorporated."[104] Although this criterion is helpful, Rule 176 provides no panacea for underwriters.[105]

(a) The type of issuer;
(b) The type of security;
(c) The type of person;
(d) The office held when the person is an officer;
(e) The presence or absence of another relationship to the issuer when the person is a director or proposed director;
(f) Reasonable reliance on officers, employees, and others whose duties should have given them knowledge of the particular facts;
(g) When the person is an underwriter, the type of underwriting arrangement, the role of the particular person as an underwriter and the availability of information with respect to the registrant; and
(h) Whether, with respect to a fact or document incorporated by reference, the particular person had any responsibility for the fact or document at the time of the filing from which it was incorporated.

In 1998, the SEC proposed amending Rule 176. *See* Securities Act Release No. 7606A (1998). To date, this proposal has not been adopted. The proposal sought to provide additional guidance for underwriters in the integrated disclosure system by setting forth six practices that, while not exclusive, would evidence the performance of requisite due diligence under Section 11. These six factors are:

- Whether the underwriter reviewed the registration statement and conducted a reasonable inquiry into any fact or circumstance that would cause a reasonable person to question whether the registration statement contains an untrue statement or material omission;
- Whether the underwriter discussed the information contained in the registration statement with the relevant executive officer(s) of the registrant (including, at minimum, the chief financial officer (CFO) or the chief accounting officer (CAO) (or designee)) and the CFO or CAO (or designee) certified that he or she has examined the registration statement and that to the best of his or her knowledge, it does not contain an untrue statement or material omission;
- Whether the underwriter received a Statement on Auditing Standards No. 72 comfort letter from the issuer's auditors;
- Whether the underwriter received a favorable opinion from issuer's counsel opining that nothing has come to its attention that has caused it to believe that the registration statement contains an untrue statement or omits to state a material fact;
- Whether the underwriter employed counsel that, after reviewing the issuer's registration statement, Exchange Act filings and other information, opined that nothing came to its attention that would lead it to believe that the registration statement contains an untrue statement or omits to state a material fact; and
- Whether the underwriter employed and consulted a research analyst that:
  - has followed the issuer or the issuer's industry on an ongoing basis for at least the six months immediately before the commencement of the offering; and
  - has issued a report on the issuer or its industry within the 12 months immediately before commencement of the offering.

[104] Rule 176(h), 17 C.F.R. § 230.176(h).

[105] The SEC commented upon these concerns in its adoption of the shelf registration rule. *See* Securities Act Release No. 6499 (1983):

Providing guidance in this setting, the SEC has suggested that an underwriter build up "a reservoir of knowledge" with respect to subject potential issuers who may retain the firm for a future public offering.[106] To do so, the Commission asserted that underwriter personnel should: review the subject company's SEC filings; attend analysts' and brokers' meetings held by the registrant; participate in the company's Exchange Act "drafting sessions"; and attend the registrant's due diligence sessions after the release of the company's quarterly earnings.[107] Attending these sessions, according to the SEC, would enable underwriters to obtain worthwhile information regarding subject issuers.[108] Nonetheless, these suggestions are not practical. It is neither efficient nor cost effective for an underwriter to send competent personnel on a regular basis to attend hundreds of sessions involving issuers who possibly may opt to retain the firm in a subsequent offering.[109]

> Concerns expressed about the quality of disclosure also relate to underwriters' ability to conduct due diligence investigations. Commentators attribute concerns about due diligence largely to fast time schedules. Under the Rule, any underwriter may be selected to handle a particular offering. Some commentators suggest that no underwriter can afford to devote the time and expense necessary to conduct a due diligence review before knowing whether it will handle an offering and that there may not be sufficient time to do so once it is selected. These commentators also indicate that they may not have the opportunity to apply their independent scrutiny and judgment to documents prepared by registrants many months before an offering.

[106] Securities Act Release No. 6335 (1981) ("Unless the underwriter intends to reserve a specified period of time for investigation after the registration statement has been prepared but before filing, it will be necessary to develop in advance a reservoir of knowledge about the companies that may select the underwriter to distribute their securities registered on short form registration statements.").

[107] *See* Securities Act Release No. 6335 (1981) (stating that: "Extensive data about seasoned companies can be obtained with little effort" (such as their Exchange Act reports) and that "analysts' and brokers' meetings allow underwriters or potential underwriters to question members of management and to evaluate their skills and abilities"); Securities Act Release No. 6499 (1983) (suggesting: the retention of law firm counsel for the prospective underwriter(s) to conduct ongoing due diligence, the holding by an issuer of "Exchange Act 'drafting sessions' [which afford] prospective underwriters and their counsel an opportunity to participate in the drafting and review of periodic disclosure documents before they are filed" as well as "periodic due diligence sessions [held by an issuer] after the release of quarterly earnings to provide prospective underwriters and their counsel an opportunity to discuss with management the most recent financial results and other events of that quarter," and scheduling individual meetings with receptive management).

Note that a number of the foregoing suggestions today possibly would violate Regulation FD. *See* 17 C.F.R. § 243.100; Securities Exchange Act Release No. 43154 (2000). Absent the existence of a confidentiality agreement, the disclosure of material non-public information to prospective underwriters during a drafting session, for example, would violate Regulation FD.

[108] *See* sources cited *supra* note 107.

[109] *See* Securities Act Release No. 6499 (1983) (Chairman Shad, Special Concurring Opinion) ("It would be very expensive for top management executives, underwriters and their counsels to spend hundreds or thousands of hours annually attending such meetings on the speculative possibility that the individual issuer will decide to do a public offering, and that one of the underwriters attending such [a] meeting will be the high bidder for the issue [and that accordingly] it therefore seems likely

Unfortunately, in many shelf offerings, little underwriter due diligence is being conducted. In the short time span available before the securities go to market, the underwriters may engage in communications with the issuer's counsel and auditor, have a conference call with other participants in the offering, and conduct an internet search focusing on such matters as litigation, regulatory developments, and financially-related matters.[110]

The SEC also has suggested that an issuer retain counsel for the underwriter to conduct due diligence on an ongoing basis.[111] The problem with this approach is that the issuer is the entity that retains the law firm for the underwriter, raising conflict of interest concerns.[112] Nonetheless, this approach is one that is being utilized apparently to a significant degree.[113]

---

that over time, few top management executives will attend such meetings and that investment bankers will begin sending junior observers, rather than qualified participants").

[110] Hence, in the automatic shelf registration framework, even when the subject underwriter does not have a previous relationship with the issuer, the following measures would be prudent for such underwriter to undertake: "holding a due diligence conference call with the issuer and its key management, the issuer's counsel, and other appropriate personnel; speaking with the company's auditor; contacting in-house counsel to the issuer or the issuer's outside counsel to inquire about material developments, including pending or ongoing litigation; inquiring about the loss or gain of material contracts, personnel, or other material changes in the issuer's business since the filing of the company's last Form 10-Q; communicating with the issuer regarding the feasibility of the offering timeline; if the company's auditor is receptive, obtaining a 'comfort letter' from such auditor; and conducting internet searches for uncovering news articles and other information about the issuer and its affiliates, including its directors, officers, and control persons." Steinberg, *supra* note 16, at 243 (and sources cited therein). *But see* Joseph K. Leahy, *The Irrepressible Myths of BarChris*, 37 Del. J. Corp. L. 411, 417 (2012) (contending that "contrary to *BarChris*'s teaching, in many securities offerings, an underwriter ought not be required to independently verify all of the issuer's material statements in the registration statement, because a prudent person would not do so").

[111] *See* Securities Act Release No. 6499 (1983) ("This technique [of appointment of a single law firm to act as underwriters' counsel] is now being followed more broadly in the shelf registration environment and represents what the Commission believes to be a sound practice because it provides for due diligence investigations to be performed continually throughout the effectiveness of the shelf registration statement.").

[112] Accordingly, the dilemma is posed that if the law firm for the underwriter asserts that certain of the company's disclosures in SEC filed documents are materially deficient or insists upon more substantial disclosures than the company or its counsel believe are warranted, the company controls whether to terminate the underwriter's representation. This dilemma is exacerbated by the generous fees earned by the law firm representing the underwriter which may induce the firm to tone down its concern over the accuracy of the issuer's disclosures.

A solution to ameliorate this conflict is that, if the company terminates the law firm for the underwriter or the firm resigns from the representation, the company must file a Form 8-K with the SEC disclosing this event and explaining the reasons for such resignation or termination. In addition, the Commission should require that the law firm in the company's Form 8-K filing explain its position regarding the resignation or termination. Implementing these requirements, if rigorously enforced, should significantly lessen the conflicts of interest posed.

[113] *See* Securities Act Release No. 6499 (1983). *But see* New York City Bar Association's Task Force on the Lawyer's Role in Corporate Governance, Executive Summary at page 14 (2007) (stating that the SEC's expectation that "many eligible issuers, in collaboration with their chosen underwriters and their lawyers, would adopt 'continuous due diligence programs' [has not occurred as] the number of companies today using such continuous due diligence programs appears not to be extensive, and

Given the deficiencies of the other alternatives that have been raised, this approach is the most attractive.

Accordingly, pursuant to SEC rule, in shelf registered offerings, issuer retention of underwriter's counsel would be required. To significantly lessen the conflict of interest concern, the law firm for the underwriter would be retained either by the subject company's audit committee or its disclosure committee. Comprised solely of independent directors, either of these committees would be charged with the retention, scope of representation, fee arrangement, and, if called for, the termination of such law firm. Upon the conducting of a shelf registered offering, the participating underwriters would incur all fees owed to the law firm. In addition, upon the execution of comprehensive nondisclosure agreements, select underwriters would be invited to attend informational sessions with the members of the independent committee and underwriter's counsel. These sessions should prove useful for generating underwriter interest in the issuer, facilitating the selection of underwriters for prospective offerings in view of meaningful interactions between the company and potential underwriters, and providing prospective underwriters with greater comfort in assuming underwriter status. Importantly, this concept facilitates the conducting of underwriter due diligence on a continuous basis, thereby enhancing the integrity of the disclosure process and providing greater protection for investors.[114]

---

opinions vary on their effectiveness"). A more recent study, however, finds that this assertion "is not supported by empirical data." Analyzing survey data gathered from over 100 securities attorneys on a nationwide basis, the author concludes that "empirical evidence [demonstrates] that underwriters have significantly adapted their due diligence investigations to the shelf registration environment and integrated disclosure system by implementing the use of underwriters' counsel." James A. Bedotto, *If It Ain't Broke, Don't Fix It: The Frequent Use of "Underwriters' Counsel" in Shelf-Registered Offerings Scraps the Need for Underwriter Due Diligence Reforms*, 42 Sec. Reg. L.J. 293, 294 (2014).

[114] Note that, with the execution of a confidentiality agreement—even if material information is conveyed to the prospective underwriter(s)—this practice is compliant with Regulation FD. *See* Rule 100(b)(2)(ii) of Regulation FD, 17 C.F.R. § 243.100(b)(2)(ii). If the underwriter were to trade on this information, such conduct would violate Rule 10b5-2, 17 C.F.R. § 240.10b5-2. *See United States v. O'Hagan*, 521 U.S. 642 (1997); discussion in Chapter 7 herein.

If underwriter's counsel resigns or is terminated by the subject company's audit or disclosure committee, the procedures set forth in *supra* note 112 would apply: first, the company must file a Form 8-K disclosing the law firm's resignation or termination and must explain the reasons for this occurrence; second, the law firm in the company's Form 8-K must explain its position regarding its resignation or termination. Effectively implemented, this procedure should further enhance the independence of counsel for the underwriter, thereby facilitating the conducting of meaningful due diligence on an ongoing basis.

To further improve this process, the subject issuer should be required to publicly identify specified potential underwriters (such as five such underwriters) that would be deemed finalists, thereby becoming eligible for being selected as the lead underwriter(s) in such issuer's forthcoming shelf registered offering(s). This process enables an issuer to obtain competitive bidding for its shelf registered offerings while incentivizing those underwriters—that are selected as "finalists"—to closely monitor developments concerning that issuer, including (after execution of confidentiality agreements) attending informational sessions with underwriter's counsel and the issuer's independent (audit or disclosure) committee. Combined with the continuous due diligence performed by underwriter's counsel and the independent committee's proactive role in the disclosure process, this measure provides an additional level of meaningful diligence.[115]

The foregoing solution proffered is not perfect. The specter of conflict of interest is diminished but not eliminated as underwriter's counsel is selected by an independent committee of the subject issuer. Other possibilities, however, such as a cooling-off period for the selected underwriter to conduct due diligence and retain its legal counsel, are problematic due to the rapid transitions of the securities markets where market windows can rapidly and unpredictably close.[116] Compared to the other proposals presented, the promulgation by SEC rule of the recommended measures set forth herein should generate a significantly higher level of due

[115] *See* Herb Frerichs, Jr., *Underwriter Due Diligence Within the Integrated Disclosure System—If It Isn't Broke, Don't Fix It*, 16 Sec. Reg. L.J. 386 (1989); Edward F. Greene, *Determining the Responsibilities of Underwriters Distributing Securities Within an Integrated Disclosure System*, 56 Notre Dame Law. 755 (1981); Comment, *Underwriter Due Diligence: It's [Not] a Whole New Ballgame*, 61 SMU L. Rev. 1633 (2008); Note, *The Impact of the SEC's Shelf Registration Rule on Underwriter's Due Diligence Investigations*, 51 Geo. Wash. L. Rev. 767 (1983).

Undoubtedly, shelf registration has accentuated the competition among underwriters. As compared to yesteryear when an issuer typically would maintain long-term relationships with its underwriter(s), the presence of competitive bidding has altered this landscape as "there no longer is assurance of a continuing relationship between issuer and underwriter." Greene, *supra*, 56 Notre Dame Law. at 791. Due to these competitive pressures, in the shelf registration setting, underwriters may take business risks without undertaking sufficient verification regarding the contents of the registration statement. *See* Marc I. Steinberg, *Securities Regulation: Liabilities and Remedies* § 5.04 (2020) (stating that "adoption of the integrated disclosure system comes at a time of intense competition among underwriters"); sources cited *supra* note 92. *See generally* Charles J. Johnson et al., *Corporate Finance and the Securities Laws* (6th ed. 2019).

[116] *See* Securities Act Release No. 6499 (1983) (stating that the flexibility of the shelf registration rule "enables a registrant to time its offering to avail itself of the most advantageous market conditions . . . by being able to meet 'market windows' ").

diligence exercised by underwriters in shelf registered offerings than currently is the practice.

V. Conclusion

This chapter has focused on the Securities Act registration framework. Key principles that should apply are that: absent sufficient business justification, all material information should be disclosed in securities offerings; the concept of materiality in narrative disclosure should be defined in a consistent manner; and incorporation by reference should be permitted only for those companies whose securities trade in an efficient market. Further, while the SEC has made commendable adjustments to facilitate capital raising and has provided market participants with greater comfort in the securities offering process, it too often has relaxed regulatory and statutory provisions to the detriment of investors. In this regard, the Commission utilizes its Section 28 exemptive authority in an unduly expansive manner without sufficient analysis whether a specified measure is consistent with investor protection. Lastly, in the context of incorporation by reference and shelf registered offerings, the dilemma faced by outside directors and underwriters in performing their due diligence functions can be largely ameliorated by: for outside directors, the presence of a vibrant disclosure committee (comprised solely of outside directors) that is actively engaged in the issuer's disclosure process; and, for underwriters, with the implementation of adequate measures as set forth herein, the retention by the subject company's audit or disclosure committee of a reputable law firm to conduct continuous due diligence on the prospective underwriter's behalf.

5

Federalization of Corporate Governance

I. Introduction

Although the federal securities laws are premised on the concept of disclosure of adequate and accurate information to enable investors and the securities markets to make informed decisions,[1] the federalization of corporate governance is a phenomenon that now is well entrenched.[2] Granted that the states (particularly Delaware) remain the primary regulators of the relations among a subject corporation, its fiduciaries, and its shareholders,[3] federal law nonetheless impacts corporate governance practices in a meaningful manner.[4] Through

[1] *See Securities and Exchange Commission v. Zandford*, 535 U.S. 813, 819 (2002) (stating that "Congress sought to substitute a philosophy of full disclosure for the philosophy of caveat emptor"); *Ernst & Ernst v. Hochfelder*, 425 U.S. 185, 195 (1976) (stating that the Securities Act of 1933 "was designed to provide investors with full disclosure of material information concerning public offerings of securities" and that the Securities Exchange Act of 1934 "was intended principally to protect against manipulation of stock prices . . . and to impose regular reporting requirements on companies whose stock is listed on national stock exchanges."). Note that the 1964 amendments extend the periodic reporting requirements to enterprises whose securities trade over the counter provided the subject company meets the asset and shareholder thresholds (§ 12(g) of the Securities Exchange Act, 15 U.S.C. § 78l(g)). *See* the Securities Acts Amendments of 1964, Pub. L. No. 88-467, 78 Stat. 565 (1964).

[2] *See infra* discussion notes 8–85 and accompanying text.

[3] *See Santa Fe Industries, Inc. v. Green* 430 U.S. 462 (1977); American Law Institute, *Principles of Corporate Governance: Analysis and Recommendations* (1994); William L. Cary, *Federalism and Corporate Law: Reflections Upon Delaware*, 83 Yale L.J. 663 (1974); Jill E. Fisch, *Leave It to Delaware: Why Congress Should Stay Out of Corporate Governance*, 37 Del. J. Corp. L. 731 (2013); Mark J. Loewenstein, *Delaware as Demon: Twenty-Five Years after Professor Cary's Polemic*, 71 Colo. L. Rev. 497 (2000).

[4] *See, e.g., infra* notes 8–85 and accompanying text. Corporate governance has been described as "a system of overlapping legal, regulatory, organizational, and contractual mechanisms designed to protect the interests of a company's owners (the shareholders) and limit opportunistic behavior by corporate managers who control the company's operations." International Organization of Securities Commissions (IOSCO), June 2009 Final Report of the Task Force, *Protection of Minority Shareholders in Listed Issuers*, and February 2005 Final Report of the Task Force, *Strengthening Capital Markets Against Financial Fraud*, available at https://www.iosco.org/library/pubdocs/pdf/IOSCOPD295.pdf and https://www.iosco.org/library/pubdocs/pdf/IOSCOPD192.pdf. Stated somewhat differently, corporate governance may be viewed as "a reaction to agency problems, associated with the separation between owners and managers" in a publicly-held corporation. Andra Beltratti, *The Complementarity Between Corporate Governance and Corporate Social Responsibility*, The Geneva Papers 373, 375 (2005), available at https://ideas.repec.org/a/pal/gpprii/v30y2005i3p373-386.html.

Rethinking Securities Law. Marc I. Steinberg, Oxford University Press. © Marc I. Steinberg 2021.
DOI: 10.1093/oso/9780197583142.003.0005

the decades, the scope of federal corporate governance has increased and likely will continue to do so.[5]

A recent book of mine published by Oxford University Press focuses on the federalization of corporate governance in this country from both historical and contemporary perspectives.[6] The book addresses the tension between state corporate law and federal securities law, examines the federal historical developments, and analyzes the impact of major federal legislation enacted since the beginning of this century.[7] The purpose of this chapter is not merely to rehash the contents of this earlier work. Rather, after setting the stage with an overview of federal corporate governance from a historical perspective, the chapter thereafter provides a critical analysis as well as recommending additional measures that should be implemented.

II. The Federalization of Corporate Governance—Historical Overview

A. Congressional and Judicial Overview

During the past two decades, Congress enacted two major Acts—The Sarbanes-Oxley Act of 2002 (SOX)[8] and the Dodd-Frank Wall Street Reform and Consumer Protection Act of 2010 (Dodd-Frank Act)[9]—that significantly enhance the presence of federal corporate governance. While these Acts intensify this federalization process, foundational components existed several decades earlier. Indeed, during the early part of the twentieth century (1903–1914), more than twenty bills were introduced in Congress aiming to

[5] *See* discussion *infra* notes 8–85 and accompanying text.

[6] Marc I. Steinberg, *The Federalization of Corporate Governance* (2018).

[7] *Id.* at 24 (concluding that "the book seeks to provide an original, historical, and contemporary analysis of this important subject [namely, the federalization of corporate governance] that impacts this country's economic well-being in a very fundamental way").

[8] The Sarbanes-Oxley Act of 2002, Pub. L. No. 107-204, 116 Stat. 745 (2002) (enhancing federal regulation by, *inter alia*, mandating that chief executive officers and chief financial officers of subject companies certify the accuracy of SEC periodic reports, federalizing aspects of corporate governance (such as the composition and functions of audit committees), mandating real-time disclosure by Exchange Act reporting companies, enhancing government enforcement, and focusing on professional (accountant and attorney) standards of conduct).

[9] The Dodd-Frank Wall Street Reform and Consumer Protection Act of 2010, Pub. L. No. 111-203, 124 Stat. 1376 (2010) (with respect to federal securities law coverage, enhancing federal corporate governance by mandating greater disclosure of executive officer compensation as well as subject company governance structure, a non-binding shareholder "say-on-pay" vote, and an independent compensation committee as a condition of national stock exchange listing).

require federal chartering and/or adherence to federal minimum substantive standards.[10] These efforts were supported by Presidents Theodore Roosevelt and William Howard Taft.[11] None of these bills were enacted. They nonetheless laid the groundwork for future federalization efforts and may have facilitated the subsequent adoption of significant measures.[12]

During the last few decades, sporadic efforts have been made to enact legislation mandating federal chartering and/or federal minimum standards.[13] For example, one bill sponsored by Senator Howard Metzenbaum in 1980 required, among other matters, that a majority of the members of the board of a publicly-held company (that meets certain financial thresholds) be comprised of independent directors and that federal law codify specified minimum standards of the duties of care and loyalty for corporate directors and officers.[14] More recently, Senator Elizabeth Warren introduced the "Accountable Capitalism Act" seeking to require the federal chartering of relatively large publicly-held companies and to regulate such matters as director conduct, board composition, securities trading, and political expenditures.[15]

---

[10] For a description of these bills, *see* Steinberg, *supra* note 6, at 28–70. Indeed, at no point in U.S. history was the concept of federal incorporation more debated in Congress than the first fifteen years of the twentieth century. *See* Martin I. Urofsky, *Proposed Federal Incorporation in the Progressive Era*, 26 Am. J. Legal Hist. 160, 176 (1982).

[11] In an address delivered to Congress in 1905, President Roosevelt asserted that effective "regulation and supervision [of corporate organizations] can only be effectively exercised by a sovereign whose jurisdiction is co-extensive with the field of work of corporations—that is, by the National Government." Federal Trade Commission, Report on Utility Corporations, No. 69A, at 18 (Sept. 15, 1934). In a similar manner, President Taft opined that federal government control over corporate enterprises was necessary to help prevent the "abuses which have arisen under state control." *Id.*

[12] Nonetheless, several provisions of these bills affected subsequent developments. For example, pursuant to a number of these bills: corporate insiders would be prohibited from serving as directors and officers at competing companies; independent auditor certification of a subject corporation's financial condition would be a requirement for the issuance of a federal charter; and there would be the implementation of federal standards to regulate executive officer compensation. By comparison, today, audited financial statements of publicly-held companies must be included in a number of SEC filings (such as the annual Form 10-K report), dual officer and director positions at competing companies are proscribed by the Clayton Antitrust Act of 1914 (15 U.S.C. § 19), and extensive disclosure as well as an advisory shareholder vote are required with respect to executive remuneration. *See* Marc I. Steinberg, *The Federalization of Corporate Governance—An Evolving Process*, 50 Loy. U. Chi. L.J. 539, 540–41 (2019).

[13] Several bills mandating federal incorporation and/or federal minimum standards also were introduced during the 1914–1930 period. For discussion of these bills, *see* Steinberg, *supra* note 6, at 71–77.

[14] "A Bill to establish Federal minimum standards relating to composition of corporate boards, duties of corporate directors, audit and nomination committees, shareholders' rights, and for other purposes." S. 2567, 96th Cong. (1980). With respect to the eligibility of independent directors, the bill sought to exclude those persons who had a significant personal or economic relationship with the subject company. For discussion of this bill, *see* Steinberg, *supra* note 6, at 77–79.

[15] S. 3348, 115th Cong. (2018). The bill applies to U.S. companies having more than $1 billion in annual revenues, thereby covering over 1,300 of the approximate 2,800 New York Stock Exchange listed companies. The bill requires these companies to:

Federalization of corporate governance efforts also have been made on the judicial level. For example, in *Santa Fe Industries, Inc. v. Green*,[16] an aggrieved shareholder alleged that the gross disparity in the price offered by the company for his stock and its fair value in a cash-out merger[17] amounted to constructive fraud and deception coming within the scope of Section 10(b) of the Securities Exchange Act.[18] Rejecting the plaintiff's position, the Supreme Court held that in order for an actionable Section 10(b) claim to be made there must be deficient disclosure.[19] Breach of fiduciary duty, standing alone, does not constitute a viable claim under the statute.[20] Pointing to the preeminence of state law in this setting, the Court asserted that substantive fairness is a matter of only tangential concern under federal law.[21] Likewise, in a subsequent case addressing the reach of Section 14(e) of the Securities Exchange Act in the tender offer

---

> [O]btain a federal charter from a newly formed Office of United States Corporations at the Department of Commerce [which would obligate] company directors to consider the interests of all corporate stakeholders—including employees, customers, shareholders, and the communities in which the company operates . . . [;] [e]mpower[] workers at United States corporations to elect at least 40% of Board members . . . [;] [r]estrict[] the sale of company shares by the directors and officers of United States corporations [by] prohibit[ing] [such] directors and officers . . . from selling company shares within five years of receiving them or within three years of a company stock buyback . . . [;] [p]rohibit United States corporations from making any political expenditures without the approval of 75% of its directors and shareholders . . . ; and [p]ermit the federal government to revoke the charter of a United States corporation if the company has engaged in repeated and egregious illegal conduct.

Press Release, Elizabeth Warren, *Warren Introduces Accountable Capitalism Act* (Aug. 15, 2018), available at https://www.warren.senate.gov/newsroom/press-releases/warren-introduces-accountable-capitalism-act.

16 430 U.S. 462 (1977).

17 Generally, a cash-out merger occurs when the subject shareholders receive solely cash as consideration for their shares. Such transactions frequently occur in the parent-subsidiary corporation setting. *See, e.g., Weinberger v. UOP, Inc.*, 457 A.2d 701 (Del. 1983).

18 *See* 430 U.S. at 466–67. Notably, the plaintiff prevailed in the U.S. Court of Appeals for the Second Circuit where the court reasoned: "Whether full disclosure has been made is not the critical inquiry since it is the merger and the undervaluation which constitutes the fraud [and that] if there is no valid purpose for the merger, then even the most brazen disclosure of that fact to the minority shareholders in no way mitigates the fraudulent conduct." *Green v. Santa Fe Industries, Inc.*, 533 F.2d 1283, 1292 (2d Cir. 1976), *rev'd*, 430 U.S. 462 (1977).

19 430 U.S. at 477–79.

20 *Id.* at 478 (stating that § 10(b) and Rule 10b-5 should not be extended "to cover the corporate universe").

21 As the Court stated: "Absent a clear indication of congressional intent, we are reluctant to federalize the substantial portion of the law of corporations that deals with transactions in securities, particularly where established state policies of corporate regulation would be overridden." *Id.* at 479. *See generally* Ralph C. Ferrara and Marc I. Steinberg, *A Reappraisal of Santa Fe: Rule 10b-5 and the New Federalism*, 129 U. Pa. L. Rev. 263 (1980). Prior to *Santa Fe*, a number of commentators posited that a federal fiduciary standard was recognized under Section 10(b). *See* Richard W. Jennings, *Federalization of Corporate Law: Part Way or All the Way*, 31 Bus. Law. 991 (1976); Donald E. Schwartz, *Federal Chartering of Corporations: An Introduction*, 61 Geo. L.J. 71 (1972).

context,[22] the Supreme Court held that, provided there is adequate disclosure, tactics undertaken by the target company to fend off a hostile bidder are not actionable under that statute.[23]

B. The SEC's Role in the Federalization of Corporate Governance

Although these federalization efforts were not successful, many other measures were implemented, largely at the behest of the Securities and Exchange Commission. Perhaps the most important is the federalization of insider trading.[24] Frustrated with state law inaction on this subject, the SEC elected to institute an insider trading enforcement action in 1961.[25] Being an administrative proceeding, there was uncertainty regarding its viability until the Second Circuit's en banc decision in *Texas Gulf Sulphur*.[26] There, the appellate

---

[22] 15 U.S.C. § 78n(e). Generally, the term "tender offer" may be defined as "a means frequently used to acquire control of a corporation characterized by active solicitation to purchase a substantial percentage of the target's stock from the target's shareholders at a premium over market price, offered for a limited period of time and that may be contingent upon the tender of a specific number of shares." Marc I. Steinberg, *Understanding Securities Law* 500 (7th ed. 2018).

[23] *Schreiber v. Burlington Northern, Inc.*, 472 U.S. 1, 8 (1985) (reasoning that "all three species of misconduct listed in Section 14(e), i.e., fraudulent, deceptive or manipulative . . . are directed at failure to disclose").

[24] Section 16 of the Securities Exchange Act, 15 U.S.C. § 78p, represents the federalization of two aspects of insider trading. First, Section 16(b) provides that directors, officers, and ten percent shareholders of an equity security must disgorge all profits when they engage in purchases and sales (or sales and purchases) within a six-month period. Second, Section 16(c) prohibits those insiders from engaging in short sales of their corporation's securities. The term "short-sale" generally means "the sale of a security that the seller does not own or that the seller owns but does not deliver." Ralph S. Janvey, *Short Selling*, 20 Sec. Reg. L.J. 270, 271 (1992). By contrast, Section 16(a) is a reporting provision, requiring such insiders timely to report their securities holdings in equity securities and their transactions in such securities to the SEC and the pertinent exchanges. *See* Steinberg, *supra* note 6, at 116–19.

[25] *In re Cady, Roberts & Company*, 40 S.E.C. 907 (1961). This frustration with state law inaction is evidenced by SEC Chairman William Cary's assertion that it is "shocking for business executives to personally profit from their inside information about the corporations they managed [and] that those actions were likely to reduce public confidence . . . in the markets." *Fair to All People, The SEC and the Regulation of Insider Trading, In the Matter of Cady, Roberts & Company*, SEC Historical Society (2006), available at https://www.sechistorical.org. *See* Donald C. Langevoort, *Rereading Cady, Roberts: The Ideology and Practice of Insider Trading Regulation*, 99 Colum. L. Rev. 1319, 1320 (1999) (commenting that "[SEC Chairman] Cary's speeches and writings during and after his chairmanship leave little doubt that he believed that state corporate law was moribund, perhaps even corrupt").

[26] *Securities and Exchange Commission v. Texas Gulf Sulphur*, 401 F.2d 833 (2d Cir. 1968) (en banc), *cert. denied sub nom., Coates v. Securities and Exchange Commission*, 394 U.S. 976 (1964). Commemorating this seminal decision on its golden anniversary, the SMU Law Review published a Symposium Issue. *See Texas Gulf Sulphur 50th Anniversary Symposium Issue*, 71 SMU L. Rev. 625 (2018).

court firmly established that impermissible insider trading constitutes deception within the meaning of the federal securities laws.[27] Although the Supreme Court in subsequent decisions has curtailed the breadth of the insider trading prohibition,[28] the issue is settled that this proscribed conduct comes within the parameters of federal law.[29]

Another key example is the SEC's adoption in 1942 of the shareholder proposal rule.[30] The manner in which shareholder meetings are called and conducted as well as items that may be permissibly placed on the agenda for such meetings have been for more than a century and continue to be within the "sweet zone" of state corporate law.[31] Yet, in what historically may be viewed as

---

[27] 401 F.2d at 848–49. From the decision, it is ambiguous whether the appellate court adopted the parity of information or the access rule. *Cf. id.* at 848 (opining that the federal securities acts' antifraud provisions seek to help ensure that "all investors trading on impersonal exchanges have relatively equal access to material information"), *with id.* at 849 (stating that "anyone in possession of material inside information must either disclose it to the investing public, or if he is disabled from disclosing it in order to protect a corporate confidence, or he chooses not to do so, must abstain from trading in or recommending the securities concerned while such information remains undisclosed").

[28] With respect to Section 10(b) and SEC Rule 10b-5, the Supreme Court has premised insider trading (and tipping) liability on a subject person's breach of fiduciary duty or relationship of trust and confidence. *See, e.g., United States v. O'Hagan*, 521 U.S. 642 (1997) (adhering to the misappropriation theory whereby one breaches a fiduciary duty or relationship of trust and confidence to the source of the information); *Dirks v. Securities and Exchange Commission*, 463 U.S. 646 (1983) (setting forth that, in the tipper-tippee context, violation is based on the tipper conveying the subject information in breach of his or her fiduciary duty or relationship of trust and confidence which is shown by the tipper tipping for personal gain or as a gift); *Chiarella v. United States*, 445 U.S. 222 (1980) (establishing that liability is premised on a breach of fiduciary duty or a relationship of trust and confidence—rejecting both the access and parity of information rationales). By contrast, in the tender offer setting, insider trading liability is based on the parity of information approach. *See* Rule 14e-3, 17 C.F.R. § 240.14e-3. Moreover, although not an insider trading violation, selective disclosure of material nonpublic information by issuers and insiders generally is proscribed by Regulation FD. *See* 17 C.F.R. § 243.100 *et seq*. Additionally, in the criminal context, interpreting the illegality of insider trading under 18 U.S.C. § 1348, the Second Circuit eliminated the *Dirks*' personal benefit test. *See United States v. Blaszczak*, 947 F.3d 19 (2d Cir. 2019), *vacated and remanded on other grounds*, 2021 WL 78043 (U.S. Sup. Ct. 2021). For the author's coauthored treatise on this subject, *see* Marc I. Steinberg and William K.S. Wang, *Insider Trading* (3d ed. 2010).

[29] *See* Steinberg, *supra* note 6, at 120–25 (describing the federalization of insider trading); Roberta S. Karmel, *Prosecution of Tippees Affirmed in Salman v. United States*, 45 Sec. Reg. L.J. 195, 199 (2017) (commenting on the importance that the Supreme Court in *Salman v. United States*, 137 S. Ct. 420 (2016), "unanimously approved insider trading prosecutions pursuant to Section 10(b) of the Exchange Act and Rule 10b-5 against remote tippees"). For further coverage of insider trading, *see* Chapter 7 herein.

[30] Rule 14a-8, 17 C.F.R. § 240.14a-8. *See* General Rules and Regulations, Solicitation of Proxies Under the Act, Securities Exchange Act Release No. 3347 (1942) (discussing shareholder proposal rule); Louis Loss and Joel Seligman, *Securities Regulation* 1939 (3d ed. 1990) (stating that the 1942 amendments to the SEC's proxy rules included "a provision under which the registrant must include in its [proxy] material a 100-word statement in support of any proposal of a security holder that it opposes").

[31] *See Schnell v. Chris-Craft Industries, Inc.*, 285 A.2d 437 (Del. 1971); *Dodge v. Ford Motor Co.*, 204 Mich. 459, 170 N.W. 668 (1919); *American Hardware Corp. v. Savage Arms Corp.*, 135 A.2d 725 (Del. Ch.), *aff'd*, 136 A.2d 690 (Del. 1957); *Mountain Manor Realty, Inc. v. Buccheri*, 55 Md. App. 185, 461 A.2d 45 (1983); William Meade Fletcher, 5 *Fletcher Cyclopedia of the Law of Private Corporations* ch. 13 (1917).

a surprising development during the midst of World War II, the Commission adopted the shareholder proposal rule.[32] With specified thresholds,[33] the rule entitles eligible shareholders to have their precatory proposals included in the subject corporation's proxy statement.[34] Although the rule today (namely, Rule 14a-8)[35] contains specified exceptions enabling a company to exclude a requested proposal from its proxy statement,[36] proponents through the decades have utilized the rule to promote their economic, political, and social causes.[37] Not surprisingly, Rule 14a-8 has both keen supporters[38] and harsh critics who seek its repeal.[39] Having celebrated its seventy-fifth anniversary in 2017, the rule

---

[32] *See* sources cited *supra* note 30.

[33] In 2020, the SEC raised the shareholder eligibility threshold and placed longer ownership time requirements. *See* Securities Exchange Act Release No. 89964 (2020). Under the revised Rule 14a-8(b), three alternative thresholds exist whereby a shareholder must show continuous ownership of at least: "[1] $2,000 of the company's securities for at least three years; [2] $15,000 of the company's securities for at least two years; or [3] $25,000 of the company's securities for at least one year." SEC Press Release No. 2020-220 (2020). The Commission also increased "the levels of shareholder support a proposal must receive to be eligible for resubmission at the same company's future shareholders meetings." *Id. See* Paul Kiernan, *SEC Adds Hurdles to Investor Proposals*, Wall St. J., Sept. 24, 2020, at A1 (stating that the SEC "raised the bar for investors to submit proposals for a vote at companies' annual meetings, a win for executives who have bristled at shareholder efforts to influence corporate policies on social and political issues."). Pursuant to the previous thresholds, in order to submit a shareholder proposal, the eligible security holder "must have continuously held at least $2,000 in market value, or 1% of the company's securities entitled to be voted on the proposal at the meeting for at least one year by the date [such security holder] submit[s] the proposal [and such security holder] must continue to hold those securities through the date of the meeting." Former Rule 14a-8(b)(1), 17 C.F.R. § 240.14a-8(b)(1).

[34] Note that the shareholder proposal may be excluded by the subject company if the shareholder does not comply with the procedural requirements or the proposal's content comes within a substantive basis for exclusion. *See* George S. Geis, *Ex-Ante Corporate Governance*, 41 J. Corp. L. 609, 614 (2016) (stating that "a corporation must include a shareholder proposal in its proxy materials unless the proposal suffers from a procedural defect or falls within one of thirteen grounds for exclusion"). Under Rule 14a-8, shareholder proposals are recommendations and not binding.

[35] 17 C.F.R. § 240.14a-8.

[36] *See* Rule 14a-8(i)(1)–(13), 17 C.F.R. § 240.14a-8(i)(1)–(13). These thirteen exclusions are summarized in Shareholder Proposals, SEC Division of Corporation Finance, Staff Legal Bulletin No. 14 (2001). For a relatively recent high-profile case where the shareholder proposal was held to be properly excluded, *see Trinity Wall Street v. Wal-Mart Stores, Inc.*, 792 F.3d 323 (3d Cir. 2015) (holding shareholder proposal recommending that the company institute a more uniform approach for its policies regarding perceived immoral or dangerous products it sells (such as guns equipped with magazines that hold greater than ten rounds of ammunition) properly excludable pursuant to Rule 14a-8(i)(7) as the proposal dealt with a matter concerning the company's ordinary business).

[37] *See* Steinberg, *supra* note 6, at 163–77 (addressing shareholder proposals during the last seventy years that recommended, for example, such measures as that the subject company abolish segregation in its business practices, enhance diversity, and refrain from making napalm). *See generally* Marilyn B. Cane, *The Revised SEC Shareholder Proxy Proposal System: Attitudes, Results and Perspectives*, 11 J. Corp. L. 57 (1985); Virginia J. Harnisch, *Rule 14a-8 after Reagan: Does It Protect Social Responsibility Shareholder Proposals?*, 6 J.L. & Pol. 415 (1990); Donald E. Schwartz, *The Public-Interest Proxy Contest—Reflections on Campaign GM*, 69 Mich. L. Rev. 419 (1971).

[38] *See* discussion in Patrick J. Ryan, *Rule 14a-8, Institutional Shareholder Proposals, and Corporate Democracy*, 23 Ga. L. Rev. 97 (1988); sources cited *supra* note 37.

[39] *See* Stephen M. Bainbridge, *Revitalizing SEC Rule 14a-8's Ordinary Business Exclusion: Preventing Shareholder Micromanagement by Proposal*, 85 Fordham L. Rev. 705 (2016); Susan W. Liebeler, *A*

is not easily rescinded. In this respect, the shareholder proposal rule is a striking illustration of the federalization of corporate governance that emanates from the near beginning of federal securities regulation.[40]

Through the decades, the SEC has taken further actions that impact corporate governance. At times, the Commission has sought to influence substantive fairness through the guise of disclosure. Two examples follow. First, dissatisfied with the Supreme Court's decision in *Santa Fe* holding that a disclosure deficiency must exist in order to state a Section 10(b) right of action,[41] the Commission adopted Rule 13e-3 that requires the subject person to disclose whether it reasonably believes that a going-private acquisition is fair or unfair to unaffiliated shareholders and the reasons supporting that position.[42] Hence, by means of disclosure, the SEC influences substantive fiduciary conduct in this setting.[43] Second, the Commission requires extensive disclosure of management compensation and related party transactions.[44] Indeed, over fifty years ago, the Commission held that the failure to disclose management self-dealing in the subject corporation's registration statement was actionable, reasoning that such information was "germane to an evaluation of the integrity of . . . management."[45] Accordingly, through the process of disclosure, applicable SEC rules seek to promote enhanced corporate governance practices.

Proposal to Rescind the Shareholder Proposal Rule, 18 Ga. L. Rev. 425 (1984); Alan R. Palmiter, *The Shareholder Proposal Rule: A Failed Experiment in Merit Regulation*, 45 Ala. L. Rev. 879 (1994).

[40] *See* Steinberg, *supra* note 6, at 190 (stating that the shareholder proposal rule "should be recognized as a vintage asset—a Rule that has symbolized for 75 years that vibrant federal corporate governance at times is an appropriate vehicle for ameliorating state law shortcomings").

[41] *Santa Fe Industries, Inc. v. Green*, 430 U.S. 462 (1977); discussion *supra* notes 16–21 and accompanying text.

[42] *See* Rule 13e-3(e), 17 C.F.R. § 240.13e-3(e); Schedule 13E-3, item 8, 17 C.F.R. § 13e-100; Regulation M-A, item 1014, 17 C.F.R. § 240.1014; Securities Exchange Act Release No. 16075 (1979). Stated succinctly, a going-private transaction occurs by merger or other acquisition whereby a publicly-held corporation becomes privately-held and its stockholders are cashed out. *See supra* note 17 for defining the term "cash-out merger." Failure to adhere to the requirements of Rule 13e-3 gives rise to private and government enforcement actions. *See, e.g.*, *Howing Co. v. Nationwide Corp.*, 826 F.2d 1470 (6th Cir. 1987); *In the Matter of FSC Corp.*, 22 SEC Docket 1374 (SEC 1981).

[43] *See* Steinberg, *supra* note 6, at 138 (stating that "although *Santa Fe* precluded Section 10(b) from being applied with respect to the substantive fairness of a going-private transaction, Rule 13e-3 indirectly accomplishes this result to a significant degree by means of its rigorous disclosure mandates"); Harold N. Iselin, Note, *Regulating Going-Private Transactions: SEC Rule 13e-3*, 80 Colum. L. Rev. 782, 787 (1980) (contending that "rule 13e-3 does in effect regulate substantive fairness through item 8's requirement that the issuer state its reasonable belief that the transaction is fair or unfair").

[44] *See* Items 402, 404 of Regulation S-K, 17 C.F.R. §§ 229.402, 229.404. This subject also is addressed in Chapter 2 herein.

[45] *In re Franchard Corp.*, 42 S.E.C. 163, [1964–1966 Transfer Binder] Fed. Sec. L. Rep. (CCH) ¶ 77,113, at 82,043 (1964) (also opining that the "quality" of executive officers is of "cardinal importance" to investors). *See Maldonado v. Flynn*, 597 F.2d 789, 796 (2d Cir. 1979) (stating that "since self-dealing presents opportunities for abuse of a corporate position of trust, the circumstances

On occasion, the Commission has gone beyond disclosure directly to impact the substance of the affected transaction. One such example is the SEC's adoption of the all-holders rule[46] in response to the Delaware Supreme Court's holding in *Unocal v. Mesa Petroleum Co.*[47] In that decision, the court held that a target company's selective tender offer excluding the hostile bidder from participating constituted an appropriate defensive measure undertaken by the board of directors.[48] Disagreeing with this position, the SEC's all-holders rule prohibits exclusionary tender offers, requiring publicly-held companies to make such offers available to all shareholders.[49] In practical effect, the Commission's mandate "reversed" a decision rendered by the preeminent state court in company law matters. In so doing, the all-holders rule provides a vivid illustration of the SEC's activism in federalizing an aspect of corporate governance nearly two decades prior to the enactment of the Sarbanes-Oxley Act.[50]

---

surrounding corporate transactions in which directors have a personal interest are directly relevant to a determination of whether they are qualified to exercise stewardship of the company"). *See generally* Ralph C. Ferrara, Richard M. Starr, and Marc I. Steinberg, *Disclosure of Information Bearing on Management Integrity and Competency*, 65 Nw. U. L. Rev. 555 (1981).

[46] *See* Rules 13e-4, 14d-10, 17 C.F.R. §§ 240.13e-4, 240.14d-10. In another context, responding to the increasing use by companies of disparate voting rights as a defensive mechanism to fend off hostile takeover bids, the SEC adopted Rule 19c-4 in 1988. With certain exceptions, Rule 19c-4 prohibited exchanges from listing the securities of companies that had such disparate rights, thereby seeking to federalize a one share, one vote rule. Invalidating the rule, the appellate court held that the SEC lacked the requisite authority. Otherwise, the court reasoned that "the Commission would be able to establish a federal corporate law by using access to national capital markets as an enforcement mechanism." *Business Roundtable v. Securities and Exchange Commission*, 905 F.2d 406, 412 (D.C. Cir. 1990). For more coverage of Rule 19c-4, *see* Chapter 8 herein.

[47] *Unocal v. Mesa Petroleum Co.*, 493 A.2d 946 (Del. 1985).

[48] *Id.* at 958 (holding that "there was directorial power to oppose the Mesa tender offer, and to undertake a selective stock exchange made in good faith and upon a reasonable investigation pursuant to a clear duty to protect the corporate enterprise").

[49] A related rule requires that the best price paid to any shareholder tendering its shares also must be paid to all other shareholders who tender their shares. *See* sources cited *supra* note 46.

[50] *See* Securities Exchange Act Release No. 23421 (1986) (reasoning that "while commentators have asserted that the Commission's authority under this provision is limited to regulating disclosure[,] [i]t is clear, however, that in adopting the Williams Act, Congress granted to the Commission broad rulemaking authority in Section 13(e) to determine the most appropriate regulatory scheme for issuer tender offers . . . [encompassing the] adoption of substantive regulations"). As another example in this context, the SEC adopted Rule 14d-2(b), 17 C.F.R. § 240.14d-2(b), defining the commencement of a tender offer, in an effort to preempt several state takeover statutes prior to the Supreme Court's decision in *Edgar v. MITE Corp.*, 457 U.S. 624 (1982). *See* Securities Exchange Act Release No. 16384 (1979). Generally, unlike many state takeover statutes which required advance disclosure of specified information prior to commencing a tender offer, Rule 14d-2(b) generally provides that a tender offer commences upon announcement of the number of shares sought to be purchased and the price to be offered. Thus, Rule 14d-2(b) created a seemingly insurmountable conflict between many state takeover statutes and federal law. *See* Comment, *The Validity of State Takeover Statutes: SEC Rule 14d-2(b) and Post-Kidwell Federal Decisions*, 38 Wash. & Lee L. Rev. 1025 (1981); discussion Chapter 8 herein.

The all-holders rule should not be viewed in isolation. For decades, enforcement proceedings instituted by the SEC have impacted corporate governance.[51] In several of these actions, the Commission successfully has obtained broad-ranging types of undertakings, including that the subject company appoint new directors,[52] legal counsel,[53] consultants,[54] and monitors,[55] all of whom must be independent. Dating back to the 1970s,[56] the SEC's use of undertakings influencing corporate governance practices continues to be invoked as an enforcement strategy.[57] In this way, the Commission's utilization of such undertakings has a positive impact on normative corporate governance practices.[58]

C. More Recent Legislation Federalizing Corporate Governance

Perhaps somewhat unnoticed from this perspective, prior to the enactment of the Sarbanes-Oxley Act in 2002, Congress passed legislation in 1990 that federalized an important aspect of corporate governance: authorizing the use

---

[51] These proceedings whereby the SEC procured meaningful ancillary relief date back to the 1970s. *See, e.g., SEC v. Mattel*, [1974–1975 Transfer Binder] Fed. Sec. L. Rep. (CCH) ¶ 94,807 (D.D.C. 1974) (mandating that the company appoint independent directors constituting a majority of its board of directors who are deemed "satisfactory" to the company and the SEC).

[52] *Id. See Securities and Exchange Commission v. Occidental Petroleum Corp.*, [1980 Transfer Binder] Fed. Sec. L. Rep. (CCH) ¶ 82,622 (SEC 1980) (among other undertakings, requiring appointment of a new director "satisfactory" to the SEC).

[53] *See, e.g., Securities and Exchange Commission v. Lockheed Aircraft Corp.*, [1975–1976 Transfer Binder] Fed. Sec. L. Rep. (CCH) ¶ 95,509 (D.D.C. 1976) (retention of special independent legal counsel tasked to investigate and report). *See generally* Samuel H. Gruenbaum and Martin A. Oppenheimer, *Special Investigative Counsel: Conflicts and Roles*, 33 Rutgers L. Rev. 965 (1981).

[54] *Securities and Exchange Commission v. Occidental Petroleum Corp.*, [1980 Transfer Binder] Fed. Sec. L. Rep. (CCH) ¶ 82,622 (SEC 1980) (ordering retention of an independent consulting firm with respect to environmental issues impacting the company).

[55] *See, e.g., In re JH Partners, LLC*, [2015–2016 Transfer Binder] Fed. Sec. L. Rep. (CCH) ¶ 81,158 (SEC 2015) (requiring retention of independent compliance monitor).

[56] *See* proceedings cited *supra* notes 51, 53.

[57] *See, e.g., In re The Port Authority of New York and New Jersey*, [2016–2017 Transfer Binder] Fed. Sec. L. Rep. (CCH) ¶ 81,573 (SEC 2017) (ordering appointment of independent consultant); *SEC v. Avon Products, Inc.*, 46 Sec. Reg. & L. Rep. (BNA) 872 (SEC 2014) (requiring appointment of a monitor). *See generally* James Doty and Brad Bennett, *Independent Consultants in SEC Enforcement Actions*, 43 Rev. Sec. & Comm. Reg. 259 (2010).

[58] These undertakings ordinarily are procured through the consent negotiation process whereby the defendant, while agreeing to the undertakings, neither admits nor denies the allegations contained in the SEC's complaint. *See generally* Marc I. Steinberg and Ralph C. Ferrara, *Securities Practice: Federal and State Enforcement* §§ 3:60–3:66 (2d ed. 2001 & ann. supp.); William B. McLucas et al., *"Neither Admit Nor Deny" Settlements from the Stanley Sporkin Era: Wise Policy or Outdated Enforcement Notion?*, 43 Sec. Reg. L.J. 29 (2015).

of an officer and director bar to be levied against an individual who violates the securities laws' antifraud provisions coupled with a finding of "substantial unfitness."[59] Notably, the imposition of a bar order may be permanent or for a period of time and extends to serving in such capacity in any publicly-held company.[60] The Sarbanes-Oxley Act modified this standard to that of "unfitness" (from that of "substantial unfitness").[61] Hence, the officer and director bar sanction preempts state corporate governance in a fundamental area—namely, the eligibility to serve in such capacity pursuant to applicable state law.

In this century, the Sarbanes-Oxley and Dodd-Frank Acts have accelerated the pace of the federalization of corporate governance. For example, among other measures,[62] these Acts, in conjunction with SEC and stock exchange rules, provide that publicly-traded companies must: (1) have a majority of independent directors;[63] (2) have an audit committee comprised solely

---

[59] The Securities Enforcement Remedies and Penny Stock Reform Act of 1990, Pub. L. No. 101-429, 104 Stat. 931 (1990) (enhancing the SEC's enforcement remedies including the levying of money penalties, cease and desist orders, and officer and director bars).

[60] *See* § 20(e) of the Securities Act, 15 U.S.C. § 77t(e); § 21(d)(2) of the Securities Exchange Act, 15 U.S.C. § 78u(d)(2). Even prior to the passage of this legislation, the SEC had success in procuring the officer and director bar sanction. *See, e.g., Securities and Exchange Commission v. Techni-Culture, Inc.*, [1973–1974 Transfer Binder] Fed. Sec. L. Rep. (CCH) ¶ 94,501 (D. Ariz. 1974). For a relatively high-profile case on this issue, *see Securities and Exchange Commission v. Posner*, 16 F.3d 520 (2d Cir. 1994).

[61] Section 305 of the Sarbanes-Oxley Act, *amending*, §§ 8A, 20(e) of the Securities Act, §§ 21(d)(2), 21C of the Securities Exchange Act. As a relatively recent example, Elon Musk pursuant to a consent decree stepped down as chairman of Tesla for a minimum three-year period. In addition, among other undertakings, Tesla agreed to the appointment of two new independent directors. *See Elon Musk Settles SEC Fraud Charges; Tesla Charged With and Resolves Securities Law Charge*, SEC Press Release No. 2018-226 (2018).

[62] As examples, other provisions are: (1) CEO and CFO certifications of SEC periodic reports; (2) executive clawback provisions; (3) specified "blackout" periods prohibiting insiders from trading; (4) auditor and management assessment of internal controls; (5) "real-time" disclosure; (6) reporting of insider transactions; (7) creation of the Public Company Accounting Oversight Board (PCAOB); (8) financial analysts' conflicts of interest; (9) disclosure as to bifurcation of the board chair and CEO positions; (10) enhanced SEC enforcement measures; and (11) greater criminal penalties. *See generally* John T. Bostelman, Robert E. Buckholz, Jr., and Marc R. Trevino, *Public Company Deskbook: Sarbanes-Oxley and Federal Government Requirements* (2d ed. 2011); James Hamilton and Ted Trautmann, *Sarbanes-Oxley Act of 2002—Law and Explanation* (2002); Steinberg, *supra* note 6, at 191–262; Symposium, 39 Loy. U. Chi. L. Rev. No. 3 (2008); Symposium, 105 Mich. L. Rev. No. 8 (2007); Kit Addleman, *The Impact of Dodd-Frank on Public Companies*, 38 Sec. Reg. L.J. 181 (2010); Charles W. Murdock, *The Dodd-Frank Wall Street Reform and Consumer Protection Act: What Caused the Financial Crisis and Will Dodd-Frank Prevent Future Crisis?*, 64 SMU L. Rev. 1243 (2011).

[63] *See* New York Stock Exchange Listed Company Manual § 303A; Nasdaq, Inc. Stock Market Rules § 5605(b); Securities Exchange Act Release No. 48745 (2003) (approving proposed stock exchange rules generally requiring that a listed company's board of directors be comprised of a majority of independent directors).

of independent directors who are to undertake specified responsibilities;[64] (3) have a compensation committee whose members are all independent directors;[65] (4) generally refrain from making company loans to directors and executive officers;[66] (5) adopt a code of ethics for its officers, directors, and employees;[67] and (6) provide their shareholders with an advisory vote on executive compensation.[68] These mandates highlight the extent to which the federal securities laws today impact substantive conduct that was previously within the exclusive purview of the states with respect to corporate governance practices.[69] They serve as a reminder that in times of crisis, where the perception exists that the states either have failed or are incapable of reigning in corporate fiduciary excesses, the invocation of federal regulation may prevail.[70]

---

[64] Section 301 of the Sarbanes-Oxley Act; Rule 10A-3, 17 C.F.R. § 240.10A-3. The audit committee of a listed company must be comprised of all independent directors who receive no compensation (including, for example, consulting fees) from the company other than their remuneration for serving as directors of such company. Rule 10A-3 directs that an audit committee undertake specified tasks, including, for example: "(1) appointing, setting the compensation for, retaining, and overseeing the company's outside auditors; (2) addressing disagreements that may arise regarding financial reporting matters between management and the outside auditor; (3) implementing procedures for the receipt, retention, and handling of complaints submitted by employees concerning questionable accounting and/or auditing matters; (4) engaging, when appropriate, independent counsel and other advisers that are deemed necessary to carry out the audit committee's duties; and (5) insisting that the company sufficiently fund payment for such advisers." Steinberg, *supra* note 6, at 196–97.

[65] Section 952 of the Dodd-Frank Act, *adding*, § 10C to the Securities Exchange Act, 15 U.S.C. § 78j-3; SEC Rule 10C-1, 17 C.F.R. § 240.10C-1. *See* discussion in Steinberg, *supra* note 6, at 208–10.

[66] Section 402 of the Sarbanes-Oxley Act, *adding*, § 13(k) of the Securities Exchange Act. Generally, some types of loans are allowed if they are provided in the ordinary course of business by the corporation and are extended to the insider on the same terms as loans made to the general public. For criticism of this provision and SOX as a whole, *see* Roberta Romano, *The Sarbanes-Oxley Act and the Making of Quack Corporate Governance*, 114 Yale L.J. 1521, 1539 (2005) (stating that "[b]ecause executive loans in many cases appear to serve their purpose of increasing managerial stock ownership, thereby aligning managers' and shareholders' interests, the blanket prohibition of executive loans in SOX is self-evidently a public policy error").

[67] *See* § 406 of the Sarbanes-Oxley Act (requiring the SEC to adopt rules requiring that a subject corporation disclose whether it has promulgated a code of ethics covering its senior financial officers); Item 406 of Regulation S-K, 17 C.F.R. § 229.406 (requiring such disclosure); New York Stock Exchange Listed Company Manual § 303A.10 (requiring that listed companies "adopt and disclose a code of business conduct and ethics for directors, officers, and employees, and promptly disclose any waivers of the code for directors or executive officers"); Nasdaq, Inc. Stock Market Rule § 5610 (adopting similar listing rule); Securities Exchange Act Release No. 48745 (2003) (approving NYSE and Nasdaq rule proposals).

[68] Section 951 of the Dodd-Frank Act, *adding*, § 14A to the Securities Exchange Act, 15 U.S.C. § 78n-1. *See* Securities Exchange Act Release No. 63768 (2011). For further discussion on this subject, *see infra* notes 147–173 and accompanying text.

[69] *See* discussion in Steinberg, *supra* note 6, 191–262.

[70] *Id.* at 292–93 (positing that "if financial debacles of significant magnitude were to ensue, accompanied by perceptions of permissive federal or state law standards (thereby leaving a gap to norms that should be remedied), this country once again may witness congressional enactment of expansive corporate governance legislation").

D. Federalization of Corporate Governance Benefitting Corporate Interests

The foregoing discussion may suggest that the federalization of corporate governance tends to favor investors over corporate interests. In times of deregulation, capital formation zeal, and disdain of perceived vexatious plaintiffs' litigation, the opposite has occurred: federalization that favors corporate fiduciaries', financial intermediaries', and promoters' interests to the detriment of investors. The use of federal preemption is the path that this process frequently undertakes. For example, seeking to expand capital formation, Congress in 1996 enacted the National Securities Markets Improvement Act of 1996 (NSMIA),[71] which preempted the states from regulating exempt offerings pursuant to the SEC Rule 506 exemption.[72] Such action was appropriate, Congress believed, due to the lack of uniformity between federal and state law and that several states imposed standards that were viewed as unduly stringent.[73] The effect of this legislation is that, although prospective investors are not as protected to the degree that they were prior to NSMIA, the prospect of capital raising is enhanced.[74]

On the litigation front, enactment of the Private Securities Litigation Reform Act of 1995 (PSLRA),[75] followed by the Securities Litigation Uniform Standards Act of 1998 (SLUSA),[76] effectively curtailed numerous investor claims.[77]

---

[71] Pub. L. No. 104-290, 110 Stat. 3416 (1996) (preempting state regulation of securities registration and exemptions thereto in regard to "covered" securities as specified therein).

[72] Section 18(b)(4)(F) of the Securities Act, 15 U.S.C. § 77r(b)(4)(F). More recently, the SEC preempted the states from regulating offerings that are exempt pursuant to Tier 2 of Regulation A. *See* SEC Rules 251–263, 17 C.F.R. §§ 230.251–263. The SEC's adoption of the Tier 2, Regulation A exemption prompted a number of states to seek its invalidation. This effort failed. *See Lindeen v. Securities and Exchange Commission*, 825 F.3d 646 (D.C. Cir. 2016) (upholding the validity of Tier 2 of Regulation A preemption). This subject is discussed in Chapter 3 herein.

[73] *See* Mark A. Sargent, *The New Regulation D: Deregulation, Federalism and the Dynamics of Regulatory Reform*, 68 Wash. U. L.Q. 225 (1990) (discussing the lack of uniformity as well as the states adhering to a more zealous regulatory approach).

[74] Another example is Section 201(a) of the JOBS Act (Jumpstart Our Business Startups Act of 2012), Pub. L. No. 112-106, 126 Stat. 306 (2012). That provision seeks to enhance capital formation by directing the SEC to amend Rule 506 to allow for the use of advertising and general solicitation in such Rule 506 offerings if all the purchasers are accredited investors. *See* Rule 506(c), 17 C.F.R. § 230.506(c); Securities Act Release No. 9415 (2013) (adopting release); discussion Chapter 3 herein.

[75] Pub. L. No. 104-67, 109 Stat. 737 (1995).

[76] Pub. L. No. 105-353, 112 Stat. 3227 (1998).

[77] Hence, no state common law or securities law claim may be brought in a class action coming within SLUSA. Another consequence is that due to the PSLRA's rigorous pleading requirements and the U.S. Supreme Court's limitation of primary liability under Section 10(b) and Rule 10b-5, collateral actors, such as bankers and attorneys, today are sued with far less frequency than was the situation prior to the Court's holding in *Central Bank of Denver v. First Interstate Bank of Denver*, 511 U.S. 164 (1994) (ruling no aider and abettor liability in private actions under § 10(b) and Rule 10b-5). Subsequent Supreme Court decisions further narrowed the reach of Section 10(b) liability. *See Janus Capital Fund, Inc. v. First Derivative Traders*, 131 S. Ct. 2296, 2302 (2011) (holding that to be liable as

Among other provisions,[78] the PSLRA imposes a discovery stay until and unless the plaintiff fends off a motion to dismiss[79] as well as creating a challenging burden for plaintiffs to hurdle with respect to contesting the veracity of forward-looking statements made by publicly-held companies.[80] Reacting to this legislation, plaintiffs increasingly instituted securities class actions in the state courts, most notably California.[81] Enacting SLUSA, Congress constrained this strategy by requiring that, with certain exceptions, securities class actions involving nationally traded securities must be brought in federal court with only federal law applying.[82] SLUSA's federal preemption is expansive, mandating that the action

the "maker" of a material misrepresentation under Rule 10b-5(b) one must have "ultimate authority over the statement, including its content and whether and how to communicate it"); *Stoneridge Investment Partners, LLC v. Scientific-Atlanta, Inc.*, 552 U.S. 148, 159 (2008) (rejecting scheme to defraud theory as plaintiffs were unable to show the requisite element of reliance and reasoning "no member of the investing public had knowledge, either actual or presumed, of respondents' deceptive acts during the relevant time"). More recently, in a government enforcement action, the Supreme Court extended Section 10(b) and Rule 10b-5(a) and (c) liability exposure to those persons who knowingly disseminate materially false statements. *See Lorenzo v. Securities and Exchange Commission*, 139 S. Ct. 1094 (2019) (also holding liability exposure under § 17(a)(1) of the Securities Act). Because of *Stoneridge*'s reliance requirement, *Lorenzo* is unlikely to be helpful to plaintiffs in the private litigation context. With respect to the PSLRA's rigorous pleading requirements, see *infra* note 79. For further discussion, *see* Chapter 6 herein.

[78] By way of example, the PSLRA contains provisions addressing plaintiff certification of the class complaint, method for determining the "most adequate plaintiff" to serve as lead plaintiff, limitation on lead plaintiff's recovery, limitation on plaintiffs' attorney fees, settlement notice to class members, attorneys' fees awarded to prevailing parties in abusive litigation, and limitation on "windfall" damages. *See Private Securities Litigation Reform Act Joint Explanatory Statement of the Committee of Conference* (1995).

[79] Section 21D(b) of the Securities Exchange Act, 15 U.S.C. § 78u-4(b). *See Tellabs, Inc. v. Makor Issues & Rights, Ltd.*, 551 U.S. 308, 314 (2007) (holding that "an inference of scienter must be more than merely plausible or reasonable—it must be cogent and at least as compelling as any opposing inference of nonfraudulent intent").

[80] Section 27A of the Securities Act, 15 U.S.C. § 77aa-1; Section 21E of the Securities Exchange Act, 15 U.S.C. § 78u-1. *See Slayton v. American Express Company*, 604 F.3d 769, 773 (2d Cir. 2010) (holding that in order to "be protected under the first prong of the safe harbor, . . . a forward-looking statement must be both identified as such and accompanied by meaningful cautionary statements identifying the important factors that could cause actual results to differ materially from those in the forward-looking statement [and, with respect to the second prong of the] safe harbor provision . . . dismissal [is required] if the plaintiffs do not prove that the forward-looking statement . . . was . . . made or approved by [an executive officer] with actual knowledge by that officer that the statement was false or misleading").

[81] *See* Joseph Grundfest et al., *Securities Class Action Litigation in 1998: A Report to NASDAQ From the Stanford Law School Securities Class Action Clearinghouse*, 1070 PLI/Corp. 69 (1998) (stating that "since passage of the [PSLRA], a substantial portion of class action litigation has shifted from federal to state court in an apparent attempt to evade the Act's provisions").

[82] *See* § 16(f) of the Securities Act, 15 U.S.C. § 28(f) of the Securities Exchange Act, 15 U.S.C. § 78bb(f). SLUSA's exceptions include individual actions, derivative suits, and class actions in the merger and acquisition contexts. *See Merrill Lynch, Pierce, Fenner & Smith, Inc. v. Dabit*, 547 U.S. 71 (2006) (applying SLUSA preemption to state law holder claims); Richard W. Painter, *Responding to a False Alarm: Federal Preemption of State Securities Fraud Causes of Action*, 84 Cornell L. Rev. 1 (1998).

must be instituted in federal court and prohibiting the attachment of ancillary state law claims.[83]

Hence, the federalization of corporate governance is an evolving process. The past century has witnessed periods of stagnation and activism. Under the Trump administration, this federalization process benefited publicly-held corporations and their fiduciaries.[84] Historically, the pendulum is likely to swing at some point due to a change in the administration or the onset of a financial crisis.[85] At that time, a more active pro-investor urgency may emerge, signaling the embracement of enhanced federal corporate governance standards. From this perspective, the next section of this chapter recommends additional corporate governance measures that should be adopted on the federal level that should prove beneficial to investors and the securities markets.

III. Recommended Federal Corporate Governance Standards

This section of the chapter addresses gaps in the corporate governance framework and recommends the implementation of improved standards on the federal level. Because of the potentially massive scope of this undertaking, the following discussion focuses on several key corporate governance enhancements. Significantly, two of these enhancements are addressed later in this book and will be covered at that time: first, the need for comprehensive legislation regulating insider trading, and, second, the propriety

[83] *See* sources cited *supra* note 82. On the other hand, securities class actions involving nationally traded companies that allege solely Securities Act claims may continue to be brought in state court. *See Cyan, Inc. v. Beaver County Employees Retirement Fund*, 138 S. Ct. 1061 (2018). In *Salzberg v. Sciabacucchi*, 227 A.3d 102 (Del. 2020), the Delaware Supreme Court upheld the validity of a provision in the subject company's certificate of incorporation providing that federal Securities Act claims must be brought exclusively in federal court. For further coverage, *see* Chapter 6 herein.

[84] *See* Binyamin Appelbaum and Jim Tankersley, *The Trump Effect: Business, Anticipating Less Regulation, Loosens Purse Strings*, N.Y. Times, Jan. 1, 2018, available at https://www.nytimes.com/2018/01/01/us/politics/trump-businesses-regulation-economic-growth.html; Greg Ip, *Donald Trump's Pro-Business Stance Inspires, But Economic Growth Isn't Assured*, Wall St. J., Jan. 4, 2017, available at https://www.wsj.com/articles/donald-trumps-pro-business-stance-inspires-but-economic-growth-isnt-assured-1483551580; Ben Protess et al., *Trump Administration Spares Corporate Wrongdoers Billions in Penalties*, N.Y. Times, Nov. 3, 2018, available at https://www.nytimes.com/2018/11/03/us/trump-sec-doj-corporate-penalties.html. According to one source, the SEC under the Trump administration "is slowly taking the shackles off corporations." Katanga Johnson, *Investors Left Exposed as Trump's SEC Gives America Inc. a Helping Hand*, Reuters, Nov. 5, 2019, available at https://www.reuters.com/article/us-usa-sec-publiccompanies-analysis/investors-left-exposed-as-trumps-sec-gives-america-inc-helping-hand-idUSKBN1XG0TA.

[85] Indeed, due to the presence of financial scandals, the Sarbanes-Oxley Act was enacted during the presidency of George W. Bush. *See* sources cited *supra* note 62.

of federalizing substantive conduct in the merger and acquisition (including tender offer) setting.

A. Composition of Boards of Directors and Board Committees

Traditionally, the composition of boards of directors and committees thereof is a matter of state corporate law.[86] To an increasing degree, however, federal law and stock exchange regulation play an important role in this function. For example, since 1977, listed companies on the New York Stock Exchange (NYSE) have been required to have an audit committee comprised entirely of independent directors.[87] Today, the stock exchanges require that listed companies have a majority of independent directors on their respective board of directors.[88] And, as mandated by the Dodd-Frank Act, compensation committees must be comprised solely of independent directors.[89] From a regulatory enforcement perspective, for decades, the SEC has successfully procured bar orders precluding corporate fiduciaries who have been subject to a fraud sanction from serving as a director or officer of any publicly-held company.[90] In addition, in undertakings entered into pursuant to the consent negotiation process, subject companies have agreed to appoint new independent directors deemed "satisfactory" to the Commission.[91] And, as a last example, pursuant to the Dodd-Frank Act, the SEC was authorized to adopt rules providing certain large shareholders access to the subject company's proxy statement to nominate a specified number of directors.[92]

---

[86] *See, e.g.*, American Bar Association, Model Business Corporation Act §§ 8.01–8.11, 8.20–8.25, 8.30–8.31; 8 Del. Gen. Corp. L. §§ 141, 144.

[87] *See* Securities Exchange Act Release No. 13346 (1977) (approving NYSE rule); Steinberg, *supra* note 6, at 141 (stating that "[r]ather than engaging in the controversial task of implementing an audit committee rule itself, the Commission 'persuaded' the NYSE to undertake this task"). For the composition and functions of audit committees post Sarbanes-Oxley, *see* discussion *supra* note 64 and accompanying text; *infra* note 95 and accompanying text.

[88] *See* NYSE Listed Company Manual § 303A.01; Nasdaq, Inc. Stock Market Rules § 5605(b).

[89] *See* § 952 of the Dodd-Frank Act, *amending*, § 10C of the Securities Exchange Act, 15 U.S.C. § 78j-3.

[90] In order for such a director or officer bar to issue, the fiduciary must have engaged in fraudulent conduct (such as a violation of § 10(b) of the Securities Exchange Act) and that such conduct demonstrates unfitness to serve in those capacities. *See supra* notes 59–61 and accompanying text.

[91] *See* proceedings cited *supra* notes 52, 61.

[92] *See* § 971 of the Dodd-Frank Act, *amending*, § 14(a) of the Securities Exchange Act, 15 U.S.C. § 78n(a); discussion *infra* notes 132–138 and accompanying text.

In certain contexts, although traditionally within the purview of state company law,[93] federal law also tasks boards of directors and committees with certain functions. For example, the Commission occasionally has brought enforcement actions against directors who allegedly failed to exercise adequate oversight with respect to their respective company's disclosure and reporting obligations.[94] With respect to board committees, federal legislation sets forth processes and standards to which audit and compensation committees must adhere.[95]

The foregoing discussion evidences that federal law is no stranger to board and committee composition and responsibilities. Therefore, engaging in the process of proffering recommendations for reform in this area is not as far-reaching as at first blush may appear to be the situation. Such recommendations are necessary due to state law deficiency in declining to prescribe appropriate norms in this context as well as failing adequately to address aberrant conduct by boards of directors. Unduly

[93] *See, e.g.*, sources cited *supra* note 86.

[94] *See, e.g.*, *Securities and Exchange Commission v. Krantz*, SEC Press Release No. 2011-238 (2011) (announcing settlement with outside directors who allegedly "ignor[ed] repeated red flags of a massive securities fraud . . . [and] abdicate[d] the duties they owed to the company and shareholders"); *Securities and Exchange Commission v. Marchese*, Securities Exchange Act Release No. 47732 (2003) (settlement whereby the SEC asserted that the subject director who served on the company's audit committee "completely failed to exercise any oversight over [the company's] financial reporting, exercising no care to ensure that the company had appropriate internal controls and that its financial records were accurate"); *In the Matter of W.R. Grace & Co.*, Securities Exchange Act Release No. 39157 (1997) (in a § 21(a) Report, emphasizing "the affirmative responsibilities of corporate officers and directors to ensure that the shareholders who they serve receive accurate and complete disclosure of information required by the . . . federal securities laws").

[95] With respect to the specified tasks that audit committees must undertake, *see* discussion *supra* note 64. It may be asserted that, provided that the corporation can afford the fees, the audit committee should retain different legal counsel than that retained by the corporation. Separately retained counsel whose sole client within the corporate enterprise is the audit committee should help ensure the rendering to the committee of independent legal advice. *See* Marc I. Steinberg, *Attorney Liability After Sarbanes-Oxley* § 9.02 (2018) (stating that after Sarbanes-Oxley, "many audit committees of publicly-held companies today rely on independent counsel"). *See generally* Frederick D. Lipman and Joseph G. Poluka, *Audit Committees Need Independent Counsel*, Directors & Boards (2016), available at https://www.blankrome.com/publications/audit-committees-need-independent-counsel.

With respect to the independence of the members of a subject company's compensation committee, that assessment is based on such factors as: "[1] the source of compensation of a member of the board of directors of an issuer, including any consulting, advisory or other compensatory fee paid by the issuer to such member of the board of directors; and [2] whether a member of the board of directors of an issuer is affiliated with the issuer, a subsidiary of the issuer or an affiliate of a subsidiary of the issuer." Section 10C of the Securities Exchange Act, 15 U.S.C. § 78j-3(a)(3). *See* SEC Rule 10C-1, 17 C.F.R. § 240.10C-1. The statute and Rule 10C-1 specify criteria that the compensation committee is to assess when determining whether to retain a compensation consultant. In addition, the committee may engage other advisers, including independent legal counsel. Applicable stock exchange rules help implement the directives set forth in the statute and SEC rule, addressing a compensation committee's composition, functions, and obligations. *See* NYSE Listed Company Manual § 303A.05; Nasdaq, Inc. Stock Market Rules § 5605(d). For further discussion, *see* Steinberg, *supra* note 6, at 208–10, 247–52.

broad application of the business judgment rule[96] as well as excessive deference to decisions made by independent directors[97] are ubiquitous. As examples: the business judgment rule is premised on concepts of gross negligence,[98] a standard that would make one potentially liable for exemplary damages in other contexts;[99] with respect to directors' inaction to engage in adequate oversight, lack of good faith is predicated on "(a) the directors *utter[] fail[ure]* to implement *any* reporting or information system or controls, or (b) having implemented such a system or controls, [they] *consciously* failed to monitor or oversee its operations thus disabling themselves from being informed of risks or problems requiring their attention"; and, with respect to related party transactions, giving excessive deference to determinations made by outside directors[100] even though acknowledging the prospect of bias by such directors favoring insider interests.[101] Aware of this lack of adequate state regulation, Congress has acted on a piecemeal basis, such as the prohibition against company loans to directors and executive officers.[102] Accordingly, providing federal standards for the criteria of independent director status thus should enhance corporate governance practices redounding to the benefit of companies and their stakeholders.[103]

Pursuant to the Dodd-Frank Act and SEC action implementing that directive, a subject company must disclose whether the same individual serves as

---

[96] Generally, the business judgment rule provides a shield from successful challenge provided that the subject board of directors (1) made a deliberative decision, (2) that was made with the board being adequately informed, (3) without a disabling conflict of interest, and (4) had a rational basis. *See Smith v. Van Gorkom*, 488 A.2d 858 (Del. 1985); *Aronson v. Lewis*, 473 A.2d 805 (Del. 1984); *Gimbal v. Signal Companies*, 316 A.2d 599 (Del. Ch.), *aff'd*, 316 A.2d 619 (Del. 1974). Any such deliberative decision made by the subject board of directors also must be lawful to come within the protection of the business judgment rule. *See Miller v. American Telephone & Telegraph Co.*, 507 F.2d 759 (3d Cir. 1974).

[97] *See, e.g.*, *Marciano v. Nakash*, 535 A.2d 400 (Del. 1987) (applying business judgment rule when interested director transaction received approval by independent directors). A number of statutes are even more expansive. For example, under Texas law, it appears that, once an interested director transaction is approved in good faith by disinterested directors after being aware of the material facts as specified in the statute, the transaction is valid and enforceable. Texas Bus. Org. Code § 21.418.

[98] *See, e.g.*, *Aronson v. Lewis*, 473 A.2d 805, 812 (Del. 1984) (holding that "under the business judgment rule director liability is predicated upon concepts of gross negligence"); *Black's Law Dictionary* 1246 (11th ed. 2019) (defining gross negligence as "[a] lack of even slight diligence or care").

[99] *See Black's Law Dictionary*, *supra* note 98, at 1246 (defining gross negligence as "[a] conscious, voluntary act or omission in reckless disregard of a legal duty and of the consequences to another party, who may typically recover exemplary damages").

[100] *Stone ex rel. AmSouth Bancorporation v. Ritter*, 911 A.2d 362, 368–69 (Del. 2006).

[101] *See, e.g.*, *Zapata Corp. v. Maldonado*, 430 A.2d 779, 787 (Del. 1981) (stating that "we must be mindful that directors are passing judgment on fellow directors in the same corporation").

[102] *See supra* note 66 and accompanying text.

[103] *See* discussion *infra* notes 104–146 and accompanying text.

chief executive officer and chair of its board of directors.[104] If so, disclosure must be made whether a lead independent director has been designated "and what specific role [such] lead director plays in the leadership of the board."[105] The company also must explain why "its leadership structure is appropriate given [its] specific characteristics or circumstances."[106]

Fortunately, an increasing number of companies are splitting the positions of CEO and board chair.[107] The benefits are clear: The CEO no longer is monitoring herself but is subject to greater independent oversight; the distinct prospect of CEO dominance is lessened with respect to his role with the board and with other internal as well as outside constituents; control of the agenda for board of directors meetings is better allocated between the CEO and board chair; the flow of internal corporate information to the outside directors, including adverse developments, is improved; significant decisions are more likely to be subject to greater scrutiny and, if deemed appropriate, challenged; and, even with the presence of committees comprised solely of independent directors (such as the audit, compensation, and nominating/corporate governance committees), independent director empowerment is reasonably likely to be enhanced.[108] Although visionary CEOs who

---

[104] Section 14B of the Securities Exchange Act, 15 U.S.C. § 78n-2; Item 407 of Regulation S-K, 17 C.F.R. § 229.407.

[105] Item 407(h) of Regulation S-K, 17 C.F.R. § 229.407(h).

[106] *Id.* As another example, the company must identify the procedures, if any, that shareholders must follow in order to communicate with the board of directors. If no such procedures exist, the company must explain the reasons for such absence.

[107] *See* Jeanne Sahadi, *Should CEOs Double as Board Chairs? Increasingly S&P Companies Are Saying No*, CNN Bus. (Oct. 31, 2019), available at https://www.cnn.com/2019/10/31/success/ceo-board-chair-split-role/index.html (stating that 53% of S&P 500 companies have separate CEOs and board chairs). Nonetheless, as set forth in a Spencer Stuart Report, with frequency, the separate board chair has a prior substantive relationship with the company, such as being a former CEO of the company. Spencer Stuart, *The Non-Executive Chairman—Offering New Solutions* 1 (2007), available at https://www.spencerstuart.com/~/media/pdf%20files/research%20and%20insight%20pdfs/cornerstone-of-the-board-the-nonexecutive-chairman_21jan2008.pdf.

[108] *See* Thomas Gryta and Theo Francis, *When Things Get Tough, Companies Split Chairman, CEO Roles*, Wall St. J., Nov. 3, 2019, available at https://www.wsj.com/articles/when-things-get-tough-companies-split-chairman-ceo-roles-11572778801?mod=searchresults&page=1&pos=2 (stating that "a record number of big U.S. companies are dividing their leadership roles—often after a crisis"); Joseph Mandato and William Devine, *Why the CEO Shouldn't Also Be the Board Chair*, Harv. Bus. Rev. (2020), available at https://hbr.org/2020/03/why-the-ceo-shouldnt-also-be-the-board-chair (stating that publicly-held companies should "be wary of giving the CEO job and the board chair job to one person" and that proposals to separate the CEO and chair roles "have become the most common type of governance proposal submitted by shareholders"); Mengqi Sun, *More U.S. Companies Separating Chief Executive and Chairman Roles*, Wall St. J., Jan. 23, 2019, available at https://www.wsj.com/articles/more-u-s-companies-separating-chief-executive-and-chairman-roles-11548288502 (stating that the move "to separate the positions is rooted in the notion a stand-alone chairman can act as a counterweight to a stand-alone chief executive").

also serve as board chair may result in impressive performance in some companies,[109] the detrimental consequences of such dual service generally outweigh the potential benefits.[110] Accordingly, Congress should enact legislation mandating that, as a condition of having its securities listed on a national stock exchange, a company must have an independent director who serves as chair of its board of directors. In view that (with few exceptions) any such enterprise already must have a majority of independent directors,[111] this mandate should not pose an unduly difficult task for the vast majority of publicly-held companies.[112]

Generally, studies have concluded that sound corporate governance practices enhance shareholder value.[113] The presence of independent

[109] *See* Michael Stockham, *Split Decisions: The Pros and Cons of Separating CEO and Chairman Roles*, Corp. Compliance Insights (2013), available at https://www.corporatecomplianceinsights.com/split-decisions-the-pros-and-cons-of-separating-ceo-and-chairman-roles/.

[110] *See* discussion in Mandato and Devine *supra* note 108.

[111] *See supra* note 63 and accompanying text. A key exception is that controlled companies where another entity, group or individual holds greater than fifty percent of the voting power are not required to have boards comprised of a majority of independent directors. *See* New York Stock Exchange Listed Company Manual § 303A; Nasdaq, Inc. Stock Market Rules § 5605(b).

[112] For smaller publicly-held companies that are challenged to recruit qualified independent directors, this mandate may prove problematic. Agreeing to serve as chair of the board of directors in such a company involves a very different analysis than serving as an outside director without the chair role. After all, both the responsibility assumed and the prospect of liability are magnified in the board chair role. After further study, if smaller publicly-held companies cannot feasibly recruit independent board chairs, then the federal statute may provide an exception for such companies that lack a specified amount of assets and number of shareholders. A suggested alternative would be to require such companies to name a lead independent director who would: act, among other functions, as an important communicator between management and the outside directors, preside over executive sessions where management ordinarily is excluded from attending, lead the performance evaluation of the CEO, and serve as a contact source for key shareholders who have issues that they want addressed. *See* Marion Plouhinec, *The Role of the Lead Independent Director*, Harv. Law School Forum on Corp. Gov. (Nov. 25, 2018), available at https://corpgov.law.harvard.edu/2018/11/25/the-role-of-the-lead-independent-director/. Nearly all S&P 500 companies appoint a lead director, assuming that the CEO also serves as board chair. *See* Spencer Stuart, *A Closer Look at Lead and Presiding Directors* 1 (2005) (stating that "as of mid-2005, 94% of S&P 500 boards had designated a lead or presiding director"), available at https://www.spencerstuart.com/~/media/pdf%20files/research%20and%20insight%20pdfs/cornerstone-of-the-board_29mar2006.pdf.

The subject of separating the CEO and board chair positions is also a pressing issue outside of the United States. *See, e.g.*, Zabihollah Rezaee, *Business Sustainability, Corporate Governance, and Organizational Ethics* 511 (Timothy Fogarty ed., 2019) (stating that "[c]orporate governance best practices in Europe support separation of the chair and CEO roles").

[113] *See, e.g.*, Paul Gompers, et al., *Corporate Governance and Equity Prices*, 118 Q.J. Econ. 107 (2003) (abstract: finding that "firms with stronger shareholder rights had higher firm value, higher profits, higher sales growth, lower capital expenditures, and made fewer corporate acquisitions"); R. Christopher Small, *The Vote Is Cast: The Effect of Corporate Governance on Shareholder Value*, Harv. Law School Forum on Corp. Gov. (May 5, 2010), available at https://corpgov.law.harvard.edu/2010/05/05/the-vote-is-cast-the-effect-of-corporate-governance-on-shareholder-value/ (stating that "our results portray a picture in which good corporate governance is rewarded by the market, and generates performance improvements in the long-run").

directors who are competent, diligent, have integrity and a good familiarity with the subject company are key criteria for financial performance.[114] Although board collegiality may be beneficial,[115] the lack of diversity all too prevalent in publicly-traded companies is unacceptable.[116] Today, pursuant to stock exchange rules, generally so long as a director does not have a "material relationship" with the subject company, he is deemed "independent."[117] The result is that outside directors frequently share the same background and views as insiders. They themselves are executives of other publicly-held

---

[114] *See generally* American Bar Association, Corporate Law Committee, *Corporate Director's Guidebook* (7th ed. 2020); American Law Institute, *Corporate Governance: Analysis and Recommendations* (1994). Nicola Faith Sharpe, *The Cosmetic Independence of Corporate Boards*, 34 Seattle U. L. Rev. 1435 (2011).

[115] *See* Arleen Jacobius, *For an Efficient Board, Mutual Respect and a Collegial Culture Are Mandatory*, Pension & Investments, Jan. 12, 2020, available at https://www.pionline.com/governance/efficient-board-mutual-respect-and-collegial-culture-are-mandatory. *But see* Paula Loop, *Is Collegiality Clouding Your Boardroom*, NACD Board Talk, Oct. 17, 2019, available at https://blog.nacdonline.org/posts/collegiality-clouding-boardroom (stating that "boards should consider balancing collegiality by having more dissenters in the room, because too much collegiality can prevent healthy debate and disagreement").

[116] *See* Elizabeth Olson, *Slow Gains for Women and Minorities on Boards of Big U.S. Firms, Study Says*, N.Y. Times, Jan. 15, 2019, available at https://www.nytimes.com/2019/01/15/business/women-minorities-corporate-boards.html (discussing study by the Alliance for Board Diversity which indicated that, while "the percentage of minorities and women on the boards of the largest public companies in the United States has edged up in the last two years, . . . the bulk of corporate directors at such firms continue to be white men").

[117] *See* NYSE Listed Company Manual § 303A.02(a)(i) (stating that a director's independence must be "affirmatively determine[d] by the subject corporation's board of directors," signifying that such director has no "material relationship with the listed company"); Nasdaq, Inc. Stock Market Rules § 5605(a)(2) (defining "independent director" in a similar manner). The rules also apply to a director's immediate family members (including, for example, a spouse, child, parent, sibling, or any other person (other than a domestic employee) who shares such director's home). *See* NYSE Listed Company Manual § 303A.02 Commentary. Both the NYSE and Nasdaq rules in a similar fashion specify situations where a director is deemed not independent. Pursuant to the NYSE framework, a director is not independent in the following situations:

(1) Being an employee or executive officer of the listed company within the last three years;
(2) Having been directly compensated (other than receipt of director and committee fees or payment of deferred compensation based on prior service) more than $120,000 by the listed company within any twelve-month period during the last three years;
(3) Being a current employee or partner of the listed company's internal or external auditor;
(4) Being or having been an executive officer within the past three years of another company where any of the listed company's current executive officers "serves or served" on such other company's compensation committee;
(5) Being a current employee of an enterprise that within any of the past three fiscal years "has made payments to, or received payments from, the listed company for property or services," provided such amount "exceeds the greater of $1 million, or 2% of such other [enterprise's] consolidated gross revenues."

Steinberg, *supra* note 6, at 235, *summarizing*, NYSE Listed Company Manual § 303A.02(b). *See* Nasdaq Stock Market Rules § 5605(a)(2).

companies, have similar life experiences, and are prone to "structural bias."[118] This absence of diversity all too often may generate greater CEO dominance, lack of critical oversight by the board, and disappointing financial performance.[119]

Although many corporations have taken steps to improve board diversity,[120] significantly more substantive measures are needed. Absent congressional directive, it is unlikely that necessary action will be implemented. Accordingly, Congress should enact legislation to enhance board diversity with the following directives. *First*, the definition of "independent director" should be expanded beyond the current definition to exclude not only those persons who have a material relationship but also individuals who have any type of financial relationship (other than securities ownership) with the company as well as those who have any type of significant family or other personal relationship (such as friendship) with an executive officer (or who has had such a relationship in the past).[121] This measure would significantly enhance board member independence and lessen the presence of structural bias. Indeed, granted that gender and racial diversity are beneficial, it is imperative that a sufficient number of directors have different backgrounds and

---

[118] Generally, structural bias means "the predilection of directors to favor those of the same social or economic class, such as fellow directors or corporate officers." Douglas M. Branson et al., *Business Enterprises: Legal Structures, Governance, and Policy—Cases, Materials, and Problems* 608 (4th ed. 2020). *See infra* note 122.

[119] *See* Neil Amato, *What to Do if Your Board Is Too Friendly*, Financial Management, Nov. 4, 2019, available at https://www.fm-magazine.com/news/2019/nov/corporate-board-refreshment-201922350.html (reporting that "forty-three percent of directors say it is difficult to express a dissenting view inside the boardroom" and that eighteen percent of directors view problematic "collegiality or personal friendships between board members").

[120] *See* Lena Eisenstein, *The Importance of Diversity on Boards*, BoardEffect, Aug. 7, 2019, available at https://www.boardeffect.com/blog/importance-diversity-boards/ (discussing greater recognition of the benefits of gender and racial diversity on corporate boards); Kathy Gurchiek, *Report: Diversity on Boards Growing Slowly But Steadily*, SHRM, June 13, 2019, available at https://www.shrm.org/resourcesandtools/hr-topics/behavioral-competencies/global-and-cultural-effectiveness/pages/report-diversity-on-boards-growing-slowly-but-steadily.aspx (reporting increase in gender and racial diversity comprising the Fortune 500 boards of directors); Subodh Mishra, *U.S. Board Diversity Trends in 2019*, Harv. Law School Forum on Corp. Gov., June 18, 2019, available at https://corpgov.law.harvard.edu/2019/06/18/u-s-board-diversity-trends-in-2019/ (surveying the Russell 3000 companies, reporting increases in the percentage of women and ethnic minorities having board seats).

[121] Hence, all independent directors, not only those who serve on the audit committee, would receive compensation solely for director and committee service. *See* Theo Francis and Joan S. Lubin, *Boards Get More Independent, But Ties Endure*, Wall St. J., Jan. 19, 2016, available at https://www.wsj.com/articles/boards-get-more-independent-but-ties-endure-1453234607 (stating that "outside directors have connections to companies and executives they oversee"). Of course, an independent director also must have the tools to achieve *substantive* independence. As stated by one source: "These tools include time, information, and knowledge, all of which have been recognized as critical to effective decision-making processes." Sharpe, *supra* note 114, at 1435.

experiences.[122] On a related point, for individuals who serve many years as a director of a subject company, there exists the specter of director lethargy as well as co-option (due to the receipt of lucrative remuneration, including attractive stock perquisites).[123] To ameliorate this dilemma, independent directors should have staggered term limits, such as for no longer than five years, with expiration scheduled for each such director in a manner so as to provide for an orderly transition—thereby having a sufficient number of incumbent independent directors in place after each election to help ensure the continuation of an adequate collective corporate knowledge base.[124]

---

[122] *See supra* note 118. For discussion on gender and racial diversity on corporate boards, *see infra* notes 125–131 and accompanying text. As poignantly stated by one source: "The women named to corporate boards may not in fact differ very much in their values, experiences, and knowledge from the men." Katherine Klein, *Does Gender Diversity on Boards Really Boost Company Performance?*, K@W, (Wharton), May 18, 2017, available at https://knowledge.wharton.upenn.edu/article/will-gender-diversity-boards-really-boost-company-performance/. For example, consider IBM's proxy statement for its 2020 annual meeting, available at https://www.ibm.com/annualreport/2019/proxy.html. IBM's board of directors recommended that shareholders vote for each of the following nominees whose employment experiences are as follows: Thomas Bubert ("chief executive officer, AXA, S.A., a multinational insurance firm"), Michael L. Eskew ("retired chairman and chief executive officer, United Parcel Service, Inc., a provider of specialized transportation and logistics services"), David N. Farr ("chairman and chief executive officer, Emerson Electric Co., a diversified manufacturing and technology company"), Alex Gorsky ("chairman and chief executive officer, Johnson & Johnson, a global healthcare products company"), Michelle Howard ("retired admiral, United States Navy"), Arvind Krisha ("chief executive officer of IBM, effective April 6, 2020"), Andrew N. Liveris ("retired chairman and chief executive officer, The Dow Chemical Company, a materials, polymer, chemicals, and biological sciences enterprise"), Frederick William McNabb III ("retired chairman and chief executive officer, The Vanguard Group, Inc., one of the world's largest investment management companies"), Martha E. Pollack ("president, Cornell University, a leading research university that creates new technologies and achieves fundamental breakthroughs in understanding and improving lives around the world"), Virginia M. Rometty ("chairman, president and chief executive officer, IBM, executive chairman of IBM, effective April 6, 2020"), Joseph R. Swedish ("senior advisor and retired chairman, president and chief executive officer, Anthem, Inc., a leading health benefits provider"), Sidney Taurel ("chairman emeritus, Eli Lilly and Company, a pharmaceutical company"), Peter R. Voser ("retired chief executive officer, Royal Dutch Shell plc, a global group of energy and petrochemical companies"), and Frederick H. Waddell ("retired chairman and chief executive officer, Northern Trust Corporation, a financial services company"). The presence of structural bias exists with respect to the vast majority of these nominees who subsequently were elected to IBM's board of directors. Out of the fourteen directors, all but three of the directors (Ms. Howard, Mr. McNabb, and Ms. Pollack) have similar work experiences.

[123] *See* PwC, *PwC's 2019 Annual Corporate Directors Survey* (2019), available at https://www.pwc.com/us/en/services/governance-insights-center/library/annual-corporate-directors-survey.html (stating that "dissatisfaction with fellow directors is at a record high—but boards aren't necessarily replacing the directors who aren't measuring up"); Diane Lerner, *Board of Directors Compensation: Past, Present and Future*, Harv. Law School Forum on Corp. Gov., March 14, 2017, available at https://corpgov.law.harvard.edu/2017/03/14/board-of-directors-compensation-past-present-and-future/ (reporting that common remuneration elements at S&P 500 companies are annual equity grants and cash retainers, with a 2015 median director total compensation of $260,000).

[124] *See* Jon Lukomnik, *Board Refreshment Trends at S&P 1500 Firms*, Harv. Law School Forum on Corp. Gov., Feb. 9, 2017, available at https://corpgov.law.harvard.edu/2017/02/09/board-refreshment-trends-at-sp-1500-firms/ (commenting on "investors' concern . . . over rising director/board tenure" observing that "average director tenure at S&P 1500 firms now stands at a level [of] 8.7 years").

Second, following the lead of California[125] as well as several foreign countries,[126] a minimum number of female directors should be required. For example, the California legislation ultimately requires that a board of directors comprised of six or more members must have a minimum of three women directors.[127] A gender-diverse board is more likely to have broader perspectives, thereby enhancing the quality of deliberations and decision-making.[128] The same also can be said for racially-diverse boards of directors.[129] Various studies evidence that, on average, boards that have women

[125] Calif. Sen. Bill 826 (2018) (applying to national stock exchange companies that are incorporated or headquartered in California). *See* Associated Press, *California Sued Again for Requiring Women on Corporate Boards*, L.A. Times, Nov. 13, 2019, available at https://www.latimes.com/business/story/2019-11-13/california-sued-for-requiring-women-corporate-boards; Rachel Feintzeig, *California Law Spurs Companies to Add Female Directors*, Wall St. J., Dec. 18, 2019, available at https://www.wsj.com/articles/california-law-spurs-companies-to-add-female-directors-11576665000; Richard Vernon Smith, *California Mandates Female Representation on Public Company Boards*, Forbes, Oct. 1, 2018, available at https://www.forbes.com/sites/allbusiness/2018/10/01/california-mandates-female-representation-public-company-boards/#22c56a521775. By the end of calendar 2021: (1) if the board size is six or more members, there must be at least three female directors; (2) if there are five members on the board, there must be at least two female directors; and (3) there must be at least one female director when there are four or fewer members on the board. The statute has been challenged as being unconstitutional under the Fourteenth Amendment's Equal Protection Clause as well as under the California constitution, thus far unsuccessfully. *See, e.g.*, *Meland v. Padilla*, 2020 WL 1911545 (E.D. Cal. 2020) (dismissal on basis of lack of standing).

[126] Countries having gender quotas requiring female directors include: Belgium, Finland, France, Iceland, Israel, Italy, Kenya, Norway, Quebec (Canada), and Spain. *See* Siri Terjesen et al., *Legislating a Woman's Seat on the Board: Institutional Factors Driving Gender Quotas for Boards of Directors*, Northeastern Univ. (online) (2014), available at https://www.academia.edu/23285395/Legislating_a_Woman_s_Seat_on_the_Board_Institutional_Factors_Driving_Gender_Quotas_for_Boards_of_Directors. In 2008, Norway required listed companies to have women comprise at least forty percent of the board, with the specter of corporate dissolution for failure to comply. *See Ten Years On From Norway's Quota for Women on Corporate Boards*, The Economist, Feb. 17, 2018, available at https://www.economist.com/business/2018/02/17/ten-years-on-from-norways-quota-for-women-on-corporate-boards. In 2011, France enacted similar legislation. *See* Claire Zillman, *Need Proof that Companies Can Have Gender Diverse Boards? Look to France*, Fortune, Dec. 3, 2018, available at https://fortune.com/2018/12/03/board-diversity-france/ (stating that out of the 200 largest European corporations, "France, far and away, has by its measure the highest share of women on company boards at 44.2%").

[127] *See* Diana C. Nicholls Mutter, *The Morals of the Women on Corporate Boards Story: Global Board Gender Diversity Efforts Still Need Fairness-Based Arguments to Move Regulation to the Next Chapter*, 53 Int'l Law. 235 (2020) (discussing quotas implemented in several countries to increase women's membership on corporate boards); discussion *supra* note 125.

[128] *See* Erica Hersh, *Why Diversity Matters: Women on Boards of Directors*, Harvard Univ. T.H. Chan School of Public Health (2015), available at https://www.hsph.harvard.edu/ecpe/why-diversity-matters-women-on-boards-of-directors/ (stating that "one way to bring diverse perspectives to an organization is through gender diversity on a board"). *See generally* Douglas M. Branson, *No Seat at the Table: How Corporate Governance and Law Keep Women Out of the Boardroom* (2008); Avivah Wittenberg-Cox, *What Do Countries with the Best Coronavirus Responses Have in Common? Women Leaders*, Forbes, April 13, 2020, available at https://www.forbes.com/sites/avivahwittenbergcox/2020/04/13/what-do-countries-with-the-best-coronavirus-responses-have-in-common-women-leaders/?sh=3914447e3dec.

[129] *See* discussion in Eisenstein, *supra* note 120; Matt Palmquist, *The Advantages of a Diverse Board*, strategy-business.com, June 18, 2015, available at https://www.strategy-business.com/blog/

directors attain higher financial performance.[130] To ensure that the boards of publicly-held companies include an appropriate composition of women members, federal legislation at this time is necessary.[131]

Third, rather than authorizing the SEC to adopt a rule (that was subsequently invalidated by a federal appellate court),[132] a statute should be enacted mandating that the largest shareholder (or group of shareholders) who beneficially owns[133] a minimum of three percent of the voting shares and who has held such shares for at least twelve months be entitled to access

The-Advantages-of-a-Diverse-Board?gko=bf646 (stating that "proponents of diversity argue that minority leaders can provide unique insights and broaden their firms' knowledge networks, bringing their varied perspectives to bear on the complex decision-making process that occurs at the board level"). In 2020, California enacted legislation requiring that all publicly-held corporations with their principal executive office located in California have a specified number of directors from "underrepresented communities." Assembly Bill 979 (2020). The legislation defines a director from an underrepresented community as "an individual who self-identifies as Black, African American, Hispanic, Latino, Asian, Pacific Islander, Native American, Native Hawaiian, or Alaska Native, or who self-identifies as gay, lesbian, bisexual, or transgender." *Id.* § 301.4(e)(1), *amending*, §§ 301, 2115.6 of the California Corporations Code. *See* Anne Steele, *California Sets Diversity Quotas for Boards*, Wall St. J., Oct. 1, 2020, at B1.

130 *See* Stephanie J. Creary et al., *When and Why Diversity Improves Your Board's Performance*, Harv. Bus. Rev., March 27, 2019, available at https://hbr.org/2019/03/when-and-why-diversity-improves-your-boards-performance (discussing benefits of gender diversity on boards of directors); Jena McGregor, *More Women at the Top, Higher Returns*, Wash. Post, Sept. 24, 2014, available at https://www.washingtonpost.com/news/on-leadership/wp/2014/09/24/more-women-at-the-top-higher-returns (stating that "researchers have long found ties between having women on a company's board of directors and better financial performance"); Nancy Sheppard, *The Benefits of Gender Diversity on the Board: The Key Research*, Directors & Boards (2015), available at https://www.directorsandboards.com/articles/singlebenefits-gender-diversity-board-key-research (stating that gender diverse boards outperform those boards having limited diversity). *But see* Klein, *supra* note 122 (stating that "rigorous, peer-reviewed academic research [shows that,] despite the intuitive appeal of the argument that gender diversity on the board improves company performance, research suggests otherwise"). *See also* Daniel J. Morrissey, *George Floyd Protests Show Corporations Must Support Racial and Economic Equality*, The Hill, June 4, 2020, available at https://thehill.com/opinion/civil-rights/501259-protests-show-corporations-must-support-racial-and-economic-equality?rnd=1591313467 (describing number of minorities on corporate boards and as C-suite executives as "dismal").

131 Significantly, several other developed countries have enacted legislation requiring a specified percentage of women directors on boards of publicly-listed companies. *See supra* note 126 and accompanying text.

132 *See* § 971 of the Dodd-Frank Act (generally authorizing the SEC to adopt rules granting shareholder access to the subject company's proxy statement and ballot for nominating director candidates for the board of directors); SEC Rule 14a-11, 17 C.F.R. § 240.14a-11. The D.C. Circuit invalidated Rule 14a-11 in *Business Roundtable v. Securities and Exchange Commission*, 647 F.3d 1144, 1148–49 (D.C Cir. 2011) (finding that "the Commission inconsistently and opportunistically framed the costs and benefits of the rule, failed adequately to quantify the certain costs or to explain why those costs could not be quantified, neglected to support its predictive judgments, contradicted itself, and failed to respond to substantial problems raised by commentators").

133 Generally, beneficial ownership entails voting and/or investment power. *See* SEC Rule 13d-3, 17 C.F.R. § 240.13d-3; Securities Exchange Act Release No. 13291 (1977); *Wellman v. Dickinson*, 682 F.2d 355, 365–66 (2d Cir. 1982).

the company's proxy statement to nominate up to twenty-five percent of the board seats up for election.[134] If such shareholder declines to do so, then the next largest shareholder who beneficially owns the requisite three percent and satisfies the one-year holding period may invoke this process.[135] Because access to the company's proxy statement is provided, such shareholders should not be permitted to utilize this avenue to effectuate a change in corporate control.[136] Although certain activist shareholders have been accused of short-termism—seeking to enhance their financial returns at the expense of the subject corporation's long-term best interests[137]—shareholders ought to make that determination on a case-by-case basis. Through the process of corporate democracy, shareholders should exercise their "voice" in their assessment whether these nominees should be elected rather than the incumbent board's candidates. After all, the right of shareholders to elect directors is a fundamental justification providing legitimacy to the separation of ownership and control in publicly-held corporations.[138]

---

[134] Rule 14a-11 "generally entitled the [subject company's] largest shareholder (or largest group of shareholders), who own at least three percent of the shares entitled to be voted and who held such shares for at least three years, to nominate the greater of one director-candidate or up to 25% of the total number of directors who serve on such company's board of directors." Marc I. Steinberg, *Understanding Securities Law* 188 (7th ed. 2018). The recommendation herein provides for a twelve-month holding period. Such a period is sufficiently long to evidence investment intent and has been employed by the SEC in a number of other settings. *See, e.g.*, SEC Rule 14a-8(b), 17 C.F.R. § 240.14a-8 (requiring a one-year holding period as a condition for being eligible to make a shareholder proposal); SEC Rule 144(d)(1)(ii), 17 C.F.R. § 230.144(D)(1)(ll) (setting forth twelve-month holding period for non-affiliates who own restricted securities of a non-reporting issuer).

[135] Stated somewhat differently, any shareholder satisfying the share ownership and holding period criteria would be entitled to access the subject company's proxy statement for this purpose if other larger shareholders decline. This approach allows another significant shareholder to invoke this process if other larger shareholders abstain. A contrary interpretation would incentivize an investor friendly to management to cumulate the largest ownership percentage without intending to invoke this process, thereby making proxy access unavailable to the next largest qualified shareholder.

[136] For those shareholders who seek a change of control, a proxy contest is an available avenue to achieve that objective. *See* Randall S. Thomas and Catherine T. Dixon, *Aranow & Einhorn on Proxy Contests for Corporate Control* (1988).

[137] *See* Harvard Kennedy School, The Hauser Institute for Civil Society, Initiative for Responsible Investment, *A Note on Short-Termism* (2015), available at https://iri.hks.harvard.edu/files/iri/files/tlf-note-on-long-term-investing.pdf (stating that "short-term investment strategies offer immediate rewards, but may have consequences for the long-term [due to that] seeking immediate high returns without accounting for long-term implications may lead to underperformance for long-term investors and, by extension, underperformance for the economy as a whole"). *See generally* Frank Zarb, *When Passive Hedge Funds Decide to Become Activist*, 52 Reg. Sec. & Comm. Reg. 247 (2019).

[138] *See, e.g.*, *Blasius Industries, Inc. v. Atlas Corp.*, 564 A.2d 651, 659 (Del. Ch. 1988) (stating that "the shareholder franchise is the ideological underpinning upon which the legitimacy of directorial power rests [and] is critical to the theory that legitimates the exercise of power by some (directors and officers) over vast aggregations of property that they do not own"); Adolphe Berle and Gardiner Means, *The Modern Corporation and Private Property* (1932) (addressing the separation of ownership and control in publicly-held companies). *See also Kurz v. Holbrook*, 989 A.2d 140, 178 (Del. Ch. 2010), *aff'd in part, rev'd in part on other grounds*, 992 A.2d 377 (Del. 2010) ("What legitimizes the

And *fourth*, a minimum of one board position should be allocated for employee representation. This measure would effectuate greater board diversity, bring different perspectives to the board, and likely improve employee morale.[139] Indeed, many of the OECD countries[140] mandate worker representation on corporate boards of publicly-held companies.[141] This approach recognizes the significant contributions that an employee representative can make to enhance board deliberations and decisions. Further, as one source has posited, "there is a conviction that in a democratic society, people in power should be accountable to those over whom power is exercised [encompassing] every social institution, including the corporation."[142]

---

stockholder vote as a decision-making mechanism is the premise that stockholders with economic ownership are expressing their collective view as to whether a particular course of action serves the corporate goal of stockholder wealth maximization").

139 The Accountable Capitalism Act, S. 3348, 115th Cong. (2018), introduced by Senator Elizabeth Warren would mandate that nearly fifty percent of NYSE listed companies would be required to have workers comprise at least forty percent of their boards of directors. *See* discussion *supra* note 15. The recommendation proffered herein is significantly milder, mandating that at least one board position be allocated for worker representation. In a number of countries, workers have representation on either a supervisory board or on the board of directors. *See* Andrea Garnero, *What We Do and Don't Know About Worker Representation on Boards*, Harv. Bus. Rev., Sept. 6, 2018, available at https://hbr.org/2018/09/what-we-do-and-dont-know-about-worker-representation-on-boards (discussing worker representation on boards and stating "employee participation on company or supervisory boards can strengthen workers' voice but, critically, it can also improve cooperation with management").

140 OECD (Organization for Economic Cooperation and Development) countries include Australia, Austria, Belgium, Canada, Chile, Czech Republic, Denmark, Estonia, France, Germany, Greece, Hungary, Iceland, Ireland, Israel, Italy, Japan, Korea, Latvia, Lithuania, Luxembourg, Mexico, Netherlands, New Zealand, Norway, Poland, Portugal, Slovak Republic, Slovenia, Spain, Sweden, Switzerland, Turkey, United Kingdom, and United States. OECD, *List of OECD Member Countries—Ratification of the Convention on the OECD* (2019).

141 *See* Garnero, *supra* note 139; Evan McGauchey, *Corporate Law Should Embrace Putting Workers on Boards: The Evidence Is Behind Them*, Harv. Law School Forum on Corp. Gov. (Sept. 17, 2018), available at https://corpgov.law.harvard.edu/2018/09/17/corporate-law-should-embrace-putting-workers-on-boards-the-evidence-is-behind-them/ (stating that "both a majority of European Union countries, and (with Norway) a majority of countries in the Organization for Economic Cooperation and Development have laws for staff on boards").

142 McGauchey, *supra* note 141 (also discussing situations where employees have sat on boards of U.S. publicly-held companies).

Another approach to give stakeholders greater voice is the emergence of stakeholders advisory councils. A number of well-known corporations reportedly have established these councils, including BP, Burger King, Coca-Cola, Nestle, Unilever, and Wells Fargo. *See* Rajesh Chhabara, *Stakeholder Panels—Reaching a Critical Mass*, June 7, 2009, available at https://www.ethicalcorp.com/business-strategy/stakeholder-panels-reaching-critical-mass. The Wells Fargo stakeholder council was formulated as a corporate governance reform arising out of a settled shareholder derivative action based on the bank's wrongful sales practices. *See In re Wells Fargo Derivative Cases*, CJC-18-0044966 (Super. Ct. Cal.); Ben Eisen, *Wells Fargo Settles U.S. Probes*, Wall St. J., Feb. 22–23, 2020, at A1 (reporting that the bank, *inter alia*, paid a $3 billion fine); Wells Fargo, *Wells Fargo Launches Stakeholder Advisory Council*, Dec. 21, 2017, available at https://newsroom.wf.com/press-release/corporate-and-financial/wells-fargo-launches-stakeholder-advisory-council (stating that the Council would "provide insight, and feedback to the Company's Board of Directors and Senior Management from a stakeholder's perspective [as well as with respect to] diversity, social inclusion

Some sources will view these proposals as an unwarranted intrusion on state corporate governance. Viewed in context, this perception is inaccurate. After all, as previously discussed, Congress and the SEC already have adopted significant measures impacting boards of directors and committees thereof.[143] Other recommendations strengthen provisions that were previously adopted[144] or implement principles that are ensconced in the laws of developed countries.[145] And, a number of recommendations elevate what may be viewed as customary corporate governance practices to the status of

---

and economic sustainability"). Provided that these stakeholder councils are comprised of diligent and objective members having adequate diversity that engage in meaningful dialogue with the board and management, this development is positive.

[143] *See* discussion *supra* notes 24–83, 87–106 and accompanying text. In this regard, the presence and obligations of independent directors in the investment company context is another example of the federalization of corporate governance. The importance and functions of independent directors in the investment company setting are set forth in *SEC Interpretation: Matter Concerning Independent Directors of Investment Companies*, Investment Company Release No. 24083 (1999):

> The critical role of independent directors of investment companies is necessitated, in part, by the unique structure of investment companies. Unlike a typical corporation, a fund generally has no employees of its own. Its officers are usually employed and compensated by the fund's investment adviser, which is a separately owned and operated entity. The fund relies on its investment adviser and other affiliates—who are usually the very companies that sponsored the fund's organization—for basic services, including investment advice, administration, and distribution.
>
> Due to this unique structure, conflicts of interest can arise between a fund and the fund's investment adviser because the interests of the fund do not always parallel the interests of the adviser. An investment adviser's interest in maximizing its own profits for the benefit of its owners may conflict with its paramount duty to act solely in the best interests of the fund and its shareholders.
>
> In an effort to control conflicts of interest between funds and their investment advisers, Congress required that at least 40% of a fund's board be composed of independent directors. Congress intended to place independent directors in the role of "independent watchdogs," who would furnish an independent check upon the management of funds and provide a means for the representation of shareholder interests in fund affairs.
>
> Independent directors play a critical role in policing the potential conflicts of interest between a fund and its investment adviser. The Act requires that a majority of a fund's independent directors: approve the fund's contracts with its investment adviser and principal underwriter; select the independent public accountant of the fund; and select and nominate individuals to fill independent director vacancies resulting from the assignment of an advisory contract. In addition, rules promulgated under the Act require independent directors to: approve distribution fees paid under rule 12b-1 under the Act; approve and oversee affiliated securities transactions; set the amount of the fund's fidelity bond; and determine if participation in joint insurance contracts is in the best interest of the fund. Each of these duties and responsibilities is vital to the proper functioning of fund operations and, ultimately, the protection of fund shareholders.

[144] The definition of independent director is such an example. *See* discussion *supra* notes 121–142 and accompanying text.

[145] Many countries, for example, require that publicly-listed companies have a specified percentage of female directors on their boards of directors. *See* discussion *supra* notes 126–131 and accompanying text.

legislative directives.[146] Implementation of these recommendations should significantly benefit investors, stakeholders, and the securities markets.

B. Shareholder Say-on-Pay and Related Issues

Pursuant to the Dodd-Frank Act, shareholders have an advisory vote on executive compensation.[147] In addition, that Act directed the SEC to require a subject company to disclose, among other items, the ratio of the CEO's annual total compensation to the median compensation paid to all employees.[148] After several years of delay, this directive went into effect in 2017.[149]

---

[146] As an example, the majority of S&P 500 companies today have different individuals serving as CEO and board chair. The recommendation herein would elevate this practice to a statutory mandate. *See* discussion *supra* notes 104–112 and accompanying text.

[147] Section 951 of the Dodd-Frank Act, *adding*, § 14A of the Securities Exchange Act, 15 U.S.C. § 78n-1. A shareholder advisory vote also must be held with respect to golden parachute compensation arrangements. This subject is discussed in Chapter 8 herein. As set forth in Section 14A, publicly-held companies are required:

> [To] conduct a separate shareholder *advisory* vote to approve the compensation of executives, as disclosed pursuant to Item 402 of Regulation S-K or any successor to Item 402. Section 14A also requires companies to conduct a separate shareholder advisory vote to determine how often an issuer will conduct a shareholder *advisory* vote on executive compensation. In addition, Section 14A requires companies soliciting votes to approve merger or acquisition transactions to provide disclosure of certain "golden parachute" compensation arrangements and, in certain circumstances, to conduct a separate shareholder advisory vote to approve the golden parachute compensation arrangements.

Shareholder Approval of Executive Compensation and Golden Parachute Compensation, Securities Exchange Act Release No. 63768 (2011).

Testimony presented by Ann Yerger, on behalf of the Counsel of Institutional Investors, presented the rationale for supporting this provision:

> [A]n annual, advisory shareowner vote on executive compensation would efficiently and effectively provide boards with useful information about whether investors view the company's compensation practices to be in shareholders' best interests. Nonbinding shareholder votes on pay would serve as a direct referendum on the decisions of the compensation committee and would offer a more targeted way to signal shareholder discontent than withholding votes from committee members. They might also induce compensation committees to be more careful about doling out rich rewards, to avoid the embarrassment of shareowner rejection at the ballot box. In addition, compensation committees looking to actively rein in executive compensation could use the results of advisory shareholder votes to stand up to excessively demanding officers or compensation consultants.

S. Rep. No. 111-176, p. 134 (2010).

[148] Section 953(b) of the Dodd-Frank Act (requiring disclosure of the annual total compensation of all company employees except for the CEO, the CEO's yearly total compensation, and the ratio of these two figures). *See* Item 402(u) of Regulation S-K, 17 C.F.R. § 229.402(u) (requiring such disclosure). *See generally* Deniz Anginer et al., *Should the CEO Pay Ratio Be Regulated?*, 45 J. Corp. L. 451 (2020). Significantly, the pay-ratio rule is inapplicable to certain types of publicly-held companies, including emerging growth companies, smaller reporting companies, and foreign private issuers. *See* § 953(b) of the Dodd-Frank Act.

[149] The pay-ratio rule was adopted by a three to two vote. *See* Securities Exchange Act Release No. 75610 (2015) (requiring pay ratio disclosure "in any annual report, proxy or information statement,

Consisting of such components as salary, bonus, equity rewards, and perquisites, the median compensation for CEOs in 2019 at the largest U.S. publicly-held companies was approximately $13 million.[150] Salary generally accounted for a relatively small fraction of total compensation,[151] with equity awards constituting by far the largest percentage.[152] As reported in the CEO-worker pay ratios, CEOs make approximately 287 times more compensation than the salaried employees in their respective companies[153] as compared to 30 times more in 1978.[154] Phrased differently, CEO compensation during the last four decades has increased approximately 1,000 percent.[155]

---

or registration statement that requires executive compensation disclosure pursuant to Item 402 of Regulation S-K"); SEC Press Release No. 2015-60, *SEC Adopts Rule for Pay Ratio Disclosure* (Aug. 5, 2015) (announcing adoption of "a final rule that requires a public company to disclose the ratio of the compensation of its chief executive officer (CEO) to the median compensation of its employees"). Since its enactment, sustained efforts have been made to repeal the price ratio rule which thus far have failed. *See* Steven A. Bank and George S. Georgiev, *Securities Disclosure as Soundbite: The Case of CEO Pay Ratios*, 60 B.C. L. Rev. 1123, 1138–39 (2019).

[150] *See* Inti Pacheco, *Coronavirus Caps Years of Rich Pay for Most CEOs*, Wall St. J., Mar. 23, 2020, available at https://www.wsj.com/articles/coronavirus-caps-years-of-rich-pay-for-many-ceos-11584960573 (also stating that the impact of the coronavirus "could wipe out hundreds of millions of dollars from executive pay packages and prompt a recalibration of how CEO compensation is set"). Larger compensation amounts were reported by a number of other sources. *See, e.g.*, Lawrence Mishel and Julia Wolfe, *CEO Compensation Has Grown 940% Since 1978*, Economic Policy Institute, Aug. 14, 2019, available at https://www.epi.org/publication/ceo-compensation-2018/ (stating that the "average pay of CEOs at the top 350 firms in 2018 was $17.2 million—or $14 million using a more conservative measure"). As reported in *The Wall Street Journal*, with some frequency, the amount of compensation that CEOs in fact make exceeds the amount that was disclosed. *See* Theo Francis, *CEO's Take-Home Pay Exceeds Disclosure*, Wall St. J., Aug. 26, 2019, at A1.

[151] *See* Chip Cutter and Theo Francis, *CEO Salaries Decline, Stock Awards Remain*, Wall St. J., June 4, 2020, at B1 (reporting that although hundreds of U.S. corporations have reduced CEO salaries due to the impact of the coronavirus, "few [companies] so far changed the equity awards that make up the bulk of executive compensation"); Craig Karmin, *Hyatt Bosses Took Pay Cut But Stand to Gain on Awards*, Wall St. J., April 1, 2020, at B1 (stating that, while Hyatt's CEO was foregoing about $200,000 in salary due to the impact of the coronavirus, his restricted stock awards granted that same month "are valued around $2.7 million, according to public filings"); Pacheco, *supra* note 150 (providing as examples salaries of three CEOs of publicly-held companies that amounted respectively to 10%, 12%, and 16% of total annual compensation).

[152] *See* John Roe and Kosmas Papadopoulos, *2019 U.S. Executive Compensation Trends*, Harv. Law School Forum on Corp. Gov., April 16, 2019, available at https://corpgov.law.harvard.edu/2019/04/16/2019-u-s-executive-compensation-trends/.

[153] See Alexia Fernandez, *CEOs Made 287 Times More Money Last Year Than Their Workers Did*, Vox, June 26, 2018, available at https://www.vox.com/policy-and-politics/2019/6/26/18744304/ceo-pay-ratio-disclosure-2018 (stating that "America's CEOs earned a staggering $14.5 million in 2018, on average, compared to the average of $39,888 that rank-and-file workers made" characterizing "the gap [as] obscene"). This pay differential significantly exceeds that of other developed countries, including Japan (67:1), United Kingdom (84:1), Australia (93:1), Germany (147:1), and Switzerland (148:1). *See* Bank and Georgiev, *supra* note 149, at 1133.

[154] *See* Mishel and Wolfe, *supra* note 150 (reporting that the ratio "was 121-to-1 in 1995, 58-to-1 in 1989, 30-to-1 in 1978, and 20-to-1 in 1965").

[155] *Id.* (reporting that, compared to 1978, 2018 CEO compensation was approximately 940% higher and, utilizing the options-granted measure, more than 1,000% higher).

Many of the CEOs who have the most lucrative compensation arrangements have drawn attention. For example, in 2018, the highest compensated CEO was Tesla's Elon Musk, who earned $513 million.[156] Walt Disney's CEO Bob Iger's compensation of $64 million (1,424 times more than the amount earned by the median Disney employee) was categorized as "insane" by Abigail Disney (granddaughter of Disney cofounder Roy Disney).[157] Walmart's CEO Doug McMillon earned nearly $23 million, while the company's median employee salary was approximately $19,000,[158] placing Walmart among the corporations with the widest pay disparity between the CEO and its employees.[159]

These wide pay gaps, in conjunction with lavish executive compensation, generate negative side effects, including worker demoralization, impairing the sense of organizational community, and perceptions of pay inequity.[160] With the advisory shareholder say-on-pay vote coupled with the internal pay equity disclosure mandate,[161] Congress sought to provide an appropriate solution to this dilemma.[162] In practical effect, however, these say-on-pay

---

[156] *See* Anders Melin et al., *A 300% Surge Makes Pot CEO No. 2 in Pay Ranking After Elon Musk*, Bloomberg, May 17, 2019, available at https://www.bloomberg.com/graphics/2019-highest-paid-ceos/ (reporting that in 2018 Elon Musk's compensation package was $513.3 million, Brendan Kennedy of Tilray, Inc. $256 million, Bob Iger of Walt Disney Co. $146.6 million, Tim Cook of Apple, Inc. $141.6 million, Nikesh Arora of Palo Alto Networks, Inc. $130.7 million, David Zaslav of Discovery, Inc. $122 million, James Heppelmann of PTC Inc. $71.5 million, Stephen Schwarzman of Blackstone Group LP $69.1 million, Tony James of Blackstone Group LP $66.2 million, and Stephen Angel of Linde PLC $66.2 million).

[157] *See* Ainsley Harris, *Disney CEO Bob Iger's Compensation Is "Insane," Says Abigail Disney*, Fast Company, April 19, 2019, available at https://www.fastcompany.com/90333082/disney-ceo-bob-igers-compensation-is-insane-says-abigail-disney.

[158] *See* Matthew Heller, *Walmart CEO's Pay Rises 2% to $22.8 Million*, CFO.com, April 20, 2018, available at https://www.cfo.com/compansation/2018/04/walmart-ceos-pay-rises-2-to-22-8-million/ (stating that the CEO's 2017 compensation was nearly 1,200 times the median Walmart salary or, stated differently, the median Walmart employee's salary was 0.015% of the CEO's annual compensation).

[159] *See* Sarah Nassauer, *At Walmart, the CEO Makes 1,188 Times as Much as the Median Worker*, Wall St. J., April 20, 2018, available at https://www.wsj.com/articles/at-walmart-the-ceo-makes-1-188-times-as-much-as-the-median-worker-1524261608 (also reporting that Walmart globally has more than 2.3 million employees, with approximately 1.5 million U.S. employees).

[160] *See* sources cited in Bank and Georgiev, *supra* note 149, at 1138–41.

[161] *See, e.g.*, Letter from Representative Keith Ellison et al. to Michael Piwowar, Acting Chairman, U.S. Securities and Exchange Commission (Mar. 14, 2017), available at https://www.sec.gov/comments/pay-ratio-statement/cll3-1660758-148835.pdf ("This pay ratio information will benefit investors by giving them valuable information for ascertaining whether company employees are fairly compensated and help them decide how to cast their 'say-on-pay' advisory votes on executive compensation.").

[162] Clearly, through the decades, the states have declined to meaningfully focus on this subject, applying relatively lax principles in this context. *See, e.g.*, *Seinfeld v. Verizon Communications, Inc.*, 909 A.2d 117 (Del. 2006) (denying shareholder's demand to inspect company's books and records regarding executive compensation paid to three executives totaling $205 million over three years

votes pass with regularity. By way of example, in 2018, only forty-nine Russell 3000 companies did not receive successful say-on-pay votes.[163] Failure to receive a successful vote often induced the subject company to make certain adjustments in executive compensation.[164] Nonetheless, lawsuits against directors for allegedly failing to make adequate adjustments in the aftermath of negative say-on-pay votes largely have been unsuccessful.[165]

Given the magnitude of this disparity in CEO and median worker salary, the evident increasing growth of this disparity, and the ineffectual impact of the advisory say-on-pay shareholder vote, more substantive action is appropriate. Three measures are suggested herein. First, Congress should enact a statute placing a ceiling on the percentage disparity between the CEO's

---

on basis that no credible basis was shown that possible wrongdoing occurred); *In re The Walt Disney Company Derivative Litigation*, 906 A.2d 27 (Del. 2006) (applying business judgment rule to hold that directors met their fiduciary obligations in approving generous employment contract and subsequently terminating senior executive without cause, thereby triggering severance payout of approximately $130 million); *Brehm v. Eisner*, 746 A.2d 244, 262 (Del. 2000) (opining that "it is the essence of business judgment for a board to determine if a particular individual warrant[s] large amounts of money, whether in the form of current salary or severance provisions"); *Zupnick v. Goizueta*, 698 A.2d 384 (Del. 1997) (applying business judgment rule upholding option grant of five million shares to CEO in gratitude for past services).

[163] *The Effects of Say on Pay Failures*, Equilar Institute, Oct. 3, 2019, available at https://www.equilar.com/blogs/428-the-effects-of-say-on-pay-failures.html. Similarly, in 2017, seven S&P 500 companies failed to receive say-on-pay approval. *See Say on Pay Vote Results (S&P 500)*, Compensation Advisory Partners, Jan. 25, 2018, available at https://www.capartners.com/cap-thinking/say-on-pay-vote-results-in-the-sp-500/. Overall, say-on-pay advisory votes receive a 92% shareholder approval average. These results, according to a number of sources, evidence that "shareholders are overwhelmingly satisfied with executive compensation packages." Thomas A. Hemphill, *Say-On-Pay Voting: A Five-Year Retrospective*, Wiley Online Library, Feb. 14, 2019, available at https://onlinelibrary.wiley.com/doi/abs/10.1111/basr.12163.

[164] These changes included reducing overall executive compensation and increasing the proportion of long-term incentive plans more strictly dependent upon the company's financial performance. *See* Equilar Institute Report, *supra* note 163.

[165] Note that the statute provides that the shareholder say-on-pay advisory vote "may not be construed to create or imply any change to the fiduciary duties of such issuer or board of directors." Section 14A(c)(2) of the Securities Exchange Act, 15 U.S.C. § 78n-1(c)(2). The overwhelming majority view is that a negative say-on-pay vote does not rebut the application of the business judgment rule. In dismissing a shareholder derivative suit, one court opined that "the Board's failure to change course in light of the [negative] say-on-pay vote does not give rise to a substantial likelihood of personal liability, nor demonstrate that the Board would have been unable objectively to evaluate a demand to bring suit." *Raul v. Rand*, 929 F. Supp. 2d 333, 346 (D. Del. 2013). For cases following this approach, *see, e.g., Laborers' Local v. Intersil*, 868 F. Supp. 2d 838 (N.D. Cal. 2012); *Swanson v. Weil*, 2012 WL 4442795 (D. Colo. 2012); *Weinberg ex. rel. BioMed Realty Trust, Inc. v. Gold*, 838 F. Supp. 2d 355 (D. Md. 2012). *But see NECA-IBEW Pension Fund ex. rel. Cincinnati Bell, Inc. v. Cox*, 2011 WL 4383368 (S.D. Ohio 2011) (denying the motion to dismiss and stating "[g]iven that the director defendants devised the challenged compensation, approved the compensation, recommended shareholder approval of the compensation, and suffered a negative shareholder vote on the compensation, plaintiff has demonstrated sufficient facts to show that there is reason to doubt these same directors could exercise their independent business judgment over whether to bring suit against themselves for breach of fiduciary duty in awarding the challenged compensation").

compensation and that of the median employee. Using a general benchmark, four decades ago this ratio was roughly 30 to 1 and three decades ago roughly 60 to 1.[166] These ratios serve as a good foundation to reign in excessive executive compensation. This objective can be achieved by placing a limit on the value of equity awards (which comprise by far the largest percentage of compensation) that can be granted to executives.[167]

The second measure, as proposed earlier in this chapter,[168] is for an employee representative to serve on the subject corporation's board of directors and also to serve as a member of the compensation committee. In determining CEO and other high-level executive compensation, it is beneficial for directors on the compensation committee (many of whom have several millions of dollars of net worth) to receive meaningful input from an employee representative. From the perspective of employees, their representative's participation in the executive remuneration process may engender a better understanding and acceptance of the challenging issues implicated.[169]

The third measure is for Congress to elevate the advisory shareholder say-on-pay vote to a binding vote. The vote required to approve would be a majority of the shares present at the meeting, with the interested shares held by the subject executives not entitled to vote on this matter.[170] Implementation of this measure hopefully should instill necessary discipline in this process. Shareholders currently vote on such matters as the

---

166 *See supra* note 154.

167 *See supra* notes 151–154 and accompanying text. Management expert Peter Drucker in 1977 believed that a ratio of 30:1 was appropriate and in 1984 had lowered that ratio to 20:1. *See* Peter F. Drucker, *Is Executive Pay Excessive?*, Wall St. J., May 23, 1977, at 20 (arguing for a ratio in the 25:1 to 30:1 range); Peter F. Drucker, *Reform Executive Pay or Congress Will*, Wall St. J., Apr. 24, 1984, at 34 (arguing for a ratio in the 15:1 to 20:1 range). On the other hand, in the past, some companies (such as Ben & Jerry's and Whole Foods) maintained a pay ratio of less than 20:1. *See* Bank and Georgiev, *supra* note 149, at 1134 (and sources cited therein).

168 *See supra* notes 139–142 and accompanying text.

169 *See* Lenore Palladino, *Worker Representation on U.S. Corporate Boards*, Harv. Law School Forum on Corp. Gov., Dec. 30, 2019, available at https://corpgov.law.harvard.edu/2019/12/30/worker-representation-on-u-s-corporate-boards/ (asserting that "workers serving on corporate boards are able to participate in business decision-making and create greater visibility and consideration for the effects of those decisions on workers [as well as allowing for] more effective information transfer from board to worker which reduces monitoring costs, creates motivation for workers, and promotes convergence of interest between shareholders and employees").

170 As the subject executive officers are the individuals to financially benefit from a vote of approval, they should be deemed interested persons and thereby recused from voting the shares they beneficially own. *Cf. Remillard Brick Co. v. Remillard-Dandini Co.*, 241 P.2d 66 (Cal. App. 1952) (interested director transaction).

Currently, the advisory say-on-pay vote focuses on the previous year's executive compensation practices. With the presence of a binding shareholder vote, the timing of executive compensation arrangements would be rescheduled to align with such shareholder vote.

ratification of the appointment of the independent auditors as well as approval with respect to exempting under SEC Rule 16b-3 certain insider transactions from short-swing trading liability.[171] A binding shareholder vote on executive compensation compares favorably to these two agenda items.[172] Elevating this matter to a binding vote may well induce institutional, activist, and ordinary shareholders to enhance their scrutiny of the subject corporation's executive compensation policies and practices. Fear of negative binding shareholder votes also may prompt companies to implement better corporate governance remuneration policies. Hence, a binding shareholder say-on-pay vote should instill a significantly higher level of discipline, better align executive pay with company performance, and improve the perception of equity in the overall corporate compensation structure.[173]

C. Undue Reliance on State Law

The last topic discussed in this section of the chapter is judicially directed. For decades, the federal courts have relied on state law principles to determine the parameters of the federal securities laws in the corporate governance sphere.[174] While this approach may have made sense fifty years ago,

[171] SEC Rule 16b-3, 17 C.F.R. § 240.16b-3 (exempting transactions between a corporation and its directors and its officers from § 16(b) short-swing trading liability provided that such transactions are approved by such corporation's board of directors, a committee comprised of outside directors, or the corporation's shareholders). Rule 16b-3 is discussed in Chapter 7 herein.

[172] For example, whether the auditor is Deloitte, Ernst & Young, KPMG or PricewaterhouseCoopers is not an important issue for many shareholders.

[173] The advisory shareholder say-on-pay vote has facilitated meaningful dialogue between management and institutional shareholders on issues of executive compensation. *See* Randall S. Thomas et al., *Dodd-Frank's Say on Pay: Will It Lead to a Greater Role for Shareholders in Corporate Governance?*, 97 Cornell L. Rev. 1213, 1256–7 (2012). On the other hand, it has been advanced that collective action problems, proxy advisers being resource constrained, and uninformed shareholders drastically limit the efficacy of the shareholder voting franchise. *See* Lucian A Bebchuk et al., *The Agency Problems of Institutional Investors*, 31 J. Econ. Persp. 89 (2017); Lucian A. Bebchuk and Scott Hirst, *Index Funds and the Future of Corporate Governance: Theory, Evidence, and Policy*, 119 Colum. L. Rev. 2029 (2019); Jill E. Fisch et al., *The New Titans of Wall Street—A Theoretical Framework for Passive Investors*, 168 U. Pa. L. Rev. 17 (2020); Sean J. Griffith, *Opt-In Stewardship: Toward an Optimal Delegation of Mutual Fund Voting Authority*, 98 Tex. L. Rev. 983 (2020). Nonetheless, it may be posited that the shareholder vote induces a subject board of directors to view its decision-making "through the lens" of shareholder interests, thereby significantly impacting board governing procedures and determinations. *See* Bernard S. Sharfman, *Enhancing the Value of Shareholder Voting Recommendations*, 86 Tenn. L. Rev. 691, 706 (2019); Leo E. Strine, Jr., *Can We Do Better for Ordinary Investors? A Pragmatic Reaction to the Dueling Ideological Mythologists of Corporate Law*, 114 Colum. L. Rev. 448, 453–55 (2014). For further discussion, *see* Chapter 8 at note 140 herein.

[174] *See* cases cited *infra* notes 178–193 and accompanying text.

it no longer retains validity. During the past thirty years, several federal statutes have been enacted that directly impact corporate governance.[175] Additionally, through the decades, SEC enforcement actions have been instituted that have significantly affected board of director and management practices.[176] Construing the federal securities laws as well as SEC rules and regulations promulgated thereunder, it is incumbent upon the federal courts to deem federal law principles premier in the corporate governance sphere.[177]

The U.S. Supreme Court's decision in *Cort v. Ash*,[178] decided in 1975, reflects the federal judicial reliance on state law in determining the propriety of corporate governance practices. There, the Court stated: "Corporations are creatures of state law, and investors commit their funds to corporate directors on the understanding that, except where federal law expressly requires certain responsibilities of directors with respect to shareholders, state law will govern the internal affairs of the corporation."[179] Five years later, in *Burks v. Lasker*,[180] in determining whether four statutorily disinterested directors under the Investment Company Act[181] had the authority to terminate a shareholders' derivative action brought for alleged violations

[175] These Acts include: Securities Enforcement Remedies and Penny Stock Reform Act of 1990, Pub. L. No. 101-429, 104 Stat. 931 (1990) (among other provisions, authorizing the SEC to seek an order barring directors and executive officers who engage in fraud and who are deemed substantially unfit from serving as a director or executive officer in any publicly-held company); National Securities Markets Improvement Act of 1996, Pub. L. No. 104-290, 110 Stat. 3416 (1996) (preempting state regulation of securities registration and exemptions thereto in regard to "covered" securities as specified therein); Securities Litigation Uniform Standards Act of 1998, Pub. L. No. 105-353, 112 Stat. 3227 (1998) (with certain carve-outs, mandating that securities class actions against nationally traded companies must be brought in federal district court with only federal law applying); Sarbanes-Oxley Act of 2002, Pub. L. No. 107-204, 116 Stat. 745 (2002) (among other provisions, enhancing federal aspects of corporate governance (such as the composition and functions of the audit committee, generally prohibiting loans being made to directors and executive officers, lowering the threshold for officer and director bars to unfitness from substantial unfitness, and focusing on senior financial officer codes of ethics)); Dodd-Frank Wall Street Reform and Consumer Protection Act, Pub. L. No. 111-203, 124 Stat. 1376 (2010) (among other provisions, enhancing federalization of corporate governance by mandating an independent compensation committee as a condition of national securities exchange listing and requiring an advisory shareholder say-on-pay vote). *See* discussion *supra* notes 8–83 and accompanying text.

[176] A number of these proceedings are addressed earlier in this chapter. *See supra* notes 51–58 and accompanying text.

[177] *See* discussion *infra* notes 178–196 and accompanying text.

[178] 422 U.S. 66 (1975).

[179] *Id.* at 80. This language was approvingly quoted by the Court in *Santa Fe Industries, Inc. v. Green*, 430 U.S. 462, 479 (1977) (holding that § 10(b) of the Securities Exchange Act and SEC Rule 10b-5 promulgated thereunder do not encompass alleged breaches of fiduciary duty unaccompanied by deficiency of disclosure). *See generally* Ralph C. Ferrara and Marc I. Steinberg, *A Reappraisal of Santa Fe: Rule 10b-5 and the New Federalism*, 129 U. Pa. L. Rev. 263 (1980).

[180] 441 U.S. 471 (1979).

[181] 14 U.S.C. §§ 80a-1 *et seq*. For discussion of the importance and functions of independent directors in the investment company setting, *see supra* note 143.

of the Investment Advisers Act,[182] the Supreme Court held that the answer depended largely on the law of the subject company's state of incorporation.[183] This standard, in essence, requires a federal court to interpret state law to ascertain the parameters of federal law. Similarly, in a subsequent decision, *Kamen v. Kemper Financial Services, Inc.*,[184] the Court ruled that the demand on the board of director requirement for a shareholder derivative action that is brought for alleged violations of the federal securities laws must be determined pursuant to the law of the subject corporation's state of incorporation[185]—once again signifying that the success of a claim based on the federal securities laws may be eviscerated by application of state law.

This misplaced reliance on state law principles by the U.S. Supreme Court is most visible in the insider trading context. There, in ascertaining the scope of the insider trading prohibition under Section 10(b) of the Securities Exchange Act[186] and SEC Rule 10b-5 promulgated thereunder,[187] the Court invoked state concepts of common law fraud.[188] Under this approach, a duty to disclose exists only if there is a fiduciary duty or a relationship of trust and confidence.[189] The Court's decision, in practical effect, overruled

---

[182] 15 U.S.C. §§ 80b-1 *et. seq.*

[183] 441 U.S. at 480, 486 (adopting a two-prong test in this assessment: first, whether the applicable state law (namely, the law of the state of the subject company's incorporation) permits the disinterested directors to terminate the derivative action, and, second, if so, whether the state rule is consistent with federal securities law policies). *See generally* Marc I. Steinberg, *The Use of Special Litigation Committees to Terminate Shareholder Derivative Suits*, 35 U. Miami L. Rev. 1 (1980).

[184] 500 U.S. 90 (1991).

[185] *Id.* at 108 (emphasis in original) (stating that "where a gap in the federal securities laws must be bridged by a rule that bears on the allocation of governing powers within the corporation, federal courts should incorporate *state* law into federal common law unless the particular state law in question is inconsistent with the policies underlying the federal statute"). The lower federal courts have applied this directive. *See, e.g., Cottrell v. Duke*, 829 F.3d 983, 990 n.5 (8th Cir. 2016) (applying the *Kamen* directive "even though some of the shareholders' claims are based on federal law").

Importantly, whether demand on the board of directors in a shareholder derivative action is required or excused frequently is determinative whether the litigation continues with settlement ordinarily the consequence or is dismissed with the defendants being relieved of liability exposure. *See Zapata Corp. v. Maldonado*, 430 A.2d 779 (Del. 1981).

[186] 15 U.S.C. § 78j(b).

[187] 15 C.F.R. § 240.10b-5.

[188] *See, e.g., Chiarella v. United States*, 445 U.S. 222, 228 (1980) (focusing on common law, stating "one who fails to disclose material information prior to the consummation of a transaction commits fraud only when he is under a duty to do so [a]nd the duty to disclose arises when one party has information 'that the other [party] is entitled to know because of a fiduciary or other similar relation of trust and confidence between them'"), *quoting*, American Law Institute, *Restatement (Second) of Torts* § 551(2)(a) (1976).

[189] This principle was first enunciated in the insider trading setting in *Chiarella v. United States*, 445 U.S. 222 (1980) (holding that silence may result in § 10(b) liability where a duty to disclose is present due to the existence of a fiduciary duty or a relationship of trust and confidence). Subsequent U.S. Supreme Court decisions adhere to this principle. *See, e.g., Salman v. United States*, 137 S. Ct. 420 (2016); *United States v. O'Hagan*, 521 U.S. 642 (1997); *Dirks v. Securities and Exchange Commission*, 463 U.S. 646 (1983).

federal appellate court decisions that had applied the parity of information and access rationales[190]—approaches to which other developed markets currently adhere.[191] As discussed in Chapter 7 of this book, the adverse consequence of these Supreme Court decisions is U.S. insider trading regulation that is vague, inconsistent, and inequitable.[192] The unacceptable status of this framework may be placed on the Supreme Court's inappropriate reliance on state law.[193]

The deference to state law principles to ascertain the parameters of the federal securities laws in the corporate governance sphere thus is unwarranted.

---

[190] *See, e.g., Securities and Exchange Commission v. Texas Gulf Sulphur Co.*, 401 F.2d 833 (2d Cir. 1968) (en banc). In *Texas Gulf Sulphur*, the Second Circuit apparently enunciated both the access and parity approaches. With respect to the possession rationale, the court stated: "Anyone in possession of material inside information must either disclose it to the investing public, or, if he is disabled from disclosing it in order to protect a corporate confidence, or he chooses not to do so, must abstain from trading in or recommending the securities concerned while such information remains undisclosed." *Id.* at 848. Earlier in that same paragraph, the court set forth the access standard, stating that the disclose-or-abstain rule "is based in policy on the justifiable expectation of the securities marketplace that all investors trading on impersonal exchanges have relatively equal access to material information." *Id.* The *Texas Gulf Sulphur* decision is viewed as one of the more important decisions in the history of the federal securities laws. *See Texas Gulf Sulphur 50th Anniversary Symposium Issue*, 71 SMU L. Rev. No. 3 (2018).

[191] For example, the parity of information standard evidently has been adopted by Australia and the European Union. *See* Corporations Act 2001 (Cth) § 1043A (Australia); Council Regulation (EU) No. 596/2014 of the European Parliament and of the Council of 16 April 2014 on Market Abuse Regulation, arts. 7, 8, 10, 14, 17. The access rationale, for example, has been adopted by Canada (Ontario) and China. *See* Province of Ontario Securities Act, R.S.O. 1990, c. S. 5, § 76; Securities Law of the People's Republic of China (2014 Amendment) (promulgated by the Standing Comm. Nat'l People's Cong., Dec. 29, 1988, rev'd Aug. 31, 2014, effective Aug. 31, 2014) art. 76.

[192] As one example, an individual who trades on material nonpublic information can legally keep her profits or go to prison based solely on whether the transaction is structured as a merger or a tender offer. In the case of a tender offer, in addition to Section 10(b) potential liability, Rule 14e-3, 17 C.F.R. § 240.14e-3, also applies. Unlike Section 10(b), Rule 14e-3 extends liability to those who trade or tip in knowing possession of material nonpublic information. This erratic treatment of similarly situated persons is addressed in Chapter 7 herein.

[193] Justice Blackmun's dissent in *Chiarella* supports this position:

> The Court continues to pursue a course, charted in certain recent decisions, designed to transform § 10(b) from an intentionally elastic "catchall" provision to one that catches relatively little of the misbehavior that all too often makes investment in securities a needlessly risky business for the uninitiated investor. Such confinement in this case is now achieved by imposition of a requirement of a "special relationship" akin to fiduciary duty before the statute gives rise to a duty to disclose or to abstain from trading upon material, nonpublic information. The Court admits that this conclusion finds no mandate in the language of the statute or its legislative history. Yet the Court fails even to attempt a justification of its ruling in terms of the purposes of the securities laws, or to square that ruling with the longstanding but now much abused principle that the federal securities laws are to be construed flexibly rather than with narrow technicality.

Id. at 246–47 (Blackmun, J., dissenting).

For two books by the author discussing this subject, *see* Marc I. Steinberg and William K.S. Wang, *Insider Trading* (3d ed. 2010); Marc I. Steinberg, *Securities and Exchange Commission v. Cuban—A Trial of Insider Trading* (2019).

The strong presence of federal corporate governance is firmly entrenched. Dating back for more than fifty years, significant federal measures have been implemented that significantly impact corporate governance.[194] This process has been accentuated by the passage of the Sarbanes-Oxley and Dodd-Frank Acts in this century.[195] Thus, no longer is reliance on state law principles justified. Although on occasion perhaps appropriate yesteryear, in recognition of today's strong presence of federal corporate governance, federal law should uniformly be the premier authority in this setting.[196]

IV. Conclusion

After examining the federalization of corporate governance from both historical and contemporary perspectives, this chapter addresses gaps in the corporate governance framework and recommends the implementation of improved standards on the federal level. First, these recommendations focus on board of director composition, advocating for splitting the positions of CEO and board chair, a more realistic definition of "independent director," greater gender and racial diversity on boards, employee representation on boards, shareholder access to the company's proxy statement to nominate a specified number of directors, and the adoption of director term limits. Second, the thorny subject of excessive executive compensation is treated. Concluding that the current status is unacceptable, remedial measures should be implemented, including binding say-on-pay votes on executive compensation, an employee representative serving as a director on the subject company's compensation committee, and placing a suitable mandatory statutory ceiling on the permissible percentage disparity between the CEO's

[194] For example, in 1964, the SEC sought indirectly to regulate management self-dealing, a matter traditionally within the purview of state law, under the guise of disclosure. *See In re Franchard Corp.*, 42 S.E.C. 163, 172 (1964) (stating that undisclosed self-dealing is material to investors as it is "germane to an evaluation of the integrity of management").

[195] *See* discussion *supra* notes 62–70 and accompanying text. For further discussion, *see* Steinberg, *supra* note 6.

[196] In appropriate circumstances, state law and the law of foreign countries may be considered as persuasive authority for determining the appropriate standard under the federal securities laws. For example, in *Morrison v. National Australia Bank Ltd.*, 561 U.S. 247 (2010), the Court took into consideration foreign law in determining the extraterritorial reach of Section 10(b): "Like the United States, foreign countries regulate their domestic securities exchanges and securities transactions occurring within their territorial jurisdiction . . . [and they] all complain of the interference with foreign securities regulation that application of § 10(b) would produce, and urge the adoption of a clear test that will avoid that consequence." *Id.* at 269–70. *See* Marc I. Steinberg and Kelly Flanagan, *Transactional Dealings—Morrison Continues to Make Waves*, 46 Int'l Law. 829 (2012).

compensation and that of the median employee. As the percentage disparity in this country is by far the largest in the world with no indication of lessening,[197] appropriate measures should be instituted to curb this excess. Third, federal court invocation of state law principles to ascertain the parameters of the federal securities laws in the corporate governance sphere is misplaced in view of the entrenched federalization of corporate governance. This misdirected approach should be discontinued, with federal law being the premier source in this context.

[197] *See* Bank and Georgiev, *supra* note 149, at 1133 (stating that "in the 1950s U.S. executives were making about 20 times more than the average employee, whereas by the early 1990s they were making 120 to 150 times more [and by] the mid-2000s, this figure had risen to 350 [with 2018 estimates] of 361:1 . . . highlight[ing] how much of an outlier the United States is compared to countries such as Australia (93:1), Germany (147:1), Japan (67:1), Switzerland (148:1), or the United Kingdom (84:1)").

6
Private Securities Litigation

I. Introduction

The private securities litigation framework in the United States is erratic and unacceptable. The litigation structure contained in the federal securities acts was based on a different era and is not suitable for today's securities markets. True, Congress subsequently has legislated on a piecemeal basis but has failed to provide a coherent liability framework.[1] In this regard, federal legislation has been enacted to address perceived shortcomings on an episodic basis, leaving gaps and inconsistencies.[2] Likewise, the federal courts, faced with this fractured statutory regimen, frequently have construed the remedial provisions of the federal securities laws in a wooden and unduly restrictive manner.[3] The consequence of these congressional and judicial actions is a disparate liability framework that lacks sound logic, consistency, and even-handed treatment for plaintiffs and defendants alike.[4] Hence, private litigation under the federal securities laws is a hodgepodge in need of clarification, greater uniformity, and better assessment of the public policy implications.

[1] For example, within a period of two years, Congress enacted the Dodd-Frank Wall Street Reform and Consumer Protection Act, Pub. L. No. 111-203, 124 Stat. 1376 (2010) (enhancing federal corporate governance), *followed by*, the Jumpstart Our Business Startups Act (JOBS Act), Pub. L. No. 112-106, 126 Stat. 306 (2012) (facilitating capital raising by relatively smaller enterprises).

[2] *See, e.g.*, Williams Act, Pub. L. No. 90-439, 12 Stat. 454 (1968) (establishing requirements in the going-private and tender offer settings); Private Securities Litigation Reform Act, Pub. L. No. 104-67, 109 Stat. 737 (1995) (focusing on class action reform, imposing stricter pleading requirements, enhancing protection for forward-looking statements by publicly-held companies, and promulgating a proportionate liability framework); Sarbanes-Oxley Act, Pub. L. No. 107-204, 116 Stat. 745 (2002) (federalizing aspects of corporate governance, strengthening disclosure requirements, and enhancing government enforcement).

[3] *See, e.g.*, *Janus Capital Fund, Inc. v. First Derivative Traders*, 564 U.S. 135 (2011) (defining the word "make" in a restrictive manner and thereby narrowing the scope of Exchange Act § 10(b) primary liability); *Gustafson v. Alloyd Company*, 513 U.S. 561 (1995) (confining the term "prospectus" in § 12(a)(2) of the Securities Act to public offerings); *Central Bank of Denver, N.A. v. First Interstate Bank of Denver, N.A.*, 511 U.S. 164 (1994) (rejecting the view unanimously held by the lower federal courts, applying a strict statutory construction, and holding no aiding and abetting liability in private actions under § 10(b)).

[4] *See* discussion *infra* notes 6–247 and accompanying text.

Rethinking Securities Law. Marc I. Steinberg, Oxford University Press. © Marc I. Steinberg 2021.
DOI: 10.1093/oso/9780197583142.003.0006

This chapter provides several examples of the inconsistencies and disparate treatment that prevail under the federal securities laws.[5] In regard thereto, recommendations for corrective measures are proffered. Rather than being an exhaustive critique of the current private litigation system—which would be a book project by itself—the discussion focuses on key situations that merit expeditious correction and sets forth proposals to reform the federal securities litigation framework. These proposals, if adopted and effectively implemented, should instill a substantially greater degree of certainty, uniformity, and equity than currently exists. The objective is to provide clear and uniform standards whereby investors receive fair treatment without imposing undue burdens upon prospective defendants irrespective of their status as entities, fiduciaries, or collateral participants.

II. The Current Federal Securities Law Framework—Needed Revisions

The following discussion highlights the disparate, inconsistent, and inequitable condition of private litigation under the federal securities laws. Recommendations for remediating this defective condition are set forth, with the objective of effectuating a substantially enhanced process.

A. Publicly-Traded Companies—Registered Offerings versus Secondary Market Trading

There exists no persuasive reason to justify why an established publicly-held company whose common stock is listed on a national securities exchange is subjected to vastly different liability regimes depending on whether it files a Securities Act registration statement versus a periodic report with the SEC pursuant to the Exchange Act. The making of a registered offering triggers the application of Section 11 of the Securities Act[6] whereby an onerous liability standard applies. With certain defenses available and conditions required to be shown by the plaintiff(s),[7] generally, if the registration statement

[5] *See* discussion *infra* notes 6–171 and accompanying text.

[6] 15 U.S.C. § 77k.

[7] For example, the plaintiff must prove that: the securities she purchased were sold in the subject registered offering; the materiality of the disclosure deficiency; and suit was brought within the

contains a material misrepresentation or omission,[8] the issuer, its directors, high-level executive officers, the underwriters for the offering, and experts are liable to purchasers of the securities sold in that public offering according to a specified damages formula.[9] Except for the issuer, all defendants may avoid liability under Section 11 by meeting the due diligence defense.[10] In addition, all defendants may invoke the loss causation defense, showing that the subject disclosure deficiency did not cause, in whole or in part, the diminution in the price of the security.[11] Lastly, the pleading burdens that must be met by plaintiffs in a Section 11 action are more relaxed than for Exchange

---

applicable statute of limitations (one year after discovery and in no event more than three years after the offering was made). Key defenses under Section 11 are the due diligence defense and lack of loss causation defense.

[8] Generally, materiality signifies that a reasonable investor would consider the misstated or omitted information important in making its investment decision. *See, e.g., TSC Industries, Inc. v. Northway, Inc.*, 426 U.S. 438 (1976). Stated in different terms, "there must be a substantial likelihood that the [accurate] disclosure of the [misstated or] omitted fact would have been viewed by the reasonable investor as having significantly altered the total mix of information made available." *Matrixx Initiatives, Inc. v. Siracusano*, 563 U.S. 27, 38 (2011). With respect to uncertain events (such as in the merger setting), the probability/magnitude standard applies whereby materiality depends "at any given time upon a balancing of both the indicated probability that the event will occur and the anticipated magnitude of the event in light of the totality of the company activity." *Securities and Exchange Commission v. Texas Gulf Sulphur Co.*, 401 F.2d 833, 849 (2d Cir. 1968) (en banc), *quoted in, Basic, Inc. v. Levinson*, 485 U.S. 224, 238 (1988). The subject of materiality is addressed extensively herein in Chapter 2.

[9] *See* § 11(a) of the Securities Act, 15 U.S.C. § 77k(a). An expert is liable under Section 11 only for that portion of the registration statement which it "expertises." Under Section 6(a) of the Securities Act, 15 U.S.C. § 77f(a), those who sign the registration statement incur Section 11 liability exposure. These persons include the subject "issuer, its principal executive officer or officers, its principal financial officer, its comptroller or principal accounting officer, and the majority of its board of directors or persons performing similar functions." *Id.* The damages formula is set forth in Section 11(e), 15 U.S.C. § 77k(e) (setting forth the damages formula as "represent[ing] the difference between the amount paid for the security (not exceeding the price at which the security was offered to the public) and (1) the value thereof as of the time such suit was brought, or (2) the price at which such security shall have been disposed of in the market before suit, or (3) the price at which such security shall have been disposed of after suit but before judgment if such damages shall be less than the damages representing the difference between the amount paid for the security (not exceeding the price at which the security was offered to the public) and the value thereof as of the time such suit was brought").

[10] The due diligence defense is set forth in Section 11(b), 15 U.S.C. § 77k(b). With respect to "the unexpertised portion of the registration statement, a subject defendant must show that, after reasonable investigation, he/she had reason to believe and did believe at the time such registration statement became effective, there was no material misstatement or omission." Marc I. Steinberg, *Understanding Securities Law* 227 (7th ed. 2018). The same standard applies to an expert with respect to the portion of the registration statement which such person expertises. In regard to the expertised portion of the registration statement, a non-expert has no duty to investigate and must establish that he/she did not have reasonable ground to believe and did not believe that such expertised portion of the registration statement contained a material misstatement or omission. *Id.* For further discussion on the due diligence defense, *see* Chapter 4 herein.

[11] *See* § 11(e), 15 U.S.C. § 77(e). For a case where the defendants successfully established the loss causation defense, *see Akerman v. Oryx Communications, Inc.*, 609 F. Supp. 363 (S.D.N.Y. 1984), *aff'd*, 810 F.2d 344 (2d Cir. 1987).

Act Section 10(b) claims where heightened fraud pleading standards apply.[12] Clearly, the Section 11 right of action is favorable to plaintiffs.[13]

Nonetheless, a number of courts have engaged in judicial activism to make the remedy less available to plaintiffs. The most pronounced limitation is the onerous tracing requirement whereby a complainant must establish to a 100 percent certainty that it purchased the securities pursuant to the defective registration statement.[14] In one case, for example, a federal appellate court denied plaintiffs standing to pursue their Section 11 claim when 99.85 percent of the subject securities in the secondary trading market could be traced to the applicable registered offering.[15] By contrast, where a defendant asserts a defense pursuant to the statute, such as the loss causation defense, the preponderance standard correctly has been applied.[16] As a second example, even though the element of reliance ordinarily is not required to be shown in a Section 11 action,[17] some courts nonetheless have ordered dismissal when this element is deemed lacking.[18] These judicial decisions represent

[12] *Cf.* Rule 8(a)(2) of the Federal Rules of Civil Procedure (FRCP), *with* FRCP Rule 9(b) and Section 21D(b) of the Securities Exchange Act, 15 U.S.C. § 78u-4. Note, however, that Section 11 claims that "sound in fraud" are subject to the heightened fraud pleading requirements. *See, e.g., Rombach v. Chang*, 355 F.3d 164, 170–71 (2d Cir. 2004).

[13] *See, e.g., Herman & MacLean v. Huddleston*, 459 U.S. 375, 381–82 (1983) (stating that § 11 "was designed to ensure compliance with the disclosure provisions of the [Securities] Act by imposing a stringent standard of liability on the parties who play a direct role in a registered offering").

[14] *See, e.g., Krim v. pcOrder.com*, 402 F.3d 489 (5th Cir. 2005). *See also Hertzberg v. Dignity Partners, Inc.*, 191 F.3d 1076 (9th Cir. 1999) (permitting tracing where 100% of the shares in the secondary market were offered in the initial public offering).

[15] 402 F.3d at 495–96. *See* Marc I. Steinberg and Brent A. Kirby, *The Assault on Section 11 of the Securities Act: A Study in Judicial Activism*, 63 Rutgers L. Rev. 1, 27 (2010) (citing cases and stating that the "already burdensome task of proving tracing has become even more onerous as a growing number of courts have rejected the use of statistical evidence to prove tracing"). The tracing requirement may pose a particularly onerous burden in the context of direct listings. *See* Securities Exchange Act Release No. 89684 (2020) (rejecting the assertion and stating that "[p]urchasers in a registered offering may face difficulty tracing their shares back to the registration statement whenever a company conducts a registered offering for less than all its shares").

[16] *See Halliburton Co. v. Erica John Fund, Inc.*, 134 S. Ct. 2398, 2417 (2014). *Cf. Herman & MacLean v. Huddleston*, 459 U.S. 375, 390 (1983).

[17] *See* § 11, 15 U.S.C. § 77k; *In re Constar International Inc. Securities Litigation*, 585 F.3d 774, 784 (3d Cir. 2009) (stating that in a § 11 action "reliance is irrelevant"); *Stark Trading v. Falconbridge Ltd.*, 552 F.3d 568, 573 (7th Cir. 2009) (stating that § 11 "does not require proof of reliance"); *In re Initial Public Offering Securities Litigation*, 483 F.3d 70, 73 n. 1 (2d Cir. 2007) (noting that no requirement exists for the plaintiff to allege reliance in a § 11 action). An exception requiring that reliance must be shown under Section 11 arises where a plaintiff purchases the securities more than twelve months subsequent to the effective date of the registration statement and if the subject company has generally made available an "earning statement" with respect to this twelve-month period. Note that "such reliance may be established without proof of the reading of the registration statement" by the complainant. Section 11(a), 15 U.S.C. § 77k(a). *See* Rule 158, 17 C.F.R. § 230.158 (for purposes of the § 11 reliance requirement, defining the terms "earning statement," "made generally available to its security holders," and "effective date of the registration statement").

[18] *See, e.g., APA Excelsior III L.P. v. Premiere Technologies, Inc.*, 476 F.3d 1261, 1277 (11th Cir. 2007) (holding that reliance under § 11 is presumed and may be rebutted such as "where it is certain

an unwarranted encroachment, thereby effecting a narrowing of this express statutory remedy authorized by Congress.[19]

As compared to the Section 11 right of action, suits alleging violations of Sections 10(b) and 18(a) of the Exchange Act present far greater challenges to plaintiffs.[20] With respect to Section 18(a), a plaintiff must prove both reliance and loss causation.[21] Because "eyeball" reliance must be shown by each complainant,[22] the fraud on the market theory,[23] recognized in Section 10(b) cases for facilitating class certification,[24] is of no avail in Section 18(a) cases. The consequence is that Section 18(a) is invoked solely in individual actions and, until recently, has not been frequently used.[25] Due to an increase in the number of opt-out actions by institutional investors who allege Section 18(a)

---

that a purchase of the securities was motivated by factors other than the registration statement"); *In re HealthSouth Corp. Securities Litigation*, 261 F.R.D. 616, 647 (N.D. Ala. 2009) (stating that reliance may be rebutted in a § 11 action); *In re Countrywide Financial Corp. Securities Litigation*, 588 F. Supp. 2d 1132, 1162 n. 34 (C.D. Cal. 2008) (stating that reliance in a § 11 action may have to be shown where "it appears from the face of the complaint that a plaintiff cannot have actually relied on the registration statement").

[19] *See* Steinberg and Kirby, *supra* note 15, at 26 ("Based on the statutory language of Section 11, the traditional interpretation of Section 11 by federal courts, and the detailed congressional history, it is abundantly clear that the Eleventh Circuit, as well as other courts that have followed its lead, is incorrect in holding that reliance is an element of a Section 11 claim.").

[20] For example, Section 10(b) requires, among other requirements, that a plaintiff in a private action prove scienter, reliance, loss causation, and damages. *See Dura Pharmaceuticals, Inc. v. Broudo*, 544 U.S. 336, 341 (2005). Section 18(a), an express private remedy, requires a plaintiff to prove direct reliance and loss causation. *See Deephaven Private Placement & Trading Ltd. v. Grant Thornton & Co.*, 454 F.3d 1168, 1171 (10th Cir. 2006). Moreover, as set forth in Section 21D(b)(4), 15 U.S.C. § 78u-4(b)(4): "In any private action arising under [the Securities Exchange Act], the plaintiff shall have the burden of proving that the act or omission of the defendant alleged to violate this [Act] caused the loss for which the plaintiff seeks to recover damages."

[21] *See, e.g., Deep Private Placement & Trading Ltd. v. Grant Thornton & Co.*, 454 F.3d 1168 (10th Cir. 2006); *In re Supreme Specialists, Inc. Securities Litigation*, 438 F.3d 256 (3d Cir. 2006); *LLDVF, L.P. v. Dinicola*, 2010 WL 3210613 (D.N.J. 2010).

[22] *See, e.g., In re Supreme Specialists, Inc. Securities Litigation*, 438 F.3d 256, 283 (3d Cir. 2006) (stating that § 18(a) requires plaintiffs "to plead actual reliance on specific statements contained in the SEC filings at issue"). Significantly, as held by a number of courts, such reliance may be established through direct reliance on the allegedly materially false or misleading statement by the plaintiff's broker or other representative. *See Gould v. Winstar Communications, Inc.*, 692 F.3d 148, 161 (2d Cir. 2012).

[23] *See, e.g., Beebe v. Pacific Trust*, 99 F.R.D. 60 (D. Ore. 1983). For this reason, typically Section 18(a) claims are not alleged in securities class actions. *But see Simpson v. Specialty Retail Concepts*, 149 F.R.D. 94 (M.D.N.C. 1993) (certifying class where § 18(a) claim alleged). *See generally* Stuart M. Grant and Megan D. McIntyre, *Class Certification and Section 18 of the Exchange Act*, 35 Rev. Sec. & Comm. Reg. 255 (2002). The fraud on the market theory is discussed *infra* notes 221–228 and accompanying text.

[24] *See, e.g., Halliburton Co. v. Erica P. John Fund, Inc.*, 134 S. Ct. 2398 (2014); *Basic, Inc. v. Levinson*, 485 U.S. 224 (1988); discussion *infra* notes 221–228 and accompanying text.

[25] *See, e.g.*, Edward F. Greene, *Determining the Responsibilities of Underwriters Distributing Securities Within an Integrated Disclosure System*, 56 Notre Dame Law. 755, 758 (1981) (stating that "there has been no reported case sustaining liability under the section").

violations in their individual suits, the situation may well be changing.[26] Nonetheless, even if more widely used, the Section 18(a) right of action poses far more challenging hurdles for plaintiffs than suits invoking Section 11 of the Securities Act.[27]

Moreover, as compared to Section 11, private actions alleging Section 10(b) violations are significantly more arduous for plaintiffs. Although the fraud on the market theory alleviates the burden of showing reliance and thereby facilitates class certification,[28] other demanding requirements apply. Most significantly, without entitlement to conduct discovery (including examining documents, posing interrogatories, and taking deposition testimony),[29] an onerous pleading standard applies.[30] The consequence is that a large percentage of cases are dismissed at the pleading stage.[31] In view that plaintiffs' counsel typically has a contingent fee arrangement, common sense would indicate that, given the time commitment incurred in the complaint drafting process, cases lacking substance ordinarily would not be undertaken even at the initial stages of the litigation. Indeed, sanctions may be levied under the federal securities laws for the filing of a frivolous complaint.[32]

---

[26] *See* Tammie Beassie Banko, *The Val(e)ant Section 18(a)*, 48 Sec. Reg. L.J. 5, 5 (2020) (citing cases and stating that "[i]nstitutional investors, particularly those opting out of highly publicized class actions involving fraudulent schemes, have awoken the sleeping giant of Section 18 by pleading the claim in the right circuit with the right set of facts against the right defendants").

[27] Unlike a Section 11 action, plaintiffs in an action under Section 18(a) must prove reliance, loss causation, and damages. *See supra* note 20.

[28] *See* cases cited *supra* note 24; discussion *infra* notes 221–228 and accompanying text.

[29] Hence, absent extraordinary circumstances, "all discovery and other proceedings shall be stayed during the pendency of any motion to dismiss." Section 21D(b)(3)(B) of the Securities Exchange Act, 15 U.S.C. § 78u-4(b)(3)(B).

[30] *See* § 21D(b)(2)(A) of the Securities Exchange Act, 15 U.S.C. § 78u-4(b)(2)(A) (stating that, with specified exceptions, "in any private action arising under [the Securities Exchange Act] in which the plaintiff may recover money damages only on proof that the defendant acted with a particular state of mind, the complaint shall, with respect to each act or omission alleged to violate this [Act], state with particularity facts giving rise to a strong inference that the defendant acted with the required state of mind"); *Tellabs, Inc. v. Makor Issues & Rights, Ltd.*, 551 U.S. 308, 314 (2007) (holding that § 21D(b)(2)(A) requires that the plaintiff plead facts that create an inference of scienter that is "cogent and at least as compelling as any opposing inference of nonfraudulent intent").

[31] *See, e.g.*, Stefan Boettrich and Svetlana Starykh, *Recent Trends in Securities Class Action Litigation: 2018 Full-Year Review* at 19 (2019), available at https://www.nera.com/content/dam/nera/publications/2018/PUB_Year_End_Trends_Report_0118_final.pdf ("Out of the motions to dismiss for which a court decision was reached, the following three outcomes classify all of the decisions: granted with or without prejudice (45%), granted in part and denied in part (30%), and denied (25%).").

[32] *See* § 21D(c) of the Securities Exchange Act, 15 U.S.C. § 78u-4(c) (providing that "in any private action arising under [this Act], upon final adjudication of the action, the court shall include in the record specific findings regarding compliance by each party and each attorney representing any party with each requirement of Rule 11(b) of the Federal Rules of Civil Procedure as to any complaint, responsive pleading, or dispositive motion . . . [and upon a finding by the court of noncompliance with Rule 11(b)] . . . shall impose sanctions on such party or attorney"). In levying such sanctions based on a party's or attorney's failure to comply with F.R.C.P. 11(b), "the court shall adopt a presumption that

Logic therefore dictates that many complaints that have some merit never proceed past the complaint stage due to the granting of motions to dismiss.[33] This burden, and to a lesser yet significant degree the loss causation requirement,[34] pose serious obstacles for plaintiffs seeking recovery pursuant to Section 10(b) and Rule 10b-5.[35]

For purposes of this discussion, a company's filing of a periodic report with the SEC triggers liability exposure under Sections 10(b) and 18(a) of the Exchange Act with their challenging requirements for plaintiffs to meet.[36] Yet, when those identical reports are incorporated by reference into a filed Securities Act registration statement,[37] the investor-friendly provisions of Section 11 apply.[38] Although a plausible argument may be made that this demarcation is appropriate because in the latter situation the issuer is seeking to raise funds from the investing public, this rationale slights the paramount importance that periodic disclosure documents play in maintaining informed and transparent securities markets.[39] To elevate the importance of a Securities Act registration statement for a seasoned company over that of its Form 10-K annual report belies reality.[40] Accordingly, for seasoned companies, the identical liability framework should apply to disclosure deficiencies whether they are contained in a Securities Act registration statement (and prospectus) or in an Exchange Act periodic filing.[41] The current option of a company "furnishing" rather than "filing" an Exchange Act report (or parts thereof), as addressed elsewhere herein, should be

the appropriate sanction . . . is an award to the opposing party of the reasonable attorneys' fees and other expenses incurred" due to such violation. *Id.*

33 *See* Marc I. Steinberg, *Pleading Securities Fraud Claims—Only Part of the Story*, 45 Loy. U. Chi. L.J. 603 (2014).

34 *See* § 21D(b)(4), 15 U.S.C. § 78u-4(b)(4) (quoted in *supra* note 20).

35 *See* Douglas M. Branson, *Running the Gauntlet: A Description of the Arduous and Now Often Fatal Journey for Plaintiffs in Federal Securities Class Actions*, 65 U. Cin. L. Rev. 3 (1996).

36 *See supra* notes 20–35 and accompanying text.

37 The subject of incorporation by reference is discussed in Chapters 2 and 4 herein.

38 *See* discussion *supra* notes 6–13 and accompanying text.

39 This position is supported by the SEC's requirement that a majority of a subject company's directors sign the Form 10-K. *See* Securities Act Release No. 6231 (1980) ("The Commission believes that just as its rules and the administrative focus of the Division of Corporation Finance are being realigned to reflect the shift in emphasis toward relying on periodic disclosure under the Exchange Act, so too the attention of the private sector, including management, directors, accountants, and attorneys, must also be refocused towards Exchange Act filings if a sufficient degree of discipline is to be instilled in the system to make it work.").

40 *Id.* (stating that the director Form 10-K signature requirement provides an "added measure of discipline [that is] vital to the disclosure objectives of the federal securities laws").

41 This liability framework is discussed later in this chapter. *See infra* notes 49–247 and accompanying text.

eliminated.[42] The proposed liability framework that should be implemented with respect to such misstatements and omissions is set forth later in this chapter.[43]

On the other hand, with respect to companies undertaking their initial public offering (IPO) or that otherwise are unseasoned (such as blank check and financially distressed issuers, companies that have been in the Exchange Act reporting system less than twelve months, and issuers having a public float of less than $75 million),[44] the provisions of Section 11 should continue to apply (with the exception, as discussed later in this chapter, that the issuer like other Section 11 defendants should have a due diligence defense).[45] Accessing the public securities markets by means of a registered offering provides issuers with an array of benefits, including enhanced capital-raising opportunities, stock liquidity, and market following. In view of these benefits and the heightened risk of misconduct when the issuer is unseasoned, Section 11 liability exposure should prevail.[46]

In addition, the onerous tracing requirement should be construed to reflect even-handed treatment: a plaintiff can invoke Section 11 only if she can establish by a preponderance of the evidence that she acquired shares pursuant to the registration statement that allegedly contained inadequacy of disclosure. Any class recovery under Section 11, however, would be limited by the percentage of shares that were outstanding in the secondary market that had been sold in the registered offering (e.g., during the class period, the class purchased ten million shares of common stock when the secondary market for that security was comprised of eighty percent of shares sold in the IPO and twenty percent of non-IPO stock, thereby signifying that eight million shares would be deemed to have been sold by means of the allegedly defective registration statement).[47] The application of Section 11 liability

[42] The liability ramifications of furnishing rather than filing an Exchange Act report are addressed in Chapters 2, 4, and 9 herein.

[43] *See* discussion *infra* notes 49–247 and accompanying text.

[44] For discussion of the different classifications of issuers, *see* Chapter 4 herein.

[45] Under current law, except for the issuer, all Section 11 defendants have the due diligence defense. *See* § 11(b) of the Securities Act, 15 U.S.C. § 77k(b). Note that a control person of a defendant who violates Section 11 is subject to liability exposure under Section 15(a) of that Act, 15 U.S.C. § 77o(a) (providing a defense if "the controlling person had no knowledge of or reasonable ground to believe in the existence of the facts by reason of which the liability of the controlled person is alleged to exist").

[46] *See generally* Charles J. Johnson et al., *Corporate Finance and the Securities Laws* (6th ed. 2019); Carl Schneider et al., *Going Public: Practice, Procedure and Consequences*, 27 Vill. L. Rev. 1 (1981).

[47] *See* discussion in Steinberg and Kirby, *supra* note 15, at 31–37. *See also id.* at 35 ("While statistical evidence has not been widely accepted as a means of establishing tracing, the statistical model offered

exposure, as set forth herein, should remain intact and thereby instill substantial discipline in the Securities Act registration process for unseasoned issuers and affected participants.[48]

B. Uniform Level of Mental Culpability

Under the current federal securities law liability framework, a person who engages in specified conduct may be subject to liability under one provision but not others. For example, a chief executive officer who negligently is responsible for a material misrepresentation in a proxy statement in connection with a merger transaction has liability exposure under Section 14(a) of the Exchange Act but not under Section 10(b), which requires proof of knowing or intentional misconduct.[49] As held by a number of courts, the same holds true in the tender offer setting where liability may be incurred for negligent conduct under Section 14(e) of the Exchange Act.[50] Similarly, as discussed earlier, a negligent material misrepresentation or omission contained in a company's Form 10-K that is incorporated by reference into its Securities Act registration statement will subject a host of participants to liability exposure under Section 11 of the Securities Act but not under Section 10(b).[51] Absent sound justification otherwise (such as with respect to an unseasoned issuer in the registration statement context discussed earlier),[52] a uniform standard of culpability should apply based on the same conduct in private federal

---

herein furthers the objectives of the Securities Act without expanding a suspect defendant's liability beyond the Act's intent.").

[48] Therefore, with respect to these unseasoned issuers and other Section 11 defendants that are sued in such registered offerings, the principles of *BarChris* remain fully applicable. *See Escott v. BarChris Construction Corporation*, 283 F. Supp. 643 (S.D.N.Y. 1968); discussion in Chapter 4 herein.

[49] *See, e.g., Ernst & Ernst v. Hochfelder*, 425 U.S. 185 (1976) (requiring scienter—knowing or intentional misconduct—to be shown in § 10(b) private damages actions); *Gould v. American Hawaiian Steamship Co.*, 535 F.2d 761 (3d Cir. 1976) (applying negligence standard in § 14(a) private action). Note that a number of courts apply a flexible duty analysis, requiring that scienter must be shown in actions against outside directors and accountants based on an alleged violation of Section 14(a). *See, e.g., Adams v. Standard Knitting Mills*, 623 F.2d 422 (6th Cir. 1980).

[50] *See, e.g., Varjabedian v. Emulex Corp.*, 888 F.3d 399 (9th Cir. 2018) (applying negligence standard in a § 14(e) action). This decision represents the minority view as the majority approach is that scienter is required in actions brought for alleged violation of Section 14(e). *See, e.g., Flaherty & Crumrine Preferred Income Fund, Inc. v. TXU Corp.*, 565 F.3d 200 (5th Cir. 2009); *Securities and Exchange Commission v. Ginsburg*, 362 F.3d 1292 (11th Cir. 2004); *In re Digital Island Securities Litigation*, 357 F.3d 322 (3d Cir. 2004). *See generally* Katlyn M. Bay, Comment, *Corporate Dualism: Applying a Dual-Standard of Liability Under Section 14(e)'s Tender Offer Antifraud Provisions*, 45 J. Corp. L. 205 (2019).

[51] *See* discussion *supra* notes 6–43 and accompanying text.

[52] *See* discussion *supra* notes 44–46 and accompanying text.

securities litigation irrespective of the remedial provisions that plaintiffs seek to invoke. Nonetheless, when a complainant seeks a court order requesting that corrective disclosure be made, the objective sufficiency and accuracy of the disclosures should be assessed without inquiry into mental culpability.[53]

As a component of its enforcement arsenal, there is justification for the SEC to have recourse to a graduated scale of enforcement provisions that range from strict liability to knowing misconduct with respect to a defendant's mental intent. After all, traditionally, registration violations are based on strict liability, akin to public welfare offenses.[54] Similarly, the SEC should have the wherewithal to institute enforcement actions premised on negligent conduct, thereby providing the Commission with greater flexibility to address deficient behavior without subjecting a target to the levying of fraud charges. SEC actions premised on negligence, if effectively implemented, deter wrongdoing while facilitating law-compliant conduct.[55] Likewise, to address knowing misconduct, the Commission may employ the antifraud provisions of the federal securities laws, such as Section 10(b).[56]

No similar justification exists with respect to private federal securities litigation. Arbitrariness prevails when a person is saddled with monetary liability under one provision of the federal securities laws but not others based on the identical conduct. The solution is that, with certain necessary exceptions, a uniform private liability standard should apply irrespective

---

[53] *See, e.g.*, *Ash v. LFE Corp.*, 525 F.2d 215 (3d Cir. 1975). *See also Beck v. Dobrowski*, 559 F.3d 680, 682 (7th Cir. 2009) (opining that "there is no required state of mind for a violation of Section 14(a) [and that] a proxy solicitation that contains a material misrepresentation or omission violates the section even if the issuer believed in perfect good faith that there was nothing misleading in the proxy materials").

[54] This position evidently is still supported today by many state courts. *See, e.g.*, *Cox v. Gorvin*, 607 S.E. 2d 549 (Ga. 2005); *Buffo v. State*, 415 So. 2d 1158 (Ala. 1982); *State v. Puckett*, 640 P.2d 1198 (Kan. 1982). *See generally* Mark A. Sargent, *A Blue Sky State of Mind: The Meaning of "Willfully" in Blue Sky Criminal Cases*, 20 Sec. Reg. L.J. 96 (2002) (discussing interpretation by several state courts that "willfully" under the applicable statute signifies that the subject person acted of his own volition without requiring proof of intent, motive, or negligence).

[55] The SEC may institute enforcement actions alleging violations of numerous statutes that require a showing of negligent, rather than intentional or knowing, wrongdoing. *See, e.g.*, § 17(a)(2), (a)(3) of the Securities Act, 15 U.S.C. § 77q(a)(2), (a)(3); §§ 13(a), 14(a) of the Exchange Act, 15 U.S.C. §§ 78m(a), n(a). *See also Aaron v. Securities and Exchange Commission*, 446 U.S. 680 (1980) (holding, *inter alia*, that the SEC need show only negligence to establish a violation of §§ 17(a)(2) and (a)(3)).

[56] Generally, knowing conduct encompasses reckless conduct that is defined as "an extreme departure from the standards of ordinary care to the extent that the danger was either known to the defendant or [was] so obvious that the defendant must have been aware of it." This language has been approvingly quoted by several federal appellate courts. *See, e.g.*, *In re Ikon Office Solutions, Inc. Securities Litigation*, 277 F.3d 658, 667 (3d Cir. 2002); *Hollinger v. Titan Capital Corporation*, 914 F.2d 1564, 1569 (9th Cir. 1990) (en banc); *Sanders v. John Nuveen & Co., Inc.*, 554 F.2d 790, 793 (7th Cir. 1977).

of the statutory or regulatory provision allegedly violated. This proposed standard is set forth later in this chapter.[57]

C. Pleading Requirements in Private Securities Litigation

The pleading requirements for Securities Act Section 11 and other non-fraud claims are based on the plausibility pleading standard enunciated by the U.S. Supreme Court in construing Rule 8(a)(2) of the Federal Rules of Civil Procedure.[58] These relatively recent decisions effectively abandoned the notice pleading standard that had received approbation for over fifty years.[59] Although presenting a greater challenge, plaintiffs

---

[57] *See* discussion *infra* notes 174–185 and accompanying text. With respect to the extraterritorial reach of Section 10(b) of the Securities Exchange Act, the U.S. Supreme Court held in *Morrison v. National Australia Bank Ltd.*, 561 U.S. 247 (1980), that, for the statute to apply, "the purchase or sale [must be] made in the United States, or [must] involve a security listed on a domestic exchange." *Id.* at 269–70. This approach has been criticized by several commentators as being unduly restrictive. *See, e.g.*, Marc I. Steinberg and Kelly Flanagan, *Transnational Dealings—Morrison Continues to Make Waves*, 46 Int'l Law. 829, 865 (2012) (stating that "the decision (1) altered the longstanding treatment of extraterritoriality as a jurisdictional issue; (2) rendered it more difficult to overcome the presumption against extraterritoriality under federal law; and (3) dramatically narrowed the scope of Section 10(b) with respect to transnational frauds"). The better approach is adherence to the "conduct" and "effects" test that had been embraced by the federal appellate courts prior to *Morrison*. The conduct analysis focuses on "whether the wrongful conduct occurred in the United States." *In re CP Ships Limited Securities Litigation*, 578 F.3d 1306, 1313 (11th Cir. 2009). The effects analysis inquires "whether the wrongful conduct had a substantial effect in the United States." *Morrison v. National Australia Bank Ltd.*, 547 F.3d 167, 171 (2d Cir. 2008), *rev'd*, 561 U.S. 247 (2010). Pursuant to statutory enactment, the conduct and effects test applies to government enforcement actions. Enacted as part of the Dodd-Frank Act, this statute provides the federal district courts with subject matter jurisdiction in government actions alleging a violation of the antifraud provisions of the securities laws involving "(1) conduct within the United States that constitutes significant steps in furtherance of the violation, even if the securities transaction occurs outside the United States and involves only foreign investors; or (2) conduct occurring outside the United States that has a foreseeable substantial effect within the United States." Dodd-Frank Wall Street Reform and Consumer Protection Act, Pub. L. No. 111-203, § 929P, 124 Stat. 1376 (2010). *See Securities and Exchange Commission v. Scoville*, 913 F.2d 1204 (10th Cir. 2019) (applying § 929P to hold that sales of securities outside of the United States were within § 10(b)'s reach). The viability of this statute is in doubt as it is focused on subject matter jurisdiction rather than the reach of Section 10(b) and other securities antifraud statutes. For purposes here, the conduct and effects test, proposed to be amended to clarify the language of Section 929P, should be extended to the private litigation setting to encompass both subject matter jurisdiction and the reach of the applicable antifraud statute.

[58] *See Ashcroft v. Iqbal*, 556 U.S. 662 (2009) (expanding the plausibility pleading standard to all federal civil claims); *Bell Atlantic Corp. v. Twombly*, 550 U.S. 544 (2007) (setting forth the plausibility pleading standard with respect to conspiracy claims brought pursuant to § 1 of the Sherman Act).

[59] *See Conley v. Gibson*, 355 U.S. 41 (1957) (adhering to the notice pleading standard). For example, in *Swierkiewicz v. Sorema, N.A.*, in applying the *Conley* standard, the Supreme Court stated that the complaint "must simply give defendant notice of what the plaintiff's claim is and the grounds upon which it rests." 534 U.S. 506, 512 (2002). Overruling this aspect of *Conley*'s pleading standards, the

in federal securities actions generally have successfully hurdled this barrier.[60]

When fraud is alleged in the complaint, however, the enhanced pleading requirements of Rule 9(b) of the Federal Rules of Civil Procedure apply, requiring that "a party must state with particularity the circumstances constituting fraud."[61] This pleading requirement has been heightened by the Private Securities Litigation Reform Act (PSLRA).[62] Pursuant thereto, a plaintiff must plead facts that give rise to an inference of scienter that is "cogent" and that is "at least as compelling" as an inference of non-fraudulent intent.[63] With the vast majority of courts rejecting group pleading and collective scienter doctrines,[64] a plaintiff's task is arduous. This challenge is severely exacerbated by the fact that no discovery is permitted until and unless a plaintiff fends off the defendants' motion to dismiss (assuming such a motion is made).[65]

These arduous pleading requirements signify that a substantial percentage of securities actions (in some years, roughly fifty percent) fail to survive the motion to dismiss stage.[66] These numbers in fact are skewed by

---

Twombly Court held that a complaint must provide "enough facts to state a claim to relief that is plausible on its face." 550 U.S. at 570.

[60] *See* discussion in Marc I. Steinberg and Diego E. Gomez-Cornejo, *Blurring the Lines Between Pleading Doctrines: The Enhanced Rule 8(a)(2) Plausibility Pleading Standard Converges With the Heightened Fraud Standards Under Rule 9(b) and the PSLRA*, 30 Rev. Litig. 1 (2010).

[61] In its entirety, Rule 9(b) provides: "In alleging fraud or mistake, a party must state with particularity the circumstances constituting fraud or mistake. Malice, intent, knowledge, and other conditions of a person's mind may be alleged generally."

[62] *See* § 21D(b)(2)(A) of the Securities Exchange Act, 15 U.S.C. § 78u-4(b)(2)(A); sources cited *supra* note 30.

[63] *Tellabs, Inc. v. Makor Issues & Rights, Ltd.*, 551 U.S. 308, 314 (2007).

[64] Generally, the group pleading doctrine posits that, for pleading purposes, statements contained in SEC filings are those of the subject corporation's directors and executive officers due to their status with the company. *See Wool v. Tanden Computers, Inc.*, 818 F.2d 1433 (9th Cir. 1987). The vast majority of federal courts have rejected the group pleading doctrine as incompatible with the PSLRA's pleading requirements. *See, e.g.*, *Winer Family Trust v. Queen*, 503 F.3d 319 (3d Cir. 2007); *Phillips v. Southland-Atlanta, Inc.*, 374 F.3d 1015 (11th Cir. 2004); *Southland Securities Corp. v. INSpire Insurance Solutions, Inc.*, 365 F.3d 353 (5th Cir. 2004). Likewise, the federal courts overwhelmingly have rejected the collective scienter theory. *See, e.g.*, *Pugh v. Tribune Co.*, 521 F.3d 686, 697 (7th Cir. 2008) (stating that "the corporate scienter inquiry must focus on the state of mind of the individual corporate official or officials who make or issue the statement . . . rather than generally to the collective knowledge of all the corporation's officers and employees acquired in the course of their employment").

[65] *See* § 21D(b)(3)(B) of the Securities Exchange Act, 15 U.S.C., § 78u4(b)(3)(B) ("In any private action arising under [the Securities Exchange Act], all discovery and other proceedings shall be stayed during the pendency of any motion to dismiss, unless the court finds upon the motion of any party that particularized discovery is necessary to preserve evidence or to prevent undue prejudice to that party."); *supra* note 29 and accompanying text.

[66] *See* statistics set forth in Boettrich and Staryk, Nera Economic Consulting Report, *supra* note 31. A more dated analysis is consistent. *See* Renzo Comolli et al., NERA Economic Consulting Report, *Recent Trends in Securities Class Action Litigation: 2012 Full-Year Review* at 16 (2013), available at

the reality that, due to these onerous pleading requirements, fewer categories of defendants today are sued than prior to the PSLRA's passage.[67] As the scienter inquiry focuses on the state of mind of each individual defendant, plaintiffs frequently find it insurmountable to adequately allege, without being afforded discovery, a "cogent" inference of fraudulent intent against collateral actors.[68] Without the availability of aiding and abetting liability in private actions,[69] the result is that these individuals ordinarily avert liability.[70]

Hence, without access to relevant documents and materials, use of interrogatories, and questioning of key witnesses by means of deposition, a plaintiff's task of adequately pleading fraud is unduly onerous. The pleading burden accordingly should be lowered to reflect the F.R.C.P. Rule 9(b) standard unadorned by the PSLRA heightened requirements. As numerous pre-PSLRA cases evidence, the Rule 9(b) standard presents a challenging task for aggrieved plaintiffs.[71] Without undue intrusion, in the discretion of the trial court, limited discovery may be ordered prior to the court's

---

https://www.nera.com/content/dam/nera/publications/archive2/PUB_Year_End_Trends_2012_1113.pdf (reporting that in 2012 over fifty percent of federal securities class action complaints were dismissed at the motion to dismiss stage).

[67] *See* Steinberg, *supra* note 33, at 607 (stating that the statistics of the percentage of cases being dismissed at the motion to dismiss stage "are artificially low due to the fact that plaintiffs today institute federal class actions against fewer types of defendants than prior to the PSLRA's enactment"). For a recent example, *see* Cornerstone Research, *Securities Class Action Settlements: 2019 Review and Analysis* at 9 (2020), available at https://www.cornerstone.com/Publications/Reports/Securities-Class-Action-Settlements-2019-Review-and-Analysis (finding that in cases settled in 2019 that involved accounting-related allegations, "only 6% involved a named auditor codefendant").

[68] *See* discussion and sources cited *supra* notes 29, 31, 61–66 and accompanying text.

[69] *See Central Bank of Denver v. First Interstate Bank of Denver*, 511 U.S. 164 (1994); discussion *infra* 73–98 and accompanying text.

[70] Although such collateral parties may be sued in state court actions, the Securities Litigation Uniform Standards Act (SLUSA) substantially limits this liability exposure. As discussed later in this chapter, with certain carve-outs, SLUSA requires that securities class actions involving a nationally traded security must be brought in federal district court with only federal law applying. Accordingly, with respect to such covered securities, only individual and derivative suits generally may be instituted in state court. *See* discussion *infra* notes 123–137 and accompanying text. In addition, although collateral parties who "cause" a material misstatement in an Exchange Act SEC filing may be sued based on an alleged violation of Section 18(a) of that Act, that statute requires direct reliance, thereby militating against class certification. *See* discussion *supra* notes 21–27 and accompanying text.

[71] *See, e.g.*, *Wexner v. First Manhattan Co.*, 902 F.2d 169 (2d Cir. 1990) (affirming dismissal of the complaint due to its failure to plead an adequate factual basis giving rise to a strong inference that the defendants acted with fraudulent intent). This pre-PSLRA strict decision was not followed by a number of other appellate courts. *See, e.g.*, *Shapiro v. UBS Financial Corp.*, 964 F.2d 272, 284 (3d Cir. 1992) (stating that "courts should be . . . 'sensitive' to the fact that application of the Rule [F.R.C.P. 9(b)] prior to discovery may permit sophisticated defrauders to successfully conceal the details of their fraud"). For literature on the Rule 9(b) pleading standard prior to enactment of the PSLRA, *see, e.g.*, William Richmond et al., *The Pleading of Fraud: Rhymes Without Reason*, 60 So. Cal. L. Rev. 959 (1987); Richard G. Himelrick, *Pleading Securities Fraud*, 43 Md. L. Rev. 342 (1984).

ruling on the motion to dismiss. After affording limited discovery, if the court finds that the complaint is frivolous, it should sanction the plaintiffs and their attorneys, including an appropriate award of attorneys' fees to the defendants.[72] This evenly balanced approach provides plaintiffs a more feasible opportunity to pursue meritorious litigation without imposing an undue burden upon defendants. In the event that plaintiffs and their counsel engage in the filing of frivolous complaints, appropriate sanctions should be ordered.

D. The Propriety of Secondary Liability in Private Securities Actions

For several decades, the lower federal courts uniformly recognized the propriety of aiding and abetting liability under Section 10(b) of the Exchange Act and Rule 10b-5.[73] This approach enabled claimants to seek the recoupment of their losses against secondary actors who allegedly knowingly and substantially assisted the commission of the alleged violations.[74] In this manner, collateral participants, including attorneys and financial intermediaries, were subject to liability exposure.[75] Application of this secondary liability principle served as a key mechanism to incentivize

[72] Current Rule 11(b) of the Federal Rules of Civil Procedure provides adequate guidance. Accordingly, under the proposed standard, the court should levy sanctions against the violating party and its attorneys if it finds that the pleading, motion, or other written document: "(1) [was] . . . presented for any improper purpose, such as to harass, cause unnecessary delay, or needlessly increase the cost of litigation; (2) . . . [was not] warranted by existing law or by a nonfrivolous argument for extending, modifying, or reversing existing law or for establishing new law; (3) . . . [did not] have evidentiary support [with respect to the factual contentions] . . . ; and (4) . . . [with respect to] denials of factual contentions [were not] warranted on the evidence." *Id.*

[73] *See, e.g.*, *Levine v. Diamanthuset, Inc.*, 950 F.2d 1478 (9th Cir. 1991); *Fine v. American Solar King Corp.*, 919 F.2d 290 (5th Cir. 1990); *ITT v. Cornfeld*, 700 F.2d 909 (2d Cir. 1980). This point is made by Justice Blackmun, dissenting in *Central Bank of Denver v. First Interstate Bank of Denver*, 511 U.S. 164, 192 (1994) (Blackmun, J., dissenting): ("In hundreds of judicial and administrative proceedings in every circuit in the federal system, the courts and the SEC have concluded that aiders and abettors are subject to liability under § 10(b) and Rule 10b-5.").

[74] As applied by the lower federal courts, there existed three conditions with respect to the levying of aider and abettor liability: (1) the commission of a primary violation by another person; (2) substantial assistance provided by the alleged aider and abettor in the perpetration of the primary violation; and (3) the alleged aider and abettor having the requisite knowledge that her conduct was improper. *See* cases cited *supra* note 73.

[75] *See, e.g.*, *Molecular Technology v. Valentine*, 925 F.2d 910 (6th Cir. 1991); *Moore v. Kayport Package Express, Inc.*, 885 F.2d 531 (9th Cir. 1989); *Edwards & Hanly v. Wells Fargo Securities Clearance Corp.*, 602 F.2d 478 (2d Cir. 1979); *Andreo v. Friedlander, Gaines, Cohen, Rosenthal & Rosenberg*, 660 F. Supp. 1362 (D. Conn. 1987).

gatekeepers to advise and insist that their clients engage in law-compliant conduct.[76]

In a surprising 1994 decision, the U.S. Supreme Court held that aiding and abetting liability under Section 10(b) is not permitted in private actions.[77] Applying a "strict statutory construction" focusing on the "scope of conduct" prohibited by Section 10(b), the Court reasoned that "the text of the 1934 Act does not itself reach those who aid and abet a § 10(b) violation [and] . . . we think that conclusion resolves the case."[78] Accordingly, as the Court concluded, "[b]ecause the text of § 10(b) does not prohibit aiding and abetting, we hold that a private plaintiff may not maintain an aiding and abetting suit under § 10(b)."[79]

In the aftermath of that decision, plaintiffs instituted actions against collateral actors asserting that their alleged misconduct brought them within the realm of Section 10(b) primary liability.[80] This effort largely has failed as the Supreme Court generally has confined the scope of primary liability to those who knowingly: make a materially false or misleading statement;[81] disseminate a materially false or misleading

[76] *See* Marc I. Steinberg, *Attorney Liability for Client Fraud*, 1991 Colum. Bus. L. Rev. 1, 7–11 (1991).

[77] *Central Bank of Denver v. First Interstate Bank of Denver*, 511 U.S. 164 (1994).

[78] *Id.* at 177.

[79] *Id.* at 191. A four-member dissent sharply disagreed with the majority's ruling. As Justice Blackmun concluded: "The principle the Court espouses today—that liability may not be imposed on parties who are not within § 10(b)'s plain language—is inconsistent with long established Commission and judicial precedent." *Id.* at 201 (Blackmun, J., dissenting). *See generally* Marc I. Steinberg, *The Ramifications of Recent U.S. Supreme Court Decisions on Federal and State Securities Regulation*, 70 Notre Dame L. Rev. 489 (1995).

[80] *See, e.g.*, *Pacific Investment Management Company v. Mayer Brown LLP*, 603 F.3d 144 (2d Cir. 2010); *Affco Investments 2001, LLC v. Proskauer Rose, LLP*, 625 F.3d 185 (5th Cir. 2010); *Ziemba v. Cascade International, Inc.*, 256 F.3d 1194 (11th Cir. 2001); *In re Software Toolworks Incorporated Securities Litigation*, 50 F.3d 615 (9th Cir. 1994). Plaintiffs premised the propriety of primary liability against collateral actors in part on the following language in the Supreme Court's *Central Bank* decision:

> The absence of § 10(b) aiding and abetting liability does not mean that secondary actors in the securities market are always free from liability under the Securities Acts. Any person or entity, including a lawyer, accountant, or bank, who employs a manipulative device or makes a material misstatement (or omission) on which a purchaser or seller of securities relies may be liable as a primary violator under 10b-5, assuming all of the requirements for primary liability under Rule 10b-5 are met.

Central Bank of Denver, 511 U.S. at 191.

[81] *See Janus Capital Fund, Inc. v. First Derivative Traders*, 564 U.S. 135, 142 (confining Rule 10b-5(b) liability to those who "make" a material misstatement or half-truth, namely, those persons who have "ultimate authority over the statement, including its content and whether and how to communicate it"). *See generally* Andrew Gilman, *Scope of Primary Liability Under Section 10(b) of the Securities Exchange Act and Rule 10b-5 Following Janus Capital Group*, 40 Sec. Reg. L.J. 269 (2012); Norman Poser, *Janus Revisited: The Lower Courts Wrestle with a Troubling Supreme Court Decision*, 45 Rev. Sec. & Comm. Reg. 211 (2012).

statement;[82] or engage in deceptive or manipulative conduct upon which the plaintiffs relied.[83] In addition, when a fiduciary duty or relationship of trust and confidence exists, primary liability under Section 10(b) may be premised on a failure to disclose the material information to those persons to whom the duty is owed.[84] This doctrine is applied in the insider trading setting (addressed in Chapter 7 herein).[85]

Hence, collateral actors ordinarily are beyond the reach of Section 10(b) primary liability in private litigation unless they themselves make a statement upon which investors rely, such as the issuance of an investment banker fairness opinion.[86] Added to this insulation from liability is the Securities Litigation Uniform Standards Act (SLUSA) of 1998,[87] which requires, with certain carve-outs, that class actions involving nationally traded securities must be brought in federal court with only federal law applying.[88] With state law ordinarily preempted in such class actions, a plaintiff's recourse typically is limited to instituting an individual federal or state court action. For the ordinary investor, who can ill afford to undertake an individual action, pursuing collateral actors is impracticable.[89]

---

[82] *See Lorenzo v. Securities and Exchange Commission*, 139 S. Ct. 1094 (2019) (in SEC enforcement action holding that those persons who knowingly disseminate to the public materially false statements are subject to liability under § 10(b) and Rule 10b-5(a) and (c)). The extent to which *Lorenzo* will be helpful to private litigants is uncertain. *See infra* note 83.

[83] *See Stoneridge Investment Partners, LLC v. Scientific-Atlanta, Inc.*, 522 U.S. 148, 159 (2008) (rejecting the "scheme" theory of liability under § 10(b) in private actions with respect to those persons who direct or orchestrate a fraudulent scheme where reliance cannot be shown, stating that "reliance by the plaintiff upon the defendant's deceptive acts is an essential element of the § 10(b) private cause of action"). This reliance requirement likely will substantially limit the applicability of *Lorenzo* (*see supra* note 82) in private Section 10(b) actions. *See* Kyle Mason, *Life After Lorenzo—The Strained Re-Emergence of Scheme Liability*, 48 Sec. Reg. L.J. 45, 59–60 (2020) (asserting that "any plaintiff attempting to use scheme liability to allege a primary violation of Rule 10b-5 in order to bring a private action would be faced with the 'tall hurdle' of reliance").

[84] *See, e.g., Chiarella v. United States*, 445 U.S. 222 (1980); *Affiliated Ute Citizens v. United States*, 406 U.S. 128 (1972).

[85] *See generally* Marc I. Steinberg and William K.S. Wang, *Insider Trading* (3d ed. 2010); discussion in Chapter 7 herein.

[86] In such event, an investment banker's fairness opinion, an auditor's opinion with respect to a subject company's financial statements, and an attorney's opinion letter are examples where, if relied upon by investors, primary Section 10(b) liability exposure arises. *See, e.g., Kline v. First Western Government Services, Inc.*, 24 F.3d 480 (3d Cir. 1994).

[87] Pub. L. No. 105-353, 112 Stat. 3227 (1998).

[88] *See* § 16(f)(2)(A) of the Securities Act, 15 U.S.C. § 77p(f)(2)(A); § 28(f) of the Securities Exchange Act, 15 U.S.C. § 78bb(f).

[89] Increasingly, institutional investors are opting out of class actions and bringing individual actions seeking redress under federal and state law. *See* 2019 Securities Class Action Settlements, *supra* note 67, at 2 (identifying "the propensity of [public pension plan] plaintiffs to opt out of class actions, including in larger cases").

Of course, certain exceptions exist. For example, as discussed herein, specified participants, including underwriters, are subject to liability exposure under Securities Act Section 11 for disclosure deficiencies contained in a registration statement.[90] In addition, with respect to individual actions, Section 18(a) of the Exchange Act may be invoked whereby persons who "cause" the making of a materially false or misleading statement contained in a 1934 Act document that is filed with the SEC may be successfully pursued.[91]

Nonetheless, other collateral liability principles recognized under the Securities Act and the Exchange Act, such as the control person provision, ordinarily are not helpful to plaintiffs who desire to hold a collateral actor accountable.[92] In this regard, the control person provision often is used by private claimants seeking to hold corporate insiders liable, including chief executive and chief financial officers, board of director chairs, and board committee chairs (such as the chair of the audit committee).[93] The end result is that, with certain exceptions, we are witnessing the vanishing of collateral participant liability under the federal securities laws. When this consequence is applied to gatekeepers, the prevalence of aberrant conduct likely will increase. This eventuality adversely impacts the objectives of law compliance, investor protection, and the integrity of the U.S. securities markets.[94]

The solution is clear: statutory reinstatement of aider and abettor liability under Section 10(b) and Rule 10b-5. The enactment of this provision would once again provide aggrieved plaintiffs with recourse to pursue collateral participants who, acting with knowing misconduct, substantially assist

---

[90] *See* § 11(a)(5) of the Securities Act, 15 U.S.C. § 77k(a)(5); discussion *supra* notes 6–13 and accompanying text.

[91] *See* § 18(a) of the Securities Exchange Act, 15 U.S.C. § 78r(a) (setting forth liability exposure upon "any person who shall make or cause to be made" any materially false or misleading statement in an Exchange Act SEC filing); discussion *supra* notes 21–27 and accompanying text.

[92] *See* § 15(a) of the Securities Act, 15 U.S.C. § 77o(a); § 20(a) of the Securities Exchange Act, 15 U.S.C. § 78t(a). In this regard, collateral actors rarely are deemed control persons. Occasionally, sufficient facts are alleged to permit the claim to go forward. *See, e.g., In re Rospatch Securities Litigation*, [1992 Transfer Binder] Fed. Sec. L. Rep. (CCH) ¶ 96,939 (W.D. Mich. 1992) (sufficient facts alleged to state control person claim against outside general counsel of the subject corporation).

[93] *See* Loftus C. Carson II, *The Liability of Control Persons Under the Federal Securities Acts*, 72 Notre Dame L. Rev. 263 (1997); Louis D. Lowenfels and Alan R. Bromberg, *Controlling Person Liability Under Section 20(a) of the Securities Exchange Act and Section 15 of the Securities Act*, 53 Bus. Law. 1 (1998); Alexander Poor and Michelle Reed, *The "Control" Quagmire: The Cumbersome Concept of "Control" for the Corporate Attorney*, 44 Sec. Reg. L.J. 101 (2016); discussion in Chapter 9 herein.

[94] This point is made by the author in a recent article. *See* Marc I. Steinberg, *Corporate Lawyers: Ethical and Practical Lawyering with Vanishing Gatekeeper Liability*, 88 Fordham L. Rev. 1575, 1596 (2020) (stating that "although ethical precepts are plentiful with respect to the corporate attorney, relatively little meaningful enforcement exists").

the primary violator in its perpetration of wrongdoing. To mount a viable claim, plaintiffs would be required to allege with adequate particularity the circumstances constituting the aider's fraudulent conduct.[95] In the discretion of the trial judge, limited discovery may be ordered to afford the plaintiff an opportunity to unearth sufficient information to withstand a motion to dismiss on this claim. If the plaintiff fails in this quest, the court should assess the substance of the claim to ascertain whether it is frivolous and levy sanctions, including attorneys' fees, when deemed appropriate.[96] Far from generating strike suits,[97] this provision evenly balances the competing interests by providing investors with a viable avenue to pursue collateral participants while imposing sanctions on plaintiffs and their lawyers for engaging in abusive litigation. Vigorous implementation of the proposed statute's mandates thus should prove beneficial to aggrieved investors while presenting the distinct risk that substantial sanctions will be ordered against miscreant plaintiffs' counsel.[98]

---

[95] The pre-PSLRA tenor expressed by the Third Circuit in *Shapiro v. UBS Financial Corp.*, 964 F.2d 272, 284 (3d Cir. 1992) (stating that "courts should be . . . 'sensitive' to the fact that application of the Rule [F.R.C.P. 9(b)] prior to discovery may permit sophisticated defrauders to successfully conceal the details of their frauds"), should be heeded.

[96] Equitable application of Rule 11 of the Federal Rules of Civil Procedure should serve the interests of litigants, counsel, and the judicial system. *See supra* note 72.

[97] Congress and the U.S. Supreme Court have expressed their distaste for the perceived proliferation of strike suits. *See, e.g.*, Private Securities Litigation Reform Act, Joint Explanatory Statement of the Committee on Conference (1995), available at https://www.congress.gov/104/crpt/hrpt369/CRPT-104hrpt369.pdf ("Professional plaintiffs who own a nominal number of shares in a wide variety of public companies permit lawyers readily to file abusive securities class action lawsuits."); *Blue Chip Stamps v. Manor Drug Stores*, 421 U.S. 723, 741 (1975) (commenting on the "potential for possible abuse of the liberal discovery provisions" available in securities litigation, including the "common occurrence" of "extensive deposition of the defendant's officers and associates and the concomitant opportunity for extensive discovery of business documents").

[98] It may be viewed as intriguing that there is great distaste for perceived strike suits and the awarding of attorneys' fees while relatively little attention is focused on the large fees that attorneys in corporate law firms receive which at times are detrimental to other meritorious interests. An excellent example is the fees that attorneys receive in the bankruptcy setting. For example, with respect to the Windstream Holdings, Inc. bankruptcy proceedings, Kirkland & Ellis LLP's fees for the month of April 2020 totaled $2,122,090.60. A number of paralegals were billed at hourly rates of $445, associates at $1,085, and partners at $1,635. *See In re: Windstream Holdings, Inc., et al., Fourteenth Monthly Fee Statement of Kirkland & Ellis LLP and Kirkland & Ellis International LLP for Compensation for Services and Reimbursement of Expenses as Counsel to the Debtors and Debtors in Possession for the Period From April 1, 2020 Through April 30, 2020 (Exhibit B)*, filed July 6, 2020 (U.S. Bkrtcy Ct. S.D.N.Y. 2020), available at https://www.kccllc.net/windstream/document/1922312200706000000000007. In connection with the city of Detroit bankruptcy, Jones Day, after "slashing" its fees by nearly $18 million, received $58 million in professional fees. *See* Martha Neil, *Judge Oks $178M in Detroit Bankruptcy Professional Fees; Jones Day Gets $58M*, ABA Journal (Feb. 12, 2015), available at https://www.abajournal.com/news/article/judge_oks_178m_in_detroit_bankruptcy_professional_fees_jones_day_gets_58m_f.

E. The Unduly Expansive Protection Given to Puffery, Statements of Belief, and Forward-Looking Statements

Corporate officers and directors owe a fiduciary duty to the corporation and, collectively, its shareholders.[99] As defined by Black's Law Dictionary, a fiduciary is an individual "who is required to act for the benefit of another person on all matters within the scope of their relationship [and who] owes to another the duties of good faith, loyalty, due care and disclosure [such as a] corporate officer [who] is a fiduciary."[100] With these principles firmly established, one may reasonably conclude that, when corporate directors and officers undertake their disclosure obligations under the federal securities laws, they must act with due care and in good faith. Failure to do so, one may posit, would subject the affected fiduciaries to the specter of liability to shareholders who were harmed by the alleged wrongdoing. This, however, is not the case. Under established law, these fiduciaries may engage in hyperbole, carelessly perform their disclosure duties, and outright lie with respect to forward-looking statements and yet not incur liability to shareholders.[101]

As an initial point, as held by the U.S. Supreme Court, corporate fiduciaries are not liable under Section 10(b) of the Exchange Act—the principal remedy for plaintiffs in securities class actions—unless they act with intentional or knowing misconduct.[102] Carelessness in performing one's disclosure obligations is not actionable under the statute.[103] This broad insulation from Section 10(b) liability is buttressed by several other doctrines. For example, under the "puffery" doctrine, corporate fiduciaries are treated akin to "used" car salespersons.[104] Making generalized optimistic statements, courts hold, is not actionable as such statements lack materiality and are not relied

---

99 *See, e.g.*, *Mills Acquisition Co. v. MacMillan, Inc.*, 559 A.2d 1261, 1280 (Del. 1989) (stating that "the directors owe fiduciary duties of care and loyalty to the corporation and its shareholders").

100 *Black's Law Dictionary* 770 (Bryan A. Garner editor-in-chief, 11th ed. 2019).

101 *See* discussion *infra* notes 102–122 and accompanying text.

102 *See Ernst & Ernst v. Hochfelder*, 425 U.S. 185 (1976) (based on the language of the statute and its legislative history, holding that intentional misconduct is required). Although the Supreme Court has not ruled on the issue, lower federal courts hold that reckless conduct is actionable under Section 10(b). *See supra* note 56. In its enforcement actions alleging violation of Section 10(b), the SEC likewise must prove scienter. *See Aaron v. Securities and Exchange Commission*, 446 U.S. 680 (1980); discussion in Chapter 9 herein.

103 In a vigorous dissent in *Hochfelder*, Justice Blackmun opined: "It seems to me . . . that an investor can be victimized just as much by negligent conduct as by positive deception, and that it is not logical to drive a wedge between the two, saying that Congress clearly intended the one but certainly not the other." 425 U.S. at 216 (Blackmun, J., dissenting).

104 This point is made in the aptly entitled article by Sarah Lee, *The Puffery Defense: From Used Car Salesman to CEO*, 30 Sec. Reg. L.J. 440 (2002).

upon by reasonable investors.[105] Frequently, these generalized statements focus on vital aspects of the subject company's business, including its culture and reputation, recent acquisitions, compliance with regulatory requirements, clinical trial data, disciplined pricing of its products, and adherence to rigorous diligence practices.[106] As another example, statements of opinion or belief made by a corporate fiduciary generally are not actionable unless the speaker in fact knows that she does not hold such opinion or belief.[107] And, last, pursuant to the PSLRA, forward-looking statements

---

[105] The use of puffery by salesmen in marketing their goods to consumers is reflected in a Sixth Circuit decision over 100 years ago. *See Harrison v. United States*, 200 F. 662, 665–66 (6th Cir. 1912) (inquiring "[w]hen does the not uncommon exaggeration of advertising become sufficient evidence of an intent to defraud? Can a business man, selling an article of merit and of value and at a fair price, be convicted of a scheme to defraud [under the mail fraud statute], because his advertising overstates the capacity and usefulness of the article?"). For cases applying the puffery doctrine in the securities law context, *see infra* note 106.

[106] *See, e.g.*, *Indiana Public Retirement System v. SAIC, Inc.*, 818 F.3d 85 (2d Cir. 2016) (laudatory statements concerning the corporation's culture and reputation deemed puffery); *Lloyd v. CVB Financial Corp.*, 811 F.3d 1200 (9th Cir. 2016) (statements touting the corporation's "sound credit culture and underwriting integrity" deemed puffery); *IBEW Local Union No. 58 Pension Trust Fund & Annuity Fund v. Royal Bank of Scotland Group, PLC*, 783 F.3d 383 (2d Cir. 2015) (generalized statements focusing on a corporate acquisition deemed puffery); *City of Edinburgh Council v. Pfizer, Inc.*, 754 F.3d 159 (3d Cir. 2014) (optimistic statements made by a pharmaceutical company regarding clinical trial data deemed puffery); *In re Aetna, Inc. Securities Litigation*, 617 F.3d 272 (3d Cir. 2010) (statements concerning corporation's disciplined pricing of insurance policies deemed puffery); *Veal v. LendingClub Corporation*, 423 F. Supp. 3d 785, 795–96 (N.D. Cal. 2019) (statements regarding the company's commitment to compliance with regulatory requirements deemed puffery). A number of decisions have limited the reach of the puffery doctrine. *See, e.g.*, *Zaghian v. Farrell*, 675 Fed. Appx. 718 (9th Cir. 2017) (holding corporation's statements that one of its products would "generate significant growth, profitability, and cash" resulting in its "largest quarter" in history deemed actionable as the statements "did not vaguely describe [the corporation's] financial health but instead addressed a particular product and the anticipated profitability of that product"); *In re Level 3 Communications, Inc. Securities Litigation*, 667 F.3d 1331 (10th Cir. 2012) (corporation's statement that its integration was "85%, 90% done" deemed actionable); *Beavers City Employees Retirement Fund v. The Shop Hold, Inc.*, 94 F. Supp. 3d 1035 (D. Minn. 2015) (CEO's statement that the corporation's "direct sourcing model [was] a material competitive advantage" deemed actionable). For commentary on the puffery doctrine, *see, e.g.*, Lee, *supra* note 104; Jennifer O'Hare, *The Resurrection of the Dodo: The Unfortunate Re-Emergence of the Puffery Defense in Private Securities Fraud Actions*, 59 Ohio St. L.J. 1697 (1998); Stefan Padfield, *Is Puffery Material to Investors? Maybe We Should Ask Them*, 10 U. Pa. Bus. & Emp. Law 339 (2008).

[107] *See Omnicare, Inc. v. Laborers District Council Construction Industry Pension Fund*, 135 S. Ct. 1318, 1326 (2015). In addition, a statement of opinion under *Omnicare* can be actionable if the opinion omits material facts with respect to the subject corporation's (or other speaker's) inquiry into or knowledge concerning such statement of opinion, and if those facts conflict with how a reasonable investor would view the statement. *Id.* at 1329. *See also Virginia Bankshares, Inc. v. Sandberg*, 501 U.S. 1083 (1991) (recognizing § 14(a) of the Exchange Act and Rule 14a-9 claim where there exists a materially false or misleading statement of belief or opinion, as well as the factual basis therefor). Although addressing statements of belief or opinion for liability purposes under Section 11 of the Securities Act, *Omnicare*'s rationale has been extended to Exchange Act Section 10(b) actions. *See, e.g.*, *City of Dearborn Heights v. Align Technology, Inc.*, 856 F.3d 605 (9th Cir. 2017). *See generally* Allison Cook, *"I Believe" Omnicare Falls Short: An Analysis of the Supreme Court's Latest Attempt to Clarify Opinion-Statement Liability*, 46 Sec. Reg. L.J. 19 (2018); James D. Cox, *"We're Cool" Statements After Omnicare: Securities Fraud Suits for Failures to Comply with the Law*, 68 SMU L. Rev. 715

by an Exchange Act reporting company are immune from private liability under the federal securities laws even if those statements are made with deliberate falsity so long as meaningful cautionary disclosures accompany such forward-looking statements.[108]

With these expansive principles recognized, it is not surprising that disclosure practices by publicly-held companies are replete with statements of cheery belief and expressions of optimism.[109] Unfortunately, all too frequently, these statements belie reality. And, with respect to unduly rosy forward-looking statements addressing such core matters as earnings, revenues, contractual undertakings, and acquisitions, liability is foreclosed in private actions if expert counsel drafts the accompanying cautionary disclosures with proficiency.[110] Although the prospects of a government enforcement action and the arousal of institutional investor and financial analyst ire may have the effect of dampening this otherwise unbridled enthusiasm,[111] shareholders are left without redress.

For corporate officers and directors to act in this manner and not be held accountable to shareholders makes a mockery of fiduciary duty principles. As the law currently stands regarding this subject, these individuals, for Section 10(b) private liability scrutiny, are fiduciaries for window-dressing purposes only, lacking substantive application. To remedy this situation, as discussed later in this chapter, culpability generally should be premised on negligent misconduct rather than scienter.[112] With respect to forward-looking statements, because of the uncertainties in accurate forecasting

(2015); Hilary A. Sale and Donald C. Langevoort, *"We Believe": Omnicare, Legal Risk Disclosure and Corporate Governance*, 66 Duke L.J. 763 (2016).

[108] *See* § 27A(c)(1), 15 U.S.C. § 77aa(c)(1); § 21E(c)(1) of the Securities Exchange Act, 15 U.S.C. § 78u-5(c)(1). Enacted as part of the PSLRA, this provision provides, with certain exceptions, a safe harbor from liability in private actions if the forward-looking statement "is identified as a forward-looking statement, and is accompanied by meaningful cautionary statements identifying important factors that could cause actual results to differ materially from those in the forward-looking statement." *Id.* If the cautionary statements are deemed insufficient, then liability for a materially false or misleading forward-looking statement is based on proof of actual knowledge. *Id. See Slayton v. American Express Company*, 604 F.3d 758 (2d Cir. 2010); *Asher v. Baxter International, Inc.*, 377 F.3d 727 (7th Cir. 2004); *Harris v. Ivax Corporation*, 182 F.3d 799 (11th Cir. 1999).

[109] *See, e.g.*, cases cited *supra* note 106.

[110] *See* sources cited *supra* note 108.

[111] *See* Donal Byard and Kenneth W. Shaw, *Corporate Disclosure Quality and Properties of Analysts' Information Environment*, 18 J. Acc., Aud. & Fin. 355 (2003), available at https://doi.org/10.1177/0148558X0301800304; Hua Cheng et al., *Corporate Disclosure Quality and Institutional Investors' Holdings During Market Downturns*, 60 J. Corp. Fin. 1 (Feb. 2020), available at https://www.sciencedirect.com/science/article/pii/S0929119919301828.

[112] *See* discussion *infra* notes 174–185 and accompanying text.

coupled with the wisdom of hindsight that plaintiffs employ, greater protection should be provided.[113] The solution is a modification of SEC rules that applied to publicly-held companies prior to the PSLRA's enactment.[114] Under this proposed standard, a forward-looking statement would be insulated from liability unless the complainant establishes that such statement was made either with gross negligence or without good faith.[115] Extending protection for "merely" negligent conduct with respect to the issuance of forward-looking statements should provide sufficient comfort to prospective defendants. Engaging in egregiously careless or bad faith predictions of corporate earnings, revenues, and other contingent developments should be actionable. After all, with this level of protection, the conduct of fiduciaries in this context still would be accorded more favorable treatment than when parties deal at arm's length in commercial settings.[116]

The same principles should apply with respect to statements of belief and puffery. There is no sound reason giving corporate fiduciaries carte blanche to act recklessly and, at times, intentionally, yet avoid liability because the false and misleading statement is viewed as an optimistic generalization or qualified as a statement of belief.[117] If the applicable statement is future-oriented or cannot otherwise be verified, then liability predicated on a complainant's showing of gross negligence or bad faith would apply. Otherwise, with respect to disclosures that are susceptible to factual verification, the culpability

---

[113] Hence, the securities laws are not investment insurance and conclusory allegations of fraud premised on hindsight must fail. *See DiLeo v. Ernst & Young*, 901 F.2d 624, 627 (7th Cir. 1990) ("The story in this complaint is familiar to securities litigation. At one time, the firm bathes itself in a favorable light. Later the firm discloses that things are less than rosy. The plaintiff contends that the differences must be attributable to fraud.").

[114] These rules are still pertinent to some degree, such as in SEC enforcement actions and in private actions where the PSLRA safe harbor for forward-looking statements is not applicable, including with respect to a subject company's initial public offering. *See* Rule 175, 17 C.F.R. § 230.175; Rule 3b-6, 17 C.F.R. § 240.3b-6. Pursuant to these rules, a forward-looking statement is not actionable "unless it is shown that such statement was made or reaffirmed without a reasonable basis or was disclosed other than in good faith." *Id.* In this regard, liability for statements of belief or opinion have been substantially relaxed due to the Supreme Court's decision in *Omnicare*. *See supra* note 107 and accompanying text.

[115] Hence, the proposal herein provides eligible issuers with greater protection than Rule 175 or Rule 3b-6 as it bases liability (in part) on a showing of gross negligence rather than a lack of reasonable basis. *See supra* note 114.

[116] For example, in arm's-length commercial settings, an action for negligent misrepresentation is recognized. *See, e.g.*, American Law Institute, *Restatement (Second) of Torts* § 552 (1977). By comparison, gross negligence is defined as the "lack of even slight diligence or care." *Black's Law Dictionary*, *supra* note 100, at 1246.

[117] Indeed, in *Virginia Bankshares, Inc. v. Sandberg*, 501 U.S. 1083 (1991), the Supreme Court held that statements contained in the corporation's proxy solicitation describing a proposed merger as providing minority shareholders a "high" value and "fair" price for their stock were actionable if specified requirements were met.

standard would be negligence.[118] When assessing the securities law disclosure obligations of corporate fiduciaries, the puffery doctrine should be dismantled and go the way of the dodo.[119]

Application of a negligence level of culpability in private actions is not foreign to the federal securities laws. After all, both Sections 11 and 12(a)(2) of the Securities Act have a more rigorous culpability standard, which in effect requires the defendant to prove its exercise of due diligence and reasonable care.[120] Also, with respect to corporate officers and directors, the proxy statute, Section 14(a) and Rule 14a-9 promulgated thereunder, impose liability in private damages actions predicated on negligent misconduct.[121] Hence, the proposals advanced herein may be viewed as consistent with certain key principles of current law. Moreover, as discussed in this chapter with respect to aider and abettor liability exposure, the requisite mental culpability level would be that of knowing misconduct.[122]

F. Federal Preemption of Securities Class Actions

As discussed earlier in this chapter, with certain carve-outs, SLUSA requires that securities class actions involving nationally traded securities must be brought in federal court with only federal law applying.[123] The Act was a congressional response to plaintiffs who zealously instituted state court class actions to avoid the rigors of the PSLRA.[124] Viewing these state lawsuits as undermining the PSLRA's objectives, Congress enacted broad preemption legislation.[125]

---

[118] *See In re Integrated Resources Real Estate Limited Partnership Securities Litigation*, 815 F. Supp. 620, 674 (S.D.N.Y. 1993) (stating "all the cautionary language in the world will not replace a true material omission or misstatement of a fact which would matter to a reasonable investor").

[119] *See* O'Hare, *supra* note 106, at 1700 (stating that "the courts have significantly expanded the scope of a powerful defense [i.e., the puffery defense] to dismiss potentially meritorious securities fraud actions with little or no analysis or consideration of the effect of their decisions").

[120] In Section 11 actions, specified defendants (other than an issuer) have the due diligence defense. In Section 12(a)(2) actions, the defendant seller has the burden of proof to show that "he did not know, and in the exercise of reasonable care could not have known" of the material "untruth or omission." 15 U.S.C. §§ 77k, l(a)(2); discussion *supra* notes 6–13 and accompanying text.

[121] *See* discussion *supra* note 49 and accompanying text.

[122] *See* discussion *supra* notes 95–98 and accompanying text; *infra* notes 206–210 and accompanying text.

[123] *See* discussion *supra* notes 87–89 and accompanying text.

[124] *See* the Securities Litigation Uniform Standards Act of 1998, S. 1260, Report of the Senate Committee on Banking, Housing, and Urban Affairs, 105th Cong., 2d Sess. at 3 (1998) (referring to "a noticeable shift in [securities] class action litigation from federal to state courts").

[125] Pub. L. No. 105-353, 112 Stat. 3227 (1998).

From a general perspective, SLUSA promotes the federal interest to enforce the PSLRA's class action reforms.[126] Otherwise, these mandates could be voided by plaintiffs filing their class actions in attractive state courts, such as the California state courts.[127] Nonetheless, SLUSA should be modified in two important ways. First, an investor's entitlement to seek state court relief should be preempted only if a federal class action was an available recourse. Under current law, as held by the U.S. Supreme Court, so long as some person on this planet was purchasing or selling the subject securities in connection with the alleged fraud, SLUSA preemption applies.[128] The result of this holding is that plaintiffs, who cannot satisfy Section 10(b)'s purchaser-seller requirement (and thereby lack standing to bring suit based on an alleged violation of that statute), nonetheless are preempted from bringing a state court class action.[129] In effect, aggrieved plaintiffs are deprived of an otherwise viable state court avenue of relief where no federal interest exists to justify such denial. Although individual actions may be initiated in state court, ordinary investors can ill afford to pursue redress absent the availability of the class action vehicle.[130]

The second modification is that, while covered class actions must be brought in federal court, state law claims should not be preempted. Prior to SLUSA's enactment, it was common practice for plaintiffs to supplement their federal claims with allegedly meritorious state claims that were consistent with class certification.[131] This strategy enabled plaintiffs to retain

---

[126] Senate Report, *supra* note 124, at 5 (stating that "the increased risk of state court class actions has had a chilling effect on the use of the 'safe-harbor' and other important provisions of the 1995 [PSLRA] Act").

[127] *See* David M. Levine and Adam C. Pritchard, *The Securities Litigation Uniform Standards Act of 1998: The Sun Sets on California's Blue Sky Laws*, 54 Bus. Law. 1 (1998).

[128] *See Merrill Lynch, Pierce, Fenner & Smith, Inc. v. Dabit*, 547 U.S. 71, 85 (2006) (opining that "it is enough that the fraud alleged 'coincide' with a securities transaction—whether by the plaintiff or someone else").

[129] In *Dabit*, the plaintiffs were holders of the subject securities and therefore lacked standing to bring a damages action alleging violation of Section 10(b). *See Blue Chip Stamps v. Manor Drug Stores*, 421 U.S. 723 (1975). As the Supreme Court in *Dabit* observed, the Second Circuit had held in the decision below that "SLUSA only pre-empts state law class action claims brought by plaintiffs who have a private remedy under federal law." *Id.* at 74, *citing*, 395 F.3d 25 (2d Cir. 2005). The Supreme Court reversed (547 U.S. 71 (2006)).

[130] A SLUSA carve-out is the initiation of individual actions in federal and state courts. In addition, class actions may be instituted in state court with respect to going-private transactions, mergers, tender offers, and the exercise of appraisal rights. *See* §§ 16(d)(1), (f)(2) of the Securities Act, 15 U.S.C. §§ 77p(d)(1), (f)(2); §§ 28(f)(3), (f)(5) of the Securities Exchange Act, 15 U.S.C. §§ 78aa(f)(3), (f)(5). There are additional SLUSA carve-outs, including with respect to derivative actions.

[131] *See, e.g., Sandberg v. Virginia Bankshares, Inc.*, 979 F.2d 332, 342–48 (4th Cir. 1992) (although defeated on their federal law securities law claims, plaintiffs awarded damages on a number of state claims). Note that the fraud on the market theory may not be invoked with respect to a number of state claims, such as common law fraud, thereby militating against class certification with respect to such claims. *See Peil v. Speiser*, 806 F.2d 1154, 1163 n. 17 (3d Cir. 1986) ("While the fraud on the

meritorious state remedies and also ensured that federal law with respect to class action mandates, including class certification, would govern.[132] In this fashion, federal interests were aptly served without substantively compromising investor remedies.[133] By precluding the bringing of state law claims in covered federal securities class actions, SLUSA halted this practice. This determination, in effect, deprived investors of important remedies without sufficient justification. Principles of federalism should have counseled otherwise.[134] The federal objective in ensuring that the provisions of the PSLRA are implemented is sufficiently met by requiring that covered class actions must be brought exclusively in federal court. The retention by plaintiffs of their state remedies provides a valuable source of redress. Unlike institutional investors who opt out of class actions to pursue their individual federal and state claims,[135] ordinary investors must remain members of the class. As much as practicable, they should be afforded similar opportunities as institutional and other well-heeled investors to the same panoply of remedies.[136] Corrective action thus should be undertaken by Congress to permit plaintiffs in covered securities class actions to institute state law claims.[137]

G. Broker-Dealers and Investment Advisers

The multi-faceted issues arising with respect to broker-dealers and investment advisers have been addressed in numerous treatises.[138] The following

---

market theory is good law with respect to the Securities Acts, no state courts have adopted the theory, and thus direct reliance remains a requirement of a common law securities fraud claim.").

[132] In this regard, a number of state securities laws do not require reliance to be proven as an element of certain claims. *See, e.g.*, § 410(b) of the Uniform Securities Act (1956). *See generally* Joseph C. Long, Michael J. Kaufman, and John M. Wunderlich, *Blue Sky Law* (2020).

[133] *See* Senate Report, *supra* note 124, Additional Views of Senators Sarbanes, Bryan and Johnson, at 14 (expressing opposition to SLUSA as it would establish the PSLRA as "the sole, uniform standard for nationally traded securities").

[134] *Id.* at 11 (stating that SLUSA's enactment would result in investors having "their state court remedies eliminated . . . [and that] such a result can only harm innocent investors, undermine public confidence in the securities markets, and ultimately raise the cost of capital for deserving American businesses").

[135] Institutional investors increasingly are opting out of class actions to pursue their individual claims. *See supra* note 89.

[136] *See* Senate Report, *supra* note 124, Additional Views at 11 ("We fear that [if SLUSA is enacted] investors will be left without any effective remedies at all").

[137] *See id.* at 14 ("As we considered the provisions of the [PSLRA] insufficiently protective of investors to be an appropriate Federal securities antifraud standard, we cannot support establishing that Act as the sole, uniform standard for nationally traded securities").

[138] *See, e.g.*, James A. Fanto, Jill I. Gross, and Norman S. Poser, *Broker-Dealer Law and Regulation* (5th ed. 2020); Tamar Frankel and Arthur B. Laby, *The Regulation of Money Managers* (3d ed. 2020).

discussion focuses on a number of important subjects. The first is the U.S. Supreme Court's upholding of pre-dispute arbitration agreements between brokerage firms and their clients.[139] As historically viewed by claimants, the arbitral forum is stacked in the industry's favor.[140] Fortunately, the overseer of this arbitration process, the Financial Industry Regulatory Authority (FINRA), has undertaken commendable measures to address this perception.[141] The most important actions are the implementation of all-public arbitration panels combined with broader exclusion of arbitrators with prior industry ties from being classified as public arbitrators.[142] Recent statistics show that approximately seventy-five percent of FINRA arbitration hearings have all-public panels, with a customer being awarded damages in fifty-three percent of such hearings.[143]

Thus, much progress has been made. Nonetheless, certain additional measures should be adopted. First, FINRA rightly is focusing on enhancing the diversity of its arbitration panels.[144] Nonetheless, greater diversity is needed in terms of age, gender, and race. The perception of fairness in the arbitration process may well be impaired when arbitration panels lack sufficient

---

[139] *See Shearson/American Express, Inc. v. McMahon*, 482 U.S. 220 (1987) (upholding enforceability of pre-dispute arbitration agreement between brokerage firm and its customers with respect to Exchange Act § 10(b) and Racketeer Influenced and Corrupt Organizations Act (RICO) claims). *See also Rodriguez De Quijas v. Shearson/American Express, Inc.*, 490 U.S. 477 (1989) (upholding enforceability of pre-dispute arbitration agreement involving Securities Act claims).

[140] *See PIABA [Public Investor Arbitration Bar Association], Other Groups Seek Data on Mandatory Arbitration*, 47 Sec. Reg. & L. Rep. (BNA) 164 (2015) ("As long as brokerage firms and investment advisers retain the ability to require investors to resolve disputes in arbitration, FINRA [Financial Industry Regulatory Authority] arbitration may be inherently biased against individuals."). *See generally* Perry Wallace, *Securities Arbitration After McMahon, Rodriguez and the New Rules: Can Investors' Rights Really Be Protected?*, 43 Vand. L. Rev. 1199 (1990).

[141] *See* Ralph S. Janvey and Hayden M. Baker, *Investor Fairness in Securities Arbitration: A Perceptional Issue?*, 45 Sec. Reg. L.J. 259, 286 (2017) (stating that FINRA has taken "commendable efforts to address the vocal concerns of investors and investor advocates").

[142] *See* Order Approving a Proposed Rule Change Relating to Revisions to the Definitions of Non-Public Arbitrator and Public Arbitrator, Securities Exchange Act Release No. 74383 (2015); Order Approving Proposed Rule Change Relating to Amendments to the Code of Arbitration Procedure for Customer Disputes Concerning Panel Composition, Securities Exchange Act Release No. 70442 (2013).

[143] *See* FINRA, 2019 Dispute Resolution Statistics (Results of All-Public and Majority Public Panels in Customer Cases), available at https://www.finra.org/arbitration-mediation/dispute-resolution-statistics/2019#resultsallpublic. By comparison in 2018, with approximately the same percentage of all-public panels, customers were awarded damages in 42% of the hearings. *Id.*

[144] *See* FINRA, *Our Commitment to Achieving Arbitrator and Mediator Diversity at FINRA*, available at https://www.finra.org/arbitration-mediation/our-commitment-achieving-arbitrator-and-mediator-diversity-finra (stating that FINRA has "bolstered" its "recruitment efforts, both in terms of increasing the numbers and diversity—in age, gender, race, and occupation").

diversity.[145] Second, the classification of industry arbitrator status should be expanded to encompass individuals who directly or indirectly (such as through their law firms) have derived fees or revenues from financial industry entities during any of the past five years of greater than $25,000. A legitimate concern of cultural bias arises in such circumstances, which should require that such persons be classified as industry arbitrators.[146] Third, to attract a qualified and diverse pool of arbitrators, the payment of honoraria to arbitrators should be substantially increased. Undertaking the assignment of serving as a FINRA arbitrator is a demanding task and should be compensated at an appropriate level.[147] Fourth, more intensive training should be implemented to enable arbitrators to have a substantially better understanding of the procedural and substantive issues involved in FINRA customer-broker arbitrations.[148] Fifth, FINRA arbitrators should be subject to compulsory periodic disclosure obligations focusing on conflicts of interest, including the receipt, directly or indirectly, of fees, revenues, or other benefits from brokerage or other financial industry entities.[149]

The sixth recommendation focuses on pre-dispute arbitration agreements. Today, unless a customer has an inordinately large account, arbitration is mandatory rather than optional.[150] For ordinary accounts, brokerage firms

[145] *See Survey Shows Some Clients See Process as Tilted Against Them*, 40 Sec. Reg. & L. Rep. (BNA) 198 (2008) (in study conducted by Professors Barbara Black and Jill Gross, finding that investors who arbitrated their broker-dealer disputes "largely believe that arbitrators were competent and understood the issues but were less sure that arbitrators were open-minded, impartial, and properly applying the law").

[146] Although FINRA has substantially improved the demarcations between industry and public arbitrators, there nonetheless remain "complaints that current FINRA rules allow the public arbitrators to hold attenuated industry ties." Janvey and Baker, *supra* note 141, at 278–80, *addressing*, FINRA Rules 12100(u), 13100(u). The proposal herein goes further than current FINRA rules in recognition of the persistent presence of cultural bias when an individual has any financial ties (other than de minimis) with the financial services industry.

[147] *See* FINRA, *Final Report and Recommendations of the FINRA Dispute Resolution Task Force* 5 (2015), available at https://www.finra.org/sites/default/files/Final-DR-task-force-report.pdf (stating that FINRA's "below-market . . . compensation acts as a disincentive in the recruitment of arbitrators and in the commitment of substantial time by arbitrators in executing their responsibilities"). Currently, FINRA arbitrators typically receive $600 per day (or $725 for chairpersons). *See* FINRA, *Become a FINRA Arbitrator*, available at https://www.finra.org/arbitration-mediation/become-finra-arbitrator.

[148] *See* Janvey and Baker, *supra* note 141, at 284–85 (commenting that, after an individual completes the basic training program, no requirement exists for continued training).

[149] *See* FINRA Dispute Resolution Task Force Report, *supra* note 147, at 13 (positing that the prompt updating of an arbitrator's disclosure should be mandated to report "material new information or a material change in status" and that each arbitrator should be "required to review, at least annually, [his or her] arbitrator disclosure report and either confirm its accuracy or update it to take account of new information").

[150] *See, e.g., De Kwiatkowski v. Bear, Stearns & Co., Inc.*, 306 F.3d 1293 (2d Cir. 2002) (reversing $111.5 million jury verdict in favor of plaintiff-customer); *infra* note 151.

ordinarily refuse to open a customer account without an executed agreement containing a mandatory arbitration clause.[151] In practical effect, for nearly all customers, pre-dispute arbitration agreements are foisted upon them. This situation is unacceptable. If arbitration in actuality is viewed as an even-handed process and less costly than pursuing a state court action,[152] customers readily will sign the agreement. After all, the financial costs borne by litigants in court proceedings ordinarily are substantially higher than those incurred in the arbitral forum.[153] The availability of contingent attorney fee arrangements does not substantially impact this analysis. Upon the opening of an account, the affected customer normally will believe that her broker and his firm will engage in lawful conduct and act consistently with her financial interests. Few customers open up brokerage accounts with the objective of subsequently suing their brokers. Accordingly, customers will likely opt for the arbitral forum at the pre-dispute stage due to its perceived lower costs and more expeditious resolution.[154] Nonetheless, to induce FINRA and the brokerage industry to improve the impartiality of the arbitration process both in actuality and perception, customer choice of forum should be implemented with respect to pre-dispute arbitration agreements. Adherence to this approach promotes the equitable resolution of litigated matters, thereby better serving the integrity of the U.S. adjudicatory process.[155]

---

[151] *See* Linda A. Fienberg and Matthew S. Yeo, *The NASD Securities Arbitration Report: View from the Inside*, 10 Insights No. 4, at 7, 8 (April 1996) ("Since [the Supreme Court's 1987 decision in] *McMahon*, broker-dealers have required almost all individual investors who open margin or option accounts to sign a pre-dispute arbitration agreement, and most broker-dealers require it for all customer accounts").

[152] *See* Norman S. Poser, *When ADR Eclipses Litigation: The Brave New World of Securities Arbitration*, 59 Brook. L. Rev. 1095, 1111 (1993) (asserting that "it would not be fair to describe [arbitration] as a deck stacked in favor of the brokerage firm").

[153] *See* Marc I. Steinberg, *Securities Arbitration: Better for Investors than the Courts?*, 62 Brook. L. Rev. 1503, 1512–14 (1996):

> Arbitration today... remains a fairly informal process. Rather than burdensome pleading requirements ..., a complainant in arbitration "need only specify the relevant facts and the remedies sought." Although discovery is permitted to an increasing extent, including written requests for information and document requests, a number of the more costly and time consuming aspects of discovery found in federal and state court litigation usually are not present. Hence, depositions are rarely permitted and dispositive motions prior to the formal hearing are not encouraged.

[154] Nonetheless, without the presence of a pre-dispute arbitration agreement, it may well be that most plaintiffs at the time that a dispute arises would opt to bring suit in a favorable state forum and have the merits of their case decided by a jury rather than a panel of arbitrators. *Id.* at 1531.

[155] Generally, an explained decision is not required unless jointly requested by the parties. FINRA Rules 12514(d), 12904(g). As stated in Rule 12904(g)(2): "An explained award is a fact-based award stating the general reason(s) for the arbitrators' decision. Inclusion of legal authorities and damage calculations is not required." Statistics evidence that parties are disinclined to request an explained

With respect to the obligations that a broker owes to its customers, the shingle theory has been recognized for over seventy-five years.[156] Among other components, the doctrine posits that any recommendation that a broker makes to its customer must have a reasonable basis and be suitable for that customer.[157] Recently, the SEC promulgated Regulation Best Interest to enhance the standard of conduct for broker-dealers beyond then existing suitability obligations.[158] As stated by the Commission, Regulation Best Interest requires broker-dealers, among other duties, to: "act in the best interest of the retail customer at the time the recommendation is made, without placing the financial or other interest of the broker-dealer ahead of the interests of the retail customer; and address conflicts of interest by establishing, maintaining, and enforcing policies and procedures reasonably designed to identify and fully and fairly disclose material facts about conflicts of interest."[159] Moreover, in situations where disclosure fails sufficiently to reasonably address the conflict, the broker-dealer must take measures to deal with this conflict, which, depending on the circumstances, requires the firm to mitigate or eliminate such conflict.[160]

---

decision. During a six-year period, there were only 37 requests for an explained decision out of approximately 5,000 eligible cases. *See* Janvey and Baker, *supra* note 141, at 274 (and authorities cited therein).

[156] *See, e.g., Charles Hughes Co. v. Securities and Exchange Commission*, 139 F.2d 434 (2d Cir. 1943).

[157] *See, e.g., Hanly v. Securities and Exchange Commission*, 415 F.2d 589, 596–97 (2d Cir. 1969) ("A securities dealer occupies a special relationship to the buyer of securities in that by his position he impliedly represents he has an adequate basis for the opinions he renders."). Other implied representations that have been recognized under the shingle theory include that of: (1) fair pricing, including any markup or markdown; (2) execution of only authorized transactions on behalf of its customers; (3) disclosing any special considerations that influence such broker-dealer's recommendation; and (4) the prompt execution of customers' orders. *See* Marc I. Steinberg and Ralph C. Ferrara, *Securities Practice: Federal and State Enforcement* § 2:17 (2d ed. 2001 & 2020–2021 supp.) (and sources cited therein).

[158] *See* Securities Exchange Act Release No. 86031 (2019) (adopting release). For the provisions of Regulation Best Interest, *see* 17 C.F.R. § 240.151-1. The SEC also adopted Form CRS (client relationship summary) mandating that investment advisers and broker-dealers provide a succinct relationship summary to their retail clients in plain English. *See* Securities Exchange Act Release No. 86032 (2019).

[159] Securities Exchange Act Release No. 86031 (2019).

[160] *Id.* Pursuant to Regulation Best Interest, a broker-dealer's (and its associated persons') general obligation to act in the best interest of the retail customer without placing their own interests ahead of the subject customer's best interest is satisfied upon compliance with four specified component obligations. These obligations are:

> (1) Providing certain prescribed disclosure before or at the time of the recommendation, about the recommendation and the relationship between the retail customer and the broker-dealer ("Disclosure Obligation"); (2) exercising reasonable diligence, care, and skill in making the recommendation ("Care Obligation"); (3) establishing, maintaining, and enforcing policies and procedures reasonably designed to address conflicts of interest ("Conflict of Interest Obligation"); and (4) establishing, maintaining, and enforcing policies and procedures reasonably designed to achieve compliance with Regulation Best Interest ("Compliance Obligation").

Id.

Regulation Best Interest has been criticized for its failure to harmonize norms of conduct that would be applicable to broker-dealers and investment advisers and to require that a broker-dealer must serve a retail client's best interests irrespective of its own financial interest.[161] Although declining to adopt the existing fiduciary standard to which investment advisers are subject,[162] the SEC nonetheless opted to enhance the obligations that broker-dealers owe to their retail customers.[163] Importantly, these duties will have substantive impact and should form the basis for negligence claims against broker-dealers and their representatives. This effect should not be minimized. By failing to adhere to mandatory regulatory standards and acting contrary to industry custom and practice, a claim based on negligence should prove an attractive source of redress for aggrieved investors (normally asserted in the arbitral forum).[164] A needed revision, however, is in order. Regulation Best Interest does not impose an obligation on the broker-dealer to monitor a retail customer's account unless such broker-dealer agrees to do so.[165] This provision slights broker-customer relations as many retail customers, paying substantial commissions, assume that the broker will monitor the account. The appropriate solution is that a broker-dealer is deemed to have a duty to monitor a retail customer's account unless the customer acknowledges in writing that the broker has no such obligation.[166]

---

[161] *See, e.g., 8 Attorneys General Sue SEC Over Regulation Best Interest*, Fed. Sec. L. Rep. (CCH) No. 2889, at 1 (2019). The effort to invalidate Regulation Best Interest thus far has been unsuccessful. *See XY Planning Network, LLC v. Securities and Exchange Commission*, 963 F.3d 244, 257 (2d Cir. 2020) (holding that certain plaintiffs lacked standing to challenge the validity of Regulation Best Interest and, for the petitioner who had standing, upholding the Regulation on the basis that its adoption "was not arbitrary and capricious").

[162] *See* Securities Exchange Act Release No. 86031 (2019) (stating that "the Commission has chosen not to create a uniform standard applicable to both broker-dealers and investment advisers"); Dave Michaels, *SEC Increases Client Obligations for Stockbrokers*, Wall St. J., June 6, 2019, at B1 (stating that broker-dealers and investment advisers "will continue to be governed by two standards").

[163] *See* Securities Exchange Act Release No. 86031 (2019) (stating that "the Commission has chosen to enhance existing obligations for broker-dealers when they make recommendations to a retail customer").

[164] Failure to act in compliance with a regulatory mandate as well as the failure to adhere to custom and practice are admissible in broker-customer arbitration proceedings and form a basis for a successful negligence claim. *See De Kwiatkowski v. Bear, Stearns & Co., Inc.*, 306 F.3d 1293 (2d Cir. 2002); *Vintila v. Drassen*, 52 S.W.3d 28 (Mo. Ct. App. 2001); *Lovett v. Estate of Lovett*, 593 A.2d 382 (N.J. Super. 1991).

[165] *See* Securities Exchange Act Release No. 86031 (2019) ("While broker-dealers will not be required to monitor accounts, in instances where a broker-dealer agrees to provide the retail customer with specified account monitoring services, it is our view that such an agreement will result in buy, sell or hold recommendations subject to Regulation Best Interest, even when the recommendation to hold is implicit.")

[166] Frequently, a customer in either a discretionary or nondiscretionary account paying substantial commissions expects his or her broker to monitor such account. Indeed, if a broker fails to do so, an astute investor would terminate her account and move her securities portfolio to another brokerage

Moreover, the emphasis on an investment adviser's fiduciary duty to its clients is overstated. Similar to the situation involving corporate directors and officers addressed earlier in this chapter,[167] the legal standard for determining whether an investment adviser's conduct constitutes a breach of fiduciary duty at times is too lax. An apt illustration is the imposition of a fiduciary duty on the investment adviser of a registered investment company "with respect to the receipt of compensation for [its] services."[168] To successfully challenge the payment of allegedly excessive compensation, a plaintiff must prove that such fees were "so disproportionately large that they bore no reasonable relationship to the services rendered."[169] This "onerous standard" for plaintiffs renders it an arduous task to mount a successful challenge and is antithetical to the financial interests of mutual fund shareholders. To call this standard suitable to assess the conduct of fiduciaries is illusory. To give substantive meaning to this obligation, the applicable standard should be that of reasonableness with the burden of proof placed on the subject investment

firm where the representative undertakes this task. The Commission's failure to recognize this reality is perplexing. The fix is straightforward: a broker-dealer that wants its representatives to refrain from assuming an obligation to monitor a subject client's account may insert language in bold print in the new account form which the client must sign as a condition to open the account.

[167] *See supra* notes 99–101 and accompanying text.

[168] Section 36(b) of the Investment Company Act, 15 U.S.C. § 80a-35(b) ("For the purposes of this subsection, the investment adviser of a registered investment company shall be deemed to have a fiduciary duty with respect to the receipt of compensation for services, or for payments of a material nature, paid by such registered investment company, or by the security holders thereof, to such investment adviser or any affiliated person of such investment adviser.").

[169] *See Jones v. Harris Associates L.P.*, 559 U.S. 335, 346 (2010) (holding that "to face liability under § 36(b), an investment adviser must charge a fee that is so disproportionately large that it bears no reasonable relationship to the services rendered and could not have been the product of arm's length bargaining"). In so holding, the Supreme Court endorsed the formulation set forth by the Second Circuit in *Gartenberg v. Merrill Lynch Asset Management, Inc.*, 694 F.2d 923 (2d Cir. 1982). *See* 559 U.S. at 345–46. In ascertaining whether a subject fee is excessive, the *Gartenberg* court set forth several non-exclusive factors as relevant, including: "the adviser-manager's cost in providing the service, the nature and quality of the service, the extent to which the adviser-manager realizes economies of scale as the fund grows larger, and the volume of orders, which must be processed by the manager." 694 F.2d at 930. Other pertinent factors are the independence, care, and expertise of the investment company's independent directors in their determination whether to approve the investment adviser's compensation; and a comparison of fee structures that other funds have. *Id.* at 930. Although adhering to the *Gartenberg* definition, the Supreme Court in *Harris* may have provided a more hospitable attitude toward Section 36(b) actions. *See* Daniel J. Morrissey, *Are Mutual Funds Robbing Retirement Savings?*, 14 N.Y.U. J. Law & Bus. 143, 167 (2017). Nonetheless, post-*Harris* Section 36(b) excessive fee litigation continues to be problematic for allegedly aggrieved mutual fund shareholders. *See* Daniel J. Morrissey, *Reforming Wall Street's Biggest Gravy Train: Making Mutual Funds Fiduciaries for Retirement Savers*, 47 Sec. Reg. L.J. 5, 13 (2019) (citing cases and stating that "excessive fee litigation after *Harris* has met with mixed success with many courts still unwilling to find obviously padded adviser compensation to be unreasonable"). *See generally* Tamar Frankel and Kenneth E. Burdon, *Investment Management Regulation* (5th ed. 2015).

adviser to establish the reasonableness of its compensation for the services provided.[170]

Hence, in determining appropriate standards to assess the conduct of broker-dealers, investment advisers, and their associated persons, emphasis should be placed on substance. Key determinants in assessing such conduct should be the exercise of due diligence by the financial intermediary, adherence to disclosure standards mandating that all material information (absent business justification) must be disclosed, the fairness of any transaction or other event that impacts the financial interests of clients, and the reasonableness of any fees or other compensation arrangement received. The disciplined application of this criteria should provide a vastly improved analytical framework than is currently in place.[171]

H. Summation

The federal securities law framework in this country is inconsistent, treats similar factual situations in a disparate manner, and is outdated. The preceding discussion identified key problematic components of this framework, addressed their shortcomings, and recommended measures that should be implemented for remediation. The adoption and faithful application of these measures should provide a substantially more coherent and equitable private securities litigation regime.

III. Replacement of the Current Private Securities Litigation Framework

In view of the fundamental deficiencies in the U.S. private securities litigation framework, sound reasons exist for its elimination. The suggested approach as set forth in this chapter is based in part on other regulatory regimes, including

---

[170] Indeed, these generous fees have been viewed as "one of the great gravy trains in financial history." Landon Thomas, Jr., *Why Are Mutual Fund Fees So High? This Billionaire Knows*, N.Y. Times (Dec. 30, 2017), available at https://www.nytimes.com/2017/12/30/business/why-are-mutual-fund-fees-so-high-this-billionaire-knows.html. Similarly, a U.S. Senator asserted: "The mutual fund industry is the world's largest skimming operation." Oversight Hearing on Mutual Funds: Hidden Fees, Misgovernance and Other Practices that Harm Investors, Hearing Before the Subcomm. On Fin. Mgmt., 108th Cong., at 3 (2004). With the large fees that investment advisers receive at the expense of public mutual fund investors, a more stringent standard is appropriate.

[171] *See* discussion *supra* notes 138–170 and accompanying text.

that of Australia, Canada (Ontario), and the state securities laws as reflected by the Uniform Securities Act.[172] The principal components of this recommended approach are set forth in the following discussion.

A. Recommended Provisions for the Revised Framework

The private remedial provisions of the federal securities laws should be revised in a coherent and equitable manner. The approach adopted should provide meaningful protection for investors who allegedly are harmed by misconduct while not saddling defendants with undue liability exposure. Although not all characteristics of a revised regime can be addressed herein, key aspects have been discussed earlier in this chapter,[173] a number of which also are the focus of the following discussion.

1. A Near Uniform Mental Culpability Standard of Negligence

As discussed earlier in this chapter, absent sound justification otherwise, a uniform standard of mental culpability should apply in private federal securities litigation regardless of the remedial provisions that plaintiffs seek to invoke.[174] Irrespective of whether the alleged material disclosure deficiency is contained in a Securities Act registration statement, Exchange Act report, proxy statement, press release, oral statement, or other communication, the same level of intent should apply. When the challenged disclosure is based on historical information or otherwise subject to verification, the appropriate standard with respect to primary participants ordinarily should be that of negligence, with the plaintiffs bearing the burden of proof on this issue.[175] In this respect, for

---

[172] *See, e.g.*, Long, Kaufman, and Wunderlich, *supra* note 132; Olivia Dixon and Jennifer G. Hill, *Australia: The Protection of Investors and the Compensation for Their Losses, in Global Securities Litigation and Enforcement* 1063 (Pierre-Henri Conac and Martin Gelter eds., 2019); Stephane Rousseau, *Canada: The Protection of Minority Investors and the Compensation for Their Losses*, in *Securities Litigation and Enforcement, supra*, at 143; Marc I. Steinberg and Alex Prescott, *The Emergence of a New Battleground: Liability for Secondary Market Violations in Ontario*, 48 Int'l Law. 17 (2014). *See also* Robin Hui Huang, *The Anatomy of Securities Class Actions in China: Functional and Comparative Approach with the United States*, 46 Sec. Reg. L.J. 365 (2018).

[173] For example, discussion earlier in this chapter addressed several key subjects, including primary and secondary liability principles, a uniform mental culpability standard, pleading requirements, and federal preemption of class actions.

[174] *See* discussion *supra* notes 49–57 and accompanying text.

[175] When information is subject to verification, it is appropriate to apply a negligence standard. After all, in many situations, the persons responsible for the applicable disclosure are fiduciaries of the recipients. This standard also is consistent with the claim of negligent misrepresentation under state law. *See supra* notes 99–101, 116 and accompanying text. Tellingly, a number of provisions of the

several decades, the negligence standard (or a stricter version thereof) has been embraced under various remedial provisions of the federal securities laws as well as the state blue sky statutes.[176]

With respect to registration violations, a negligence standard likewise should apply. In view of the complexity of many of the issues surrounding exemptions from registration and the propriety of certain conduct when a company is in registration,[177] strict liability may be incurred even when the defendant acts with due care.[178] With rescission normally the remedy of choice for plaintiffs who want out when the deal heads south,[179] a violation committed while acting with due care can nix the entire venture. In view of these severe consequences, a negligence standard of culpability in this context is appropriate.

On the other hand, as discussed earlier in this chapter, the current Securities Act Section 11 liability scheme should apply to specified registered offerings, with the modification that the issuer also should have the due diligence defense.[180] Strict liability in private litigation should no longer exist under the federal securities laws. When a subject issuer has requisite due diligence performed on its behalf, imposing monetary liability is too harsh a standard and impairs capital-raising incentives.[181] Hence, in regard to enterprises undertaking their

---

federal securities laws, such as Exchange Act Section 14(a), have a negligence standard of culpability. *See supra* note 49 and accompanying text.

[176] *See* §§ 11, 12(a)(2) of the Securities Act, 15 U.S.C. §§ 77k, l(a)(2); § 14(a) of the Securities Exchange Act, 15 U.S.C. § 78n(a); Uniform Securities Act 410(b) of the Uniform Securities Act; discussion *supra* notes 6–13, 49–53 and accompanying text. In addition, negligence is actionable in private actions under numerous foreign securities laws, including Australia and Ontario. *See* sources cited *supra* note 172.

[177] For example, in private offerings such as pursuant to Rule 506(b) of Regulation D, 17 C.F.R. § 230.506, general solicitation voids the exemption. Determining whether certain actions constitute general solicitation can be problematic. *See* Marc I. Steinberg, *Understanding Securities Law* § 3.08 (7th ed. 2018) (and sources cited therein).

[178] *See Securities and Exchange Commission v. Ralston Purina Co.*, 346 U.S. 119 (1953). In construing the strict liability parameters of the statutory private offering exemption, the Supreme Court asserted that "the issuer's motives, laudable though they may be, fade into irrelevance." *Id.* at 126.

[179] *See* § 12(a)(1) of the Securities Act, 15 U.S.C. § 77l(a)(1) (with a one-year statute of limitation, imposing liability upon any person "who offers or sells a security in violation of section 5"). *See Wigand v. Flo-Tek, Inc.*, 609 F.2d 1028, 1035 (2d Cir. 1979) ("if [the] plaintiff owns the stock, he is entitled to rescission but not damages. If [the] plaintiff no longer owns the stock, he is entitled to damages but not rescission.")

[180] *See* discussion *supra* notes 36–46 and accompanying text.

[181] Elimination of strict liability would be consistent with other legislative and regulatory actions that have sought to enhance capital raising. *See, e.g.*, National Securities Markets Improvement Act of 1996 (NSMIA), Pub. L. No. 104-290, 110 Stat. 3416 (1996) ("To amend the Federal securities laws in order to promote efficiency and capital formation in the financial markets."); Jumpstart Our Business Startups Act of 2012 (JOBS Act), Pub. L. No. 112-106, 126 Stat. 306 (2012) ("To increase American job creation and economic growth by improving access to the public capital markets for emerging growth companies."); Securities Act Release No. 8591 (2005) (regulatory reform measures

IPOs or that otherwise are unseasoned (including companies that have less than a $75 million public float, have been in the Exchange Act reporting system for less than twelve months, are financially distressed, or are blank check), the provisions of Section 11 (with the issuer having its due diligence defense) should remain applicable. The continuation of Section 11 liability in this setting should instill needed discipline in the Securities Act registration process for unseasoned issuers.[182]

With respect to forward-looking statements or statements that otherwise are not subject to factual verification, a more relaxed standard should apply, but such standard should not be nearly as permissive as current law provides.[183] As discussed earlier in this chapter, "soft" statements should be insulated from liability unless the plaintiff proves that any such statement was made either with gross negligence or without good faith.[184] This standard should extend to statements of belief and puffery that cannot be verified.[185] Engaging in egregiously careless or bad faith statements regarding prospective corporate earnings, revenues, and other key company-related information should not be countenanced.

2. Primary Liability Principles

Primary liability principles should be simplified. This approach would lessen the pleading burdens, provide more certainty, and narrow the liability gaps. When a corporation, for example, makes an allegedly materially false statement in an SEC filing or other communication that is disseminated to investors, specified individuals should be subject to primary liability exposure,

---

adopted in the Securities Act registered offering setting to enhance capital formation, relax regulatory impediments, and instill greater certainty in the securities offering process).

This elimination of strict liability under the federal securities laws would extend to all situations, including, for example, liability of the short-swing insider trading prohibitions of Section 16(b) of the Securities Exchange Act, 15 U.S.C. § 78p(a). Provided that the reforms recommended herein are adopted in the insider trading context, strict liability may be eliminated. Indeed, as addressed in Chapter 7 herein, provided that the recommendations in that chapter are implemented, Section 16(b) should be rescinded. *See* discussion in Chapter 7 herein.

[182] *See Herman & MacLean v. Huddleston*, 459 U.S. 375, 381–82 (1983) (stating that § 11 "was designed to assure compliance with the disclosure provisions of the [Securities] Act by imposing a stringent standard of liability on the parties who play a direct role in a registered offering"); discussion *supra* notes 6–13, 44–48 and accompanying text.

[183] *See* discussion *supra* notes 99–122 and accompanying text.

[184] *See* discussion *supra* notes 113–116 and accompanying text.

[185] *See* discussion *supra* notes 117–119 and accompanying text. In this regard, if such statements of puffery and/or belief do not proximately cause investor losses, the SEC nonetheless would have authority to institute enforcement action and seek appropriate sanctions. *See* discussion in Chapter 9 herein.

including its high-level executive officers (e.g., its chief executive officer, chief financial officer, and chief operating officer).[186] Outside directors should not be subject to primary liability unless they sign the subject document or otherwise give their explicit approbation to an oral or written communication.[187] A stricter standard likely would deter proficient individuals from serving as outside directors.[188]

In the Securities Act registration setting, irrespective of the status of the company as an unseasoned, seasoned, or well-known seasoned issuer,[189] the underwriters for the offering should be subject to primary liability exposure. After all, the underwriters serve as gatekeepers with respect to the registration statement's veracity[190] and derive substantial fees for their contributions.[191] Even though this role has sought to be minimized in the shelf registration

---

[186] *Cf.* § 410(b) of the Uniform Securities Act (in addition to the defendant "seller," subjecting control persons, "every partner, officer, or director of such a seller [and] every person occupying a similar status or performing similar functions" to liability exposure, without requiring proof that such person materially aided the sale); Ontario Securities Act §§ 138.3(1), 138.3(3) (with respect to a document containing a material misstatement, subjecting the issuer as well as other specified persons, including its directors and certain officers, to liability exposure).

[187] Although other regulatory frameworks, including that of the Uniform Securities Act and Ontario (*see supra* note 186), subject directors to primary liability exposure, the better policy to induce proficient individuals to serve as outside directors is, but for the exceptions set forth in the text, to adopt a secondary liability approach whereby such persons may be held liable if they act with reckless or intentional misconduct. *See infra* notes 200–210 and accompanying text.

[188] *Cf. Smith v. Van Gorkum*, 488 A.2d 858 (Del. 1985) (holding directors subject to money damages for breach of the duty of care). This decision stunned the corporate world, generating fears that the decision signaled the onslaught of shareholder actions resulting in large judgments against outside directors, among others. With director and officer insurance becoming less available and more costly after the decision, the specter of outside directors declining to serve on corporate boards was manifest. Reacting to this situation, Delaware and other states enacted statutes permitting corporations to adopt provisions eliminating a director's monetary liability for breach of the duty of care. *See, e.g.*, Del. Gen. Corp. Law § 102(b)(7). For further discussion, *see, e.g.*, Symposium, *Van Gorkum and the Corporate Board: Problem, Solution or Placebo?*, 96 Nw. U. L. Rev. No. 2 (2002); Bayless Manning, *Reflections and Practical Tips on Life in the Boardroom After Van Gorkum*, 41 Bus. Law. 1 (1985); Marc I. Steinberg, *The Evisceration of the Duty of Care*, 42 Sw. L.J. 919 (1988).

[189] The status of an issuer as a seasoned issuer or well-known seasoned issuer is discussed in Chapters 2 and 4 herein.

[190] *See, e.g.*, *In re Worldcom, Inc. Securities Litigation*, 346 F. Supp. 2d 628, 670 (S.D.N.Y. 2004) (referring to the SEC's "intent to maintain high standards for underwriter due diligence"); *Feit v. Leasco Data Processing Equipment Corp.*, 332 F. Supp. 544, 581–82 (E.D.N.Y. 1971) (stating that "underwriters are supposed to assume an opposing posture with respect to management" and in view of "this adverse position . . . must be expected to be alert to exaggerations and rosy outlooks and chary of assurances by the issuer"); *Escott v. BarChris Construction Corporation*, 283 F. Supp. 643, 697 (S.D.N.Y. 1968) (stating that "underwriters must make some reasonable attempt to verify the data submitted to them"); Securities Exchange Act Release No. 26100 (1988) (stating that, "occup[ying] a vital role in an offering . . . [an] underwriter stands between the issuer and the public purchasers").

[191] *See, e.g.*, M. Szmigiera, *Underwriter Fees in U.S. IPO, 2014–2017, by Deal Size* (Dec. 12, 2019), available at https://www.statista.com/statistics/533357/underwriter-fees-in-usa-ipo-by-deal-size/ ("In 2017, the underwriting fees of companies undergoing [the] initial public offering (IPO) process, where the deal was valued between 500 million and 1 billion U.S. dollars, amounted to 5.4% of gross proceeds from the offering.").

framework,[192] underwriters should retain responsibility for the accuracy of the registration statement.[193] This approach incentivizes the participating underwriters to act with reasonable care, thereby enhancing the likelihood that accurate disclosure will be made.

Like current law, primary liability exposure also should extend to those persons who make an allegedly materially false or misleading statement[194] or engage in fraudulent or manipulative conduct.[195] Hence, the auditor who certifies a company's financial statements that are contained in a Securities Act registration statement or a Form 10-K annual report would be subject to liability exposure as a primary violator as would an investment banker who renders a fairness opinion contained in a subject company's proxy statement.[196] And, of course, one who engages in insider trading or stock manipulation likewise would incur primary liability.[197]

There likely exist other situations where primary liability is appropriate.[198] Nonetheless, the key point is that primary liability exposure is based on two distinct categories: first, those persons who themselves make a materially false or misleading statement to the investing public or otherwise engage in actionable misconduct; and second, those persons who have a specified status as set forth in the applicable statute (such as an executive officer of a corporation or an underwriter in a registered offering by a well-known seasoned issuer).[199] This two-fold structure provides greater certainty, enhances

---

[192] *See, e.g.*, *In re Worldcom, Inc. Securities Litigation*, 346 F. Supp. 2d 628 (S.D.N.Y. 2004); discussion in Chapters 2 and 4 herein.

[193] As the SEC stated when it adopted Rule 176, 17 C.F.R. § 230.176, the integrated disclosure process seeks to "simplify disclosure and reduce unnecessary repetition and redelivery of information" rather than to "modify the responsibility of underwriters and others to make a reasonable investigation." Securities Act Release No. 6335 (1981). *See* discussion in Chapters 2 and 4 herein.

[194] *See, e.g.*, *Janus Capital Group, Inc. v. First Derivative Traders*, 564 U.S. 135 (2011); *supra* note 81 and accompanying text.

[195] *See, e.g.*, *Lorenzo v. Securities and Exchange Commission*, 139 S. Ct. 1094 (2019); *Stoneridge Investment Partners LLC v. Scientific-Atlanta, Inc.*, 522 U.S. 148 (2008); *supra* notes 82–83 and accompanying text.

[196] *See, e.g.*, *Hershkowitz v. Nutri/System, Inc.*, 857 F.2d 179 (3d Cir. 1988) (investment banker); *Cooper v. Pickett*, 137 F.3d 616 (9th Cir. 1997) (auditor).

[197] *See, e.g.*, § 9 of the Securities Exchange Act, 15 U.S.C. § 78i (securities manipulation); *United States v. O'Hagan*, 521 U.S. 642 (1997) (insider trading); *ATSI Communications, Inc. v. The Shaar Fund, Ltd.*, 493 F.3d 87 (2d Cir. 2007) (stock manipulation); discussion in Chapter 7 herein.

[198] For example, prior to the U.S. Supreme Court's decision in *Janus Capital*, 564 U.S. 135 (2011) (*see supra* notes 81, 194 and accompanying text), a number of lower courts held that one who is integrally involved in orchestrating a fraudulent scheme or knowingly drafts disclosure documents central to the subject transaction was subject to Section 10(b) primary liability exposure. *See, e.g.*, *Molecular Technology v. Valentine*, 925 F.2d 910 (6th Cir. 1991); *supra* notes 81–83 and accompanying text.

[199] *See* discussion *supra* notes 186–198 and accompanying text.

investor protection, and does not unduly expand the parameters of primary participant liability exposure.

3. Secondary Liability Principles

Prior to the U.S. Supreme Court's 1994 decision in *Central Bank of Denver*,[200] aiding and abetting liability in private Section 10(b) actions was firmly entrenched.[201] This form of secondary liability should once again comprise an important component of the private securities remedial landscape. This measure is necessary to ensure that collateral actors, who knowingly and substantially assist primary violators, are held accountable in private actions.

Today, a broad array of misconduct by collateral actors does not give rise to private liability exposure in class actions under the federal securities laws.[202] For example, the bankers in the Enron scandal, who allegedly orchestrated sham transactions, were beyond Section 10(b)'s private liability reach.[203] Likewise, an attorney who, unbeknownst to investors, knowingly drafts materially false offering or disclosure documents on her client's behalf is not subject to Section 10(b) liability in private actions.[204] This state of the law is unacceptable. It brazenly permits bad actors to avoid private securities law liability, impairs the efficacy of gatekeeping functions, harms market transparency, and denies injured investors the opportunity to seek recompense against blameworthy persons.[205]

---

[200] *Central Bank of Denver v. First Interstate Bank of Denver*, 511 U.S. 164 (1994). *See* discussion *supra* notes 73–98 and accompanying text.

[201] *See supra* note 73 and accompanying text.

[202] *See* discussion *supra* notes 80–94 and accompanying text.

[203] The federal district court in *Enron* gave its approbation to more flexible liability criteria with respect to investment bankers and others in that litigation. *See In re Enron Securities, Derivative & ERISA Litigation*, 235 F. Supp. 2d 549 (S.D. Tex. 2002). This approach subsequently was rejected by the Fifth Circuit. *See Affco Investments 2001, LLC v. Proskauer Rose, LLP*, 625 F.3d 185 (5th Cir. 2010); *Regents of University of California v. Credit Suisse First Boston*, 482 F.3d 372 (5th Cir. 2007). Similar to the district court in *Enron*, the Ninth Circuit stated that "substantial participation or intricate involvement in the preparation of financial statements is grounds for primary liability even though that participation might not lead to the actor's actual making of the statement." *Howard v. Everex Systems, Inc.*, 228 F.3d 1057, 1061 n. 5 (9th Cir. 2000). The Supreme Court's decision in *Stoneridge* rejected the version of scheme liability that had been embraced by a number of lower federal courts. *See* 552 U.S. 148 (2008); discussion *supra* notes 82–83, 195 and accompanying text.

[204] *See, e.g., Janus Capital Group, Inc. v. First Derivative Traders*, 564 U.S. 135 (2011); *Affco Investments 2001, LLC v. Proskauer Rose, LLP*, 625 F.3d 185 (5th Cir. 2010); *Pacific Investment Management Co. v. Mayer Brown LLP*, 603 F.3d 144 (2d Cir. 2010).

[205] In this regard, Professor Steven Ramirez sets forth the following "virtues" of private securities litigation, including:

> First, private enforcement operates in a depoliticized context. Senators and even presidents have no ability to influence private securities litigation through appropriations, informal influence over government agents, or promises of career advancement.... Second,

Accordingly, those persons who knowingly and substantially assist a primary violator should be held accountable in private actions. Unlike primary violations proposed herein that generally are premised on negligence,[206] aiding liability should require proof that the defendant acted with intentional or reckless misconduct.[207] As fraud is being alleged, heightened pleading standards should apply.[208] As discussed earlier in this chapter, in the discretion of the district court, the plaintiff may be afforded limited discovery prior to the court's ruling on a motion to dismiss.[209] With respect to actions that are instituted frivolously against a collateral party, the levying of sanctions (including the payment of the defendant's legal fees) would be appropriate.[210]

Of course, a subject person also can be held secondarily liable on the basis of the control person provision of the 1933 and 1934 Acts.[211] Limited in its reach to those persons who control primary violators, the provision has been useful in private securities litigation to ensnare high-level executive officers within the liability net.[212] In this regard, pursuant to Section 20(a) of the Exchange Act, a control person is subject to liability unless it is shown that he "acted in good faith and did not directly or indirectly induce the act or acts constituting the violation or cause of action."[213] This amorphous standard has led to permissive interpretations by some courts, enabling control

---

> private claims of securities fraud require no government bureaucracy or other government funding support, other than the routine operation of a court system. . . . Third, only private litigation both strips the fraudfeasor of the benefits of their wrongdoing and compensates the victim. . . . Fourth, private remedies allow a reduced reliance upon ex ante government regulation.

Steven A. Ramirez, *The Virtues of Private Securities Litigation: An Historic and Macroeconomic Perspective*, 45 Loy. U. Chi. L. Rev. 669, 722–25 (2014) (*id.* at 721—asserting that "the entire war on private securities litigation rests on a weak foundation").

206 *See* discussion *supra* notes 49–57, 174–185 and accompanying text.

207 *See* discussion *supra* notes 73–98 and accompanying text.

208 *See* discussion *supra* notes 58–72 and accompanying text.

209 *See* discussion *supra* notes 71–72 and accompanying text.

210 *See* discussion *supra* note 72 and accompanying text.

211 *See* discussion *supra* notes 92–94 and accompanying text. Control person liability also is addressed in the context of SEC enforcement actions in Chapter 9 herein.

212 *See* Marc I. Steinberg and Forrest C. Roberts, *Laxity at the Gates: The SEC's Neglect to Enforce Control Person Liability*, 11 U. Va. L. & Bus. Rev. 201, 211 (2017) ("With regularity, courts have allowed control person claims in private litigation to proceed against executive officers, including CEOs, CFOs, COOs."), *citing*, *Maverick Fund v. Converse Technology*, 801 F. Supp. 2d 41 (E.D.N.Y. 2011); *Puskala v. Koss Corp.*, 799 F. Supp. 2d 941 (E.D. Wis. 2011); *In re Tronox, Inc. Securities Litigation*, 769 F. Supp. 2d 202 (S.D.N.Y. 2011). *See also* discussion in Chapter 9 herein (control person liability exposure in the SEC enforcement setting).

213 15 U.S.C. § 78t(a).

persons to avoid liability without sufficient justification.[214] Hence, it should be rejected in favor of the approach adopted by the Uniform Securities Act, which provides the control person with an affirmative defense that she "did not know and in the exercise of reasonable care could not have known" of the liability-producing facts.[215] This standard is consistent with the policy objective of inducing a control person to engage in active and prudent oversight.[216] Although by no means a guarantor of a controlled person's conduct, the control person's adherence to the reasonable care standard should result in a higher degree of law compliance within the enterprise.[217]

Likewise, an entity, such as a broker-dealer firm or a publicly-held corporation, would be subject to the reasonable care defense under the control person provision.[218] Implementation of this standard should signify that the common law doctrine of respondeat superior be abandoned under the federal securities laws.[219] Saddling an enterprise with strict liability for the

---

[214] A minority of courts adhere to the "culpable participant" test, requiring a plaintiff alleging a control person claim to "plead facts showing either conscious misbehavior or recklessness." *In re Vivendi Universal, S.A.*, 387 F. Supp. 2d 158, 189 (S.D.N.Y. 2003). *See In re Lehman Brothers Mortgage-Backed Litigation*, 650 F.3d 167 (2d Cir. 2011).

[215] Section 410(b) of the Uniform Securities Act.

[216] In this fashion, the statute is similar to the due diligence defense of Section 11 and the reasonable care defense of Section 12(a)(2) of the Securities Act, 15 U.S.C. §§ 77k, l(a)(2). Both statutes, like Section 410(c) of the Uniform Securities Act, require the defendant to prove the statutory defense. To satisfy this standard, the control person must engage in affirmative action to oversee (directly or indirectly) the controlled person's conduct as a reasonable person would act in like circumstances. *See Connecticut National Bank v. Giacomi*, 699 A.2d 101 (Conn. 1997).

[217] This is due to the state statutory provision that "imposes absolute liability upon the director[, officer, or control person] of a corporation to purchasers of securities sold in violation of the [Indiana] Securities Act based on his position . . . unless he proves the statutory defense." *Kirchoff v. Selby*, 701 N.E.2d 644, 651 (Ind. 1998).

[218] *See Hines v. Data Systems, Inc.*, 787 P.2d 8, 14 (Wash. 1990) (stating that once the plaintiff shows a primary violation of the Washington securities laws and that the defendant "controlled the person or entity committing the primary violation . . . the defendant has the burden of showing that it acted in good faith and did not directly or indirectly induce the act or acts constituting the violation or cause of action"). *Cf. Haynes v. Anderson & Strudwick, Inc.*, 508 F. Supp. 1303, 1314 (E.D. Va. 1981) (holding that the complaint sufficiently alleged a control person claim against the defendant brokerage firm and stating that "the courts are in general agreement that a more stringent supervisory duty should be imposed upon a broker-dealer than upon an officer or director [and that accordingly] in practice it will be more difficult for a broker-dealer to exculpate [itself] using the good faith defense than for an officer or director").

[219] Under the doctrine of respondeat superior, "an employer or principal [is held] liable for the employee's or agent's wrongful acts committed within the scope of employment or agency." *Black's Law Dictionary, supra* note 100, at 1569. A number of courts have rejected the doctrine of respondeat superior under the securities laws, reasoning that its application would negate the controlling person provisions. *See, e.g., Carpenter v. Harris, Upham & Co., Inc.*, 594 F.2d 388 (4th Cir. 1979). On the other hand, several courts adhere to the respondeat superior doctrine in the securities law setting on the basis that the controlling person provisions were designed to supplement rather than supplant this common law principle. For example, in *Hollinger v. Titan Capital Corp.*, 914 F.2d 1564, 1577 (9th Cir. 1990) (en banc), the court held that the controlling person provision of Section 20(a) of the Securities Exchange Act "was intended to impose liability on controlling persons, such as controlling

misdeeds of its officers and employees, when due care has been exercised, is unwarranted. Moreover, if the damages incurred exceed the insurance proceeds, current shareholders will bear the costs even though the subject corporation acted with prudence. The suggested approach therefore is to: elevate the control person defense to the level of reasonable care; and eliminate respondeat superior liability under the securities laws.[220]

4. Elimination of the Reliance Requirement

The element of reliance in securities law private damages actions should be eliminated. The advent of the fraud on the market theory[221] and its subsequent embracement by the U.S. Supreme Court[222] have proven essential to the certification of class actions.[223] While recognizing the propriety of the theory in creating a presumption of reliance, the Court held in *Halliburton* that this presumption can be rebutted before class certification "through evidence that an alleged misrepresentation did not actually affect the market price of the stock."[224] After *Halliburton*, an inordinate amount of time and

---

shareholders and corporate officers, who would not be liable under respondeat superior because they were not the actual employers."

220 This approach should enhance law-compliant conduct and limit the monetary exposure of the business enterprise, irrespective of whether it be a corporation, financial intermediary firm, or other commercial entity. Moreover, the placement of a cap on damages proposed herein should substantially limit the monetary exposure of those persons who act with negligence rather than with knowing misconduct. *See infra* notes 232–247 and accompanying text.

221 As stated by the U.S. Supreme Court, the fraud on the market theory "holds that the market price of shares traded on well-developed markets reflects all publicly available information, and, hence any material misrepresentations." *Basic, Inc. v. Levinson*, 485 U.S. 224, 246 (1988), *quoted with approval, Halliburton Co. v. Erica P. John Fund Inc.*, 573 U.S. 258, 268 (2014). As a federal appellate court succinctly stated:

> The fraud on the market theory is based on the hypothesis that, in an open and developed securities market, the price of a company's stock is determined by the available material information regarding the company and its business. . . . Misleading statements will therefore defraud purchasers of stock even if the purchasers do not directly rely on the misstatements.

Peil v. Speiser, 806 F.2d 1154, 1160 (3d Cir. 1986).

222 *See Halliburton Co. v. Erica P. John Fund Inc.*, 573 U.S. 258 (2014); *Amgen v. Connecticut Retirement Plans and Trust Funds*, 568 U.S. 455 (2013); *Erica P. John Fund, Inc. v. Halliburton Co.*, 563 U.S. 804 (2011); *Basic, Inc. v. Levinson*, 485 U.S. 224 (1988).

223 *See Halliburton*, 573 U.S. at 268 (recognizing that "requiring proof of individualized reliance," in practical effect, would prevent plaintiffs from "proceeding with a class action in Rule 10b-5 suits" and that, if every plaintiff were required to prove direct reliance on the allegedly materially misleading statements, individual issues would outweigh the common ones, "making certification under [F.R.C.P.] 23(b)(3) inappropriate").

224 *See Halliburton*, 573 U.S. at 284. *See also id.* at 284 (Ginsburg, J., concurring) ("Advancing price impact consideration from the merits stage to the certification stage may broaden the scope of discovery available at certification. But the Court recognizes that it is incumbent upon the defendant to show the absence of price impact.").

money have been expended, through the use of event studies and contentious lawyering, to ascertain whether this presumption has been rebutted.[225]

Logic dictates that the reliance requirement should be eliminated. The fraud on the market theory may be described in this context as a fiction whereby the reliance requirement is met even though investors did not read or even receive the communication containing the alleged disclosure deficiency.[226] It is a necessary fiction as otherwise individualized reliance would be required, thereby militating against class action certification.[227] It is time that the reliance requirement is no more. This reform would be consistent with the approach adopted by other developed markets as well as state securities laws.[228]

Moreover, eliminating the reliance requirement would not provide a windfall for investors. Significantly, plaintiffs would still be required to prove that the actionable misconduct caused financial loss (loss causation)[229] as well as the amount of damages suffered thereby.[230] In addition, as addressed

---

[225] *See* Alon Bray and J.B. Heaton, *Event Studies in Securities Litigation, Low Power, Confounding Effects, and Bias*, 93 Wash. U. L. Rev. 583 (2015) ("An event study is a statistical method for determining whether some event—such as the announcement of earnings or the announcement of a proposed merger—is associated with a statistically significant change in the price of a company's stock." The authors question the reliability of event studies.); Jill E. Fisch et al., *The Logic and Limits of Event Studies in Securities Fraud Litigation*, 96 Tex. L. Rev. 553 (2018) (observing that "event studies have become increasingly important in securities fraud litigation" and opining that "courts and litigants widely misunderstand the event study methodology"); Michael J. Kaufman and John M. Wunderlich, *Regressing: The Troubling Dispositive Role of Event Studies in Securities Fraud Litigation*, 15 Stan. J.L. Bus. & Fin. 183, 184 (2010) (asserting that "the dispositive role now played by event studies . . . is inconsistent with the Seventh Amendment and the federal securities laws [thereby] pos[ing] an unconstitutional and unwarranted barrier to meritorious securities fraud suits").

[226] *See Halliburton*, 573 U.S. at 297 (Thomas, J., concurring in the judgment) (asserting that the Court in its adoption of the fraud on the market theory resolved the "policy problem" of how investors in impersonal markets prove reliance by turning to "nascent economic theory and naked intuitions about investment behavior in efforts to fashion a new, easier way to meet the reliance requirement" and that "actual reliance, not the fictional 'fraud on the market' version" should be the applicable standard).

[227] *See* discussion *supra* note 223 and accompanying text.

[228] *See, e.g.*, Ontario Securities Act, R.S.O. 1990, c. S.5, §§ 138.3(1)–(4); Uniform Securities Act § 410; sources cited *supra* note 172. Note that a number of remedial provisions under current law do not require a plaintiff to prove reliance, including Sections 11 and 12(a)(2) of the Securities Act, 15 U.S.C. §§ 77k, l(a)(2).

[229] Accordingly, consistent with current law, as set forth in Section 21D(b)(4) of the Securities Exchange Act, 15 U.S.C. § 78u-4(b)(4), loss causation must be proven by the plaintiff. *See Dura Pharmaceuticals, Inc. v. Broudo*, 544 U.S. 336, 346 (2005) (holding that plaintiffs must "prove proximate causation and economic loss").

[230] The out-of-pocket measure of damages is the most frequently used by courts in Section 10(b) actions. *See, e.g.*, *Estate Counseling Service, Inc. v. Merrill Lynch, Pierce, Fenner & Smith, Inc.*, 303 F.2d 527, 533 (10th Cir. 1962) (defining the out-of-pocket measure as "the difference between the contract price, or the price paid, and the real or actual value at the date of the sale, together with such outlays as are attributable to the defendant's conduct"). *See generally* Michael J. Kaufman, *Securities Litigation: Damages* (2019).

in the following discussion, a cap on damages would apply in the absence of knowing misconduct.[231]

5. Cap on Damages

Unless it is shown that the defendant engaged in knowing misconduct, a cap on damages in corporate litigation should apply. Monetary liability for negligent conduct should be capped at the greater of that individual's: (1) total annual compensation (including equity compensation benefits), (2) fees and other revenues derived from the engagement, or (3) $100,000.[232] With respect to the limitation of damages for a subject company,[233] irrespective whether the litigation is settled prior to trial or knowing misconduct is alleged and proven, such amount should be capped at an amount that is not excessive. An exception exists if the other wrongdoers, including the parent corporation, have substantial ownership interests in such company.[234] Otherwise, the liability of a publicly-held corporation should be capped at the greater of: $1 million or two percent of its market capitalization.[235] Absent the availability of insurance, current shareholders will incur the impact of these damages.[236] This consequence should be minimized as much as practicable, thereby calling for the aforementioned cap on damages.[237]

---

[231] *See* discussion *infra* notes 232–247 and accompanying text.

[232] *Cf.* Ontario Securities Act, R.S.O. 1990, c. S.5, §§ 138.1(b), (d) (capping the amount of damages upon an individual officer, director, and other insider at the greater of fifty percent of such person's total annual compensation or $25,000). With respect to experts, the damages cap is the greater of $1 million or "the revenue that the expert and its affiliates . . . have earned from the responsible issuer and its affiliates during the 12 months preceding the misrepresentation." *Id.* § 138.1(f). With respect to an "influential person" that is not an individual, such as a parent corporation, capping damages at "the greater of 5% of its market capitalization . . . and $1 million." *Id.* § 138.1(c). Note that these caps do not apply if the violations are committed with knowing misconduct. § 138.7(2).

[233] The Department of Justice and the SEC have levied astronomical fines upon publicly-held companies for their alleged violations of securities and related laws. As the discussion in Chapter 9 addresses, this approach frequently is detrimental to shareholder interests.

[234] In such event, damages should be capped at a higher amount. For example, absent knowing misconduct, the Ontario Securities Act caps damages at "the greater of 5% of [such parent corporation's] market capitalization . . . and $1 million." Similar caps should apply to collateral enterprise participants who act with negligence, such as accounting firms and financial intermediaries. If the enterprise or firm is privately-held, net asset value rather than market capitalization should be applied. *See supra* note 232.

[235] Although this amount may seem unduly minimal, at least two considerations support this approach: first, current shareholders of the corporation will bear the cost of such damages beyond the amount insured; second, the median settlement amount in 2019 was $11.5 million (*see* 2019 Securities Class Action Settlements, *supra* note 67, at 1), signifying that companies whose market capitalization is $1 billion, for example, would pay no more than $20 million which substantially exceeds the median 2019 settlement amount.

[236] *See* discussion in Chapter 9 herein.

[237] Note that Section 21D(e) of the Securities Exchange Act, 15 U.S.C. § 78u-4(e), places a cap on damages for actions brought under that Act when the plaintiff seeks to prove damages by reference

Of course, rarely does a private securities action proceed to trial.[238] If not dismissed, nearly all suits thereafter are settled. In this regard, many of these settlements will be at monetary amounts above the recommended statutory caps.[239] With no finding of fraud or intentional misconduct, defendants will seek indemnification of the amounts paid in settlement that exceed insurance coverage.[240] In view of flexible state indemnification statutes,[241] coupled with the cultural bias of nondefendant directors,[242] indemnification ordinarily

to the subject security's market price. In such actions, the statute caps damages by reference to "the difference between the purchase or sale price paid or received, as appropriate, by the plaintiff for the subject security and the mean trading price of that security during the 90-day period beginning on the date on which the information correcting the misstatement or omission that is the basis for the action is disseminated to the market." *Id.* This cap "does not function as intended." Julia Pashin, *The PSLRA Cap on Securities Fraud Damages: An Empirical Evaluation of the 90-Day "Bounce-Back,"* 41 Sec. Reg. L.J. 169, 188–89 (2013) (stating that "a broad range of company-specific disclosures released during the [90-day] period may cause the [stock] price to rise or fall, even though these disclosures are not remotely connected to the alleged fraud").

[238] *See* Alexander "Sasha" Aganin, Cornerstone Research, *Securities Class Action Filings—2019 Year in Review*, Harv. Law School Forum Corp. Gov. (Feb. 14, 2020), available at https://corpgov.law.harvard.edu/2020/02/14/securities-class-action-filings-2019-year-in-review/ (stating that from 1997 to 2019, "less than 1% of core federal [securities] filings have reached a trial verdict"); Kevin M. LaCroix, *Rare Securities Class Action Lawsuit Trial Results in Partial Verdict for Plaintiffs*, The D&O Diary (Feb. 2, 2019), available at https://www.dandodiary.com/2019/02/articles/securities-litigation/rare-securities-class-action-lawsuit-trial-results-partial-verdict-plaintiffs/ ("Since 1996, there have been more than 5,200 securities class action lawsuits filed, but . . . fewer than 25 cases during that time have gone to trial.").

[239] For example, the average settlement in 2018 exceeded $69 million, elevated due to the Petrobras $3 billion settlement. *See* 2018 Full-Year Review, *supra* note 31, at 28–29. In 2019, the average settlement was $27.4 million. *See* 2019 Securities Class Action Settlements, *supra* note 67, at 1.

[240] *See* Del. Gen. Corp. Law § 145; *Waltuch v. ContiCommodity Services, Inc.*, 88 F.3d 87 (2d Cir. 1996); *Senior Tour Players 207 Management Co. v. Golftown, 207 Holding Co.*, 853 A.2d 124 (Del. Ch. 2004); *Merritt-Chapman & Scott Corp. v. Wolfson*, 321 A.2d 138 (Del. Super. Ct. 1974); Paul J. Lockwood, *Legal and Practical Limits on Indemnification and Advancement in Delaware Corporate Entities*, Harv. Law School Forum Corp. Gov. (July 2, 2018), available at https://corpgov.law.harvard.edu/2018/07/02/legal-and-practical-limits-on-indemnification-and-advancement-in-delaware-corporate-entities/.

[241] *See, e.g.*, E. Norman Veasey et al., *Delaware Supports Directors with a Three-Legged Stool of Limited Liability, Indemnification, and Insurance*, 42 Bus. Law. 399 (1987). *See also* Kurt A. Mayr II, *Indemnification of Directors and Officers: The Double Whammy of Mandatory Indemnification in Waltuch v. Conticommodity Services, Inc.*, 42 Vill. L. Rev. 223 (1997).

[242] The cultural or structural bias of nondefendant directors is accentuated when their fellow directors are sued in shareholder actions, including derivative suits. To some extent, a number of courts have recognized this bias. *See Zapata v. Maldonado*, 430 A.2d 779, 787 (Del. 1981) ("[N]otwithstanding our conviction that Delaware law entrusts the corporate power to a properly authorized committee [comprised of independent directors], we must be mindful that directors are passing judgment on fellow directors in the same corporation."); *Einhorn v. Culea*, 612 N.W. 2d 75, 81 (Wis. 2000) (holding that a court "should determine whether, considering the totality of the circumstances, a reasonable person in the position of a member of the special litigation committee can base his or her decision on the merits of the issue rather than on extraneous considerations or influences"). Law journal commentators have focused on the cultural or structural bias of nondefendant directors in the litigation context. *See, e.g.*, Kenneth Davis, *Structural Bias, Special Litigation Committees, and the Vagaries of Director Independence*, 90 Iowa L. Rev. 1305 (2005); Marc I. Steinberg, *The Use of Special Litigation Committees to Terminate Shareholder Derivative Suits*, 35 U. Miami L. Rev. 1 (1980); Julian Velasco, *Structural Bias and the Need for Substantive Review*, 82 Wash.

will be approved.[243] In actuality, the corporation and its shareholders thus would incur the costs of these settlement payments.

The recommended course of action in this setting is that, while advancement and indemnification of expenses may be provided pursuant to applicable state law,[244] monetary amounts paid in settlement may be indemnified only if the corporation's disinterested shareholders at a duly called meeting authorize the payment of such indemnification.[245] An exception to this approach would be made for outside directors who may be indemnified pursuant to state law. Otherwise, the prospective lack of adequate insurance, coupled with the risk that disinterested shareholder approval for indemnification may not be obtained, would deter large numbers of proficient individuals from serving as outside directors on corporate boards.[246] With respect to corporate executives, financial intermediaries (such as underwriters), and others who seek indemnification, disinterested shareholder approval would be required. Such approval by the disinterested shareholders gives substance to the indemnification process. It also helps to ensure that shareholder litigation is not a zero-sum (or worse) "game" whereby the financial benefits that are derived by investor-plaintiffs from the litigation do not exceed the costs that they indirectly incur due to the expenditure of corporate funds and perhaps the diminution in the value of their stock.[247]

U. L.Q. 821 (2004); Note, *The Business Judgment Rule in Derivative Suits Against Directors*, 65 Cornell L. Rev. 600 (1980).

[243] *See* Veasey et al., *supra* note 241, at 406–17; *see id.* at 413 (pointing out that pursuant to Del. Gen. Corp. Law § 145(f), "statutory rights and procedures regarding indemnification are not exclusive, thus permitting a corporation to indemnify a litigant [e.g., a defendant director or officer] pursuant to intracorporate policies under circumstances not defined in the statute").

[244] *See* Del. Gen. Corp. Law § 145(e) (permitting the advancement of expenses, including legal fees, "upon receipt of an undertaking by [the defendant director or officer] or on behalf of such director or officer to repay such amount if it shall ultimately be determined that such person is not entitled to be indemnified by the corporation as authorized in this section"). As stated by Chief Justice Veasey and his coauthors, the policy underlying this provision is to encourage directors and officers "to accept positions of responsibility and to make good faith decisions without fear of undue penalty." Veasey et al., *supra* note 241, at 411.

[245] Pursuant to Delaware law, shareholder approval is one means by which indemnification may be authorized. This method is disfavored by insiders. *See* Veasey et al., *supra* note 241, at 409 (stating that "most corporations are understandably reluctant to submit the question to stockholders and this method is rarely used"). Under Section 145(d) of the Delaware General Corporation Law, the determination of whether indemnification is authorized for a subject director or officer may be made by a court, or "[b]y a majority vote of the directors who are not parties to such action, suit or proceeding, even though less than a quorum; or [b]y a committee of such directors designated by majority vote of such directors, even though less than a quorum; or [i]f there are no such directors, or if such directors so direct, by independent legal counsel in a written opinion; or [b]y the stockholders."

[246] *See* Veasey et al., *supra* note 241, at 406 (pointing out that a key policy supporting the availability of indemnification is to induce qualified individuals to serve as corporate directors).

[247] *See* Susan Beck, *Summary Judgment: Until Directors and Officers Start Paying Some of Their Legal Fees, Corporate Accountability Is a Myth*, The Amer. Law., Feb. 3, 2010, available at https://www.law.com/americanlawyer/almID/1202441941788/summary-judgment-until-directors-and-officers-start-paying-some-of-their-legal-fees-corporate-accountability-is-a-myth/ (opining that

Accordingly, in these contexts, the institution of a cap on damages, along with disinterested shareholder approval of contemplated indemnification payments to specified defendants, should provide a superior approach as compared to current practice.

B. Summation

The replacement of the current private securities law regime is past due. The approach recommended herein instills greater uniformity and certainty. While providing substantially enhanced protection for allegedly injured investors, it does not impose upon defendants unwarranted liability exposure. In addition to the recommendations that are made in this section of the chapter, other suggestions are proffered throughout this book (including earlier in this chapter).[248] This section focuses on several reforms that should be instituted. As elaborated upon in this chapter, these reforms are: the implementation of a uniform mental culpability standard regardless of the provision allegedly violated; the application of primary liability principles that are more equitable and less arbitrary; the recognition of secondary liability standards that promote law-compliant conduct and that appropriately ensnare culpable collateral actors within the liability net; the elimination of the reliance requirement and thereby dispensing with time-consuming and costly litigation with respect to class certification; and the adoption of an appropriate cap on damages that seeks to preserve the subject enterprise's assets as well as limit the liability exposure of outside directors. Implementation

"[t]here's a moral hazard in corporate boardrooms and executive suites, [namely,] . . . ridiculously cushy indemnification contracts that insulate directors and officers from responsibility for their own actions"). Clearly, meritorious securities class actions are an important and integral component of the corporate governance framework. *See* Daniel Morrissey, *Private Lawsuits Are Essential for Defrauded Shareholders*, The Hill (Aug. 11, 2020), available at https://thehill.com/opinion/finance/511530-private-lawsuits-essential-for-defrauded-shareholders ("While the SEC can be effective in getting sanctions against fraudsters, the real financial benefit to investors comes from class actions brought on their behalf."); Ramirez, *supra* note 205, at 737 ("Robust private enforcement of the federal securities laws should operate as a fundamental element of sound legal infrastructure.").

248 Recommendations that have been proffered herein focus, for example, on the continuous disclosure framework, due diligence in the integrated disclosure process, concepts of materiality, insider trading revisions, federalized corporate governance enhancements, substantive conduct in the merger and acquisition context, and SEC enforcement and regulatory practices. For discussion of the recommendations made earlier in this chapter, *see supra* notes 6–171 and accompanying text.

of these measures should vastly improve our country's securities litigation framework.

IV. Conclusion

The private securities litigation framework should be revised in a meaningful and substantial way. This chapter has provided several examples of the inconsistencies, disparate treatment, and unsound policy ramifications of the current regime. When addressing key concrete situations where these deficiencies prevail, the chapter focuses on specific proposals to correct these shortcomings. If adopted and faithfully implemented, these proposals should instill a substantially greater degree of certainty, uniformity, and equity than currently exists. In this manner, the analysis herein has sought to recommend clear and uniform standards whereby allegedly aggrieved investors are accorded fair treatment without the imposition of unwarranted liability exposure upon prospective defendants.

7

Insider Trading

I. Introduction

The U.S. securities law framework with respect to the regulation of insider trading is abysmal. Uncertainties and inconsistencies prevail resulting in disparate treatment for similarly situated actors. Other developed countries, while applying principles of U.S. securities law to their securities markets,[1] have rejected the U.S. approach in the insider trading context.[2] To redress this situation, Congress should enact comprehensive legislation that meaningfully and clearly addresses the contours of the insider trading prohibition.[3]

For decades, the Securities and Exchange Commission (SEC) has focused on combatting insider trading.[4] Enforcement actions alleging illegal insider trading annually comprise a component of the SEC's docket.[5] Criminal prosecutions are instituted by the U.S. Department of Justice with regularity charging illegal insider trading,[6] making this offense one of the

[1] The U.S. federal securities law's emphasis on disclosure is the most prominent principle applied by developed markets outside of this country. *See* Marc I. Steinberg, *International Securities Law—A Contemporary and Comparative Analysis* 1–51 (1999).

[2] *See* discussion *infra* note 22 and accompanying text.

[3] Through the years, there have been efforts to enact comprehensive insider trading legislation. The most recent effort is the passage by the U.S. House of Representatives in 2019 of the Insider Trading Prohibition Act, H.R. 2534, 116th Cong. (Dec. 5, 2019). This bill was referred to the U.S. Senate Committee on Banking, Housing, and Urban Affairs (Dec. 9, 2019). For further discussion on this bill, *see infra* note 130 and accompanying text.

[4] Nearly forty years ago, SEC Chairman John Shad stated: "In order to curtail and deter insider trading, the Commission has sharply increased the number of enforcement actions against such conduct." Written Statement of the Honorable John S.R. Shad, Chairman, Securities and Exchange Commission, Before the Subcommittee on Telecommunications, Consumer Protection and Finance of the Energy and Commerce Committee Concerning the Insider Trading Sanctions Act, U.S. House of Representatives, at 3 (April 13, 1983). The Commission's enforcement priorities continue to focus on illegal insider trading. *See* SEC Division of Enforcement 2019 Annual Report at 24–25 (2019), available at https://www.sec.gov/files/enforcement-annual-report-2019.pdf (describing enforcement actions in fiscal year 2019 brought for alleged insider trading violations). *See also* David A. Vise and Steve Coll, *Eagle on the Street* 49 (1991) (discussing "the SEC's war on insider trading").

[5] In 2019, insider trading cases comprised six percent of the SEC's standalone enforcement actions and four percent of its total actions. *See* 2019 Annual Report, *supra* note 4, at 28–29.

[6] *See* Marc I. Steinberg and Ralph C. Ferrara, *Securities Practice: Federal and State Enforcement* § 7:11 (2d ed. 2001 & 2020–2021 supp.) (stating that "a large number of criminal prosecutions brought for violating Section 10(b) have involved insider trading" and citing cases in support thereof).

Rethinking Securities Law. Marc I. Steinberg, Oxford University Press. © Marc I. Steinberg 2021.
DOI: 10.1093/oso/9780197583142.003.0007

more prominent white-collar crimes.[7] While the government merits kudos to some extent for its vigilance, it unfortunately has created a number of loopholes that facilitate insider wrongdoing.[8]

Much of the blame for the unacceptable state of insider trading regulation in this country rests with the U.S. Supreme Court. In two decisions four decades ago, the Court rejected the parity and access rules that were embraced by the lower federal courts[9] (and which today are adhered to by developed securities markets outside of the United States[10]), opting to adopt a restrictive approach premised on state law fiduciary duty principles. These two decisions—*Chiarella v. United States*[11] and *Dirks v. Securities and Exchange Commission*[12]—paved the way for the incongruous insider trading framework that exists in this country.

This chapter explores the deficient insider trading regimen in this country. In far too many situations, ambiguity, laxity, and disparate treatment prevail. Thereafter, recommendations for reform are proffered, seeking the adoption and implementation of a vastly improved regulatory framework.

II. The Unacceptable Current Insider Trading Framework

A. Setting the Stage

Insider trading became federalized under the antifraud provisions with the SEC's decision in *Cady, Roberts*[13] and the U.S. Court of Appeals subsequent decision in *Texas Gulf Sulphur*.[14] Viewed by a number of sources as the single most important decision in the history of the federal securities

---

[7] The substantial number of movies whose plot focuses on insider trading provide support for this statement. *See, e.g.*, *Equity* (2016); *The Price* (2017); *Trading Places* (1983); *Wall Street* (1987).

[8] *See* discussion *infra* notes 22, 84–96 and accompanying text.

[9] *See, e.g.*, *Securities and Exchange Commission v. Texas Gulf Sulphur Co.*, 401 F.2d 833 (2d Cir. 1968) (en banc).

[10] *See* discussion *infra* note 22 and accompanying text.

[11] 445 U.S. 222 (1980).

[12] 463 U.S. 646 (1983). For the author's treatise on insider trading, *see* Marc. I. Steinberg and William K.S. Wang, *Insider Trading* (3d ed. 2010).

[13] *In re Cady, Roberts & Company*, 40 S.E.C. 907, 911 (1961) (applying the access theory, stating "insiders must disclose material facts which are known to them by virtue of their position"). Note that Section 16 of the Securities Exchange Act expressly focuses on the reporting of insider transactions, disgorgement of short-swing profits by insiders, and the prohibition of insiders engaging in short sales. *See* 15 U.S.C. § 78p; discussion *infra* notes 79–89 and accompanying text.

[14] 401 F.2d 833 (2d Cir. 1968) (en banc). The federalization of insider trading is addressed in the author's recent book published by Oxford University Press, Marc. I. Steinberg, *The Federalization of Corporate Governance* 120–25 (2018).

laws,[15] the appellate court in *Texas Gulf Sulphur* enunciated two broad principles with respect to the insider trading proscription: First, the parity of information rationale provides that "[a]nyone in possession of material inside information must either disclose it to the investing public, or, if he is disabled from disclosing it in order to protect a corporate confidence, or he chooses not to do so, must abstain from trading in or recommending the securities concerned while such information remains undisclosed."[16] Second, pursuant to the access principle, "anyone who . . . has access, directly or indirectly, to information intended to be available only for a corporate purpose and not for the personal benefit of anyone may not take advantage of such information knowing it is unavailable to those with whom he is dealing, [namely,] the investing public."[17]

Eventually, the access approach emerged as the preferred rationale of the lower federal courts.[18] With respect to "tipping" liability, the general approach was that the tippee stood in the shoes of its tipper.[19] Upon the knowing receipt of material nonpublic information[20] from an insider or from another person who had access to such confidential information, the tippee likewise was subject to the prohibition against trading until there was adequate dissemination of the information to the investing public.[21]

---

[15] In addition to focusing on insider trading, the *Texas Gulf Sulphur* decision also addressed concepts of materiality, the impact that information disclosed has on the market price of a subject security, the timing of insider's trades, company affirmative disclosure obligations, and company liability based on misleading disclosure in the secondary securities markets. In commemoration of the fiftieth-year anniversary of this historic decision, the *SMU Law Review* published a Symposium Issue with over twenty prominent academicians authoring articles. *See Texas Gulf Sulphur 50th Anniversary Symposium Issue*, 71 SMU L. Rev. No. 3 (2018).

[16] 401 F.2d at 848.

[17] *Id.* (also stating that the disclose-or-abstain rule "is based in policy on the justifiable expectation of the securities marketplace that all investors trading on impersonal exchanges have relatively equal access to material information").

[18] *See, e.g., United States v. Chiarella*, 588 F.2d 1358, 1365 (2d Cir. 1978), *rev'd*, 445 U.S. 222 (1980) ("Anyone corporate insider or not who regularly receives material nonpublic information may not use this information to trade in securities without incurring an affirmative duty to disclose.").

[19] *See, e.g., Elkind v. Liggett & Myers, Inc.*, 635 F.2d 156 (2d Cir. 1980); *Securities and Exchange Commission v. Geon Industries, Inc.*, 531 F.2d 39 (2d Cir. 1976); *Shapiro v. Merrill Lynch, Pierce, Fenner & Smith, Inc.*, 495 F.2d 228 (2d Cir. 1974).

[20] Knowing conduct should encompass both intentional and reckless conduct. The widely accepted definition of reckless conduct under the federal securities laws is conduct that is "highly unreasonable" representing "an extreme departure from the standards of ordinary care to the extent that the danger was either known to the defendant or [was] so obvious that the defendant must have been aware of it." *In re Ikon Office Solutions, Inc. Securities Litigation*, 277 F.3d 658, 667 (3d Cir. 2002).

[21] This principle was sufficiently established for the authors of one law school textbook to conclude that this "prohibition almost certainly extends to the immediate 'tippees' of the insiders who, by trading on such information, participate in the wrong committed in the giving of the tip." Lewis Solomon, Russell Stevenson, and Donald Schwartz, *Corporations: Law and Policy* 908 (1982).

B. Supreme Court Decisions

The parity and access principles, as set forth in the foregoing discussion, represent the prevailing approach adhered to by developed securities markets outside of the United States.[22]

[22] For example, the European Union and Australia adhere to the parity of information approach while Canada (Ontario) and China follow the access standard. *See* Corporations Act 2001 (Cth) § 1043A (Australia) (setting forth proscribed conduct for any person in possession of material non-public information); Province of Ontario Securities Act, R.S.O. 1990, c S. 5, § 76 (Canada) (providing for access standard); Securities Law of the People's Republic of China (2014 Amendment) (promulgated by the Standing Comm. Nat'l People's Cong., Dec. 29, 1998, *rev'd* Aug. 31, 2014, effective Aug. 31, 2014) art. 76 (setting forth access standard); Regulation (EU) No. 596/2014 of the European Parliament and of the Council of 16 April 2014 on Market Abuse Regulation, art. 8 (Insider Dealing) (promulgating possession standard). In this regard, the European Regulation provides:

1. For the purposes of this Regulation, insider dealing arises where a person possesses inside information and uses that information by acquiring or disposing of, for its own account or for the account of a third party, directly or indirectly, financial instruments to which that information relates. . . .
2. For the purposes of this Regulation, recommending that another person engage in insider dealing, or inducing another person to engage in insider dealing, arises where the person possesses inside information and:
   (a) recommends, on the basis of that information, that another person acquire or dispose of financial instruments to which that information relates, or induces that person to make such an acquisition or disposal, or
   (b) recommends, on the basis of that information, that another person cancel or amend an order concerning a financial instrument to which that information relates, or induces that person to make such a cancellation or amendment.
3. The use of the recommendations or inducements referred to in paragraph 2 amounts to insider dealing within the meaning of this Article where the person using the recommendation or inducement knows or ought to know that it is based upon inside information.
4. This Article applies to any person who possesses inside information as a result of:
   (a) being a member of the administrative, management or supervisory bodies of the issuer or emission allowance market participant;
   (b) having a holding in the capital of the issuer or emission allowance market participant;
   (c) having access to the information through the exercise of an employment, profession or duties; or
   (d) being involved in criminal activities.
   This Article also applies to any person who possesses inside information under circumstances other than those referred to in the first subparagraph where that person knows or ought to know that it is inside information.
5. Where the person is a legal person, this Article shall also apply, in accordance with national law, to the natural persons who participate in the decision to carry out the acquisition, disposal, cancellation or amendment of an order for the account of the legal person concerned.

EU Regulation No. 596/2014 at art. 8. *See* Directive 2014/57/EU of the European Parliament and Council of 16 April 2014 on Criminal Sanctions for Market Abuse, art. 3, para. 3, 2014 O.J. (L 173) 179–89 (providing, *inter alia*, that a person engages in improper insider dealing when one has access to material nonpublic information by means of one's profession, employment, or duties or otherwise "has obtained [such] inside information under [other] circumstances where that person

In this country, however, the U.S. Supreme Court rejected these principles in *Chiarella v. United States*.[23] There, applying state law concepts, the Court reasoned that silence may incur liability under Section 10(b) of the Securities Exchange Act[24] only if there is a duty to disclose based on a fiduciary relationship or a relationship of trust and confidence.[25] Deemed the "classical" approach, this rationale prohibits corporate fiduciaries as well as temporary insiders[26] from trading while aware of material nonpublic information because these persons have a relationship of trust and confidence to the shareholders of the subject corporation.[27]

---

knows that it is inside information"). *See generally Market Abuse Regulation—Commentaries and Annotated Guide* (Marco Ventoruzzo & Sebastian Mocks eds., 2017) (providing excellent commentaries on the EU Market Abuse Regulation); Franklin A. Gevurtz, *The Road Not Taken: A Comparison of the E.U. and U.S. Insider Trading Prohibitions*, 56 Wash. U. J.L. & Pol'y 31, 36 (2018) (providing comparisons and also explaining that "a regulation under E.U. law is directly binding law, whereas a directive is an instruction to member nations of the European Union as to what their national laws must contain"); Marc I. Steinberg, *Insider Trading Regulations—A Comparative Analysis*, 37 Int'l Law. 153 (2003) (addressing insider trading regulation in the United States as well as other developed markets).

Even though several countries have insider trading provisions that are stricter than the United States, the level of enforcement and private redress have been relatively minimal. One example is New Zealand which adheres to a parity of information standard. *See* George R. Walker and Andrew F. Simpson, *Insider Conduct Regulation in New Zealand; Exploring the Enforcement Deficit*, 2013 New Zealand L. Rev. 521, 536 (2013) (stating that no insider trading prosecutions and few civil proceedings have been brought for several years revealing "the lack of successful enforcement action against insider conduct").

23 445 U.S. 222 (1980).

24 15 U.S.C. § 78j(b).

25 445 U.S. at 230 (stating that such liability premised on a defendant's silence "is premised upon a duty to disclose arising from a relationship of trust and confidence between parties to a transaction").

26 In *Dirks v. Securities and Exchange Commission*, 463 U.S. 646, 677 n. 14 (1983), the Court recognized the temporary insider principle. The Court stated:

> Under certain circumstances, such as where corporate information is revealed legitimately to an underwriter, accountant, lawyer, or consultant working for the corporation, these outsiders may become fiduciaries of the shareholders. The basis for recognizing this fiduciary duty is not simply that such persons acquired nonpublic corporate information, but rather that they have entered into a special confidential relationship in the conduct of the business of the enterprise and are given access to information solely for corporate purposes.... [W]hen such a person breaches his fiduciary relationship, he may be treated more properly as a tipper than as a tippee.... For such a duty to be imposed, however, the corporation must expect the outsider to keep the disclosed nonpublic information confidential, and the relationship at least must imply such a duty.

27 *See* 445 U.S. at 230. Interestingly, under corporate law principles, directors and officers generally owe a fiduciary duty to the corporation and its shareholders collectively, not to any particular shareholder. *See, e.g., Mills Acquisition Co. v. Macmillan, Inc.*, 559 A.2d 1261, 1280 (Del. 1989) ("It is basic to our law that the board of directors has the ultimate responsibility for managing the business and affairs of a corporation. In discharging this function, the directors owe fiduciary duties of care and loyalty to the corporation and its shareholders."). Moreover, a number of states take the position that a fiduciary's obligation is owed to the corporation, not to its shareholders. *See, e.g., Ritchie v. Rupe*, 443 S.W. 3d 856 (Tex. 2014). For commentary on *Chiarella* and its aftermath, *see, e.g.*, Donald C. Langevoort, *Insider Trading and the Fiduciary Principle: A Post-Chiarella Restatement*, 70 Cal.

In a subsequent decision, *United States v. O'Hagan*,[28] the Court extended this rationale by adopting the misappropriation theory. Pursuant to this approach, a person commits securities fraud by misappropriating confidential information for securities trading purposes, thereby breaching a relationship of trust and confidence to the source of the information.[29] Hence, this theory focuses on a subject enterprise's outsiders who become privy to material nonpublic information but who do not owe a fiduciary duty to its shareholders. As strange as it may appear, because this duty is owed to the information's source, the subject person may avoid Section 10(b) liability by disclosing to the source that she plans to trade the securities.[30] In such event, no deception has been perpetrated within the meaning of Section 10(b).[31]

This baffling holding illustrates the condition of U.S. insider trading laws. By way of example, an attorney representing the prospective acquirer in a merger transaction who receives material confidential information from his client can avoid Section 10(b) liability by disclosing to his law firm and his client that he intends to purchase the target's common stock prior to public announcement of the transaction.[32] Hence, the miscreant's advance disclosure of his wrongdoing is compliant with Section 10(b).[33]

L. Rev. 1 (1982); Donna M. Nagy, *Insider Trading and the General Demise of Fiduciary Principles*, 94 Iowa L. Rev. 1315 (2009); William K.S. Wang, *Insider Trading on Material Nonpublic Information on Impersonal Stock Markets: Who Is Harmed and Who Can Sue Whom Under SEC Rule 10b-5*, 54 So. Cal. L. Rev. 1217 (1981).

28 521 U.S. 642 (1997).

29 *Id.* at 652 ("The misappropriation theory holds that a person commits fraud 'in connection with' a securities transaction, and thereby violates § 10(b) and Rule 10b-5, when he misappropriates confidential information for securities trading purposes, in breach of a duty owed to the source of the information.").

30 *Id.* at 655 (stating that "full disclosure [to the source of the information] forecloses liability under the misappropriation theory").

31 *Id.* at 659 n. 9 (reasoning that "the textual requirement of deception precludes liability when a person trading on the basis of nonpublic information has disclosed his trading plans to, or obtained permission from, the principal—even though such conduct may affect the securities markets in the same manner as the conduct reached by the misappropriation theory [and] [m]oreover, once a disloyal agent discloses his imminent breach of duty, his principal may seek appropriate equitable relief under state law").

32 *See* Kimberly D. Krawiec et al., *Don't Ask, Just Tell: Insider Trading After United States v. O'Hagan*, 84 Va. L. Rev. 153 (1998).

33 That the misappropriator who gives advance notice of his contemplated trades may be liable under other civil and criminal provisions mitigates the laxity of this approach. Nonetheless, this conduct falls outside the scope of Section 10(b), the premier antifraud provision of the federal securities laws.

It is challenging to fathom a public policy rationale that justifies this approach.[34]

With respect to tipping liability, the U.S. Supreme Court likewise rejected the position adhered to by the lower courts that the tippee stands in the shoes of the tipper,[35] opting instead for an approach premised on breach of fiduciary duty. In *Dirks v. Securities and Exchange Commission*,[36] the Court held that liability under Section 10(b) exists in this context only if the tipper breaches his fiduciary duty by conveying the material nonpublic information to the recipient. This breach is shown by the tipper's communication of such information for his personal benefit or for the purpose of making a gift to the recipient.[37] By conditioning tipping liability on a breach of fiduciary duty with the grafting of a motivational requirement, the Court further muddled the law of insider trading and made its effective enforcement more arduous.[38]

C. The SEC's Responses to Court Decisions

Faced with judicial decisions restricting the scope of insider trading liability, the SEC has responded by adopting rules and regulations that ameliorate their impact. While the Commission's efforts have been successful to a significant extent, the consequence of these administrative

---

[34] *See* Krawiec et al., *supra* note 32, at 187 ("Given the Court's insistence that trading covered by the misappropriation theory harms members of the investing public, it is difficult to understand how the Court can exclude from the theory's reach such conduct that has an identical effect on the investing public.").

[35] *See* cases cited *supra* note 19.

[36] 463 U.S. 646 (1983).

[37] *Id.* at 662. More recently, the Court reaffirmed *Dirks* in *Salman v. United States*, 137 S. Ct. 420 (2016). Employing *Dirks*' "gift" rationale, the Court stated: "By disclosing confidential information as a gift to his brother with the expectation that he would trade on it, Mayer [the temporary insider who tipped] breached his duty of trust and confidence to [his employer] Citigroup and its clients—a duty that Salman [the defendant-tippee] acquired, and breached himself, by trading on the information with full knowledge that it had been improperly disclosed." *Id.* at 428. The *Salman* decision thus "was a missed opportunity by the Court . . . as the law of insider trading remains . . . vague and disparate." Marc I. Steinberg, *From the Editor-in-Chief*, 45 Sec. Reg. L.J. 5, 6 (2017). *See* Eric C. Chaffee, *The Supreme Court as Museum Curator: Securities Regulation and the Roberts Court*, 67 Case W. Res. L. Rev. 847, 863 (2018) (commenting that *Salman* provided "an opportunity to remake federal securities regulation in the area of insider trading, and once again the Court chose to preserve the status quo created by existing precedent").

[38] *See* 463 U.S. at 668 (Blackmun, J., dissenting) (asserting that the majority opinion "engrafts a special motivational requirement on the fiduciary duty doctrine [and] excuses a knowing and intentional violation of an insider's duty to shareholders if the insider does not act from a motive of personal gain"). The making of a gift also satisfies the *Dirks*' test. *See id.* at 664 (stating that "[t]he tip and trade resemble trading by the insider himself followed by a gift of the profits to the recipient"); *supra* note 37.

determinations has been to instill further uncertainty and arbitrariness in this setting. Three examples are provided.

1. Insider Trading in the Tender Offer Context—Adoption of Rule 14e-3

Upset with the Supreme Court's decision in *Chiarella*,[39] the SEC lessened its impact by adopting Rule 14e-3.[40] Limited to tender offers, the rule adheres to a broad parity of information prescription coupled with an expansive anti-tipping provision.[41] Hence, under Rule 14e-3, with certain exceptions, it is illegal for any person in possession of material information—which she knows or has reason to know is nonpublic and knows or has reason to know that such information has been received, directly or indirectly, from an offeror, target, or financial intermediary—to purchase or sell securities in connection with a tender offer.[42] With its broad parity of information approach coupled with an expansive anti-tipping provision, Rule 14e-3 is nearly the antithesis of Section 10(b) in the insider trading context—namely, a parity rule not conditioned on principles of fiduciary duty.[43]

Due to the critical distinctions between Section 10(b) and Rule 14e-3, disparate treatment exists for similarly situated persons. If a transaction is structured as a merger, Rule 14e-3 is inapplicable, thereby signifying that the Section 10(b) fiduciary relationship rationale is the governing

---

[39] *Chiarella v. United States*, 445 U.S. 222 (1980).

[40] 17 C.F.R. § 240.14e-3. *See* Securities Exchange Act Release No. 17120 (1980).

[41] *See* Rule 14e-3(a), (d). Rule 14e-3 applies when "a substantial step or steps to commence . . . a tender offer" are taken—even if no tender offer ultimately occurs. *See Securities and Exchange Commission v. Mayhew*, 121 F.3d 44 (2d Cir. 1997).

[42] *See* Rule 14e-3(a). An exception is provided for multi-service financial firms, including broker-dealers, that can establish that "the individual(s) making the investment decision on behalf of [another] person to purchase or sell any security . . . did not know the material nonpublic information [and that the financial firm] had implemented . . . policies and procedures, reasonable under the circumstances, . . . to ensure that [its personnel] making investment decision(s) would not violate [the rule]." Rule 14e-3(b). With respect to measures undertaken by financial institutions that seek to preclude subject personnel from learning or using material nonpublic information, *see* Division of Market Regulation, Securities and Exchange Commission, Broker-Dealer Policies and Procedures Designed to Segment the Flow and Prevent the Misuse of Material Nonpublic Information, [1989–1990 Transfer Binder] Fed. Sec. L. Rep. (CCH) ¶ 84,520 (1990).

[43] Limiting its holding to the circumstances at bar, the *O'Hagan* Court upheld the validity of Rule 14e-3. The Court reasoned:

> [I]t is a fair assumption that trading on the basis of material, nonpublic information will often involve a breach of a duty of confidentiality to the bidder or target company or their representatives. The SEC, cognizant of the proof problem that could enable sophisticated traders to escape responsibility, placed in Rule 14e-3(a) a "disclose or abstain from trading" command that does not require specific proof of a breach of fiduciary duty. That prescription, we are satisfied, applied to this case, is a "means reasonably designed to prevent" fraudulent trading on material, nonpublic information in the tender offer context.

521 U.S. at 672–73.

standard.[44] If the dealmakers, however, opt for the tender offer route, the expansive parameters of Rule 14e-3 apply.[45] With some frequency, persons privy to material inside information who engage in trading or tipping are clueless how the transaction is structured. The consequence is that in certain instances an individual engaging in trading or tipping acts lawfully if the transaction is structured as a merger yet is subject to liability if the transaction is structured as a tender offer. The result is that the very same conduct can result in widely disparate consequences: the lawful retention of profits in a merger transaction as contrasted with in a tender offer the incurrence of liability pursuant to a government enforcement action, including the specter of criminal liability. This disparity in treatment lacks adequate justification and is incompatible with investor protection, market integrity, and principles of fairness.[46]

2. The Misappropriation Theory—Adoption of Rule 10b5-2

As discussed in the foregoing, the Supreme Court in *O'Hagan* gave its approbation to the misappropriation theory premised on a breach of a relationship of trust and confidence to the source of the information.[47] In a subsequent surprising decision, the U.S. Court of Appeals, applying *O'Hagan*, held that marriage, standing alone, does not constitute a fiduciary relationship.[48] Responding to this decision, the SEC adopted Rule 10b5-2.[49] In addition to setting forth that an individual having a specified relationship (such as that of marriage) is presumed to have a duty of trust or confidence under the misappropriation theory, the Commission also included as coming within that prescription "a person [who] agrees to maintain information in

---

[44] *See, e.g.*, *Securities and Exchange Commission v. Switzer*, 590 F. Supp. 756 (W.D. Okla. 1984) (alleging University of Oklahoma football coach and his friends traded on material nonpublic information regarding a merger transaction—held not liable under § 10(b)).

[45] *See supra* notes 40–43 and accompanying text.

[46] I have made this point on numerous occasions. *See, e.g.*, Steinberg, *supra* note 14, at 127–28. Note that the SEC occasionally has invoked Section 17(a)(3) of the Securities Act, 15 U.S.C. § 77q(a)(3), in its insider trading enforcement actions. *See, e.g.*, *In re Bolan*, 2015 SEC LEXIS 2201 (SEC 2015). Unlike Section 10(b) and Section 17(a)(1), the culpability level of Section 17(a)(3) is negligence. *See Aaron v. Securities and Exchange Commission*, 446 U.S. 680 (1980). For further discussion, *see* Marc I. Steinberg and Abel Ramirez, Jr., *The SEC's Neglected Weapon: A Proposed Amendment to Section 17(a)(3) and the Application of Negligent Insider Trading*, 19 U. Pa. J. Bus. L. 239 (2017).

[47] *See* discussion *supra* notes 28–34 and accompanying text.

[48] *United States v. Chestman*, 947 F.2d 551 (2d Cir. 1991). Other courts have disagreed. *See, e.g.*, *Securities and Exchange Commission v. Yun*, 327 F.3d 1263 (11th Cir. 2003) (in view that husband and wife had a practice of sharing and keeping business confidences, reasonable expectation of confidentiality existed premised on a relationship of trust and confidence).

[49] 17 C.F.R. § 240.10b5-2. *See* Securities Exchange Act Release No. 43154 (2000).

confidence."[50] In so doing, the SEC inappropriately transformed a contractual agreement into a fiduciary relationship: That the entering into of a nondisclosure agreement (NDA) or confidentiality agreement forms a relationship of trust or confidence belies commercial reality.[51] Ordinarily, parties to these agreements deal at arm's length with the objective of serving their own or their principal's best interests.[52] Absent unusual circumstances, these parties neither have a close relationship nor trust another. Customarily, they are fastidious to execute written agreements that are designed to safeguard the confidentiality of their proprietary information.[53] If the agreement is violated, a breach of contract action may well ensue. However, a contractual breach is of a very different character than one premised on a breach of a relationship of trust or confidence. Hence, pursuant to custom and practice, NDA or confidentiality agreements should not be characterized as fiduciary in nature. The SEC's determination to do so in Rule 10b5-2, and its application by a number of courts, contravenes Supreme Court precedent.[54]

---

[50] Pursuant to Rule 10b5-2, "a duty of trust or confidence exists in the following circumstances, among others: (1) Whenever a person agrees to maintain information in confidence; (2) Whenever the person communicating the material nonpublic information and the person to whom it is communicated have a history, pattern, or practice of sharing confidences, such that the recipient of the information knows or reasonably should know that the person communicating the material nonpublic information expects that the recipient will maintain its confidentiality; or (3) Whenever a person receives or obtains material nonpublic information from his or her spouse, parent, child, or sibling; provided, however, that the person receiving or obtaining the information may demonstrate that no duty of trust or confidence existed with respect to the information."

[51] As stated in a brief of amici curiae filed by five prominent law professors in *Securities and Exchange Commission v. Cuban*, Case No. 3:08-CV-02050-D (N.D. Tex.):

> In the context of a business relationship, a confidentiality agreement alone is insufficient to create a fiduciary or similar relationship of trust and confidence between the parties. Under both state and federal common law, a confidentiality agreement alone creates only an obligation to maintain the secrecy of the information, not a fiduciary or fiduciary-like duty to act loyally to the source of the information. In the absence of any other facts or circumstances indicating the existence of a fiduciary or similar relationship of trust and confidence, there can be no insider trading liability based on the misappropriation theory pursuant to Section 10(b).

This brief is contained in Marc I. Steinberg, *Securities and Exchange Commission v. Cuban—A Trial of Insider Trading* 49 (2019).

[52] Steinberg, *supra* note 51, at 329 (author stating that "to elevate a non-disclosure agreement to the status of constituting a relationship of trust and confidence between the contracting parties belies economic reality").

[53] *See* Richard Harroch, *The Key Elements of Non-Disclosure Agreements*, Forbes, March 10, 2016, available at https://www.forbes.com/sites/allbusiness/2016/03/10/the-key-elements-of-non-disclosure-agreements/#29addf3b627d. *See generally* Gary Lawrence, *Due Diligence in Business Transactions* (2019).

[54] *See Securities and Exchange Commission v. Cuban*, 620 F.3d 551 (5th Cir. 2010). *Securities and Exchange Commission v. Cooperman*, [2017 Transfer Binder] Fed. Sec. L. Rep. (CCH) ¶ 99,653 (E.D. Pa. 2017); *supra* note 50. The *Cuban* case focused on the alleged breach of an oral nondisclosure agreement by Mark Cuban and his subsequent sale of the subject company's securities prior to public

From a different perspective, the SEC's activism illustrates another shortcoming of the current insider trading framework. Clearly, parties to confidentiality agreements should be required to adhere to insider trading compliance. Either approach—the parity of information or access approach—accomplishes this objective. The fiduciary relationship rationale embraced by the Supreme Court, however, fails to encompass such agreements. Nonetheless, utilizing a result-oriented perspective, the SEC defines these relationships as constituting a relationship of trust or confidence. The Commission's activism to do so exemplifies its quest to mold its administrative rules and enforcement actions to purportedly come within the scope of Supreme Court precedent. By expanding the reach of the fiduciary relationship rationale beyond its boundaries, the Commission with frequency has sought to vigorously implement insider trading prohibitions while portraying that its actions are consistent with Supreme Court precedent.[55]

3. Selective Disclosure—Adoption of Regulation FD

The Supreme Court's decision in *Dirks* permits insiders under Section 10(b) to convey material nonpublic information to financial analysts and other favored persons so long as such communications are not for personal gain or to make a gift.[56] *Dirks* thus leaves a large void in regard to improper tipping under Section 10(b), including situations involving "loose lip" executives[57] as well as the deliberate conveyance of selective disclosure by company spokespersons to financial analysts with the objective that their respective companies receive more favorable reviews from these analysts.[58] Prior to *Dirks*,

disclosure of the allegedly material nonpublic information. The author was retained as an expert witness on behalf of Mr. Cuban. The jury found Mr. Cuban not liable. For an experiential book on this litigation, *see* Steinberg, *supra* note 51.

[55] *See, e.g.*, Steinberg, *supra* note 51, at 47 (In its memorandum of law opposing the defendant's motion to dismiss, the SEC stated: "This case involves the application of well-settled insider trading principles to straightforward allegations of fraud [and presents] a textbook example of unlawful misappropriation."). Nonetheless, during the Trump administration, the number of insider trading enforcement actions decreased. *See* Tom Dreisbach, *Under Trump, SEC Enforcement of Insider Trading Dropped to Lowest Point in Decades*, NPR, All Things Considered (Aug. 14, 2020), available at https://www.npr.org/2020/08/14/901862355/under-trump-sec-enforcement-of-insider-trading-dropped-to-lowest-point-in-decade.

[56] *Dirks v. Securities and Exchange Commission*, 463 U.S. 646 (1983); discussion *supra* notes 35–38 and accompanying text.

[57] *See Elkind v. Liggett & Myers, Inc.*, 635 F.2d 156 (2d Cir. 1980) (decided prior to *Dirks*, holding liability under § 10(b) due to "loose lip" corporate executive communicating material nonpublic information to financial analyst).

[58] *See, e.g.*, Fred Barbash, *Companies, Analysts a Little Too Cozy*, Wash. Post, Oct. 31, 1999, at H1; Susan Pulliam, *Abercrombie & Fitch Ignites Controversy over Possible Leak of Sluggish Sales Data*, Wall St. J., Oct. 14, 1999, at C1. The SEC did initiate one enforcement action in this context alleging that the

tipping of material nonpublic information to financial analysts ran afoul of Section 10(b)'s insider trading prohibition as did trading on the basis of that information.[59]

With such selective disclosure no longer being actionable under Section 10(b), the SEC chose a different path. Viewing that this widespread practice benefited market professionals at the expense of ordinary investors, contravening "principles of integrity and fairness,"[60] the Commission adopted Regulation FD (Fair Disclosure).[61] This Regulation thus seeks to fill much of the gap that *Dirks* left open. Its principal premise is that "when an issuer, or person acting on its behalf, discloses material nonpublic information to [selective] persons, . . . it must make public disclosure of this information."[62] By promulgating Regulation FD outside the contours of Section 10(b)'s insider trading proscription, the SEC astutely charted a course that largely addresses the concerns at issue without contravening Supreme Court authority.[63]

Nonetheless, insider trading and Regulation FD are not one and the same. Unlike Section 10(b), Regulation FD is not an antifraud provision and does

---

Dirks standard was met. The case subsequently was settled. *See Securities and Exchange Commission v. Stevens*, SEC Litigation Release No. 12813 (1991) (settlement whereby Commission alleged that the subject company's board chairman and chief executive officer received "direct, tangible benefit in his status as a corporate manager" by selectively conveying material nonpublic information to analysts).

[59] *See* cases cited *supra* note 19.

[60] *See* Michael Schroeder and Randall Smith, *Disclosure Rule Cleared by the SEC*, Wall St. J., Aug. 11, 2000, at C1 (quoting SEC Chairman Arthur Levitt).

[61] *See* Securities Exchange Act Release No. 43154 (2000).

[62] *Id.* As stated by the SEC in that Release:

> Regulation FD (Fair Disclosure) is a new issuer disclosure rule that addresses selective disclosure. The regulation provides that when an issuer, or person acting on its behalf, discloses material non-public information to certain enumerated persons (in general, securities market professionals and holders of the issuer's securities who may well trade on the basis of the information), it must make public disclosure of that information. The timing of the required public disclosure depends on whether the selective disclosure was intentional or non-intentional; for an intentional selective disclosure, the issuer must make public disclosure simultaneously; for a non-intentional disclosure, the issuer must make public disclosure promptly. Under the regulation, the required public disclosure may be made by filing or furnishing a Form 8-K, or by another method or combination of methods that is reasonably designed to effect broad, non-exclusionary distribution of the information to the public.

[63] For more extensive coverage of Regulation FD, *see* Michael D. Guttentag, *Selective Disclosure and Insider Trading*, 69 Fla. L. Rev. 519 (2019); Marc I. Steinberg and Jason B. Myers, *Lurking in the Shadows: The Hidden Issues of the Securities and Exchange Commission's Regulation FD*, 27 J. Corp. L. 173 (2002).

not provide a private right of action for allegedly aggrieved investors.[64] Moreover, the SEC's utilization of Regulation FD may be viewed as sporadic with relatively milder sanctions as compared to insider trading enforcement actions.[65] Overall, however, the Commission has aptly achieved the key objective underlying Regulation FD—providing an enforcement resource to invoke against companies and their spokespersons who selectively communicate material nonpublic information to financial analysts, market professionals, and current shareholders.[66]

4. Summation

The foregoing examples illustrate the SEC's activism to counteract restrictive Supreme Court decisions in the insider trading realm. In practicality, the Commission has achieved significant success in this quest. The consequence, however, is the presence of disparate treatment of similarly situated persons, transforming a contractual undertaking to that of a fiduciary relationship, and creating further ambiguity in this area of the law.

---

[64] *See* Securities Exchange Act Release No. 43154 (2000) (stating that Regulation FD "is not designed to create new duties under the antifraud provisions of the federal securities laws or in private rights of action").

[65] *See, e.g., In re TherapeuticsMD, Inc.*, Securities Exchange Act Release No. 86708 (2019) (settlement involving alleged tipping of material nonpublic information by company executives to research analysts with company agreeing to a cease and desist order and $200,000 civil penalty); *In re Polizzotto*, SEC Press Release No. 2013-174 (SEC 2013) (settlement whereby corporation's former investor relations spokesperson consented to cease and desist order and $50,000 monetary penalty); *Securities and Exchange Commission v. Flowserve Corp.*, SEC Press Release No. 2005-41 (D.D.C. 2005) (settlement whereby company and its chief executive officer consented to cease and desist order and payment of monetary penalties (the company $350,000, the CEO $50,000)); *In re Schering-Plough Corp.*, SEC Litigation Release No. 18330 (SEC 2003) (settlement whereby company and its former chief executive officer settled to cease and desist order and payment of monetary penalties (the company $1 million, the CEO $50,000)). On the other hand, in one case, *Securities and Exchange Commission v. Siebel Systems, Inc.*, 384 F. Supp. 2d 694, 704 (S.D.N.Y. 2005), the Commission was criticized for its overzealous use of Regulation FD under the facts of that case:

> The SEC . . . scrutinized, at an extremely heightened level, every particular word used in the statement, including the tense of verbs and the general syntax of each sentence. No support for such an approach can be found in Regulation FD. . . . Such an approach places an unreasonable burden on a company's management and spokespersons to become linguistic experts, or otherwise live in fear of violating Regulation FD should the words they use later be interpreted by the SEC as connoting even the slightest variance from the company's public statements.

[66] *See* Steinberg and Myers, *supra* note 63, at 208 (contending that "the Regulation does fill a gap in an issuer's disclosure duties that had been left open by the federal securities laws, and at least in some small regard, brings the U.S. laws in line with other established markets abroad").

D. The Elimination of the Improper Benefit Test in Criminal Cases

Recently, the Department of Justice has invoked the wire fraud statute and the general criminal securities fraud statute enacted by Congress pursuant to the Sarbanes-Oxley Act of 2002 (SOX).[67] The SOX criminal statute (18 U.S.C. § 1348) was passed to "supplement the patchwork of existing technical securities law violations with a more general and less technical provision."[68] Interpreting this statute as well as the federal wire fraud statute (which also is a Title 18 provision), a number of courts have handed down decisions that significantly expand the scope of criminal liability for insider trading.[69]

The Second Circuit's decision in *United States v. Blaszczak*[70] charts new territory for federal prosecutors to pursue actions against tippers and tippees. In that case, the appellate court ruled that the *Dirks* personal benefit test has no application under these Title 18 criminal statutes. Holding that the Title 18 securities and wire fraud statutes have broader reach than the Title 15 Section 10(b) provision, the court accordingly reasoned that the government can invoke these more expansive statutes in securities fraud prosecutions, including those alleging illegal insider trading.[71] More specifically, the appellate court declined "to graft the *Dirks* personal benefit test onto the elements of Title 18 securities fraud."[72] Hence, in these Title 18 cases, criminal convictions can be procured in cases involving tippers and tippees without any showing of personal benefit. As the Second Circuit opined, the "government may avoid the personal benefit test altogether by prosecuting insider trading with less difficulty under the Title 18 fraud statutes—particularly the Title 18 securities fraud statute."[73]

The result of this decision illustrates the absurdity of the insider trading framework in this country: Except for the standard of proof,[74] a criminal

---

[67] 18 U.S.C. §§ 1343, 1348. *See, e.g.*, *United States v. Blaszczak*, 947 F.3d 19 (2d Cir. 2019); *United States v. Melvin*, 143 F. Supp. 3d 1354 (N.D. Ga. 2015).

[68] The Corporate and Criminal Fraud Accountability Act of 2002, S. Rep. No. 107-146, at 14, 187th Cong., 2d Sess. (2002).

[69] *See* cases cited *supra* note 67.

[70] 947 F.3d 19 (2d Cir. 2019), *vacated and remanded on other grounds*, 2021 WL 78043 (U.S. Sup. Ct. 2021).

[71] 947 F.3d at 35–37.

[72] *Id.* at 37.

[73] *Id.* ("Accordingly, we hold that the personal-benefit test does not apply to the wire fraud and Title 18 securities fraud statutes.").

[74] The criminal standard, of course, is beyond a reasonable doubt while the standard in SEC and private actions is preponderance of the evidence. *See Herman & MacLean v. Huddleston*, 459 U.S. 375 (1983) (holding that preponderance of the evidence standard applies in § 10(b) private damages

prosecution under the Title 18 fraud statutes is an easier case than a civil proceeding in the tipper-tippee setting because, unlike pursuant to Section 10(b), no personal benefit by the tipper need be proven. Hence, the government now can more readily obtain a criminal conviction than for a private claimant or the SEC to win a civil case. Nonetheless, with the specter of a criminal referral being made by the SEC to the Justice Department, this prospect may induce alleged violators to expeditiously negotiate settlements with the Commission whereby they neither admit nor deny wrongdoing.[75] Prompt and relatively amicable resolution of a SEC enforcement matter frequently lessens the risk of criminal referral.[76] The key point remains that in this country today, or at least in the Second Circuit where a large percentage of federal criminal securities prosecutions are instituted, the procurement of a criminal conviction for illegal insider trading is easier than for the SEC to win its civil case. This situation indeed is bewildering but such is the state of the insider trading law in this country.

E. Loopholes Created by the SEC

This discussion focuses on two major loopholes that the SEC created that facilitate insider trading by corporate fiduciaries. The first situation addresses the Commission's relaxation of insider liability under Section 16(b) of the Securities Exchange Act.[77] The second situation examines the SEC's approbation of Rule 10b5-1 trading plans that provide a safe harbor from Section 10(b) insider trading liability.[78]

---

actions); *Steadman v. Securities and Exchange Commission*, 450 U.S. 91 (1981) (holding preponderance of the evidence standard applies in SEC actions alleging violation of the antifraud provisions of the federal securities laws).

[75] *See* discussion in Marc I. Steinberg and Ralph C. Ferrara, *Securities Practice: Federal and State Enforcement* § 7.18 (2d ed. 2001 & 2020–2021 supp.) (setting forth one of the strategies used to decrease the likelihood of a criminal referral is to negotiate a prompt settlement with the SEC).

[76] Depending upon the circumstances however, it may be necessary for a target to litigate tenaciously with the SEC, including resisting the staff's broad investigative demands and asserting the Fifth Amendment privilege against self-incrimination. *Id.*

[77] *See* Securities Exchange Act Release No. 28869 (1991); discussion *infra* notes 79–89 and accompanying text.

[78] *See* Securities Exchange Act Release No. 43154 (2000); discussion *infra* notes 90–96 and accompanying text.

1. Relaxation of Insider Liability under Section 16(b)

Section 16 of the Securities Exchange Act may be viewed as federalizing an aspect of insider trading.[79] Going beyond disclosure, the statute attempts to deter corporate fiduciaries from engaging in insider trading.[80] Section 16 has three components: first, Section 16(a) requires that officers, directors, and shareholders owning more than ten percent of a class of equity security of an Exchange Act company report to the Commission their holdings and transactions in these securities;[81] second, Section 16(b) mandates that these insiders disgorge all profit realized from engaging in purchases and sales or sales and purchases within a six-month period ("short-swing" transactions) in such securities;[82] and Section 16(c) prohibits these insiders from engaging in short sale transactions in their company's equity securities.[83]

---

[79] 15 U.S.C. § 78p. *See* Steinberg, *supra* note 14, at 116–17 (pointing out that, although disclosure rather than substantive fairness was an important focus of the Exchange Act, "Congress elected to federalize an aspect of corporate governance by means of Section 16 of that Act").

[80] As the language of Section 16(b) provides, its objective is to "*prevent . . . the unfair use of information* which may be obtained by such beneficial owner [of greater than ten percent of a class of such company's equity securities], director or officer by reason of his relationship to the issuer." 15 U.S.C. § 78p(b) (emphasis supplied).

[81] 15 U.S.C. § 78p(a). Each such report generally must be filed within two business days. In addition to officers and directors, Section 16 covers persons who beneficially own more than ten percent of a class of equity security of an Exchange Act company. *See* Securities Exchange Act Release No. 18114 (1981) ("Section 16(a) . . . provides that every person who is directly or indirectly the beneficial owner of more than 10% of any class of equity security (other than an exempted security) registered pursuant to Section 12 [of the Exchange Act], or who is an officer or director of the issuer of such securities shall file with the Commission an initial report disclosing the amount of all equity securities of such issuer of which he is a beneficial owner"); Securities Exchange Act Release No. 28869 (1991) (covering a subject insider's subsequent filing of ownership reports regarding such insider's transactions in the issuer's securities).

The term "beneficial owner" is defined in Rule 16a-1(a)(2) as "any person who directly or indirectly, through any contract, arrangement, understanding, relationship or otherwise has or shares direct or indirect pecuniary interest in the equity securities." For court decisions ascertaining the parameters of this term, *see, e.g.*, *CBI Industries, Inc. v. Horton*, 682 F.2d 643 (7th Cir. 1982); *Whiting v. Dow Chemical Co.*, 523 F.2d 680 (2d Cir. 1975).

[82] Profit realized is expansively construed for Section 16(b) purposes to "squeeze all possible profits out of stock transactions and thus to establish a standard so high as to prevent any conflict between the selfish interest of a fiduciary officer, director, or stockholder and the faithful performance of his duty." *Smolowe v. Delendo Corp.*, 136 F.2d 231, 239 (2d Cir. 1943). Strict liability is the standard. *See, e.g.*, *Bershad v. McDonough*, 428 F.2d 693, 696 (7th Cir. 1970) (stating that a subject insider is "deemed capable of structuring his dealings to avoid any possibility of taint and therefore must bear the risks of any miscalculation"). The statute has generated a plethora of litigation and legal commentary. An action under Section 16(b) may be brought by the subject issuer, or if it declines to do so, by a shareholder on such issuer's behalf. *See* § 16(b). For discussion of Supreme Court and other applicable case law as well as SEC rules and regulations in this area, *see, e.g.*, Peter J. Romeo and Alan L. Dye, *Section 16 Treatise* (2019).

[83] 15 U.S.C. § 78p(c). Short-selling generally may be described as "the sale of a security that the seller does not own or that the seller owns but does not deliver." Ralph Janvey, *Short-Selling*, 20 Sec. Reg. L.J. 270, 271 (1992). *See Short-Selling in the Stock Market*, H.R. Rep. No. 102–414, at 8 (1991) (stating that complaints regarding short-selling "have alleged that short-sellers, after establishing a major short position in a particular stock, have aggressively circulated false rumors about the

Prior to the SEC's 1991 rule amendments, the exercise of an option followed by a sale of the underlying securities was deemed a purchase and sale that were matched pursuant to Section 16(b).[84] Departing from judicial precedent,[85] the Commission rejected this principle, determining that the acquisition of an option or other derivative security, rather than the exercise thereof, be defined as a purchase for Section 16(b) purposes.[86] Accordingly, six months after acquiring an option, an insider may exercise the option and immediately thereafter sell the securities. Hence, under the 1991 amendments, insiders may freely sell their equity securities so long as the underlying option or other derivative security was held for six months, subject to the antifraud provisions.[87] Subsequently, in 1996, the Commission went further by amending Rule 16b-3, providing broad exemptive relief through an additional avenue: the transaction's prior approval "by the board of directors, a committee comprised solely of no less than two non-employee directors, or shareholders, or later ratification by shareholders . . . provides a direct exemption [under Section 16(b)] both for the grant itself and any subsequent acquisition of the underlying shares."[88] Hence, upon learning of adverse financial information regarding the subject company, an insider under Section 16(b) whose transaction has received the requisite approval under

---

company's financial condition, problems with its products, or the health or integrity of its officers in an effort to drive down the stock price").

[84] *See* Marc I. Steinberg, *Securities Regulation: Liabilities and Remedies* § 4.06[3] (2020) ("This approach reverses the SEC's previous regulatory approach and differs from cases that have held that the exercise of the option (rather than its acquisition) is the purchase of an equity security under Section 16(b)."), *citing*, *Colan v. Monumental Corp*., 713 F.2d 330 (7th Cir. 1983); *Morales v. Mapco*, 541 F.2d 333 (10th Cir. 1976); *Silverman v. Landa*, 306 F.2d 422 (2d Cir. 1962).

[85] *See, e.g.*, cases cited *supra* note 84.

[86] The Commission evidently sought to restrict Section 16 insiders from using material nonpublic information in transactions involving derivative securities. *See* Securities Exchange Act Release No. 28869 (1991) ("Just as an insider's opportunity to profit commences when he purchases or sells the issuer's common stock, so too the opportunity to profit commences when the insider engages in transactions in options or other derivative securities that provide an opportunity to obtain or dispose of the stock at a fixed price.").

[87] As a U.S. Senator lamented in response to this change, "by the time a CFO is eligible to exercise an option, the six-month period is long gone and the CFO can buy and sell immediately." Comments by U.S. Senator Carl Levin, Fed. Sec. L. Rep. (CCH) No. 1485, at 7 (1992). *See* Marc I. Steinberg, and Daryl L. Landsdale, Jr., *The Judicial and Regulatory Constriction of Section 16(b) of the Securities Exchange Act*, 68 Notre Dame L. Rev. 33, 65 (1992) ("The increased potential for abuse under the new regulatory scheme comes from the ability of insiders to exercise options and sell the underlying stock immediately, as long as the option has been held for at least six months.").

[88] Frederic W. Cook & Co., Inc., *SEC Adopts a Radically Different Rule 16b-3* (Aug. 2, 1996), available at https://www.fwcook.com/content/documents/publications/8-2-96_SEC_Adopts_a_Radically_Different_Rule_16b-3.pdf. Note that discretionary transactions are excluded from Rule 16b-3's exemptive coverage. *See* 17 C.F.R. § 240.16b-3; Securities Exchange Act Release No. 37261 (1996).

Rule 16b-3 or who has held the subject option for six months, may exercise that option and promptly sell her securities prior to public disclosure of such information. The creation of these loopholes by the SEC, which enables this type of conduct to be outside of Section 16(b)'s parameters, is antithetical to the objectives underlying that statute.[89]

2. Insider Trading Plans under Rule 10b5-1

Pursuant to Rule 10b5-1, a purchase or sale of a security is deemed to be "on the basis of" material nonpublic information if the subject person was "aware" of such information at the time of the transaction.[90] Pursuant to that rule, an affirmative defense is recognized if the subject person engages in the transaction(s) pursuant to a preexisting contract, plan, or instruction that is specific and binding.[91] Seemingly, the rule, coupled with the affirmative defense, enables corporate

---

[89] As another example, pursuant to the 1991 amendments, the SEC no longer requires that pre-insider trades by directors and officers be disclosed pursuant to Section 16(a) or subject to the short-swing liability provision of Section 16(b). *See* Rule 16a-2(a), 17 C.F.R. § 240.16a-2(a); Securities Exchange Act Release No. 28869 (1991). When adopted, the lower courts held that Section 16 applied if the subject director or officer held this status at the time of either the purchase or the sale. *See, e.g., Arrow Distributing Corp. v. Baumgartner*, 783 F.2d 1274, 1279 (5th Cir. 1986); *Feder v. Martin Marietta Corp.*, 406 F.2d 260, 266 (2d Cir. 1969). For a critical assessment, *see* Steinberg and Landsdale, *supra* note 87, at 74 (asserting that "the inherent access to inside information that directors and executive officers enjoy, in conjunction with the statute's policy of deterring fiduciaries from making improper use of information gained in their representative capacity, requires that the statute be interpreted as subjecting pre-insider transactions by such insiders to Section 16").

[90] Rule 10b5-1(b), 17 C.F.R. § 240.10b5-1(b). *See* Securities Exchange Act Release No. 43154 (2000).

[91] Pursuant to Rule 10b5-1(c), a pre-existing contract, plan, or instruction generally would have three aspects:

> First, a person [e.g., an executive officer] must demonstrate that prior to becoming aware of the inside information, he/she had entered into a binding contract to purchase or sell the security, had provided instructions to another person to execute the trade for the instructing person's account, or had adopted a written plan for trading securities. Second, the person must demonstrate that, with respect to the purchase or sale, the contract, instructions, or plan: expressly specified the amount(s), price(s), and date(s); provided a written formula, algorithm, or computer program for determining the amount(s), price(s), and date(s); or did not permit the person to exercise any influence over how, when, or whether to execute the trade(s) (and in the event that any other person exercised such influence that person was not aware of the material, nonpublic information). Third, the person must demonstrate that the trade(s) that occurred were pursuant to the previously established contract, instructions, or plan.

Marc I. Steinberg, *Understanding Securities Law* 390 (7th ed. 2018). With respect to entities, Rule 10b5-1 provides an affirmative defense if it is established that the individuals making the investment decision on the subject entity's behalf were not aware of the material nonpublic information and that such entity "had implemented reasonable policies and procedures . . . to ensure that [the] individuals making investment decisions would not violate the laws prohibiting trading on the basis of material nonpublic information." Rule 10b5-1(c)(2), 17 C.F.R. § 240.10b5-1(c)(2).

fiduciaries to engage in legitimate securities trading without the specter of impropriety.[92]

Unfortunately, the Commission declined to promulgate an airtight provision, leaving loopholes that have been abused.[93] For example, there is no requirement that these Rule 10b5-1 plans must be publicly disclosed. As a consequence, verification is lacking. No outside check exists, for example, whether these plans are implemented with executives taking advantage of material nonpublic information regarding future stock movements of their companies' equity securities. Moreover, existing plans can be modified or canceled by insiders when beneficial to their financial interests without disclosure to the SEC or investors. Further, having knowledge of the specific dates when their securities are to be purchased or sold, executives can withhold disclosure of material developments for a desired period of time in order to enhance their profits from these transactions.[94]

Various studies and articles have highlighted the abuses that have occurred by insiders invoking their respective company's Rule 10b5-1 plan as a shield against alleged wrongdoing.[95] Responding to this concern, proposals have been advanced by Congress and the SEC to alleviate the misconduct that is transpiring under these plans.[96] Thus far, no corrective action has been taken.

---

[92] *See* Daniel J. Morrissey, *Taming Rule 10b5-1: The Unfinished Business of Texas Gulf Sulphur*, 71 SMU L. Rev. 883, 886 (2018) ("These programs would . . . be available as a safe harbor to charges of insider trading, even if executives made purchases or sales of their shares when they knew of privileged information that might otherwise subject them to liability.").

[93] *See* discussion *infra* notes 94–96 and accompanying text.

[94] Indeed, a corporation may have multiple Rule 10b5-1 plans simultaneously in effect. *See* Alan D. Jagolinzer, *SEC Rule 10b-1 and Insiders' Strategic Trade*, 55 Mgmt. Sci. 224, 226–27 (2009); Taylan Mavruk and H. Nejat Seyhun, *Do SEC's Rule 10b5-1 Safe Harbor Rules Need to Be Rewritten?*, 2016 Colum. Bus. L. Rev. 133 (2016); Morrissey, *supra* note 92.

[95] *See, e.g.*, M. Todd Henderson et al., *Hiding in Plain Sight: Can Disclosure Enhance Insiders' Trade Returns?*, at 2–3, Coarse-Sandor Working Paper Series in Law & Econ. No. 411 (2012), available at, https://chicagounbound.uchicago.edu/cgi/viewcontent.cgi?article=1646&context=law_and_economics; Jagolinzer, *supra* note 94, at 232–33. Reporting on these two studies, Professor Morrissey stated that: the Jagolinzer study found, among other findings, that "46% of the plans involving preordained sales were terminated in advance of positive news so that officials could keep their shares and enjoy the gains resulting from the release of that information"; and the Henderson et al. study found that "individuals with Rule 10b5-1 plans [had] abnormal profits . . . [with insiders] . . . strategically engaging in purchases and sales using their programs as cover against charges of illegal activity . . . call[ing] this tactic 'hiding in plain sight.'" Morrissey, *supra* note 92, at 888. *See generally* Allan Horwich, *The Legality of Opportunistically Timing Public Company Disclosures in the Context of SEC Rule 10b5-1*, 71 Bus. Law. 1113 (2016).

[96] For example, in 2019, the U.S. House of Representatives passed H.R. 624—Promoting Transparent Standards for Corporate Insiders Act. If enacted, the Act would require that the SEC study Rule 10b5-1 plans in view of current trading plan practices to ascertain gaps in coverage. The Commission would be required "to consider whether to limit trading to issuer-adopted trading windows, to curb the use of multiple . . . trading plans, to mandate a delay between adoption of a trading

F. Conclusion

The foregoing discussion focuses on the unacceptable insider trading framework that exists in the United States. Federal court decisions, coupled with SEC actions, have resulted in an ambiguous, disparate, and inconsistent regimen with the presence of loopholes accentuating this situation. The discussion that ensues recommends several measures that should considerably improve insider trading regulation in this country.

III. Recommendations for Improved Insider Trading Regulation

There are several measures that should be implemented to provide a more coherent and effective insider trading framework in the United States. The following discussion highlights the reforms that should be adopted.

A. Requiring Company Disclosure of All Material Information

As discussed in Chapter 2 of this book, the SEC declines to require that all material information that is known to the subject company be disclosed.[97] The failure to mandate the disclosure of such information (absent the existence of a justifiable business reason) signifies that, with frequency, the securities of even premier stock exchange listed companies do not trade at prices that accurately reflect their value. This situation thus adversely affects the integrity of the securities markets—namely, that while the market price of a company's stock in an efficient market reflects all publicly available material information,[98] that price does not reflect undisclosed

---

plan and the first executed trade under the plan, to restrict an insider's ability to modify or cancel a trading plan, to require companies and insiders to make certain filings with the Commission, and to mandate that company boards adopt relevant policies and monitor for compliance." Fed. Sec. L. Rep. (CCH) No. 2860, at 6–7 (2019). With respect to the SEC, the Commission has proposed but declined to adopt the requirement that Rule 10b5-1 plans be publicly reported. *See* Securities Exchange Act Release No. 45742 (2002).

[97] *See* discussion in Chapter 2 herein, at notes 140–170 and accompanying text.

[98] *See, e.g., Halliburton Co. v. Erica P. John Fund, Inc.*, 134 S. Ct. 2398, 2408 (2014), *quoting, Basic, Inc. v. Levinson*, 485 U.S. 224, 246 (1988) (stating that "the market price of shares traded on well-developed markets reflects all publicly-available information").

significant information that has a reasonable likelihood of price impact. The appropriate solution to this deficiency is to require that publicly-traded companies (absent meritorious business justification) disclose by means of a SEC filing and press release (or other suitable form of communication) all material information within one business day after becoming aware of the materiality of such information. To buttress this mandate in the insider trading context, during the interval between the occurrence of a reportable event and the making of a SEC filing (such as a Form 8-K), the subject company's directors, executive officers, and other persons having access to such information would be barred from trading.[99]

The implementation of this mandate would drastically reduce opportunities for illegal insider trading. By considerably closing the window for the lawful nondisclosure of material information, incidents of impermissible insider trading (and tipping) should drastically decrease. By providing a narrow exception for permitting nondisclosure due to a recognized business justification,[100] all other material information would be promptly disclosed by the issuance of a press release and the filing of a Form 8-K with the SEC. With nearly all material information more expeditiously reaching the securities markets, price efficiency should be enhanced and opportunities for illegal insider trading should be dampened. Of course, this recommendation assumes that the SEC will undertake effective enforcement against Exchange Act reporting companies and

---

[99] *See* 8-K Trading Gap Act of 2019, H.R. 4335 (2019). This bill passed by the U.S. House of Representatives in 2019 would prohibit corporate officers and directors from trading in the subject corporation's stock during the window prior to the filing or furnishing of a Form 8-K with the SEC. This bill seeks to curb insider trading by corporate fiduciaries during this window period. *See* Fed. Sec. L. Rep. (CCH) No. 2905, at 6 (2020) (quoting a sponsor of the bill, Representative Carolyn Maloney, stating that "[t]here has been research from academics at Columbia Law School and Harvard Law School that shows that executives do actually trade in this 4-day gap and profit significantly from it"). The proposal herein goes significantly further, proposing that all material nonpublic information (absent business justification otherwise) be publicly disclosed within one business day coupled with insiders being prohibited from trading during this period.

[100] This adequate business justification exception should be narrow, such as when "immediate disclosure is likely to prejudice the legitimate interests of the issuer." Market Abuse Regulation (MAR) art. 17(4). *See* European Securities and Markets Authority, *MAR Guidelines Delay in the Disclosure of Inside Information* (2016), available at https://www.esma.europa.eu/sites/default/files/library/2016-1478_mar_guidelines_-_legitimate_interests.pdf. (A non-exhaustive list of such possible situations was issued by the European Securities and Markets Authority (ESMA) to include negotiations focusing on major transactions (such as a merger), plans to acquire a substantial equity interest in another enterprise, and required approval of a contemplated contract by an unrelated party where confidentiality is necessary.); Timothy J. Johnson, *Is Real-Time Disclosure Really Mandatory? A Comparison of Real-Time Disclosure Frameworks and Enforcement*, 47 Sec. Reg. L.J. 49, 58 (2019) (discussing situations where disclosure of material information may be delayed pursuant to the EU MAR Regulation).

their insiders irrespective of their assets and reputations. That is an assumption that may be unwarranted.[101]

B. Advance Notice of Insider Trades, Revision of Insider Trading Plans, Repeal of Section 16(b)

Under current law, insiders who are subject to Section 16(a) of the Securities Exchange Act must report their trading of equity securities to the SEC by the end of the second business day after the execution of the subject transaction.[102] This provision was enacted pursuant to the Sarbanes-Oxley Act of 2002,[103] drastically shortening the filing deadline of insider transactions that had previously been prescribed.[104] This revision effectively curtails the opportunity of insiders to engage in stock option backdating practices[105] and provides far more timely notice to the securities markets of insider transactions.[106]

A more encompassing approach, however, is needed to effectively combat insider trading by corporate fiduciaries. On occasion, the SEC has taken the position that knowledge of an insider's trades before those trades are publicly known by itself constitutes material information.[107] This position

---

[101] The SEC's failure to take meaningful action is illustrated by the insider abuse of Rule 10b5-1 plans and the frequency that executives trade during the Form 8-K window. The U.S. House of Representatives has passed bills seeking to address this inappropriate conduct. *See supra* notes 95, 99.

[102] *See* Securities Exchange Act Release No. 46421 (2002) (stating that, with certain exceptions, Form 4 is required to be filed "before the end of the second business day following the day on which the subject transaction has been executed"). *See also* Securities Exchange Act Release No. 47809 (2003) (requiring the electronic filing and website posting of these § 16(a) reports). Item 405 of Regulation S-K, 17 C.F.R. § 229.405, requires companies to disclose delinquent Section 16(a) reports identifying its insiders who failed to timely file these reports.

[103] *See* § 403 of the Sarbanes-Oxley Act, *amending*, § 16(a)(2)(C), 15 U.S.C. § 78p(a)(2)(C).

[104] Prior to this amendment, the subject insider was required to file the requisite form with the SEC by the tenth day of the month following the trade. *See* former Rule 16a-3.

[105] *See Ryan v. Gifford*, 918 A.2d 341, 345 (Del. Ch. 2007) (stating that the practice of stock option backdating "involves a company issuing stock options to an executive on one date while providing fraudulent documentation asserting that the options were actually issued earlier"). Providing a windfall for executives, stock option backdating practices "coincide with market lows . . . thereby increasing management compensation." *Id.*

[106] *See supra* notes 102–103 and accompanying text. *See also* Comment, *The Hidden Contradiction Within Insider Trading Regulation*, 53 UCLA L. Rev. 1275 (2006) (stating that § 16(a) filings by insiders enhance market efficiency).

[107] The SEC took this position, for example, in its insider trading enforcement action against Martha Stewart. Ms. Stewart settled the case, agreeing without admitting or denying the SEC's allegations to significant sanctions. *See* SEC Litigation Release No. 19794 (2006). (Ms. Stewart's broker "illegally tipped" her "with the nonpublic information that the then CEO of ImClone Systems, Samuel D. Waksal, and his daughter were selling their ImClone stock [and that] based on this information, Stewart sold all of her ImClone stock." Ms. Stewart agreed "to disgorge $45,673, representing the losses avoided from her insider trading, plus prejudgment interest of $12,389 . . . and a civil

is not to suggest that all such trades are material, but, clearly, the securities markets consider this information relevant.[108] Going further, the approach recommended herein is for Congress to enact a statute requiring that an insider *prior* to engaging in any purchase or sale of a subject security (such as common stock) make a filing with the SEC that becomes available that same day on the Commission's publicly accessible internet site. The subject fiduciary then would be permitted to engage in the otherwise lawful contemplated transaction the following business day. Coupled with the mandate that corporate directors and executive officers would be barred from trading the subject company's securities during the interval between a reportable event and the making of a SEC filing (such as a Form 8-K), opportunities to engage in impermissible insider trading would be significantly reduced.[109]

Consistent with the foregoing recommendation, Congress should enact legislation focusing on insider trading plans. Current Rule 10b5-1 no longer should be in effect. In its stead, in order for an insider trading plan to be deemed a defense to allegations of unlawful insider trading, the following measures should be required. First, disclosure of the plan and its contents must be provided to the subject company's shareholders in a proxy statement, annual report, or other suitable SEC filing. The plan itself

penalty of $137,019, representing three times the amount of the losses avoided." In addition, she "agreed to a five-year bar from serving as a director of a public company, and a five-year limitation on her service as an officer or employee of a public company by prohibiting her from participating in certain activities, including financial reporting, financial disclosure, monitoring compliance with the federal securities laws, internal controls, audits or Commission filings."). In the criminal proceeding, this author, retained as an expert witness on behalf of Ms. Stewart, opined that the government's position that knowledge of the CEO's trade itself constituted material nonpublic information was contrary to custom and practice. *See* Declaration of Marc I. Steinberg, *United States v. Martha Stewart* (dated Feb. 19, 2004) ("If the fact that a corporate insider (such as a CEO) were seeking to sell his/her stock were itself material information, then every insider trade (such as by a CEO) would itself violate the law."). *See also* Jeanne L. Schroeder, *Envy and Outsider Trading: The Case of Martha Stewart*, 26 Cardozo L. Rev. 2023, 2025 (2005) ("[S]he was a tippee of her broker who 'stole' the fact that insiders were selling their stock—a novel theory that goes far beyond any other application of the misappropriation theory to date."). The U.S. Court of Appeals upheld Ms. Stewart's conviction of conspiracy, making false statements to government officials, and obstructing an agency proceeding. *See United States v. Stewart*, 433 F.3d 273 (2d Cir. 2006).

[108] *See, e.g.*, Caitlin McCabe, *Insiders Snap Up Stock, Betting on Recovery*, Wall St. J., March 27, 2020, at B1 ("Because insiders typically know the most about their companies' outlook, evidence of buying can signal corporate optimism and reassure investors, especially in times of turmoil").

[109] *See* Walker and Simpson, *supra* note 22, at 542, *quoting* Study by, Ahmad Etebari et al., *Disclosure Regulation and the Profitability of Insider Trading: Evidence from New Zealand*, 12 Pacific-Basin Fin. J. 479, 481 (2004) (stating that the study found that "large abnormal gains to insiders came 'largely from transactions involving delayed disclosure' whereas 'transactions involving immediate disclosure earn insignificant returns'" and that accordingly "[a]n effective continuous disclosure regime reduces the incidence of insider conduct by narrowing the information asymmetry between insiders and the market generally").

should be required to be posted on the company's website.[110] Second, in a duly called shareholder meeting, the plan must be approved by a majority of the shares present at the meeting, not counting the shares beneficially owned by the insiders who would benefit from the plan.[111] Third, absent a national emergency or other catastrophic event, the plan could not be modified or canceled by the subject company's board of directors absent the requisite shareholder consent.[112] Fourth, after approval of the plan (or amendment thereto) by a company's shareholders, there should be a mandatory waiting period, such as three months, before it becomes operational.[113] Fifth, the company's audit, corporate governance, or other appropriate committee should monitor compliance with the plan and provide an annual report to shareholders that is filed with the SEC attesting to whether the plan's requirements were followed.[114] Last, technical compliance with an authorized plan should not insulate as a matter of law corporate fiduciaries from insider trading liability.[115] Rather, such compliance would create a presumption of lawful conduct that the complainant could rebut by proving by clear and convincing evidence (or beyond a reasonable doubt in criminal proceedings) that, irrespective of the plan, the subject

---

[110] For example, current SEC rules and regulations mandate that Exchange Act companies post on their respective website specified SEC filings as well as other materials. By way of example, Section 16(a)(4) requires that reports filed pursuant to that statute be made accessible on the SEC's internet site as well as on the subject company's website. As another example, with respect to a subject company's code of ethics, one method of compliance is for that company to "[p]ost the text of such code of ethics on its Internet website and disclose, in its annual report, its Internet address and the fact that it has posted such code of ethics on its Internet Web site." Item 406(c)(2) of Regulation S-K, 17 C.F.R. § 229.406(c)(2). This approach should be the required means by which shareholders and the securities markets may access a subject company's insider trading plan.

[111] This voting structure would be similar to an interested party transaction where the votes of the financially-interested fiduciaries are not counted in determining the outcome. *Cf. Kahn v. M & F Worldwide Corp.*, 88 A.3d 635 (Del. 2014) (applying more relaxed standard of the business judgment rule if controller buyout is approved by an independent and aptly functioning special committee as well as by a majority of the minority shareholders with no coercion being exerted).

[112] *Cf.* Rule 16b-3(d)(2), 17 C.F.R. § 240.16b-3(d)(2) (providing that one method to exempt specified transactions between the issuer and an officer or director from § 16(b) of the Exchange Act is pursuant to shareholder approval).

[113] *See* Marvuk and Seyhun, *supra* note 94, at 136 (proposing that a plan's initial trades "must be scheduled no less than six months after the plan is filed," with that six-month period being reset after any amendment to the plan).

[114] *See* H.R. 624, *supra* note 96 (mandating that the SEC consider, among other requirements, whether corporate boards must implement relevant policies and oversee compliance with the respective Rule 10b5-1 plan's provisions).

[115] This view is seen in a number of SEC rules and regulations. *See, e.g.*, Regulation D, Note (f) (stating that "Regulation D is not available to any issuer for any transaction or chain of transactions that, although in technical compliance with Regulation D, is part of a plan or scheme to evade the registration provisions of the Act").

insiders traded or tipped while knowing or having reason to know of material nonpublic information.[116]

If effectively implemented, the foregoing recommendations should substantially reduce the frequency of insider trading by corporate executives and directors. As a final point, Section 16(b) has lost much of its vigor and should be repealed. Adherence to Section 16(b) has become a technical and cumbersome process. With the SEC's creation of loopholes and the employment of customary corporate policies that are compliant with this provision, Section 16(b) provides relatively little deterrent to unlawful insider trading.[117]

C. Adoption of a Comprehensive Access Approach

The U.S. Supreme Court's approach to insider trading should be a relic of the past. From its inception, the fiduciary duty rationale has been problematic. To condition the presence of a federal securities law disclosure duty on the application of state law principles is misplaced.[118] In conjunction with this narrow construction of Section 10(b) is the SEC's embracement of an expansive insider trading prohibition in the tender offer setting pursuant to Rule 14e-3.[119] As the discussion earlier in this chapter detailed, the law of insider trading currently existing in this country is unacceptable.

The United States should enact legislation that is consistent with the insider trading laws of other developed markets. Those persons who are in a

---

[116] Of course, in a criminal proceeding, beyond a reasonable doubt would be the applicable standard. In civil proceedings, a clear and convincing standard provides substantially greater protection to a defendant than the preponderance of the evidence standard. *See Black's Law Dictionary* 698 (11th ed. 2019) (defining clear and convincing evidence as "indicating that the thing to be proved is highly probable or reasonably certain").

[117] A number of commentators have recommended that Section 16(b) be repealed. *See, e.g.*, Michael H. Dessent, *Weapons to Fight Insider Trading in the 21st Century: A Call for the Repeal of Section 16(b)*, 33 Akron L. Rev. 481 (2000); Marleen A. O'Connor, *Toward a More Efficient Deterrence of Insider Trading; The Repeal of Section 16(b)*, 58 Fordham L. Rev. 309 (1989); Ellen Taylor, *Teaching an Old Law New Tricks: Rethinking Section 16*, 39 Ariz. L. Rev. 1315 (1997). As Professor Taylor asserted, Section 16(b) should be repealed because, among other reasons, "it is ineffective at preventing or punishing insider trading." 39 Ariz. L. Rev. at 1318.

[118] Dissenting in *Chiarella*, Justice Blackmun opined that the majority's decision "fails even to attempt a justification of its ruling in terms of the purposes of the securities laws, or to square that ruling with the longstanding but now much abused principle that the federal securities laws are to be construed flexibly rather than with narrow technicality." 445 U.S. at 246–47 (Blackmun, J. dissenting). *See also* Charles W. Murdock, *The Future of Insider Trading after Salman: Perpetuation of a Flawed Analysis or a Return to Basics*, 70 Hastings L.J. 1547, 1608 (2019) (asserting that Justice Powell, writing for the Court in *Chiarella* and *Dirks*, misinterpreted case law and, with respect to *Dirks*, the decision contained a "severely flawed analysis.").

[119] *See* discussion *supra* notes 40–46 and accompanying text.

position to have access to material nonpublic information should be prohibited from trading on or tipping others such information.[120] In addition, those persons who know or have reason to know that they are receiving, directly or indirectly, material nonpublic information from a source that is privy to such information due to such source's access status likewise would be subject to the insider trading prohibition.[121] While application of this rationale occasionally will produce harsh results,[122] overall this approach is far more preferable. Its scope is limited to: any person whose position comes with the mutual understanding that she is to receive material nonpublic information with the commitment that it remain confidential and not be used for trading or tipping purposes until and unless such information is adequately disseminated to the investing public; any person who acquires access to material nonpublic information through dishonest or illegal means; and any person who, directly or indirectly, receives material nonpublic information knowing or having reason to know that it was conveyed by a person having access to such information.[123]

This rationale thus permits securities analysts to undertake their investigative tasks to unearth pertinent information regarding specific companies without undue concern of fraud liability.[124] On the other hand, if a financial analyst or any other individual knowingly receives material nonpublic

---

[120] This approach generally was employed by the lower federal courts prior to the Supreme Court's decision in *Chiarella. See, e.g., United States v. Chiarella*, 588 F.2d 1358, 1365 (2d Cir. 1978) ("Anyone corporate insider or not who regularly receives material nonpublic information may not use this information to trade in securities without incurring an affirmative duty to disclose."), *rev'd*, 445 U.S. 222 (1980).

[121] *See* cases cited *supra* note 19.

[122] An example is the *Dirks* case. It may be posited that the SEC exercised poor prosecutorial discretion in pursuing Dirks, who revealed a massive fraud which eluded the SEC and other regulators. Indeed, the Equity Funding fraud is reminiscent of the Commission's ineptness with respect to the Madoff scandal. *See Dirks*, 463 U.S. at 649 (commenting that a former Equity Funding employee had stated that "various regulatory agencies had failed to act on similar charges [of fraud] made by Equity Funding employees"); David Stout, *Report Details How Madoff's Web Ensnared SEC*, N.Y. Times, Sept. 2, 2009, available at https://www.nytimes.com/2009/09/03/business/03madoff.html (stating that the SEC's inspector general found that, "despite numerous credible and detailed complaints, [the Commission failed to take] the necessary, but basic, steps to determine if Madoff was operating a Ponzi scheme").

[123] Thus, this prohibition would apply to those persons who access material nonpublic information by means of computer hacking or by otherwise purloining such information. This approach is far superior than stretching the misappropriation theory under current law to encompass this conduct. *See Securities and Exchange Commission v. Dorozhko*, 574 F.3d 42 (2d Cir. 2009) (computer hacker deemed to have misappropriated material nonpublic information concerning subject corporation's quarterly earnings release).

[124] *See* Bruce A. Hiler, *Dirks v. SEC—A Study in Cause and Effect*, 43 Md. L. 292, 317–18 (1984) (commenting that the Court justified its decisions in *Dirks* by reference to two objectives—"enhancement of certainty for insiders and analysts in dealing with disclosure of material information, and assurance of prompt reflection of important information in the securities markets").

information from an access person, the insider trading prohibition applies.[125] The breadth of this rationale is also limited by its exclusion of individuals who, without having access to or being tipped by a person who has such access, become privy to material inside information. Although Rule 14e-3 and a number of foreign countries adhere to the parity of information approach,[126] this mandate sweeps too broadly. To subject individuals who learn of inside information through their diligence or in an inadvertent manner (and without having reason to know of the source of the information) to the panoply of insider trading sanctions may be viewed as overreach. In any event, with the customary practice by corporations, financial intermediaries, and other advisers (including legal counsel) of undertaking extensive procedures to maintain the confidentiality of material nonpublic information,[127] there ordinarily will be relatively few individuals who become privy to such information in this manner.[128]

The access approach thus is the preferred approach. It commendably supports the integrity of the securities markets, perceptions of fairness, and effective enforcement.[129] Unlike current law, this approach is consistent and even-handed.[130] The degree of its impact would be determined to a large

---

[125] Under *Dirks*, tipping is prohibited under Section 10(b) only if the tipper conveys the material nonpublic information for personal pecuniary gain or as a gift. *See* 463 U.S. at 682; *supra* notes 35–38 and accompanying text. Of course, if the information relates to a tender offer, Rule 14e-3's broad parity of information approach would apply. *See supra* notes 39–46 and accompanying text.

[126] *See* discussion *supra* notes 22, 39–46 and accompanying text.

[127] *See* Marc I. Steinberg and John Fletcher, *Compliance Programs for Insider Trading*, 47 SMU L. Rev. 1783, 1835 (1994) (over twenty-five years ago, stating that "any organization that comes into possession of inside information with respect to publicly-held enterprises would be prudent to adopt and implement a law compliance program designed to prevent insider trading").

[128] Generally, persons who could legally trade under this approach would include persons who lack access but through their own research and acumen identify material nonpublic information; persons who inadvertently become privy to such information and who have no reason to know that the information was received, directly or indirectly, from an individual who enjoyed access; and tippees who have no reason to know that they received the information, directly or indirectly, from a person who had access.

[129] Although not as expansive as the parity of information rule, this principle enhances the fundamental principle that the trust of investors "is a foundation of the securities system." Tarmar Frankel, *Insider Trading*, 71 SMU L. Rev. 783, 789 (2019).

[130] *See* discussion *supra* notes 8–96 and accompanying text. In an effort to clarify the law of insider trading, the U.S. House of Representatives in 2019 passed the Insider Trading Prohibition Act, H.R. 2534. The Act would codify much of existing law, including conditioning improper use of material nonpublic information on a breach of a fiduciary duty (including contractual breaches) or the perpetration of such misconduct as theft (through electronic or other means), conversion, and misappropriation. *See* H.R. 2534, at § 16A(c)(1). By implication, the Act seemingly would equate a contractual breach with that of a breach of fiduciary duty. *See id.* at § 16A(c)(1)(D) (emphasis supplied) (including within the definition of "wrongful" conduct is "a breach of fiduciary duty, a breach of a confidentiality agreement, a breach of contract, or a breach of *any other personal or other relationship of trust and confidence*"). This approach is criticized earlier in this chapter. *See supra* notes 40–54 and accompanying text. As passed, the bill retains a personal benefit test with respect to tipper-tippee

extent by the SEC in its enforcement practices and by the federal courts in construing the parameters of the prohibition. Clearly being far superior to the present regimen, the access approach as proposed herein should be adopted.

IV. Conclusion

This chapter highlights the abysmal condition of the insider trading framework in the United States. Ambiguity, inconsistency, and disparate treatment prevail. To significantly enhance this framework, this chapter recommends that: publicly-held companies must promptly disclose to the SEC and the securities markets all material information (absent business justification otherwise); directors, executive officers, and other access persons are barred from trading in the subject company's securities during the interval between the occurrence of a reportable event and the making of a SEC filing (such as a Form 8-K); insiders subject to Section 16(a) of the Securities Exchange Act are required to provide advance notice of their contemplated trades in the subject company's equity securities; a subject company's insider trading plan, consistent with the criteria set forth herein, creates a rebuttable presumption that the securities transactions effected pursuant to the plan are compliant with the securities laws' antifraud provisions; and a comprehensive access approach is adopted to govern the legality of trading and tipping on the basis of material nonpublic information. Enactment of these recommended provisions would significantly improve this country's insider trading framework.

liability. *See House Passes Potentially Historic Bill that Would Codify Law of Insider Trading*, Fed. Sec. L. Rep. (CCH) No. 2900, at 9–13 (2019).

8
Mergers and Acquisitions

I. Introduction

This chapter focuses on mergers and acquisitions (M&A), entailing going-private transactions, tender offers, proxy contests, mergers, and similar types of transactions. The discussion that follows addresses key issues that arise in this setting and formulates proposals for reform. Hence, rather than providing a broad overview of this subject,[1] the analysis contained herein is directed toward examining the current framework and providing recommendations for implementation.

The next section of the chapter discusses specific subjects within the M&A statutory and regulatory framework. Thereafter, several recommendations will be proffered that, if effectuated, should prove beneficial to investors, the securities markets, and the U.S. economy.

II. Critique of the Current M&A Framework

As with other areas of securities regulation, the M&A process is primarily focused on disclosure to enable investors to make informed voting and investment decisions.[2] While state corporate law in this setting addresses the fairness of these transactions pursuant to the duties of care and loyalty,[3] federal law also enters the fairness arena by setting forth the processes by

[1] For books and treatises that focus on mergers and acquisitions, *see, e.g.*, Arthur M. Borden and Joel A. Yunis, *Going Private* (2019); Arthur Fleischer, Alexander R. Sussman, and Gail Weinstein, *Takeover Defense: Mergers and Acquisitions* (2017); Martin Lipton and Erica H. Steinberger, *Takeovers & Freezeouts* (2019); Simon M. Lorne and Joy M. Bryan, *Acquisitions and Mergers: Negotiated and Contested Transactions* (2020); Randall S. Thomas and Catherine T. Dixon, *Aranow & Einhorn on Proxy Contests for Corporate Control* (1998); Michael D. Walters, *Proxy Regulation* (1993).

[2] *See, e.g.*, *Schreiber v. Burlington Northern, Inc.*, 472 U.S. 1 (1985) (holding that § 14(e) of the Securities Exchange Act encompasses only the accuracy and adequacy of disclosure).

[3] *See, e.g.*, *Versata Enterprises, Inc. v. Selectica, Inc.*, 5 A.3d 586 (Del. 2010); *Omnicare, Inc. v. NCS Healthcare, Inc.*, 818 A.2d 914 (Del. 2003); *Unitrin, Inc. v. American General Corp.*, 651 A.2d 1361 (Del. 1995); *MacAndrews & Forbes Holdings v. Revlon, Inc.*, 506 A.2d 173 (Del. 1986); *Unocal Corp. v. Mesa Petroleum Co.*, 493 A.2d 946 (Del. 1985); *Weinberger v. UOP, Inc.*, 457 A.2d 701 (Del. 1983).

Rethinking Securities Law. Marc I. Steinberg, Oxford University Press. © Marc I. Steinberg 2021.
DOI: 10.1093/oso/9780197583142.003.0008

which these "deals" are undertaken.[4] Granted that these federal fairness provisions are more procedural than substantive, by regulating the "tournament" between insurgents and target companies, they have substantial influence in helping to improve equitable treatment for market participants and investors.[5]

Nonetheless, with respect to principles of disclosure, a glaring gap prevails. As discussed in Chapter 2 herein, there currently is no requirement under the federal securities laws (except in the insider trading context) that the subject party disclose all material information (unless an appropriate business justification is established).[6] This policy is antithetical to the maintenance of efficient markets and informed decision-making as well as contrary to the approach adopted by other developed markets.[7]

Otherwise, within the disclosure and procedural fairness spheres, Congress and the SEC merit kudos for establishing an M&A framework that generally functions in an efficient and equitable manner. In addition to extensive disclosure required to be made by specified parties as called for by provisions of the Securities Exchange Act and SEC rules,[8] a number of these disclosures seek to substantively enhance equitable treatment for shareholders. Three examples are provided.

First, when the right of appraisal under the applicable state law is available in a transaction,[9] the registrant or other person who files the disclosure document must inform security holders of this right and the procedures that must be satisfied in order for a dissenting security holder to perfect its right to appraisal.[10] Although focused solely on disclosure, this mandate has the

---

[4] *See, e.g.*, § 14(d) of the Securities Exchange Act, 15 U.S.C. § 78n(d); discussion *infra* notes 29–36 and accompanying text.

[5] *See* discussion *infra* notes 29–71 and accompanying text.

[6] *See* discussion in Chapter 2 herein, at notes 149–170 and accompanying text.

[7] *Id.* (and sources cited therein).

[8] *See, e.g.*, Regulation M-A, 17 C.F.R. §§ 229.1000 *et seq.*; Schedule 13D, 17 C.F.R. § 240.13d-101; Schedule 13E-3, 17 C.F.R. § 240.13e-100; Schedule 14A, 17 C.F.R. § 240.14a-101; Schedule TO, 17 C.F.R. § 240.14d-100.

[9] *See, e.g.*, 8 Del. Gen. Corp. L. § 262 (generally providing the right of appraisal in mergers and consolidations). Many other states extend the right of appraisal generally to sales of substantially all assets and exchange of shares transactions as well as to certain amendments of the articles of incorporation. *See, e.g.*, Model Bus. Corp. Act § 13.02(a)(1). *See generally* Mary Siegel, *An Appraisal of the Model Business Corporation Act's Appraisal Rights Provisions*, 74 L. & Contemp. Prob. 231 (2011).

[10] *See* Schedule 14A, Item 3, 17 C.F.R. § 240.141-101 (dissenter's right of appraisal). Generally, pursuant to state law, the failure to comply with the procedures required to perfect the appraisal right results in loss of the remedy. *See* Randall S. Thomas, *Revising the Delaware Appraisal Statute*, 3 Del. L. Rev. 1 (2000):

> The appraisal remedy is procedurally complex. There are several strict deadlines that a shareholder must satisfy in order to perfect her appraisal right. To begin, the shareholder

salutary effect of alerting uninitiated security holders of the procedures that they are required to follow under state law in order to invoke their appraisal right.[11]

Second, in response to a tender offer, the subject company is required to disclose to shareholders its position concerning the takeover bid and the reasons supporting that position.[12] Moreover, if a material change occurs with respect to this disclosure, the company must promptly convey to shareholders such material change.[13] Based on disclosure, this mandate promotes informed securities markets, enhances the efficient market objectives of the securities laws, and provides shareholders with important information to enable them to more effectively evaluate their alternatives.[14]

Third, as elaborated upon later in this chapter,[15] after the U.S. Supreme Court's decision in *Santa Fe Industries*,[16] foreclosing a Section 10(b) right of action premised on "mere" unfairness unadorned by deficiency of disclosure,[17] the SEC adopted Rule 13e-3.[18] Stated succinctly, a provision of this rule requires that the subject party disclose whether it reasonably believes that the going-private transaction is fair or unfair to unaffiliated minority

---

> must deliver a written appraisal demand to the corporation before the vote on the transaction informing the company of her desire to seek appraisal. Failure to do so eliminates the shareholder's ability to seek appraisal. The purpose of this requirement is to ensure that the corporation receives notice of the number of shareholders that will seek appraisal.

Id. at 30.

[11] *See* Thomas, *supra* note 10, at 30 (stating that the "procedural requirements [for perfecting the appraisal remedy] seem quite burdensome on smaller shareholders").

[12] *See* Schedule 14D-9, item 4, 17 C.F.R. § 240.14d-9; Rule 14e-2, 17 C.F.R. § 240.14e-2. Pursuant to Rule 14e-2, the subject company must convey to its shareholders within ten business days after the tender offer is received whether it: "(1) Recommends acceptance or rejection of the bidder's tender offer; (2) Expresses no opinion and is remaining neutral toward the bidder's tender offer; or (3) Is unable to take a position with respect to the bidder's tender offer; [and in such case] [s]uch statement shall include the reason(s) for the position (including the inability to take a position) disclosed therein."

[13] *See* Schedule 14D-9(b); Rule 14e-2(b).

[14] As stated by this author: "What the rule does seemingly accomplish is that it compels target management to articulate its position in a conscientious manner with the theoretical objective of permitting shareholders to make their investment decisions after hearing all sides." Marc I. Steinberg, *Securities Regulation: Liabilities and Remedies* § 11.07 (2020). *See* Richard L. Gelfond and Steven B. Sebastian, *Reevaluating the Duties of Target Management in a Hostile Tender Offer*, 60 Bos. U. L. Rev. 403, 410 (1980) (stating that this disclosure obligation is consistent "with the Act's goal of informing the investing public . . . [and] furthers the efficient market purposes of the Act").

[15] *See* discussion *infra* notes 54–61 and accompanying text. This subject also is addressed in Chapter 2 herein, at notes 35–39 and accompanying text.

[16] *Santa Fe Industries, Inc. v. Green*, 430 U.S. 462 (1977).

[17] *Id.* at 474 (holding that the transaction "was neither deceptive nor manipulative and therefore did not violate either § 10(b) of the [Securities Exchange] Act or Rule 10b-5").

[18] 17 C.F.R. § 240.13e-3. *See* Securities Exchange Act Release No. 16075 (1979) (adopting release).

security holders and the material factors upon which such belief is based.[19] Hence, utilizing the guise of disclosure, the SEC seeks to enhance minority shareholder interests in going-private transactions.[20] Accordingly, at times, the Commission mandates disclosure evidently with the principal objective of benefiting minority shareholder well-being.[21]

In Chapter 2 of this book, the recommendation is made that companies must promptly disclose all material information unless a justifiable business reason exists.[22] The M&A setting provides an example of how this process would function. Under Item 303 of SEC Regulation S-K (Management's Discussion and Analysis of Financial Condition and Results of Operation (MD&A)),[23] disclosure must be made, among other contingencies, of any known event or uncertainty that is reasonably likely to occur and, if it comes to fruition, that a material effect on the company's financial condition or results of operations is reasonably likely to occur.[24] By its terms, MD&A disclosure would encompass preliminary merger negotiations that have reached a sufficiently advanced stage. Premature disclosure of such negotiations, however, may well have the effect of jeopardizing consummation of the prospective transaction.[25] Accordingly, unless the company already has disclosed the existence of the negotiations[26] or such disclosure otherwise is

---

19 *Id. See* Schedule 13E-3, Item 8; SEC Regulation M-A, Item 1014. Interestingly, proposed Rule 13e-3 required both procedural and substantive fairness in going-private transactions. *See* Securities Exchange Act Release No. 14185 (1977). When the rule was ultimately adopted in 1979, the SEC opined that "the views expressed in the 1977 release are sound and therefore [we] specifically affirm those views." Securities Exchange Act Release No. 16075 (1979).

20 *See* Marc I. Steinberg, *The Federalization of Corporate Governance* 138 (2018) (commenting that "although *Santa Fe* precluded Section 10(b) from being applied with respect to the substantive fairness of a going-private transaction, Rule 13e-3 indirectly accomplishes this to a significant degree through its rigorous disclosure mandates").

21 Violation of Rule 13e-3 gives rise to both private and government liability exposure. *See, e.g., Howing Co. v. Nationwide Corp.*, 826 F.2d 1470 (6th Cir. 1987); *In the Matter of FSC Corp*, 22 SEC Docket 1374 (SEC 1981). *See generally* Ndiva Kofele-Kale, *Some Unfinished Business, Some Unresolved Issues: Section 13(e) and the Going-Private Rules*, 20 Toledo L. Rev. 625 (1989).

22 *See* discussion in Chapter 2 herein, at notes 149–170 and accompanying text.

23 Regulation S-K, Item 303, 17 C.F.R. § 229.303.

24 *Id. See In the Matter of Caterpillar, Inc.*, Administrative Proceeding No. 3-7692 (SEC 1992); Securities Act Release No. 9106 (2010); SEC Financial Reporting Release No. 36 (1989).

25 *See* SEC Financial Reporting Release No. 36 (1989) ("While Item 303 could be read to impose a duty to disclose otherwise nondisclosed preliminary merger negotiations, as known events or uncertainties reasonably likely to have material effects on future financial condition or results of operation, the Commission did not intend to apply and has not applied Item 303 in this manner.").

26 *See, e.g., Basic, Inc. v. Levinson*, 485 U.S. 224 (1988) (stating that, once the subject company elects to speak and the merger negotiations are at a material stage, a duty not to mislead exists).

required,[27] an adequate business justification exists for nondisclosure of preliminary merger negotiations irrespective of the MD&A mandates.[28]

Unlike other areas of securities regulation, federal statutes and SEC rules go beyond mandating disclosure to address procedural fairness.[29] Pursuant to these directives, federal law plays a primary role in specifying the rules by which M&A deals must be "played." Several examples follow:

(1) If the company seeks to solicit proxies in connection with a shareholder meeting, it must, upon the written request of any record or beneficial holder of the subject securities, either supply such holder with a list of shareholders or mail to such shareholders the holder's materials (or use other prompt methods of dissemination).[30]

(2) It is impermissible for a putative bidder to announce a tender offer without having the wherewithal to initiate and complete such offer.[31]

---

[27] *See, e.g.*, Schedule 14D-9, Item 7, 17 C.F.R. § 240.14d-101 (requiring the target company to disclose the undertaking of negotiations in response to the tender offer).

[28] *See* SEC Financial Reporting Release No. 36 (1989):

> [W]here disclosure is not otherwise required, and has not otherwise been made, the MD&A need not contain a discussion of the impact of such negotiations where, in the registrant's view, inclusion of such information would jeopardize completion of the transaction. Where disclosure is otherwise required or has otherwise been made by or on behalf of the registrant, the interests in avoiding premature disclosure no longer exist. In such case, the negotiations would be subject to the same disclosure standards under Item 303 as any other known trend, demand, commitment, event or uncertainty. These policy determinations also would extend to preliminary negotiations for the acquisition or disposition of assets not in the ordinary course of business.

[29] *See infra* notes 30–36 and accompanying text.

[30] *See* Rule 14a-7, 17 C.F.R. § 240.14a-7. The security holder must reimburse the reasonable expenses incurred by the company, including the mailing costs. *See* Rule 14a-7(e). If the insurgent security holder is successful in gaining control in a proxy contest, its expenses ordinarily will be reimbursed. *See Jana Master Fund, Ltd. v. CNET Networks, Inc.*, 954 A.2d 335, 341 (Del. Ch. 2008) ("Generally, although management is reimbursed for its proxy expenses from the corporate coffers, insurgent shareholders finance their own bid and can hope for reimbursement if that bid is successful."); *Johnson v. Tago, Inc.*, 233 Cal. Rptr. 503, 506 (Cal. Ct. App. 1986) (stating that "repayment is generally given [to] . . . successful insurgents"); Lucian Arye Bebchuk and Marcel Kahan, *A Framework for Analyzing Legal Policy Towards Proxy Contests*, 78 Cal. L. Rev. 1073, 1106 (1990) (stating that "companies generally pay all the expenses for the reelection campaign of incumbents, but reimburse challengers only if they gain control over the board"). Except for roll-up and going-private transactions, the company has the option either to furnish the security holder list or to mail the materials. On the other hand, where the prospective transaction is subject to the SEC's roll-up or going-private rules, the security holder, upon satisfaction of specified conditions, has the option to be provided with the security holder list. *See* Rule 14a-7(b). *See generally* Randall J. Thomas and Catherine T. Dixon, *Aranow v. Einhorn on Proxy Contests for Corporate Control* (3d ed. 1998).

[31] *See* Rule 14e-8, 17 C.F.R. § 240.14e-8 (declaring it is "a fraudulent, deceptive or manipulative act or practice within the meaning of section 14(e) of the [Securities Exchange] Act for any person to publicly announce that the person (or a party on whose behalf the person is acting) plans to make a tender offer that has not been commenced if the person: (a) is making the announcement

(3) Shareholders are entitled to have their securities purchased on a pro rata basis by the bidder during the entire time period that the offer is open,[32] with such offer being required to remain open for a minimum of twenty business days.[33]

(4) Tender offers must be open to all shareholders. Discriminatory tender offers that exclude specified shareholders are prohibited.[34]

(5) Shareholders generally are entitled to withdraw the shares previously tendered to a bidder during the entire period that the tender offer remains open.[35]

(6) And, as a last example, the consideration paid by the bidder to any shareholder who tenders its shares must be paid to all other tendering security holders. Stated differently, all security holders are entitled to the best price offered to any other security holder who tenders its shares pursuant to the tender offer.[36]

---

of a potential tender offer without the intention to commence the offer within a reasonable time and complete the offer, (b) intends, directly or indirectly, for the announcement to manipulate the market price of the stock of the bidder or subject company, or (c) does not have the reasonable belief that the person will have the means to purchase securities to complete the offer").

[32] Rule 14d-8, 17 C.F.R. § 240.14d-8. The rule extends the ten-calendar day period that is set forth in Section 14(d)(6) of the Securities Exchange Act, 15 U.S.C. § 78n(d)(6). Chairman Shad and Commissioner Treadway dissented, asserting that the SEC lacked the authority to adopt the rule. *See* Securities Exchange Act Release No. 19336 (1983). In that release, the Commission stated that "extension of proration rights throughout the term of the offer is essential to assure security holders the time necessary to consider the merits of an offer and to obtain sufficient information upon which to base their investment decisions and to minimize the potential security holder confusion and misunderstanding generated by changing proration periods and multiple proration pools." *Id.*

[33] Rule 14e-1, 17 C.F.R. § 240.14e-1. An exception exists for certain roll-up transactions which must be open for a minimum of sixty calendar days. *Id.* Note that application of several state takeover statutes will result in many tender offers being held open for significantly longer than twenty business days. *See CTS v. Dynamics Corp. of America*, 481 U.S. 69 (1987) (upholding the constitutionality of the Indiana Control Share Acquisitions statute).

[34] *See* Rules 13-4, 14d-10, 17 C.F.R. §§ 240.13e-4, .14d-10. This rule adoption was in response to the Delaware Supreme Court's decision in *Unocal Corp. v. Mesa Petroleum Co.*, 493 A.2d 949 (Del. 1985) (upholding under the business judgment rule an exclusionary issuer self-tender offer). For further discussion, *see infra* notes 49–53 and accompanying text.

[35] *See* Rule 14d-7, 17 C.F.R. § 240.14d-7. Note, however, that if there is a subsequent offering period, no withdrawal rights are available. *See id.*; Rule 14d-11, 17 C.F.R. § 240.14d-11. Rule 14d-7 extends the statutory withdrawal period provided by Section 14(d)(5) of the Securities Exchange Act, 15 U.S.C. § 78n(d)(5), from that of seven days to the entire initial offering period. The statute provides authority for the Commission to extend this time period setting forth the statutory time period and then stating "except as the Commission may otherwise prescribe by rules, regulations, or order as necessary or appropriate in the public interest or for the protection of investors."

[36] *See* Rules 13e-4(f)(8), 14d-10, C.F.R. §§ 240.13e-4(f)(8), 14d-10. Thus, Rule 14d-10 states in relevant part: "No bidder shall make a tender offer unless . . . the consideration paid to any security holder for securities tendered in the tender offer is the highest consideration paid to any other security holder for securities tendered in the tender offer." In 2006, the SEC amended the best price rule to clarify that it applies solely to the consideration paid for the tendered securities and does not

The foregoing examples evidence that frequently in the M&A setting SEC regulation extends beyond disclosure to specify rules by which the deal process is to be played. At times, the Commission has become even more proactive in an effort to ensure greater consistency and fairness in the takeover forum. Although not of recent vintage, this activism evidences the SEC's willingness at times to stretch its statutory authority to the utmost extent. While a number of these measures ultimately were invalidated by courts,[37] others remain valid and comprise key aspects of the takeover landscape.[38] Examples follow.

Prior to the U.S. Supreme Court's decision in *Edgar v. MITE Corporation*,[39] which declared unconstitutional the Illinois Business Takeover Act,[40] many of the state statutes required advance disclosures as well as a specified waiting period before a tender offer was allowed to begin.[41] These statutes impaired the efficiency of the takeover process, increased compliance costs, and tilted the neutrality objective of the Williams Act[42] in favor of target

extend to employment compensation, severance, or other kinds of employee benefit arrangements. *See* Securities Exchange Act Release No. 54684 (2006); Emmanuel U. Obi, *SEC Rule 14d-10(e)(2) Amendment: Is This the Optimal Solution to the Tender Offer "Best-Price Rule" Dilemma?*, 35 Sec. Reg. L.J. 355 (2007).

[37] *See* discussion *infra* notes 62–71 and accompanying text.

[38] *See* discussion *infra* notes 39–61 and accompanying text.

[39] 457 U.S. 624 (1982).

[40] *Id.* at 643 (declaring the Illinois Act unconstitutional on interstate commerce grounds due to that it "imposed a burden on that commerce [that was] excessive in relation to the local interests served by the statute"). Another portion of Justice White's opinion, not joined in by a majority of the Court, reasoned that the Illinois Act also was unconstitutional under the Supremacy Clause. *Id.* at 630–34. *See generally* Mark A. Sargent, *On the Validity of State Takeover Regulation: State Responses to MITE and Kidwell*, 42 Ohio St. L.J. 689 (1981).

[41] The Illinois statute, for example, applied to target entities having a sufficient Illinois presence. As stated by the Court: "A target company [under the Illinois Act] is defined as a corporation or other issuer of securities of which shareholders located in Illinois own 10% of the class of equity securities subject to the offer, or for which any two of the following three conditions are met: the corporation has its principal executive office in Illinois, is organized under the laws of Illinois, or has at least 10% of its stated capital and paid-in surplus represented within the State." 457 U.S. at 627.

The Illinois statute provided for a twenty-day waiting period. In addition, the Illinois Secretary of State had the authority "to call a hearing at any time during the 20-day waiting period to adjudicate the substantive fairness of the offer if he believes it is necessary to protect the shareholders of the target company, and a hearing must be held if requested by a majority of a target company's outside directors or by Illinois shareholders who own 10% of the class of securities subject to the offer." 475 U.S. at 627. *See* Comment, *The Validity of State Tender Offer Statutes: SEC Rule 14d-2(b) and Post-Kidwell Decisions*, 38 Wash. and Lee L. Rev. 1025, 1026 (1981) (citing thirty-six states that had enacted statutes regulating takeover bids).

[42] The neutral position adhered to by the Williams Act, Pub. L. No. 90-439, 12 Stat. 454 (1968), was emphasized by Senator Harrison Williams, the Act's primary sponsor: "We have taken extreme care to avoid tipping the scales either in favor of management or in favor of the person making the takeover bid." 113 Cong. Rec. 24664 (1967). *See* sources cited *infra* note 48.

companies.[43] Responding to this state action, the SEC adopted Rule 14d-2 in 1979,[44] generally providing that a bidder's public announcement of the tender offer that sets forth the number of shares sought to be acquired and the price to be offered for such shares triggers the commencement of such tender offer.[45] By presenting a direct conflict with the pre-commencement requirements of many state takeover statutes,[46] Rule 14d-2 effectively preempted these state statutes.[47] The SEC's authority to engage in this preemption was upheld by numerous federal courts.[48]

A second example is the SEC's adoption of the all-holders rule.[49] The rule's promulgation was a swift response to the Delaware Supreme Court's decision in *Unocal Corp. v. Mesa Petroleum Co.*,[50] where an issuer self-tender offer that excluded the hostile bidder was upheld.[51] By requiring that issuer and third-party tender offers must be open to all shareholders, the all-holders rule in effect nullifies the Delaware Supreme Court's

---

[43] *See, e.g.*, William C. Tyson, *The Proper Relationship Between Federal and State Law in the Regulation of Tender Offers*, 66 Notre Dame L. Rev. 241, 249–60 (1990).

[44] *See* Securities Exchange Act Release No. 16384 (1979).

[45] Rule 14d-2, 17 C.F.R. § 240.14d-2 (with certain exceptions, in its present form, stating that "[a] bidder will have commenced its tender offer for purposes of section 14(d) of the Act and rules under that section at 12:01 a.m. on the date when the bidder has first published, sent or given the means to tender to security holders"). To lessen the regulatory challenges of securities exchange offers, the Commission authorizes these offers to commence upon the filing of a registration statement. Significantly, however, the bidder is precluded from purchasing securities that are tendered until the effectiveness of the subject registration statement and providing security holders with a prospectus supplement that includes all material changes. *See* Securities Exchange Act Release No. 42055 (1999).

[46] This direct conflict was due to that a tender offer under federal law generally commences upon public announcement of the offer while the pre-notification requirements that were contained in many state statutes had significant waiting periods after public announcement.

[47] *See* Securities Act Release No. 16384 (1979).

[48] *See, e.g.*, *Kennecott Corp. v. Smith*, 637 F.2d 181 (3d Cir. 1980); *Great Western United Corp. v. Kidwell*, 577 F.2d 1256 (5th Cir. 1978), *rev'd on other grounds*, 443 U.S. 173 (1979); *Canadian Pacific Enterprises, Inc. v. Krouse*, 506 F. Supp. 1192 (S.D. Ohio 1981); *G.M. Sub. Corp. v. Liggett Group, Inc.*, [1979–1980 Transfer Binder] Fed. Sec. L. Rep. ¶ 97,389 (D. Del. 1980). Holding that Rule 14d-2 preempted the New Jersey statute, the Third Circuit in *Kennecott* stated:

> Kennecott has shown that it pursued a course authorized under federal law, and that this course conflicted with state law, and that it was not possible to comply with both schemes. It has also demonstrated that the effect of the state law has been to prevent prompt disclosure of crucial information to the shareholders, and through delay, to shift the advantage in this struggle to incumbent management. A primary purpose of the Williams Act, as well as the regulations under it, is to ensure that full information is conveyed to the shareholders of a target company as soon as possible, so that they may exercise a knowledgeable and an unfettered choice. The Act is also designed to preserve a balance between management and challenging groups, so that neither has an unfair advantage.

637 F.2d at 187–88, *citing*, *Rondeau v. Mosinee Paper Corp.*, 422 U.S. 49 (1975).

[49] *See* Rules 13e-4, 14d-10, 17.C.F.R. §§ 240.13e-4, 14d-10.

[50] 493 A.2d 949 (Del. 1985).

[51] *Id.* at 958 (concluding that "there was directorial power to oppose the Mesa tender offer, and to undertake a selective stock exchange made in good faith and upon a reasonable investigation pursuant to a clear duty to protect the corporate enterprise").

decision with respect to publicly-held companies.[52] Recognizing that the rule adopted goes beyond regulating disclosure, the SEC asserted that Congress granted the Commission expansive authority in this context to adopt substantive regulations in order to help ensure the adoption of the most appropriate framework.[53]

As discussed earlier in this chapter, a third example is the SEC's adoption of Rule 13e-3[54] in the aftermath of the U.S. Supreme Court's decision in *Santa Fe Industries*.[55] In that decision, the Court held that matters of substantive fairness entailing alleged breaches of fiduciary duty unaccompanied by deficient disclosure are outside the scope of Section 10(b) of the Securities Exchange Act and Rule 10b-5 prescribed thereunder.[56] The SEC responded by promulgating Rule 13e-3.[57] The rule mandates that in a going-private transaction[58] the subject party must disclose whether it "reasonably believes that the Rule 13e-3 transaction is fair or unfair to unaffiliated security holders" as well as communicating the "material factors" upon which this belief is based.[59] Although premised on disclosure principles, the rule clearly has a substantive objective. Hence, by means of its rule-making authority, the Commission, in actuality, has enhanced the fairness of the going-private process. Along with Delaware Supreme Court decisions with respect to cash-out long-form mergers,[60] the SEC's

---

[52] *See* Steinberg, *supra* note 20, at 141 (stating that "[t]he Commission's proactive rule-making signifies that discriminatory tender offers for shares of publicly-held companies no longer are an available defensive strategy").

[53] *See* Securities Exchange Act Release No. 23421 (1986) (reasoning that "in adopting the Williams Act, Congress granted to the Commission broad rule-making authority in section 13(e) to determine the most appropriate regulatory scheme for issuer tender offers, and that the exercise of this authority could include adoption of substantive regulations").

[54] 17 C.F.R. § 240.13e-3.

[55] *Santa Fe Industries, Inc. v. Green*, 430 U.S. 462 (1977). *See* discussion *supra* notes 15–21 and accompanying text.

[56] 430 U.S. at 473, 477–79 (focusing on § 10(b)'s statutory language, its legislative history, the objective of the securities laws to effectuate adequacy of disclosure, the primary role of the states to govern fiduciary standards for officers and directors, and the danger of vexatious litigation).

[57] *See* Securities Exchange Act Release No. 16075 (1979).

[58] Generally, a going-private transaction is "a transaction or series of transactions in a publicly-held company whereby the controlling (or other) group substantially reduces or eliminates entirely the number of shares held by the public by inducing shareholders to exchange their stock for cash, thereby causing the company to attain privately-held status." Marc I. Steinberg, *Understanding Securities Law* 486 (7th ed. 2018).

[59] *See* Schedule 13E-3, Item 8; SEC Regulation M-A, Item 1014.

[60] *See, e.g.*, *Kahn v. M & F Worldwide Corp.*, 88 A.3d 635 (Del. 2014); *McMullin v. Beran*, 765 A.2d 910 (Del. 2000); *Weinberger v. UOP, Inc.*, 457 A.2d 701 (Del. 1983). On the other hand, in short-form mergers (where the controlling shareholder owns at least 90% of the subject company's shares), "absent fraud or illegality, appraisal is the exclusive remedy available to a minority stockholder." *Glassman v. Unocal Exploration Corp.*, 777 A.2d 242, 248 (Del. 2001). *See* Marc I. Steinberg, *Short-Form Mergers in Delaware*, 27 Del. J. Corp. L. 489 (2002).

activism has redounded to the benefit of investors by advancing both procedural and substantive fairness in this setting.[61]

On the other hand, the SEC's activism met with a resounding defeat in its attempt to federalize a one share, one vote rule.[62] The issue arose in the early 1980s when an increasing number of corporations, as a means to fend off hostile takeover bids, adopted dual-class capital structures (also called disparate voting rights plans). While the listing rules of the Nasdaq and American Stock Exchange did not address disparate voting rights, the New York Stock Exchange (NYSE) had a long-standing rule providing one vote per share of common stock.[63] Fearful that the then takeover craze would impel concerned companies to transfer their listings to the Nasdaq, the NYSE sought SEC approval of a rule that, under certain conditions, would permit the listing of classes of shares with disparate voting rights.[64] Rather than acting on the NYSE's request, the Commission adopted its own rule—Rule 19c-4.[65] With certain exceptions, Rule 19c-4 prohibited—even with shareholder approval—the self-regulatory organizations from listing the common stock of corporations that disparately reduced the per-share voting rights of existing shareholders.[66]

Ultimately, the U.S. Court of Appeals vacated Rule 19c-4 in *Business Roundtable v. Securities and Exchange Commission*[67] on the rationale that the rule exceeded the SEC's authority under Section 19 of the Securities Exchange Act.[68] Rejecting the Commission's position that it had

---

[61] *See* discussion in Steinberg, *supra* note 20, at 113–56.

[62] *See* discussion *infra* notes 63–71 and accompanying text.

[63] *See* Joel Seligman, *Equal Protection in Shareholder Voting Rights: The One Common Share, One Vote Controversy*, 54 Geo. Wash. L. Rev. 687, 692–93, 700 (1986).

[64] Securities Exchange Act Release Nos. 23724, 23803 (1986). *See* Stephen M. Bainbridge, *The Short Life and Resurrection of Rule 19c-4*, 69 Wash. U. L.Q. 565, 576 (1991) ("Given the ability of disparate voting rights plans to insulate management from the threat of hostile takeovers, it is not surprising that a substantial number of NYSE-listed firms demanded the right to adopt such plans.").

[65] Securities Exchange Act Release No. 25891 (1988).

[66] *See Business Roundtable v. Securities and Exchange Commission*, 905 F.2d 406, 407 (D.C. Cir. 1990), *quoting*, SEC Rule 19c-4 (stating that, as adopted, Rule 19c-4 "bar[s] national securities exchanges and national securities associations, together known as self-regulatory organizations (SROs), from listing stock of a corporation that takes any corporate action 'with the effect of nullifying, restricting or disparately reducing the per share voting rights of [existing common stockholders]' . . . even where approved by a shareholder vote conducted on one share/one vote principles").

[67] 905 F.2d 406 (D.C. Cir. 1990).

[68] Quoting the language of Section 19(c) of the Securities Exchange Act, the appellate court recognized that this provision "allows the Commission on its own initiative to amend the rules of a self-regulatory organization as it 'deems necessary or appropriate [1] to insure the fair administration of the self-regulatory organization, [2] to conform its rules to requirements of [the Securities Exchange] Act and the rules and regulations thereunder applicable to such organization, or [3] otherwise in furtherance of the purposes of [the Securities Exchange Act].'" The third catch-all provision was the one

"immensely broad" authority to do what it deemed necessary to "protect investors and the public interest,"[69] the appellate court responded: "If Rule 19c-4 were validated on such broad grounds, the Commission would be able to establish a federal corporate law by using access to national capital markets as its enforcement mechanism."[70] Holding that the SEC lacked the authority to amend securities exchange rules to mandate a one share, one vote rule, the appellate court vacated Rule 19c-4.[71]

The discussion in this section of the chapter illustrates that overall the SEC has done a commendable job in the M&A setting in seeking to protect investors, providing sufficiently concrete and practical standards for market participants, and enhancing the transparency of the securities markets. Going beyond disclosure, the Commission has been successful in adequately specifying the processes and procedures of M&A transactions and has, at times, positively impacted the substantive fairness of certain matters. Nonetheless, the current framework needs significant improvement. The next section of this chapter focuses on new measures in the M&A setting that should be implemented on the federal level.

---

offered by the SEC for upholding its authority to promulgate Rule 19c-4—which the appellate court rejected. *Id.* at 408–09.

[69] *Id.* at 412.

[70] *Id. See id.* at 413 ("We read the [Securities Exchange] Act as reflecting a clear congressional determination not to make any such broad delegation of power to the Commission.").

[71] *Id.* at 412–13. Today, an increasing number of companies going-public utilize dual-class shares which give the corporation's founders and executives more votes per share than that granted to public shareholders. *See* Speech, Rick Fleming (Investor Advocate), *Dual-Class Shares: A Recipe for Disaster* (SEC Oct. 15, 2019); Vijay Govindarajan et al., *Should Dual-Class Stock Be Banned?*, Harv. Bus. Rev. (Dec. 3, 2018). *See generally* Robert B. Thompson, *Collaborative Corporate Governance: Listing Standards, State Law and Federal Regulation*, 38 Wake Forest L. Rev. 961 (2003). With respect to the importance of listing standards on securities exchanges, the Commission more recently commented:

> The development, implementation, and enforcement of standards governing the initial and continued listing of securities on an exchange are activities of critical importance to financial markets and the investing public. Listing requirements, among other things, serve as a means for an exchange to provide listed status only to companies that meet certain initial and continued quantitative and qualitative criteria that help to ensure that fair and orderly markets can be maintained once the company is listed. The corporate governance standards embodied in the listing standards of national securities exchanges, in particular, play an important role in assuring that exchange-listed companies observe good governance practices, including that listed companies provide adequate disclosure to allow investors to make informed investment and voting decisions. The Commission has long encouraged exchanges to adopt and strengthen their corporate governance listing standards in order to, among other things, provide greater transparency into the governance processes of listed issuers and enhance investor confidence in the securities markets.

Securities Exchange Act Release No. 78223 (2016).

III. Necessary Revisions for Implementation in the M&A Setting

Significant revisions should be implemented in the M&A context. The most glaring concern is that the state internal affairs doctrine governs M&A transactions having global ramifications and involving several billions of dollars.[72] Matters of great importance in this process, such as the legitimacy of defensive tactics adopted to fend off hostile bidders, should be determined by the federal government. Comprehensive legislation should be passed by Congress with the SEC being the regulator overseeing the M&A process. That is not to say that the states would not have a key part to play. For example, such issues as procedures relating to the call of shareholder and board of director meetings, the requisite quorum for board and shareholder meetings to be conducted, the list of shareholders of record, and the application of the appraisal remedy would remain matters of state company law.[73]

The principal objective of this change would be that, with respect to companies whose shares are listed on a national securities exchange, federal law would govern substantive issues arising in the M&A setting. Having ramifications affecting national and international policies, the federal government should be the principal regulator. These matters should not be determined by the premier state of company law—Delaware[74]—that has less than one million residents[75]—or, for that matter, by any other state.[76]

---

[72] Generally, the internal affairs doctrine applies the law of the state of the subject company's incorporation to govern the relations between and among the company, its shareholders, and its fiduciaries. *See CTS Corp. v. Dynamics Corp. of America*, 481 U.S. 69 (1987). *See generally* Richard Buxbaum, *The Threatened Constitutionalization of the Internal Affairs Doctrine in Corporate Law*, 75 Cal. L. Rev. 29 (1987). An expansive application of this doctrine recently occurred in *Salzberg v. Sciabacucchi*, 227 A.3d 102 (Del. 2020). There, the Delaware Supreme Court upheld the validity of a charter provision in a subject company's certificate of incorporation requiring that private lawsuits brought for alleged violations of the Securities Act of 1933 must be initiated exclusively in federal court. The court's decision thus authorizes companies incorporated in Delaware to prescribe charter provisions that regulate matters that are deemed within the "outer band" of "intra-corporate affairs," thereby encompassing matters that are beyond the "universe of internal affairs." *Id.* at 109.

[73] These matters currently are within the purview of state company law. *See, e.g.*, Del. Gen. Corp. Law; Model Bus. Corp. Act; Edward P. Welch et al., *Folk on the Delaware General Corporation Law* (6th ed. 2020).

[74] *See* Delaware Division of Corporations, *Annual Report Statistics, A Message from the Secretary of State—Jeffrey W. Bullock*, available at https://corp.delaware.gov/stats (2020) (stating that "Delaware remains the home of the vast majority of top U.S. companies, including more than two thirds of the Fortune 500 and 80% of all firms that go public").

[75] As estimated, Delaware in 2020 has a population of 983,000 individuals. *See Delaware Population 2020*, available at https://worldpopulationreview.com/states/delaware-population.

[76] Other states have sought to attract major companies to incorporate in their respective state. Nevada is known as the Delaware of the west. *See* J. Weston Phippen, *Nevada, a Tax Haven for Only $174*, The Atlantic, April 6, 2016 (stating that in 1991 "Nevada loosened its corporation

A. Recommendations for Reform

The following discussion focuses on several recommendations that should be adopted by Congress and overseen by the SEC. The implementation of these changes would transfer M&A regulation for publicly-held companies to a significantly greater degree to the federal level. The recommendations follow.

1. Disclosure of Beneficial Ownership

Currently, Section 13(d) of the Securities Exchange Act and SEC rules generally require any person (or group) who acquires more than five percent beneficial ownership interest in an equity security of a publicly-held company to file a Schedule 13D with the SEC within ten days after attaining this ownership percentage.[77] A key objective of the statute is to alert the marketplace to potential changes of control in a subject company.[78] During the ten-day period prior to filing, additional purchases can be made under the federal securities laws.[79] Although the requirements of the Hart-Scott-Rodino Antitrust

---

laws . . . hoping to make it a Delaware of the West and attract corporations with its low taxes and high secrecy"), available at https://www.theatlantic.com/national/archive/2016/04/panama-papers-nevada/476994/.

[77] *See* § 13(d) of the Securities Exchange Act, 15 U.S.C. § 78m(d); Rule 13d-1, 17 C.F.R. § 240.13-1; Schedule 13D, 17 C.F.R. § 240.13d-101. As stated by one source: "Schedule 13D requires disclosure of the identity of the issuer and the security, the identity, background, and citizenship of the reporting persons, the source and amount of funds used to acquire the securities, the purpose of the transactions, the reporting person's interest in the securities including trading history for the last 60 days, and any contracts, arrangements, understandings or relationships with respect to the securities to which the reporting person or group is a party." Kenneth J. Bialkin et al., *Why, When and How to Conduct a Proxy Fight for Corporate Control, Proxy Contests and Battles for Corporate Control* 117 (Practising Law Institute 1981).

Generally, in order for there to be a "group" under Section 13(d), two conditions must exist: first, the persons must agree to act in concert; and, second, these persons cumulatively must be beneficial owners of more than five percent of a class of equity securities in a publicly-held company. *See Wellman v. Dickinson*, 682 F.2d 355 (2d Cir. 1982) (setting forth criteria for the meaning of "group" under § 13(d)); Rule 13d-5, 17 C.F.R. § 240.13d-5 (defining "group" as "two or more persons [that] agree to act together for the purpose of acquiring, holding, voting or disposing of equity securities of an issuer"). For a more recent case addressing this subject, *see Lowinger v. Nelson*, 841 F.3d 122 (2d Cir. 2016).

[78] *See Treadway Companies v. Care Corp.*, 638 F.2d 357, 380 (2d Cir. 1981) (stating that "the goal of § 13(d) is to alert the marketplace to every large, rapid aggregation or accumulation of securities . . . which might represent a potential shift in corporate control"). Certain investors, including passive investors, may file a Schedule 13G, which calls for less burdensome disclosure than a Schedule 13D. *See* § 13(g) of the Securities Exchange Act, 15 U.S.C. § 78m(g); Schedule 13G, 17 C.F.R. § 240.13d-102; Securities Exchange Act Release No. 39538 (1998) (stating that the Schedule 13G "applies only to persons not seeking to acquire or influence control of the issuer and who own less than 20% of the class of securities").

[79] *See* Steinberg, *supra* note 58, at 442 (asserting that this loophole enables the accumulation of shares, possibly resulting in a potential change in corporate control, without sufficient notification and disclosure of requisite information to investors and the securities markets).

Improvements Act frequently will limit these purchases,[80] the federal securities laws should close this loophole by lowering this five percent threshold to three percent and by prohibiting accumulation above the three percent level until one business day after a Schedule 13D filing has been made.[81]

In this setting, three percent accumulation should be sufficient to mandate a Schedule 13D filing. Whether a buyer is contemplating holding for investment, becoming an active shareholder, or launching a takeover bid, the market frequently will value that information and deem it material.[82] In this situation, the buyer in fact may be legally trading on material nonpublic information that it has generated. Although this practice arguably should be entirely prohibited, an effective solution is to lower the ownership threshold to three percent. Absent the presence of a controller,[83] three percent ownership in a national securities exchange listed company is significant.[84] Accordingly, once a person reaches that level, it should be required to file within twenty-four hours a Schedule 13D with the SEC and thereafter wait at least one business day before being permitted to make additional purchases.[85]

---

[80] The Hart-Scott-Rodino Antitrust Improvements Act of 1976, Pub. Law 94-435, 15 U.S.C. § 18a. The HSR Act requires that a pre-acquisition notification filing be made with the Federal Trade Commission and Department of Justice if specified monetary thresholds are met and provides that the subject acquisition must be delayed until the waiting period for agency review expires. The threshold amounts to trigger the HSR filing requirements are adjusted annually. The HSR Act applies to mergers, tender offers, and similar acquisitions. For 2020, among other requirements, the size-of-threshold transaction generally is $94 million. *See* Federal Trade Commission, *FTC Announces Annual Update of Size of Transaction Thresholds for Premerger Notification Filings and Interlocking Directorate* (Jan. 28, 2020), available at https://www.ftc.gov/news-events/press-releases/2020/01/ftc-announces-annual-update-size-transaction-thresholds-premerger. *See generally* Stephen M. Axinn, *Acquisitions Under the Hart-Scott-Rodino Antitrust Improvements Act* (3d ed. 2008).

[81] *See* Martin Lipton and Erica Steinberger, *Takeovers and Freezeouts* § 7.02[5] (2019) (stating that "an accumulation of stock prior to making a hostile raid may trigger the obligation to file a Form [under the HSR Act], and thereby compel the raider to surface and disclose its intentions, even if it does not meet the five-percent threshold for the filing of a Schedule 13D"). Note, however, that many purchasers of securities are uncertain whether they will launch a takeover bid. Such purchasers may be content for the present to be active shareholders and perhaps seek a board seat. In this situation, it may well be that these purchasers can acquire more than a five percent ownership during this ten-day interval.

[82] That a company is deemed "in play" ordinarily has a significant impact on the price of its stock. *See, e.g., Basic, Inc. v. Levinson*, 485 U.S. 224 (1988).

[83] For example, a publicly-traded subsidiary corporation is controlled by its parent shareholder. *See, e.g., Weinberger v. UOP, Inc.*, 457 A.2d 701 (Del. 1983). In this situation, a three percent shareholder ordinarily would not be able to exert significant influence.

[84] This three percent ownership level requiring disclosure has been adopted by a number of countries, including the United Kingdom. *See* Financial Conduct Authority (FCA), Disclosure Guidance and Transparency Review, Chapter 5, available at http://www.handbook.fca.org.uk/handbook/DTR.pdf. In this country, by analogy, with respect to the shareholder access rule, the SEC placed an ownership threshold of three percent in order for the largest shareholder to nominate directors. *See* Rule 14a-11, 17 C.F.R. § 240.14a-11. This rule was invalidated by the D.C. Circuit in *Business Roundtable v. Securities and Exchange Commission*, 647 F.3d 1144 (D.C. Cir. 2011), discussed in Chapter 5 herein.

[85] This one-business day is comparable to the time period provided by Regulation FD when public disclosure must be made by the subject company if the selective disclosure was non-intentional. *See* 17 C.F.R. § 243.101(d) (providing that, in situations where the selective disclosure was non-intentional,

2. Golden Parachutes

Golden parachutes, lucrative severance agreements for executive officers, have been a subject of contention for decades.[86] The Dodd-Frank Act of 2010 requires that an advisory shareholder vote be held with respect to these arrangements.[87] Ordinarily, this advisory vote (accompanied by disclosures pertaining to such golden parachute arrangements that are included in executive compensation disclosures) occurs when shareholders cast their "say-on-pay" votes.[88] Otherwise, this non-binding vote may take place at the time a subject corporation seeks shareholder approval of a merger or similar transaction.[89]

Based on the analysis set forth in Chapter 5 on the say-on-pay executive compensation vote,[90] rather than being advisory, this shareholder vote should be binding and should be required to be conducted at the time that shareholder approval is sought for the subject acquisition. In view of the generous benefits provided to executive officers by golden parachute arrangements as they "exit" their respective companies and that many workers of these enterprises no longer will have positions post-acquisition,[91] a meaningful and binding shareholder vote should be mandated. At that time, after being adequately apprised of the parameters of these arrangements, shareholders should have ample opportunity to focus and exercise their voice.[92]

---

the company must publicly disclose information "as soon as reasonably practicable (but in no event after the later of 24 hours or the commencement of the next day's trading on the New York Stock Exchange)").

[86] *See* Securities and Exchange Commission, *Advisory Committee on Tender Offers—Report of Recommendations* (July 8, 1983), available at SEC Historical Society Papers (dissenting view of Justice Arthur J. Goldberg), republished in 43 Md. L. Rev. 225, 230 (1984) (asserting that "[g]olden parachutes should be prohibited [as they] have become a scandal and a discredit to sound fiscal corporate governance").

[87] Dodd-Frank Act § 951, *amending*, § 14A of the Securities Exchange Act, 15 U.S.C. § 78n-1. As stated by the SEC:

> [C]ompanies are required to provide . . . disclosure regarding compensation arrangements with executive officers in connection with merger transactions, known as "golden parachute" arrangements. Disclosure is required of all agreements and understandings that the acquiring and target companies have with the named executive officers of both companies.

Securities Exchange Act Release No. 63768 (2011).

[88] *See* § 14A(b)(2) of the Securities Exchange Act, 15 U.S.C. § 78n-1(b)(2).

[89] *Id.*

[90] *See* discussion in Chapter 5 herein, at notes 68, 147–173 and accompanying text.

[91] *See, e.g.*, Alana Semuels, *The Downsides of Efficiency*, The Atlantic (March 2, 2017) (stating that "businesses often cut jobs after mergers"), available at https://www.theatlantic.com/business/archive/2017/03/mergers-eficiency/518031/.

[92] Generally, this approach with respect to termination payments is adopted by the United Kingdom's City Code on Takeover and Mergers (Rules 16.2, 24.6 of the City Code), available at http://www.thetakeoverpanel.org.uk/download-links/the-takeover-code. By analogy, in this country,

3. Greenmail

Generally, greenmail is a potentially hostile bidder's acquisition of a substantial block of a subject company's common shares with a key objective of inducing that company to purchase those shares at a premium over the amount that the "bidder" paid.[93] This practice enables a supposed corporate bidder to threaten the initiation of a proxy contest or takeover bid without an intention of actually following through.[94] By application of the business judgment rule under Delaware law, the subject company may repurchase these shares.[95] Being deemed inadequate, more forceful measures have been implemented, including the enactment of state statutes placing restrictions on this practice[96] and the levying of an excise tax of fifty percent on short-term "investors" who engage in greenmail.[97] Other than outright prohibition, one additional measure should be implemented: In order for a greenmail

---

golden parachute arrangements should be treated akin to related party transactions under state company law where shareholder approval is sought with some frequency to help authorize the transaction. *See, e.g.*, *Weinberger v. UOP, Inc.*, 457 A.2d 701, 707–08 (Del. 1983).

[93] *See Unocal Corp. v. Mesa Petroleum Co.*, 493 A.2d 946, 957 (Del. 1985) (referring to "the payment of greenmail to a raider or dissident posing a threat to the corporate enterprise"). *See* Jonathan R. Macey and Fred S. McChesney, *A Theoretical Analysis of Corporate Greenmail*, 95 Yale L.J. 13, 13–14 (1985) (stating that "greenmail payments are more frequent and more controversial [and during a one-year period] corporations paid over four billion dollars to repurchase blocks of stock from individual shareholders").

[94] 493 A.2d at 956 (referring to the threat "posed by a corporate raider with a national reputation as a greenmailer"). *See generally* Ronald J. Gilson, *Drafting an Effective Greenmail Prohibition*, 88 Colum. L. Rev. 329 (1988); Roberta S. Karmel, *Greenmail, The Control Premium and Shareholder Duty*, 48 Wash. & Lee L. Rev. 939 (1991).

[95] The *Unocal* two-prong test would apply in this situation: first, the board of directors must establish that there were "reasonable grounds for believing that a danger to corporate policy and effectiveness existed [and, second, that any such action taken was] reasonable in relation to the risk posed." *Unocal*, 493 A.2d at 954.

[96] *See* Karmel, *supra* note 94, at 945 (stating that state anti-greenmail statutes generally prohibit "a corporate repurchase of a significant block of stock (in some cases 3%, in some 5%, and, in New York, as high as 10%) that has been held for a short period of time (ranging from 6 months to 3 years) without a majority shareholder vote or an equal offer to all shareholders") (citing statutes). Another approach is to prohibit the payment of greenmail pursuant to a provision in the subject company's certificate of incorporation or bylaws. *See* David M. Duree, *How Your Company Can Avoid Becoming the Victim of Greenmail* (Nov. 18, 2019), available at https://www.dmduree.net/blog/2019/11/how-your-company-can-avoid-becoming-the-victim-of-greenmail/ (stating that "companies can include provisions in their corporate charter to help prevent becoming the victims of greenmail").

[97] 26 U.S.C. § 5881(a) (levying a 50% tax on greenmail profits); 26 I.R.C. § 162(k) (limiting the deductibility by subject companies of greenmail payments). Today, greenmail is more frequently used when a supposed insurgent threatens the launching of a proxy contest. Note, moreover, that "due to the narrow definition of greenmail, the excise tax is easy to avoid." Noam Noked, *Greenmail Makes a Comeback*, Harv. Law School Forum on Corp. Gov., Jan. 22, 2014, available at https://corpgov.law.harvard.edu/2014/01/22/greenmail-makes-a-comeback/.

payment to be made by a subject corporation, its shareholders must approve such payment and the terms thereof pursuant to a binding vote.[98]

4. The Acquirer's Shareholders

All too often under state law, shareholders of the bidder or acquiring corporation have little or no "say" with respect to major acquisitions undertaken by such company. Two prime examples are triangular mergers[99] and tender offers. In each such case, the shareholders of the acquiring corporation have no vote under state law.[100] It is an affront to principles of corporate governance that an acquirer can undertake a triangular merger or launch a tender

---

[98] This recommendation thus adopts the position by a number of states as well as congressional legislative proposals with respect to this practice. *See supra* note 96. The alternative of making an equal offer to all shareholders ordinarily is not practical unless the subject company seeks dissolution and possible liquidation. During the mid-1980s, greenmail was a subject of proposed congressional action that sought to impose restrictions in this setting. None of these proposals were enacted. *See* Linda C. Quinn and David B.H. Martin, Jr., *The SEC Advisory Committee on Tender Offers and Its Aftermath—A New Chapter in Change-of-Control Regulation*, contained in *Tender Offers—Developments and Commentaries* 9, 28 (M. Steinberg ed., 1985) (stating that "greenmail was the subject of action not only in the Commission's legislative initiative but also in separate pieces of [proposed] legislation, most of which included the same provision as in the Commission's legislative package, that is, a requirement that any repurchase of shares at a price above market, from any person who holds more than 3% of the class to be purchased and who has held the securities for less than two years, be approved by a majority of the shareholders or be made on equal terms to all shareholders") (citing S. 2700, 2754, 2777, 2779).

[99] *See* Douglas M. Branson et al., *Business Enterprises—Legal Structures, Governance, and Policy* 868–69 (4th ed. 2020):

> Triangular mergers involve three or more corporations. In a three-corporation triangular merger, the acquiror creates a shell subsidiary—a subsidiary that holds no assets and conducts no business—that becomes a party to a merger with the company to be acquired (target). . . . By using a subsidiary of the acquiror (rather than the acquiror itself) as the constituent corporation in the merger, the acquiror can effectively acquire the target as a wholly owned subsidiary.

[100] Note that, pursuant to New York Stock Exchange mandate, if twenty percent or more of the acquirer's shares are sought to be issued pursuant to the merger, approval of such issuance by the acquirer's shareholders is required. *See* New York Stock Exchange Company Manual § 312.03. In *Paramount Communications, Inc. v. Time, Inc.*, 571 A.2d 1140 (Del. 1990), the Delaware Supreme Court observed that the voting rights that Time shareholders had, if the transaction had been effected as initially planned, were required by the New York Stock Exchange rather than Delaware law. *Id.* at 1146. Responding to this statement, this author commented:

> The [Delaware Supreme Court] states that . . . the Time board did not deprive the corporation's shareholders of any right that they had under Delaware law. Approval of the initially-planned merger by Time shareholders was mandated by the New York Stock Exchange, not Delaware law. The court's statement is correct. Nonetheless, it is a poignant commentary on corporate governance that a board of directors can cause a subsidiary to be formed, have a party to the transaction merged into the subsidiary, and thereby deny the corporation's shareholders their right to vote on such a fundamental issue directly impacting upon their economic interest. In this case, but for the rules of the New York Stock Exchange, former Warner shareholders, if the merger had proceeded, would have owned 62% of Time-Warner without Time shareholders having a voice in the transaction.

offer incurring billions of dollars in costs and debt with its shareholders having no voice in the transaction.[101] Due to the neglect of the states to remedy this prolonged inadequacy, the solution is the federalization of shareholder voting rights in M&A transactions. Pursuant to this framework, M&A deals involving nationally traded companies that constitute twenty percent or more of a respective company's net assets ordinarily would be deemed "extraordinary" transactions. In addition to the acquired company's shareholders tendering their shares or voting their approval, a majority of the outstanding shares of the publicly-held (direct or indirect) acquirer corporation (provided that such twenty percent threshold is met) would be required to approve the subject transaction. This recommendation accordingly would grant voting rights to the shareholders of publicly-held corporations in triangular mergers, tender offers, and similar types of transactions that under state law would preclude such shareholder "voice."[102]

5. Repeal of State Takeover Statutes

The presence of state anti-takeover statutes impacting prospective acquisitions involving nationally traded companies is prevalent.[103] Seeking to further various stakeholder interests, including that of employees and communities, these statutes tilt the level playing field between bidders and targets approved by Congress[104] to favor in-state target companies.[105] While this favoritism may be permitted when confined to local companies

Marc I. Steinberg, *Nightmare on Main Street: The Paramount Picture Horror Show*, 16 Del. J. Corp. L. 1, 14 (1991). *See* American Law Institute, *Principles of Corporate Governance: Analysis and Recommendations* § 6.01(b) (1994) (requiring shareholder approval in, *inter alia*, triangular statutory mergers).

[101] *See* Goldberg, *supra* note 86, at 234 (stating that "before a tender offer is made, it should be approved by shareholders of the offeror [as this] requirement is simply an application of corporate democracy"); discussion *supra* note 100.

[102] By contrast, under state corporation law, the approval by a majority of the outstanding shares of each affected corporation generally is required in long-form merger transactions. *See, e.g.*, Del. Gen. Corp. Law § 251(c).

[103] *See, e.g.*, Thomas Lee Hazen, *State Anti-Takeover Legislation: The Second and Third Generations*, 23 Wake Forest L. Rev. 77 (1988); Alan R. Palmiter, *The CTS Gambit: Stanching the Federalization of Corporate Law*, 69 Wash. U. L.Q. 445 (1991); Arthur R. Pinto, *The Constitution and the Market for Corporate Control: State Takeover Statutes After CTS Corp.*, 29 Wm. & Mary L. Rev. 699 (1988).

[104] The Williams Act sought to provide a level playing field between bidders and targets. *See supra* note 42.

[105] *See CTS Corp. v. Dynamics Corp. of America*, 481 U.S. 69 (1987) (upholding the constitutionality of an Indiana statute (applicable to Indiana incorporated companies that have certain other connections with that state) that permits the exercise of voting rights by a purchaser of specified percentages of stock of the subject company being dependent upon receiving the approval of a majority of the disinterested shares); *Edgar v. MITE Corporation*, 457 U.S. 624 (1982) (declaring Illinois

whose securities are not listed on a national securities exchange, state legislation should not substantially interfere with national policy.[106] Even if a particular state statute may be deemed beneficial to shareholders, the securities markets, and the public interest, that determination should be made by Congress rather than the individual states acting pursuant to their own agendas.[107] Accordingly, there should be federal preemption of state takeover statutes that regulate companies whose securities are nationally traded.

6. Shareholder Ownership Threshold Requiring Takeover Bid for All Outstanding Voting Shares

Although several proposals have been advanced[108] and the practice is adhered to in numerous foreign countries,[109] there exists no requirement under federal law that a shareholder must make a tender offer after acquiring

---

takeover statute that required pre-notification and waiting periods prior to commencement of a tender offer unconstitutional on interstate commerce grounds); *Amanda Acquisition Corporation v. Universal Foods Corporation*, 877 F.2d 496 (7th Cir. 1989) (upholding constitutionality of Wisconsin statute generally providing, unless the target corporation's board of directors agrees in advance to the contemplated transaction, that the bidder, after purchasing the shares, must wait three years to effectuate a follow-up merger); sources cited *supra* note 103.

[106] *See* Recommendation 4 of the SEC Advisory Committee Report on Tender Offers, in *Tender Offers*, *supra* note 98, at 31 ("Regulation of takeovers should recognize that such transactions take place in a national securities market.").

[107] Then SEC Chairman David S. Ruder reasoned:

> Limitations on the free transferability of securities of corporations which are owned by shareholders nationwide diminish the efficiency, depth, and liquidity of the nation's securities markets. Accordingly, I believe that federal law should control in that area by preempting state statutes that unduly interfere with the free transferability of securities. I believe that corporations whose activities and ownership are national in scope should not be given protection against takeovers by the states where their primary production facilities are located. Just as I believe it to be imprudent for Congress to regulate internal corporate affairs through tender offer regulation, I believe it is imprudent for states to use their authority over matters of internal governance as a means of regulating the interstate market for corporate control.

Remarks of SEC Chairman David S. Ruder, *Federal Preemption of State Anti-Takeover Legislation*, before the 26th Annual Corporate Counsel Institute, at 8–9 (Chicago Oct. 7, 1987), *reported in* Fed. Sec. L. Rep. (CCH) No. 1256, at 8–9 (1987).

[108] *See, e.g.*, SEC Advisory Committee Report on Tender Offers Recommendation 14, discussed *infra* note 115 and accompanying text.

[109] *See, e.g.*, *European Directive on Takeover Bids*, 2004/25/EC (May 20, 2004) (providing that, once a person reaches a Member-State established threshold, such person must make a tender offer for all of the target company's outstanding stock). *See also Baker McKenzie Takeovers Guide*, Australia (2018), available at https://www.bakermckenzie.com/-/media/files/people/lustig-richard/bk_australia_ takeoversguide_jan2018.pdf?la=en; International Organization of Securities Commissions, Emerging Markets Committee, *Takeover Regulation in the Jurisdictions of Some IOSCO EMC Members* (2006), available at https://www.iosco.org/library/pubdocs/pdf/IOSCOPD210.pdf; sources cited *infra* note 118. Note that the Pennsylvania anti-takeover law has a provision mandating, with certain exceptions, that a person who acquires twenty percent or greater of voting stock of a subject corporation must pay in cash the "fair value" for the shares held by other

a specified percentage of the subject company's shares.[110] Although piecemeal accumulations of stock are required to be disclosed pursuant to Schedule 13D,[111] this technique may permit an acquirer to gain control through stock market purchases and privately-negotiated transactions. In such private purchases, a premium to market price is likely to be paid.[112] Because control may be viewed as a corporate asset, all shareholders under this rationale should have the opportunity to share in the premium an acquirer pays for this asset.[113] Mandating the circumstances in which an acquirer must launch a tender offer provides a means to help ensure that these substantive protections are effectuated.[114] In this respect, the SEC's Advisory Committee Report on Tender Offers recommended that, with the SEC being given broad exemption authority, "[n]o person may acquire voting securities of an issuer, if immediately following such acquisition, such person would own more than 20% of the voting power of the outstanding voting securities of that issuer unless such purchases were made (1) from the issuer or (2) pursuant to a tender offer."[115] This recommendation, or one calling for

---

stockholders who object to that person's acquisition. *See* Pa. Bus. Corp. Law Sub. 25E. §§ 2541–2548, at § 2546.

Note that European governments have "strengthen[ed] protections against foreign business takeovers as concerns grow that companies whose share prices have slumped because of the coronavirus outbreak are vulnerable." Simon Clark and Ben Drummatt, *EU Beefs Up Takeover Protections*, Wall St. J., April 11–12, 2020, at B1.

[110] There have been proposals to require that a tender offer be made to all shareholders once a person acquires a specific percentage of the subject company's voting shares. *See* discussion *infra* notes 115–118 and accompanying text.

[111] Such piecemeal acquisitions by a director, officer, or ten percent beneficial shareholder of an equity security also must be reported pursuant to Section 16(a), with the filing of the requisite Form 4 with the SEC. *See* § 16(a) of the Securities Exchange Act, 15 U.S.C. § 78p(a). With respect to Schedule 13D, *see supra* notes 77–85 and accompanying text.

[112] This statement assumes that the prospective sellers are aware of the prospective buyer's beneficial ownership percentage. This information would be available pursuant to Form 4 and Schedule 13D filings. Recognizing that the prospective purchaser plans to amass a larger position, these prospective sellers ordinarily should be successful in bargaining for a premium over the market price. *See supra* notes 77–85, 111 and accompanying text. Moreover, in certain circumstances, privately-negotiated transactions accompanied by widespread shareholder solicitation offering to purchase a fixed number of shares at a premium over the prevailing market price may constitute a tender offer. *See Hanson Trust PLC v. SCM Corporation*, 774 F.2d 47 (2d Cir. 1985).

[113] *See* Quinn and Martin, *supra* note 98, at 18 (stating that, underlying the SEC Advisory Committee's proposal generally requiring an acquirer of more than twenty percent of a subject company's voting stock to make a tender offer for all shares, "was the view that control is essentially a corporate asset and that shareholders should have an equal opportunity to share in any premium paid for such asset"); *infra* note 115 and accompanying text.

[114] *Id.* (stating the SEC's opinion that enhanced improvement "would be best assured by imposing the substantive protections of the tender offer process").

[115] *SEC Advisory Committee Report on Tender Offers*, Recommendation 14, *contained in Tender Offers, supra* note 98, at 34.

a lower ownership threshold, such as fifteen percent, should be enacted by Congress.[116] In addition, because partial bids generally are disfavored and rarely utilized today,[117] the making of a tender offer should be for all outstanding voting shares—hence, precluding partial takeover bids.[118]

---

[116] *See* Goldberg, *supra* note 86, at 234 (asserting that "[a]n acquisition of shares in a company resulting in ownership of fifteen percent or more of its outstanding securities should be required to make a tender offer for all shares"); Louis Lowenstein, *Pruning Deadwood in Hostile Takeovers: A Proposal for Legislation*, 83 Colum. L. Rev. 249, 317 (1983) (generally proposing that acquisition of twenty percent beneficial ownership should require that a tender offer be made for hostile purchases exceeding five percent of the target's shares); sources cited *infra* note 118.

[117] The decrease in the frequency of partial tender offers is due to several reasons, including that proration and withdrawal rights now extend to the entire offering period (thereby minimizing the stampede effect whereby shareholders rush to tender their shares to prevent all their shares from being relegated to the back-end likely lower-priced transaction) and the presence of state anti-takeover statutes that impose significant waiting periods for effecting a back-end transaction. Hence, the dissipation of the "stampede" effect coupled with waiting three years or more to effectuate a cash-out merger dissuades the making of two-tier offers. In addition, numerous state statutes have "fair price provisions" generally mandating that, absent disinterested shareholder approval, the same price must be paid in the second step transaction as was paid in the front-end tender offer. *See* Md. Gen. Corp. Law § 3-202; L.P. Scriggins and David Clarke, Jr., *Takeovers and the 1983 Maryland Fair Price Legislation*, 43 Md. L. Rev. 266 (1984). In addition, many corporations have adopted fair price charter amendments which provide similar protection. *But see* Mark S. Johnson and Ramesh P. Rao, *The Impact of Anti-Takeover Charter Amendments on Expectations of Future Earnings and Takeover Activity*, 20 Managerial and Decision Economics No. 2, at 75 (1999) (finding that anti-takeover charter amendments neither impact takeover activity nor premiums offered). *See generally* Richard A. Booth, *The Promise of State Takeover Statutes*, 86 Mich. L. Rev. 1635 (1988).

[118] Extraordinary circumstances may call for the propriety of permitting a partial tender offer in a particular situation. In such event, the SEC should be authorized to issue an exemption, thereby authorizing the conducting of a partial offer in that situation.

The requirement of all share tender offers is the approach adopted in many countries. *See, e.g., The European Directive on Tender Offers, supra* note 109 (mandating that an acquirer must make a tender offer for all of the subject company's outstanding shares upon attaining a specified ownership threshold set forth by a Member State); Marco Ventoruzzo, *Europe's Thirteenth Directive and U.S. Takeover Regulation: Regulatory Means and Political and Economic Ends*, 41 Tex. Int'l L.J. 171, 191 (2006) (stating that "most European countries required compulsory tender offers on all outstanding shares when a specified controlling threshold was acquired"). In the United Kingdom, the specified ownership threshold generally is thirty percent. *See* City Code on Takeovers and Mergers, Rules 5, 9, *supra* note 92; Hong Kong, Securities and Futures Commission, The Codes on Takeovers and Mergers and Share Buy-Backs (July 13, 2018), available at https://www.sfc.hk/media/EN/assets/components/codes/files-current/web/codes/the-codes-on-takeovers-and-mergers-and-share-buy-backs.pdf (30%); Singapore, Monetary Authority of Singapore, The Singapore Code on Take-Overs and Mergers (Jan. 24, 2019), available at https://www.mas.gov.sg-media/MAS/resource.sic/The_Singapore_Code_on_Take_Overs_and_Merger_24-January-2019.pdf?la=en&hash=8DCB4A29BF6DDA17527EC7E54A8CB5CFEDDAEE7D (30%). On the other hand, a number of countries (such as China, Japan, and South Korea) adhere to a mandatory partial bid approach whereby an acquirer, upon reaching a securities ownership threshold (such as 20%), "is obligated to launch a partial bid to acquire the number of target shares which it plans to purchase." Robin Hui Huang and Charles Cho Wang, *The Monetary Bid Rule under China's Takeover Law: A Comparative and Empirical Perspective*, 53 Int'l Law. 195, 208 (2020). *See* Yueh-Ping (Alex) Yang and Pin-Hsien (Peggy) Lee, *Is Moderation the Highest Virtue? A Comparative Study of a Middle Way of Control Transactions Regimes*, 41 Del. J. Corp. L. 393 (2017). *See also* Goldberg, *supra* note 86, at 233–34 (asserting that "[p]artial and two-tier tender offers generally should be prohibited . . . [as these offers leave] shareholders who, for one

7. Measures in Response to Takeover Bids

With certain exceptions,[119] the propriety of defensive tactics to fend off unwanted takeover bids is within the province of state law.[120] That determination was made by the U.S. Supreme Court in *Schreiber v. Burlington Northern, Inc.*,[121] holding that a deficiency of disclosure must be shown in order to prove an actionable claim under the tender offer antifraud provision—Section 14(e) of the Securities Exchange Act.[122] In ascertaining the reach of that provision, the Court opined: "All three species of misconduct listed in Section 14(e), i.e., fraudulent, deceptive or manipulative, are directed at failure to disclose."[123]

The Court's holding thus signifies that the business judgment rule under state law ordinarily applies to fiduciary conduct in this setting.[124] Although Delaware courts embrace an enhanced business judgment rule standard when the subject company seeks to maintain its independence (i.e., the *Unocal* standard),[125] in effect, *Unocal*'s application frequently resembles that of the "plain vanilla" version.[126] In sale of control situations, the inquiry shifts to whether the subject board of directors, applying the business judgment rule, satisfied its obligation to maximize shareholder return.[127] Pursuant to

---

reason or another, do not tender to the mercy of the market which often declines after the partial bid is consummated").

[119] Two exceptions previously discussed are the SEC's best price and all holders rules. *See supra* discussion notes 34, 36, 49–53 and accompanying text.

[120] *See infra* notes 121–132 and accompanying text.

[121] 472 U.S. 1 (1985).

[122] 15 U.S.C. § 78n(e). Prior to the Supreme Court's decision in *Schreiber*, a number of lower federal courts held that, even though sufficiently disclosed, certain defensive tactics constituted manipulation under Section 14(e). *See, e.g.*, *Mobil v. Marathon Oil Co.*, 669 F.2d 366 (6th Cir. 1981) (target company's grant to white knight of option to purchase company's crown jewel held manipulative); *Data Probe Acquisition Corp. v. Datatab, Inc.*, 568 F. Supp. 1538 (S.D.N.Y.), *rev'd*, 722 F.2d 1 (2d Cir. 1983) (attractive option grant to third party to purchase target company's shares was manipulative). *See generally* Mark J. Loewenstein, *Section 14(e) of the Williams Act and the Rule 10b-5 Comparisons*, 71 Geo. L.J. 1311 (1983).

[123] 472 U.S. at 8.

[124] *Cf. Gearhart Industries v. Smith International, Inc.*, 741 F.2d 707 (5th Cir. 1984) (applying traditional business judgment rule under Texas law), *with Unocal Corp. v. Mesa Petroleum Co.*, 493 A.2d 946 (Del. 1985) (applying modified business judgment rule); discussion *infra* notes 125–130 and accompanying text.

[125] There are two prongs under the *Unocal* modified business judgment rule: first, the board of directors must establish that there were "reasonable grounds for believing that a danger to corporate policy and effectiveness existed [and, second, that any such action was] reasonable in relation to the risk posed." 493 A.2d at 954. Note that this showing is more easily made when the target corporation's board of directors is comprised of a majority of independent directors. *See, e.g.*, *Paramount Communications, Inc. v. Time, Inc.* 571 A.2d 1140, 1152 (Del. 1990).

[126] As stated by this author, the *Unocal* standard "may well be of cosmetic value, having little substantive impact." Marc I. Steinberg, *Tender Offer Regulation: The Need for Reform*, 23 Wake Forest L. Rev. 1, 15 (1988). *See* sources cited *infra* note 132.

[127] *See Lyondell Chemical Co. v. Ryan*, 970 A.2d 235, 242 (Del. 2009) (stating that "there is only one Revlon duty—to [obtain] the best price for the stockholders at a sale of the company"); *MacAndrews*

these standards, Delaware courts have given business judgment rule protection to extraordinary defensive maneuvers under the *Unocal* standard, including the incurrence of $10 billion in debt,[128] the undertaking of major corporate recapitalizations,[129] and the adoption of poison pill provisions.[130] Proponents assert that Delaware merits kudos for its allegedly insightful approach to this challenging dilemma,[131] while critics contend that Delaware's approach unduly favors fiduciaries of the target corporation over shareholder interests.[132] Irrespective of which position is correct, the more important

---

& Forbes Holdings v. Revlon, Inc., 506 A.2d 173, 182, 185 (1986) (holding that, once a company is for sale, the duty of the target corporation's board of directors "change[s] from the preservation of [the company] as a corporate entity to the maximization of the company's value at a sale for the stockholders' benefit", and that, if such duty is undertaken, the board's action is "entitled to the deference accorded it by the business judgment rule"). In *Paramount*, while not excluding other situations, the Delaware Supreme Court identified two scenarios where *Revlon* applies: "The first and clearer one, is when a corporation initiates an active bidding process seeking to sell itself or to effect a clear breakup of the company [and the second situation is that] *Revlon* duties also may be triggered where, in response to a bidder's offer, a target abandons its long-term strategy and seeks an alternative transaction also involving the breakup of the company." *Paramount Communications, Inc. v. Time, Inc.*, 571 A.2d 1140, 1150 (Del. 1990). A third scenario arises where a change of control of the corporation occurs. *See Paramount Communications, Inc. v. QVC Network, Inc.*, 637 A.2d 34 (Del. 1993). Moreover, as the Delaware courts have ruled, maximization of value does not necessarily require that an auction among competing bidders be held. *See, e.g., Barkan v. Armsted Industries, Inc.*, 579 A.2d 1279 (Del. 1989).

128 *See Paramount Communications, Inc. v. Time, Inc.*, 571 A.2d 1140, 1155 (Del. 1990) (ruling that Time's incurrence of debt amounting to $7–$10 billion to finance its Warner acquisition pursuant to a long-term business strategy was permissible because the board "could reasonably perceive its debt load not to be so injurious to the corporation as to jeopardize its well-being"). *Accord, Unocal Corp. v. Mesa Petroleum Co.*, 493 A.2d 946, 950 (Del. 1990) (under modified business judgment rule, upholding Unocal's incurrence of over $6 billion of additional debt to finance self-tender offer to its shareholders and explaining that "[t]he directors were told that the primary effect of this obligation would be to reduce exploratory drilling, but that the company would nonetheless remain a viable entity").

129 *See Unitrin, Inc. v. American General Corp.*, 651 A.2d 1361, 1368 (Del. 1995) (holding that "if the board of directors' response is not draconian (preclusive or coercive) and within a 'range of reasonableness,' a court must not substitute its judgment for the board's"); cases cited *supra* note 128.

130 *See, e.g., Moore Corp. v. Wallace Computer Services, Inc.*, 907 F. Supp. 1545 (Del. 1995) (applying Delaware law) (giving approbation to the "just say no" defense when target company's board of directors opted to retain the poison pill when faced with a non-coercive all share all cash offer by a hostile bidder); *Versata Enterprises, Inc. v. Selectica, Inc.*, 5 A.3d 586 (Del. 2010) (upholding shareholder rights plan that had a 4.99% trigger); *Air Products & Chemicals, Inc. v. Airgas, Inc.*, 16 A.3d 48 (Del. Ch. 2011) (upholding under facts at bar decision by target company's board of directors to maintain a poison pill that had a 15% trigger when responding to a non-coercive unfriendly takeover bid).

131 *See, e.g.*, Stephen M. Bainbridge, *Unocal at 20: Director Primacy in Corporate Takeovers*, 31 Del. J. Corp. L. 769 (2006); Martin Lipton, *Takeover Bids in the Target's Boardroom*, 35 Bus. Law. 101 (1979).

132 *See* Jennifer J. Johnson and Mary Siegel, *Corporate Mergers: Redefining the Role of Corporate Directors*, 136 U. Pa. L. Rev. 315, 330 (1987) (viewing *Unocal* as a "toothless standard"); Mark J. Loewenstein, *Unocal Revisited; No Tiger in the Tank*, 27 J. Corp. L. 1, 3 (2001) (describing *Unocal* as a "toothless tiger"); Steinberg, *supra* note 100, at 11–29 (discussing inadequacy of shareholder protection under Delaware law in the tender offer setting). *See also* A.A. Sommer, Jr., *Whom Should the*

point in this context is that takeover policies involving national and global companies should not be within the province of state company law. Rather, the federal government should establish the parameters with respect to the legitimacy of defensive maneuvers in the takeover sphere.[133]

In developing a national policy, one guiding principle should apply: When a board of directors seeks to adopt a substantial tactic to fend off prospective as well as ongoing takeover bids or to entice a friendly suitor, the shareholders of the subject corporation must vote to approve this requested action. By way of example, with respect to fending off a hostile takeover bid, these maneuvers include adopting poison pills, engaging in recapitalizations (such as stock repurchases, uncustomary cash distributions, and issuer self-tender offers), and undertaking restructurings (such as material debt restructurings). The same approach should be applied when lock-ups are extended by target corporations to friendly suitors in the white knight setting or other negotiated transactions. In this context, such actions as the issuance of securities, the sale of crown jewels, and the grant of options to purchase attractive assets of the target corporation, should be permitted only after receiving shareholder approval. Hence, irrespective whether the contemplated conduct is undertaken by amendment of the charter or bylaws or by other means, an affirmative shareholder vote is required. Applying both to defensive measures to fend-off unwanted bidders and to lock-ups extended to suitors in negotiated deals, this approach supports shareholder

Corporation Serve? The Berle-Dodd Debate Revisited Sixty Years Later, 16 Del. J. Corp. L. 33, 49 (1990) (former SEC Commissioner commenting that the Delaware Supreme Court in *Unocal* "blurred the distinction between the interests of the corporation and those of the shareholders").

For cases upholding a target company's board of directors decision to maintain a shareholder rights plan or poison pill where a non-coercive all share all cash hostile bid has been made, *see* cases *supra* note 130. Prior to these decisions, Chancellor Allen analyzed this situation in very different terms:

> To acknowledge that directors may employ the recent innovation of "poison pills" to deprive shareholders of the ability effectively to choose to accept a noncoercive offer, after the board has had a reasonable opportunity to explore or create alternatives, or attempt to negotiate on the shareholders' behalf, would, it seems to me, be so inconsistent with widely shared notions of appropriate corporate governance as to threaten to diminish the legitimacy and authority of our corporation law.

City Capital Associates v. Interco, Inc., 551 A.2d 787, 799–800 (Del. Ch. 1988).

133 *See* Ted Fiflis, *Of Lollipops and Law—A Proposal for a National Policy Concerning Tender Offer Defenses*, 19 U.C. Davis L. Rev. 303, 306 (1986) (addressing whether "it is appropriate for Delaware, which conceivably may not be the abode of a single Unocal [or other global company] shareholder, to fix national policy in the international securities market, while Congress and the federal courts, Nero-like, abdicate a policymaking role").

empowerment in order to harmonize the separation of ownership and control in publicly-held companies.[134]

Adherence to this approach would allow a target corporation's board of directors to consider the interests of employees, communities, and other stakeholders.[135] Nonetheless, because the bidder's offer is made directly to the shareholders of the target impacting the alienability of one's stock ownership,[136] maneuvers that are sought to be undertaken by the target's board of directors that would impede that interest should be subject to shareholder approval.

With frequency, due to time limitations and the pressures prevalent in the context of takeover bids, certain maneuvers that a target company's board of directors would seek to implement during the midst of a takeover battle would not be available if shareholder approval would be required at that time. Thus, this approach stresses advanced planning of the strategies that an incumbent board would be inclined to implement and receipt of shareholder approval before a takeover bid is launched by a hostile or so-called friendly third-party.[137] Taking its rationale to the shareholders, the board can set forth the company's position regarding the asserted soundness of these maneuvers. This position is likely to be disputed by certain shareholders.

---

[134] *See Conoco, Inc. v. Seagram Co.*, 517 F. Supp. 1299, 1303 (S.D.N.Y. 1981) ("What is sometimes lost sight of in these tender offer controversies is that the shareholders, not the directors, have the right of franchise with respect to the shares owned by them."); *Blassius Industries, Inc. v. Atlas Corp.*, 564 A.2d 651, 659 (Del. 1988) (stating that "[t]he shareholder franchise is the ideological underpinning upon which the legitimacy of directorial power rests [and that] [g]enerally, shareholders have only two protections against perceived inadequate business performance . . . [namely,] [t]hey may sell their stock . . . or they may vote to replace incumbent board members"). With respect to certain defensive maneuvers, such as amending a subject company's articles of incorporation to provide for a staggered board of directors or removal of directors only for cause, shareholder approval under state law already is mandated. *See* § 10.03 of the Model Business Corporation Act. Under the recommended approach herein, this shareholder vote would be a matter of federal law.

[135] A majority of the states have enacted constituency statutes. Other stakeholders include customers, employees, and suppliers. For discussion of these statutes, *see, e.g.*, American Bar Association, Committee on Corporate Laws, *Other Constituencies Statutes: Potential for Confusion*, 45 Bus. Law. 2253 (1990); Marleen A. O'Connor, *Corporate Malaise—Stakeholder Statutes: Cause or Cure?*, 21 Stetson L. Rev. 3 (1991); Brett McDonnell, *Corporate Constituency Statutes and Employee Governance*, 30 Wm. Mitchell L. Rev. 1227 (2004).

[136] *See* Goldberg, *supra* note 86, at 234 (former U.S. Supreme Court Justice stating "shareholders own corporations, management does not . . . [and] are entitled to make the ultimate decision on matters directly affecting the future of the offeror and target companies"); cases cited *supra* note 134.

[137] Advanced planning and implementation for obtaining shareholder approval for maneuvers, such as poison pills, would be prudent in the event that general economic conditions or a national/global catastrophe, such as the coronavirus pandemic, should occur. Such conditions present the added takeover risk of "opportunistic activism." *See* Aaron Bertinetti, Glass, Lewis & Co., *Poison Pills and Coronavirus: Understanding Glass Lewis' Contextual Policy Approach*, Harv. Law School Forum on Corp. Governance (April 11, 2020), available at https://corpgov.law.harvard.edu/2020/04/11/poison-pills-and-coronavirus-understanding-glass-lewis-contextual-policy-approach/.

To help ensure that shareholders are better informed, the shareholder (or group) that owns the largest percentage of voting common stock (or the next largest shareholder if others decline) should be entitled to present its position (with an appropriate maximum word limit) on the company's disclosure statement.[138] Effectuating this "game plan" would enable shareholders to be better apprised of the multi-faceted issues that are at stake. Also, engaging in this dialogue prior to the onset of a takeover bid enables the affected persons to present their positions in a more deliberate and reasoned manner. Once shareholders vote to approve each maneuver after receiving sufficient disclosure (including adequate explanation of the provisions for each such maneuver), the target's board of directors would be authorized to deploy the maneuvers if appropriate—namely, when such board of directors, after being sufficiently informed without a disabling conflict of interest, reasonably determines that a particular maneuver's utilization serves the best interests of the subject corporation and, collectively, its shareholders.[139]

---

[138] *Cf.* Rule 14a-8, 17 C.F.R. § 240.14a-8 (shareholder proposal rule whereby eligible shareholders may present their resolutions in the company's proxy statement) (discussed in Chapter 5 herein); former Rule 14a-11 (proxy access rule, allowing largest shareholder owning at least three percent of the company's voting stock to nominate a specified number of directors utilizing the company's proxy statement). Rule 14a-11 subsequently was declared invalid. *See Business Roundtable v. Securities and Exchange Commission*, 647 F.3d 1144 (D.C. Cir. 2011). For discussion, *see supra* note 84 and accompanying text; Chapter 5 herein.

[139] The proposal in the text finds support in the United Kingdom's City Code on Takeovers and Mergers. Under the Code, a target company's board of directors, absent shareholder approval, cannot engage in tactics that may result in a bona fide offer being impaired or that prevent shareholders from determining whether to accept the bidder's offer. For example, poison pills may not be adopted. *See* City Code, *supra* note 92, General Principle 3 (providing that "[t]he board of an offeree company must act in the interests of the company as a whole and must not deny the holders of securities the opportunity to decide on the merits of the bid"); Rule 21 of the City Code; Steve Cooke et al., Slaughter and May, *A Guide to Takeovers in the United Kingdom* 30–31 (2020), available at https://my.slaughterandmay.com/insights/client-publications/a-guide-to-takeovers-in-the-united-kingdom/. *See also* Ventoruzzo, *supra* note 118, at 194 (stating that "the European approach freezes directors' powers once a public offer has been launched and requires any action that might adversely affect the outcome of the takeover to be approved by the shareholders . . . [thereby] directly empower[ing] shareholders on the issue of defensive measures"). *But see* Clark and Drummatt, *supra* note 109 (reporting that European governments are strengthening protection for their "home" companies against foreign takeovers).

Through the decades, there have been proposed several different approaches regarding the use of defensive maneuvers in tender offers. Two of the more far-reaching proposals are: (1) requiring that the target company's board of directors and management must be totally passive (*see* Frank Easterbrook and Daniel Fischel, *The Proper Role of Target Management in Responding to a Tender Offer*, 94 Harv. L. Rev. 1161 (1981)); and (2) upon receiving a bona fide tender offer, the target corporation is required to put itself up for auction in an attempt to obtain more favorable bids from other potential acquirers (*see generally* Lucian Bebchuk, *The Case for Facilitating Competing Tender Offers*, 95 Harv. L. Rev. 1028 (1982)). Another approach advanced is to require a "freeze" period for a significant amount of time, such as six months. During that period, absent shareholder approval, no structural change (such as the grant of an option to sell a key asset to a friendly suitor) would be allowed. *See* Lowenstein, *supra* note 116. For one of the early articles on this subject, *see* Gary G. Lynch and Marc I. Steinberg, *The Legitimacy of Defensive Tactics in Tender Offers*, 64 Cornell L. Rev. 901 (1979).

The protection of the business judgment rule is not appropriate in the tender offer setting. With respect to a maneuver that has received shareholder approval for its possible use, the target corporation's board of directors must act reasonably with respect to its deployment. Having a cache of weapons does not give the board carte blanche to launch them. Rather, upon a showing that the subject directors are sufficiently informed, disinterested, and independent, the use of a particular maneuver is justified—provided that such deployment serves the corporation's and, collectively, the shareholders' best interests.

B. Summation

In addition to addressing specific defensive and offensive tactics that may change over time due to responses to judicial, legislative, and regulatory developments as well as the implementation of innovative techniques,[140] the recommendations herein generally apply on a uniform basis regardless of the particular maneuver at issue. This approach enhances commercial certainty, providing participants with a clearer vision of measures that must receive shareholder approbation. Importantly, shareholder interests are duly protected as the adoption of any substantive tactic can be legally undertaken only if shareholder approval is obtained. This approach thus strikes a proper balance and should be implemented.[141]

[140] *See* Statement by Stanley Sporkin in *Tender Offers*, *supra* note 98, at 329 (stating that "[o]ne of the major problems [in takeover regulation] . . . is the tremendous creative ability of the specialists that perform in this field [as they] always seem to come up with a new offensive tactic or new defensive response").

[141] The efficacy of the shareholder vote has been questioned on several grounds. These reasons include: the collective action shareholder voting problem that exists in publicly-held companies; the failure of proxy advisers, due to their constrained resources, to provide more meaningful voting recommendations tailored to specific companies; and the lack of incentives to induce actively managed funds and other institutional investors to expend the resources necessary to make sufficiently informed decisions that enhance shareholder value. For literature on this subject, *see, e.g.*, Lucian A. Bebchuk et al., *The Agency Problems of Institutional Investors*, 31 J. Econ. Persp. 89 (2017); James D. Cox et al., *Understanding the (Ir)Relevance of Shareholder Votes in M&A Deals*, 69 Duke L.J. 503 (2019); sources cited in Chapter 5 herein, at note 173. Nonetheless, it may be posited that the shareholder vote provides the key basis for supporting the legitimization of the separation of ownership and control and has the beneficial effect of focusing a subject board of directors' attention on the propriety of its decision-making "through the lens of shareholder interests," thereby significantly improving board governing processes and determinations. *See* Bernard S. Sharfman, *Enhancing the Value of Shareholder Voting Recommendations*, 86 Tenn. L. Rev. 691, 697 (2019); Leo E. Strine, Jr., *Can We Do Better for Ordinary Investors? A Pragmatic Reaction to the Dueling Ideological Mythologists of Corporate Law*, 114 Colum. L. Rev. 449, 453–55 (2014). The ultimate result should be the effectuation of decisions that further the subject corporation's and, collectively, the shareholders' best interests.

IV. Conclusion

This chapter generally reviews the current regulatory aspects for M&A transactions and thereafter proffers necessary revisions for implementation. While the SEC and Congress merit kudos for establishing an overall admirable M&A framework, significant gaps prevail. The discussion herein addresses these shortcomings and their importance. The solutions recommended focus on the federal government's deserved status to serve as the principal regulator overseeing the M&A process and its substantive impact. Among other suggestions, state anti-takeover statutes should be federally preempted and the legitimacy of measures undertaken in response to takeover bids should be within the province of federal law. As discussed herein, an essential condition whether any such defensive or offensive maneuver is permissible and given effect is whether shareholder approval is obtained. The recommendations advanced herein: do not materially impede M&A deals; facilitate a neutral playing field; recognize that shareholder voice merits a primary role; and correctly place matters of national policy with the federal government.

9

The Securities and Exchange Commission

I. Introduction

The Securities and Exchange Commission (SEC) and the U.S. Department of Justice (DOJ) have far-reaching authority to enforce the federal securities laws. While the DOJ pursues alleged criminal violators, the SEC regulates the multi-faceted aspects of federal securities law. In addition, the Commission oversees the self-regulatory organizations, including the stock exchanges and the Financial Industry Regulatory Authority (FINRA).[1] While the SEC is to be commended for the diligence of its staff and the propriety of many of its practices,[2] the Commission's zeal for the vigorous enforcement of the securities laws and its principal mission of protecting investors has dissipated over the past few decades.[3] In previous chapters, several examples of these failures have been addressed.[4]

This chapter focuses on key policy determinations made by the SEC during the last two decades that are unacceptable and should be highlighted. Once uncovered, the challenge presented is to provide a justifiable explanation for

---

[1] *See, e.g.*, § 15A of the Securities Exchange Act, 15 U.S.C. § 78o-3 (FINRA); § 19 of the Securities Exchange Act, 15 U.S.C. § 78s (national securities exchanges).

[2] Earlier chapters of this book addressed several positive actions by the Commission. Examples include: the adoption of an integrated disclosure framework; the focus on qualitative economic materiality; adaptability with respect to insider trading regulation; the promulgation of the all holders rule; and addressing concerns in going-private transactions. *See* discussion in Chapters 2, 4, 5, 7, and 8 herein. The Commission's diligent staff is widely acknowledged. *See, e.g.*, SEC Report on the 38th Annual Government-Business Forum on Small Business Capital Formation, Omaha NE, Aug. 14, 2019, available at https://www.sec.gov/files/small-business-forum-report-2019.pdf (referring to "the hardworking staff at the SEC").

[3] *See, e.g.*, Steve Coll and David A. Vise, *Eagle on the Street* (1992) (focusing on the SEC's efforts to protect investors, often unsuccessful, during the 1980s); Jesse Eisinger, *The Chickenshit Club: Why the Justice Department Fails to Prosecute Executives* 296 (2017) (stating that three years after the financial crisis the SEC had hardly instituted any enforcement actions and mainly focused on low-level tangential offenders).

[4] Examples include the SEC's focus on capital formation rather than investor protection in the exempt offering context (Chapter 3), enabling disclosure gaps in SEC filings (Chapters 2 and 4), and adopting an excessive safe harbor for insider trading plans (Chapter 7).

Rethinking Securities Law. Marc I. Steinberg, Oxford University Press. © Marc I. Steinberg 2021.
DOI: 10.1093/oso/9780197583142.003.0009

the Commission's conduct. After all, the SEC's primary objectives should be to enhance transparency, market integrity, and investor protection.[5] After addressing the Commission's numerous failures to engage in meaningful regulation and enforcement, the chapter recommends a fundamental solution that should substantially ameliorate the current unpalatable situation.

II. The SEC's Unacceptable Focus

The following discussion addresses key failures by the SEC during the past several decades. A number of these shortcomings involve SEC inaction, even when the Commission has clear statutory authority (and at times congressional direction) to undertake appropriate regulation. Other measures have been proactively pursued by the Commission to favor corporate interests at the expense of investors. Viewed cumulatively, the Commission's policies evidence misplaced priorities that poorly reflect on an agency that historically has been viewed as preeminent.[6]

A. Adoption of a Current Reporting System

Prior to the adoption of the Sarbanes-Oxley Act of 2002,[7] a black hole existed in the mandatory disclosure framework in this country. During the interim between periodic reports, with certain exceptions,[8] no disclosure of material information was mandated by the federal securities

[5] Another Commission objective is to facilitate capital formation. *See* Securities and Exchange Commission, *The Mission of the SEC* (2020), available at https://www.sec.gov/about/what-we-do. The SEC is widely perceived as an agency foremost concerned with investor protection. *See* History.com Editors, *SEC: Securities and Exchange Commission* (Dec. 6, 2019), available at https://www.history.com/topics/us-government/securities-and-exchange-commission ("The Securities and Exchange Commission, or SEC, is an independent federal agency tasked with protecting investors and capital, overseeing the stock market and proposing and enforcing federal securities law.").

[6] *See* discussion *infra* notes 7–126 and accompanying text. This point has been made at various points in the book. *See, e.g.*, Chapters 2, 3, and 4 herein.

[7] Pub. L. No. 107-204, 116 Stat. 745 (2002). Aspects of the Sarbanes-Oxley Act are addressed in other chapters, including, for example, in Chapters 2 and 5 herein.

[8] Prior to the Sarbanes-Oxley Act and the Commission's amendments to Form 8-K, 17 C.F.R. § 249.308, the following five items were required to be disclosed under Form 8-K: "Changes in Control of Registrant (Item 1), Acquisition or Disposition of Assets [Not Within the Normal Course of Business] (Item 2), Bankruptcy or Receivership (Item 3), Changes in Registrant's Certifying Accountant (Item 4), and Resignations of Registrant's Directors (Item 6)." Marc I. Steinberg, *Understanding Securities Law* 193 n. 125 (1989).

laws.[9] Although stock exchange rules generally call for disclosure of such information,[10] investors lack a private remedy for violation of SRO rules and the exchanges themselves rarely take enforcement action against listed companies for such failures to disclose.[11]

Recognizing this deficiency, Congress directed the SEC in the Sarbanes-Oxley Act to remedy this situation, providing that an Exchange Act reporting company "shall disclose to the public on a rapid and current basis such additional information concerning material changes in the financial condition or operations of the issuer, in plain English, which may include trend and qualitative information and graphic presentations, as the Commission determines, by rule, is necessary or useful for the protection of investors and the public interest."[12] Pursuant to this statute, the Commission was given the authority to promulgate timely disclosure standards that were comparable to other developed markets whereby, absent justifiable business reason, all material information must be publicly and promptly disclosed.[13] This approach is favored by this author as discussed in Chapters 2 and 4 herein. Rather than seizing this opportunity, however, the Commission delayed until 2004 to implement this directive and did so in a manner favorable to listed companies.[14]

While the SEC's adoption of a current reporting framework expands the scope of matters that must be disclosed within an inordinately long four

---

[9] *See* Marc I. Steinberg, *Insider Trading, Selective Disclosure, and Prompt Disclosure: A Comparative Analysis*, 22 U. Pa. J. Int'l Econ. L. 635, 658 (2001) (stating that the "black hole in the U.S. continuous disclosure framework, in practical effect, occurs most frequently where adverse financial information exists relating to the subject company"). In this regard, the SEC made a number of statements urging publicly-held companies to make accurate and prompt disclosure of material developments. *See, e.g.*, Timely Disclosure of Material Corporate Developments, Securities Act Release No. 5092 (1970) ("Notwithstanding the fact that a company complies with [its] reporting requirements, it still has an obligation to make full and prompt announcements of material facts regarding the company's financial condition"). Nonetheless, these pronouncements were hortatory. *See* Chapter 2 herein for further discussion.

[10] *See, e.g.*, New York Stock Exchange (NYSE), Listed Company Manual §§ 202.01–.06; Nasdaq Listing Rules, Disclosure of Material Information Rule, IM-5250(b)(1); discussion in Chapter 2 herein.

[11] *See, e.g.*, *Harris v. TD Ameritrade, Inc.*, 805 F.3d 664 (6th Cir. 2015); *Walck v. American Stock Exchange*, 687 F.2d 778 (3d Cir. 1982); *State Teachers Retirement Board v. Fluor Corp.*, 654 F.2d 843 (2d Cir. 1981); *Jablon v. Dean Witter & Co.*, 614 F.2d 677 (9th Cir. 1980). Over fifty years ago, a number of courts implied a private right of action in this setting. *See, e.g.*, *Buttrey v. Merrill Lynch, Pierce, Fenner & Smith, Inc.*, 410 F.2d 135 (7th Cir. 1969). These cases evidently no longer are followed. *See* discussion in Chapter 2 herein.

[12] Section 409 of the Sarbanes Oxley Act, *codified at* § 13l of the Securities Exchange Act, 15 U.S.C. § 78m(l).

[13] The continuous disclosure mandates adopted by other developed markets are discussed in Chapters 2 and 4 herein.

[14] *See* Securities Exchange Act Release No. 49424 (2004).

business days in the Form 8-K,[15] the Commission declined to mandate the disclosure of all material information. Inexplicably, for example, the loss of a major contract by a subject company need not be disclosed in the Form 8-K—even when the loss of such contract is irretrievable and certain.[16] Such material information may remain embargoed until the filing of the next periodic report, thereby adversely impacting transparency, the efficient market for that security, and investor knowledge.[17] As another example, although the departure of an executive officer must be disclosed in the Form 8-K, the reasons for such resignation, retirement, or removal need not be disclosed.[18] This rule makes no sense. Clearly, institutional and other active investors as well as the financial community will want to know more. Yet, if the company provides more detailed information selectively, it risks violating Regulation FD.[19] The consequence all too frequently is general "sanitized" disclosure being contained in the Form 8-K with investors and the securities markets being ill informed.[20]

B. Insulating Liability Exposure for Companies and Their Insiders

As discussed in the foregoing, with respect to implementing the continuous disclosure mandate prescribed by the Sarbanes-Oxley Act, the SEC opted for a scaled-back version. In so doing, the Commission provided key accommodations to Exchange Act reporting companies—namely, declining

---

[15] *See* 17 C.F.R. § 249.308; discussion in Chapter 2 herein. This four business day period is far too long. *Cf.* Regulation FD, discussed in Chapters 2 and 7 herein, whereby the called for disclosure must be made generally within one business day.

[16] *See* Securities Exchange Act Release No. 49424 (2004) (reasoning that it could be difficult for the registrant to ascertain when the contract terminated and that mandating such disclosure could be used as a negotiation tactic by contracting parties).

[17] If material, the terminated contract would be required to be disclosed pursuant to Item 303 (MD&A) of Regulation S-K. *See* discussion in Chapter 2 herein.

[18] *See* Item 5.02 of Form 8-K. The SEC reasoned that disclosure of the supposed reasons for the executive officer's departure may embarrass the officer or result in the officer bringing a defamation action against the company. *See* Securities Exchange Act Release No. 49424 (2004).

[19] 17 C.F.R. § 243.100 *et seq. See* Securities Exchange Act Release No. 43154 (2000) (adopting Release). With certain exceptions, Regulation FD prohibits a subject corporation or a person acting on its behalf from selectively disclosing material nonpublic information concerning that corporation or its securities. Regulation FD is discussed in Chapters 2 and 7 herein.

[20] An example of a generalized disclosure in this context is that the subject officer "resigned for personal and professional reasons." In the author's experience as an expert witness, this language was used in two different cases explaining an executive officer's departure, both of which culminated in a settlement whereby the plaintiffs recovered damages.

to adopt a continuous disclosure framework requiring the immediate disclosure (absent the existence of meritorious business justification) of all material information and providing loopholes where clearly material information need not be disclosed in the Form 8-K (such as the irretrievable loss of a major contract).[21] Perhaps somewhat unnoticed, however, the Commission went significantly further by insulating from Section 10(b) liability reporting companies and their insiders for their failure to disclose specified items within a Form 8-K.[22] Pursuant to this safe harbor provision, a subject company and its insiders, knowing of material nonpublic information that is required to be disclosed pursuant to Form 8-K, may deliberately decline to file a Form 8-K as to that information and thereby avoid Section 10(b) liability for such failure in both government and private actions.[23]

What can possibly be the Commission's rationale for adopting this safe harbor provision? After all, establishing a meritorious Section 10(b) case is arduous due to the mandate that such criteria as scienter, materiality, reliance, loss causation, and damages must be shown.[24] The only plausible explanation is clear: to deprive investors of their right to institute a class action under the federal securities laws for such a blatant disclosure violation.[25]

---

[21] *See* discussion *supra* notes 15–20 and accompanying text; discussion in Chapters 2 and 4 herein.

[22] *See* Rule 13a-11(c), 17 C.F.R. § 240.13a-11(c) ("No failure to file a report on Form 8-K that is required solely pursuant to Item 1.01, 1.02, 2.03, 2.04, 2.05, 2.06, 4.02(a), 5.02(e) or 6.03 of Form 8-K shall be deemed to be a violation of Section 10(b) and Rule 10b-5."). *See generally* Allan Horwich, *A Call for the SEC to Adopt More Safe Harbors that Limit the Reach of Rule 10b-5*, 74 Bus. Law. 53 (2018).

[23] *See* Securities Exchange Act Release No. 49424 (2004). This safe harbor includes the following Items of Form 8-K:

Item 1.01 Entry into a Material Definitive Agreement

Item 1.02 Termination of a Material Definitive Agreement

Item 2.03 Creation of a Direct Financial Obligation or an Obligation under an Off-Balance Sheet Arrangement of a Registrant

Item 2.04 Trigger Events that Accelerate or Increase a Direct Financial Obligation or an Obligation under an Off-Balance Sheet Arrangement

Item 2.05 Costs Associated with Exit or Disposal Activities

Item 2.06 Material Impairments

Item 4.02(a) Non-Reliance on Previously Issued Financial Statements or a Related Audit Report or Completed Interim Review (in the case where a company makes the determination and does not receive a notice described in Item 4.02(b) from its independent accountant)

Item 5.02(c) Executive Officer Employment and Compensation Arrangements

Id.

[24] *See* discussion in Chapter 6 herein. Of course, in a government proceeding, reliance, loss causation, and damages are not required to be proven.

[25] Provided that the materially misleading information in the Form 8-K is "filed" (and not "furnished"), an Exchange Act Section 18(a) private right of action is available. However, this statute has not successfully been invoked in class actions because of its individualized reliance requirement. *See* Chapter 6 herein. Note, moreover, that depending on the applicable state law, a right of action may exist under state securities or common law. Nonetheless, the Securities Litigation Uniform

As for the SEC, even with the safe harbor, the Commission may bring an enforcement action against a subject defendant pursuant to a number of alternative provisions, such as a reporting violation of Section 13(a) of the Securities Exchange Act[26] and a fraud violation under Section 17(a) of the Securities Act.[27] Under both of these provisions, no private right of action is recognized.[28] For investors, however, without the availability of the Section 10(b) remedy, they are left without class action redress under the federal securities laws.[29] The adoption of this safe harbor provision speaks volumes as to the Commission's flexibility toward insulating corporate miscreants from being held liable in private actions to ordinary investors—a position that is untenable for a government agency charged with investor protection.

The Commission's solicitousness in this respect also is illustrated by its adoption of a "filed" versus "furnished" distinction. Under several SEC rules, a subject company may elect to "furnish" rather than to "file" certain information contained in its SEC required documents. For example, specified items called for in the Form 10-Q (quarterly report)[30] and Form 8-K (current report)[31] may be furnished rather than filed with the

---

Standards Act of 1998 (SLUSA), Pub. L. No. 105-353, 112 Stat. 3227 (1998), preempts state law (with certain carve-outs) for class actions involving nationally traded securities. This subject is addressed in Chapter 6 herein.

[26] 15 U.S.C. § 78m(a) (requiring Exchange Act reporting companies to file with the SEC reports "as the Commission may prescribe as necessary or appropriate for the proper protection of investors and to insure fair dealing in the security").

[27] 15 U.S.C. § 77q(a) (prohibiting misstatements, schemes to defraud, and conduct which operates as a scheme to defraud in the offer or sale of securities). *See Aaron v. Securities and Exchange Commission*, 446 U.S. 680 (1980) (holding that the SEC is required to prove scienter in actions instituted for alleged violation of § 17(a)(1) of the Securities Act and § 10(b) of the Exchange Act but need not prove scienter with respect to § 17(a)(2) and 17(a)(3)).

[28] *See, e.g., Northstar Financial Advisors, Inc. v. Schwab Investments*, 618 F.3d 1106 (9th Cir. 2010) (holding no private right under § 13(a) of the Exchange Act); *Landry v. All American Assurance Co.*, 688 F.2d 381 (5th Cir. 1982) (holding no private right of action under § 17(a) of the Securities Act); Marc I. Steinberg, *Securities Regulation: Liabilities and Remedies* §§ 6.05[2], 9.03(2020) (and cases cited therein).

[29] Under certain circumstances, a state remedy may be available. *See supra* note 25; discussion in Chapter 6 herein.

[30] With respect to the Form 10-Q: "The information required by Items 1 (Financial Statements), 2 (Management's Discussion and Analysis of Financial Condition and Results of Operations) and 3 (Quantitative and Qualitative Disclosures About Market Risk) of Part I of the Form 10-Q is not deemed to be filed for purposes of Section 18 of the Exchange Act." Securities Exchange Act Release No. 84842 at n. 61 (2018). *See* Rule 13a-13(d), 17 C.F.R. § 240.13a-13(d) (stating that "the financial information required by Part I of Form 10-Q shall not be deemed to be 'filed' for the purpose of section 18 of the [Exchange] Act or otherwise subject to the liabilities of that section of the Act but shall be subject to all other provisions of the Act").

[31] Pursuant to Form 8-K, information called for by Items 2.02 ("Results of Operations and Financial Condition") and 7.01 ("Regulation FD Disclosure") may be furnished. *See* General Instructions at B.2. of Form 8-K, 17 C.F.R. § 249.308 (providing that "[t]he information in a

Commission.[32] By electing to furnish the SEC report, an issuer and other prospective defendants avert both Securities Act Section 11 and Exchange Act Section 18(a) liability exposure.

By its terms, Section 18(a) imposes liability upon any person who makes or causes to be made a materially false or misleading statement contained in a document (such as a Form 10-Q) that is "filed" pursuant to the Exchange Act (or pursuant to any rule or regulation thereunder), subject to certain conditions.[33] With respect to Section 11, pursuant to the integrated disclosure framework as discussed in Chapters 2 and 4 herein, specified SEC "filed" Exchange Act reports are incorporated by reference into the subject Securities Act registration statement.[34] If the affected issuer is undertaking a continuous shelf registered offering, it may well opt to "file" (rather than "furnish"). For example, as the SEC has observed, a company conducting an ongoing registered offering "may choose to file" earnings release information contained in its Form 8-K "to ensure that a registration statement currently in use does not contain a material omission of the information contained in an earnings release."[35] Such incorporation by reference signifies that these filings are assessed pursuant to the investor-friendly provisions of Section 11, thereby substantially increasing the liability exposure of the issuer, its directors and officers, as well as the underwriters and experts for the registered offering.[36]

On the other hand, if an Exchange Act reporting company elects to furnish rather than file specified information when it is permitted to do so, no Securities Act Section 11 or Exchange Act Section 18(a) liability will ensue. In this fashion, the SEC has eviscerated important remedies that investors would otherwise be entitled to invoke. Although plaintiffs may bring suit alleging violations of Section 10(b), this provision presents a more difficult

---

report furnished pursuant to Item 2.02 . . . or Item 7.01 . . . shall not be deemed to be 'filed' for purposes of Section 18 of the Exchange Act or otherwise subject to the liabilities of that section, unless the registrant specifically states that the information is to be considered 'filed' under the Exchange Act or incorporates it by reference into a filing under the Securities Act or the Exchange Act").

32 *See supra* notes 30, 31. As another example, a company's annual report to its security holders is not deemed a "filed" report. *See* Securities Exchange Act Release No. 3380 (1943).

33 15 U.S.C. § 78r(a). Section 18(a) is discussed in Chapter 6 herein.

34 *See* discussion in Chapters 2 and 4 herein.

35 Securities Exchange Act Release No. 84842 at n. 35 (2018).

36 *See* 15 U.S.C. § 77k. The concept of due diligence and its ramifications in the shelf registration setting are addressed in Chapter 4 herein.

challenge.[37] Moreover, unlike Sections 11 and 18(a) where there may be a wide range of collateral actors who are subject to liability,[38] only primary violators may be sued in Section 10(b) private actions.[39]

Proponents who support the Commission's approach assert that applying the strict provisions of Section 11 to a reporting company's Exchange Act periodic reporting obligations is inappropriate.[40] Given Section 11's strict due diligence defense (with no such defense provided to the issuer) as well as its lack of reliance and loss causation requirements,[41] this position has some appeal. But there are stronger counterarguments. First, if this diminution in investor remedies is implemented, such action should be effectuated by congressional action.[42] Second, it is improper for a regulatory agency charged with investor protection to proactively divest aggrieved investors of remedies that they otherwise would be able to assert.[43] Third, shelf registered offerings benefit Exchange Act reporting companies by enabling these companies to more successfully access the public markets with less expense due in part to incorporation by reference.[44] As a quid pro quo for this substantial benefit, the rigorous Section 11 provisions should apply to instill greater discipline to be exercised by directors, officers, and underwriters in the shelf registration framework.[45]

---

[37] *See* 15 U.S.C. § 78j(b). Section 10(b) and Rule 10b-5 promulgated thereunder are discussed in Chapters 2 and 6 herein.

[38] Under Section 11, liability exposure extends to the issuer, signatories of the registration statement (including the issuer's chief executive officer and its chief financial officer), the issuer's directors, underwriters for the offering, and experts (with respect to that part of the registration statement that the expert "expertises"). Generally, under Section 18(a), those persons who "make or cause to be made" a materially false or misleading statement that is contained in an Exchange Act filing are subject to liability exposure under that statute.

[39] *See Central Bank of Denver v. First Interstate Bank of Denver*, 511 U.S. 164 (1994) (foreclosing aiding and abetting liability in private actions under § 10(b)). For further discussion, *see* Chapter 6 herein.

[40] *See* discussion in David B.H. Martin and Graham Robinson, *Securities Disclosure: To Be or Not To Be "Filed,"* 17 Insights No. 8, at 16 (Sept. 2003).

[41] *See* discussion in Chapters 4 and 6 herein.

[42] Although the Commission has broad exemptive authority under Section 28 of the Securities Act, 15 U.S.C. § 78bb, expansive diminution in investor remedies should be outside the parameters of this provision. This statute also limits the SEC's exemptive authority to the Securities Act and its rules and regulations. Moreover, as a matter of policy, such administrative activism, altering the statutory framework to the detriment of investors, should be disfavored.

[43] As the Commission is deemed to be the "guardian" of the investing public, divesting plaintiffs of key remedies is unacceptable. *See* Securities and Exchange Commission, *The "Work" We Do* (2013), available at https:www.sec.gov/about/what-we-do.

[44] *See* discussion in Chapters 2 and 4 herein.

[45] In an effort to instill greater discipline in the preparation of the Form 10-K, the SEC requires that a majority of the registrant's directors sign the Form 10-K. *See* Securities Exchange Act Release No. 6231 (1980) ("The Commission believes that just as its rules and administrative focus of the Division of Corporation Finance are being realigned to reflect the shift in emphasis toward relying on periodic

Fourth, the number of Section 11 actions on an annual basis is not so large as to warrant as a matter of policy its elimination in this setting. During 2019, with many lawsuits involving relatively smaller companies (including with respect to their initial public offerings (IPOs)), there were a total of sixty-five filings in federal and state courts alleging violations of Section 11.[46] And fifth, the onerous tracing requirement that federal courts apply in Section 11 cases drastically limits the pool of prospective plaintiffs when an active secondary trading market for the subject securities exists.[47]

More baffling is the SEC's divestment of the Exchange Act's Section 18(a) remedy when an Exchange Act reporting company chooses to furnish rather than file specified information.[48] In this setting, the Commission's rationale evidently is to eliminate the Section 18(a) right of action as it may impose undue hardship on a subject issuer, its insiders, and affected collateral participants.[49] For the SEC to proactively eviscerate a remedy that Congress adopted in its enactment of the 1934 Act is disconcerting.

Accordingly, the SEC should eliminate the filed versus furnished distinction. A publicly-held company should not be able to choose the liability ramifications of its faulty disclosures when it provides periodic reports to the Commission that are relied upon by the investing public and the securities

---

disclosure under the Exchange Act, so too the attention of the private sector, including management, directors, accountants, and attorneys, must also be refocused towards Exchange Act filings if a sufficient degree of discipline is to be instilled in the system to make it work.").

[46] *See* Cornerstone Research, *Securities Class Action Filings: 2019 Year in Review* at 22 (2020), available at https://www.cornerstone.com/Publications/Reports/Securities-Class-Action-Filings-2019-Year-in-Review ("In 2019, the combined number of federal Section 11 filings and state 1933 Act filings was 65 [consisting of] 22 parallel filings, 27 state-only filings, and 16 federal-only filings.") *See also Salzberg v. Sciabacucchi*, 227 A.3d 102, 114–15 (Del. 2020) (citing and quoting the Cornerstone Research 2019 Year in Review).

[47] *See, e.g., Krim v. pcOrder.com*, 402 F.3d 489 (5th Cir. 2005) (requiring tracing to be established with 100% certainty even when the pool of stock in the aftermarket was comprised of 99.85% of shares that were traced to the applicable registered offering). This onerous requirement has been criticized by this author. *See* Marc I. Steinberg and Brent A. Kirby, *The Assault on Section 11 of the Securities Act: A Study in Judicial Activism*, 63 Rutgers L. Rev. 1 (2010).

[48] Section 18(a)'s scope is limited to a subject "application, report, or document" being "filed" with the SEC pursuant to the Exchange Act "or any rule or regulation thereunder or any undertaking contained in a registration statement as provided in subsection (d) of section 15." 15 U.S.C. § 78r(a). Likewise, certain materials may be furnished rather than filed to avoid liability exposure under the proxy statute, Section 14(a) of the Securities Exchange Act (15 U.S.C. § 78n(a)) and Rule 14a-9 (17 C.F.R. § 240.14a-9). *See* Martin and Robinson, *supra* note 40, at 18 (stating that "the purpose of deeming disclosure to be 'not filed' was to eliminate liability under Section 18 of the Exchange Act (and, when applicable, under Section 14(a) of the Exchange Act and Rule 14a-9 thereunder)" and that, with that objective, the Commission did not require the filing of the "proxy statement disclosure of the compensation committee report relating to executive compensation"), *citing*, Securities Act Release No. 6962 (1992).

[49] *See* Martin and Robinson, *supra* note 40, at 18; *supra* note 48.

markets. Benefitting from accessing the public markets and raising capital thereby, these companies should not be extended favored treatment at the expense of aggrieved investors. Hence, the liability provisions of the federal securities laws should remain intact without the SEC engaging in undue regulatory activism. If this liability framework should be altered, that task suitably is left for Congress.[50]

C. Enforcement Policies, Practices, and Priorities

The SEC settles a vast majority of its enforcement actions pursuant to the consent negotiation process whereby the defendant agrees to specified sanctions without admitting or denying wrongdoing.[51] These consent decrees, a practice that largely originated from my mentor then SEC Enforcement Director Stanley Sporkin,[52] generally have aptly served the Commission's interests. In this manner, pending matters can be more expeditiously resolved with the SEC procuring much of the relief desired without an undue expenditure of its resources.[53]

When enforcement actions are instituted in federal court, consent decrees must receive judicial approval to become effective.[54] Perhaps due to harsh criticism by a number of judges who considered the SEC's requested relief as inadequate in view of the seriousness of the alleged misconduct,[55] the

[50] *See* discussion *supra* notes 42–49 and accompanying text.

[51] *See* William R. McLucas et al., *"Neither Admit Nor Deny" Settlements from the Stanley Sporkin Era: Wise Policy or Outdated Enforcement Notion?*, 43 Sec. Reg. L.J. 29, 29 (2015) ("Over the last 40 years, the Commission's standard approach has been to permit defendants to enter into a settlement without admitting or denying the allegations against them (i.e., on a 'neither admit nor deny' basis).").

[52] *See* Theodore A. Levine and Edward D. Herlihy, *The Father of Enforcement*, 43 Sec. Reg. L.J. 7, 9 (2015) ("Judge Sporkin's greatest achievement in leading the Commission's expanding enforcement program was the use of the consent decree."). *See also* Arthur M. Mathews, *Effective Defense of SEC Investigations: Laying the Foundation for Successful Disposition of Subsequent Civil, Administrative, and Criminal Proceedings*, 24 Emory L.J. 567 (1975).

[53] *See* Levine and Herlihy, *supra* note 52, at 9 ("These consent decrees, which normally included various forms of equitable relief, were the most effective way to resolve an enforcement matter because they avoided the expense and risk of litigation, allowed the Commission to get the relief it had sought, and allowed defendants to avoid collateral estoppel consequences.").

[54] *See, e.g.*, *Securities and Exchange Commission v. Citigroup Global Markets, Inc.*, 752 F.3d 285 (2d Cir. 2014); *Securities and Exchange Commission v. Randolph*, 736 F.2d 525 (9th Cir. 1984).

[55] For example, Judge Jed Rakoff called the SEC's "neither admit nor deny" consent process "hallowed by history, but not by reason." *Securities and Exchange Commission v. Citigroup Global Markets, Inc.*, 827 F. Supp. 2d 328, 332 (S.D.N.Y. 2011), *rev'd*, 752 F.3d 285 (2d Cir. 2014). In rejecting the proposed settlement, which was reversed on appeal, Judge Rakoff opined that "a proposed Consent Judgment that asks the Court to impose substantial injunctive relief, enforced by the Court's

Commission is bringing an increasingly larger percentage of its proceedings in the administrative forum where no judicial approval is required to effectuate the settlement.[56] A substantial number of these cases are settled with a civil money penalty, disgorgement of profits, a non-scienter-based alleged violation, and no charges against individuals.[57]

Indeed, for the last two decades, the SEC has levied large civil money penalties against entities as standard fare, including in some cases the levying of hundreds of millions, if not billions, of dollars of penalties, since the aftermath of the financial crisis of 2008.[58] Opponents, including some SEC Commissioners, have criticized this practice as harmful to the very shareholders who were

---

own contempt power, on the basis of allegations unsupported by any proven or acknowledged facts whatsoever, is neither reasonable, nor fair, nor adequate, nor in the public interest." 827 F. Supp. 2d at 335. Reversing, the Second Circuit held that "the district court abused its discretion by applying an incorrect legal standard in assessing the consent decree." 752 F.3d at 289.

In 2013, the SEC announced that it would require admissions of wrongdoing in especially egregious cases. Factors that the Commission assess are "the need for public acknowledgment and accountability, the egregiousness of the offense, and the amount of harm to investors." *[Chair] White Announces Revisions of SEC "No Admit" Settlement Policy*, 45 Sec. Reg. & L. Rep. (BNA) 1150 (2013). Since its adoption, the SEC's "policy of requiring admissions has been used sparingly . . . [with] admissions . . . obtained in settlements . . . [in] well under two percent of the individuals and entities charged." David Rosenfeld, *Admissions in SEC Enforcement Cases: The Revolution That Wasn't*, 103 Iowa L. Rev. 113, 116 (2017) (*id.* at 117—stating that it "appears that the SEC is typically seeking admissions from large financial institutions in cases where no individuals are being charged and where there is no realistic possibility of collateral consequences such as criminal charges, private class actions, or regulatory sanctions"). *See* Verity Winship and Jennifer K. Robbennolt, *An Empirical Study of Admissions in SEC Settlements*, 50 Ariz. L. Rev. 1, 1 (2017) (stating that the "number of settlements including admissions is low").

56 *See* Jean Eaglesham, *SEC Steers More Trials to Judges It Appoints*, Wall St. J., Oct. 21, 2014, at A1. *See also Securities and Exchange Commission v. Citigroup Global Markets, Inc.*, 752 F.3d 285, 295 (2d Cir. 2014) (stating "to the extent that the S.E.C. does not wish to engage with the courts, it is free to eschew the involvement of the courts and employ its own arsenal of remedies instead").

57 *See* David Rosenfeld, *Civil Penalties Against Public Companies in SEC Enforcement Actions: An Empirical Analysis*, 22 U. Pa. J. Bus. L. 135, 135–36 (2019). *See also* Marc I. Steinberg and Ralph C. Ferrara, *Securities Practice: Federal and State Enforcement* (2d ed. 2001 and 2020–2021 supp.).

58 *See, e.g.*, Press Release, U.S. Dep't of Justice, No. 14-884, *Bank of America to Pay $16.65 Billion in Historic Justice Department Settlement for Financial Fraud Leading Up To and During the Financial Crisis* (Aug. 21, 2014), available at https://www.justice.gov/opa/pr/bank-america-pay-1665-billion-historic-justice-department-settlement-financial-fraud-leading; Press Release, U.S. Department of Justice, *Goldman Sachs Agrees to Pay More than $5 Billion in Connection with Its Sale of Residential Mortgage Backed Securities* (April 11, 2016), available at https://www.justice.gov/opa/pr/goldman-sachs-agrees-pay-more-5-billion-connection-its-sale-residential-mortgage-backed; Ben Eisen, *Wells Fargo Settles U.S. Probes*, Wall St. J., Feb. 22–23, 2020, at A1 (payment of $3 billion); *In the Matter of JP Morgan-Chase Bank, N.A.*, Securities Exchange Act Release No. 76694 (Dec. 18, 2015) (settlement with payment of $307 million); *In the Matter of Citigroup Alternative Investments LLC & Citigroup Global Markets LLC*, Securities Exchange Act Release No. 75710 (Aug. 15, 2015) (settlement with payment of $180 million); *In the Matter of Deutsche Bank AG*, Securities Exchange Act Release No. 75040 (May 26, 2015) (settlement with payment of $55 million); Patrick Thomas, *Mylan Settles SEC Lawsuit*, Wall St. J., Sept. 28–29, 2019, at B3 (settlement with payment of $30 million).

victimized by the misconduct.[59] The SEC counters by asserting that, along with the amounts disgorged by alleged wrongdoers,[60] money penalties can be deployed pursuant to the "fair funds" provision to compensate injured persons.[61] Statistics evidence that the Commission distributes substantial amounts pursuant to the fair funds provision. For example, in its 2019 Annual Report, the Division of Enforcement stated that $4.3 billion in disgorgement and penalties had been collected, with approximately $1.2 billion being returned to harmed persons.[62] Although not beyond dispute, another study lauds the SEC's success in its use of the fair funds provision.[63]

---

[59] *See, e.g.*, SEC Commissioner Paul S. Adkins, Remarks Before the Atlanta Chapter of the National Association of Corporate Directors (Feb. 23, 2005) ("Corporations fined for disclosure-based transgressions use shareholder money to pay for behavior of which the shareholders were victims."), available at https://www.sec.gov/news/speech/spch022305psa.htm; SEC Commissioner Cynthia A. Glassman, *SEC in Transition: What We've Done and What's Ahead* (June 15, 2005), available at https://www.sec.gov/news/speech/spch061505cag.htm; Rosenfeld, *supra* note 57, at 149 (quoting the preceding sources and stating that the propriety of levying money penalties against publicly-held enterprises contributed "to a deep division at the Commission.").

In 2006, the SEC issued the Penalty Statement to clarify the circumstances with respect to which the Commission will levy money penalties. *See* SEC Press Release 2006-4, available at https://www.sec.gov/news/press/2006-4.htm. The Penalty Statement looked to two principal factors: (1) "The presence or absence of a direct benefit to the corporation as a result of the violation"; and (2) "The degree to which the penalty will recompense or further harm the injured shareholders." Moreover, several additional factors are enumerated in the Penalty Statement, generally focusing on deterrence, the level of intent of the violator(s), remedial measures undertaken, and cooperation with law enforcement authorities, including the SEC. The Penalty Statement is not binding policy. Since its adoption, the Penalty Statement has been implemented by the Commission with varying degrees of enthusiasm. *See* discussion in Rosenfeld, *supra* note 57, at 149–54.

[60] The SEC's remedy of disgorgement was upheld by the U.S. Supreme Court in *Liu v. Securities and Exchange Commission*, 140 S. Ct. 1936, 1940 (2020) (generally upholding an award of disgorgement if such award "does not exceed a wrongdoer's net profits and is awarded" to victims of the wrongdoing).

[61] The fair funds provision was enacted pursuant to the Sarbanes-Oxley Act of 2002. *See* § 308 of the Sarbanes-Oxley Act, 15 U.S.C. § 7246. In addition to the fair funds provision, the SEC distributes funds to investors by means of disgorgement of the proceeds of unlawful gains, receivership actions, clawback actions, and coordinated government proceedings. *See generally* Andrew Kull, *Common-Law Restitution and the Madoff Liquidation*, 92 Bos. U. L. Rev. 939 (2012).

[62] *See* SEC Press Release 2019-233 (Nov. 6, 2019) at 4, available at https://www.sec.gov/news/press-release/2019-233 ("Through these [enforcement] actions, the SEC obtained judgments and orders totaling more than $4.3 billion in disgorgement and penalties . . . [and] also returned roughly $1.2 billion to harmed investors as a result of enforcement actions."); SEC Division of Enforcement, 2019 Annual Report at 16–17 (2019), available at https://www.sec.gov/files/enforcement-annual-report-2019.pdf (stating that in fiscal year 2019, the SEC obtained orders amounting to $3.248 billion in disgorgement and $1.101 billion in money penalties, with nearly $1.2 billion of funds being returned to injured investors).

[63] *See* Urska Velikonja, *Public Compensation for Private Harm: Evidence from the SEC's Fair Fund Distributions*, 67 Stan. L. Rev. 331, 334 (2015) (in a study of fair funds between 2002 and 2013, stating that the SEC distributed greater than 75% of all collected money penalties pursuant to fair funds and that "two-thirds of fair funds compensate investors for what can best be described as customer fraud or anticompetitive behavior by financial intermediaries . . . [thereby] compensat[ing] investors for losses where a private lawsuit is either unavailable or impractical"). *But see* U.S. Government Accountability Office (GAO) Letter dated April 22, 2010 to Honorable Dennis Moore, Chairman of the Subcommittee on Oversight and Investigations of the U.S. House of Representatives Committee on Financial Services at 3, available at https://www.gao.gov/assets/100/96667.pdf ("Since 2007, fewer

When settling with the SEC, it is common practice for defendants to seek waivers from disqualification provisions that otherwise would apply upon the effectiveness of the Commission's order.[64] As these disqualifiers would adversely impact the subject defendant's business operations, they are a key component of the consent negotiation process.[65] As statistics evidence, these waivers are disproportionately granted to large financial firms (even if they are recidivists) than to smaller financial firms.[66] This practice reinforces the

---

Fair Funds have been established and the collection and distribution of Fair Funds have increased, but many Fair Funds continue to remain open and active for years."). *See generally* Richard M. Buxbaum, *From TGS Conservatorships to Sarbanes-Oxley Fair Funds*, 71 SMU L. Rev. 653 (2018); Verity Winship, *Fair Funds and the SEC's Compensation of Injured Investors*, 60 Fla. L. Rev. 1103 (2008).

[64] *See* Urska Velikonja, *Waiving Disqualification: When Do Securities Violators Receive a Reprieve?*, 103 Cal. L. Rev. 1081 (2015). Generally, ineligible-issuer and bad actor disqualifiers bar individuals and entities from utilizing specified exemptions from Securities Act registration as well as from more favorable securities offering and disclosure treatment. For example, a bad actor disqualifier, absent grant of a waiver, automatically disqualifies a subject issuer from relying on the Rule 506 exemption (which is the exemption from Securities Act registration pursuant to which the largest amount of capital is raised—*see* discussion in Chapter 3 herein). As another example, absent grant of a waiver, a bad actor is barred from being classified as a well-known seasoned issuer (*see* discussion in Chapter 4 herein). Bad actor disqualification events include, for example: criminal convictions in connection with securities transactions; a court issued injunction restraining or enjoining such person from engaging in specified conduct in connection with the purchase or sale of a security; an order issued by a state securities commission barring the person from engaging in the business of insurance, banking, or securities; an order by the SEC suspending or revoking a person's registration as a broker or dealer; and a cease and desist order involving a scienter-based antifraud provision (such as Section 10(b) of the Securities Exchange Act). *See, e.g.*, Rule 262, 17 C.F.R. § 230.262. In this regard, absent grant of a waiver, "firms and individuals convicted of securities fraud cannot serve as investment advisors, investment fund managers, or fund underwriters for a period of ten years." Velikonja, *supra*, at 1090, *citing*, 15 U.S.C. § 80a-9(a). Note that pursuant to Regulation A and Regulation D, the bad actor disqualifier is triggered if "any of the issuer's directors, officers, general partners, promoters, or 10% owners, or the underwriter's partners, directors, or officers are subject to such a conviction, order, injunction, . . . bar [or cease and desist order based on violation of the antifraud provisions of the federal securities laws, violation of Section 5 of the Securities Act, or final order of specified federal and state regulatory authorities.]" Velikonja, *supra*, at 1092. For the disqualification to be waived, a showing of "good cause" must be established by the person seeking the waiver. *See, e.g.*, Rule 262(b), 17 C.F.R. § 230.262(b).

[65] *See* Mary Jo White, Chair of the Securities and Exchange Commission, *Understanding Disqualifications, Exemptions and Waivers Under the Federal Securities Laws*, Remarks at the Corporate Counsel Institute (March 12, 2015), available at https://www.sec.gov/news/speech/031215-spch-cmjw.html (stating that "the potential scope of disqualifications under the federal securities laws is quite wide and can have a very significant impact on market participants").

[66] *See* Velikonja, *supra* note 64, at 1081 (stating that the study shows that "large financial firms received a large majority of waivers, 81.6%"). With respect to the SEC's frequent granting of waivers to recidivists, *see* SEC Commissioner Kara M. Stein, Dissenting Statement Regarding Certain Waivers Granted by the Commission for Certain Entities Pleading Guilty to Criminal Charges Involving Manipulation of Foreign Exchange Rules (May 21, 2015), available at https://www.sec.gov/news/statement/stein-waivers-granted-dissenting-statement.html (dissenting and highlighting "the recidivism of these institutions," including granting Citigroup its fourth waiver since 2006, Barclays its third waiver since 2007, UBS its seventh waiver since 2008, JP Morgan

long-standing assertion that the SEC unjustifiably favors the large firms and excessively punishes smaller firms.[67]

As a final general observation, individuals are not ordinarily charged in SEC enforcement actions involving publicly-held companies or financial service firms. For example, from fiscal year 2014 through fiscal year 2018, in roughly seventeen percent of actions involving publicly-held companies were one or more individuals charged.[68] Moreover, in fiscal year 2018, in approximately five percent of proceedings involving financial institutions were one or more individuals charged.[69] Hence, pursuant to the consent negotiation process, entities usually are successful in persuading the SEC to refrain from charging their executives. As discussed later in this chapter, the failure of the Commission to pursue meritorious enforcement actions against executives and other high-level officials in large enterprises is unacceptable.[70]

In view of the foregoing observations, several corrective measures should be implemented. First, money penalties against corporations and other enterprises should be levied only if a substantial percentage of the

Chase its sixth waiver since 2008, and Royal Bank of Scotland Group its third waiver since 2013). More recently, then SEC Chairman Jay Clayton expressed the position that "a settling entity can request that the Commission consider an offer of settlement that simultaneously addresses both the underlying enforcement action and any related collateral disqualifications . . . includ[ing] a simultaneous waiver request." SEC Chairman Jay Clayton, Statement Regarding Offers of Settlement (July 3, 2019), available at https://www.sec.gov/news/public-statement/clayton-statement-regarding-offers-settlement.

[67] *See* Stavros Gadinis, *The SEC and the Financial Industry: Evidence from Enforcement Against Broker-Dealers*, 67 Bus. Law. 679 (2012). Providing an empirical account of the Commission's enforcement actions against brokerage firms and investment banks, Professor Gadinis found the following:

> The analysis shows that big-firm defendants fared better. . . . [W]hen big firms and their staff were engaged in misconduct, the SEC often brought actions based exclusively on corporate liability without naming any specific individuals as defendants. . . . [Moreover, in Commission] administrative proceedings, big-firm defendants were more likely than small-firm defendants to receive no industry ban. . . . The gap between big and small firms persists when the analysis is limited to the individual employees of such firms.

Id. at 728. Rather than being of recent vintage, this disparity has existed for several decades. *See, e.g.*, Helen L. Miller and Jeffrey Rasansky, *A Slap on the Wrist or a Punch in the Face: The SEC's Disproportionate Treatment of NYSE Member and Non-NYSE Member Firms*, 19 Sec. Reg. L.J. 243, 243 (1991) ("The SEC has consistently imposed harsher broker-dealer sanctions on non-NYSE member firms than on NYSE member firms for securities violations that appear fairly similar").

[68] *See* Rosenfeld, *supra* note 57, at 171 (With respect to the SEC charging individuals in cases involving publicly-held companies, from "FY 2014 through FY 2018, individuals were charged in 63 of the 360 actions (or in related actions) or 17.5%.").

[69] *Id.* at 172 (stating that for FY 2018, individuals were charged by the SEC in two of the thirty-seven SEC enforcement actions involving financial institutions amounting to 5.4% of such actions).

[70] *See infra* discussion notes 109–124 and accompanying text.

proceeds will be distributed to victims of the misconduct.[71] Otherwise, innocent shareholders will incur further financial harm due to the wrongdoing committed by insiders.[72] In situations, however, where the individual wrongdoers own a large equity interest in the subject enterprise, the imposition of a large money penalty may be more warranted.[73] Second, the SEC's frequent grant of waivers from disqualification consequences to large financial firms should undergo thorough review, with the adoption of a transparent policy that is more balanced and limited.[74] Third, financial firms, irrespective of their size, should receive comparable treatment when the SEC levies sanctions. Undue favoritism to larger financial firms and

[71] *See* Rosenfeld, *supra* note 57, at 135 (explaining the controversy of money penalties being imposed against publicly-held companies in that shareholders, who were not responsible and may have already incurred harm by the misconduct, indirectly bear the costs of the financial penalties).

[72] *See* sources cited *supra* note 59.

[73] Hence, owning a substantial percentage of the entity, the wrongdoers may well have indirectly profited from the wrongdoing. However, these individuals may not have the personal financial wherewithal to pay a large money penalty. Where the entity's revenues and earnings increased because of the wrongdoing perpetrated by such insiders, a substantial corporate money penalty is more warranted.

[74] The SEC's waiver policy has drawn criticism from members of both Houses of Congress. *See* Letter dated June 13, 2014 from Senator Sherrod Brown, Chairman of the Banking Subcommittee on Financial Institutions and Consumer Protection, to SEC Chair May Jo White, available at https://www.brown.senate.gov/newsroom/press/release/sen-brown-urges-sec-chair-to-stop-granting-waivers-from-securities-law-to-banks-with-civil-or-criminal-settlements-or-enforcement-actions (stating that the Commission's recent actions "imply that the SEC's policy appears to make waivers the rule rather than the exception . . . [and expressing the] hope that the SEC will reconsider and revise a process that has now been questioned by the public, lawmakers, and a sitting Commissioner"). Faced with the SEC's evident refusal to modify its waiver policy, Congresswoman Maxine Waters has introduced legislation to improve this process. Pursuant to the Bad Actor Disqualification Act, the Commission would be prevented from automatically granting waiver requests by:

> [1] Requiring the waiver process to be conducted and voted on at the Commission level, rather than at the staff level;
> [2] Requiring the Commission to consider whether granting a waiver would be in the public interest, protect investors, and promote market integrity;
> [3] Requiring the Commission to publish notice and afford the public an opportunity to comment and present their views at a public hearing on whether a particular waiver should be granted or denied; and
> [4] Requiring SEC staff to keep complete, public records of all waiver requests (formal and informal) and create a public database of all disqualified bad actors.

Press Release, *Waters Introduces Legislation to Improve SEC Process for Holding Bad Actors Accountable* (July 27, 2017), available at financialservices.house.gov/news/documentsingle.Aspx?DocumentID=400728 (Congresswoman Waters, Ranking Member of the House of Representatives Committee on Financial Services, also asserting that "[t]his commonsense legislation will subject waiver requests to public scrutiny and robust SEC review so that the law protects investors, the markets, and the public [signifying that] no one is above the law, including large financial firms"). In 2019, Congresswoman Waters introduced a discussion draft of this proposed legislation. *See* Robert Bergen et al., *The Bad Actor Disqualification Act and Expected Impact on SEC Settlements*, Harv. Law School Forum on Corp. Gov. (July 20, 2019), available at https://corpgov.law.harvard.edu/2019/07/20/the-bad-actor-disqualification-act-and-expected-impact-on-sec-settlements/ (asserting that enactment of the proposed legislation would complicate the SEC's enforcement program, including decreasing incentives for targets to settle rather than litigate and

their insiders should be eliminated.[75] And fourth, the Commission should utilize the statutory resources at hand to pursue meritorious enforcement actions against officers and directors of large publicly-held corporations and large financial firms.[76] The SEC's laxity in pursuing these individuals poorly reflects on the Commission's mission as an effective and even-handed law enforcement agency.[77]

While the Commission's continued use of the consent negotiation process and administrative forum are acceptable strategies in view of the realities of its limited resources,[78] the SEC should not employ these techniques to enter into disparate consent decrees favoring so-called reputable targets with no judicial review applicable. Unfortunately, as addressed later in this chapter, the Commission's cultural bias in this regard is so firmly entrenched that evidently only more zealous reform will substantially ameliorate this dilemma.[79]

D. Declining to Implement Statutory Directives

With some frequency, the SEC declines to implement directives legislated by Congress. As an administrative agency charged with adhering to statutory mandates, this intransigence is troubling. Perhaps not surprisingly, such refusal has arisen when congressional mandates direct the Commission to promulgate rules that may adversely impact corporate executives and gatekeepers.[80] For example, pursuant to the Dodd-Frank Act of 2010,[81] the

---

thereby impairing the Commission's ability to bring as many enforcement actions due to its limited resources).

[75] *See* sources cited *supra* notes 66, 67, 74.

[76] *See* discussion *infra* notes 109–124 and accompanying text.

[77] *See* discussion *infra* notes 109–154 and accompanying text.

[78] For example, during fiscal year 2020, the Commission instituted 89% of its enforcement actions involving publicly-held corporations and subsidiaries as administrative proceedings. *See* Cornerstone Research, *SEC Enforcement Activity: Public Companies and Subsidiaries—Fiscal Year 2020 Update*, available at https://www.cornerstone.com/Publications/Reports/SEC-Enforcement-Activity-FY-2020-Update.pdf. *See also* Gretchen Morgenson, *Quick, Call Tech Support for the S.E.C.*, N.Y. Times, Dec. 16, 2007, available at https://www.nytimes.com/2007/12/16/business/16gret.html ("It's no secret that the Securities and Exchange Commission is terrifically understaffed and wildly underfunded compared with the populous and wealthy Wall Street world it is supposed to police."). Given the SEC's limited resources, a significant increase in the number of litigated enforcement actions and contested collateral issues in administrative proceedings and the federal courts would signify a likely reduction in the number of enforcement actions that the Commission could institute.

[79] *See* discussion *infra* notes 127–154 and accompanying text.

[80] *See* discussion *infra* notes 81–108 and accompanying text.

[81] The Dodd-Frank Wall Street Reform and Consumer Protection Act, Pub. L. No. 111-203, 124 Stat. 1376 (2010).

Commission is tasked with adopting a rule that requires Exchange Act reporting companies to disclose the correlation (or lack thereof) between a subject corporation's financial performance and the amount of executive compensation that has been paid.[82] Disclosure under this statute must include "information that shows the relationship between executive compensation actually paid and the [corporation's] financial performance, taking into account the change in the value of the shares of stock, . . . dividends . . . and any distributions."[83] Implementation of this directive would enable shareholders and the securities markets to better evaluate increases in the level of executive compensation when the company's financial performance is falling.[84] More generally, such disclosures would facilitate the drawing of comparisons between the amount of executive compensation and the corporation's overall financial performance. Notably, the Commission proposed a rule to implement this statutory directive in 2015;[85] six years later, no action has been taken.[86]

Similarly, another provision of the Dodd-Frank Act mandates that, as a condition of having its securities listed on a national securities exchange, a company is required to adopt and implement an internal "clawback" policy whereby, in the event of an accounting restatement, its executives would pay back to the company incentive-based compensation that was erroneously awarded to them.[87] Significantly, however, the statute is not self-executing.

---

[82] *See* § 953 of the Dodd-Frank Act, *adding*, § 14(i) to the Securities Exchange Act, 15 U.S.C. § 78n(i).

[83] *Id.* Emerging growth companies are exempted from this statute. *Id.* For discussion on emerging growth companies, *see* Chapter 4 herein.

[84] *See* Senate Report No. 111-176, Committee on Banking, Housing and Urban Affairs, 111th Cong., 2d Sess., The Restoring American Financial Stability Act of 2010, at 135 (2010). *See Dodd-Frank Wall Street Reform and Consumer Protection Act: Law, Explanation, and Analysis* 425 (CCH Attorney-Editor Publ. 2010). *See also* Theo Francis and Joann S. Lublin, *Should Bar Be Lifted on CEO Bonuses?*, Wall St. J., June 2, 2017, at B3 (stating the concern of some investors that boards of directors set performance goals too low, thereby triggering executive bonuses upon meeting these goals without having to attain excellent performance as compared to similar companies).

[85] *See* Pay versus Performance, Securities Exchange Act Release No. 74835 (2015) (proposing amendments to Regulation S-K, item 402).

[86] *See* Marc I. Steinberg, *The Federalization of Corporate Governance* 221 (2018) (stating that "to date, the SEC has proposed but not adopted a rule implementing this statute").

[87] *See* § 954 of the Dodd-Frank Act, *adding*, § 10D to the Securities Exchange Act, 15 U.S.C. § 78j-4. Note that Section 304 of the Sarbanes-Oxley Act, 15 U.S.C. § 7243, also contains a clawback provision which in some ways is narrower and in others more extensive than its Dodd-Frank counterpart. For example, while Section 954 provides for the recovery of incentive-based compensation "in excess of what would have been paid to the executive officer under the accounting restatement," Section 304 is more expansive encompassing executive reimbursement of seemingly all categories of compensation (including incentive- and equity-based remuneration as well as stock profits). On the other hand, while Section 304 limits the clawback provision to the subject corporation's CEO and CFO, Section 954 applies to "any current or former executive officer." As another example, while Section 304 has a look back period of twelve months, Section 954's period is three years. *See* discussion in Steinberg, *supra* note 86, at 200–02.

Rather, its effectiveness is dependent upon the Commission prescribing a rule that directs the national securities exchanges to prohibit the listing of any such company's securities due to its non-compliance with the statute.[88] In 2015, the SEC proposed a rule to implement this congressional directive but has declined to take final action.[89]

Indeed, as stated in an article published in 2018 that continues to be the situation today, "[t]en years after the fall of Lehman Brothers, and eight years after the passage of Dodd-Frank, 5 of 12 mandatory executive compensation rules remain to be approved."[90] Moreover, at times, even when the SEC follows Congress's directive by adopting a specified rule, its enforcement of that rule is nonexistent. The SEC's implementation of its Standards of Professional Conduct for Attorneys serves as such an example.

In the aftermath of the financial crisis of 2008, Congress believed that attorneys failed to aptly perform their role as gatekeepers.[91] From a general perspective, gatekeepers are intermediaries who are in a position to detect and deter fraud.[92] By exercising adequate diligence in evaluating, certifying, or verifying facts surrounding the applicable transaction or other event, gatekeepers frequently stand in a position to deter and sometimes prevent

---

[88] *See* § 954(a) of the Dodd-Frank Act, *adding*, § 10D(a) to the Securities Exchange Act, 15 U.S.C. § 78j-4(a) (emphasis supplied) ("The Commission *shall, by rule*, direct the national securities exchanges and any national securities associations to prohibit the listing of any security of an issuer that does not comply with the requirements of this section.").

[89] *See* Listing Standards for Recovery of Erroneously Awarded Compensation, Securities Exchange Act Release No. 75342 (2015) (proposing Exchange Act Rule 10D-1); SEC Press Release No. 2015-136 (July 1, 2015), available at https://www.sec.gov/news/pressrelease/2015-136.html. ("Under the proposed new Rule 10D-1, listed companies would be required to develop and enforce recovery policies that, in the event of an accounting restatement, 'claw-back' from current and former executive officers [without regard to fault] incentive-based compensation they would not have received based on the restatement.") Significantly, several corporations voluntarily have adopted clawback policies. *See* American Accounting Association, *Executive Pay Clawbacks* (Jan. 30, 2015), available at https://aaahq.org/Outreach/Newsroom/Press-Release/1-30-15-Executive-Pay-Clawbacks-Mandated. *See generally* Terrance Gallogly, *Enforcing the Clawback Provision: Preventing the Erosion of Liability under Section 954 of the Dodd-Frank Act*, 42 Seton Hall L. Rev. 1229 (2012); Rachel E. Schwartz, *The Clawback Provision of Sarbanes-Oxley: An Underutilized Incentive to Keep the Corporate House Clean*, 64 Bus. Law. 1 (2008).

[90] Francine McKenna, *A Decade After the Crisis, the SEC Still Hasn't Passed Executive Compensation Rules*, MarketWatch—Capitol Report, Sept. 14, 2018, available at https://www.marketwatch.com/story/a-decade-after-the-crisis-the-sec-still-leaves-executive-compensation-rules-unwritten-2018-09-10 (describing mandatory rules that the SEC is required to adopt pursuant to the Dodd-Frank Act but to date has declined to do so).

[91] *See* The Corporate and Criminal Fraud Accountability Act of 2002, U.S. Senate Committee on the Judiciary, 187th Cong., 2d Sess., S. Rep. No. 107-146, at 2 (2002) (stating that, among others, attorneys serve as "gatekeepers who detect and deter fraud").

[92] *See Lawson v. FMR, LLC*, 571 U.S. 429, 449 (2014) ("Emphasizing the importance of outside professionals as 'gatekeepers who detect and deter fraud,' the Senate Report concludes: 'Congress must reconsider the incentive system that has been set up that encourages accountants and lawyers who come across fraud in their work to remain silent.'") (quoting S. Rep. No. 107-146, at 2 (2002)).

wrongdoing.[93] Seeking to impel attorneys to proficiently perform their gatekeeper role, Congress in its enactment of the Sarbanes-Oxley Act of 2002[94] directed the SEC to promulgate a rule that requires legal counsel to "go-up-the-ladder" when confronted with evidence of a material violation of the securities laws or a breach of fiduciary duty by the corporate client or any of its agents.[95]

Following this congressional directive, the SEC adopted its Standards of Conduct for Attorneys.[96] Generally, these Standards largely mirror existing ethical rules embraced by the American Bar Association and the overwhelming majority of the states.[97] While adhering to the "up-the-ladder" mandate set forth in the Sarbanes-Oxley Act,[98] the Commission declined to

---

[93] *See, e.g.*, John C. Coffee, Jr., *The Attorney as Gatekeeper: An Agenda for the SEC*, 103 Colum. L. Rev. 1193 (2003); Marc I. Steinberg and James Ames, *From the Regulatory Abyss: The Weakened Gatekeeping Incentives Under the Uniform Securities Act*, 35 Yale L. & Pol. Rev. 1 (2016); Fred Zacharias, *Lawyers as Gatekeepers*, 41 San Diego L. Rev. 1387 (2004). All too often, gatekeepers do not adequately respond when faced with client fraud. As the eminent Judge Stanley Sporkin lamented in one well-known case:

> Where were these professionals, a number of whom are now asserting their rights under the Fifth Amendment, when these clearly improper transactions were being consummated? Why didn't any of them speak up or disassociate themselves from the transactions? Where also were the outside accountants and attorneys when these transactions were effectuated? What is difficult to understand is that with all the professional talent involved (both accounting and legal), why at least one professional would not have blown the whistle to stop the overreaching that took place in this case.

Lincoln Savings & Loan Association v. Wall, 743 F. Supp. 2d 901, 910 (D.D.C. 1990).

[94] Pub. L. No. 107-204, 116 Stat. 745 (2002).

[95] *See* § 307 of the Sarbanes-Oxley Act, 15 U.S.C. § 7245. Pursuant to this statute, the Commission was directed to adopt a rule:

> (1) requiring [a subject] attorney to report evidence of a material violation of securities law or breach of fiduciary duty or similar violation by the company or any agent thereof, to the chief legal counsel or the chief executive officer of the company (or the equivalent thereof); and (2) if the counsel or officer does not appropriately respond to the evidence (adopting, as necessary, appropriate remedial measures or sanctions with respect to the violation), requiring [such] attorney to report the evidence to the audit committee of the board of directors of the issuer or to another committee of the board of directors comprised solely of directors not employed directly or indirectly by the issuer, or to the board of directors.

[96] *See* 17 C.F.R. Part 205; Securities Exchange Act Release No. 47276 (2003).

[97] *See, e.g.*, American Bar Association, *Model Rules of Professional Conduct*, Rules 1.2(d), 1.6, 1.13, 4.1 (2020); American Law Institute, *Restatement (Third) of the Law Governing Lawyers* § 67 (2000). *See also* Marc I. Steinberg, *Attorney Liability After Sarbanes-Oxley* § 3.02 n. 6 (2018) ("Today, over forty states permit or require an attorney to reveal a client's crime or fraud that threatens substantial financial loss.").

[98] In this regard, the SEC Standards of Professional Conduct for Attorneys:

- require an attorney to report evidence of a material violation, determined according to an objective standard, "up-the-ladder" within the issuer to the chief legal counsel or the chief executive officer of the company or the equivalent;

require that legal counsel make a "noisy withdrawal" when faced with client fraud.[99] Instead, the Standards give the subject attorney discretion to make such a noisy withdrawal when deemed reasonably necessary to prevent or rectify the client's wrongful conduct.[100]

These SEC Standards of Conduct have been addressed previously by this author[101] and many other sources.[102] The point of this discussion, however, is not to analyze the content and propriety of these Standards. Rather, it is to highlight the stark reality that in the nearly two decades since the Standards

---

- require an attorney, if the chief legal counsel or the chief executive officer of the company does not respond appropriately to the evidence, to report the evidence to the audit committee, another committee of independent directors, or the full board of directors;
- clarify that the rules cover attorneys providing legal services to an issuer who have an attorney-client relationship with the issuer, and who have notice that documents they are preparing or assisting in preparing will be filed with or submitted to the Commission;
- allow an issuer to establish a "qualified legal compliance committee" (QLCC) as an alternative procedure for reporting evidence of a material violation. . . . One way in which an attorney could satisfy the rule's reporting obligation is by reporting evidence of a material violation to a QLCC;
- allow an attorney, without the consent of an issuer client, to reveal confidential information related to his or her representation to the extent the attorney reasonably believes necessary (1) to prevent the issuer from committing a material violation likely to cause substantial financial injury to the financial interests or property of the issuer or investors; (2) to prevent the issuer from committing an illegal act; or (3) to rectify the consequences of a material violation or illegal act in which the attorney's services have been used; [and]
- state that the rules govern in the event the rules conflict with state law, but will not preempt the ability of a state to impose more rigorous obligations on attorneys that are not inconsistent with the rules.

SEC Press Release No. 2003-13 (Jan. 23, 2003), available at https://www.sec.gov/news/press/2003-13.htm.

[99] Generally, a "noisy withdrawal" occurs when the attorney resigns from representing the client and informs a regulator (such as the SEC) or investors that the withdrawal was due to professional reasons (and also may communicate that she no longer can stand behind her work product). While the SEC proposed a "noisy withdrawal" mandate, it declined to adopt this provision. *See* Securities Exchange Act Release No. 46868 (2002) (proposing a "noisy withdrawal" requirement).

The SEC's approach follows the overwhelming majority view. With respect to a minority of states, a small number require that legal counsel make a "noisy withdrawal" under certain circumstances (*see, e.g.*, Tennessee Rules of Professional Conduct, Rule 4.1), while a few states prohibit a lawyer's disclosure of client confidences and secrets where there is financial (and not physical) harm (*see, e.g.*, California Business and Professional Code § 6068(e)).

[100] *See supra* notes 95–99 and accompanying text.

[101] *See, e.g.*, Marc I. Steinberg, *Lawyering and Ethics for the Business Attorney* 15–38 (5th ed. 2020). Marc I. Steinberg, The Fouston Siefkin Lecture, *The Corporate/Securities Attorney as a "Moving Target"—Client Fraud Dilemmas*, 46 Washburn L.J. 1 (2006).

[102] *See, e.g.*, Karl A. Groskaufmanis, *Climbing Up the Ladder: Corporate Counsel and the SEC's Reporting Requirements for Lawyers*, 89 Cornell L. Rev. 511 (2004); Thomas L. Hazen, *Administrative Law Controls on Attorney Practice—A Look at the Securities and Exchange Commission's Lawyer Conduct Rules*, 55 Admin. L. Rev. 323 (2003); Lisa H. Nicholson, *SarbOx 307's Impact on Subordinate In-House Counsel: Between a Rock and a Hard Place*, 2004 Mich. St. L. Rev. 559 (2004).

have been prescribed, the Commission has not brought a single proceeding based on an attorney's alleged failure to comply therewith. In spite of the continuing presence of financial scandals and private lawsuits against premier law firms for their alleged misconduct for facilitating their clients' frauds,[103] the SEC has sat on the sidelines with its helmet off acting as if it were a spectator rather than a government regulator that is tasked with upholding the law. The Commission's inaction appropriately may be portrayed as an undue abstention to act in accordance with its administrative authority.[104]

The SEC's inaction with enforcing its Standards of Conduct is consistent with the Commission's refusal to bring disciplinary or enforcement proceedings against major law firms. For several decades, the Commission has not initiated such an action[105] even though it does so with some frequency with respect to major accounting firms.[106] In view that attorneys today are

---

[103] Due to the Supreme Court's denial of aiding and abetting liability under Section 10(b) and Rule 10b-5 (*see Central Bank of Denver v. First Interstate Bank of Denver*, 511 U.S. 164 (1994)), the Supreme Court's restrictive definition of primary liability under these provisions (*see Janus Capital Group, Inc. v. First Derivative Traders*, 564 U.S. 135 (2011)); *Stoneridge Investment Partners, LLC v. Scientific-Atlanta, Inc.*, 552 U.S. 148 (2008)), the challenging pleading requirements of the Private Securities Litigation Reform Act (*see* § 21D(b) of the Exchange Act; *Tellabs, Inc. v. Makor Issues & Rights, Ltd.*, 551 U.S. 308 (2007)), and the requirement pursuant to the Securities Litigation Uniform Standards Act that, with certain carve-outs, class actions involving nationally traded securities must be brought in federal court with only federal law applying (*see* § 28(f) of the Securities Exchange Act; *Merrill Lynch, Pierce, Fenner & Smith, Inc. v. Dabit*, 547 U.S. 71 (2006)), attorneys today are not sued with frequency in federal class actions. Nonetheless, they have incurred substantial monetary liability in receivership actions and in state court lawsuits. *See* Marc I. Steinberg, *Attorney Liability After Sarbanes Oxley* (2018); Marc I. Steinberg, *Corporate Lawyers: Ethical and Practical Lawyering with Vanishing Gatekeeper Liability*, 88 Fordham L. Rev. 1575 (2020); Marc I. Steinberg and Chris Claassen, *Attorney Liability Under the State Securities Laws: Landscapes and Minefields*, 3 U. Cal. Berk. Bus. L.J. 1 (2005).

[104] Another example is the SEC's adoption of Rule 14a-11 pursuant to the Dodd-Frank Act. That Act empowered the Commission to promulgate appropriate rules enabling specified large shareholders to designate in a subject company's proxy statement a certain number of director-nominee candidates for board election. *See* § 971 of the Dodd-Frank Act, *codified at*, § 14(a)(2) of the Securities Exchange Act, 15 U.S.C. § 78(n)(a)(2). Seeking to fulfill this legislative directive, the Commission promulgated Rule 14a-11 which authorized certain eligible large shareholders access to the company's proxy statement in order to nominate a specified number of directors. *See* Securities Exchange Act Release No. 62764 (2010). Subsequently, the rule was invalidated by the U.S. Court of Appeals. *See Business Roundtable v. Securities and Exchange Commission*, 647 F.3d 1144 (D.C. Cir. 2011). Rather than modifying and reissuing the rule, the Commission elected to abandon this task. *See* discussion in Steinberg, *supra* note 86, at 186–88.

[105] One of the more recent such actions against a law firm was four decades ago. *See In re Keating, Muething & Klekamp*, Securities Exchange Act Release No. 15982, [1979 Transfer Binder] Fed. Sec. L. Rep. (CCH) ¶ 82,124, at 81,989 (SEC 1979) (pursuant to settlement, law firm ordered to adopt, maintain, and implement adequate procedures).

[106] Unlike with respect to law firms, the SEC institutes proceedings with some frequency against major accounting firms. *See, e.g.*, *In re PricewaterhouseCoopers LLP*, Securities Exchange Act Release No. 87052 (2019) (pursuant to settlement, PwC consented to auditor independence violations and payment of approximately $8 million); *In re KPMG LLP*, Securities Exchange Act Release No. 86118 (2019) (settlement involving firm's alleged alteration of its past audit work as well as cheating by a number of its employees on internal training exams, with payment of $50 million and undertakings

rarely sued in federal securities class actions due in large part to the onerous pleading requirements and the impracticability of establishing primary liability,[107] the SEC should be vigilant to help ensure that, acting in the role of gatekeeper, attorneys engage in law-compliant conduct.[108]

E. Lack of Enforcement against Insiders of Large Enterprises

The Commission's refusal to bring enforcement actions against directors and executive officers of large publicly-held corporations and financial firms is well known and has been subject to extensive criticism.[109] With the exception of insider trading and similar types of blatant self-dealing misconduct,[110] SEC enforcement actions against such insiders are rare. For example, in the aftermath of the financial crisis, during the Obama administration, the Commission brought one enforcement action against a high-level executive officer.[111] This abstention continues today.[112]

---

to be implemented); *In re Grant Thornton LLP*, Securities Exchange Act Release No. 76536 (2015) (settlement with admission of wrongdoing regarding violation of professional standards, with firm disgorging $1.5 million of fees and paying a $3 million penalty).

[107] *See supra* note 103; discussion in Chapter 6 herein.

[108] During the first decade of this century, the SEC instituted a number of enforcement actions against attorneys. *See, e.g., Securities and Exchange Commission v. Mintz*, SEC Litigation Release No. 20866 (2008); *Securities and Exchange Commission v. Heinen*, SEC Litigation Release No. 20683 (2006); *Securities and Exchange Commission v. Isselmann*, SEC Litigation Release No. 18896 (2004).

[109] *See, e.g.*, Eisinger, *supra* note 3, at 296 (stating that three years after the financial crisis the SEC had hardly instituted any enforcement actions against corporate executives and mainly "charged low-level, tangential miscreants"); Jed Rakoff, *Why Have No High Level Executives Been Prosecuted in Connection with the Financial Crisis?*, CLS Blue Sky Blog (Nov. 15, 2013), available at https://clsbluesky.law.columbia.edu/2013/11/15/why-have-no-high-level-executives-been-prosecuted-in-connection-with-the-financial-crisis/ (stating that "not a single high level executive has been successfully prosecuted in connection with the recent financial crisis").

[110] Corporate officers and directors as well as attorneys and other professionals have been the subject of several SEC enforcement actions alleging illegal insider trading. *See* cases cited in Marc I. Steinberg and William K.S. Wang, *Insider Trading* (3d ed. 2010).

[111] *See Final Judgment as to Defendant Angelo Mozillo*, No. CV 09-3994-JFW (MANx), 2010 WL 3656068 (C.D. Cal. Sept. 16, 2010) (former CEO of Countywide Financial settled SEC enforcement action agreeing to permanent bar from serving as an officer or a director of any publicly-held company and paying $45 million in disgorgement as well as $22.5 million in money penalties). With respect to enforcement actions against corporate directors, then SEC Commissioner Luis Aguilar observed that "these matters are so infrequent that the agency does not currently maintain statistics on cases that are brought against directors." Luis A. Aguilar, SEC Commissioner, Remarks at the 12th Annual Boardroom Summit and Peer Exchange: The Important Work of Boards of Directors (Oct. 14, 2015), available at https://www.sec.gov/news/speech/important-work-of-boards-of-directors.html.

[112] *See, e.g.*, Ben Eisen, *Wells Fargo Settles U.S. Probes*, Wall St. J., Feb. 22–23, 2020, at A1 (reporting that Wells Fargo paid $3 billion to settle DOJ and SEC investigations with no executives being charged—subsequently, the Commission brought a proceeding against the company's

The Commission's inaction has been defended with the assertion that proving fraud by C-suite executives and directors in this context ordinarily is an insurmountable task. Under this rationale, senior executive officers and outside directors are unaware of the wrongdoing that is transpiring within the organization.[113] Assuming the validity of this approach, this inaction fails to explain the Commission's refusal to deploy the controlling person provision of the Securities Exchange Act.[114] Pursuant to Section 20(a), any person who controls another person who engages in a violation of the Exchange Act or any rule or regulation adopted thereunder also is liable unless the control

CEO); Rosenfeld, *supra* note 57, at 172 (noting that in twenty-six enforcement actions brought against financial institutions during FY 2017, no individuals were charged); U.S. Senator Elizabeth Warren, Facebook (Jan. 15, 2016), available at https://m.facebook.com/senatorelizabethwarren/posts/546470835515414 ("Seven years later. No admission of guilt. No individuals are going to jail. . . . That's not justice."); sources cited *supra* note 109. Occasionally, the SEC will pursue high-level executives of major publicly-held companies, typically with mild sanctions being entered into by consent. *See, e.g., In the Matter of John G. Stumpf*, Securities Act Release No. 10887 (2020) (settlement whereby cease and desist order entered against Wells Fargo former CEO for alleged violations of §§ 17(a)(2) and 17(a)(3) (based on negligence) and payment of $2.5 million civil money penalty); *In the Matter of Valeant Pharmaceuticals International, Inc.* et al., Securities Act Release Nos. 10809-10811 (2020) (settlement whereby company paid $45 million civil penalty, with former executives paying $425,000 in civil penalties, reimbursing the company $560,000 in compensation clawbacks, and company controller being suspended from practicing before the SEC as an accountant having the option to seek reinstatement after one year); *In the Matter of Walgreens Boots Alliance, Inc.*, Securities Act Release No. 10562 (2018) (pursuant to consent agreement, CEO and CFO each agreed to entry of cease and desist order and money penalty of $160,000 allegedly for failing to disclose material information that caused an approximate 15% decrease in the price of the stock when that information became publicly known—by contrast, the company agreed to a cease and desist order and levying of a $34.5 million money penalty). On the other hand, pursuant to a settlement agreement, the U.S. Comptroller of the Currency charged former Wells Fargo executives individually, including a fine of $17.5 million and lifetime ban levied upon the company's former CEO. *See* Rachel Louis Ensign and Ben Eisen, *Wells Fargo Ex-CEO Is Banned for Life*, Wall St. J., Jan. 24, 2020, at A1. *See also* David Michaels and Ben Eisen, *Wells Fargo's Ex-CEO Settles with SEC*, Wall St. J., Nov. 14–15, 2020, at B10 (settlement involving far lesser sanctions than those imposed by the Comptroller of the Currency). Outside of this country, "U.K. prosecutors charged Barclays PLC's former chief executive officer with fraud and illegal payments, the most prominent and most senior banker to be charged with crimes relating to the global financial crisis." Max Colchester and Margot Patrick, *Barclays Hit with Fraud Charges*, Wall St. J., June 21, 2017, at B1.

[113] *See* Daniel C. Richman, *Corporate Headhunting*, 8 Harv. L. & Pol'y Rev. 265 (2014) (discussing challenges in bringing government enforcement actions against executive officers and directors). *See also* Brandon Garrett, *The Corporate Criminal as a Scapegoat*, 101 Va. L. Rev. 1789, 1790 (2015) ("The corporation appears to be a kind of scapegoat: perhaps not entirely blameless, as in the traditional concept, but literally impossible to jail—yet capable of receiving the brunt of blame and punishment, while the individual culprits go free."). Prior to enactment of the Sarbanes-Oxley Act and well before the financial crisis, one of the major exceptions to this abstention was the SEC's enforcement action against high-level executives in the Salomon Brothers proceeding. *See In re Gutfreund*, Securities Exchange Act Release No. 31554 (1992).

[114] Section 20(a) of the Securities Exchange Act, 15 U.S.C. § 78t(a). Pursuant to Rule 405, 17 C.F.R. § 230.405, the term "control" means "the possession, direct or indirect, of the power to direct or cause the direction of the management and policies of a person."

person shows that she "acted in good faith and did not directly or indirectly induce the act or acts constituting the violation."[115] This far-reaching provision should extend, as a matter of corporate structure, to an enterprise's chief executive officer and the chair of its board of directors.[116] Moreover, with respect to alleged financial disclosure illegality, the corporation's chief financial officer as well as the chair of its audit committee ordinarily should be defined as control persons.[117]

In the aftermath of the financial crisis, the Commission assessed huge monetary penalties against several publicly-held corporations. For example, Bank of America and Goldman Sachs each paid billions of dollars in penalties.[118] Yet, inexplicably, despite its rhetoric, the SEC refused to invoke the control person provision in its enforcement actions against the insiders of any of these enterprises.[119] Contrasted with the Commission's abstention, the control person provision is invoked with regularity in private securities actions to the degree that claims are routinely brought

---

[115] 15 U.S.C. § 78t(a). *See In re Stone & Webster, Inc. Securities Litigation*, 424 F.3d 24 (1st Cir. 2005); *Harrison v. Dean Witter Reynolds, Inc.*, 974 F.2d 873 (7th Cir. 1992); *Titan v. Hollinger Titan Capital Corp.*, 914 F.2d 1564 (9th Cir. 1990) (en banc); *G.A. Thompson & Co., Inc. v. Partridge*, 636 F.2d 945 (5th Cir. 1981). Nonetheless, a minority of courts require the plaintiff adequately to plead "culpable conduct," showing that "the controlling person was in some meaningful sense a culpable participant" with respect to the securities law violation(s) committed by the controlled person. *See Sharp v. Coopers & Lybrand*, 649 F.2d 175 (3d Cir. 1981).

[116] *See, e.g., Maverick Fund v. Converse Technology*, 801 F. Supp. 2d 41 (E.D.N.Y. 2011) (denying a motion to dismiss § 20(a) claims against several directors, chief financial officer, and general counsel); *Puskala v. Koss Corp.*, 799 F. Supp. 2d 941 (E.D. Wis. 2011) (denying motion to dismiss § 20(a) claim against corporate director); *In re Tronox, Inc. Securities Litigation*, 769 F. Supp. 2d 202 (S.D.N.Y. 2011) (denying officer-defendants motion to dismiss § 20(a) claims); *In re Proxima Corp Securities Litigation*, 1994 U.S. Dist. LEXIS 21443 (N.D. Cal. 1994) (holding § 20(a) control person claim adequately pleaded against outside directors).

[117] *See* cases *supra* note 116.

[118] *See* proceedings cited *supra* note 58. *See also* Warren, *supra* note 112 ("In the 2008 financial crisis, we lost trillions in wealth and millions of people lost their homes and their jobs because of Wall Street recklessness. Today, Goldman Sachs announced it will pay $5.1 billion for its role in precipitating the economic collapse by misleading investors about the quality of the junk mortgage securities they peddled.... No admission of guilt. No individuals are going to jail.").

[119] Such rhetoric was used by Chair White during the Obama Administration. *See* SEC Chair Mary Jo White, Speech at the Council of Institutional Investors Fall Conference, Chicago, Deploying the Full Enforcement Arsenal (Sept. 26, 2013), available at https://www.sec.gov/News/Speech/Detail/Speech/1370539841202:

> Another core principle of any strong enforcement program is to pursue responsible individuals wherever possible. That is something our enforcement division has always done and will continue to do. Companies, after all, act through their people. And when we can identify those people, settling only with the company may not be sufficient. Redress for wrongdoing must never be seen as "a cost of doing business" made good by cutting a corporate check.

against corporate officers and directors alleging such liability.[120] For whatever reason, which the Commission has not articulated, it has declined to invoke this provision.

More recently, in 2018, the SEC in a settled enforcement action utilized the control person provision against a corporation's chief executive officer and chief financial officer.[121] At this time, the Commission's invocation of the control person provision in that litigation appears to be an exception. That is unfortunate. Although the Commission frequently has exhorted corporate fiduciaries to engage in law-compliant conduct,[122] it all too often fails to pursue these insiders with sufficient vigor. The control person provision significantly alleviates the SEC's task by imposing liability against a subject officer and director unless he shows good faith and noninducement.[123] It is incumbent upon the Commission to deploy the resources in its "tool chest." As a law enforcement agency, the SEC should invoke the control person provision against appropriate officers and directors of major corporations and financial firms in a reasoned and fair way. By exercising its statutory authority in this manner, greater discipline and ethics will be instilled in the C-suite and boardroom, thereby effectuating

[120] *See* Marc I. Steinberg and Forrest C. Roberts, *Laxity at the Gates: The SEC's Neglect to Enforce Control Person Liability*, 11 Va. L. & Bus. Rev. 201, 238 (2017) (stating that "within the last three years, cases have been filed in every U.S. circuit alleging Section 20(a) control person liability") (citing cases).

[121] *See Securities and Exchange Commission v. ITT Educational Services, Inc.*, SEC Litigation Release No. 24188 (2018) (in settlement, invoking the control person provision of § 20(a) against former CEO and CFO of corporation, barring each from serving as an officer or director of a publicly-held company for a five-year period as well as levying money penalties). With respect to the monetary penalties of $200,000 and $100,000 levied respectively against the former CEO and CFO, four U.S. Senators in a letter to SEC Chairman Jay Clayton asserted that these "measly" fines "amount to nothing more than a parking ticket." Letter dated July 20, 2018 from Senators Richard J. Durbin, Sherrod Brown, Elizabeth Warren, and Richard Blumenthal to SEC Chairman Jay Clayton, available at https://www.durbin.senate.gov/newsroom/press-releases/durbin-brown-warren-blumenthal-blast sec-for-weak-settlement-with-former-for-profit-college-executive.

[122] *See, e.g.*, SEC Chair Mary Jo White, Remarks at the Securities Enforcement Forum (Oct. 9, 2013), available at https://www.sec.gov/News/Speech/Detail/Speech/1370539872100#_ftnref6 (stating that "investors in our markets want to know there is a strong cop on the beat [and] . . . I believe the SEC should strive . . . to be the agency that covers the entire neighborhood and pursues every level of violation"); *In the Matter of W.R. Grace & Co.*, Securities Exchange Act Release No. 39157 (1997) (pursuant to settlement, emphasizing in a § 21(a) Report "the affirmative responsibilities of corporate officers and directors to ensure that the shareholders who they serve receive accurate and complete disclosure of information required by the . . . federal securities laws"); *supra* note 119.

[123] *See* Steinberg and Roberts, *supra* note 120, at 239–48. As one U.S. Senator has stated: "The SEC doesn't always use all of the penalties at its disposal, and it should." Senator Chuck Grassley, Press Release, *Bill Seeks Tougher Penalties for Wall Street Fraud* (July 9, 2015), available at http://www.grassley.senate.gov/news/news-releases/bill-seeks-Tougher-penalties-wall-street-fraud.

a greater adherence to legal norms and enhanced corporate governance conduct.[124]

F. Summation

The foregoing discussion, along with the subjects addressed earlier in this book,[125] highlights the SEC's failure to implement its statutory authority in a manner befitting an agency that decades ago was viewed as premier.[126] The Commission's refusal to adopt and meaningfully implement legislative directives, its neglect to pursue high-level executives of major enterprises for unlawful conduct, its divestment of plaintiffs' remedies, and its undue favoritism for capital formation to the detriment of investor protection are antithetical to the SEC's mission. Strong action is necessary to rectify the imbalance that has occurred. The following section of this chapter recommends that a new framework for the composition of SEC Commissioners be implemented.

III. Reconstituting the Securities and Exchange Commission

Severe criticism has been directed at the SEC and the Department of Justice for their failures to effectively enforce federal law against insiders of major enterprises.[127] While this book is focused on the SEC, the DOJ's abstention

---

[124] *See* Steinberg and Roberts, *supra* note 120, at 247–48 ("Without explanation, the Commission has declined to meaningfully utilize [the control person] provision and instead has tended to pursue gatekeepers only if they commit or aid in a primary violation [and that] with respect to the 'big players' on Wall Street, the SEC has declined to pursue any individual liability at all, except on rare occasions.").

[125] *See* discussion in Chapters 2–8 herein; *supra* note 4.

[126] *See* Judith Miller, *S.E.C.: Watchdog 1929 Lacked*, N.Y. Times, Oct. 31, 1979, at D1 (stating that "the agency created in 1934 to enforce the [federal securities] laws, the Securities and Exchange Commission, is still widely regarded as the nation's best independent regulatory agency"); David L. Ratner, *The SEC at Sixty*, 16 Cardozo L. Rev. 1765, 1779 (1995) ("The SEC is one important reason why the securities industry is in so much better shape than other financial service industries, and why the U.S. securities markets are the best securities markets in the world.").

[127] *See* Stephen Lebaton, *S.E.C. Facing Deeper Trouble*, N.Y. Times, Dec. 1, 2002, at D1 (stating that the SEC "is plagued by problems that go deeper than its leadership difficulties and have undermined its ability to police companies and markets"); discussion *supra* notes 3, 109, 112, 113, 120, 122 and accompanying text.

to institute a single criminal prosecution against a high-level executive in the aftermath of the financial crisis shows that the SEC and the DOJ share a similar cultural bias problem.[128] As for the SEC, the Commission brought merely one enforcement action against a boardroom-level executive in connection with the financial crisis. Unquestionably, the SEC's traditional image as the guardian of the investing public and a tough enforcer has become minimized, with popular culture deriding the agency as being feckless and fearful of pursuing high-level executives of major publicly-held companies and financial firms.[129]

A. The Revolving Door Challenge

The failure to engage in meaningful enforcement against high-level executives of major firms is due, many critics assert, to the "revolving door" whereby regulators seek to leave the government to enter lucrative private-sector employment.[130] Aware that their use of perceived overzealous regulatory and enforcement practices may well be viewed as detrimental to their future employment prospects, government attorneys are incentivized to perform in a highly proficient manner yet not to the degree that they will lose their appeal to potential employers. As stated by one source: "If you

---

[128] *See* John C. Coffee, Jr., *Corporate Crime and Punishment—The Crisis of Underenforcement* 3 (2020) (commenting that "no senior executive on Wall Street or at a major financial firm was convicted (or even prosecuted)"); Eisinger, *supra* note 3, at xvi–xvii (stating that "the government failed" and that "no top bankers from the top financial firms went to prison for the widespread malfeasance that led to the 2008 financial crisis"); Michael H. Hurwitz, *Focusing on Deterrence to Combat Financial Fraud and Protect Investors*, 75 Bus. Law. 1519, 1520 (2020) (observing that one top executive went to prison in the aftermath of the 2008 financial meltdown).

[129] *The Big Short* (2015), *based on* Michael Lewis, *The Big Short* (2010); *Billions* (Short Squeeze 2016) (for example, one actor stating that "[t]he SEC may be feckless, but they're not incompetent"). In this regard, Senator Elizabeth Warren has called the SEC "particularly feeble." Senator Elizabeth Warren, *Rigged Justice 2016: How Weak Enforcement Lets Corporate Offenders Off Easy* at 1 (Jan. 2016), available at http://www.warren.senate.gov/files/documents/Rigged_Justice_2016.pdf.

[130] *See, e.g.*, Peter J. Henning, *The Revolving Door and S.E.C. Enforcement*, N.Y. Times: Dealbook (April 8, 2010), available at https://dealbook.nytimes.com/2010/04/08/the-revolving-door-and-s-e-c-enforcement/ (discussing whether the revolving door adversely affects the effectiveness of the SEC's Enforcement Division); Andrew Ross Sorkin, *Revolving Door at S.E.C. Is Hurdle to Crisis Cleanup*, N.Y. Times: Dealbook (Aug. 1, 2011), available at https://dealbook.nytimes.com/2011/08/01/revolving-door-at-s-e-c-is-hurdle-to-crisis-cleanup/ (observing that "the revolving door" for many years has been "a dominant fact" at the SEC raising questions about Washington and Wall Street). *See also* James D. Cox and Randall S. Thomas, *Revolving Elites: The Unexplored Risk of Capturing the SEC*, 107 Geo. L.J. 845, 849, 860 (2019) (stating that many commentators viewed "the tenure of former SEC Chair Mary Jo White as the paradigmatic example of the revolving door" and that "the revolving door is a fact of life at the SEC").

work for the enforcement division of the S.E.C. you probably know in the back of your mind, and in the front too, that if you maintain good relations with Wall Street you might soon be paid huge sums to be employed by it."[131] This perception also applies to SEC attorneys in other divisions, such as the Division of Corporation Finance, where an attorney's zealous application of SEC rules and policies may become known in the private sector and alienate prospective employers. The end game for many SEC attorneys is to become a partner in a premier law firm, representing clients who they may have once regulated.[132]

The revolving door also is problematic on a senior staff level where law firm partners and other experienced individuals from the private sector join the SEC staff, frequently as division heads or other high-level staff positions.[133] The cultural bias problem is particularly poignant in this setting. Successful individuals who have worked for years, if not decades, in prominent law firms and other premier positions in the private sector normally lack affinity for vigorous government regulation and enforcement. Once their tenure with the Commission is over, they are likely to return to their law firms and continue their practice.[134] They often will be even more attractive to their clients as a result of procuring greater know-how, insights, and staff accessibility due to their government service. The consequence is a lack of fervor for rigorous government regulation and enforcement. As one SEC staffer stated at his retirement reception, the Commission "polices the broken windows on the street level and rarely goes to the penthouse floors."[135]

---

[131] Michael Lewis and David Einhorn, *The End of the Financial World as We Know It*, N.Y. Times (Jan. 3, 2009), available at https://www.nytimes.com/2009/01/04/opinion/04lewiseinhorn.html.

[132] *See* discussion in Cox and Thomas, *supra* note 130, at 848–51. On the other hand, the door between the SEC staff and law firms that represent plaintiffs in securities class actions does not revolve. *See* Alexander I. Pratt, *The Non-Revolving Door*, 46 J. Corp. L. (forthcoming 2021), available at https://ssrn.com/abstract=3674179.

[133] *See* Cox and Thomas, *supra* note 130, at 869 (asserting that "a focus on division directors, where they come from and where they return, is a far more significant issue than where their subordinates migrate [and that accordingly the] important issue in the revolving door debate should be on the agency's division heads and not the staff").

[134] It is commonplace for such SEC division heads as the Enforcement Director, Director of the Division of Corporation Finance, and the General Counsel to assume law firm partnerships after their tenure at the Commission ends. The same frequently is true with other high-level staff in those divisions. *See* Cox and Thomas, *supra* note 130, at 901–10. One notable exception was my mentor SEC Enforcement Director Stanley Sporkin who, upon his departure from the Commission, became General Counsel of the Central Intelligence Agency and thereafter a federal district judge. After his retirement from the bench, Judge Sporkin joined the law firm of Weil, Gotshal & Manges.

[135] Eisinger, *supra* note 3, at 267 (quoting James Kidney). The term "broken windows" refers to the policy pursued under SEC Chair Mary Jo White that any violation, however minor, should draw SEC enforcement scrutiny. *See* Remarks of SEC Chair Mary Jo White, Securities Enforcement Forum (Oct. 9, 2013), available at https://www.sec.gov/news/speech/spch100913mjw (stating that "even the

The revolving door problem is not easily solved. In order to attract astute junior attorneys, mobility is essential. Without opportunities to migrate to law firms and other attractive positions in the private sector, premier junior attorneys and other relatively inexperienced astute professionals would be reluctant to join the SEC staff. By gaining sought-after skills through their government employment with the lure of mobility to obtain appealing positions in the private sector, the SEC remains an attractive employment option for these individuals.[136]

In addition, the movement of experienced attorneys and other professionals from the private sector to the SEC staff may be beneficial. These knowledgeable individuals provide valuable practical experience, keen insights from private sector sources, and experienced assessments as to the feasibility of contemplated SEC policies and actions. Moreover, once these individuals return to the private sector, they may help instill in their respective clients a better adherence to regulatory requirements and thereby enhance law compliance.[137]

B. Reconstituting the Composition of SEC Commissioners

The solution therefore is not to erect greater barriers to the revolving door for junior-level SEC personnel or deter experienced professionals in the private sector from engaging in meritorious government service. Rather, the answer lies in the composition of the SEC Commissioners. After all, the tone is set at the top. And this tone during the past few decades has been one of favoring capital formation over enhancing investor protection accompanied by a

---

smallest infractions have victims, and that the smallest infractions are very often just the first step toward bigger ones down the road").

[136] Indeed, this position is manifested in the Model Rules of Professional Conduct where screening mechanisms may be implemented to avoid firm-wide disqualification when a personally disqualified government lawyer migrates to private practice. *See* American Bar Association, Model Rules of Professional Conduct, Rule 1.11. The rationale is that, if screening were prohibited in this context, the government's ability to recruit proficient attorneys would be substantially impaired. *See, e.g., Armstrong v. McAlpin*, 625 F.2d 433 (2d Cir. 1980) (en banc); Thomas D. Morgan, *Appropriate Limits on Participation by a Former Agency Official in Matters Before an Agency*, 1980 Duke L.J. 14 (1980); Robert Mundheim, *Conflict of Interest and the Former Government Employee: Rethinking the Revolving Door*, 14 Creighton L. Rev. 707 (1981).

[137] *See* Cox and Thomas, *supra* note 130, at 861–62, *citing*, U.S. Government Accountability Office (GAO), GAO-11-654, *Securities and Exchange Commission: Existing Post-Employment Controls Could Be Further Strengthened* at 11 (2011).

general refusal to initiate enforcement actions against high-level executives of large companies and financial firms. In this regard, a substantial number of SEC Commissioners (as well as SEC Chairs) during the past three decades previously had been partners at prestigious corporate law firms and financial firms.[138] In addition, several of the Commissioners who had been law professors or who held other government positions (such as congressional staff) were associated with major law firms previously in their careers.[139] Moreover, once their tenure ended, many SEC Commissioners migrated as partners to major law firms or joined large publicly-held companies in high-level positions.[140]

What is evident is the seeming disqualification of qualified individuals having certain affiliations. For example, many experienced securities litigators who represent investors in class actions would bring a different perspective to Commission deliberations; yet, insofar as I am aware, not one has ever been appointed.[141] The same can be said for knowledgeable individuals

[138] *See* Paul Kierman, *SEC Director Says He Will Step Down*, Wall St. J., Oct. 28, 2020, at A2 ("Top positions in the agency have typically been held by former corporate lawyers."). From 1990 to 2020, approximately thirty-two individuals have been appointed as SEC Commissioners. The following SEC Commissioners in chronological order from 1990 to 2020 were appointed to the Commission having significant experience at large corporate law firms and financial firms: Philip R. Lochner, Jr. (General Counsel of Time, Inc.); J. Carter Beese (partner at Alex, Brown & Sons); Steven Wallman (partner at Covington & Burling); Norman S. Johnson (partner at Van Cott, Bagley, Cornwell & McCarthy); Harvey L. Pitt (Chair) (partner at Fried, Frank, Harris, Shriver & Jacobson); William H. Donaldson (Chair) (Chairman and CEO of Donaldson, Lufkin & Jenrette); Paul S. Atkins (associated at Davis Polk & Wardwell); Christopher Cox (Chair) (partner at Latham & Watkins); Annette L. Nazareth (managing director at Smith Barney); Luis A. Aguilar (partner at McKenna Long & Aldridge); Daniel M. Gallagher (partner at WilmerHale); Mary Jo White (Chair) (partner at Debevoise & Plimpton); Jay Clayton (Chair) (partner at Sullivan & Cromwell); Allison H. Lee (partner at Sherman & Howard). In addition, several recent SEC Chairs had strong corporate law firm or industry ties, including Harvey Pitt, William Donaldson, Christopher Cox, Mary Jo White, and Jay Clayton. *See* GAO Report, *supra* note 137, at 4, 6. Information for notes 138–140 was derived from publicly available sources. Noteworthy, fourteen former SEC Commissioners authored U.S. Supreme Court briefs supporting the defendants' position in *Stoneridge Investment Partners LLC v. Scientific-Atlanta, Inc.*, 552 U.S. 148 (2008), which severely limited the scope of primary liability under Section 10(b) of the Securities Exchange Act. *See* Eisinger, *supra* note 3, at 255.

[139] For example, in chronological order (from 1990 to 2020), SEC Commissioners who were law professors or held other government positions prior to their respective appointment and who had been affiliated with a major corporate law firm at an earlier stage in his or her career include: Richard C. Breedan (Chair); Roel C. Campos; Elisse B. Walter; Troy A. Paredes; Kara M. Stein; Robert J. Jackson, Jr.; Hester M. Peirce; and Elad L. Roisman.

[140] For example, SEC Commissioners in chronological order (from 1990 to 2019) who became partners at major corporate law firms or joined large publicly-held companies in high-level positions after their tenure ended include: Richard C. Breeden; Philip R. Lochner, Jr.; Richard Y. Roberts; J. Carter Beese, Jr.; Norman S. Johnson; Roel C. Campos; Christopher Cox; Annette L. Nazareth; Daniel M. Gallagher; and Mary Jo White.

[141] There are several premier plaintiffs' securities litigation law firms, yet none of their attorneys have been appointed a Commissioner—at least for the last forty years, if not since the inception of

who serve in high-level capacities at public pension funds whose beneficiaries are ordinary individual investors, such as The California Public Employees' Retirement System (better known as CALPERS). Moreover, private non-profit organizations (such as AARP) whose membership is comprised of millions of Americans, many of whom invest in the securities markets, have never had one of their high-level officers serve on the Commission. As a last example, employees who belong to a labor union and who own securities through their respective company's pension fund have never had one of their proficient persons (such as sophisticated in-house counsel from the AFL-CIO) appointed to the Commission.[142]

Instead, for several decades, there has been an abundance of corporate lawyers and executives who have been appointed SEC Commissioners.[143] It is therefore no surprise that the SEC's resounding failure to meaningfully engage in investor protection is the end result. By setting the policy and tone at the top, SEC Commissioners have signaled, for example, that facilitating capital formation is a priority over investor protection and that high-level corporate executives and directors of large publicly-held companies and financial firms are not to be pursued in enforcement actions for engaging in their ordinary fare (such as their conduct with respect to the subject company's disclosure practices).[144] Taking the cue from the top, the SEC staff dutifully implements the Commission's implied agenda.

The situation would be drastically different if the Commission were to implement, rather than exhort, the investor protection policies underlying the federal securities laws.[145] The SEC's meaningless rhetoric would be a relic of a bygone era. Receiving direction from the Commission, the SEC staff would be charged with effectuating these objectives. As a widely known characteristic

---

the SEC in 1934. For example, five well-known plaintiffs' securities litigation law firms are: Bernstein Litowitz Berger & Grossmann; Grant & Eisenhofer; Kasowitz Benson & Torres; Labaton Sucharow; and Robbins Geller Rudman & Dowd.

[142] Hence, the pool of seemingly eligible individuals to serve as SEC Commissioners has generally been narrow, drawing principally from major law firms, financial service firms, and the government, especially individuals from Capitol Hill. *See supra* note 138–140.

[143] *See supra* notes 138–140. *See also* Eisinger, *supra* note 3, at 224 (referring to SEC Chair Mary Jo White as "one of the premier defense lawyers in the country").

[144] These points have been discussed throughout the book, including earlier in this chapter. Note that, on occasion, the SEC brings an enforcement action against such a high-level executive. *See, e.g., supra* note 112.

[145] *See* Eisinger, *supra* note 3, at 296 (stating that in response to the financial crisis the SEC had hardly instituted any individual enforcement actions and, when brought, were against "low-level, tangential miscreants"); *supra* notes 119, 122.

of Commission employment, staff attorneys would retain their attractiveness to law firms and other private sector enterprises. Vigorous and even-handed enforcement, along with disclosure and market regulation practices benefitting investors and the integrity of the securities markets, would be deemed foremost. For seasoned outside attorneys and other professionals who would abhor the SEC's revitalized focus, they would not be suitable to migrate to the Commission staff to serve as division heads or other positions. Nonetheless, scores, if not hundreds, of other experienced professionals would be eager to procure high-level SEC staff positions in order to serve the public interest and to develop a thorough comprehension of the Commission's practices and culture to enable them to return to the private sector (such as law firms) being more valued by their colleagues and clients.[146]

To effectuate these objectives, the composition of SEC Commissioners must be far more diverse than is current practice. First, the federal securities laws should be amended to increase the size of the Commission from five to seven members.[147] Second, the statute should provide that no more than four Commissioners may be from the same political party, with the President designating the Commissioner who would serve as SEC Chair.[148] Third, pursuant to statute, the Commission would be comprised of one individual each from: (1) a corporate law firm, a publicly-held corporation, or a registered financial firm, (2) an accounting firm that is registered with the Public Company Accounting Oversight Board (PCAOB), (3) a law firm that represents investors in securities class actions, (4) academia or the government (including from Capitol Hill) whose expertise is in the securities area, (5) an institutional investor which manages a public pension plan, (6) a nonprofit organization whose membership is comprised of at least tens of thousands of Americans who invest in the securities markets, and (7) an organization whose members or beneficiaries are employees of publicly-held corporations. Appointment of SEC Commissioners in this manner would greatly enhance the diversity and perspective than currently exist. Although these seven classifications may be modified to some degree,

---

[146] *See* discussion in Cox and Thomas, *supra* note 130, at 861–62 (setting forth the view that "the revolving door may positively impact performance in both the private- and public-sector by promoting a greater understanding of regulatory requirements and increased levels of compliance").

[147] *See* § 4(d)(a) of the Securities Exchange Act, 15 U.S.C. § 78d(a) (setting forth that the SEC is "to be composed of five commissioners to be appointed by the President by and with the advice and consent of the Senate").

[148] *Id.* (stating that "[n]ot more than three of such commissioners shall be members of the same political party"). *See supra* note 147.

they must retain their specifications of qualified individuals with a diversity of views who come from organizations whose members, clients, or operations are connected with the securities laws or the securities markets. Key considerations that are to be included within these specifications are gender and racial diversity.[149] Adoption of this framework would help enable the Commission to return to its glory of yesteryear as an effective and feared law enforcement agency whose primary mission is investor protection. With the continuation of the current system, irrespective of whether the Democrats or Republicans are in power, the erosion of the SEC's prowess likely will continue.[150] If unchecked, this eventuality bodes ill for investors and the integrity of the U.S. securities markets.

IV. Conclusion

Fundamental changes must be made at the SEC. As discussed in this chapter, the Commission has lost its luster. It no longer is viewed as a champion of investor protection or feared by high-level executives of blue-chip companies who engage in aberrant behavior in the ordinary course of performing their responsibilities. Addressing several of the SEC's failures during the past few decades, the foregoing discussion recommends corrective measures that should be implemented. Unfortunately, however, the Commission's misguided practices and policies are not piecemeal. They are systemic, calling for comprehensive action. The most feasible way to generate a revitalized SEC is to set the appropriate tone at the top by reconstituting the composition of SEC Commissioners as advanced herein. Undertaking this reform in an effective manner should energize the SEC to engage in more balanced regulation and to reassume its role as a champion of investor protection.

---

[149] The discussion focusing on gender and racial diversity on corporate boards of directors contained in Chapter 5 herein is relevant to the appointment of SEC Commissioners.

[150] Indeed, it should be emphasized that the SEC's failures to institute enforcement actions against high-level executives of large financial firms in the aftermath of the financial crisis of 2008 occurred during the Obama administration. With respect to the Trump administration, as anticipated, any perception that there would be tougher corporate enforcement by the SEC was misplaced. *See* Eisinger, *supra* note 3, at 325.

10

Summary of Recommendations for Adoption

I. Introduction

This chapter summarizes key recommendations that are proffered throughout this book. Of course, not all recommendations made herein are restated in this chapter. The analyses underlying these recommendations are contained in the respective chapters where such recommendations are made. Hopefully, the compilation of the following list of recommendations in this relatively succinct manner provides substantial benefit to the overall objectives of this challenging project.

II. Recommendations for Adoption

A. The Disclosure Regimen of the Federal Securities Laws

1. Propriety of Federal Law Regulating Substantive Fairness

When appropriate, the federal securities laws should regulate substantive fiduciary conduct. This approach is beneficial as it signals to state legislatures and courts that unduly permissive treatment favoring corporate officers and directors may trigger federal action that either preempts or significantly regulates matters that previously had been within the purview of state law. Federal action also may be necessitated to resolve important issues that the states either decline or fail adequately to address.

2. The Concept of Materiality

a. Undue reliance on quantitative standards of materiality should be rejected in favor of applying fluid qualitative and quantitative

Rethinking Securities Law. Marc I. Steinberg, Oxford University Press. © Marc I. Steinberg 2021.
DOI: 10.1093/oso/9780197583142.003.0010

materiality thresholds consistent with judicial precedent and the SEC's disclosure pronouncements.

b. A narrative disclosure misrepresentation or omission should be judged by identical materiality standards irrespective of the statutory or regulatory provisions that are at issue. For example, a material disclosure deficiency in the MD&A setting should be deemed material for purposes of Section 10(b) and other antifraud provisions of the securities laws.
c. Judicial interpretations of the SEC's disclosure mandates with respect to qualitative materiality in the corporate governance setting, particularly with respect to officer and director conduct, frequently have been unduly narrow. A more robust approach is merited to promote market integrity and shareholder interests.

3. The Mandatory Disclosure Framework

a. The mandatory disclosure framework is firmly ensconced in the securities law framework and its fundamental importance should receive the highest priority.
b. The use by registrants and fiduciaries of laudatory language known as puffery and optimistic statements of belief is unduly insulated from liability under the securities laws. Fiduciaries who owe duties of care and loyalty to their respective corporations and shareholders should be held to a higher standard of accountability.
c. "Overload" of information that clearly is not material prevails in the SEC disclosure framework. The length of disclosure documents should be significantly shortened while implementing the mandate that, absent the existence of justifiable business reason, all material information must be promptly and sufficiently disclosed.
d. A mandatory Summary Section should be required in a subject company's SEC filings, including its Securities Act registration statements and Exchange Act periodic reports. The presence of a sufficiently comprehensive Summary in SEC registration statements and periodic reports should facilitate a more disciplined disclosure process and provide ordinary investors with better access to the material information necessary to make informed decisions.
e. Each Exchange Act reporting company should be required to have a disclosure committee comprised solely of independent directors who may retain separate legal counsel on the committee's behalf.

f. The SEC has inappropriately dismantled the mandatory disclosure framework with respect to Rule 506 offerings made to accredited investors. Unless these investors have adequate monetary wealth as well as financial sophistication, the mandatory disclosure framework should apply, entitling such investors to the receipt of registration-type information.

g. The failure of the SEC to require that subject companies disclose, absent a justifiable business reason, all material information signifies that, with frequency, the securities of these companies do not trade at prices that accurately reflect their value. To alleviate this situation, publicly-traded companies should be required to disclose (absent meritorious justification) all material information within one business day after becoming aware of the materiality of such information.

B. Issuer Exemptions from Securities Act Registration

1. Regulation D

   a. In order for an individual to be deemed an accredited investor, in addition to having the requisite monetary wherewithal, the investor or its purchaser representative should be required to be financially sophisticated. Likewise, entities, in addition to meeting specified monetary levels (such as having $5 million in total assets), should be required to be financially sophisticated.

   b. The requisite financial amounts for qualification as an accredited investor should be based upon the monetary levels as they were adopted by the SEC in 1982 when Regulation D (including Rule 506) was promulgated, adjusted annually since 1982 for inflation.

   c. In addition to one's primary residence being excluded from calculating an individual's net worth in determining qualification as an accredited investor, certain other irreplaceable assets, including amounts vested in pension and retirement accounts, also should be excluded.

   d. Advertising and general solicitation should be permitted only to accredited investors and qualified institutional buyers (QIBs) and only after these investors are deemed qualified (pursuant to the criteria proposed herein) as having that status.

e. Once disclosure of substantive information is made to any accredited investor, the identical information should be required to be provided to all investors.
f. A Form D should be required to be filed with the SEC and with each applicable state at least 72 hours before: the use of advertising and general solicitation (in Rule 506(c) offerings); and the making of any offer or sale (in Rule 504, Rule 506(b) offerings); as well as at the closing of the offering.
g. Rule 506(c) should be rescinded as its objectives would be largely met by the proposals herein that have greater investor safeguards.

2. Enhanced Funding of State Securities Regulatory Agencies

The funding for state securities regulatory agencies should be substantially improved. The solution proposed is for the North American Securities Administrators Association (NASAA) to adopt a recommended schedule of fees for the state securities commissions to charge their users, including issuers, financial intermediaries, and investment companies. The respective state securities agencies would implement this recommended schedule and retain all or a sufficient amount of these fees to fund their operating costs.

3. Regulation A

a. Serious consideration should be given to whether Tier 1 of Regulation A should be rescinded. With the increase in the Rule 504 offering amount to $10 million in a twelve-month period, smaller issuers can engage in mini-public offerings under the purview of state registration requirements. Issuers seeking to raise a larger amount of capital in a public offering, frequently accessing larger pools of investors, would be subject to the more rigorous mandates of Regulation A, Tier 2.
b. There should be no state preemption of Regulation A offerings. Nonetheless, to ensure that uniform disclosure requirements would apply without the presence of additional state mandates, such as merit regulation, federal standards would govern the exemption's parameters on the state level.
c. The use of advertising and general solicitation (as well as testing-the-waters communications) should be limited to only accredited investors and QIBs after they are deemed qualified (pursuant to the criteria proposed herein) as having that status.

d. In Regulation A, Tier 2 offerings, there should be no limit on the monetary amount that a non-accredited investor may purchase in such an offering.

4. Intrastate Offerings

The intrastate offering exemption should be rescinded. The benefits of the exemption would be outweighed by the availability of alternative exemptions recommended herein that would better meet issuer and investor needs.

5. Integration of Primary Exempt Offerings

a. Provided that the allegedly separate offerings are not for the same general purposes, the offerings should not be integrated.
b. If the allegedly separate offerings are for the same general purposes, a ninety-day safe harbor should apply.
c. Where purportedly separate offerings are made within ninety days of one another and are made for the same general purposes, the traditional five-factor test should apply to determine whether they would be integrated and deemed a single offering.

C. Exemptions for Resales of Securities

1. Public Resales of Securities

a. With respect to Exchange Act reporting companies, because there is an abundance of information in the public domain regarding these companies and their securities generally trade in more developed markets, resales of securities of these companies should be permitted with no holding period, irrespective whether such securities are restricted or non-restricted.
b. With no holding period, the quantity limitations set forth in Rule 144 with respect to the equity securities of Exchange Act reporting companies during any three-month period should not exceed the greater of: (a) three percent of the shares of the class outstanding; or (b) the average weekly trading volume that is reported on the exchanges and/or reported by means of the automated quotation system for a registered securities association for the four weeks preceding the trade.

c. With respect to securities of enterprises that are not Exchange Act reporting companies, Rule 15c2-11 should be revised to provide more complete and updated information. The information called for by the revised Rule 15c2-11 would be required to be updated every three months and would be accessible on the subject company's website or by other electronic means.
d. Provided that the Rule 15c2-11 information and delivery requirements are updated and complied with as recommended, no holding period for either restricted or non-restricted securities would apply with respect to the securities of non–Exchange Act reporting enterprises.
e. Pursuant to revised Rule 144, resales of equity securities of privately-held enterprises during a three-month period would be limited to the greater of one percent of the enterprise's outstanding equity securities or the average weekly trading volume during the four weeks prior to the trade.

2. Private Resales of Securities

a. In order for non-reporting companies to invoke the private resale exemption of Section 4(a)(7), the information called for by revised Rule 15c2-11 would be provided to the prospective purchasers.
b. For an Exchange Act reporting company, timely compliance by the subject enterprise with its Exchange Act reporting mandates would be sufficient.
c. If the informational requirements are met, Section 4(a)(7) as revised would permit offers and sales to both accredited and non-accredited investors of both Exchange Act reporting companies and privately-held enterprises, provided that such investors (either themselves or through their representatives) are qualified as being financially sophisticated.
d. In view of these revisions to Section 4(a)(7), the informal Section "4(1–1/2)" exemption would be rescinded.

3. Resales to Qualified Institutional Buyers

With one exception, the requirements set forth in Rule 144A are appropriate. That one exception is that, upon request to the subject issuer, certain basic information regarding such issuer as well as its financial statements must be provided to the security holder and to the prospective purchaser. As these "big players" can fend for themselves, Rule 144A's provision of information requirement would be rescinded.

D. The Securities Act Registration Framework

1. Disclosure—Securities Act Registration Statements

   a. In Securities Act registration statements, absent the existence of justifiable business reason, all material information should be required to be disclosed.
   b. Incorporation by reference from Exchange Act reports into a subject company's registration statement should be permitted only for those companies whose securities in fact trade in an efficient market.
   c. In view that ordinary investors (particularly, many individual investors) do not read the Exchange Act periodic reports that are incorporated by reference into the Securities Act registration statement, there should be required a sufficiently comprehensive Summary Section in the prospectus.

2. The Registration Process—Time Periods

   a. The current definition of "accredited institutional investor" is unduly broad. The total asset standard does not equate with financial sophistication. Accordingly, absent these investors being qualified as having the requisite financial sophistication, "testing the waters" or otherwise engaging in offers to sell in the pre-filing period should be prohibited by issuers that are not well-known seasoned issuers.
   b. A number of securities law provisions facilitate smaller publicly-held companies and market participants to condition the market for a forthcoming registered offering. To deter these companies and participants from engaging in such activities, more rigorous standards should be applied.
   c. To the extent that scaled-disclosure for smaller publicly-held companies substantially eases regulatory costs and investor overload, it makes good sense. However, scaled disclosure should not result in the withholding of material information from investors and the securities markets. Consistent with principles of disclosure, absent justifiable

business reason, prompt and sufficient disclosure of all material information should be mandatory irrespective of the size of the subject company.

3. The SEC's Misapplication of Section 28 of the Securities Act

With respect to the Commission's adoption of rules in the private and public offering settings, it has invoked Section 28 of the Securities Act as the basis of its authority. On several occasions, the SEC has misapplied the directives of Section 28, namely, that the exercise of its exemptive authority "is necessary or appropriate in the public interest and is consistent with the protection of investors." To comply with these directives, the SEC should apply two overriding principles: first, if investors would be worse off were the contemplated measure adopted, then such measure should not be adopted as it is not consistent "with the protection of investors"; and, second, if any proposed reduction in disclosure signifies that certain material information no longer will be available to investors and the securities markets, that proposed measure likewise should not be adopted.

E. Due Diligence in Registered Offerings

1. Outside Directors

As a condition of listing on a national securities exchange, publicly-held companies should be required to have a disclosure committee of the board of directors comprised solely of independent directors. Similar to the audit committee mandate, the disclosure committee should have the authority to retain its own advisers, including legal counsel. The disclosure committee should hold sessions attended by the other outside directors who do not serve on the committee (along with support personnel, including legal counsel).

2. Underwriters

a. Many of the SEC's suggestions focusing on the steps that an underwriter should take to build up "a reservoir of knowledge" with respect to prospective issuers of registered securities are not practical. On the other hand, the Commission's suggestion that an issuer retain counsel for the underwriter to conduct due diligence on an ongoing basis is the most attractive of the alternatives feasibly available. This recommendation should be elevated to a mandate; namely, issuer retention of underwriter's counsel would be required in shelf registered offerings.

b. To significantly lessen the conflict of interest concerns, the law firm for the underwriter would be retained by the subject company's audit committee or its disclosure committee, with each such committee being comprised entirely of independent directors.
c. Such audit or disclosure committee would be charged with the retention, scope of representation, fee arrangement, and, if called for, the termination of the law firm for the underwriter.
d. Upon the execution of comprehensive nondisclosure agreements, a specified number of prospective underwriters would be invited to attend informational sessions with the members of the audit or disclosure committee.
e. A subject issuer would be required to publicly identify specified potential underwriters (such as five such underwriters) that would be deemed finalists, thereby becoming eligible for selection as the lead underwriter(s) in such issuer's forthcoming shelf registered offering(s).

F. Federalization of Corporate Governance

Gaps in the corporate governance framework exist, calling for the implementation of improved standards on the federal level. Two of these enhancements are addressed elsewhere in the book: the need for enactment of comprehensive legislation regulating insider trading; and the federalization of substantive conduct in the merger and acquisition setting.

1. Composition of Boards of Directors and Board Committees

In view of developments during the last several decades, federal law has impacted board of director and board committee composition and responsibilities. Additional measures are necessary due to state law failure to prescribe appropriate norms of conduct and to adequately address aberrant conduct by corporate fiduciaries.

a. Congress should enact legislation requiring that, as a condition of having its securities listed on a national stock exchange, a subject company must have an independent director who serves as chair of its board of directors.

b. Congress should enact legislation to enhance board composition with respect to both the background of directors and their diversity, including gender and racial diversity. At least one board position should be allocated for employee representation. Adoption of this measure would enhance board member independence and lessen the presence of structural bias.

c. Independent directors should have staggered term limits in order to reduce the specter of director lethargy and co-option.

d. The largest shareholder (or group of shareholders) who beneficially owns at least three percent of the voting shares of a subject company and who has held such shares for a minimum of twelve months should be entitled to access such company's proxy statement to nominate up to twenty-five percent of the board seats up for election.

2. Shareholder Say-on-Pay and Related Issues

a. With respect to corporations whose securities trade on a national securities exchange, Congress should enact a statute placing a ceiling on the percentage disparity between the CEO's compensation and that of the median employee.

b. The employee representative who serves on a subject company's board of directors (pursuant to the recommendation set forth in the foregoing) also should serve as a member of that company's compensation committee.

c. The current advisory shareholder say-on-pay vote with respect to executive compensation should be elevated to a binding shareholder vote. A binding shareholder vote would instill a significantly higher level of discipline, better align executive pay with company performance, and improve the perception of equity in the overall corporate compensation structure.

3. Undue Reliance on State Law Principles

The deference to state law principles to ascertain the parameters of the federal securities laws is unwarranted. In view of today's strong presence of federal corporate governance, federal law should uniformly be the controlling source when construing the meaning and scope of the federal securities laws.

G. Private Securities Litigation

The private securities litigation framework in the United States is unacceptable and in need of clarification, greater uniformity, and better assessment of the public policy issues implicated.

1. Publicly-Traded Companies—Registered Offerings versus Secondary Market Trading

    a. There exists no persuasive reason to justify why an established publicly-held company whose common stock is listed on a national securities exchange is subjected to vastly different liability regimes depending on whether it files a Securities Act registration statement versus a periodic report pursuant to the Exchange Act. Accordingly, for seasoned companies, the identical liability framework should apply to disclosure deficiencies irrespective whether they are contained in a Securities Act registration statement (and prospectus) or in an Exchange Act periodic filing.
    b. With respect to companies undertaking their initial public offering or that otherwise are unseasoned (e.g., issuers having a public float of less than $75 million), the current provisions of Securities Act Section 11 should apply, with the exception that the issuer (like other Section 11 defendants) should have a due diligence defense.
    c. Section 11's onerous tracing requirement should be interpreted to reflect even-handed treatment: a plaintiff can invoke Section 11 only if she can establish by a preponderance of the evidence that she acquired shares pursuant to the registration statement that allegedly contained inadequacy of disclosure. Any class recovery under Section 11, however, would be limited by the percentage of shares that were outstanding in the secondary market that had been sold in the subject registered offering.

2. Uniform Level of Mental Culpability

    a. Absent sound justification otherwise, a uniform standard of culpability should apply based on the same conduct in private federal securities litigation irrespective of the remedial provisions that a plaintiff seeks to invoke.

b. Generally, with respect to disclosures that are susceptible to factual verification, the culpability of defendants should be premised on negligent misconduct rather than scienter.
c. If the applicable statement is future-oriented or cannot otherwise be verified, liability predicated on a complainant's showing of gross negligence or bad faith should apply.
d. Strict liability should be eliminated in private securities litigation.

3. Pleading Requirements in Private Securities Litigation

a. The onerous pleading standards in private securities actions alleging fraud should be lowered to reflect the FRCP 9(b) standard unadorned by the Private Securities Litigation Reform Act (PSLRA) heightened requirements.
b. Without undue intrusion, in the discretion of the trial court, limited discovery may be ordered prior to the court's ruling on the motion to dismiss.
c. After affording limited discovery, if the court finds that the complaint is frivolous, it should sanction the plaintiffs and their attorneys, including an appropriate award of attorneys' fees to the defendants.

4. Primary Liability Principles

Primary liability principles should be simplified. The recommended approach herein would lessen the pleading burdens, provide more certainty, and narrow the liability gaps.

a. Like current law, primary liability exposure should extend to those persons who make an allegedly materially false or misleading statement or who engage in fraudulent or deceptive conduct.
b. When an entity, such as a corporation, makes an allegedly materially false or misleading statement in an SEC filing or other communication that is disseminated to investors, specified individuals having the requisite status with such entity should be subject to primary liability exposure, including its high-level executive officers.
c. Outside directors should not be subject to primary liability unless they sign the subject document or otherwise give their approbation to an oral or written communication that is disseminated to the investing public.

d. With respect to Securities Act registration statements, irrespective of the status of the company, the underwriters for the offering as well as the auditors should be subject to primary liability exposure.

5. Elimination of the Reliance Requirement

The element of reliance in securities law private damages actions should be eliminated. Rather than engaging in the efficient market theory analysis whereby undue time and resources are expended, the better course is to follow other developed markets (and state securities laws) that dispense with a reliance requirement. Nonetheless, plaintiffs would be required to prove loss causation and the amount of damages.

6. Secondary Liability in Private Securities Actions

a. Aider and abettor liability in private actions should be statutorily reinstated with the culpability standard being that of intentional or reckless misconduct.
b. The control person liability provisions should be modified to provide for an affirmative defense if the subject control person acted with reasonable care, thereby implementing the standard set forth in the Uniform Securities Act adhered to by many states.
c. The common law doctrine of respondeat superior liability should be abandoned under the securities laws.

7. Puffery, Statements of Belief, and Forward-Looking Statements

a. When assessing the securities law disclosure obligations of corporate fiduciaries, the puffery doctrine should be dismantled.
b. The protections extended to forward-looking statements by the PSLRA should be curbed. Under the revised standard, a forward-looking statement would be insulated from liability unless the plaintiff proves that such statement was made either with gross negligence or without good faith.
c. Likewise, with respect to statements of belief, if the applicable statement is future-oriented or cannot otherwise be verified, liability should be predicated on a plaintiff proving that the defendant acted with gross negligence or without good faith.

8. Federal Preemption of Securities Class Actions

    a. With certain exceptions, federal preemption of securities class actions of nationally traded securities as mandated by the Securities Litigation Uniform Standards Act (SLUSA) should be retained.
    b. SLUSA preemption, however, should not apply with respect to plaintiffs who cannot satisfy Section 10(b)'s standing requirement because they neither are purchasers nor sellers of the subject securities.
    c. While SLUSA preemption should require that covered class actions must be brought in federal court, state law claims should not be preempted. Corrective action thus should be undertaken by Congress to authorize plaintiffs in covered class actions to institute their state law claims in a properly brought class action in federal court.

9. Broker-Dealers and Investment Advisers

    a. With respect to securities arbitration, the Financial Industry Regulatory Authority (FINRA) should: expand its arbitrator pool to obtain greater diversity in terms of age, gender, and race; engage in more rigorous classification of those persons who qualify as public arbitrators; increase the level of honoraria paid to arbitrators; require more intensive arbitrator training; and enhance the compulsory periodic disclosure obligations of FINRA arbitrators.
    b. Although pre-dispute arbitration agreements should remain enforceable, they should not be compulsory as a condition for a customer to open an account. Rather, customer choice of forum should be implemented with respect to pre-dispute arbitration agreements.
    c. Regulation Best Interest should be modified to require that a broker-dealer must monitor a retail customer's account unless the customer acknowledges in writing that the broker has no such obligation.
    d. An investment adviser's fiduciary duty to its clients has been interpreted in a lax manner. For example, with respect to an investment adviser's receipt of compensation for its services, the applicable standard should be that of reasonableness with the burden of proof placed on the subject investment adviser to establish the reasonableness of its compensation for the services provided. The current unduly permissive "so disproportionately large" standard thus should be rejected.

10. Cap on Damages

A cap on damages would apply unless a plaintiff proves that the subject defendant engaged in knowing misconduct.

a. With respect to monetary liability for an individual defendant's negligent conduct, damages should be capped at the greater of that individual's: total annual compensation (including equity compensation benefits); fees and other revenues derived from the engagement; or $100,000.
b. Generally, the liability of a publicly-held corporation should be capped at the greater of: $1 million; or two percent of its market capitalization.
c. With respect to indemnification, the advancement of expenses as provided by state law should be allowed. However, with respect to amounts paid in settlement or pursuant to adverse judgment, indemnification for corporate executives and financial intermediaries would be permitted only if approval is received from the disinterested shareholders. Outside directors would continue to be indemnified pursuant to the standards set forth under current applicable state law.

H. Insider Trading

The U.S. securities law framework with respect to the regulation of insider trading is abysmal. Uncertainties and inconsistencies prevail resulting in disparate treatment for similarly situated persons. To redress this situation, Congress should enact comprehensive legislation that meaningfully and clearly addresses the contours of the insider trading prohibition.

1. Requiring Company Disclosure of All Material Information

As addressed elsewhere in this book, publicly-held companies (absent meritorious business justification) should be required to disclose by means of a SEC filing and press release (or other suitable form of communication) all material information within one business day after becoming aware of the materiality of such information. During the interval between the occurrence of a reportable event and the making of a SEC filing, company insiders and others having access to the subject information would be barred from trading and tipping. The implementation of this mandate would drastically reduce opportunities for illegal insider trading.

2. Advance Notice of Insider Trades

Congress should enact a statute requiring that insiders subject to Section 16(a) of the Securities Exchange Act provide advance notice of their contemplated transactions in a subject company's equity securities. Such advance notice would be made in a filing with the SEC that would become available that same day on the Commission's publicly available internet site. The insider then would be permitted to engage in the otherwise lawful contemplated transaction the following business day.

3. Revision of Insider Trading Plans

SEC Rule 10b5-1 should be repealed. In its place, Congress should enact legislation focusing on the propriety of insider trading plans. As proposed herein, in order for an insider trading plan to constitute a meritorious defense to allegations of unlawful insider trading, the adoption and effective implementation of several substantive measures set forth herein would be required.

4. Repeal of Section 16(b) of the Securities Exchange Act

Section 16(b) has lost much of its vigor and should be repealed. Adherence to the statute has become a technical and cumbersome process. With the SEC's creation of loopholes in its interpretations of Section 16(b) and the employment of customary corporate policies that are compliant with this statute, Section 16(b) provides relatively little deterrent to unlawful insider trading. This assertion particularly holds true if the other recommendations set forth herein with respect to insider trading are adopted.

5. Adoption of the Access Approach

The United States should enact legislation that is consistent with the insider trading laws of other developed markets.

a. Those persons who are in a position to have access to material nonpublic information should be prohibited from trading on or tipping others with respect to such information.
b. Likewise, those persons who know or have reason to know that they are receiving, directly or indirectly, material nonpublic information from a source that is privy to such information due to such source's access status would be subject to the insider trading prohibition.

c. The access approach accordingly should be the preferred approach. It commendably supports the integrity of the securities markets, perceptions of fairness, and effective enforcement.

I. Mergers and Acquisitions

1. Federal Law Should Govern Substantive Issues in the M&A Setting

With respect to companies whose shares are listed on a national securities exchange, federal law should govern substantive issues arising in the M&A setting. Having ramifications affecting national and international policies, the federal government should be the principal regulator.

2. Disclosure of Beneficial Ownership

The federal securities laws should be amended to require that any person (or group) that beneficially owns more than three percent of an equity security of an Exchange Act reporting company must file within twenty-four hours a Schedule 13D with the SEC and be prohibited from further accumulating its holdings until one business day after such Schedule 13D filing has been made.

3. Golden Parachute Arrangements

The shareholder vote with respect to the approval of golden parachute arrangements should be binding rather than advisory. The vote should be conducted at the time that shareholder approval is sought for the subject acquisition. Accordingly, as proposed herein, shareholder votes on say-on-pay executive compensation and golden parachute arrangements should be treated in a similar manner.

4. Greenmail

In order for a greenmail payment to be made by a subject corporation, shareholder approval of the contemplated payment and its terms should be required.

5. The Acquirer's Shareholders

Due to the neglect of the states in M&A transactions to provide the shareholders of the acquiring corporation with a meaningful voice, the federalization of shareholder voting rights in this context is appropriate. Pursuant to this recommendation, M&A deals involving nationally traded companies that constitute twenty percent or more of a respective company's net assets ordinarily would be deemed "extraordinary" transactions. In addition to the acquired company's shareholders tendering their shares or voting their approval, a majority of the outstanding shares of the publicly-held (direct or indirect) acquirer (provided that such twenty percent threshold is met) would be required to approve the subject transaction. Accordingly, this recommendation would grant voting rights to such shareholders in triangular mergers, tender offers, and similar types of transactions.

6. Repeal of State Takeover Statutes

There should be federal preemption of state takeover statutes that regulate companies whose securities are nationally traded. Even if a particular state statute may be deemed beneficial to shareholders, the securities markets, and the public interest, that determination should be made by Congress rather than the individual states acting pursuant to their own agendas.

7. Shareholder Ownership Threshold Requiring Takeover Bid for All Outstanding Shares

   a. The recommendation set forth in the SEC's Advisory Committee Report on Tender Offers should be implemented—namely, that, upon acquisition by a person of twenty percent (or alternatively fifteen percent) of the voting power of a subject issuer's outstanding securities, additional purchases may be made only from the issuer or pursuant to a tender offer.
   b. Partial bids should be prohibited, thereby requiring that a tender offer must be made for all outstanding voting shares.

8. Measures in Response to Takeover Bids

Takeover policies involving national and global companies should not be the province of state company law. Rather, the federal government should establish the parameters with respect to the legitimacy of defensive measures in the takeover sphere.

   a. When a board of directors seeks to adopt a substantive tactic to fend off prospective as well as ongoing takeover bids or to entice a friendly suitor, the shareholders of the subject corporation should be entitled to vote to approve the requested action. Applying both to defensive maneuvers to fend off unwanted bidders and to lock-ups extended to suitors in negotiated deals, this approach supports shareholder empowerment in order to harmonize the separation of ownership and control in publicly-held companies.

b. This recommended approach stresses advanced planning of the defensive strategies that an incumbent board would be inclined to implement and receipt of shareholder approval before a takeover bid is launched by a third party.
c. To help ensure that shareholders are better informed, the shareholder (or group) that owns the largest percentage of voting common stock should be entitled to present its position (with an appropriate word limit) in the company's disclosure statement regarding the contemplated maneuver(s).
d. Application of the business judgment rule is not appropriate in the tender offer setting. With respect to a maneuver that has received shareholder approval for its possible use, the target corporation's board of directors must act reasonably with respect to its deployment—mandating that such deployment serves the corporation's, and collectively, the shareholders' best interests.

J. The Securities and Exchange Commission

The SEC's zeal for the vigorous enforcement of the federal securities laws and its principal mission of protecting investors has dissipated over the past several decades. This failure calls for the implementation of strong measures to ameliorate the current unacceptable situation.

1. Failure to Adopt an Acceptable Continuous Disclosure Framework

Pursuant to the Sarbanes-Oxley Act, Congress directed the SEC to promulgate a current disclosure framework for Exchange Act reporting companies. Instead of adopting disclosure standards that are comparable to other developed markets whereby (absent justifiable business reason) all material information must be publicly and timely disclosed, the Commission prescribed additional disclosure items under Form 8-K. As a result, substantial gaps remain permitting subject companies to refrain from making disclosure of material information on a timely basis. This glaring deficiency should be remedied by the SEC adopting a continuous disclosure framework consistent with that embraced by other developed markets.

2. Unduly Insulating Liability Exposure for Companies and Their Insiders

The SEC proactively has limited the liability exposure of subject companies and their insiders under the federal securities laws. For a regulatory agency charged with investor protection, such conduct is unacceptable. The actions approved by the Commission that should be reversed include the following:

a. Insulating from Section 10(b) liability reporting companies and their insiders for the failure to disclose specified items within a Form 8-K, even if done intentionally with intent to harm investors and perpetrate fraud.
b. Adopting a "filed" versus "furnished" distinction with respect to certain information contained in SEC required documents of Exchange Act reporting companies. By electing to furnish rather than file the subject document, a subject company and other defendants avoid private liability exposure both under Section 11 of the Securities Act and Section 18(a) of the Exchange Act.

3. Enforcement Policies, Practices, and Priorities

Several of the SEC's enforcement policies, practices, and priorities are misguided and should be corrected. Measures that should be adopted to remedy these shortcomings include the following:

a. Money penalties against corporations and other enterprises ordinarily should be levied only if a substantial percentage of the proceeds will be distributed to victims of the misconduct.
b. The SEC's frequent grant of waivers from disqualification provisions to large financial firms should undergo thorough review, with the adoption of a transparent policy that is balanced and limited.
c. Financial firms, irrespective of their size, should receive comparable treatment when the SEC levies sanctions. Undue favoritism to larger financial firms and their insiders should be eliminated.
d. The Commission should invoke its statutory authority with greater vigor to pursue meritorious enforcement actions against officers and directors of large publicly-held corporations and large financial firms.

4. Declining to Implement Statutory Directives

With some frequency, the SEC declines to implement directives legislated by Congress. As an administrative agency charged with adhering to statutory mandates, this intransigence is unacceptable. This inaction appropriately may be portrayed as an undue abstention to act in accordance with its administrative authority. The Commission should expeditiously and faithfully implement these congressional directives. Examples include the following:

a. Pursuant to the Dodd-Frank Act, Congress tasked the Commission with promulgating several rules, a number of which the SEC to date has declined to adopt. The Commission expeditiously should adopt these congressionally-mandated rules.
b. Although adopting its Standards of Conduct for Attorneys in 2003 as prescribed by the Sarbanes-Oxley Act, in the nearly two decades since the adoption of these Standards, the SEC has not brought even a single proceeding based on an attorney's alleged failure to comply therewith. Accordingly, the Commission should invoke these Standards when appropriate.
c. The Commission has refused to invoke the control person provision of the Securities Exchange Act to pursue high-level executive officers and directors. With this provision readily available during the financial crisis, the SEC did not utilize this provision against a director or officer on even one occasion. Clearly, the Commission should vigorously utilize this important enforcement measure.
d. As a law enforcement agency, the Commission should adhere to congressional directives and dutifully implement its statutory authority.

5. Reconstituting the Securities and Exchange Commission

The SEC's traditional image as the guardian of the investing public and a tough enforcer has become minimized. Popular culture has derided the Commission as being feckless and fearful of vigorously pursuing high-level executives of major publicly-held companies and large financial firms. Although the revolving door for SEC personnel has been a reason given for this demise, the solution lies in the composition of the SEC Commissioners. This reconstitution of SEC Commissioners should be accomplished in the following manner:

a. The federal securities laws should be amended to increase the size of the Commission from five to seven members.
b. No more than four Commissioners may be from the same political party, with the President designating the Commissioner, who serves as SEC Chair.

c. The Commission should be comprised of one individual each from: a corporate law firm, publicly-held corporation, or registered financial firm; an accounting firm that is registered with the Public Company Accounting Oversight Board (PCAOB); a law firm that represents investors in securities class actions; academia or the government; an institutional investor which manages a public pension plan; a nonprofit organization whose membership is comprised of at least tens of thousands of Americans who invest in the securities markets; and an organization whose members are employees of publicly-held corporations.
d. Although the foregoing classifications may be modified to some degree, they should retain their specifications of qualified individuals with a diversity of views who come from organizations whose members, clients, or operations are connected with the securities laws or the securities markets. Key considerations that should be included within these specifications are gender and racial diversity.

III. Conclusion

The analysis and recommendations set forth in this book hopefully will prove beneficial to legislators, policymakers, the practicing bar, academics, and students. Insofar as I am aware, this project is the first effort to "rethink" the securities laws since the American Law Institute's Restatement several decades ago. It has been a challenging and enjoyable endeavor. Although a number of the recommendations proposed herein likely will meet with disagreement, the fact remains that many facets of the current framework are unacceptable. This book thus has identified these problematic areas, analyzed their shortcomings, and recommended solutions that should ameliorate the deficiencies that exist. With the adoption and implementation of the recommendations made in this book, the U.S. securities framework should become more transparent, evenhanded, and investor-oriented without imposing undue burdens on legitimate business practices. After all, the stature of the U.S. securities markets in their efficiency, transparency, and integrity should be preeminent. The focus of this book is that this prominent distinction should continue as reality.

Index

For the benefit of digital users, indexed terms that span two pages (e.g., 52–53) may, on occasion, appear on only one of those pages.

CPSIA information can be obtained
at www.ICGtesting.com
Printed in the USA
BVHW021259170523
663897BV00010B/6

9 780197 583142